Applying Business Intelligence Initiatives in Healthcare and Organizational Settings

Shah J. Miah
Victoria University, Australia

William Yeoh
Deakin University, Australia

A volume in the Advances in Business Strategy and Competitive Advantage (ABSCA) Book Series

IGI Global
DISSEMINATOR OF KNOWLEDGE

Published in the United States of America by
IGI Global
Business Science Reference (an imprint of IGI Global)
701 E. Chocolate Avenue
Hershey PA, USA 17033
Tel: 717-533-8845
Fax: 717-533-8661
E-mail: cust@igi-global.com
Web site: http://www.igi-global.com

Library of Congress Cataloging-in-Publication Data

Names: Miah, Shah J., 1974- editor. | Yeoh, William, 1979- editor.
Title: Applying business intelligence initiatives in healthcare and organizational settings / Shah J. Miah and William Yeoh, editors.
Description: Hershey, PA : Business Science Reference, [2018]
Identifiers: LCCN 2017052805| ISBN 9781522557180 (hardcover) | ISBN 9781522557197 (ebook)
Subjects: LCSH: Business intelligence. | Strategic planning.
Classification: LCC HD38.7 .A67 2018 | DDC 658.4/72--dc23 LC record available at https://lccn.loc.gov/2017052805

This book is published in the IGI Global book series Advances in Business Strategy and Competitive Advantage (ABSCA) (ISSN: 2327-3429; eISSN: 2327-3437)

British Cataloguing in Publication Data
A Cataloguing in Publication record for this book is available from the British Library.

Advances in Business Strategy and Competitive Advantage (ABSCA) Book Series

Patricia Ordóñez de Pablos
Universidad de Oviedo, Spain

ISSN:2327-3429
EISSN:2327-3437

Mission

Business entities are constantly seeking new ways through which to gain advantage over their competitors and strengthen their position within the business environment. With competition at an all-time high due to technological advancements allowing for competition on a global scale, firms continue to seek new ways through which to improve and strengthen their business processes, procedures, and profitability.

The **Advances in Business Strategy and Competitive Advantage (ABSCA) Book Series** is a timely series responding to the high demand for state-of-the-art research on how business strategies are created, implemented and re-designed to meet the demands of globalized competitive markets. With a focus on local and global challenges, business opportunities and the needs of society, the **ABSCA** encourages scientific discourse on doing business and managing information technologies for the creation of sustainable competitive advantage.

Coverage

- Core Competencies
- Tacit Knowledge
- Small and Medium Enterprises
- Entrepreneurship & Innovation
- Balanced Scorecard
- Strategic alliances
- Value Creation
- Customer-Orientation Strategy
- Competitive Strategy
- Foreign Investment Decision Process

IGI Global is currently accepting manuscripts for publication within this series. To submit a proposal for a volume in this series, please contact our Acquisition Editors at Acquisitions@igi-global.com or visit: http://www.igi-global.com/publish/.

The Advances in Business Strategy and Competitive Advantage (ABSCA) Book Series (ISSN 2327-3429) is published by IGI Global, 701 E. Chocolate Avenue, Hershey, PA 17033-1240, USA, www.igi-global.com. This series is composed of titles available for purchase individually; each title is edited to be contextually exclusive from any other title within the series. For pricing and ordering information please visit http://www.igi-global.com/book-series/advances-business-strategy-competitive-advantage/73672. Postmaster: Send all address changes to above address.

Titles in this Series

For a list of additional titles in this series, please visit: www.igi-global.com/book-series

Handbook of Research on Strategic Innovation Management for Improved Competitive Advantage
George Leal Jamil (InesTec, Portugal) João José Pinto Ferreira (InesTec, Portugal) Maria Manuela Pinto (InesTec, Portugal) Cláudio Roberto Magalhães Pessoa (Universidade Fumec, Brazil) and Alexandra Xavier (InesTec, Portugal)
Business Science Reference • copyright 2018 • 772pp • H/C (ISBN: 9781522530121) • US $465.00 (our price)

Utilizing Consumer Psychology in Business Strategy
Tevfik Dalgic (University of Texas at Dallas, USA) and Sevtap Unal (Izmir Katip Celebi University, Turkey)
Business Science Reference • copyright 2018 • 340pp • H/C (ISBN: 9781522534488) • US $215.00 (our price)

Ethical Standards and Practice in International Relations
F. Sigmund Topor (Keio University, Japan)
Information Science Reference • copyright 2018 • 364pp • H/C (ISBN: 9781522526506) • US $195.00 (our price)

Applications of Conscious Innovation in Organizations
Jesus Enrique Portillo Pizana (Tecnológico de Monterrey University, Mexico) Sergio Ortiz Valdes (Tecnológico de Monterrey University, Mexico) and Luis Miguel Beristain Hernandez (Tecnológico de Monterrey University, Mexico)
Business Science Reference • copyright 2018 • 296pp • H/C (ISBN: 9781522540236) • US $205.00 (our price)

Business Strategies and Advanced Techniques for Entrepreneurship 4.0
Jose Manuel Saiz-Alvarez (Tecnológico de Monterrey, Mexico)
Business Science Reference • copyright 2018 • 231pp • H/C (ISBN: 9781522549789) • US $195.00 (our price)

Ethics and Decision-Making for Sustainable Business Practices
Ionica Oncioiu (Titu Maiorescu University, Romania)
Business Science Reference • copyright 2018 • 308pp • H/C (ISBN: 9781522537731) • US $215.00 (our price)

Handbook of Research on Entrepreneurial Ecosystems and Social Dynamics in a Globalized World
Luísa Cagica Carvalho (Universidade Aberta, Portugal & Universidade de Évora, Portugal)
Business Science Reference • copyright 2018 • 601pp • H/C (ISBN: 9781522535256) • US $345.00 (our price)

Start-Up Enterprises and Contemporary Innovation Strategies in the Global Marketplace
Rajagopal (EGADE Business School, Tecnologico de Monterrey, Mexico) and Ramesh Behl (International Management Institute Bhubaneswar, India)
Business Science Reference • copyright 2018 • 341pp • H/C (ISBN: 9781522548317) • US $235.00 (our price)

IGI Global
DISSEMINATOR OF KNOWLEDGE

701 East Chocolate Avenue, Hershey, PA 17033, USA
Tel: 717-533-8845 x100 • Fax: 717-533-8661
E-Mail: cust@igi-global.com • www.igi-global.com

Table of Contents

Preface xv

Section 1
BI Foundational Understanding and Their Specialized Fields and Applications

Chapter 1
A Framework and Architecture for Performance Management in Virtual Organizations 1
Amin Kamali, IBM Canada, Canada
Gregory S. Richards, University of Ottawa, Canada
Bijan Raahemi, University of Ottawa, Canada
Mohammad H. Danesh, University of Toronto, Canada

Chapter 2
The Rise of Embedded Analytics: Empowering Manufacturing and Service Industry With Big Data 21
Mohsen Attaran, California State University – Bakersfield, USA
Sharmin Attaran, Bryant University, USA

Chapter 3
Business Intelligence Maturity Framework 44
Chee-Sok Tan, Universiti Tunku Abdul Rahman, Malaysia
Wai-Khuen Cheng, Universiti Tunku Abdul Rahman, Malaysia
Jie Ren, Fordham University, USA
Siew Fan Wong, Sunway University, Malaysia

Chapter 4
Opportunities and Challenges of Implementing Predictive Analytics for Competitive Advantage 64
Mohsen Attaran, California State University – Bakersfield, USA
Sharmin Attaran, Bryant University, USA

Chapter 5
Developing Business Intelligence Product and Metacontent Map (BIP-Map) 91
Chin-Hoong Chee, Universiti Teknologi PETRONAS, Malaysia

Chapter 6
Business Intelligence Implementation Critical Success Factors 112
Ahad Zare Ravasan, Kharazmi University, Iran
Sogol Rabiee Savoji, Mehralborz Institute of Higher Education, Iran

Chapter 7
Integration of Knowledge Management and Business Intelligence for Lean Organizational Learning by the Digital Worker 130
Selvi Kannan, Victoria University, Australia
Shah J. Miah, Victoria University, Australia

Section 2
Diversified Business Aspects and BI or Analytics Applications

Chapter 8
Culturally Sensitive Data Visualizations 142
Michael Gendron, Central Connecticut State University, USA

Chapter 9
Building a Maturity Framework for Big Data Cybersecurity Analytics 164
Chi Minh Pham, Deakin University, Australia

Chapter 10
Developing Strategic Capability Through Business Intelligence Applications: A Case Study From the German Healthcare Insurance Industry 184
Martin George Wynn, University of Gloucestershire, UK
Daniel Brinkmann, University of Gloucestershire, UK

Chapter 11
Factors Influencing Managers' Use of Mobile Tablets: An Exploratory Study 202
Shijia Gao, Monash University, Australia
William Yeoh, Deakin University, Australia
Siew Fan Wong, Sunway University, Malaysia
Edgar Alexander Bruno Kautzner, Monash University, Australia

Chapter 12
Mind the Gap: From Analytics to Action in Student Retention 218
Qing Huang, La Trobe University, Australia
Nilupulee Nathawitharana, La Trobe University, Australia
Kok-Leong Ong, La Trobe University, Australia
Susan Keller, La Trobe University, Australia
Damminda Alahakoon, La Trobe University, Australia

Section 3
Emerging Areas of BI Research and Its Growth

Chapter 13
Tailorable Technologies for Improving Business Intelligence Systems: Small Business Decision Maker's Perspective 238
Shah J. Miah, Victoria University, Australia

Chapter 14
Design Methods of Strategic Decision Support Solutions for B2C Business Managers 254
Madhury Khatun, Victoria University, Australia
Shah J. Miah, Victoria University, Australia

Section 4
Emerging Large and Huge BI Platforms and Applications

Chapter 15
Transformative Analytics and Logistics Pricing: How Business Intelligence Can Inform Logistics 275
Jeffrey Drue Peck Jr., Central Connecticut State University, USA
Michael S. Gendron, Central Connecticut State University, USA
Tera Black, Central Connecticut State University, USA

Chapter 16
Depicting Data Quality Issues in Business Intelligence Environment Through a Metadata Framework 291
Te-Wei Wang, University of Illinois at Springfield, USA
Yuriy Verbitskiy, University of South Australia, Australia
William Yeoh, Deakin University, Australia

Chapter 17
Strategy, Action Plan, and Approaches for Business Intelligence in Banking and Mining 305
Hafeez Niazi, University of South Australia, Australia

Chapter 18
A Study of Business Intelligence Strategy Development by Large Organizations 326
Carmine Sellitto, Victoria University, Australia
Paul Hawking, Hawking Solutions, Australia

Compilation of References 340

About the Contributors 377

Index 383

Detailed Table of Contents

Preface xv

Section 1
BI Foundational Understanding and Their Specialized Fields and Applications

Chapter 1
A Framework and Architecture for Performance Management in Virtual Organizations 1
Amin Kamali, IBM Canada, Canada
Gregory S. Richards, University of Ottawa, Canada
Bijan Raahemi, University of Ottawa, Canada
Mohammad H. Danesh, University of Toronto, Canada

Virtual organizations are becoming common in the new world of work characterized by modern data exchange capabilities. These organizations face new challenges in information sharing that traditional approaches cannot address. This research proposes a framework and architecture for providing performance data to partners in virtual organizations. The framework aligns the activities of partners in a virtual organization at three different layers and defines common performance measurement indicators at each layer. It also proposes an implementation architecture that enables inter-organizational performance management in collaborative environments. The proposed architecture is validated through a prototype developed using IBM business process and business intelligence products.

Chapter 2
The Rise of Embedded Analytics: Empowering Manufacturing and Service Industry With Big Data 21
Mohsen Attaran, California State University – Bakersfield, USA
Sharmin Attaran, Bryant University, USA

The internet revolution, cloud computing, and the evolution to self-service analytics have all contributed to the changing dimensions of business intelligence. To compete effectively in a digitally driven world, business leaders must understand and address the critical shifts taking place in the field of analytics, and how these shifts impact their overall strategy. The key objective of this chapter is to propose a conceptual model for successful implementation of embedded analytics in organizations. This chapter also covers some of the potential benefits of analytics, explores the changing dimensions of analytics, and provides a guide to some of the opportunities that are available for using embedded analytics in business. Furthermore, this study reviews key attributes of a successful modern analytics platform and illustrates how to overcome some of the key challenges of incorporating embedded analytics into an analytic strategy in business. Finally, this study highlights successful implementation of analytics solutions in manufacturing and service industry.

Chapter 3
Business Intelligence Maturity Framework 44
Chee-Sok Tan, Universiti Tunku Abdul Rahman, Malaysia
Wai-Khuen Cheng, Universiti Tunku Abdul Rahman, Malaysia
Jie Ren, Fordham University, USA
Siew Fan Wong, Sunway University, Malaysia

This chapter builds an enterprise-level business intelligence maturity (EBIM) model that facilitates an improved view of the path in business intelligence (BI) implementation. The authors adopted a two-stage qualitative approach, namely a Delphi study followed by case studies. The findings reveal that a comprehensive EBIM model enables organizations to plan, assess, and manage their BI initiatives more effectively than previously. In addition, this study lists important key process areas (KPAs) that influence BI implementation success. The authors found that the KPAs in different levels and dimensions help organizations identify critical areas in need of maximum attention and channel their scarce resources to improve those areas. Further, the entire EBIM framework fosters better use of limited resources in critical areas, which is likely to have a greater effect at the right time.

Chapter 4
Opportunities and Challenges of Implementing Predictive Analytics for Competitive Advantage 64
Mohsen Attaran, California State University – Bakersfield, USA
Sharmin Attaran, Bryant University, USA

Predictive analytics has become an increasingly hot topic in analytics landscape. As a result, predictive analytics deployments are gaining momentum. Yet, the adoption rate is slow, and organizations are only beginning to scratch the surface in regard to the potential applications of this technology. Implemented properly, the business benefits can be substantial. However, there are strategic pitfalls to consider. The key objective of this chapter is to propose a conceptual model for successful implementation of analytics in organizations. This chapter highlights the importance of predictive analytics, identifies determinants of implementation success, and covers some of the potential benefits of this technology. Furthermore, this study reviews key attributes of a successful predictive analytics platform and illustrates how to overcome some of the strategic pitfalls of incorporating this technology in business. Finally, this study highlights successful implementation of analytics solutions in manufacturing and service industry.

Chapter 5
Developing Business Intelligence Product and Metacontent Map (BIP-Map) 91
Chin-Hoong Chee, Universiti Teknologi PETRONAS, Malaysia

A business intelligence (BI) system provides users with multi-dimensional information (a so-called "BI product") to support decision making. However, existing BI systems overlook the lineage metadata which supports individual data quality dimensions such as data believability and ease of understanding. Using a design science research paradigm, this chapter proposes and develops an integrated framework (known as BI product and metacontent map – "BIP-Map") to facilitate the traceability and accountability of BI products. Specifically, the business workflow layer of the integrated framework is modelled using business process modelling notation, and an information product map is used to model the second layer's information manufacturing process, whilst the third layer represents the metacontent detail of the data validation stage, from source system through to ETL, to the data warehousing stage. The integrated framework addresses individual-related data quality issues and builds user confidence by enhancing the traceability and accountability of a BI product.

Chapter 6
Business Intelligence Implementation Critical Success Factors.. 112
Ahad Zare Ravasan, Kharazmi University, Iran
Sogol Rabiee Savoji, Mehralborz Institute of Higher Education, Iran

Many organizations take business intelligence (BI) systems to improve their decision-making processes. Although many organizations have adopted BI systems, not all of these implementations have been successful. This chapter seeks to identify critical success factors (CSFs) that impact on the successful implementation of BI systems in organizations. So, at first, through literature review, 26 CSFs were identified. Following that, a questionnaire was developed and then filled out by domain experts who had at least three years of experience in BI implementation projects. Robust exploratory factor analysis (EFA) was run for data analysis, which finally classified 26 CSFs into four distinct groups termed as "organizational," "human," "project management," and "technical." The results of this study provide a very useful reference for scholars and managers to identify the relevant issues of BI projects in Iran.

Chapter 7
Integration of Knowledge Management and Business Intelligence for Lean Organizational Learning by the Digital Worker.. 130
Selvi Kannan, Victoria University, Australia
Shah J. Miah, Victoria University, Australia

The polarization of global labor market, hunt for talent, need to adapt quickly to changing environment is pressuring businesses more than ever before on their performance. This is further snowballed with the development of digitalization, automation, robotization, and artificial intelligence that offer approaches for addressing enormous industry challenges. These challenges create a push for organizational decision makers to rethink on the management of work. Knowledge management (KM) is understood to encourage content management, collaboration with inclusion of organizational behavioral science, and of course technologies. Complementing BI with knowledge management (KM) system in an organization can account for lean and accelerated performance. In this chapter, the authors present their position and insights in the integration of KM and BI suited for the worker in the digital world which possibly encourages lifelong learning with the focus on adaptability.

Section 2
Diversified Business Aspects and BI or Analytics Applications

Chapter 8
Culturally Sensitive Data Visualizations 142
Michael Gendron, Central Connecticut State University, USA

Organizations are undergoing significant changes in their business environment. Competing on a global scale means that organizations must better understand cultural issues of their customers, employees, and key stakeholders. As business analytics grows in importance, managers are sharing data visualizations to a variety of different cultures and beliefs. When creating culturally sensitive data visualizations, a set of best practices is required to assist managers to make timely and accurate decisions with the least possible cultural bias. This chapter aims to develop these best practices by analyzing cultural traits, communication habits, and other differences between the western and eastern global regions.

Chapter 9
Building a Maturity Framework for Big Data Cybersecurity Analytics 164
Chi Minh Pham, Deakin University, Australia

In recent years, big data analytics has become widely applied in cybersecurity, leading to the novel approach of big data cybersecurity analytics. While some organizations have been adopting this new approach in tackling cybercrime, there are limited guidelines to which companies can refer. Therefore, the renowned maturity model concept, which offers a systematic approach for an organization to measure and improve its maturity level, is applied in this study. On the basis of a comprehensive literature review, this chapter proposes a maturity framework for big data cybersecurity analytics. This synthesized comprehensive maturity framework comprises seven dimensions across five stage levels—namely organization, human, infrastructure, data management, analytics application, governance, and security dimensions. Knowing which dimensions need to be improved and which pathway to follow ensures the successful implementation of big data cybersecurity analytics within organizations.

Chapter 10
Developing Strategic Capability Through Business Intelligence Applications: A Case Study From the German Healthcare Insurance Industry 184
Martin George Wynn, University of Gloucestershire, UK
Daniel Brinkmann, University of Gloucestershire, UK

Company performance can be measured at all levels across an organization, and in the German healthcare industry, business intelligence systems play a crucial role in achieving this. For one major health insurance company (discussed here as an alias – AK Healthcare), the deployment of business intelligence applications has supported sustained growth in turnover and market share in the past five years. In this chapter, these tools are classified within an appropriate conceptual framework which encompasses the organization's information infrastructure and associated processes. Different components of the framework are identified and examples are given: systems infrastructure, data provision/access control, the BI tools and technologies, report generation, and information users. The use and integration of business intelligence tools in the strategy development process is then analyzed, and the key functions and features of these tools for strategic capability development are discussed. Research findings encompass system access, report characteristics, and end-users' capabilities.

Chapter 11
Factors Influencing Managers' Use of Mobile Tablets: An Exploratory Study................................. 202
Shijia Gao, Monash University, Australia
William Yeoh, Deakin University, Australia
Siew Fan Wong, Sunway University, Malaysia
Edgar Alexander Bruno Kautzner, Monash University, Australia

In recent years mobile tablets are being used by many managers. Yet hitherto there is a lack of research on managerial use of the new mobile technology. Hence, this study aims to explore the factors that influence the use of mobile tablets by managers and how mobile tablets impact the use of other digital devices. Semi-structured interviews were conducted with a panel of mid- to high-level managers who had incorporated mobile tablets into their work routine. The findings reveal that mobile tablets are suitable for managerial tasks due to nine main factors: non-routineness, collaborative nature, time-critical, information-centric, mobility, user friendliness of the interface, reliability, connectivity, and autonomy. Also, the use of mobile tablets has significant impact on the use of other digital devices as well as traditional manual process of using pens and papers. This study fills in the research gap and provides a foundation to help managers establish a business case for or against mobile tablet use.

Chapter 12
Mind the Gap: From Analytics to Action in Student Retention.. 218
Qing Huang, La Trobe University, Australia
Nilupulee Nathawitharana, La Trobe University, Australia
Kok-Leong Ong, La Trobe University, Australia
Susan Keller, La Trobe University, Australia
Damminda Alahakoon, La Trobe University, Australia

The issue of student attrition is a complex one and has been an area of research interest among education researchers. Recently, education researchers are proposing to tap into the large amount of student data that are housed within the institution's data warehouse. This big student data of demography, learning journey, and their interactions with the institution presents a rich source of insights that can be discovered using advanced analytics. Consequently, education researchers have put forward predictive models, suggest the use of data triggers and dashboards aimed at improving student retention. This however has been met with limited success to date. From experience, there remains a gap between the analytics and the operationalization of the analytics. Consequently, this gap needs to be addressed to achieve student retention. The authors propose a dual framework to close this gap. While this framework was developed in the context of creating a solution for student attrition, it is sufficiently generalizable to analytical solutions for problems around student learning.

Section 3
Emerging Areas of BI Research and Its Growth

Chapter 13
Tailorable Technologies for Improving Business Intelligence Systems: Small Business Decision Maker's Perspective 238
Shah J. Miah, Victoria University, Australia

The Australian farm-based businesses can be benefited from specially designed applications for cost-effective operation while maximizing profits to survive in economic and environmental crises. For decision support, existing business intelligence systems (BIS) approaches scarcely deal with specific user's provisions to adjust changing situations in decision making, without extra technical exertions. In this chapter, the authors describe a conceptual framework of tailorable BIS solution that is based on case study findings in that the highlighted requirements are relevant to address changing situations through enhancing end user's engagement. The activities of end user's engagement supported through the use of tailorable features that reinforce a shift from the traditional BIS process to a new provision where business owners can actively involve in adjusting their features to their decision support.

Chapter 14
Design Methods of Strategic Decision Support Solutions for B2C Business Managers.................... 254
Madhury Khatun, Victoria University, Australia
Shah J. Miah, Victoria University, Australia

This chapter reviews methods to develop a decision support system (DSS) for small business managers. The primary objective is to support managers, making strategic decisions for achieving competitive advantages in the business-to-consumer (B2C) e-commerce environment. Many researchers in the DSS domain utilized various methods to design information systems (IS) solution, mostly intended for large businesses. None of the researchers have considered the business environment as a knowledge source for DSS development of small business strategic decision support needs. User-centered design (UCD) and design science research (DSR) method were adopted for DSS development. DSR was appropriate because it addresses the real-world application environment where research problem or opportunity are defined. Multiple case studies and web content analysis were carried out for understanding business problems, needs, and system requirements. This study used the qualitative and descriptive data analysis methods. The findings suggested developing a DSS solution to meet the small business strategic needs.

Section 4
Emerging Large and Huge BI Platforms and Applications

Chapter 15
Transformative Analytics and Logistics Pricing: How Business Intelligence Can Inform Logistics.................... 275
Jeffrey Drue Peck Jr., Central Connecticut State University, USA
Michael S. Gendron, Central Connecticut State University, USA
Tera Black, Central Connecticut State University, USA

Raw materials and products are moved and created globally through complex supply chains. Within those supply chains, logistics is what enables the goods to move through distribution and reach the end consumer. Being such a widely used process, this is what motivates the researchers to examine the logistics portion of the supply chain from an analytical perspective and attempt to determine the relationship between various market forces and their impact on the cost of logistics. This will be accomplished with transformative analytics techniques, such as multivariate regression modeling focusing on areas such as directionality and precipitation. That should enable logistics managers, researchers, and others to better understand the factors that go into the cost of logistics services, and thus impact pricing of goods dependent on those services. In a world where logistics managers rely heavily on "gut feel," utilizing business intelligence and analytics can better enable decision making.

Chapter 16
Depicting Data Quality Issues in Business Intelligence Environment Through a Metadata Framework.................... 291
Te-Wei Wang, University of Illinois at Springfield, USA
Yuriy Verbitskiy, University of South Australia, Australia
William Yeoh, Deakin University, Australia

Modern business intelligence systems depend highly on high quality data. The core of data quality management is to identify all possible sources of data quality problems. To achieve this goal, an extensive metadata infrastructure is the most promising solution. Through theoretical metadata model investigation, the authors identified a set of data quality dimensions by carefully examining the data quality management principles and applied those principles to current BI environment. They summarize the analysis by proposing a BI data quality framework.

Chapter 17
Strategy, Action Plan, and Approaches for Business Intelligence in Banking and Mining 305
Hafeez Niazi, University of South Australia, Australia

This case study will analyze the critical success factors and key matters related to the deployment of BI deployment in different organizations. Different organizations have different approaches to making BI available for different business users, divisions, and departments. Data visualization is also one of the important factors which will provide user better reflection of data rather than make them confuse about organization data with too much information in the reports and dashboards. Data quality and diverse standards, which make BI famous in the different organizations, are also analyzed during the investigation of both organizations used in this case study. The case study analysis also shows how BI maturity, governance, and framework are key factors involved in the successful deployment of the BI in different organizations.

Chapter 18
A Study of Business Intelligence Strategy Development by Large Organizations 326
Carmine Sellitto, Victoria University, Australia
Paul Hawking, Hawking Solutions, Australia

Organizations have adopted business intelligence solutions with a mixed degree of benefits. Some businesses highlight significant outcomes, while others identify limitations or shortfalls in the benefits derived. Notably, the alignment of business strategy with the adoption of business intelligence processes has been an important predictor of firms being able to achieve organizational wide benefits. The chapter uses a case study approach to document the informational needs achieved through aligning organizational strategy and the adoption of business intelligence solution at two distinct companies. The adoption approaches used by each firm, although different, reflect the important areas in which business intelligence is most useful—strategic alignment, governance, and information presentation.

Compilation of References 340

About the Contributors 377

Index 383

Preface

This book titled *Applying Business Intelligence Initiatives in Healthcare and Organizational Settings* incorporates emerging concepts, methods, models and relevant applications of business intelligence (BI) systems within problem contexts of healthcare and other organizational boundaries. According to Gartner's (2018) definitions, the term *Business Intelligence* represents applications, methods, models and techniques, as well as the best practices that enable access to and analysis of information to improve and optimize decisions and/or business performance. In this book, we express the focal interest and its meaning which has been reflected on different promising research that are diversified in relevant application areas.

Emerging Business Intelligence techniques, decision support methods such as analytics technologies involving mobility, locational decision support, big-data analytics both on cloud and non-cloud computing environment have been of paramount mainstream technologies in processing, analyzing and handling varieties of internal and external business data both for real-time decision support and production of intelligence that may directly contribute to managerial decision making and improving business performance. The example application areas can be for instance, healthcare management, operational management for businesses, workforce management and agricultural management.

BI has been an essential application in enterprises or any types of business and non-profit organizations for improving business decision support. Therefore, BI implementation is critical for them and their internal and external performance improvement, measurement and forecasting. Currently BI application has extensively been proliferated because of its prominence use for both strategic and operational decision support in order to achieve various benefits, such as competitive advantages, cost reduction, improved efficiency and profitability (Isık et al., 2013). Many organizations have been invested in BI innovations and/or developing BI-oriented problem-solving methods, decision support mechanisms, models and instantiations to leverage their soft assets for the management of day-to-day data, transaction logs, social media data, and any form of stored information to achieve effective decision support to transform their business strategies, operational processes, optimization of production and customer value propositions. Data-driven discovery or intelligence and analytics around demand-oriented technologies for effective information support services already reinforced to change traditional system development practices, and as a result, newer forms of business intelligence, analytics, knowledge-based and decision-support development and acquisition practices are emerging to leverage new technologies. Although recent information systems studies have discussed relevant issues, approaches and methodologies around the use of these technologies within a context of BI development, it is still an emergent task for articulating requirements and new knowledge for combining overall ideas, approaches, methods and any other forms of effective studies that focused on meeting the demand of decision support and creation of intelligence in this current era of the big data exploration. Although this task is quite challenging, but an initiative can reinforce researchers, BI developers, BI consultants and information service providers for improving effective practices and relevant theories for designing powerful BI, Business Analytics (BA), Data or Knowledge-based Analytics, and any forms of decision support systems (DSS) techniques and applications as integral portions of the current dynamic digital ecosystems. The core motivation came from these aspects for covering in this book.

Grossmann and Stefanie Rinderle-Ma (2015) presented a book called "Fundamentals of Business Intelligence" focusing on transforming process-oriented data into information about the underlying business process. While Sherman (2014) edited a book called "Business Intelligence Guidebook: From Data Integration to Analytics" for focusing on high level of BI technical knowledge such as architecture, design and process in organizations. These books didn't cover any practical aspects and emerging applications of BI and other relevant data-driven technologies. It is important for articulating new knowledge for connecting thoughts, concepts and applications to design and guide purposeful knowledge creation in the BI field of study. In this research book, we would inform about connecting elements of BI technologies and different problem spaces to design and create artificial large-scaled or small-scaled systems for human operations and businesses.

We have edited the book keeping in mind that we will be continuously filling the gap by articulating and providing useful knowledge that contributes into the aforementioned aspects for the enhancement of current body of BI practical knowledge within the organizational boundaries. Authors of each chapter in this book bring their individual research and relevant contributions considering their own topic area of interests relevant to BI applications. We haven't had any control or imposed them to follow any directed pathway. Within our capacity as editor, we look over the quality and rigorousness of their research as well as overall suitability of the works the authors presented in their chapters. We would like to take the opportunity to thank all of the authors for their significant contributions to this book.

The book has been produced for the BI researchers, BI Application designers, BI investors and industry practitioners who are interested in achieving latest BI design and applications-oriented knowledge that may offer insights and case-based learning situations in relation to different emerging fields of BI. The book has been structured in four sections. Section 1 (BI Foundational Understanding and Their Specialized Fields and Applications) provides induced technical and non-technical concepts to decision-oriented problem solving in organizations. Section 2 (Diversified Business Aspects and BI or Analytics Applications) includes organizational and technical concepts for various business aspects and areas of applications. Section 3 (Emerging Areas of BI Research and Its Growth) includes emerging approaches and concepts for effective and efficient BI system design and development. Finally, Section 4 (Emerging Large and Huge BI Platforms and Applications) includes emerging technologies such as cloud computing for web-based decision service design and relevant applications and issues.

We will be pleased if this book contributes to human community or in developing human systems in this planet.

Sincerely

Shah J. Miah
Victoria University, Australia

William Yeoh
Deakin University, Australia

REFERENCES

Garter. (2018). *IT Glossary*. Retrieved from https://www.gartner.com/it-glossary/business-intelligence-bi/

Grossmann, W., & Rinderle-Ma, S. (2015). *Fundamentals of Business Intelligence, Data-Centric Systems and Applications*. Springer. doi:10.1007/978-3-662-46531-8

Işık, Ö., Jones, M. C., & Sidorova, A. (2013). Business intelligence success: The roles of BI capabilities and decision environments. *Information & Management*, *50*(1), 13–23. doi:10.1016/j.im.2012.12.001

Sherman, R. (2015). *Business Intelligence Guidebook: From Data Integration to Analytics* (1st ed.). Kindle Edition.

Section 1

BI Foundational Understanding and Their Specialized Fields and Applications

Chapter 1
A Framework and Architecture for Performance Management in Virtual Organizations

Amin Kamali
IBM Canada, Canada

Gregory S. Richards
University of Ottawa, Canada

Bijan Raahemi
University of Ottawa, Canada

Mohammad H. Danesh
University of Toronto, Canada

ABSTRACT

Virtual organizations are becoming common in the new world of work characterized by modern data exchange capabilities. These organizations face new challenges in information sharing that traditional approaches cannot address. This research proposes a framework and architecture for providing performance data to partners in virtual organizations. The framework aligns the activities of partners in a virtual organization at three different layers and defines common performance measurement indicators at each layer. It also proposes an implementation architecture that enables inter-organizational performance management in collaborative environments. The proposed architecture is validated through a prototype developed using IBM business process and business intelligence products.

INTRODUCTION

In recent years, organizational forms known as collaborative networks (CNs) have emerged that are information driven and characterized by extensive multi-partner arrangements in complex value chains and global business ecosystems (Camarinha-Matos, 2009). Within the CN category, a subtype referred to as a Virtual Organization (VO) has been noted. One of the distinguishing features of a VO is that it

DOI: 10.4018/978-1-5225-5718-0.ch001

shares resources among multiple partners to respond to temporary opportunities (Camarinha-Matos, Afsarmanesh, Galeano, & Molina, 2009). This type of organization is important because it provides a means for partners to collaborate to quickly seize opportunities, but managing the multiple alliances involved has proven to be a challenge (Graser, Jansson, Eschenbacher, Westphal, & Negretto, 2005).

An essential prerequisite for effective VO management is the availability of performance data emanating from the activities of the various partners involved. Yet, each of the partners is autonomous, each has information that it may not want to share especially given that the VO is a temporary alliance. How then, can the information needed to manage the VO effectively be provided while at the same time ensuring that the autonomy of each partner is respected?

Traditional performance management (PM) methodologies are designed to assess efficiency of intra-organizational processes. For example, approaches such as the Balanced Scorecard, Benchmarking, Six Sigma, and EFQM are generally appropriate for intra-organizational purposes (Graser, Jansson, Eschenbacher, Westphal, & Negretto, 2005). Although the SCOR model was developed by the Supply Chain Council to address interactions among organizations within a supply chain, it supports static and stable interactions and does not address the dynamic nature of VOs.

From the perspective of data sourcing and Business Intelligence (BI), several IT solutions such as extended Enterprise Resource Planning (ERP) systems have been proposed to specifically address inter-organizational coordination. These systems, however, are not flexible enough to adapt to rapid changes noted in most VOs. For instance, the goal of an extended ERP is to consolidate business functions throughout different systems of each business partner. The process of customization, implementation, and adoption of such systems is highly time and resource intensive. Once implemented, system change is difficult meaning that the flexibility needed by VOs to disband and reform as current opportunities are met and new ones emerge is difficult to achieve.

The Service Oriented Architecture (SOA) technology along with Business Process Management (BPM) approaches have been identified as a viable solution for integrating inter-organizational information systems in dynamic situations. Studies show that incorporation of SOA-based BPM with enterprise systems enables more standardized and flexible integration and management of different systems (Wang, Chu, & Xu, 2010). BPM provides the standardized business process modeling and management, while SOA enables flexible integration across various system components. Therefore, a dynamic solution suitable for VOs can be created based on an SOA infrastructure using the concept of services as a foundation for building business processes.

This paper introduces a PM framework for VOs that extracts key performance indicators from their SOA-based BPM collaboration infrastructure. The research follows the Design Science Research (DSR) methodology for information systems (March & Storey, 2008; Peffers, Tuunanen, Rothenberger, & Chatterjee, 2008). This approach includes design, creation, and evaluation of IT artifacts intended to solve identified organizational problems. The rest of this paper is organized into 7 sections. Section 2 discusses the literature related to Collaborative Networked Organizations (CNOs), VOs, collaborative performance measurement, and reference frameworks for performance measurement. Section 3 addresses the concept of a Service Oriented Virtual Organization (SOVO) which is partially developed during this research. In Section 4, the proposed framework for collaborative performance measurement in a SOVO is outlined. The implementation architecture that enables aggregation and monitoring of collaborative performance from different sources of information is proposed in Section 5. To validate the proposed framework and architecture, the implementation of a prototype is described in Section 6. This is followed by Section 7 in which analysis of different parameters of the proposed solution against the design requirement specifications is discussed. Finally, conclusions are presented in Section 8.

BACKGROUND

The Characteristics of Virtual Organizations

Small and medium sized enterprises (SMEs) with limited resources and skills need to collaborate with others to overcome their individual limitations. In fact, their capability to form temporary, goal-driven associations enables dynamic adjustment to the needs of the market. Although collaboration through supply chains has a long history in the manufacturing environment, such collaboration assumes relatively stable and well-defined roles, responsibilities and interaction among principals. However, facing further complicated and more dynamic markets, new forms of collaboration over networks of entities have emerged. These new forms, referred to as collaborative networks (CNs) (Camarinha-Matos & Afsarmanesh, 2005), are information-driven instead of data-driven.

A (CN) is a network consisting of a variety of entities (e.g. organizations, people, and machines) that are largely autonomous, geographically distributed, and heterogeneous in terms of their operating environment, culture, social capital and goals, but who collaborate to better achieve common or compatible goals, and whose interactions are supported by computer networks (Camarinha-Matos & Afsarmanesh, 2005). Most forms of CNs feature governance rules and imply the existence of an organizing framework over constituents, their roles, and activities. These CNs are generally called collaborative networked organizations (CNOs) (Camarinha-Matos, 2009).

A specific sub-type of a goal-oriented CNO is a Virtual Organization (VO). A VO is a temporary alliance of enterprises or organizations that come together to share core competencies and resources in order to better respond to temporary business opportunities, and whose cooperation is supported by computer networks (Camarinha-Matos, Afsarmanesh, Galeano, & Molina, 2009).

Various typologies of VOs exist including supply chain, star or peer-to-peer networks (Karvonen, Salkari, & Ollus, 2005). Regardless of the typology, the continual creation and dissolution of VOs is one of the defining features of this organizational form. Although typical organizations spend only a negligible fraction of their lifetime in the creation and dissolution stages, in VOs these two phases are common, complex and take up considerable effort (Camarinha-Matos & Afsarmanesh, 2007). The full cycle of VO formation however, includes creation, operation, evolution, dissolution or metamorphosis (Camarinha-Matos & Afsarmanesh, 2008).

Measuring the Performance of VOs

Two characteristics of a VO create challenges for performance measurement. The first is impermanence of the VO and its typically short life cycle, and the second is inter-organizational issues and complexities (Westphal, Thoben, & Seifert, 2010).

VOs are temporary arrangements, which means they spend only a limited time in the operation and evolution phases. After the opportunity has been exploited, there is no reason to continue the collaboration. The VO therefore begins dissolution. This temporary nature implies that the typical strategic objectives, which are meant to measure long term performance of organizations, would not be necessarily be used to measure overall performance. Therefore, success factors for a short-term alignment should be identified and used as the basis for performance measurement.

In addition, each instance of a VO would have specific performance measures, which are not necessarily the same as the measures of previous VO instances. Despite the fact that each VO could have a unique PM framework, each instance should be comparable in terms of performance to other VOs. This implies the need for some level of standardization of performance measures which can generally be done a high-level such as by considering overall task accomplishment. Yet, even if the measures are defined clearly at this level with some degree of standardization, performance of the VO is context sensitive. That is, as will be explained in more detail later, the high-level performance indicators can only be interpreted by considering the lower level components.

The second characteristic of a VO that complicates PM is inter-organizational relationships and collaborations among partners. Each partner has its own objectives which may not all be necessarily aligned with those of the other partners in the VO. Therefore, any successful PM solution must support alignment of the partners' goals and objectives in a way that satisfies the VO's purposes. In addition, the partners may not feel comfortable sharing their individual performance data with others in the group. This implies that the PM system must support the partners' privacy for data they wish to keep internal to their own companies.

Another issue is related to the point of measurement. Should the measurements be performed only at the interface of different organizations, or also within the companies themselves? This decision will influence the degree to which harmonization of internal business processes of different partners is required. Accordingly, one of the most important questions to consider is the need for specific measures that are not limited to the operations of the VO partners. These measures must assess capability and productivity of the *collaboration*. Therefore, the PM system must provide standardized measures at the level of collaboration, which support sound and easy comparison of the partners' contributions. At the same time, internal measures from each of the partners might contribute to these standardized measures.

SERVICE-ORIENTED VIRTUAL ORGANIZATIONS

To respond to the specific needs of VO performance measurement, the VO performance measurement model is situated within an appropriate technological context. In previous related work (Danesh, Raahemi, & Kamali, 2011; Danesh M. H., Raahemi, Kamali, & Richards, 2013; Kamali, Richards, Danesh, & Raahemi, 2012), the framework and architecture of a Service Oriented Virtual Organization (SOVO) using the concept of service zones was discussed. In a SOVO, different organizations address a business opportunity by composing their services to create a more complex service that provides more value to the customer. To enable collaboration, an SOA-based BPM infrastructure that enables dynamic creation and evolution of virtual organizations was defined (Danesh, Raahemi, & Kamali, 2011; Danesh M. H., Raahemi, Kamali, & Richards, 2013; Kamali, Richards, Danesh, & Raahemi, 2012). Using this technology, SOVO partners can publish their business processes as services without threatening their privacy or comprising aspects that form their own competitive advantage.

Based on this architecture, the performance measurement framework for SOVOs is modeled in three layers that reflect the operations and collaborative strategies of the partners. These layers are the value network, collaborative processes, and partners' services; each is discussed in more detail in the following sections.

When organizations gather together to produce value added services, they typically engineer their processes using functional or process-oriented models. However, this approach is inadequate when alignment with the overall value co-production of the VO is necessary (Shu & Chuang, 2007). Therefore, in this research the concept of value networks is used to model the business value creation mechanism. Business Value Networks "are ways in which organizations interact and share values forming complex chains including multiple providers and administrators to derive increased business value" (Haq & Schikuta, 2010). This helps the VO to identify service participants and their value expectations and value exchange relations.

The E3-Value (Gordijn & Akkermans, 2003) ontology was employed to conceptualize, map, and model the VO's value network layer. This ontology defines partnership linkages in a supply chain that might include for example, business partners (manufacturer, wholesaler, and store) as well as the consumer (Kort & Gordijn, 2007).

One of the characteristics that differentiates VOs from traditional organizations is *collaboration*. Collaboration is defined as "… acting in an incompletely determined and non-hierarchic way to enable joint processes with other independent organizations and human actors that are performed to reach common goals" (Westphal, Thoben, & Seifert, 2010). The collaborative processes in our framework are modeled using the concept of service choreography. The choreography model focuses on partner collaboration and service interactions. It specifies each party's role and activities and the sequences of service invocations. The level of information provided in the choreography model is decided on by the VO management consortium. The service choreography model defines the agreement among the participating business partners (Mohamed, Galal-Edeen, & El-Zoghbi, 2010).

Figure 1 illustrates the three modeling layers of SOVO. Layer 1 defines the value network that is related to the strategic objectives of the alliance. Layer two defines relationships among the partners, while layer 3 defines the specific services delivered by each partner. This modelling paradigm permits identification of the relationships between the three layers as a prerequisite to identifying performance indicators and the mathematical relationships among them. For example, Figure 1, depicts the relation-

Figure 1. Three modeling layers of SOVO

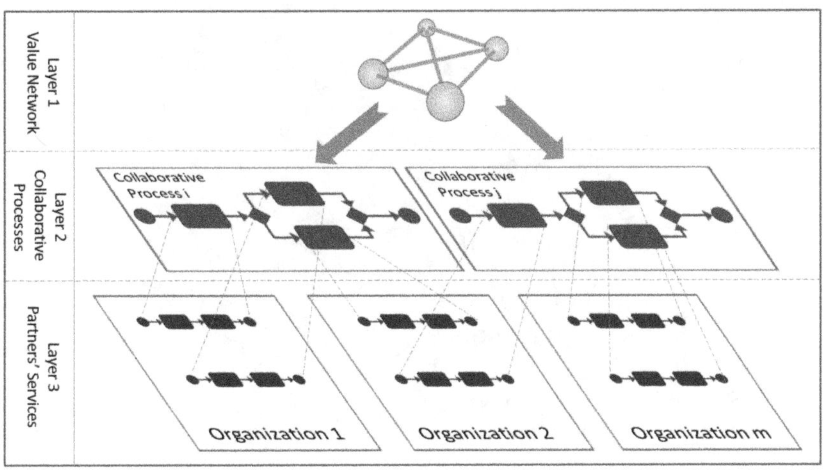

ship between processes in the third layer and sub-processes in the second layer. These sub-processes are services delivered within each of the partners' organization.

As such, each instance of a collaborative process in the second layer calls one or more instances of sub-processes (partners' services). Accordingly, the cardinality between the collaborative process and partner services is one-to-many: one instance of a collaborative process calls many instances of partner services. Therefore, the relationship between the second and the third modeling layers is well-defined, allowing for aggregation of performance indicators between these two layers.

The relationship between the first and the second layers is not easily identifiable as the sequence in which value objects are exchanged is required for developing the service choreography model. As such, a method is proposed in (Kamali, Richards, Danesh, & Raahemi, 2012) to extract the choreography model from the value network.

PROPOSED PERFORMANCE MEASUREMENT FRAMEWORK

In collaborative environments, inter as well as intra-organizational performance indicators must be defined to fully assess performance of the alliance. In other words, from a SOVO partner's point of view, the performance measurement structure must be balanced considering both internal and external factors (Folan & Browne, 2005). To address this requirement, following the model discussed in Figure 1, a a three-layer *structural* framework for performance measurement that includes indicators for the value network, collaboration performance, and service performance is proposed. These performance categories can be interpreted as layers of a SOVO performance pyramid at different levels of strategic importance as depicted in Figure 2.

In the bottom layer (Service Performance), performance data would be used to assess the effectiveness and efficiency of services provided by a specific partner. The specification of each service, their

Figure 2. SOVO performance indicator pyramid

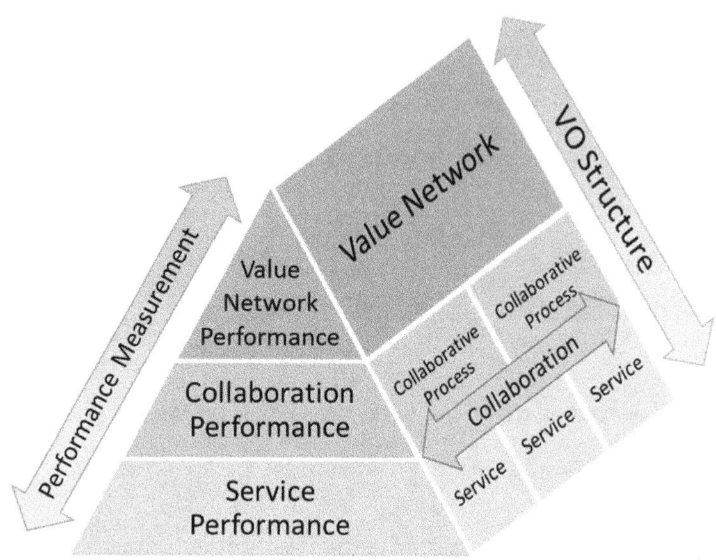

target level and the responsibilities of the service provider must be agreed upon among partners and be documented in the form of a Service Level Agreement (SLA) (Long, 2008).

The Information Technology Infrastructure Library (ITIL) V3 suggests that the following performance indicators be documented in an SLA (Office of Government Commerce, 2007a):

1. **Availability:** The percentage of the times that a service is available to be invoked.
2. **Responsiveness:** The time it takes for response to a service invocation.
3. **Reliability:** Maximum number of service breaks that can be tolerated in a specific period (the definition of what constitutes a 'break' is also included in SLA).

The definition of the indicators "availability" and "responsiveness" is based on the ITIL framework. The definition of "reliability", however, is extended to include all expectations from the service throughput. In fact, the operational parameters of partners are reflected in the services such as quotation service, ordering service, billing service, etc. These parameters include the cost of the products or services, the quantity to be delivered, the quality measures to be satisfied, and the duration of service or product delivery. Therefore, the definition of "reliability" in the lower level is case-specific and must be defined based on the requirements of product or service production and delivery. This extension of the definition of reliability is also suggested by ITIL guidelines to meet the business needs as much as possible.

Layer 2 (Collaboration Performance) involves measuring the performance of the partners' collaboration, an essential factor in managing the VO (Camarinha-Matos, Afsarmanesh, & Ollus, 2008). Meeting the targets of collaboration performance enables merging of SOVO partners' processes to accomplish a common task in a non-hierarchical manner (Graser, Westphal, & Eschenbaecher, 2005). Collaboration performance indicators assess the effectiveness and efficiency of partner collaboration. Accordingly, this layer is critical for coordination across the VO.

The Supply Chain Operation Reference (SCOR) model (Supply Chain Council, 2010), the European Collaborative Networked Organizations Initiative (ECOLEAD) (Camarinha-Matos, Afsarmanesh, & Ollus, 2008, p. 250) and ITIL V3 (Office of Government Commerce, 2007) are used as reference frameworks for this layer. The SCOR model proposes five dimensions to measure the overall performance of supply chains: cost, asset, reliability, responsiveness, and agility. Three of these dimensions (reliability, responsiveness, and agility) are intended to measure collaboration performance. ECOLEAD builds its collaboration performance dimensions based on SCOR and extends it with the two additional dimensions of communication and commitment. Definitions of the above five performance dimensions based on SCOR and ECOLEAD are as follows:

1. **Responsiveness:** The speed at which collaborative tasks are performed such as cycle-time metrics;
2. **Reliability:** The ability to deliver material, information, and services within agreed upon quality, quantity, time and cost;
3. **Communication:** The ability to communicate, which includes the aspect of using ICT as a means of communication;
4. **Flexibility:** The ability to respond to internal or external changes and the ability to adapt to new situation; and
5. **Commitment:** The willingness of partners to predict, prevent, and solve the critical situations.

Level 3 (Value Network Performance), focuses on the effectiveness of management and strategic decision making (Rabelo, Gusmeroli, Arana, & Nagellen, 2006). In typical organizations, this category of performance indicators usually addresses high-level, long-term goals and objectives. However, the VO is a "temporary" network of organizations which collaborate to address a business opportunity, through providing value-added products or services. This layer can be considered as the most strategic level of performance indicators as it has the strongest ties to the SOVO's overall purpose.

The literature provides several different approaches to assessing value networks. The *E3-Value* (Kort & Gordijn, 2007) approach focuses on modeling the interaction of partners, value exchanges, and the feasibility of value networks. Others such as *ValueNet Works* (Allee & Schwabe, 2011), introduce indicators to evaluate the structure and vitality of the value network. The *ValueNet Works* (Allee & Schwabe, 2011) approach was adopted to analyze the efficiency of the SOVO value creation network. This approach is socially-based seeking to identify the role of human perception in assigning value to different objects. It takes intangible (e.g. knowledge, brand) as well as tangible (e.g. money, product, service) values into account. It also tries to describe the relationships between asset utilization and the value creation process. This approach integrates classic network analysis indicators such as social networks and informational networks, with value network specific indicators. The resulting framework includes the following four major categories of indicators:

1. Value Creation
2. Value Flow Optimization
3. Value Network Structure
4. Value Network Vitality

In the SOVO environment, the primary focus is on tangible values that include products, services, money, and information. Therefore, not all the above considerations (e.g. human interactions in social networks) are applicable in the context of SOVO. As such, the recommendations and guidelines of ValueNet research was employed to identify the indicators and to customize them to suit SOVO requirements.

Indicators in the value creation and value flow optimization dimensions are identified to evaluate how *efficiently* the value is created and the degree to which value flow is optimized. These indicators are subject to change during the operation and evolution phase of the VO. However, the frequency of change is less than would be expected in the partner service layer.

The dimensions of value network structure and vitality describe the characteristics of the structure of value network roles, value objects, and value transactions. These indicators are used in the creation and evolution phase of the VO to evaluate the *effectiveness* of the structure of the B2B alignment, and the importance of each object in the value network to the success of the VO.

The performance data are useful to the degree that they provide information linked to specific targets. In this case, the framework uses a multi-level Service Level Agreement (SLA) structure that captures expectations among partners covering all three layers of the SOVO framework (service, collaboration and value).

PROPOSED SOVO PM IMPLEMENTATION MODEL

Architecture

The architecture must enable gathering of performance data from different data sources throughout the partners' infrastructure, re-structuring the metadata, integrating the performance data, publishing the resulting information, and enabling collaborative performance monitoring. We describe this architecture in three layers: SOA based BPM, local performance monitoring, and global performance monitoring.

The following products are used to implement this architecture:

1. IBM WebSphere Service Registry and Repository (WSRR)
2. IBM WebSphere Enterprise Service Bus
3. IBM Service Federation Management Feature Pack (SFM)
4. IBM WebSphere Application Server (WAS)
5. IBM Business Process Manager (BPM) Advance
6. IBM Business Monitor
7. IBM Cognos BI
8. IBM Cognos Framework Manager (FM)
9. IBM Cognos Transformer
10. IBM Cognos Report Studio

Figure 3 provides an overview of the implementation architecture which is discussed in more detail in the sections that follow.

Figure 3. SOVO PM implementation architecture

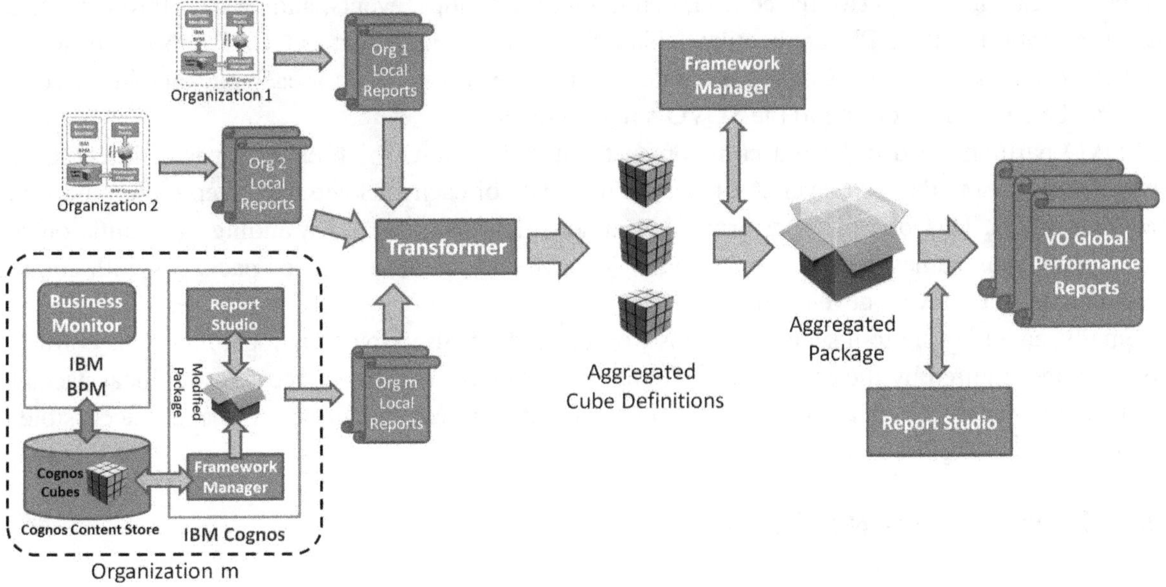

An SOA-based Business Process Management (BPM) system is the operational system for the SOVO partners through which they can perform the assigned tasks. Partners have the flexibility to perform their tasks using their own infrastructure, but they are still required to publish the applications as web services to facilitate integration of their services within the SOVO environment.

The collaborative processes created in BPM are published as applications on Websphere Application Server (WAS). This layer of the architecture facilitates integration of business process management systems of the partners through mediation, federation, and integration of the partners' services. As such, each partner publishes its services on the web service registry and repository (WSRR). Mediation of the services to the appropriate partner is done through the federated Enterprise Service Bus (ESB). This component facilitates integration of new composite SOA and BPM applications. It provides capabilities such as complex integration logic and adapters needed for composing and mediating services. Services published by each partner need to be accessible by specific partners, according to the topology of the SOVO. Service Federation Manager (SFM) is a feature pack added to WSRR that supports sharing information and services between service domains and handles the connectivity setup required to make services useable between domains. Although SFM is a feature pack installed on WSRR, it needs ESB installed to have proper functionality.

This layer supports dynamic creation and operation of a SOVO. The detailed specifications of this layer and the way to configure it is discussed thoroughly in prior work (Danesh M., 2012).

Local Performance Monitoring

The role of this layer is to monitor the performance of services and collaborative processes hosted by each partner. This job is performed by IBM Business Monitor, which is a feature pack installed on IBM BPM. This component facilitates definition of the monitor model and structure of the OLAP cube, including performance dimensions, measures, performance indicators, and query subjects. The IBM Business Monitor model is created for each collaborative process and is published on the WAS. This component captures the performance data, including time stamps, events, and process throughput, during the operation of the BPM application. This information is published as OLAP cubes and stored as Cognos Packages in the IBM Cognos BI content store. The access level for each package in the content store can be defined according to the SOVO's requirements.

SOVO partners need to have a common metadata definition which enables easier integration of performance data in the next layer. As such, the metadata of each package may need to be modified to match the others. This job can be performed in Framework Manager (FM) by adding a presentation layer with agreed-upon namespaces to the package. Consequently, a set of Cognos packages with common meta-data definition were developed.

Finally, an authoring tool such as Cognos Report Studio is used to create local reports according to the structure required by the SOVO. The Cognos reports have real-time access to the local packages. The level of access to each report in the Cognos content store can be defined to make it accessible for external modeling tools.

Global Performance Monitoring

The role of this layer is to aggregate the local performance indicators and provide global integrated reports. Definition of the aggregated KPIs is provided in the SOVO PM Structural Framework, which includes aggregation per collaborative process and per partner. To perform the data integration, a standalone installation of a Cognos Server and its tools including Transformer and FM is required. This installation can be done on a virtual machine hosted by any of the partner organizations.

The local reports of the partners are made accessible to the modeling tools in this layer, therefore they are accessed by an instance of IBM Cognos Transformer to define aggregated cubes. The structure of these cubes supports aggregation of the performance indicators according to the structural framework. The cubes created in Transformer are published as an IBM Cognos package in the content store. This package can be further modified for representation purposes by FM. This modification includes defining new query subjects and performance indicators based on the measures included in the package.

The global reports then are designed based on the modified package using an authoring tool. Report Studio is used in our prototype to create the final reports. Access level to these reports for each partner is set according to their SLA view specification (discussed in the SOVO PM Structural Framework). A series of OLAP cube design specifications were created to ensure that the correct data would be captured and displayed through the system.

PROTOTYPING

A scenario was created to design and implement a working prototype of the proposed framework. In this scenario, there are two organizations: a wireless service provider and a cell phone provider. They want to bundle their services to provide a value-added service package to the customer that includes a cell phone with activated wireless service. Through this collaboration, they can provide a more cost-efficient product/service that saves clients' time while making the process of purchase and activation more convenient for them. They provide the service bundle with a new brand that will be referred to as "VOWireless".

The client submits a request for quotation with the specification of the cell phone and the wireless service. Each of the two partners receives the related information, processes the request, and provides an aggregated quotation to the client. Then the client submits an order based on the received quotation. The cell phone provider initiates the shipment of the cell phone with a SIM card and instructions to the customer. The wireless service provider must activate the service upon delivery of the cell phone so that when the client receives the order, the phone is ready to use.

Modelling

The value network of the collaboration between wireless service provider and cell phone provider has been mapped using the E3-Value ontology. The value objects are any objects of economic value exchanged between the roles of the value network. These value objects can be of any type: product, service, money, and information. The model is shown in Figure 4. The overall process included definition of the value network, the relationships between and among the partners, and the multi-level SLAs for each layer in the model as discussed in more detail below.

Transformation of the value network model to operational business processes is performed by using the method discussed in Danesh (2012). The resulting choreography model is shown in Figure 5.

After identifying the value network, choreography model, and business processes, the multi-level SLA structure of the VOWireless is defined according to the guidelines of ITIL V3.

Figure 4. VOW ireless E3-value model

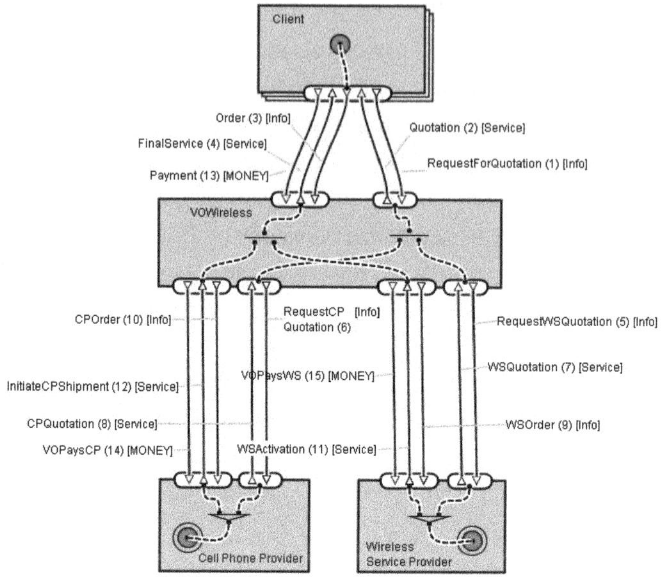

Figure 5. VOWireless service choreography model

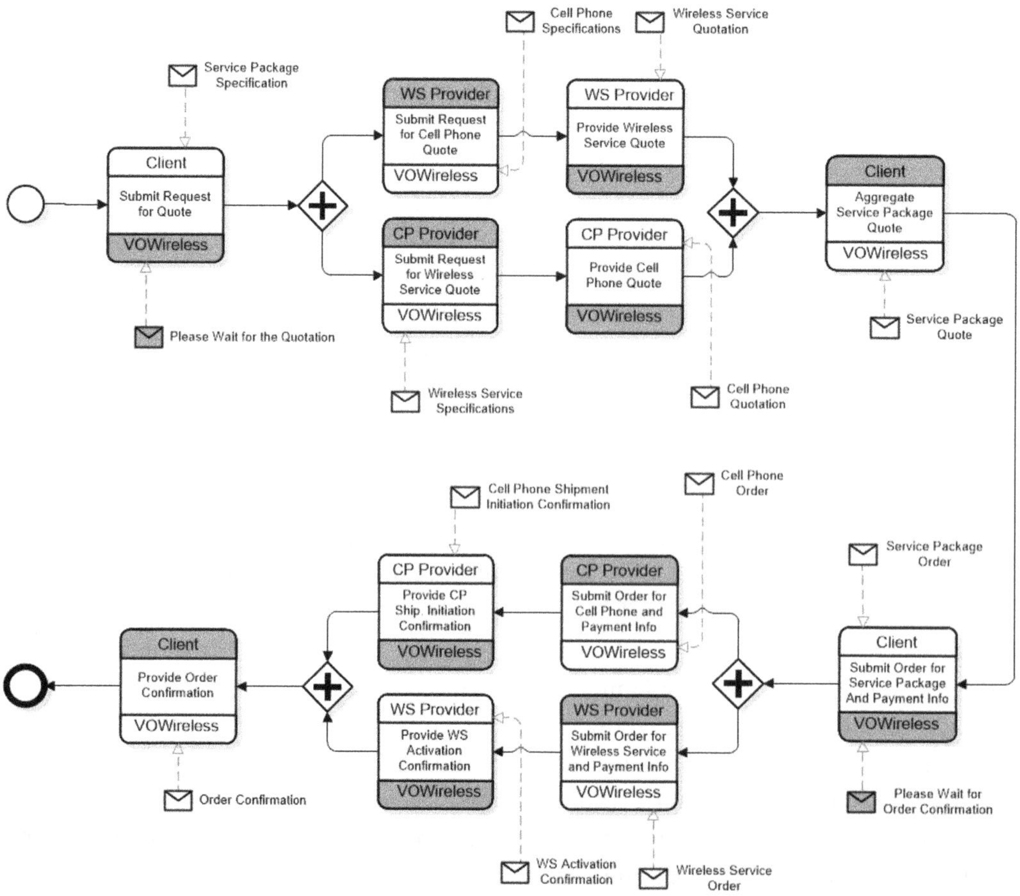

The terms of the SLAs must be negotiated and documented accordingly. The terms for each SLA shown in Figure 6 have been identified using the SOVO PM Structural Framework. The SLAs in the figure document the terms of the services as follows:

- **SLA1-1:** The quotation service provided by WS Provider.
- **SLA1-2:** The order fulfillment service provided by WS Provider.
- **SLA2-1:** The quotation service provided by CP Provider.
- **SLA2-2:** The order fulfillment service provided by CP Provider.
- **CP1-SLA:** The aggregated quotation service provided by collaborative process 1.
- **CP2-SLA:** The aggregated order fulfillment service provided by collaborative process 2.
- **Client-SLA:** The final service provided by VOWireless to the Client.

IBM's BPM process designer was used to implement the collaborative processes. Integration of the collaborative processes with the underlying services of the partners is done in BPM Integration designer. As such, the services of the partners are published as web services. The VOWireless Collaborative Process has access to the WSDL interfaces and imports them into BPM Integration Designer.

After implementing and integrating the collaborative process and the underlying services, monitor models are generated using IBM Business Monitor. These models include the definition of the dimensions, sub-dimensions, measures, events, and performance indicators associated with each process. The monitor model must be published as an application on the IBM Web Application Server. This application listens to the events inside each process application and captures the information defined in the monitor model project.

The performance indicator model is used to define and formulate the indicators and set the control limits for each. The structure of the cube including dimensions, sub-dimensions, and measures are designed and modified in the dimensional model. After publishing the monitor model, IBM Cognos cubes

Figure 6. SLA Aggregation for VOWi reless

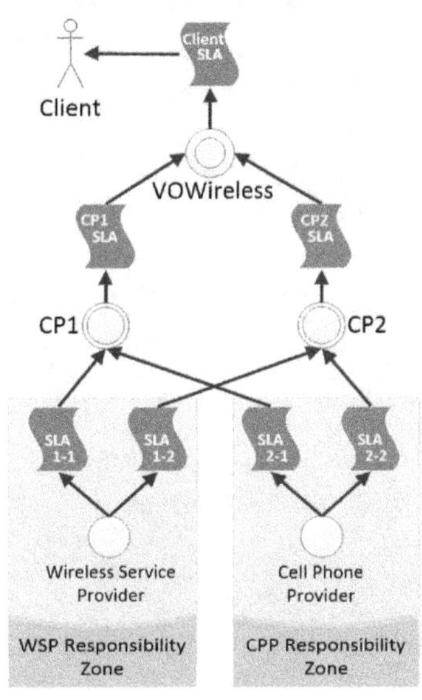

are generated automatically and published as Packages in the IBM Cognos content store (in this case implemented using the DB2 Express database).

The metadata of the stored packages can then be modified, if needed, to follow common namespaces in the VO. This is required to enable integration of performance information. In this example the modification is implemented using FM. To do so, a presentation model (also called presentation layer) is created from the original model (called native layer) of the package (Figure 7).

The aggregated IBM Cognos Cubes are designed and published as packages using Transformer, according to the SOVO PM Structural Framework. Figure 8 shows the cube definition in the Transformer environment.

This cube is repopulated and republished at the frequency with which the local reports are generated. This frequency depends on the requirement of the SOVO partners and available resources. In this case, the refresh frequency was set to thirty minutes. As such, the partners could republish the local reports to the common directory with the same frequency. This frequency can be reduced by using more computing resources.

Various authoring tools can be used to create reports, charts, and dashboards based on the published IBM Cognos package. IBM Cognos Report Studio was used to design reports with drill down/up capability. Figure 9 shows drilling down on a sample chart to show the service availability performance indicator.

ANALYSIS OF THE PROPOSED SOLUTION

The proposed framework and implementation architecture is evaluated based on the implemented prototype according to the criteria defined in Table 1. The overall concept shown on the left side of this table is inter-organizational performance management. The next column depicts three key operational

Figure 7. Adding the Presentation Model to the Package in Framework Manager

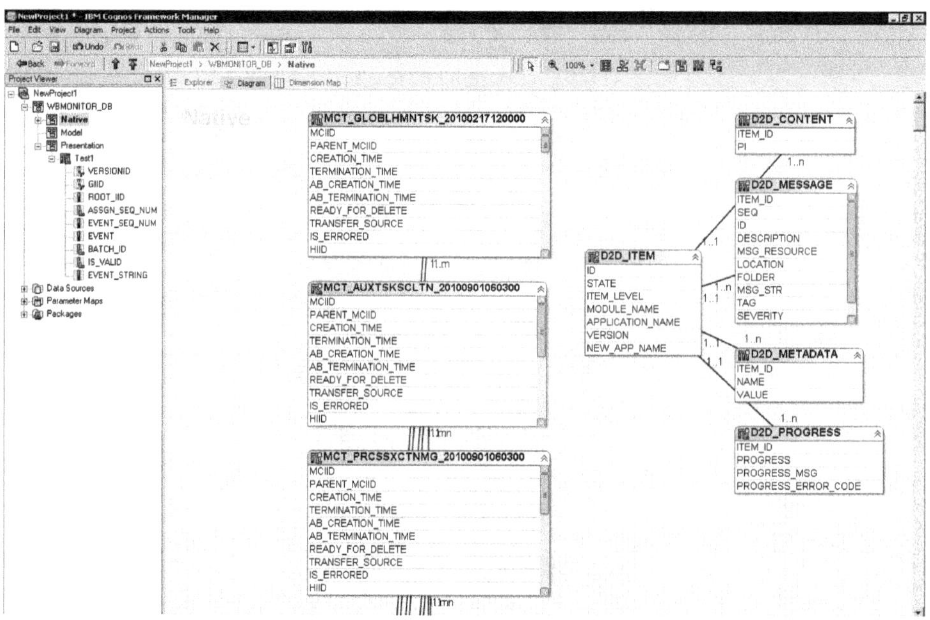

Figure 8. Cube definition in IBM Cognos Transformer

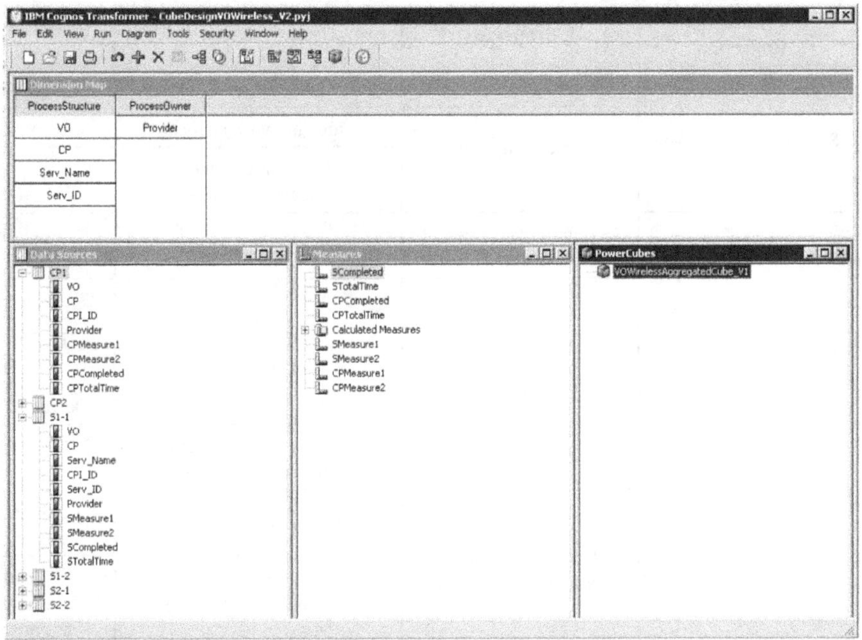

Figure 9. Drill-down through structural dimensions for service availability chart

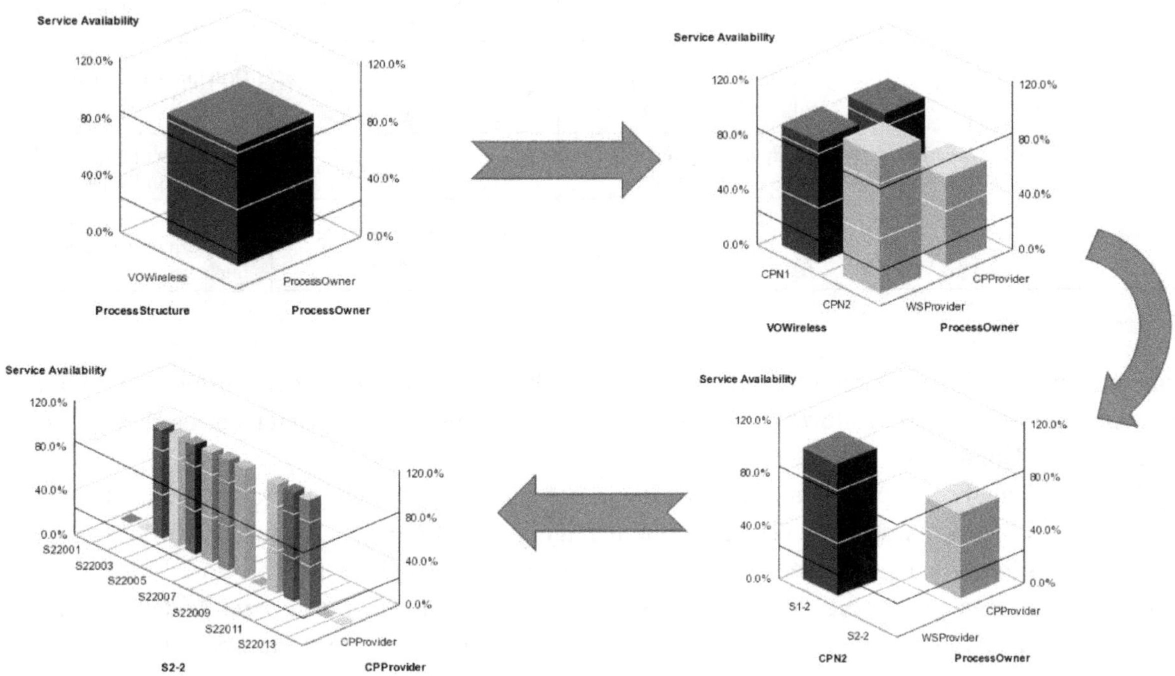

Table 1. SOVO PM framework success criteria

1. Concepts	2. Operational Concepts	3. Properties	4. Criteria	5. Proposed Mechanism/ Solution
Inter-Organizational Performance Measurement	Strategic coordination	Goal consistency	Value proposition alignment	E3-Value model
		Strategic alignment efficiency	Value network analysis	VNA indicators
			Customer centric measurement	Multi-layer SLA structure
	Collaboration	Common measurement logics	Common KPI formulation	Providing definition of collaboration KPIs
		Joint Processes	Process inter-operability	Define availability indicators
				Define responsiveness indicators
				Define reliability indicators
			Interdependencies among partners' services	BPMN service choreography model
		Decentralized PM (Partners' Autonomy)	Distributed measurement	Integrate global and local performance measurement
			Distributed monitoring	Providing dashboard capabilities over the aggregated OLAP cube
		Mutual trust	Providing transparency at an agreed- upon level	Defining SLA view zones
		Commitment	Support both pro-active and re-active aspects	Define proactive and reactive commitment indicators
		Flexibility	Evaluate effort needed for change	Define flexibility indicators
	Performance Improvement	Integrity of performance structure	Traceability of root causes of unsatisfactory performance levels	Drill through the multi-layer SLA structure
		Supporting improvement action plans	Identify authority of change	Definition of responsibility zones of the partners
		Providing Agile improvement	Real-time performance monitoring	Inter-organizational performance monitoring implementation architecture

concepts that need to be monitored and evaluated. Column 3 identifies specific properties related to these operational concepts followed by the assessment criteria in Column 4 and features of the proposed framework in Column 5.

The operational concept of strategic coordination of partners in CNOs generally and in VOs specifically is one of the most important challenges in managing such alliances. The proposed PM framework addresses this important issue through coordination of partners' value creation network. The framework illustrates the common goal, i.e. providing value-added services to the customer while defining the collaboration and service agreements along with delivery of data to evaluate overall performance.

The VO cannot operate well without well-defined and executed collaboration processes. The proposed framework provides several features to enhance collaboration. The challenge of different measurement frameworks used by partners is addressed by the definition of common performance indicators to measure partnership effectiveness and efficiency. The proposed framework also addresses interdependencies among partners' services by mapping collaboration performance linked to service performance. As discussed earlier, despite the need for common indicators, these alliances also need the capability for decentralized performance measurement and monitoring. This has been answered by integration of local performance information into the aggregated OLAP cube and by providing monitoring capabilities over the aggregated cube.

Mutual trust between partners is enabled by providing transparency of the SLAs in place. Trust builds when partners do what they say they are going to do. The use of the performance framework provides visibility into the agreements in place and the results achieved from service delivery therefore providing a touchstone for trust and continued collaboration. The dynamic nature and rapid changes of VO alliances can be handled by referring to the related layer of the performance structure. The degree to which the VO enables flexibility can also be evaluated by defining a series of flexibility indicators.

Finally, the ultimate goal of a PM solution is to drive performance improvements in the VO in a distributed manner. This implies traceability of the unsatisfactory levels of SLA terms, which is enabled by using the drill-down capability over the range of SLA aggregation patterns. Improvement action plans are supported by the identification of responsible parties through the creation of responsibility zones for each partner. Finally, the agility of performance improvement can be guaranteed by real-time monitoring.

CONCLUSION

To keep pace with the growth of the global economy and increasingly competitive markets, organizations, especially SMEs, tend to form strategic alliances to deliver value to their customers more effectively and efficiently. These alliances, when formed with the main purpose of temporary collaborative value creation, have evolved into Virtual Organizations (VO).

Current studies on virtual organizations do not provide concrete definitions for performance indicators nor do they provide an architecture that can deal with the temporary and dynamic nature of the alliance. The framework proposed is derived from basic definitions of performance indicators and best practices in the literature (such as E3-Value, ValueNet, SCOR, ECOLEAD, and ITIL) but customized to meet the specific requirements of VOs. This approach provides a set of consistent indicators in the three layers of value network, collaborative processes, and services.

From an implementation point of view, the proposed architecture was tested through development of a scenario that required collaborative performance measurement and monitoring. The proposed architecture integrates performance information from different data sources into aggregated OLAP cubes. Cube dimensions and measures were designed considering the structure of the collaborative processes and services of the VO to support aggregation of information based on this structure.

Ultimately, VOs that can monitor, measure and adapt at all three levels of the value network should be able to perform better. More importantly, for those companies considering formation of a VO or of multiple VOs, the existence of a standardized framework for assessing performance should provide more confidence that the partners can manage the alliance effectively.

ACKNOWLEDGMENT

This project was jointly funded by the MITACS Accelerate program and the IBM Center for Business Analytics and Performance (CBAP) at the University of Ottawa.

REFERENCES

Allee, V., & Schwabe, O. (2011). *Value Networks and the true nature of collaboration*. ValueNet Works and Verna Allee Associates.

Camarinha-Matos, L. M. (2009). Collaborative networked organizations: Status and trends in manufacturing. *Annual Reviews in Control*, *33*(3), 199–208. doi:10.1016/j.arcontrol.2009.05.006

Camarinha-Matos, L. M., & Afsarmanesh, H. (2005). Collaborative networks: A new scientific discipline. In *Collaborative Networks and their Breeding Environments* (pp. 193–204). New York: Springer-Verlag. doi:10.1007/0-387-29360-4

Camarinha-Matos, L. M., & Afsarmanesh, H. (2005). Collaborative networks: A new scientific discipline. *Journal of Intelligent Manufacturing*, 4–5.

Camarinha-Matos, L. M., & Afsarmanesh, H. (2007). A comprehensive modeling framework for collaborative networked organizations. *Journal of Intelligent Manufacturing*, *18*(5), 529–542. doi:10.100710845-007-0063-3

Camarinha-Matos, L. M., & Afsarmanesh, H. (2008). On reference models for collaborative networked organizations. *International Journal of Production Research*, *46*(9), 2453–2469. doi:10.1080/00207540701737666

Camarinha-Matos, L. M., Afsarmanesh, H., Galeano, N., & Molina, A. (2009). Collaborative networked organizations - Concepts and practice in manufacturing enterprises. *Computers & Industrial Engineering*, *57*(1), 46–60. doi:10.1016/j.cie.2008.11.024

Camarinha-Matos, L. M., Afsarmanesh, H., & Ollus, M. (2005). *Virtual Organizations: Systems and Practices*. New York: Springer. doi:10.1007/b102339

Camarinha-Matos, L. M., Afsarmanesh, H., & Ollus, M. (2008). *Methods and Tools for Collaborative Networked Organizations*. New York: Springer. doi:10.1007/978-0-387-79424-2

Danesh, M. (2012). Design and implementation of a framework for process management in service oriented organizations using service zones. Ottawa: Academic Press.

Danesh, M. H., Raahemi, B., & Kamali, M. A. (2011). A frameweork for process management in service oriented virtual organizations. *7th International Conference on Next Generation Web Services Practices*, 12-17.

Danesh, M. H., Raahemi, B., Kamali, S. M., & Richards, G. (2013). A framework for process and performance management in service oriented virtual organizations. *IJCISIM*, 203-215.

Feo, J. D., & Barnard, W. (2003). *Juran Institute Six Sigma Breakthrough and Beyond: Quality Performance and Breakthrough Methods*. McGraw-Hill Professional.

Fiammante, M. (2009). *Dynamic SOA and BPM: Best Practices for Business Process Management and SOA Agility*. IBM Press.

Folan, P., & Browne, J. (2005). A review of performance measurement: Towards performance management. *Computers in Industry*, *56*(7), 663–680. doi:10.1016/j.compind.2005.03.001

Franco-Santos, M., Kennerley, M., Micheli, P., Martinez, V., Mason, S., Marr, B., ... Neely, A. (2007). Towards a definition of a business measurement system. *International Journal of Operations & Production Management*, *27*(8), 784–801. doi:10.1108/01443570710763778

Gordijn, J., & Akkermans, J. M. (2003). Value-based requirements engineering: Exploring innovative e-commerce ideas. *Requirements Engineering*, 114–134.

Graser, F., Jansson, K., Eschenbacher, J., Westphal, I., & Negretto, U. (2005). Towards Performance Measurement in Virtual Organizations. In *Collaborative Networks and Their Breeding Environments* (pp. 301–310). New York: Springer-Verlag. doi:10.1007/0-387-29360-4_31

Graser, F., Westphal, I., & Eschenbaecher, J. (2005). *Roadmap on VOPM challenges on operational and strategic level*. ECOLEAD.

Haq, I., & Schikuta, E. (2010). Aggregation patterns of service level agreements. *8th International Conference on Frontiers of Information Technology*, 1-40.

Kamali, S. M., Richards, G., Danesh, M. H., & Raahemi, B. (2012). A framework for performance measurement in service oriented virtual organizations: A value network approach to collaborative performance measurement. SciTePress.

Karvonen, I., Salkari, I., & Ollus, M. (2005). *Collaborative Networks and their Breeding Environments*. New York: Springer-Verlag. doi:10.1007/0-387-29360-4_20

Kort, C., & Gordijn, J. (2007). *Handbook of Ontologies for Business Interaction*. IGI Global.

Long, J. (2008). *ITIL Version 3 at a Glance*. New York: Springer.

March, S. T., & Storey, V. C. (2008). Design science in the information systems discipline: An introduction to the special issue on design science research. *Management Information Systems Quarterly*, *32*(4), 725–730. doi:10.2307/25148869

Mohamed, U. A., Galal-Edeen, G. H., & El-Zoghbi, A. A. (2010). Building integrated oil and gas B2B e-commerce hub architecture based on SOA. *International Conference on e-Education, e-Business, e-Management, and e-Learning*, 599-608. 10.1109/IC4E.2010.138

Office of Government Commerce. (2007). *Service Design*. London: UK Government, Cabinet Office.

Office of Government Commerce. (2007a). *Continual Service Improvement*. London: Cabinet Office, UK Government.

Peffers, K., Tuunanen, T., Rothenberger, M., & Chatterjee, S. (2008). A Design Science Research Methodology for Information Systems Researc. *Journal of Management Information Systems*, 45–77.

Rabelo, R. J., Gusmeroli, S., Arana, C., & Nagellen, T. (2006). The Ecolead ICT infrastructure for collaborative networked organizations. In *Network-Centric Collaboration and Supporting Frameworks* (pp. 451–460). Boston: Springer. doi:10.1007/978-0-387-38269-2_47

Shu, W., & Chuang, M. Y. (2007). Service Innovation in the Context of Business Web: Enterprise Web Resource Planning as a Strategic Tool for Inreasing Service Value. *Service Science*, 45–77.

Supply Chain Council. (2010). *Supply Chain Operations Reference model overview: Version 10.* Author.

Wang, Z., Chu, D., & Xu, X. (2010). Value network based service choreography design and evolution. In *E-Business Engineering, IEEE International Conference*, (pp. 495-500). Los Alamitos, CA: IEEE.

Westphal, I., Thoben, K. D., & Seifert, M. (2007). Measuring Collaboration Performance. In *Virtual Organizations: Establishing The Foundation Of Collaborative Networks* (Vol. 243, pp. 33–42). Boston: Springer. doi:10.1007/978-0-387-73798-0_4

Westphal, I., Thoben, K. D., & Seifert, M. (2010). Managing collaboration performance to govern virtual organizations. *Journal of Intelligent Manufacturing*, *21*(3), 311–320. doi:10.100710845-008-0182-5

Chapter 2
The Rise of Embedded Analytics:
Empowering Manufacturing and Service Industry With Big Data

Mohsen Attaran
California State University – Bakersfield, USA

Sharmin Attaran
Bryant University, USA

ABSTRACT

The internet revolution, cloud computing, and the evolution to self-service analytics have all contributed to the changing dimensions of business intelligence. To compete effectively in a digitally driven world, business leaders must understand and address the critical shifts taking place in the field of analytics, and how these shifts impact their overall strategy. The key objective of this chapter is to propose a conceptual model for successful implementation of embedded analytics in organizations. This chapter also covers some of the potential benefits of analytics, explores the changing dimensions of analytics, and provides a guide to some of the opportunities that are available for using embedded analytics in business. Furthermore, this study reviews key attributes of a successful modern analytics platform and illustrates how to overcome some of the key challenges of incorporating embedded analytics into an analytic strategy in business. Finally, this study highlights successful implementation of analytics solutions in manufacturing and service industry.

INTRODUCTION

The past few years have seen an explosion in business use of analytics. Corporations around the world are using analytical tools, including business intelligence (BI), dashboards and data mining, to gain a better understanding of their present customers and to predict who will potentially become customers. It was predicted that 2017 would mark the rapid proliferation of enterprises using business intelligence

DOI: 10.4018/978-1-5225-5718-0.ch002

and analytics to predict the future with an acceptable level of reliability (IDC, 2017). With the help of new analytics tools that leverage analytics for specific purposes enterprises can leverage analytics to drive a host of business objectives, from better decision making to streamlined operations, to improved customer relations. In fact, Big Data analytics will transform virtually every business activity, and bring businesses benefits including enhanced customer service, optimized production levels, superior capacity planning, reduced repair and maintenance costs, and improved working capital utilization. Several research studies have documented the advantages and widespread applications of analytics tools in corporations around the world (Evelson and Bennett, 2015; Gaitho, 2017; Lebied, 2016; Eckerson, 2016; Henke, at al., 2016; Minelli, et al., 2013).

According to a 2016 Forester study of 116 professionals with knowledge of business intelligence in their organizations, 35 percent of correspondents enjoyed an ROI of 25-100 percent on their analytics investment whereas 13 percent enjoyed and ROI of 100-300 percent. According to the same research study, 19 percent of respondents had the estimated payback time period on their analytics investment of less than a year, 32 percent had payback period of 1-3years, and 15 percent realized a payback period of 3 or more years. Professionals who participated in the study identified resource utilization to increase yield, IT cost savings/avoidance, risk avoidance, and human resource utilization as typical cost savings/cost avoidance of implementing analytics in their organizations. The top three tangible analytics benefits were identified as: increased margin, profitability, and increased gross sales (Evelson and Bennett, 2015).

In a similar study, McKinsey investigated the returns on Big Data and analytics investments for a random sample of 714 companies around the world. The results indicated that these companies gained competitive intelligence on future market conditions, targeted customers more successfully, and optimized operations and supply chains. Data-analytics investments significantly increased value-added or operating profits in the 6 percent range. Another important finding of this study is that putting analytics tools in the hands of as many different kinds of frontline employees as possible (democratizing usage) will yield broad performance improvements (Bughin, 2016).

Traditional business analysis is undergoing major changes. We are evolving from static and passive reports of what happened to proactive analytics with real-time dashboards to see what is happening every second. The factors that have contributed to underlying shifts include large volumes of data, the Internet, the evolution to the Cloud, and the changing demands of customers. The Internet revolution has created an environment where consumers want even more information and have greater expectations. Management wants fast answers, and analysts expect the data now, without latency. A new genre in BI tools has emerged. Modern BI tools offer data exploration and rapid prototyping. These new tools empower users to choose when, where, and how they interact with an organization.

According to Gartner (2018), "Embedded analytics is the use of analytic and reporting capabilities in transactional business applications." Although most organizations already empower their employees with analytics tools to access data and improve decision making, many are now embedding analytics into their core business applications. The objective is twofold; first, to broaden their reach and second, to improve the timeliness of insights. Embedded analytics is not a new concept. However, the technology for the integration of reports, charts, dashboards, and self-service tools has evolved rapidly over the past 30 years.

Although the current users of embedded analytics are primarily large corporations, there are numerous additional industries and organizations where embedded analytics tools could advantageously assist decision makers. Therefore, it is important to explore the opportunities and challenges of implementing big analytics and embedded analytics into the core business applications of organizations and present the findings for enterprise leaders, administrators, managers, and policymakers to consider. Additionally, a conceptual implementation model is presented to help business leaders justify their analytics expenditures, create value tied directly to data visibility, and rip the benefits of analytics process.

BIG DATA EXPLOSION IN THE ANALYTIC LANDSCAPE

The Rise of Big Data

Data is growing faster than ever before and is everywhere – documents, Internet, social networks, appliances, devices, sensors, etc. In 1986, just three Exabyte (1 Exabyte = 10^{18} bytes) of data existed. Fast forward twenty-five years later to 2011, and that figure was up to more than 300 Exabytes. More than 1200 Exabytes of new data is brought about each year from a variety of sources including social media, mobile devices, and the Internet of Things (IOT). Eighty percent of this data is unstructured and is hard to store, process and analyze with commonly used tools (Feki, et al, 2016). According to an estimate, the U.S. has more than 2,000 Exabytes of data and that volume is projected to double every three years (Getz and Reinsel, 2013). According to Gartner Research, data volume will grow 800 percent over the next 5 years. Several trends have contributed to this data explosion. Each of these activities, listed below, leaves a rich data trail at every turn (Marr, 2015; Perrin, 2015):

- A massive growth in video and photo data, 20 hours of video uploaded to YouTube every minute, and 50 million tweets per day.
- A staggering usage of smart phones, all packed with sensors capable of collecting all kinds of data.
- 42 percent of Americans use the Internet several times a day.
- 2.9 million emails are sent every second.
- There are 50 billion smart connected devices in the world.
- Facebook ingests 500 terabytes of new data every day - Social interactions and feeds - a staggering number of messages, updates, and images posted to social networks –SMS, MMS, speech-to-text.
- Business data feeds- widespread usage of CRM, ERP, and product/service logs.
- A massive growth in Spatial and GPS coordinates data.
- Stock ticker data and financial transactions.

A recent article by McAfee and Brynjolfsson published in Harvard Business review claimed that growing numbers of companies are collecting data from their customers. Wal-Mart collects more than 2.5 quadrillion bytes of data every hour from customer transactions. As of 2012, about 2.5 billion gigabytes of data are created each day, and that number is doubling every 40 months. This trend will continue in the future. By the year 2020, about 1.7 megabytes of new information will be created every second for every human being on the planet. By then, our accumulated universe of data will reach 44 trillion gigabytes (McAfee and Brynjolfsson, 2012).

Big Data Defined

The act of gathering and storing large amounts of information for eventual analysis is not new. The term "Big Data" was coined by John Mashey of Silicon Graphics Inc. in mid 1990s. The first significant academic reference is arguably Weiss and Indurkhya (1998). The concept gained momentum in the early 2000s when Doug Laney at Gartner enriched the concept significantly and articulated the definition of Big Data as the "three V's." (Diebold, 2012). According to Gartner, Big Data is comprised of high Volume, high Velocity, and high Variety data.

Big Data is defined as data that is too large, complex, and dynamic, and exceeds the processing capacity of conventional database architectures of an organization. More specifically, the data is too big and cannot be handled easily, it moves with excessive speed flowing in and out, making

it difficult to analyze. Finally, the range and type of data sources are too great to assimilate (Figure 1). Data draws from multiple sources and transactions and contains valuable patterns and information that could be from people-to-people, people-to-machine, and machine-to-machine interactions. Typically, organizations cannot manage the data effectively with current database architectures, rather they should choose an alternative way to process Big Data to gain value from it. A well-defined data management strategy is essential to successfully utilize Big Data in corporations around the world.

Big Data and Analytics

The right use of Big Data can enable analysts to find trends and give big insights that help create value and drive operational efficiencies for the enterprise. Big Data can bring important benefits to organizations such as: enabling new products and services, helping to better meet customer demands, and facilitating growth and analytics use. Insights hidden previously by data too costly to process can help in the creation of new products and in the discovery of ways to gain competitive advantage. Similarly,

Figure 1. 3 V's of big data

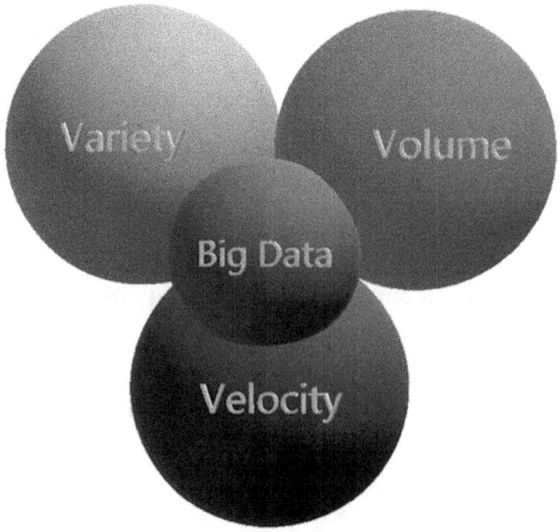

the ability to process every item of data in reasonable time and successfully exploiting the value in Big Data removes the troublesome need for sampling and promotes an investigative approach to data.

By using the right analytics, Big Data can deliver richer insights and uncover hidden patterns and relationships. More data could translate into more possibilities for a business only if it can discover the meaning inside of it. In today's fast-paced business world, monthly reports and specialized research tools simply aren't good enough. One needs technology that helps people transform data into actionable insights, giving everyone in the organization the power to find answers quickly and making decisions when they matter most.

THE CHANGING DIMENSIONS AND EVOLUTION OF ANALYTICS

The Rise of Business Analytics

Analytics is "the science of analysis." A practical definition of analytics is how a business arrives at an optimal or realistic decision based on existing data. The Institute for Operations Research and the Management Sciences defines analytics as "a set of technologies, processes, and techniques that use data to understand and analyze business performance and guide decision making." (Koushik, 2011). Analytics have been used in business since the era of Scientific Management that was initiated by Frederick Taylor in the late 19th century. For example, Henry Ford measured pacing of the assembly line, thus revolutionizing manufacturing. Today, businesses of all sizes use analytics (Strickland, 2015).

Thomas Davenport identified three eras in the use of analytics—Analytics 1.0, 2.0 and 3.0. They are also referred to as before big data and after big data. These eras are described below and summarized in Figure 2 based on writings of Davenport and Phillips (Davenport, 2013; Phillips, 2014):

1. Analytics 1.0—the Era of "Business Intelligence" (1950s to mid-2000s)- In the mid-1950s, descriptive analytics and reporting activity were used for internal data analysis. The purpose was for internal decision support and to gain an objective, deep understanding of important business phenomena. Spreadsheets and other tools were used that could produce and capture a larger quantity of information and discern patterns in it far more quickly than the human mind ever could.

Data sources were relatively small and structured, and mostly from internal systems. Data about production processes, sales, customer interactions and more were recorded, aggregated, and analyzed. Analysts spent a good deal of their time on data preparation and relatively little time on the analysis itself. Analytics picked up in the late 1960s when computers were used in decision support systems. Since then, analytics have evolved with the development of a wide variety of hardware and software tools and applications. Information systems were at first custom-built by large companies and later were commercialized by several vendors in generic forms. This era is characterized by the enterprise data warehouse, used to capture information, and of business intelligence software, used to query and report it (Philips, 2014).

2. Analytics 2.0—the Era of "Big Data" (mid 2000s to 2015) – Big Data gained momentum in the mid-2000s when internet-based companies such as Google and eBay began to collect and analyze new kinds of information, captured from their social networks. Big data was externally sourced,

Figure 2. The evolution of business analytics

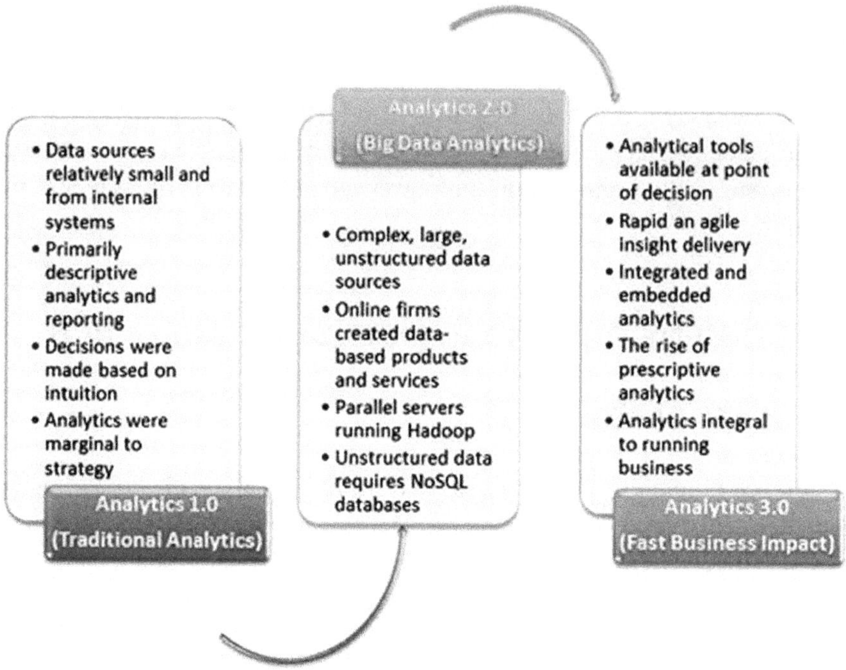

coming from the internet, sensors of various types, and audio and video recordings. Big Data necessitated rapid storage and processing and was the only focus of analytics. Big Data brought important benefits to organizations, such as enabling new products and services, helping to better meet customer demands, and facilitating growth and analytics use. Companies rushed to build new capabilities and powerful new analytics to harness the information embedded in the Big Data. The right use of Big Data enabled analysts to find trends and give big insights that help create value and drive operational efficiencies for the enterprise. Insights hidden previously by data too costly to process helped in the creation of new products and in the discovery of ways to gain competitive advantage. Similarly, the ability to process every item of data in reasonable time and successfully exploiting the value in Big Data removes the troublesome need for sampling and promotes an investigative approach to data. According to Davenport, many technologies were introduced during this period including Hadoop—an open source software for fast batch data processing across parallel servers; NoSQL — a new class of database to deal with unstructured data; Machine-Learning methods, and powerful reports and dashboards for complex visuals (Davenport, 2013).

3. Analytics 3.0—the Era of "Data-Enriched Offerings" (2015-Today) – Over the past decade data exploded and became big. Widespread access to the Cloud, insightful data visualizations, interactive business dashboards, and the rise of self-service analytics make the technology available and affordable for businesses of all sizes. Suddenly advanced analytics is not just for the analysts. According to Davenport, "Today it's not just information firms and online companies that can create products and services from analyses of data. It's every firm in every industry." (Davenport, 2013). During the 1.0 era, firms used data warehouses for analysis. In the 2.0 era, they focused on Hadoop clusters and NoSQL databases. Analytics 3.0 uses data warehouses, big data analytics,

environments that combine traditional database approaches with Hadoop, vertical and graph databases, and more. Analytics 3.0 uses descriptive, predictive and prescriptive analytics to harness the information embedded in Big Data. However, it emphasizes prescriptive analytics for embedding analytics into key processes and employee behaviors (Phillips, 2014). The new benefits that modern data analytics brings to the table are speed and efficiency. Models in Analytics 3.0 are often embedded into operational and decision processes, dramatically increasing their speed and impact. The ability to work faster – and stay agile – gives organizations a competitive edge that they didn't have before.

Benefits of Using Analytics

Most people rely on their gut instinct when faced with important decisions. Human biases and heuristics are predominant in decision making. Human error and physical limitations often lead to mistakes. Henke et al. (2016) claimed that analytics overcomes limitations and improves four aspects of decision making:

1. **Speed:** When real time responses are needed, analytics can react in an instant. Analytics visualization tools can deliver results at the speed-of-thought and it is well suited to working with a very large volume of data coming from a variety of sources.
2. **Accuracy:** Provided with the right data, predictive models are able to provide a cleaner view of the future. They can make forecasts and predictions more accurate and precise.
3. **Reliability and Consistency:** Machines and analytics are reliable and predictable. Analytics tools can seamlessly connect with a wide range of structured, semi-structured, and unstructured traditional data sources enabling users to gain insight in a reliable and consistent way.
4. **Transparency:** Machines and algorithms improve transparency which allows for decisions to be reviewed and improved upon in the future.

Today's Landscape for Analytics

In today's business environment, analytics is increasingly strategic and is now central to most business roles. A recent study by Gartner, published in 2015, identified a shift in focus from IT-led reporting to business-led self-service analytics. Traditional reporting-based BI platforms are not designed to handle the exponential growth in terms of the sources, volume, and complexity of data. The traditional platforms enforce strict data and report governance, only allowing access by specialized reporting groups. In contrast, the modern approach views data governance as an important step in creating self-service analytics. Traditional BI platforms are being augmented with more agile solutions. Where traditional systems could take months to implement, the modern approach takes as little as a few hours. Latency is no longer tolerated. The advances in the Internet have resulted in greater expectations and less patience. Modern BI platforms support organizational needs for greater accessibility, agility, and analytical insight from a diverse range of data sources. Every business process is an analytics process, and every business user is an analytics user. To meet the time-to-insight demands of today's competitive business environment, many organizations changed the traditional BI model and end-user requirements. The modern BI platform aims to democratize analytics with self-service capabilities. It is characterized by agility, flexibility, and ease of use (Table 1) (Gartner Report, 2015).

Table 1. Traditional vs modern analytics

Analytic Workflow Component	Traditional Platform	Modern Platform
Data ingestion and preparation	IT-produced	IT-Enabled
Content authoring	Primarily IT staff-limited usage	Business users-comprehensive governance
Analysis	Predefined, ad hoc reporting, based on predefined model	Free-form exploration
Insight delivery	Distribution and notifications via scheduled reports or portal	Sharing and collaboration, storytelling, open APIs

Factors Fueling Progress

In the past five years, technology has set off waves of change in the BI landscape. Advances in data collection, computational power, machine learning, and deep learning have expanded the field of BI well beyond what was forecasted before. More sophisticated algorithms are being devised by scientists. Moreover, the growth of cloud-based platforms has given companies elastic scalability, up-to-date security, and the tools and storage capacity to conduct advanced analytics. Henke et al. (2016) found that the following technology trends and developments have contributed to a breakthrough in the field of BI and are helping rapid advances as they converge:

- Exponential growth in the volume of available data
- Advances in algorithms such as deep learning
- Greater computational power
- Increased data storage capacity at reduced costs
- The growth of cloud-based platforms

Categories of Analytics

Analytics is constantly evolving, has changed dramatically over the years and is advancing rapidly today. There are five categories of analytics: descriptive, diagnostics, predictive, prescriptive, and cognitive. These categories build on each other and enable enterprises to make faster and smarter decisions. As organizations evolve, they move from focusing on historical "what" and "why" questions to a more forward-looking predictive, and prescriptive predictions, and finally to cognitive analytics that automate decision. The advanced analytics maturity path is summarized in Table 2 and shown on Figure 3 (Intel, 2017).

Descriptive analytic are valuable for answering questions about what happened in the past and uncovering patterns that offer insight. Such data provide an opportunity for business enterprise to review data to understand the state of affairs of their operations. Business decision makers can drill into specific areas of their business to identify anomalies and root causes of problems or issues. Descriptive analytics tools include data modeling, reporting, visualization, and regression to collect and store data in an efficient way, to create reports and presentation information, and to find trends in the data. Since data is scattered in large numbers of disparate data sources, analyzing all relevant data can be a challenge for most organizations.

Diagnostic analytics are used for discovery. They examine data or content to answer the question why did it happen. Diagnostic analytics takes a deeper look at data to attempt to understand the root causes of events and behaviors in an organization. To optimize diagnostic analytics, it needs to be extended to operational employees of the organization. The result of the diagnostic analytics is often an analytic dashboard that is used for discovery or to determine why something happened.

Predictive analytics analyze current and historical data to provide insights into what will happen and why will it happen in the future with an acceptable level of reliability. It attempts to accurately project the future condition and states. It uses data, text, media mining, forecasting, and predictive modeling to identify probabilities of potential outcomes and/or likely results of specific operations. Predictive Analytics is an extension of Data Mining technology. Both are based on a huge amount of mathematical theory dating back several decades. Data mining technology helps to examine large amounts of data. One can sift through all the chaotic and repetitive noise in data to discover patterns and use that information to assess likely outcomes, and then make informed decisions. Data Mining refers only to past data and uncovers relationships between measurable variables. Despite being around for such a long time, Data

Mining has not yet reached the business mainstream. Predictive analytics can help businesses with a wide range of problems. Lebied (2016) claimed that businesses are using Predictive Analytics to analyze historical data and facts in order to better understand clients' needs, market potentials, products, suppliers, and partners and to identify potential risks and opportunities for a company Other businesses use this type of analytics for predicting which customers are most valuable, scheduling preventive maintenance, and detecting fraud. Airlines use analytics to decide how many tickets to sell at what discounted price for a flight. Hotels use it to predict the number of guests they can expect to book on any given night to increase revenue (Adelman, 2015).

Table 2. Categories of Business Analytics

Business Analytics	Questions	Tools	Outcomes	Focus
Descriptive (Hindsight)	• What happened? • What is happening?	• Data modeling • Business reporting • Visualization • Dashboard • Regression	Well defined business problems or opportunities	Uncovering patterns that offer insight
Diagnostic (Insight)	Why did it happen?	• Enterprise data warehouse • Data discovery • Data mining and correlations • Drill-down/roll-up	Accurate projections of the future conditions and states	Identify past patterns to predict the future
Predictive (Foresight)	• What is likely to happen? • What will happen? • Why will it happen	• Data mining • Text/media mining • Predictive modeling • Artificial Neural Networks (ANN)	Accurate projections of the future conditions and states	Identify past patterns to predict the future
Prescriptive (Automation)	• What should I do? • Why should I do it?	• Decision modeling • Optimization • Simulation • Expert systems	Optimization-Best possible business decisions	Focus on decision making and efficiency
Cognitive	• What should I do? • Why should I do it?	• Machine and deep learning • Data lakes • Human thought Simulation	Better decisions for everyone	Self-service analytics

Figure 3. Moving up the analytics value chain

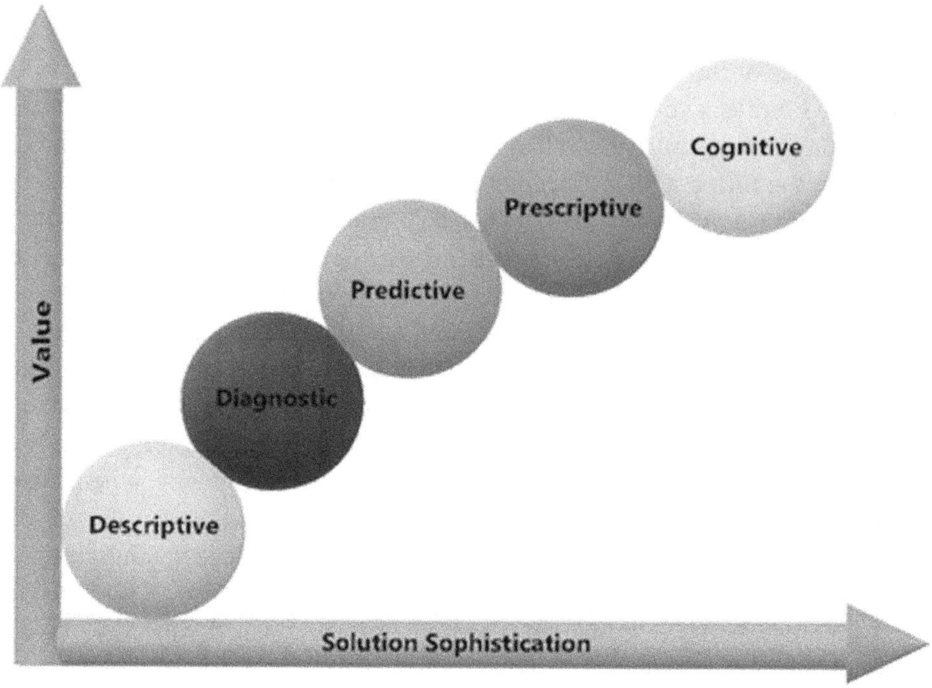

Prescriptive analytics goes beyond predicting future outcomes. It not only anticipates what will happen and when it will happen, but also why it will happen. It employs data techniques such as decision modeling, graph analysis, simulation, neural networks, heuristics, and machine learning to suggest actions that the organization could take to achieve the desired outcome. Prescriptive analytics tries to evaluate the effect of future decisions in order to adjust the decisions before they are actually made. Future outcomes are taken into consideration in the prediction. Prescriptive analytics are commonly used in organizations to optimize scheduling, production, inventory and supply chain design, and other organizational activities to deliver what the customers want, and meet and exceed customers' expectations (Riabacke, Danielson, and Love, 2012). Prescriptive analytics is the most valuable kind of analytics and usually results in rules and recommendations for next steps. A 2012 surveys by Gartner shows most analytics users still focus on measurement of the past, with only 13 percent of users making extensive use of predictive analytics. Less than 3 percent of analytics users are using prescriptive analytics tools such as decision/mathematical modeling, simulation and optimization. Another study shows that by 2020, 40 percent of new investment in analytics tools will be in predictive and prescriptive analytics (Intel, 2017).

Cognitive analytics employs technologies such as machine and deep learning and other high performance analytics tools to automate human-like decision making. It could also augment human decisions with help from smart machines. In this type of analytics, incoming data is translated into action without human intervention.

THE EVOLUTION OF EMBEDDED ANALYTICS

Embedded Analytics vs. Business Intelligence (BI)

Traditional BI is a set of technologies, applications, infrastructure, and best practices that aggregate data from multiple sources, prepare that data for analysis, and then provide reporting and analysis on that data to optimize decisions and performance. These systems are specifically developed to be operated by an organizations' analyst and optimized for supporting managerial decisions that require aggregated views of information from across a department, unit, or entire organization.

Traditional BI platforms focus on data preparation and integration and provide analysis via scripting, reports, interactive visualizations, and static dashboards. An important shortcoming of traditional BI is its latency in receiving reports. By the time the decision maker received the reports, it typically is too late to undertake any action. Embedded analytics facilitate dealing and addressing that latency by shifting from reactive analytics to proactive analytics. Embedded analytics inserts intelligence or a set of tightly integrated capabilities inside the everyday systems or applications (such as CRM, ERP, marketing or financial systems) that employees or customers use to improve the analytics experience. This makes users more productive by combining insight and action in the same application. There is no need for users to switch between multiple applications to derive insights and take action. Figure 4 shows the relationship between embedded analytics, traditional BI and business applications (Harris, 2017).

Decker (2017) concluded that Embedded analytics is built based on three principles:

1. **Synthesis:** Enabling the rapid integration of multiple sources and large volumes of data.
2. **Enabling in-the-Moment Analysis:** Analytics is available within users familiar business applications and for a wide range of scenarios. Embedding makes analytics available when and where needed, providing users a powerful experience.
3. **Democratizing Analytics:** Allowing a wide population of users to understand and use analytics results in easy-to-use, easy-to-share interface.

Figure 4. Traditional BI vs predictive analysis

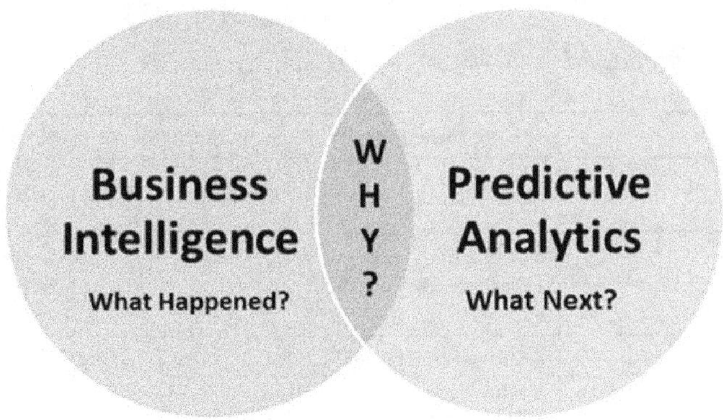

The Rise of Embedded Analytics

The concept of embedding reports inside software applications is not new. It has been around as long as there has been BI software. What has changed by the 2000s is the report tool that software vendors included into their commercial software packages. Static reports of the 1990s have evolved to interactive reports and dashboards in the 2000s and self-service and blended analytics today. Furthermore, relational databases were predominant data source of the 1990s. In the 2000s, BI tools could access a much broader range of data than traditional data sources. Today, many BI tools support Big Data sources; Cloud applications and Cloud file systems, server logs, event streams, and search indexes. Today, the best analytics are characterized by being repeatable, shareable, scalable, and transferrable. Eckerson (2016) summarized the evolution of embedded analytics as shown on Table 3.

Technology companies, software companies, financial services, manufacturing, and retails are among the highest users of the embedded analytics. The adoption of embedded analytics continues to grow and exceed that of standard data recovery. Logi Analytic conducted a 2017 survey of 500 executives and managers and found that 93 percent of respondents are currently embedding analytics in their applications. Companies now go beyond simply adding open-source charts or static visualizations. They are willing to spend the time and resources to embed sophisticated analytics to impress end users. Investment in embedded analytics continues to grow. Ninety percent of respondent plan to invest in embedded analytics going forward. Additionally, 60 percent of end users leverage embedded analytics on a regular basis, and 98 percent said embedded analytics contributed to revenue growth. Respondents also reported that embedded analytics plays a critical role in improving customer satisfaction and user experience. Executives and managers are paying more attention as their competitors use embedded analytics to win and retain customers (Butler, 2017).

Forces Driving Embedded Analytics

Today, business leaders are looking for analytics solutions that are flexible, saleable, and embeddable. They must provide easy-to-implement solutions. Business analysts, power users, and customer alike should be able to apply the analytics tools for their specific analytics needs. There are three forces driving embedded analytics: technology, people, and business as shown on Figure 5.

Table 3. The Evolution of Embedded Analytics

Decades	User Functionality	Platform	BI Software	Pricing
1980s **Report**	Static reports	Desktop	Desktop	User-based
2000s **Analyze**	• Interactive reports • Dashboards • OLAP	Web	Web	Server-based
2010s **Monitor**	• Self-service visual • Interactive • Predictive • Blended analytics • Data-storytelling	Cloud	Platform	Value- based

Figure 5. Forces driving embedded analytics

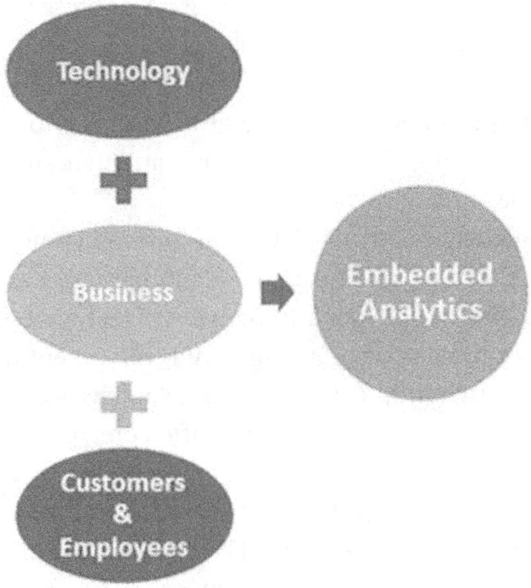

1. **Technology:** The increasing volume and availability of data, advances in data collections, computational power and storage capacity, advances in analytical techniques and technologies are all leading to the formation of new business models and reshaping industry competition.
2. **Business:** Today, businesses are looking for real-time analytics that can be turned into actionable insights, helping them stay agile and competitive in their industry. To make data-driven decisions, enterprise leaders are demanding platforms to store and analyze massive amount of data from variety of disparate data sources. They also demand the ability to:
    a. Access data with extreme speed
    b. Blend and seamlessly connect with a wide range of data from multiple data sources
    c. Analyze massive amount of data using complex data science algorithms
    d. Provide the outputs of analytics in a visualized, easy-to-use, customizable interface.
    e. Integrate market data with real-time network feeds (Twitter, Facebook, etc.) to correlate market activity with social reaction.
3. **Customers and Employees:** Customers are looking for visual analytics that requires no training nor technical expertise. These visual analytics must also be available from a variety of data sources. Internal employees desire a solution that allows them to push data in, and return easy-to-read analytics, allowing them to quickly produce results and solve problems.

Benefits of Embedded Analytics

Traditional analytics require significant development time and are accessible only within an analytics silo that must be accessed separately. On the other hand, embedded analytics are reports and visualizations that are inserted directly into existing websites and applications. They are fast and inexpensive to develop and can be inserted into virtually any application. More organizations are beginning to leverage analytics within applications as a part of their operational processes. Many of the benefits offered by embedded analytics are specific to business applications where analytics is seamlessly integrated. However, the following benefits are common for many users of embedded analytics platform (Decker, 2017; Harris, 2017; Eckerson, 2016):

1. **Seamlessness of User Experience:** Users do not have to rely on separate tools and software to make decisions. A user can simply log into the application and make data-driven decisions using tools embedded within the suite.
2. **Data Blending:** Blending and analyzing data from different sources is a technical challenge for many companies. Embedded analytics make this daunting task easy and simple for the end user.
3. **Reduced Development Time and Speed to Market:** Deployments of analytics platform would normally require weeks or months of planning and development time. Embedded analytics tools enable end users to connect to multiple disparate data sources and create visualizations and reports via one user-friendly interface. Business users can often create the visualizations themselves, with minimal technical knowledge.
4. **Lower Initial Creating Cost:** The initial cost of creating embedded analytics is often lower than that of standalone or custom-coded solutions. The embedding process is often simple, and it can be completed by the developers in a matter of minutes.
5. **Lower Ongoing Maintenance, Upgrades, and Support Costs:** The maintenance cost for embedded analytics is often lower than that of custom-coded solutions. Visualizations are intuitive and simple to update. In many cases, business users can continue to support much of the visualizations themselves with minimal assistance from developers.
6. **Lower Opportunity Cost:** Embedded analytics can be developed and deployed fairly quickly without requiring much time and resources from internal development staff. This allows development and support staff to focus on the organization's core competencies and other needs that aid in its growth.
7. **Improved Strategic Planning:** Having embedded analytics with constant visibility into operations creates constant insight and allows decision makers to identify whether overall goals are met and how to adjust them as necessary and on an ongoing basis.
8. **Gained Competitive Advantage:** Embedded analytics tools enable businesses to know more about their customers and their competitors. The knowledge gained from powerful, context-specific analytical insights enables organizations gain distinct competitive advantage.
9. **Process Optimization:** Embedded analytics tools facilitate process optimization. An organization that is using embedded analytics can plan and build processes more proactively, creating an agile environment in which processes can be adjusted and resources can be shifted to quickly respond to changes in the market. Business leaders can ask complex questions about processes, create what-if scenarios, and evaluate possible outcomes without affecting live processes and waiting for the results of their changes.

BI Functionality Embedded in Applications

As we explained in this paper, BI turns data into insights and actions, and helps businesses run more intelligently. BI evolved into two major categories: Reporting and Analysis. Reporting geared to casual users and analysis geared to power users and analysts. Both categories are now converging in an embedded analytics market. Organization and software vendors embed reports, dashboards, and analytics functionality into applications to turn insights into action. This creates a seamless user experience, turning client facing applications into powerful tools for reducing costs, growing revenues, increasing efficiencies, and improving customer satisfaction.

Most organizations support a myriad of BI functionality that run on different systems and platforms. Eckerson (2016) and Wong (2016) found that the common BI functionality that organizations embed inside applications ranges from charts, and dashboards, to predictive analytics. Table 4 provides a summary of these embedded functionalities.

A CONCEPTUAL MODEL FOR DEPLOYING EMBEDDED ANALYTICS

Common Deploying Practices

Embedded analytics should be deployed whenever and wherever organizations have the opportunity to provide their users analytical information. Decker (2017) identified the following common deployment models:

1. **Customer Portals:** Provides customers with analytic access whenever customers interact with a company via its web site. This provides an opportunity for the company to engage with the customers, to help cross-sell or up-sell additional products, services, or to answer questions more effectively.
2. **Analytics Portals:** Provides users with websites, tools, or applications that are dedicated only to reporting and analytic results. This type of deployment is common choice for an information provider where analytics is its premier offering.
3. **Business Applications:** Helps internal employees make decisions in a timely manner by embedding analytics in many categories of business applications. Those business applications include CRM systems that front-line employees use or ERP systems that procurement managers use to place orders.

Table 4. Functionalities embedded in applications

Functionality	Description
Charts and reports	charts, tables, maps, metrics, and graphics with a connection to a predefined data source
Dashboards or interactive reports	A collection of interconnected reports (charts, tables, graphics) that provide end-user with an easy-to-use analytics solution.
Self-Service analytics	Allows users to analyze massive amount of data from a wide range of sources with extreme speed, then enables users to visualize the report in an easy-to-use, easy-to-share, customizable interface.
Predictive analytics	Embeds self-service analytics tools such as forecasting, regression, data mining, text, and media mining, and other advanced predictive analytics algorithms to provide foresight and recommendations.
Benchmarking	Enables comparing performance metrics against best practices
Mobile reporting	Enables interactive functionality on mobile devices by taking advantage of capabilities specific to mobile devices
Transactions	A collection of tools that execute transactions

A Proposed Conceptual Model for Implementation

Data-driven businesses are looking to deploy embedded analytic solutions as value-added offerings to their internal and external customers. The adoption of embedded analytics, when done right, leads to organizations being able to justify their analytics expenditures and create value tied directly to data visibility. Opportunities for deploying embedded analytics capabilities continue to evolve and grow with the broader adoption of technologies. Implementing a successful embedded analytics program takes time and effort. Many parts of the company will be affected, there are complex decisions to be made, and various stakeholders must be involved. It requires engagement and support from business users across the data analytics landscape. Some companies have not been successful with deployment of embedded analytics process due to the failure of developing an analytics strategy rooted in the delivery of IT services linked to their business outcomes. Furthermore, many enterprises do not know how to initiate their analytics projects. When it comes to embedding analytic solutions, there are a few key considerations. A range of recently published research literature on the implementation of business intelligence, predictive analytics and embedded analytics is reviewed to explore their current state, issues and challenges learned from their practice (McNeill, 2014; Asllani, 2015; Loshin,, Aug-2017 ; Loshin,, Dec-2017). It is argued that before deploying embedded analytics process in a company, the need to determine where analytics will add business value needs to be identified and a scalable deployment approach must be planned.

We have modified steps suggested by these researches and added more to create a practical implementation steps for successful deployment of predictive analytics process. Figure 6 summarizes our recommended implementation steps. Following is a brief summary:

1. **Top Management Involvement:** Obtaining the support and backing of top management is crucial in providing the necessary funding and ensuring that the organization supports the analytics process. To manage Big Data and analytics in today's information economy, progressive organizations have created two new senior executive positions: the Chief Data Officers (CDO) and the Chief Analytics Officers (CAO). The CDO focuses on data strategies for the organization, whereas the CAO find ways to optimize the use of analytics throughout the organization. These senior executives need to be provided with what they need, both in terms of technology and data.
2. **Proper Planning and Scoping:** It is necessary to understand the organizations key business objectives and concentrate on building analytics models that can have the maximum impact in meeting those objectives.
    a. **Create a Compelling Business Case:** A business case needs to be created and communicated clearly wherever appropriate across the organization. A business case presents the reasoning for initiating analytics process. A compelling business case communicates the nature of the proposed project and the arguments, both quantified and unquantifiable, for its deployment.
    b. **Use Experienced Workers:** Hire a competent team composed of data analysts, business analysts, data scientists and statisticians.
    c. **Give Analysts Access to Relevant and Trustworthy Data:** Collect and store inventory of relevant technical and business data sets and make sure analytics applications have access to the right data.
3. **Identify Business Processes That Can Be Improved:** Embedded Analytics tools will help organizations identify business processes that can be improved. It is necessary to get managers and workers on board with putting those findings into action.

Figure 6. A conceptual model for deploying embedded analytics

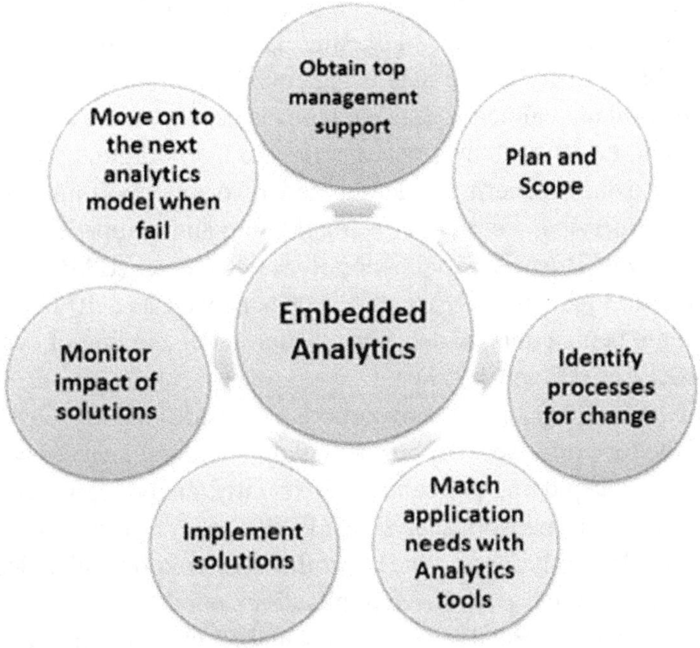

4. **Match Application Needs With Analytics Tools:** Look for predictive analytics tools that provide capabilities matching application needs. There are plenty of tools to choose from either from open source or from commercial markets. Among important factors to consider when choosing predictive analytics tools are the ability to handle structured, semi-structures, and unstructured data, compatibility with a variety of Big Data platforms, and integration with data visualization tools.
5. **Implement Solutions:** Incorporate solutions and maintain a solid data governance program. We are living in a world of constantly changing data. Internal and external data sets are continuously being captured and integrated. Make sure to institute solid data governance practices to guarantee that the quality and consistency of the data sets in your analytics systems remain at an acceptable level.
6. **Monitor Impact of Solutions:** Embedded Analytics not only influence changes in business processes, but also can have a measurable impact on business performance. Create metrics that can be used to quantify the business value of employing the analytics models.
7. **Move on to the Next Analytics Model When Fail:** If your analytics model did not deliver useful information to the business, move on to the next model.

ANALYTICS IN PRACTICE- BUSINESS APPLICATIONS OF EMBEDDED ANALYTICS

BI and analytics go beyond the technology for gathering and analyzing data. They are about having the mindset of an experimenter- being willing to let data guide a company's decision- making process. Businesses are using predictive analytics to analyze historical data and facts in order to better understand clients' needs, market potentials, products, suppliers, and partners. Predictive analytics is also utilized to identify potential risks and opportunities for a company (Lebied, 2016).

Analytics is commonly used in Finance, Marketing, Human Resources, Health Care, Government Policies and every possible industry where data is generated (Analytics Vidhya, 2015). From banking to manufacturing, from retail to healthcare, data analytics is used to make breakthrough discoveries, to deliver better services, and enrich the customer experience. Corporations around the world are using analytics to gain various business benefits, including new revenue opportunities, improved operational efficiency, better customer service, more effective marketing, and competitive advantages over rivals. According to a recent study by Business Application Research Center (BARC), organizations that used Data Analytics reported an 8 percent increase in revenues as well as a 10 percent reduction in costs. Other benefits reported are better strategic decisions, better understanding of customers, and improved control of operation processes (Lebied, 2017).

Most often Data Analytics is associated with corporate decision-making. However, analytics has applications well beyond the for-profit world of business. Application of analytics in public service is well documented. Examples are: Deploying police more efficiently, analyzing traffic violations, predictive modeling to catch criminals, social network analysis to identify potential terrorists, etc. (Wetherbee, 2014).

Many companies have already harnessed the capabilities offered by embedded analytics to improve their core operations. Many are using packaged applications purchased from software vendors, while others are using tools developed internally. Some are available only from desktop computers inside the company, while others can be accessed via a web browser or a mobile device from anywhere. For example, UPS uses embedded analytics to determine the most efficient routs for its drivers. According to the company's estimate, the system reduces the number of miles its vehicles travel each year by 100 million, with annual saving of more than 300 million (Rosenbush and Steven, 2015). Google is experimenting with different analytics tools to reduce time for search queries since a few milliseconds can translate into additional millions of dollars in revenue (Bughin, 2016). Netflix has used embedded analytics to improve its recommendation engine for its global customers. Netflix estimates that the analytics platform brings in one billion dollars in annual revenue (Carlos et al., 2016). T-Mobile uses embedded analytics to improve customer satisfaction. T-Mobile merges information obtained from social media with its own transaction data from CRM and cuts customer defections in half in a single quarter (Tylor, 2012). Amazon distinguished itself as an innovative company that provides fast shipping, low prices, and great customer service. Amazon uses embedded analytics tools to satisfy customer's informational needs by providing product ratings, video reviews, and suggested products. Amazon has added tremendous value to support the ecommerce experience and has created a superior customer experience by providing relevant analytic information at the point of transaction. Ford has embedded dashboards in the parts and services division to keep managers up-to-date with the latest sales figures. These embedded analytics dashboards also streamline operations in manufacturing, finance, purchasing, warranty department, customer service, and labor relations (Wong, 2013). Nissan Motor Company uses easy-to-use embedded analytics platform powered by Google Analytics that features Ecommerce Reporting and Custom Reports to gain deep insights into users' product preferences (Bulygo, 2015). Honda France wanted to boost the performance of its sales force and increase the efficiency of its IT department. The company decided to replace its existing resource-intensive and expensive analytics platform with easy-to-use embedded analytics that provide access to its sales and customer data via a trustworthy web-based platform. The platform should provide Honda's sales team with access to efficient analytics anywhere, anytime via any device enabling them to make better decisions in real time. Moreover, the platform should enable the IT department to maintain and manage reporting and analytics solution via a range of devices, quickly and efficiently. The company purchased an embedded analytics platform from Yellofin. The platform provides a hassle free web based analytics solutions, enabling administrators, sales force and IT personnel to independently access up-to-date visual analytics at the right time on the desktop or iPad, whether they are at their desk or on-the-move. The self-service nature of the analytics portal also enables Honda's IT personnel to maintain and manage reporting and analytics environment effectively (Honda France, 2013).

Table 5 at the end of this chapter (see appendix), highlights embedded analytics examples in different industries.

SUMMARY AND CONCLUSION

For decades, business leaders around the world have focused on using analytics techniques to empower decision makers in their organizations and to compete effectively in a digitally driven world. Over the past five years, the sheer volume of data has grown exponentially, and new analytics tools have been developed to turn this flood of unstructured, semi-structured, and structured data into insights. Embedded analytics, a term that encompasses a range of algorithmic approaches, or a set of tightly integrated capabilities inserted inside the applications, has rapidly advanced to the forefront of the analytics landscape. Embedded analytics delivers live, interactive and contextual analytical insights from the transactional business applications. Organizations are discovering the power of embedded analytics which accelerate time to insight, deliver greater value for end users, and provide a greater strategic value for the organization.

As highlighted in this paper, there are several factors fueling the evolution of embedded analytics. Advances in data collection, analytics solutions, hardware and software, and computational power have revolutionized the field. Additionally, business users within organizations need more than personal productivity tools, and more than analytic engines understood only by expert data scientists. They demand, more than ever, autonomy, agility, and self-service analytic capabilities. They need a thoughtfully designed analytics platform that empowers everyone within these organizations to make data an integral part of their day-to-day processes and decisions. Progressive organizations are building analytics data models that run without IT support, answering complex questions with powerful analytics, and designing intuitive guided analytic experiences all within a centralized enterprise environment that allows them to securely scale business intelligence capabilities.

This paper proposed a conceptual model for successful implementation of Embedded Analytics in organizations. Moreover, this paper argued that embedded analytics adoption, if done well, leads to organizations being able to justify their analytics expenditures and create value tied directly to data visibility. This paper also discussed many of the benefits offered by embedded analytics and showed how embedded analytics are deployed in customer portals, analytics portals and in various business applications including CRM, ERP, and marketing and financial systems.

Organizations should consider analytics a strategic investment because adding new analytic functions affect an organization's existing applications, devices, services, and web sites. Important decisions such as the best way to deliver analytic content and reports to customer, and ensuring that embedded content is engaging must be made. Business leaders must also evaluate how an embedded analytics initiative will affect users (external and internal), existing applications and interfaces, and multiple stakeholders such as executives, managers, marketing and sales personnel.

REFERENCES

Adelman, S. (2015). Why Big Data Means Big Opportunity for the Travel Industry. *Forbes*. Retrieved from https://www.forbes.com/sites/ibm/2015/07/09/why-big-data-means-big-opportunity-for-the-travel-industry/#5528576b21a5

Vidhya, A. (2015). *13 Amazing Applications/Uses of data Science Today*. Retrieved from https://www.analyticsvidhya.com/blog/2015/09/applications-data-science/

Asllani, A. (2015). *Business Analytics with Management Science Models and Methods*. Upper Sadler River, NJ: Pearson Education, Inc.

Bughin, J. (2016). Big Data, Big Bang? *Journal of Big Data, 3*(2).

Bughin, J. (2016). Big Data: Getting a Better Read on Performance. *McKinsey Quarterly*. Retrieved from https://www.mckinsey.com/industries/high-tech/our-insights/big-data-getting-a-better-read-on-performance

Bulygo, Z. (2015). How Netflix Uses Analytics To Select Movies, Create Content, and Make Multimillion Dollar Decisions. *Kiss Metrics*. Retrieved from https://blog.kissmetrics.com/how-netflix-uses-analytics/

Butler, C. (2017). 2017 State of Embedded Analytics Report. *Logi Analytics*. Retrieved from http://go.logianalytics.com/rs/793-ECD-841/images/2017%20State%20of%20Embedded%20Analytics_Logi_final.pdf

Carlos, A., Gomez-Uribe, & Hunt, N. (2016). The Netflix recommender system: Algorithms, business value, and innovation. *ACM Transactions on Management Information Systems*, *6*(4).

Davenport, T. (2013, December). Analytics 3.0. *Harvard Business Review*, 13.

Decker, J. (2017). *Embedded Analytics for Dummies*. John Wiley & Sons, Inc.

Diebold, F. X. (2012). *On the Origin(s) and Development of the Term "Big Data," PIER Working Paper 12-037.* Penn Institute for Economic Research, Department of Economics, University of Pennsylvania. Retrieved from https://economics.sas.upenn.edu/sites/economics.sas.upenn.edu/files/12-037.pdf

Eckerson, W. (2016). *Embedded Analytics: The Future of Business Intelligence*. Eckerson Group. Retrieved from https://www3.technologyevaluation.com/research/white-paper/embedded-analytics-the-future-of-business-intelligence.html

Evelson, B., & Bennett, M. (2015). Quantify Tangible Business Value of BI. *Forrester*. Retrieved from http://www.lavastorm.com/assets/2015-Forrester-Quantify-Tangible-Business-Value-of-BI.pdf

Feki, M., Boughzala, I., & Wamba, S. F. (2016). Big Data Analytics-enabled Supply Chain Transformation: A Literature Review. *49th Hawaii International Conference on System Sciences*.

Gartner I. T. Glossary. (2018). *Embedded Analytics*. Retrieved from https://www.gartner.com/it-glossary/embedded-analytics

Gartner Report. (2015). Retrieved from http://www.gartner.com/newsroom/id/3130817

Gaitho, M. (2017). How Applications of Big Data Drive Industries. *SimpliLearn*. Retrieved from https://www.simplilearn.com/big-data-applications-in-industries-article

Gets, J., & Reinsel, D. (2013). *The Digital Universe in 2020*. IDC.

Harris, D. (2017). A Guide to Embedded Analytics: Use Cases and Benefits. *Software Advice*. Retrieved from https://www.softwareadvice.com/resources/embedded-analytics-definition-and-examples/#benefits

Henke, N., Bughin, J., Chui, M., Manyika, J., Saleh, T., Wiseman, B., & Sethupathy, G. (2016). *The Age of Analytics: Competing in a Data-Driven World*. McKinsey Global Institute.

France, H. (2013). *Case Study*. Yellowfin International Pty Ltd. Retrieved from https://portal.yellowfinbi.com/Document.i4?DocumentId=242108

Intel. (2017). *Guide to Getting Started with Advanced Analytics*. Intel Planning Guide. Retrieved from https://www.intel.com/content/www/us/en/analytics/getting-started-advanced-analytics-planning-guide.html

IDC. (2017). *Worldwide Semiannual Big Data and Analytics Spending Guide*. Retrieved from https://www.idc.com/getdoc.jsp?containerId=prUS42371417

Koushik, R. (2011). Analyze This! Analytics Explained and Applied. *Capgemini*. Retrieved from https://www.capgemini.com/gb-en/2011/05/analyse-this-analytics-explained-and-applied/

Lebied, M. (2016). Top 11 Business Intelligence and Analytics Trends for 2017. *Business Intelligence*. Retrieved from http://www.datapine.com/blog/business-intelligence-trends-2017/

Loshin, D. (2017). *Five Steps to Build Better Predictive Analytics Applications*. Retrieved from http://searchbusinessanalytics.techtarget.com/tip/Five-steps-to-build-better-predictive-analytics-applications

Loshin, D. (2017). *Ten Steps to Start Using Predictive Analytics Algorithms Effectively*. Retrieved from http://searchbusinessanalytics.techtarget.com/tip/Ten-steps-to-start-using-predictive-analytics-algorithms-effectively

Marr, B. (2015). Big Data: 20 Mind-Boggling Facts Everyone Must Read. *Forbes*. Retrieved from https://www.forbes.com/sites/bernardmarr/2015/09/30/big-data-20-mind-boggling-facts-everyone-must-read/#56a1b34e17b1

McAfee, A., & Brynjolfsson, E. (2012). Big Data: The Management Revolution. *Harvard Business Review*. Retrieved from https://hbr.org/2012/10/big-data-the-management-revolution

McNeill, D. (2014). *Analytics in Healthcare and the Life Sciences: Strategies, Implementation Methods and Best Practices*. Upper Sadler River, NJ: International Institute for Analytics.

Minelli, M., Chambers, M., & Dhiraj, A. (2013). *Big Data, Big Analytics: Emerging Business Intelligence and Analytic Trends for Today's Businesses*. Hoboken, NJ: John Wiley & Sons. doi:10.1002/9781118562260

Perrin, A. (2015). *One-fifth of Americans Report Going Online-Almost Constantly*. Pew Research Center.

Phillips, J. (2014). *Analytics 3.0: The Era of Impact*. International Institute for Analytics. Retrieved from https://www.sas.com/content/dam/SAS/en_us/doc/event/The-Era-of-Impact-127837.pdf

Riabacke, M., Danielson, M., & Love, E. (2012). State-of-the-Art Prescriptive Criteria Weight Elicitation. *Advances in Decision Sciences, 2012*, 1–24. doi:10.1155/2012/276584

Rosenbush, S., & Stevens, L. (2015). At UPS the Algorithm is the Driver. *The Wall Street Journal*. Retrieved from https://www.wsj.com/articles/at-ups-the-algorithm-is-the-driver-1424136536

Strickland, J. (2015). *Analytics: is it more than a buzzword?* Retrieved from https://bicorner.com/2015/09/16/analytics-is-it-more-than-a-buzzword/

Taylor, P. (2012, June 19). Crunch Time for Big Data. *The Financial Times*.

Weiss, S. M., & Indurkhya, N. (1998). *Predictive Data Mining: A Practical Guide*. Morgan Kaufmann Publishers, Inc.

Wetherbee, C. (2014). *Optimizing Your Agency's Business Processes through Analytics*. Retrieved from http://slideplayer.com/slide/1606960/

Wong, A. (2013). What is Embedded Analytics? *Logi Analytics*. Retrieved from https://www.logianalytics.com/bi-trends/what-is-embedded-analytics/

APPENDIX

Table 5. Embedded analytics applications in different industries

Industry	Applications
Financial Institutions	• Analyze the probabilities of risk and default • Compliance and regulatory reporting • Trade surveillance • Credit worthiness evaluation • Detects the misuse of credit and debit cards • Cross-selling and up-selling
Manufacturing	• Demand forecasting • Process optimization • Predictive maintenance • Condition monitoring
Retail	• Predictive inventory planning • Determine customer responses or purchases and set up for upselling and cross selling opportunities • Market segmentation and targeting • Predict trends, recommend new products – and boost profitability • Customer ROI and lifetime value
Travel and Hospitality	• Social media-consumer feedback and interaction analysis • Customer complaint resolution • Dynamic pricing • Traffic patterns and congestion management
Healthcare	• Analyze large amounts of information quickly to provide lifesaving diagnoses or treatment options almost immediately. • Alerts and diagnostics from real-time patient data • Disease identification and risk evaluation • Healthcare provider sentiment analysis • Proactive health management
Energy and Utilities	• Power usage analytics • Carbon emissions and trading • Smart grid management • Energy supply and demand optimization
Web and Digital Media	• Clickstream analysis • Ad targeting, forecasting and optimization • Social graph analysis and profile segmentation • Campaign management and loyalty programs • Abuse and click-fraud prevention
eComerce and Customer Service	• Cross-channel analytics • Event analytics • Next best offer or next best action • Recommendation module
Online & Physical Security	• Identify suspicious activity or behavior. • Reduce fraud with real-time monitoring of user behavior and network activity. • Trigger alarms when analytics picks up on irregular activity.

Chapter 3
Business Intelligence Maturity Framework

Chee-Sok Tan
Universiti Tunku Abdul Rahman, Malaysia

Wai-Khuen Cheng
Universiti Tunku Abdul Rahman, Malaysia

Jie Ren
Fordham University, USA

Siew Fan Wong
Sunway University, Malaysia

ABSTRACT

This chapter builds an enterprise-level business intelligence maturity (EBIM) model that facilitates an improved view of the path in business intelligence (BI) implementation. The authors adopted a two-stage qualitative approach, namely a Delphi study followed by case studies. The findings reveal that a comprehensive EBIM model enables organizations to plan, assess, and manage their BI initiatives more effectively than previously. In addition, this study lists important key process areas (KPAs) that influence BI implementation success. The authors found that the KPAs in different levels and dimensions help organizations identify critical areas in need of maximum attention and channel their scarce resources to improve those areas. Further, the entire EBIM framework fosters better use of limited resources in critical areas, which is likely to have a greater effect at the right time.

INTRODUCTION

In this era of data explosion, companies have become more aware of the importance of business intelligence (BI). BI is a broad category term encompassing technologies, applications, and processes for gathering, storing, accessing, and analyzing data to facilitate and improve decision-making (Wixom & Watson, 2010). Its main elements are integration processes, namely, processes to move data from different sources into one integrated place, and storing, analyzing, and presenting data to end users. It means

DOI: 10.4018/978-1-5225-5718-0.ch003

that BI is technology that allows business analysts to use data collected from various sources across an organization for analysis and other business purposes. Hence, BI offers a comprehensive view across different organizational functions (Wixom & Watson, 2010). Actionable information from BI may yield competitive advantage in an ever-changing business environment.

However, BI implementation involves a considerable amount of resources and is hence a costly and complex undertaking. Thus, it must be monitored prudently. To identify the strengths and weaknesses of BI initiatives, managers need to assess the maturity of their BI efforts. For this purpose, BI academics and practitioners have developed multiple maturity models to assess organizations' BI implementation toward improving and reaping increased benefits. Maturity models serve as a tool to measure and categorize organizational capabilities against established benchmarks (de Bruin, Rosemann, Freeze, & Kulkarni, 2005).

BI maturity models help stakeholders to understand holistically the issues that affect BI implementation. The models allow BI stakeholders to optimize the use of scarce resources by focusing on key areas more likely to have a greater impact than other areas. These reasons underscore the value of a BI maturity model in aiding BI implementation. However, many organizations are yet to reap the full benefits of BI implementation (Klynveld Peat Marwick Goerdeler, 2009), although their managements have devoted considerable attention to the implementation process. This failure to harvest the full benefits results in a significant loss to organizations.

More importantly, studies that present systematic guidelines for, and assessment of, BI initiatives are limited. Academics and practitioners have proposed numerous BI maturity models, but the reliability and underlying maturity concept of these are unclear and questionable (Lahrmann, Marx, Winter, & Wortmann, 2011; Shaaban, Helmy, Khedr, & Nasr, 2011). Moreover, most of the studies examining these models did not discuss model evaluation. In addition, guidelines on technical issues are absent in the related literature. Lahrmann et al. (2011) also observed two other weakness of these models: the models target specific clients and focus less on BI. However, Lahrmann et al. (2011) did not explain the specific groups of clients targeted by the models and this question remains unanswered. Moreover, the criticism that the existing models' focus on BI is limited is inaccurate because these models cover only some topics under the umbrella term BI.

Further, most prior studies emphasized certain topics such as data and infrastructure and rarely addressed important business areas such as strategic business alignment, organizational structures, and strategy (Lahrmann et al., 2011). Overall, the links between BI technology and BI organizational performance were not specified clearly. Although BI is a broad category that spans a wide spectrum of topics, from technology-related to business-related topics, the current literature is yet to present a comprehensive coverage of the entire spectrum. Lahrmann, Marx, Winter, and Wortmann (2010) recognized this lack of comprehensiveness as a weakness of the existing BI maturity models after comparing 10 such models.

Therefore, a more comprehensive BI maturity model is needed. The main objective of the present study was to develop an enterprise-level business intelligence maturity (EBIM) model to help organizations plan, assess, or undertake large-scale BI initiatives. The overarching research question was "How can a more comprehensive BI maturity model be developed?" To answer this question, we first explored the existing literature and developed the EBIM model. Next, we explored the views of certain BI experts on this model. By building the EBIM model, this study offers three contributions. First, it has developed a more comprehensive EBIM model for BI stakeholders than existing models.

Second, this study presents a clearer pathway to BI stakeholders to increase BI maturity in their organization. By using the EBIM model, they will be able to recognize the current position of their organization in the maturity hierarchy and also determine actions to be taken to move to a higher level of BI maturity (Burton, 2009). In addition, this study provides guidelines for organizations to achieve higher maturity levels and to enhance the efficiency of their BI initiatives. Finally, it has produced a more comprehensive BI maturity model that supports easy self-assessment by users. Users will be able to evaluate BI implementation maturity at their convenience. This should enable them to monitor the BI maturity level closely and take necessary steps to enable their organizations to attain a higher level within a short period.

LITERATURE REVIEW

Business Intelligence and Its Benefits

Recently, business intelligence (BI) applications have been dominating the technology priority list of many Chief Information Officers (Gartner, 2016). BI is a combination of technologies (e.g., mining tools, dashboards, and scorecards) and architectures (e.g., data warehouse, data mart, and Online Analytical Processing (OLAP)) that supports data manipulation (i.e., gathering, analyzing, storing, and sharing data) to provide meaningful information and insights for better decision-making. As supported by Turban et al. (2008), "The process of BI is based on the transformation of data to information, then to decisions, and finally to actions." Additionally, BI allows interactive access to the right information by the right person at the right time. Thus, BI improves business performance and helps organizations achieve competitive advantage.

According to Thompson (2004), the major benefits of BI are faster, more accurate reporting, improved decision-making, improved customer service, increased revenue, and reduction in IT and non-IT-related costs. Moreover, Thompson (2004) recognized that the most common applications areas for BI are general reporting, sales and marketing analysis, planning and forecasting, financial consolidation, statutory reporting, budgeting, and profitability analysis. Table 1 presents the BI applications in multiple domains.

Maturity Studies

The word maturity describes a "state of being complete, perfect or ready" (Simpson & Weiner, 1989). To reach a desired state of maturity, organizations must progress on an evolutionary transformation path from an initial to a target stage (Fraser, Moultrie, & Gregory, 2002). Maturity models are used to guide this transformation process. Hence, maturity models are developed to measure and categorize the capabilities of an organization against established benchmarks.

Maturity models were initially proposed in the 1970s (Gibson & Nolan, 1974), and numerous such models have been published in the field of Information Systems (IS) to date (Mettler & Rohner, 2009). As these high numbers led to a certain arbitrariness in the design process (de Bruin et al. 2005; Mettler & Rohner, 2009), methods to design maturity models were developed. The important characteristics of maturity models are the maturity concept, dimensions, levels, maturity principle, and assessment approach.

A maturity model typically consists of multiple maturity levels, stages, or phases for a class of objects and it is designed in sequential and predictable ways. Lahrmann et al. (2010) summarized the properties of maturity models in detail as concept, dimensions, levels, principle, and assessment approach. Each level contains a set of key requirements called key process areas (KPAs) to be achieved (Chamoni

Table 1. BI applications

Industry	Objectives
Retail industry	• ***Forecasting***. Using scanning data to forecast demand, and based on the forecast, defining inventory requirements more accurately • ***Ordering and replenishment***. Using information to make faster decisions about items to order and to determine optimum quantities • ***Marketing***. Providing analyses of customer transactions (products sold and customer information) • ***Quick response***. Using quick response technologies to help speed merchandise to the shelf and reduce inventory levels needed to increase turns; requires powerful information system and strong communications backbone • ***Merchandising***. Defining the right merchandise for the market at any point in time, planning store level, and refining inventory • ***Distribution and logistics***. Helping distribution centers manage increased volumes; can use advance shipment information to schedule and consolidate inbound and outbound freight • ***Transportation management***. Developing optimal load consolidation plans and routing schedules • ***Inventory planning***. Helping identify the level of inventory needed, ensuring a given grade of service • ***Stock location planning***. Helping warehouse planners assign products to locations to minimize distances and improve efficiency • ***Finished goods deployment***. Balancing supply, demand, and capacity to determine how to allocate limited quantities of finished goods • ***Space management.*** Using planograms developed at headquarters to automatically adjust to reflect store-specific sales patterns and category space • ***Card technology***. Through proprietary and frequent-shopper cards "swiped" at a POS device, instantly capturing customer and transaction information, from which customer purchase patterns can be projected
Insurance	• ***Claims and premium analysis***. Analyzing detailed claims and premium history by product, policy, claim type, and other specifics • ***Customer analysis***. Analyzing client needs and product usage patterns, developing marketing programs on client characteristics, and conducting risk analysis, improving client service • ***Risk analysis***. Identifying high-risk market segments and opportunities in specific segments, relating market segments, and reducing frequency of claims
Banking, finance and securities	• ***Customer profitability analysis***. Determining the overall profitability of individual customers, current and long term, providing the basis for high-profit sales and relationship banking, maximizing sales to high-value customers, reducing costs to low-value customers, and providing the means to maximize profitability of new products and services
Telecommunications Manufacturing industry	• ***Customer profiling and segmentation***. Determine high-profit product profiles and customer segments, provide detailed integrated customer profiles, develop individualized frequent-caller programs, determine future customer needs. • ***Customer demand forecasting***. Forecast future product needs or service activity, provide basis for churn analysis and control for improving customer retention. • ***Sales***. Provide analyses of customer-specific transaction data. • ***Forecasting.*** Forecast demand, define inventory requirements. • ***Ordering and replenishment.*** Order optimum quantities of items. • ***Purchasing***. Help distribution centers manage increased volumes. • ***Distribution and logistics.*** Use advance shipment information to schedule and consolidate inbound and outbound freight. • ***Transportation management.*** Develop optimal load consolidation plans and routing schedules. • ***Inventory planning.*** Identify the inventory level needed, ensure a given grade of service.

& Gluchowski, 2004). However, KPAs differ between models depending on the problem domain. A particular maturity level is attained by accomplishing all KPAs in that level.

Comparison of BI Maturity Models

We conducted a rigorous search in the scholarly databases to identify existing BI maturity models in the literature and obtained a list of 18 models. One model was excluded from the comparison because it is only a theoretical model and there is limited information on it. We then evaluated the remaining 17 models on the basis of 13 components: data, architecture, tools, impact, performance management, behavior, sponsorship and funding, change management, processes, staff, strategy, organizational structure, and efficiency. Synonyms were matched during examination of extant literature on BI maturity models. For example, the terms "Technology" and "IT" were treated as the same term as both actually address a similar aspect.

Table 2 outlines the comparison of the models. Some models appear in more than one year because they were modified and updated periodically. They differ from each other in terms of the concept, number of maturity levels or stages, key dimensions, and characteristics. Each of the models has some limitations. The most noticeable limitation detected from the comparison table is a lack of comprehensiveness. The components listed in Table 2 cover both business- and technology-related issues. However, none of the models covers all components. This finding is equivalent to that of Lahrmann et al. (2010).

The 17 models are arranged in chronological order in Table 2. It is apparent that business-related aspects receive more attention from academics and practitioners than technology-related issues. For instance, performance management, sponsorship, and funding have been highlighted significantly in many BI maturity models since 2006. This shows that academics and practitioners have begun to be aware of the broad scope of BI, which covers business aspects and IT aspects, since 2006.

Conversely, processes have received lesser attention from the authors who proposed the models. Processes refer to the sequences of actions or steps to which BI-related activities are performed. It is essential to emphasize processes in BI maturity models because the processes serve as practical guidelines to BI

Table 2. Comparison of BI maturity models

Scope	Year	2001	2004				2005		2006		2007				2008		2009	2010		2012		
	Component \ Model	Watson et al. (2001)	SAS	Eckerson	SMC		Cates et al.	Dataflux	Sen et al.	AMR Research	Davenport and	Deng	William and William	Eckerson	Kasnik	Teradata	HP	Sacu and Spruit	Gartner	Sen et al.	Raber et al.	Σ
Technology	Data	•					•	•	•			•	•	•		•	•		•	•	•	12
	Architecture	•	•	•	•			•	•		•			•			•	•		•	•	12
	Tools	•		•	•						•			•	•	•	•	•	•			10
Business	Impact	•		•				•	•					•		•	•		•	•	•	10
	Performance management									•	•	•		•			•	•	•		•	8
	Behavior		•	•					•		•			•					•	•		7
	Sponsorship and funding			•							•			•			•		•		•	6
	Change management	•							•		•						•		•	•		6
	Processes		•		•			•					•									4
	Staff	•									•						•		•			4
	Strategy										•						•				•	3
	Organizational structure				•									•					•			3
	Efficiency	•																				1

stakeholders to improve their chances of gaining increased benefits from BI. Absence of processes in a maturity model may increase time taken by the stakeholders to search for ways to improve and achieve a higher BI maturity level.

Further, efficiency was mentioned only in the model proposed by Watson, Ariyachandra, and Matyska (2001). Efficiency is the ratio of resource input to resource output. In other words, it indicates the costs and benefits of BI initiatives. This aspect typically draws attention from organizations, but not from academic authors of the models. This is because the intangible benefits of BI initiatives are rather difficult to measure using BI maturity models. Therefore, efficiency is less likely to receive academic attention.

Notably, the models have rarely addressed components such as organizational structure, staff, and strategy. These components are highly pointed out in the information system literature (Watson et al., 2001). The term organizational structure refers to the characteristics, structure, and placement of the system across the enterprise. Staff refers to the experience, skills, and specialization of BI staff in the organization, while strategy refers to the strategic alignment of BI—for instance, on corporate, business, or IT objectives. The three components are vital contributors to successful BI implementation. Therefore, an effective BI maturity model should include these components.

Components that are well addressed in the models are behavior, change management, performance management, sponsorship, and funding. These are components of business-related issues. It is important to include components from the business side of BI to develop a comprehensive BI maturity model. The aforementioned components increase the effectiveness and efficiency of BI implementation across the organization. Thus, they should not be overlooked.

The comparison reveals the extensive attention on classic IT topics such as tools, architecture, and data' be acceptable. IT topics are always the first to be recollected in discussions on BI. However, IT is only a part of BI because BI is an umbrella term that encompasses architectures, tools, database applications, methodologies, and business-related topics. Hence, business-related topics must be included in BI maturity models. Further, many models also focus on impact as it is vital to measure impact (organizational impact and individual impact) in BI maturity models.

In sum, the comparison of different BI maturity models highlighted a few issues. IT-related topics, such as on tools, architecture, and data, remain the most popular topics. Conversely, business-related topics, such as on behavior, change management, performance management, sponsorship, and funding, attracted increased attention from academics and practitioners during 2001–2012. However, a few components—efficiency, organizational structure, staff, and strategy—were rarely discussed. The present study recommends incorporating all IT- and business-related components in a comprehensive BI maturity model to ensure coverage of the broad business-to-IT scope of BI.

METHOD

We adopted a two-stage qualitative approach. In Stage 1, we conducted an exploratory Delphi study to identify the EBIM factors through group consensus of 15 BI experts. According to Linstone and Turoff (2002), Delphi is "a method for structuring a group communication process so that the process is effective in allowing a group of individuals, as a whole, to deal with a complex problem" (pg. 3). This method fits the exploratory nature of our study because expert opinion is significant in defining the research framework when knowledge and theory are incomplete. Further, the anonymity in a Delphi method encourages respondents to be truthful (Linstone & Turoff, 2002).

The Delphi study consisted of two iterations. In the first iteration, we distributed a list of the 43 factors that we compiled from the literature to the experts and asked them to rate the importance of these factors on a 5-point Likert scale. We also informed the experts that they could add new factors to the list. In the second iteration, we presented the experts a comparison of their own responses and the group's responses (i.e., the group median and interquartile range). We also gave them the same questionnaire used in the first iteration and asked them to rate the importance of the factors again. The only additions to this questionnaire were the new factors added by the experts in the first iteration. We once again told the experts that they could add new factors. We finalized the list of factors according to these experts' feedback.

Table 3 shows the background of these experts. These individuals were selected on the basis of their position in the organization, their BI experience, and BI initiatives in their companies. Four of them were from the academic field and the others, from different industries such as consulting/professional

Table 3. Stage 1: participants' background and company information

Expert	Position	Expert's BI experience (years)	Company type	Lengths of company's BI initiative (years)	Number of BI applications used in the company	BI investment from company's annual revenue (%)
1	Managing Director	1 to 3	SME	1 to 3	1 to 2	1
2	Academic (Lecturer)	1 to 3	SME	1 to 3	1 to 2	1
3	Deputy General Manager	4 to 6	SME	5 to 10	3 to 5	2 to 3
4	Senior Product Manager	1 to 3	MNC	1 to 3	3 to 5	0.01
5	Chief Technology Officer	14 years and above	LPL	5 to 10	6 to 10	2 to 3
6	Partner of a firm	20 years and above	SME	10 to 20	21 or more	1
7	Academic (Deputy Director)	7 to 10	SME	5 to 10	21 or more	4 to 5
8	Academic (Head of School)	7 to 10	SME	5 to 10	21 or more	4 to 5
9	Application Engineer	1 to 3	MNC	1 to 3	1 to 2	2 to 3
10	IT Assistant Manager	4 to 6	SME	5 to 10	1 to 2	1
11	Manager	1 to 3	MNC	3 to 5	3 to 5	6 to 10
12	Assistant Manager	4 to 6	MNC	10 to 20	3 to 5	4 to 5
13	Academic (Lecturer)	4 to 6	SME	1 to 3	1 to 2	1
14	Team Lead, Information Management	4 to 6	MNC	5 to 10	21 or more	4 to 5
15	Manager	4 to 6	MNC	1 to 3	1 to 2	11 or more

Note: SME: Small and medium-sized enterprise; MNC: Multinational corporation; LPL: Local public listed company services (three experts), financial services (four experts), software/Internet services (two experts), telecommunications (one expert) and construction/architecture/engineering (one expert). Most of the industry experts were at the management level and had many years of BI experience. Their companies actively invested in BI by directing some percentage of annual revenues to BI projects. The companies were also located in different regions, with one each in the United Kingdom, the United States, Singapore, and Indonesia, two in Australia, and nine in Malaysia. The diverse participant backgrounds ensured that our study reflected the view of experts from different industries, regions, and company sizes.

In Stage 2, we performed case studies to corroborate the findings from Stage 1. In the absence of extensive academic literature, the Stage 1 Delphi study was used to reduce the number of factors. Therefore, the case study methodology was used because it provides better explanations, insights, and understanding on the examined phenomena and allows rich descriptions (Miles & Huberman, 1994; Yin, 2003). In case selection, relevance rather than representativeness is prioritized because, essentially, a case study is an empirical investigation following replication logic that leads to analytic generalization (Yin, 2003). Therefore, the multiple case studies that we used in this study should be regarded as multiple experiments and not as responses from multiple respondents in a survey (Yin, 2003).

In this study, we selected four cases—two in the high BI maturity Level 5 (C1 and C3) and one each in the moderate Level 3 (C4) and the low maturity Level 1 (C2). C1 and C3 supported more BI applications compared with C4 and C2. Since the cases included a variety of companies in different countries (see Table 4), the sampling was deemed to be rich in information and appropriate for theoretical replication.

Semi-structured interviews were conducted with the BI experts. At the beginning of the interview session, we distributed a set of questionnaires to the interviewees to assess the current BI initiative of their companies. The assessment result served as the foundation for subsequent interview questions. We also used a guiding list of predefined questions. The interview questions revolved around five themes: accuracy of the proposed EBIM model, its comprehensiveness, satisfaction level with the organization's BI maturity, motivating factors to move on or remain in the current BI maturity level, and shift of focus as the organization's BI maturity increased.

Data Analysis

The Delphi data from Stage 1 were analyzed using descriptive statistics. In particular, standard deviation (SD), median, and interquartile range were calculated. Interquartile ranges are used in Delphi studies to show the degree of group consensus. When using a 5-point Likert scale, responses with a quartile

Table 4. Stage 2: information on the participating companies

Case	Years of BI initiative in the company	Number of BI applications in the company	Company type	BI investment from the company's annual revenues (%)	Location of the company
C1	10	21 or more	SME	4 to 5	England
C2	1	1 to 2	SME	1	Malaysia
C3	10	21 or more	MNC	4 to 5	United States
C4	2	1 to 2	MNC	11 or more	Singapore

deviation less than or equal to 0.6 are considered high consensus; those greater than 0.6 and less than or equal to 1.0, moderate consensus; and those greater than 1.0, low consensus (Raskin, 1994). Hasson et al. (2000) opined that consensus is achieved when standard deviation (SD) is 1.2 or less, because one standard deviation from the mean contains 68% of all scores. Therefore, only factors with SD of 1.0 or less were selected as KPAs. Based on the recommended procedures, the thresholds of SD less than 1.0 and interquartile range less than or equal to1.0 support the resultant KPAs. The existence of Critical Success Factors (CSFs) in Iteration 3 of the Delphi study signaled a critical point to terminate the study. The interview data from Stage 2 were analyzed in line with Miles and Huberman's (1994) three major concurrent processes of data reduction, data display, and conclusion drawing/verification.

RESULTS

Stage 1 Findings

Table 5a shows the results for Iteration 1. The consensus regarding five KPAs was high; three of these are from the Organization dimension and one each, from Technology and Process. This implies that the experts have been paying more attention to the Organization dimension. The consensus on BI as key revenue generator was the highest. In fact, almost all experts agreed that it belongs to Level 4–Optimize because BI can be the key revenue generator only after successful BI implementation. Additionally, after consolidation and integration at the previous levels, BI is optimized in Level 4. The consensus on 10 KPAs was low. The consensus on Spreadsheets and Define BI vision and roadmap was the least. It is interesting to find that the consensus on the latter KPA was low.

Table 5a. Results for the Delphi study: Iteration 1

KPA	Median	SD	Interquartile
Master Data Management (MDM) architecture	*3*	*0.88*	*0.5*
Multiple BI applications developed	*3*	*0.83*	*0.5*
Little/No BI awareness	*1*	*0.99*	*0.5*
Cross-departmental BI governance	*3*	*0.74*	*0.5*
BI as key revenue generator	*4*	*0.88*	*0.0*
Spreadsheets	2	1.36	2.0
Senior-level management actively sponsors BI	4	1.11	1.5
Define BI vision and roadmap	3	1.18	2.0
BI Service-Oriented Architecture (SOA)	5	1.44	1.5
Key Performance Indicators (KPI)	4	1.18	1.5
Advanced analytics	4	1.10	1.5
Program management	4	1.18	1.5
Operational BI	3	1.03	1.5
Change management	3	1.01	1.5
Balanced scorecard	4	1.13	1.5

Note: Italics are used for KPAs with high consensus and plain font for KPAs with low consensus

On comparing the results for Iteration 1 with those in the literature, we found that the level in which the experts positioned Spreadsheets and Key Performance Indicators (KPI) differed. Four experts from the financial services industry placed the former in Level 3 or above, while the literature has argued it should be in Level 1. The rest of the Delphi participants categorized it into either Level 1 or Level 2. Since Database, which is meant to replace spreadsheets, is present in Level 2 of the Technology dimension, it does not make logical sense to place Spreadsheets in Level 3.

Based on the literature, Key Performance Indicators (KPI) should be in Level 3. However, it was placed in Level 4 under the Organization dimension. All four academic experts on the panel categorized it as Level 4 or Level 5, while the practitioners placed it into different levels ranging from the lowest to the highest.

In Iteration 2, there were more KPAs with high consensus (see Table 5b), implying increased agreement among the experts on the factors. We included all these KPAs in the EBIM model. There was high or moderate consensus on KPAs with low consensus in Iteration 1. In other words, there was no KPA with low consensus in Iteration 2.

The KPA Little/No BI awareness has an interquartile value of 0. In Iteration 1, some experts categorized it into Level 3 and Level 4, thus contributing to its high interquartile value. In this iteration, all experts positioned it in Level 1 as it precedes any BI effort within organizations. The KPA Spreadsheets was also moved from Level 2 to Level 1 as the experts agreed that it belongs to the lowest level, which is the beginning of any BI initiative. The SD for KPA Key Performance Indicators (KPI) is lower than

Table 5b. Results for the Delphi study: Iteration 2

KPA	Median	SD	Interquartile
Little/No BI awareness	1	0.00	0.0
BI as key revenue generator	4	0.88	0.0
Spreadsheets	1	0.46	0.5
Centralized data warehouse	3	0.46	0.5
Senior-level management actively sponsors BI	4	0.70	0.5
Multiple BI applications developed	3	0.70	0.5
Define BI vision and roadmap	3	0.93	0.5
BI Service-Oriented Architecture (SOA)	5	0.83	0.5
BI Competency Center	4	0.88	0.5
Separated analytical process	2	0.83	0.5
Cross-departmental BI governance	3	0.88	0.5
Master Data Management (MDM) architecture	3	0.88	0.5
Key Performance Indicators (KPI)	*4*	*0.68*	*1.0*
Program management	*4*	*0.68*	*1.0*
Advanced analytics	*4*	*0.63*	*1.0*
Operational BI	*3*	*0.88*	*1.0*
Change management	*3*	*0.74*	*1.0*
Balanced scorecard	*4*	*0.51*	*1.0*

Note: Italics are used to indicate KPAs for which the consensus changed in Iteration 2 from that of Iteration 1 in Iteration 1 although it remained in Level 4. Although this result is different from that in the literature, the KPA seems to fit reasonably well into the EBIM model and was thus retained.

Next, we proposed an EBIM model containing three dimensions and five levels (see Table 5c) based on the Stage 1 results. The three dimensions are Process, Organization, and Technology. Level 1 is the lowest level and an organization would progressively move to the highest level. Each lower level is a

Table 5c. The proposed model following stage 1 results

<table>
<tr><th>Dimension</th><th>Level</th><th>KPA</th></tr>
<tr><td rowspan="5">Process</td><td>5 (Innovate)</td><td>Fully embedded advanced analytics and BI</td></tr>
<tr><td>4 (Optimize)</td><td>• Established a standard for best practices
• Advanced master data management (MDM)</td></tr>
<tr><td>3 (Integrate)</td><td>• Sophisticated data governance
• Integrated analytics and BI within systems and workflows
• Change management
• Operational BI
• Metadata management</td></tr>
<tr><td>2 (Consolidate)</td><td>• Start master data management (MDM)
• Separated analytical process
• Ad hoc BI</td></tr>
<tr><td>1 (Initial)</td><td>• Analytics is undefined
• Inconsistent data</td></tr>
<tr><td rowspan="5">Organization</td><td>5 (Innovate)</td><td>High quality information easily accessible</td></tr>
<tr><td>4 (Optimize)</td><td>• Align BI with business strategy
• Maximum alliance between business and IT team
• BI in R&D
• Program management
• Senior-level management actively sponsors BI
• BI Competency Center
• KPI</td></tr>
<tr><td>3 (Integrate)</td><td>• Executive sponsors BI
• Enterprise wide performance metric framework
• Cross-departmental BI governance
• Project-based roles and skills
• Defined BI vision and roadmap</td></tr>
<tr><td>2 (Consolidate)</td><td>• Defined BI goals and scope
• Begin to provide BI training
• BI expertise remains in individuals
• Low involvement from management level
• Limited insight into customers, markets, and competitors</td></tr>
<tr><td>1 (Initial)</td><td>Little/No BI awareness</td></tr>
<tr><td rowspan="5">Technology</td><td>5 (Innovate)</td><td>BI Service-Oriented Architecture (SOA)</td></tr>
<tr><td>4 (Optimize)</td><td>• Enterprise data warehouse
• Advanced analytics
• Balanced scorecard</td></tr>
<tr><td>3 (Integrate)</td><td>• Centralized data warehouse
• Master data architecture
• ETL & OLAP</td></tr>
<tr><td>2 (Consolidate)</td><td>Data silos</td></tr>
<tr><td>1 (Initial)</td><td>Spreadsheets</td></tr>
</table>

prerequisite for the next higher one, which means a higher maturity level will encompass the KPA from all previous lower levels. The five levels are defined as follows:

- **Level 5–Innovate:** The organization and BI is in oneness and effort of actively seeking innovation and breakthrough is carried out.
- **Level 4–Optimize:** BI becomes a strategic enterprise resource and the organization continues to optimize BI implementation to the fullness.
- **Level 3–Integrate:** Connect and combine segmented BI efforts across the organization.
- **Level 2–Consolidate:** The organization dynamically adopts BI and constructs BI practices and systems.
- **Level 1–Initial:** BI is a strange concept to the organization or it has just become aware of BI.

Stage 2 Findings

The results around the five themes were as follows.

Accuracy of Model

Interviewees were questioned to determine their consensus on the assessment results. All experts agreed and were satisfied with the assessment results. They believed that the results matched their perception of the BI maturity level in their organizations. They were able to identify the maturity level of their organizations with the KPAs. In other words, the EBIM model accurately reflected their organizations' current BI maturity and efforts through the KPA in every cell (the intersection of level and dimension). For instance, the C4 interviewee agreed with the result showing that his organization was at Level 3 in the "Technology" dimension. Overall, none of the experts raised any objections to the assessment results. Through the process, they verified the accuracy of the model in presenting the identified KPAs and the BI maturity or their organizations.

Moreover, the results show that all of the four cases were doing exceptionally well in the Technology dimension. They had achieved Level 4 or Level 5. This finding shows that organizations put a great deal of effort into developing the technological dimension in BI implementation. Although the Technology dimension is important, organizations should not emphasize only this dimension and exclude the others, because they can ensure successful BI implementation only by focusing on all the dimensions.

Satisfaction Level of Organization's BI Maturity

The C1, C3, and C4 interviewees were satisfied with their current BI maturity in every dimension as well as with the overall maturity in the EBIM model. However, they also indicated their desire to move to a higher maturity level. An interviewee commented, "Being good is not enough—it is essential to do better." Organizations must continuously direct their efforts toward BI implementation to realize the desire to attain a higher maturity level.

The desire to perform better is not in individuals alone but is also propagated across organizations through refined company vision, mission, and plans. In the C1 organization, the sponsorship of senior-level management became a significant driver for the BI initiative. Senior-level management was excited to observe "what is coming up" by applying advanced analytics. Similarly, in C4, the organization continually aligned its goals and vision for improving BI implementation. The EBIM model revealed unfinished tasks (unfulfilled KPA) to the companies in the case studies. According to an interviewee, this motivated them to increase their effort to achieve the highest level in all dimensions. Additionally, the C4 interviewee stated that they were working on the KPA about Sophisticated data governance while pursuing higher BI maturity. He pointed out that people were the main barrier in implementing data governance in the organization because of the work culture in certain departments, which impeded data sharing across the organization. For instance, the Finance Department was reluctant to share sensitive financial data, although the senior-level management had encouraged data sharing for the BI initiative. Organizations must reassure employees that it has eliminated the risk of sensitive data being leaked.

Conversely, the C2 organization, while obtaining Level 4 in the Technology dimension, was able to achieve only Level 1 in the Process and Organization dimensions. The C2 organization was consolidating its BI initiative and had channeled substantial effort and resources to the dimensions in which its maturity level was low for some KPAs. During the interview, the C2 interviewee conveyed his desire to move the C2 organization to a higher level of BI maturity. Nevertheless, he was unclear about how to align the organization so that it could move to a higher level of BI maturity. He also said that the EBIM model presented a clear pathway of actions the organization should take to move on to the next level. Therefore, this finding proves the usability of the EBIM model in the business world.

Shift of Focus as Organization's BI Maturity Increases

The interviewees were asked to identify the most essential KPA in each level and were told that the KPA could be from any dimension. All four interviewees agreed that organizations must first focus on Inconsistent data in Level 1. An interviewee stressed that data inconsistency is a painful fact in many companies and it adversely affects management decisions. Without consistent data, an organization could stagnate for a long time and its competitors might overtake it. Another interviewee claimed that it is proven that an organization experiences considerable improvement by having consistent data. It is undeniable that data are vital for the BI initiative because data serve as the foundation of BI. We agree that data significantly influence (i.e., either a beneficial influence or an adverse one) BI implementation, as highlighted by the interviewee.

In Level 2–Consolidate, interviewees identified Start Master Data Management (MDM), Defined BI goals and scope, Limited insight into customers, markets, and competitors, and Low involvement from management level as the most essential KPAs. Most of the interviewees advocated that the KPAs in the Organization dimension should be the first priority because management support for the BI initiative is the main factor to ensure the initiative is successful. If the BI initiative lacks management support, having advanced technologies and sophisticated processes will not help organizations ensure successful BI implementation. All three elements are required to achieve this goal.

One of the interviewees emphasized the importance of MDM. In other words, ensuring data consistency allows senior management to trust and rely on such data for decision-making. Further, other interviewees also stressed that the involvement of chief management is critical. They need to be educated about the importance of reports and leveraging data to gain insights into customer behaviors, markets, and competitors. Insights generated by the reporting system would assist management in drilling down to the root problem quickly. "Limited insight into customer behaviors, markets, and competitors" and "Low involvement from management level" contribute to the "Start to define BI goals and scope" KPA. Management, on realizing the importance of gaining insights into customer behaviors, markets, and competitors, will begin defining BI goals and scope. Clear BI goals and scope help the organization and employees to observe the direction of the BI implementation and the corresponding actions to be taken.

The interviewees selected many KPAs from Level 3–Integrate as the most essential. Most of these are from the Organization dimension. The selected KPAs are Executive Sponsors BI, Project-based roles and skills, Define BI vision and roadmap, Change management, ETL & OLAP, and Centralized data warehouse. Obviously, this dimension receives extensive attention from practitioners and academics. Executive sponsorship of the BI initiative is considered significant once again. The level of executive sponsorship is higher in this level compared with management sponsorship in Level 2. The BI initiative must be actively promoted by an executive to drive its implementation. Subsequently, this individual will also help to define the BI vision and roadmap. The direction of BI initiative development would depend on the defined BI vision and roadmap. Moreover, project-based roles and skills need to be clearly defined. A list of guidelines must be prepared for the benefit of employees seeking assistance during BI implementation on designated experts they can contact, topics on which information is available, links at which this information is available, and methods of searching for information.

In addition to the aforementioned KPAs, one interviewee chose Change management as one of the most essential KPAs in Level 3. She explained that this KPA guaranteed a certain degree of transparency to people in her organization. For example, KPIs previously stored in individual computers were now always easily accessible to superiors who desired to use these to evaluate their subordinates. She believed that transparency is necessary to smoothen the processes of BI implementation. Further, another interviewee suggested that Extract, Transform, Load (ETL) & Online Analytical Processing (OLAP) is also essential in Level 3 because it is correlated to the selected KPA. Yet another interviewee proposed that Centralized data warehouse (in the "Technology" dimension) should be included among the most essential KPA. We noticed that the interviewee was biased toward this dimension.

The most essential KPAs in Level 4–Optimize are Align BI with business strategy, Advanced Master Data Management (MDM), and Advanced analytics. BI is aligned with business strategy to drive enterprise and industry transformation. Their BI initiative is becoming a critical requirement for organizations and is closely related to their business activities. One of the interviewees remarked that advanced MDM is important as it enables global consolidation and standardization of data within the organization. With advanced features, advanced MDM increases the efficiency of data management and quality. Advanced analytics is in the Technology dimension and it refers to a grouping of tools and technologies used to perform predictive analytics. It allows anticipation of future outcomes and preparation of actions to address these outcomes. For instance, it helps to identify latent market demand and innovate products to fulfill such demand.

KPAs such as Fully embedded advanced analytics and BI in processes and BI service-oriented architecture (SOA) are chosen by interviewees for Level 5–Innovate. According to two of the interviewees, Level 4–Optimize and Level 5–Innovate are actually interrelated. Actions in Level 4 affect Level 5; however, these two levels differ. Organizations would seek innovation in using BI in Level 5. As suggested by its definition, at Level 5, organizations would seek to explore new methods of using advanced analytics and BI to maximize profits. There is active effort in the organization to understand more about customers from the behavioral aspect to improve customer engagement. For instance, advanced analytics is integrated with business processes to offer recommendations on related products after customers purchase a certain product. Further, data mining and advanced analytics technologies such as data visualization are used to communicate information and insights clearly and efficiently to BI users through the information graphics selected, such as tables and charts. Therefore, management is able to take precise decisions based on easily accessible, rich, real-time information.

The C2 interviewee suggested BI service-oriented architecture (SOA) is the most essential KPA in Level 5 because it enables seamless integration and delivery of data across the organization. Organizations must work on the speed with which they are able to deliver new analytics to users as well as on understanding how emerging technologies affect the way users receive and process information. SOA provides automated analytical processes with lesser human interaction, which could result in quick delivery of information to supporting decision-making.

Overall, most of the interviewees were in favor of the Organization dimension as their organization's BI maturity increased. This finding highlights the significance of organizational support in implementing BI. Management sponsorship would influence the success of BI initiatives tremendously. As indicated by one interviewee, without a supportive management, the organization cannot implement its BI initiative even if it uses sophisticated processes and advanced technology. However, this finding does not suggest that the KPAs in other dimensions are unimportant. The focus in this discussion is on priority. Another interviewee prioritized the three dimensions in the following order: Process, Organization, and Technology. She mentioned that a process must be developed to produce data. Next, management sponsorship is vital in bringing in technology to work with the established process. Failure is guaranteed if any one of these dimensions is missing.

The C1, C3, and C4 interviewees were aware that the Organization dimension is the key driver of a successful BI initiative. At the outset, data must be handled carefully because these are sources of useful information and valuable insights that later facilitate improved decision-making. Therefore, all interviewees agreed that organizations must first focus on data cleansing, to ensure inconsistency is eliminated. As the maturity level increases, interviewees highlighted KPAs mostly from the Organization dimension up to Level 4–Optimize. Further, a few KPAs were selected from the Process dimension as most essential. The interviewee who selected these process-related KPAs emphasized the Process dimension more than the other dimensions. This could be related to her position in managing data within her organization. However, she also stressed the importance of Organization by selecting a few KPAs from this dimension.

The Technology dimension had the least number of KPAs chosen as the most essential. Most were chosen by the C2 interviewee who was in the organization that achieved the lowest BI maturity (Level 1) among the four companies studied. The C2 assessment result and the interview data indicated the development of the BI initiative of this organization was imbalanced in three dimensions. The Technology Dimension was the most developed. C2 had obtained Level 4 in this dimension, while it was at Level 2 in the other two dimensions. Analysis of the interview data reveals that C2 was similar to other organizations that failed to harvest the full benefits of their BI initiative because they mistook technology to be the sole driver of a successful BI initiative. Business users saw data warehousing as an IT solution without clear business objectives and goals. Business needs in BI initiative were not addressed. This explains the bias of the C2 interviewee in selecting most of the essential KPAs from the Technology dimensions. He also revealed that the business owner and management had lost confidence in their BI initiative because of the lack of improvement after investment in BI. The BI initiative must be developed again together with other dimensions (Process and Organization) to ensure successful BI implementation.

Regardless of organization scale, Technology was the first and most developed dimension. According to the interviewees, management decisions dictated the direction of BI initiatives. The shift of focus of the four companies as BI maturity increases also reflects the importance of management decisions. In C2, the negligence of KPAs in Process and Organization dimensions was the outcome of management shortsightedness in considering data warehousing the IT solution to their problems. In conclusion, the three dimensions together with the KPA in each cell were discussed sufficiently during the interviews. Interviewees reflected that the EBIM model showed the evolutionary path of BI maturity accurately and in a systematic manner. They also proved that KPAs in lower maturity levels are prerequisites for KPAs in higher maturity levels.

Comprehensiveness of EBIM Model

Generally, all of the interviewees were pleased with the EBIM model. The KPAs were well grouped in every level, said an interviewee. Further, KPAs in every level matched the descriptive name of the levels. Overall, the EBIM model measures the BI maturity of organizations efficiently.

Further, another interviewee mentioned that the KPAs of the EBIM model provide a clearer and better view of different BI maturity levels. Previously, the interviewee only saw technology as the BI solution for his organization, but now he saw that a BI initiative requires support from the Process and Organization dimensions as well. Moreover, the EBIM model provides specific KPAs as guidelines for his organization to move on to a higher maturity level, especially in the two dimensions neglected by his organization (C2). For example, the organization needs to first involve management and draw insights into customer behaviors, markets, and competitors and then define its BI goals and scope.

In addition, one of the interviewees commented that KPAs related to people need to be included and she said that the Organization dimension already encompasses such KPAs about people. A people-centric dimension is necessary because a BI initiative involves people and is significantly affected by people such as BI users, customers, suppliers, and other BI stakeholders. In addition to these points, interviewees offered further suggestions, which are discussed in the next subsection.

Interviewees also commented on the correlation between KPAs in and across dimensions. Positive feedback was received from interviewees. For example, Level 1 KPAs in Organization (Analytics is undefined and Inconsistent data), Process (Little/No BI awareness), and Technology (Spreadsheets) are correlated. In the absence of a BI initiative, excel spreadsheets are used to store data on individual computers. This causes data inconsistency, as there are several copies of the same data on different devices.

Another example is the correlation between Level 4 KPAs in the Organization (Program management, Senior-level management actively sponsors BI, BI Competency Center (BICC), and KPI), Process (Established a standard for best practices and Advanced Master Data Management (MDM)), and Technology dimensions (Enterprise data warehouse and Advanced analytics). Program management is executed to manage several BI projects with the intention of improving the organization's performance and this KPA is correlated to the KPAs in the Technology dimension that benefited from program management in establishing a standard set of project development methodologies and technologies that incorporate best practices. It is certain that active support from senior-level management is expected to approve and perform activities related to the aforementioned KPAs in the Process and Technology dimensions. KPI is implemented together with advanced analytics such as predictive analysis and data mining. BICC is established to consolidate all information-centric disciplines such as BI, data warehousing, and content. The consolidation process needs to be implemented along with advanced MDM and enterprise data warehouse to achieve a single version of the truth across the organization.

Last, the EBIM model is well-designed and covers BI maturity in terms of levels and dimensions. KPAs in the model span the spectrum of BI from technology-related topics to business-related topics. Therefore, the comprehensiveness of the EBIM model is recognized with the commendation from interviewees.

Additional Suggestions

During the interviews, interviewees offered a few suggestions concerning extra KPAs, KPA outliers, and the EBIM model in general. First, the interviewee who focused on the Process dimension added an extra KPA, namely Utilization. She explained that the KPA should be placed in Level 5–Innovate of the Process dimension. Utilization refers to usage of the structure and efforts made for the entire BI initiative by the users. She further stated that if organizations do not define a comprehensive process of utilization of all the BI technologies, the BI initiative would be unsuccessful and thus of no benefit to organizations. We agreed with her view; however, we consider that it can be grouped as a sub-KPA in the EBIM model and it should be placed under the BI service-oriented architecture (SOA) KPA because utilization is already considered in building BI SOA in the Technology dimension.

Further, another interviewee commented that a new KPA, Data product, should be added to the proposed model. A data product refers to products and services created using analytics on data assets. The interviewee gave the example of suggestive selling by Amazon.com that systematically keeps its customers in a buying mood when they have committed to their primary purchases, which is a true path to retail profitability. Later, the interviewee stated that "Data product" was already included in BI SOA from a technological perspective. Therefore, no change was made to the EBIM model based on this suggestion.

Outliers are the KPAs whose level in the Delphi study result did not match their original levels in literature from which they were extracted. We obtained the opinions of the interviewees on every outlier discussed. There are two outliers, namely, Spreadsheets and Key Performance Indicators (KPI). The first outlier was placed in the correct level (Level 1) after the review by the BI experts in Iteration 2 of the Delphi study. However, we sought confirmation through interviews. All interviewees agreed that spreadsheets should be moved from Level 2 to Level 1. Two of the interviewees initially categorized it into Level 2 during round one of Delphi study and then re-categorized the KPA into Level 1 during Iteration 2 of the Delphi study. They admitted the initial categorization was an error when we enquired about the change they made. The interviewees further added that spreadsheets are the first tool used by organizations before introduction of any BI effort. For the second outlier, the interviewees did not change their decision that it should belong to Level 4 in the Organization dimension. They indicated that KPI should be in Level 4 because this is the stage in which organizations expend maximum efforts toward BI initiative optimization using tools such as advanced analytics, and thus, must use KPI to measure organization performance.

In addition, an interviewee commended the completeness and comprehensiveness of the EBIM model in presenting all crucial KPAs systematically, but he was concerned about the practicality of the model in industry. Organizations that lack information about the benefits offered by BI and the ways in which BI could help the organization may not be keen to adopt it. Hence, they continue to use their current way of conducting business. With the aim of helping organizations understand the power of BI, agile BI has been developed to motivate business users to commence searching for insights from their data after viewing the quick analysis generated by agile BI. Then, the organization will open to BI adoption. Further, the interviewee elaborated that the EBIM model is mostly applicable to organizations that have started BI implementation but may not attract attention from organizations that have not. We acknowledged the suggestion and clarified that the objective of the EBIM model is to provide a more comprehensive way to measure BI maturity in organizations and the study did not focus on promoting BI adoption. Hence, the practicality issue raised by the interviewee is not applicable to this study.

CONCLUSION

The main goal of this study was to develop a comprehensive BI maturity model for BI stakeholders to enable them to improve the maturity level of organizational BI initiatives. It was accomplished through a two-stage research methodology. This study listed important KPAs that influence the success of the BI implementation process. The KPAs were further grouped systematically into different levels and dimensions based on a literature review, Delphi study, and case study. The literature review and Delphi study helped to construct the EBIM model, and it was consolidated and validated through the case study.

This study offers three important research contributions. First, the proposed maturity model is more comprehensive than existing BI maturity models because it provides wider coverage, ranging from technology-related topics to business-related topics. Lack of comprehensiveness is a significant problem of the existing BI maturity models. The more comprehensive EBIM model would enable BI stakeholders to gauge BI initiative maturity in their organizations more accurately.

Second, the EBIM model presents a clearer pathway for organizations to attain higher BI maturity. Organizations can plan, assess, and undertake large-scale BI initiatives efficiently, because the model reveals the current stage of their BI implementation and steps they can take to improve it. Moreover, guidelines (KPAs) are provided for organizations to achieve higher maturity levels and to enhance the efficiency of their BI initiatives.

Finally, a comprehensive EBIM model allows users to perform self-assessment easily without third-party assistance. Only a few existing BI maturity models offer this feature, but these either lack guidelines or offer insufficient guidelines. By using the proposed EBIM model, users would be able to evaluate the maturity of their BI implementation conveniently. Thus, they can closely monitor their BI maturity level and take necessary actions to obtain higher levels of BI maturity.

This study had some limitations. The chosen research approach—qualitative approach—and research method—action research—present limitations in terms of generalizability. The findings of this research open up a number of avenues for future research. First, a people-centric dimension can be studied further to discover more KPAs about people. People are the key factor that affects BI initiative in organizations. In addition, a software system can be developed for BI stakeholders to better measure and visualize the maturity levels of respective BI initiatives. It serves as an automated tool to help users in self-assessment without third-party assistance and offers useful guidelines.

REFERENCES

Burton, B. (2009). *Toolkit: Maturity checklist for business intelligence and performance management*. Stamford, CT: Gartner Research.

Chamoni, P., & Gluchowski, P. (2004). Integration trends in business intelligence systems: An empirical study based on the business intelligence maturity model. *Wirtschaftsinformatik*, *46*(2), 119–128. doi:10.1007/BF03250931

de Bruin, T., Rosemann, M., Freeze, R., & Kulkarni, U. (2005, November–December). *Understanding the main phases of developing a maturity assessment model.* Paper presented at the Australasian Conference on Information Systems (ACIS), Sydney, Australia.

Fraser, P., Moultrie, J., & Gregory, M. J. (2002). The use of maturity models/grids as a tool in assessing product development capability. *IEEE International Engineering Management Conference (IEMC 2002): Managing Technology for the New Economy*. 10.1109/IEMC.2002.1038431

Gartner. (2011, April 20). *Gartner says worldwide business intelligence, analytics and performance management software market surpassed the $10 billion mark in 2010*. Retrieved from https://www.gartner.com/newsroom/id/1642714

Gartner. (2016, October 17). *Gartner survey of more than 2,500 CIOs charts the rise of the digital ecosystem* [Press release]. Retrieved from https://www.gartner.com/newsroom/id/3481117

Gibson, C., & Nolan, R. (1974). Managing the four stages of EDP growth. *Harvard Business Review, 1*, 76–88.

Hasson, F., Keeney, S., & McKenna, H. (2000). Research guidelines for the Delphi survey technique. *Journal of Advanced Nursing, 32*(4), 1008–1015. PMID:11095242

Klynveld Peat Marwick Goerdeler. (2009). *Does your business intelligence tell you the whole story?* Academic Press.

Lahrmann, G., Marx, F., Winter, R., & Wortmann, F. (2010). Business intelligence maturity models: An overview. *Proceedings of the VII Conference of the Italian Chapter of AIS*.

Lahrmann, G., Marx, F., Winter, R., & Wortmann, F. (2011). Business intelligence maturity: Development and evaluation of a theoretical model. In *44th Hawaii International Conference on* (pp. 1–10). IEEE.

Lincoln, Y. S., & Guba, E. G. (1985). *Naturalistic inquiry*. Newbury Park, CA: Sage.

Linstone, H. A., & Turoff, M. (2002). *Delphi method: Techniques and applications*. Addison-Wesley.

Mettler, T., & Rohner, P. (2009). Situational maturity models as instrumental artifacts for organizational design. *Proceedings of 4th International Conference on Design Science Research in Information Systems and Technology*. 10.1145/1555619.1555649

Miles, M. B., & Huberman, A. M. (1994). *Qualitative data analysis* (2nd ed.). Thousand Oaks, CA: Sage.

Shaaban, E., Helmy, Y., Khedr, A., & Nasr, M. (2011). Business intelligence maturity models: Toward new integrated model. In *Proceedings of The International Arab Conference on Information Technology (ACIT '11)*. Riyadh, Saudi Arabia: Academic Press.

Simpson, E. S. C., & Weiner, J. A. (Eds.). (1989). *The Oxford encyclopaedic English dictionary*. Oxford, UK: Clarendon Press.

Thompson, O. (2004). *Business intelligence success, lessons learned*. Retrieved from http://www.technologyevaluation.com/Research/ResearchHighlights/ExecutiveView/2004/01/research_notes/MI_EV_XOT_01_29_04_1.asp

Turban, E., & Sharda, R. (2008). Introduction to business intelligence. In E. Turban, R. Sharda, D. Delen, & D. King (Eds.), *Business intelligence* (2nd ed.; pp. 9–16). New York, NY: Pearson Prentice Hall.

Watson, H. J., Ariyachandra, T. R., & Matyska, R. J. Jr. (2001). Data warehousing stages of growth. *Information Systems Management*, *18*(3), 42–50. doi:10.1201/1078/43196.18.3.20010601/31289.6

Wixom, B. H., & Watson, H. J. (2010). The BI-based organization. *International Journal of Business Intelligence Research*, *1*(1), 13–28. doi:10.4018/jbir.2010071702

Yin, R. K. (2003). *Case Study Research: Design and Methods*. Newbury Park, CA: Sage.

Chapter 4
Opportunities and Challenges of Implementing Predictive Analytics for Competitive Advantage

Mohsen Attaran
California State University – Bakersfield, USA

Sharmin Attaran
Bryant University, USA

ABSTRACT

Predictive analytics has become an increasingly hot topic in analytics landscape. As a result, predictive analytics deployments are gaining momentum. Yet, the adoption rate is slow, and organizations are only beginning to scratch the surface in regard to the potential applications of this technology. Implemented properly, the business benefits can be substantial. However, there are strategic pitfalls to consider. The key objective of this chapter is to propose a conceptual model for successful implementation of analytics in organizations. This chapter highlights the importance of predictive analytics, identifies determinants of implementation success, and covers some of the potential benefits of this technology. Furthermore, this study reviews key attributes of a successful predictive analytics platform and illustrates how to overcome some of the strategic pitfalls of incorporating this technology in business. Finally, this study highlights successful implementation of analytics solutions in manufacturing and service industry.

INTRODUCTION

Data is growing faster than ever before from a variety of sources including social media, mobile devices, and the Internet of Things (IOT). According to Gartner Research, data volume will grow 800 percent over the next 5 years and 80 percent of that data will be unstructured (Feki, et al, 2016). Several trends have contributed to this data explosion including massive growth in video and photo data, staggering usage of smart phones, 50 billion smart connected devices in the world, widespread usage of CRM, ERP,

DOI: 10.4018/978-1-5225-5718-0.ch004

and product/service logs (Marr, 2015; Perrin, 2015). Additionally, growing numbers of companies are collecting data from their customers. This trend will continue in the future. By the year 2020, about 1.7 megabytes of new information will be created every second for every human being on the planet. By then, our accumulated universe of data will reach 44 trillion gigabytes (McAfee and Brynjolfsson, 2012).

The majority of Big Data (unstructured data) doesn't offer a lot of value in its unprocessed state. Of course, one can pull powerful insights from this stockpile of data by applying the right set of tools and analytics. One can also see patterns and build a model of how these data work. Once you build a model, you can predict. The right use of Big Data can enable analysts to find trends and give big insights that help create value and drive operational efficiencies for the enterprise. Moreover, Big Data can bring other important benefits to organizations such as: enabling new products and services, helping to better meeting customer demands, and facilitating growth and analytics use. Insights hidden previously by data too costly to process can help in the creation of new products and in the discovery of ways to gain competitive advantages. Similarly, the ability to process every item of data in reasonable time and successfully exploiting the value in Big Data removes the troublesome need for sampling and promotes an investigative approach to data.

After years of slow adoption, Big Data and business analytics solutions have finally hit mainstream. Among all analytics tools, Predictive Analytics has become an increasingly hot topic in analytics circle as more organizations realize that predictive modeling of customer behavior and business scenarios is the big way to gain insights out of Big Data. Predictive Analytics is also considered as one of the key pillars of enabling digital transformation efforts across industries and business processed globally. Furthermore, heightened development and commercialization of analytics tools by IT vendors has also helped expand predictive analytics capabilities. As a result, there has been an increase in adoption levels.

When implemented properly, the technology can enable organizations to tap their collection of data to gain business benefits. Although the current users of predictive analytics are primarily large corporations, there are numerous additional industries and organizations where predictive analytics tools could advantageously assist decision makers.

In spite of the apparent advantages of using predictive analytics, a 2015 study by the MHI/Deloitte revealed that less than one-quarter of companies surveyed have adopted predictive analytics, though that number is expected to climb to nearly 70 percent by 2020 (DeAngelis, 2015). Therefore, it is important to explore the opportunities and challenges of implementing predictive analytics into the core business applications of businesses, and present the findings for enterprise leaders, administrators, managers, and policymakers to consider.

THE EVOLUTION OF BIG DATA AND ANALYTICS

The Rise of Big Data

The term "Big Data" was coined in mid 1990s and is defined as data that is too large, complex, and dynamic, and exceeds the processing capacity of conventional database architectures of an organization (Weiss and Indurkhya, 1998). According to Gartner, Big Data is comprised of high Volume, high Velocity, and high Variety data, which he calls 3V's. The data is too big and cannot be handled easily, it moves with excessive speed flowing in and out, making it difficult to analyze. Finally, the range and type of data sources are too great to assimilate (Figure 1). (Diebold, 2012)

The act of gathering and storing large amounts of data for eventual analysis is not new. Since 1950s, businesses were using basic analytics to uncover hidden patterns and trends, show changes over time, and confirm or challenge theories. As enterprises have amassed broader pools of data in big data platforms, it has created increased opportunities for them to mine that data for predictive insights. Typically, organizations cannot manage the data effectively with current database architectures rather they should choose an alternative way to process Big Data to gain value from it. A well-defined data management strategy is essential to successfully utilize Big Data in corporations around the world. Data and analytics are playing important roles in improving competitive advantage. (Taylor, 2012).

The Rise of Business Analytics

Analytics, in the form of business intelligence, is defined as a set of technologies, processes, and tools that use data to predict likely behavior by individuals, machinery or other entities.

By using the right analytics, Big Data can deliver richer insights and uncover hidden patterns and relationships. More data could translate into more possibilities for a business only if it can discover the meaning inside of it (Minelli, et al., 2013).

Since the 1950s, decades before anyone used the term "Big Data," businesses were using basic analytics to uncover hidden patterns and trends, show changes over time, and confirm or challenge theories. The new benefits that modern data analytics brings to the table are speed and efficiency. The ability to work faster – and stay agile – gives organizations a competitive edge that they didn't have before. Over the past decade data exploded, and became big and business intelligence has been revolutionized. Widespread access to the Cloud, insightful data visualizations, interactive business dashboards, and rise of self-service analytics made the technology available and affordable for businesses of all sizes. Suddenly advanced analytics is not just for the analysts (Gaitho, 2017). Analytics is commonly used in Finance, Marketing, Human Resources, Health Care, Government Policies and every possible industry where data is generated (Analytics Vidhya Content Team, 2015).

The past few years have seen an explosion in business use of analytics. Corporations around the world are using analytical tools, including business intelligence (BI), dashboards and data mining to gain a better understanding of their present customers and to predict who will potentially become customers,

Figure 1. 3 V's of Big Data

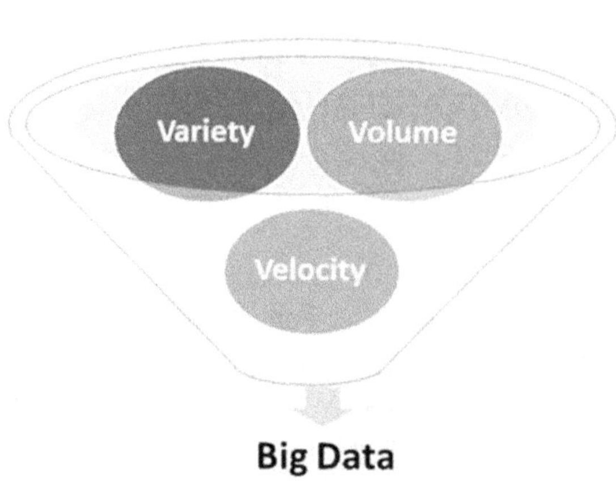

and what their need are. With the help of new analytics tools, enterprises can leverage Big Data analytics to drive a host of business objectives, from streamlined operations to improved customer relations (Henke, et al, 2016). In fact, Big Data analytics will transform virtually every business activity, and bring businesses benefits including enhanced customer service, optimized production levels, superior capacity planning, reduced repair and maintenance costs, and improved working capital utilization (Bughin, 2016). According to a 2016 Forester study, the top three tangible analytics benefits were identified as: increased margin, profitability, and increased gross sales (Evelson and Bennett, 2015). Several research studies have documented the advantages and widespread applications of analytics tools in corporations around the world (Evelson and Bennett, 2015; Gaitho, 2017; Lebied, 2016; Eckerson, 2016; Henke, at al., 2016; Minelli, et al., 2013).

Traditional vs. Modern Analytics

In the past five years, technology has set off waves of changes in the BI landscape. Advances in data collection, computational power, machine learning, and deep learning have expanded the field of BI well beyond previous forecasts. More sophisticated algorithms are being devised by scientists (Henke et al, 2016). Moreover, the growth of cloud-based platforms has given companies elastic scalability, up-to-date security, and the tools and storage capacity to conduct advanced analytics (Attaran, 2017).

In today's business environment, analytics is increasingly strategic and is now central to most business roles. A recent study by Gartner, published in 2015, identified shift of focus from IT-led reporting to business-led self-service analytics (Gartner Report, 2015). Traditional reporting-based BI platforms are not designed to handle the exponential growth in terms of the sources, volume, and complexity of data. The traditional platforms enforce strict data and report governance, only allowing access by specialized reporting groups. In contrast, the modern approach views data governance as an important step in creating self-service analytics. Traditional BI platforms are being augmented with more agile solutions. Where traditional systems could take months to implement, the modern approach takes as little as a few hours. Latency is no longer tolerated. The advances in the Internet have resulted in greater expectations and less patience.

Modern BI platforms support organizational needs for greater accessibility, agility, and analytical insight from a diverse range of data sources. Every business process is an analytics

process, and every business user is an analytics user. To meet the time-to-insight demands of today's competitive business environment, many organizations changed the traditional BI model and end-user requirements. The modern BI platform aims to democratize analytics with self-service capabilities. It is characterized by agility, flexibility, and ease of use (Gartner Report, 2015).

Categories of Analytics

Analytics is constantly evolving and has changed dramatically over the years and is advancing rapidly today. There are four categories of analytics: descriptive, diagnostics, predictive, and prescriptive (Table 1). These categories build on each other and enable enterprises to make faster and smarter decisions. As organizations evolve, they move from focusing on historical "what" and "why" questions to a more forward-looking predictive, and prescriptive predictions. The advanced analytics maturity path is shown on Figure 2 (Intel, 2017). Descriptive analytics is the simplest class of analytics. It allows you to con-

Table 1. Categories of business analytics

Business Analytics	Questions	Tools	Outcomes	Focus
Prescriptive (Automation)	• What should I do? • Why should I do it?	• Decision modeling • Optimization • Simulation • Expert systems	Optimization-Best possible business decisions	Focus on decision making and efficiency
Predictive (Foresight)	• What is likely to happen? • What will happen? • Why will it happen	• Data mining • Text/media mining • Predictive modeling • Artificial Neural Networks (ANN)	Accurate projections of the future conditions and states	Identify past patterns to predict the future
Diagnostic (Insight)	Why did it happen?	• Enterprise data warehouse • Data discovery • Data mining and correlations • Drill-down/roll-up	Accurate projections of the future conditions and states	Identify past patterns to predict the future
Descriptive (Hindsight)	• What happened? • What is happening?	• Data modeling • Business reporting • Visualization • Dashboard • Regression	Well defined business problems or opportunities	Uncovering patterns that offer insight

Figure 2. Moving up the analytics value chain

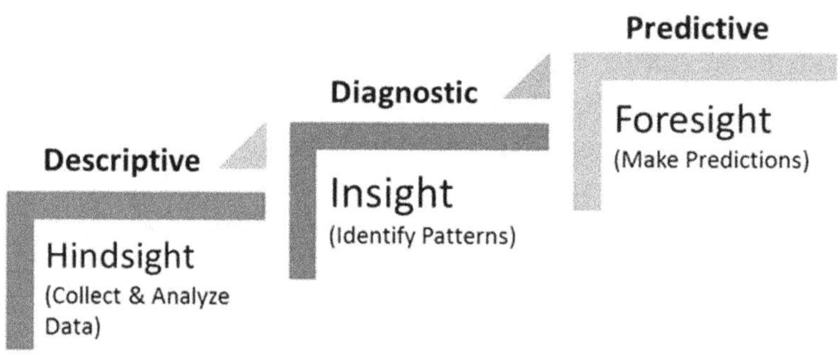

dense big data into smaller, more useful nuggets of information. The purpose of descriptive analytics is to summarize what happened in the past and uncover patterns that offer insights. It uses data modeling, reporting, visualization, and regression to collect and store data in an efficient way, to create reports and presentation information, and to find trends in the data. Since data is scattered in large numbers of disparate data sources, analyzing all relevant data can be a challenge for most organizations. Most descriptive analytics are exact (number of likes, number of clicks, etc.) because they are defined by a single, deterministic model which does not allow contradicting results. It is estimated that more than 80% of business analytics, most notably social analytics are descriptive.

Diagnostic analytics is the next step up in data reduction and it is used for discovery. It examines data or content to answer the question why did it happen. Diagnostic analytics takes a deeper look at data to attempt to understand the root causes of events and behaviors in an organization. To optimize diagnostic analytics, it needs to be extended to operational employees of the organization. The result of the diagnostic analytics is often an analytic dashboard that is used for discovery or to determine why something happened.

Predictive analytics analyze current and historical data to provide insights into what will happen and why will it happen in the future with an acceptable level of reliability. It attempts to accurately project the future condition and states. It does not predict one possible future, but rather multiple futures based on the decision-maker's actions. It utilizes a variety of statistical, modeling, data mining, text, media mining, forecasting, and predictive modeling to identify probabilities of potential outcomes and/or likely results of specific operations. Predictive analytics can only forecast what might happen in the future, because all predictive analytics are probabilistic in nature. Predictive analytics can help businesses with a wide range of problems. Businesses are using Predictive Analytics to analyze historical data and facts in order to better understand clients' needs, market potentials, products, suppliers, and partners and to identify potential risks and opportunities for a company (Lebied, 2016). Other businesses use this type of analytics for predicting which customers are most valuable, scheduling preventive maintenance, and detecting fraud. Airlines use this analytics to decide how many tickets to sell at what discounted price for a flight. Hotels use it to predict the number of guests they can expect to book on any given night to increase revenue.

The emerging technology of prescriptive analytics goes beyond descriptive and predictive models and shows the likely outcome of each decision. It goes a step further in the future and attempt to answers about what should be done and why. It employs data techniques such as decision modeling, graph analysis, simulation, neural networks, heuristics, and machine learning to suggest actions that the organization could take to achieve the desired outcome. Prescriptive analysis tries to evaluate the effect of future decisions in order to adjust the decisions before they are actually made. Future outcomes are taken into consideration in the prediction. Prescriptive analytics are commonly used in organizations to optimize scheduling, production, inventory and supply chain design, and other organizational activities to deliver what the customers want, and meet and exceed customers' expectations. Prescriptive analytics is the most valuable kind of analytics and usually results in rules and recommendations for next steps. However, it is largely not used. A 2012 surveys by Gartner shows most users still focus on measurement of the past, with only 13 percent of users making extensive use of predictive analytics. Less than 3 percent of users are using prescriptive analytics tools such as decision/mathematical modeling, simulation and optimization. Another study shows that by 2020, 40 percent of new investment in analytics tools will be in predictive and prescriptive analytics (Intel, 2017).

The Evolution of Predictive Analytics

Predictive Analytics is an extension of Data Mining technology. Both are based on a huge amount of mathematical theory dating back to several decades. Data mining technology helps to examine large amounts of data. One can sift through all the chaotic and repetitive noise in data to discover patterns and use that information to assess likely outcomes, and then make informed decisions. Data Mining refers only to past data and uncovers relationships between measurable variables. Despite being around for such a long time, Data Mining has not yet reached the business mainstream.

Business Intelligence vs. Predictive Analytics

Traditional BI is a set of technologies, applications, infrastructure, and best practices that aggregate data from multiple sources, prepare that data for analysis, and then provide reporting and analysis on that data to optimize decisions and performance. These systems are specifically developed to operate by organizations' analyst and optimized for supporting managerial decisions that require aggregated views of information from across a department, unit, or entire organization.

Predictive analytics is the natural evolution of BI processes, tools and technologies to forecast future activities, behavior and trends. While BI focuses on historical analysis, analytics builds upon this set of technologies and techniques to re-focus on the future. Traditional BI platforms focus on data preparation and integration and provide analysis via scripting, reports, interactive visualizations, and static dashboards. An important shortcoming of traditional BI is its latency in receiving reports. By the time the decision maker received the reports, it typically was too late to undertake any action. Embedded analytics facilitate in dealing and addressing that latency by shifting from reactive analytics to proactive analytics. Embedded analytics inserts intelligence or a set of tightly integrated capabilities inside the everyday systems or applications such as (CRM, ERP, marketing or financial systems) that employees or customers use to improve the analytics experience. This makes users more productive by combining insight and action in the same application. There is no need for users to switch between multiple applications to derive insights and take action. Figure 3 shows the relationship between traditional BI and predictive analytics.

Predictive Analytics Process

Predictive Analytics allows organizations to become forward looking, anticipating and deciding based upon the data not on assumptions. The following processes summarize steps taken to implement Predictive Analytics (Figure 4.):

Figure 3. Traditional BI vs predictive analytics

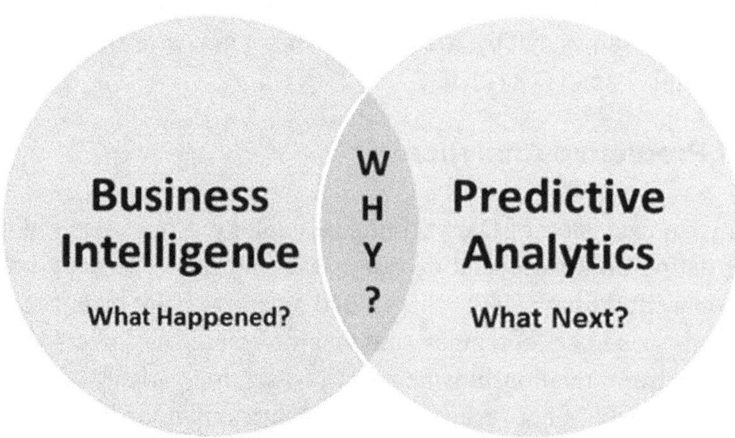

Figure 4. Predictive analytics process

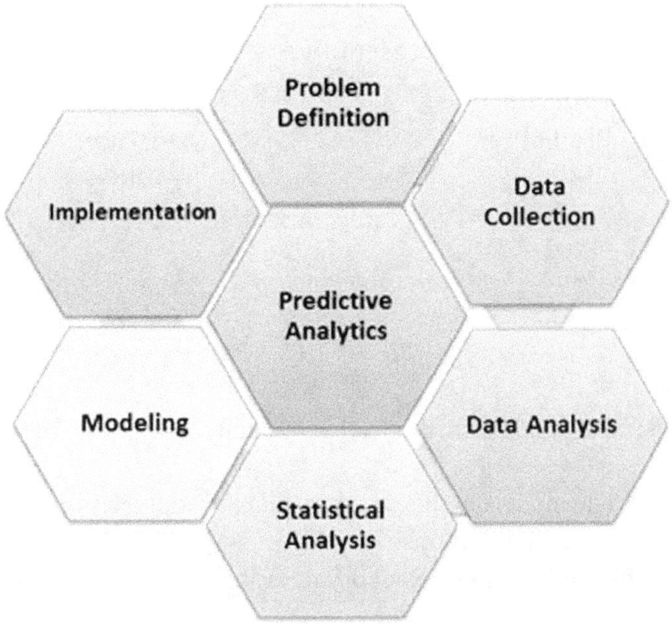

1. **Problem Definition:** Define the project outcomes and business objectives. Identify the data sets which are going to be used.
2. **Data Collection:** Collect data (structured or unstructured data) from multiple sources for analysis.
3. **Data Analysis:** Analyze data using different processes including inspecting, cleaning, modeling, and transforming data. The objective is to discover useful information.
4. **Statistical Analysis:** Use standard statistical models to validate and test the hypotheses and the assumptions.
5. **Modeling:** Use predictive modeling to create accurate predictive models or the best solutions about future.
6. **Implement Actions:** Deploy the analytical results in every day decision making process. Monitor and review the model performance to ensure the it provides the expected results.

Predictive Modeling Process

Predictive Analytics uses a number of modeling methods including statistics, artificial intelligence, and machine learning. The model is chosen on the basis of testing, validation, and evaluation of an outcome. Each model has its strength and weakness and is best suited for specific types of problems. Predictive modeling is the process of running one or more algorithms on the historical data where prediction is going to be carried out. The process involves training the model and using multiple models on the same data set and arriving on the best fit model.

Predictive Analytics utilizes three categories of modeling (Figure 5):

Figure 5. Predictive analytics modeling

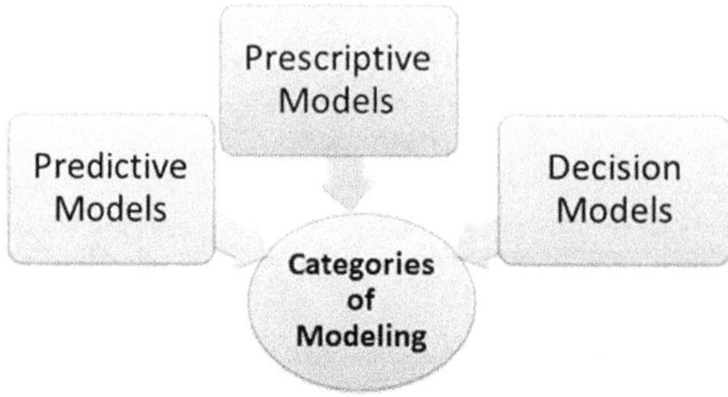

- **Predictive Models:** The models in this category analyze the past performance to predict the future.
- **Descriptive Models:** The models in this category quantify the relationships in data. These models are used to classify data sets into groups.
- **Decision Models:** The models in this category describe the relationship between all the variables of a decision in order to predict the results.

Algorithms perform statistical analysis and data mining and determine trends and patterns in historical structured and unstructured data. Most of the predictive analytics solutions have built

in algorithms such as time series, decision trees, regression, neural networks, and clustering. Table 2 summarizes these algorithms.

The Rise of Predictive Analytics

The concept of building predictive analytics algorithms to boost business's bottom line is not new. It has been around as long as there has been BI software. Figure 6 shows analytical platform evolution where we have been, where we are and where we need to go in terms of our analytics capability. The transition in major companies is evident. From Business Reporting using KPI Metrics to Business Intelligence and Data Visualization and Dashboards to Descriptive Analytics and finally to Predictive Analytics. As we move, from Reporting to Predictive Analytics, the quality and value of analytics improves. Static reporting of 1980s was extremely inefficient and impractical at helping determine and guide decision-making Static reports of 1980s have evolved to the simplest class of analytics "descriptive analytics" of 1990s. Descriptive analytics provided clarity as to where an organization stands related to defined business measures. This leap forward came as a result of an explosion in the quantity of data and advances in the computer technology. At the next stage, there was a growing trend among businesses to use predictive analytics algorithms to boost their bottom line. Extracting information from data in order to classify data and predict data patterns based on statistical modeling became popular. Moreover, what has changed by the 2000s is the report tool that software vendors included into their commercial software packages. Static reports of 1980s have evolved to interactive reports and dashboards in the 2000s and self-service and blended analytics today. Furthermore, relational databases were predominant data source of 1990s. In the 2000s, BI tools could access a much broader range of data than traditional data sources. Today, many

Table 2. Predictive modeling algorithms

PA Core Techniques	Methodologies Used
Predictive Modeling	• Statistical techniques for analysis and pattern detection • linear and logistic regression • Linear and nonlinear mathematical programming algorithms • Constrained optimization • Neural Networks • Bayesian and Monte Carlo Statistics • Matrix operations • Constrained optimization
Decision Analysis and Optimization	• Decision trees • Time-series analysis • Proprietary mathematical modeling & optimization technology • Data analysis • Cluster analysis • Association rules
Transaction Profiling	• Neural network models • Computational linguistics • Matrix and graph algorithms • Unsupervised clustering • Data mining
Predictive Search (supervised learning)	• Machine learning • Language processing • Text analytics • Primary components analysis • Scripting and development tools • Market basket analysis

BI tools support Big Data sources; Cloud applications and Cloud file systems, server logs, event streams, and search indexes. Today, the best analytics are characterized by being repeatable, shareable, scalable, and transferrable. Figure 6 summarizes the evolution of analytics over the decades (Eckerson, 2016).

Technology companies, software companies, financial services, manufacturing, and retails are among the highest users of the embedded analytics. The adoption of embedded analytics continues to grow and exceed that of standard data recovery. A 2017 survey of 500 executives and managers found that 93 percent of respondents are currently embedding analytics in their applications (Butler, 2017). Companies now go beyond simply adding open-source charts or static visualizations. They are willing to spend the time and resources to embed sophisticated analytics to impress end users. Investment in embedded analytics continues to grow. Ninety percent of respondents plan to invest in embedded analytics going forward. Additionally, 60 percent of end users leverage embedded analytics on a regular basis, and 98 percent said embedded analytics contributed to revenue growth. Respondents also reported that embedded analytics plays a critical role in improving customer satisfaction and user experience. Executives and managers are paying more attention as their competitors use embedded analytics to win and retain customers (Butler, 2017).

Forces Driving Predictive Analytics Adoption

Today, enterprise around the world store large volumes of diverse data from many sources. The insights hidden within this Big Data hold tremendous business value. The highest value is achieved through pre-

Figure 6. The rise of predictive analytics

dictive analytics which apply advanced analytical techniques to predict future events and drive decisions or actions. Predictive analytics has been around for decades, however, is now has entered the mainstream business decision-making. A recent IBM-sponsored study by Ventana Research has revealed that Predictive Analytics has emerged as the highest priority from the response of all participants regarding the top capabilities of Big Data Analytics (Ventana Research, 2015).

Today, business leaders are looking for analytics solutions that are flexible, saleable, and easy-to-implement. Business analysts, power users, and customer alike should be able to apply the analytics tools for their specific analytics needs. There are a variety of market forces driving predictive analytics including the advent of Big Data, an increase in computing power, a better understanding of the value of the technology, and the rise of certain economic forces (Figure 7). The increasing volume and availability of data, advances in data collections, computational power and storage capacity, advances in analytical techniques and technologies are all leading to formation of new business models and reshaping industry competition. Companies are looking to use the technology to predict trends and understand behavior for better business performance. Predictive analytics utilizes data mining, business intelligence tools, and statistics and modeling techniques to make predictions. Additionally, the emergence of enormous amount of structured and unstructured data and ground-breaking technology deployments are the major drivers for the predictive analytics market. Furthermore, the heightened level of competition is forcing enterprises to adjust their operations to compete in a global market. Customers are looking for visual analytics that requires no training nor technical expertise. These visual analytics must also be available from a variety of data sources. Internal employees desire a solution that allows them to push data in, and return easy-to-read analytics, allowing them to quickly produce results and solve problems.

Benefits of Predictive Analytics

Traditional analytics require significant development time and are accessible only within an analytics silo that must be accessed separately. Traditional BI tools quantify and compare historical data to uncover

Figure 7. Forces driving predictive analytics

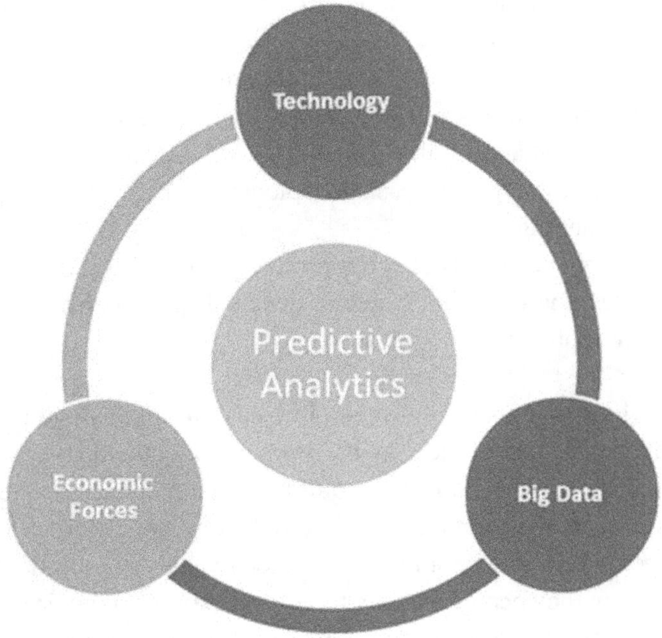

what has happened in the past. On the other hand, predictive analytics uses that same information to enable quick and accurate forecasting. Many of the benefits offered by predictive analytics are specific to business applications where analytics is seamlessly integrated. However, organizations of all sizes are using Predictive Analytics to support business core functions such as marketing, merchandising, sales, and risk management. According to several recent studies, organizations that incorporate predictive analytics tools into their business strategies can realize significant benefits including (Siegel, 2016; Stedman, 2017; Angelis, 2015; Kalakota, 2014):

- Optimize productivity and cost efficiency.
- More rapid identification of emerging opportunities.
- Higher levels of profitability.
- Greater customer loyalty and retention.
- Faster detection and corrections of problems.
- Increase competitive advantage.
- Reduce risk, eliminate waste, and accelerate time to improvement.
- Determine true process capacity.
- Reduce process cycle time.
- Optimize resources especially staffing levels and schedules.
- Improve equipment maintenance and reliability.
- Real-time insights of equipment health and performance.
- Improve availability, reliability and decision-making.
- Better insight into both large and small communities of interest.
- Identify market gaps, turning them into revenue.

- Achieve better accuracy in sales forecasts.
- Increase asset utilization and the ability to identify underperforming assets.
- Identify market gaps, turning them into revenue.
- Proactively identify and target customers at risk of churning well before the loss.
- More targeted and effective promotions and campaigns, increase usage of value-added services.
- Better insight into both large and small communities of interest.
- Create forecasts for assortment planning, shelf replenishment, pricing and promotion analysis, and sales and purchasing planning.
- Select specific promotional channels for your products and services.
- Dynamically price what you're selling (football tickets, low-cost airline seats, etc.).
- Detect false claims or applications.

Predictive analytics solutions transform raw data into easy-to-understand and actionable insights. It helps plant personnel take advantage of the massive amounts of data and use it to make real-time decisions that have a significantly positive impact on equipment maintenance and reliability. Early warning detection and diagnosis of equipment problems help employees work more effectively- plan necessary maintenance and avoid potential equipment failure. Predictive analytics solutions can identify problems days, weeks or months before they occur, creating time for personnel to be proactive. Organizations can leverage predictive asset analytics solutions to spend less time looking for potential issues and more time taking actions to get the most out of every asset. Several recent studies have documented the key benefits of incorporating predictive analytics into organization's business intelligence strategies. A recent empirical study of 205 Indian manufacturing organizations found that Predictive Analytics had significant impact on social performance and environmental performance (Dube et al, 2017). Another IBM-sponsored study by Ventana Research found that 68 percent of organizations that have implemented predictive analytics have gained a competitive advantage from it (Rajpurohit, 2014). Other significant advantages included finding new revenue opportunities, increased profitability and customer service, and gained operational efficiencies (Figure 8).

EFFECTIVE DEPLOYMENT AND USE OF PREDICTIVE ANALYTICS

Challenges of Implementing PA

Predictive Analytics faces numerous implementation challenges. A Predictive Analytics Benchmark Research conducted by Ventana Research on behalf of IBM identified several challenges organizations have encountered in their use of predictive analytics. The study also identified the largest business barrier to the effective deployment and use of predictive analytics.

These challenges fall in two categories of technical and organizational challenges as highlighted in Table 3 and summarized below (Ventana Research, 2013):

1. Difficulty of integrating predictive analytics into organization's information architecture.
2. Difficulty of accessing source data.
3. Difficulty of using the results.
4. Lack of resources including budget and skills.

Figure 8. Reported benefits of predictive analytics

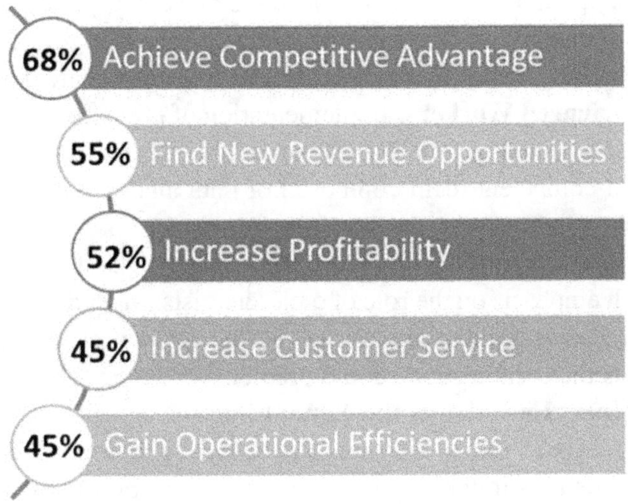

Table 3. Implementation challenges

Technical	Organizational
• The volume of required data • Difficulty of accessing source data • Difficulty of using the results • Difficulty of integrating predictive analytics into IT systems	• Lack of resources including budget and skills • Lack of awareness - how to apply • Lack of in-house experts • Low accuracy of results

5. Lack of awareness - an understanding of how to apply predictive analytics to business problems.
6. Lack of in-house experts to implement the results.
7. Focusing on past pattern.
8. The data is too expensive to measure.
9. Low accuracy of results.

Strategic Pitfalls

Organizations should not approach predictive analytics like they do other IT projects. When predictive analytics is implemented properly, the business benefits can be substantial. But there are some mainly strategic pitfalls to watch out for:

1. **Plan Ahead:** Companies looking to take advantage of PA tools should think strategically about implementation upfront. Companies need to start with a comprehensive assessment of analytics needs, and internal resources and skills.

2. **Make Data Accessible for Analysis:** As with other types of business intelligence and business analytics initiatives, predictive analytics applications must incorporate effective data management strategies in order to integrate, unify and standardize data coming from different source systems. Without an effective data management strategy, analytics efforts are wasted.
3. **Do Not Use Inexperienced Workers:** Implementation of predictive analytics requires knowledge of statistics, regression, and other analytics tools and techniques that might not be found inside the organization. Hire a competent team composed of data analysts, business analysts, statisticians, and data engineers.
4. **Define the Role of Data Scientists:** Organizations often give data scientists too much responsibility and put too much emphasis on the role of data scientists. Most data scientists do not understand business practices. Business managers should be the ones in charge of identifying the kind of behaviors and trends the organization should predict.
5. **Focus on One Business Initiative at the Time:** Limit the number of metrics you track and focus on one business initiative at a time. One needs to be tightly focused. Tracking too many indicators and tracing several business initiatives can become a distraction because the human brain simply can't make sense of continually increasing pieces of information at one time.

Predictive Analytics Deployments

Adoption of predictive analytics, when done correctly, leads to organizations being able to justify their analytics expenditures and create value tied directly to data visibility. Opportunities for deploying predictive analytics capabilities continue to evolve and grow with the broader adoption of technologies. Implementing a successful predictive analytics program takes time and effort. Many parts of the company will be affected, there are complex decisions to be made, and various stakeholders must be involved. It requires engagements and support from business users across the data analytics landscape. Some companies have not been successful with deployment of predictive analytics process due to the failure of developing an analytics strategy rooted in the delivery of IT services linked to their business outcomes. Furthermore, many enterprises do not know how to initiate their analytics projects. A range of recently published research literature on the implementation of business intelligence and predictive analytics is reviewed to explore their current state, issues and challenges learned from their practice.

(McNeill, 2014; Asllani, 2015; Loshin, Aug-2017 ; Loshin, Dec-2017). It is argued that before deploying analytics process in a company, one must first determine where analytics will add business values. Then a scalable deployment approach must be planned. We have modified steps suggested by these researches and added more to create a practical implementation steps for successful deployment of predictive analytics process:

1. **Top Management Involvement:** Obtaining the support and backing of the top management is crucial in providing the necessary funding and ensuring that the organization supports the predictive analytics process. To manage Big Data and analytics in today's information economy, progressive organizations have created two new senior executive positions: the Chief Data Officers (CDO) and the Chief Analytics Officers (CAO). The CDO focuses on data strategies for the organization, whereas the CAO find ways to optimize the use of analytics throughout the organization. These senior executives need to be provided with what they need, both in terms of technology and data.

2. **Proper Planning and Scoping:** It is necessary to understand the organization's key business objectives and concentrate on building analytics models that can have the maximum impact in meeting those objectives.
3. **Create a Compelling Business Case:** A business case needs to be created and communicated clearly wherever appropriate across the organization. A business case presents the reasoning for initiating Predictive Analytics process. A compelling business case communicates the nature of the proposed project and the arguments, both quantified and unquantifiable, for its deployment.
4. **Identify Business Processes That Can Be Improved:** Predictive Analytics tools will help organizations identify business processes that can be improved. It is necessary to get managers and workers on board with putting those findings into action.
5. **Define Measurable Business Benefits:** Predictive Analytics not only influence changes in business processes, but also can have a measurable impact on business performance. One must create metrics that can be used to quantify the business value of employing the analytics models.
6. **Use Experienced Workers:** Hire a competent team composed of data analysts, business analysts, data scientists, and statisticians.
7. **Match Application Needs With Analytics Tools:** Look for predictive analytics tools that provide capabilities matching application needs. There are plenty of tools to choose from either from open source or from commercial markets. Among important factors to consider when choosing predictive analytics tools are: the ability to handle structured, semi-structured, and unstructured data, compatibility with a variety of Big Data platforms, and integration with data visualization tools.
8. **Maintain a Solid Data Governance Program:** We are living in a world of constantly changing data. Internal and external data sets are continuously being captured and integrated. Make sure to institute solid data governance practices to guarantee that the quality and consistency of the date sets in your analytics systems remain at an acceptable level.
9. **Give Analysts Access to Relevant and Trustworthy Data:** Collect and store the inventory of relevant technical and business data sets and make sure predictive analytics applications have access to the right data.
10. **Move on to the Next Analytics Model When Fail:** If your analytics model did not deliver useful information to the business, move on to the next model.

Analytics Solutions Available to Organizations

Finding a right Predictive Analytics solution for your organization can be challenging. There is no one-size-fits-all option and no plug-and-play. There is a wealth of new tools that leverage analytics for specific purposes and independent standards are developing rapidly by vendors. Several companies are providing Predictive Analytics solutions including SAP AG, Tableau Software, SAS Institute Inc., International Business Machines Corporation (IBM), and TIBCO Software Inc., among others. Table 4 has the summary of these services.

ANALYTICS IN PRACTICE: BUSINESS APPLICATIONS OF ANALYTICS

BI and analytics go beyond the technology for gathering and analyzing data. They are about having the mindset of an experimenter- being willing to let data guide a company's decision making process. Busi-

Table 4. Predictive analytics solutions available to organizations

Service Providers	Markets Served	Services Provided
Tableau Software	**Tableau** Colleges and Universities	• Student performance management • Enrollment movement • Donor Relations and Federal Funding • Financial aid administration • Teaching analysis, class scheduling
Detica	• Insurance and healthcare solutions • Banking market	• Credit scoring • Fraud solutions • Collections and recovery solutions
Fair Issac Corporation (FICO)	**FICO® Score** • Banking and financial • Insurance and healthcare solutions	• Credit scoring • Fraud solutions • Collections and recovery solutions
ViPS	Insurance and healthcare solutions	Sarah Lawrence College
KXEN	**InfiniteInsight™** Customer lifecycle	Help companies to optimize every step in customer acquisition, cross-sell, up-sell, retention and next best activity
IBM	**IBM Business Analytics** • Fraud solutions • Healthcare market • Commercial, government and academic customers	• Delivers information that decision-makers trust to improve business performance • Provides clear, immediate and actionable insights into current performance and the ability to predict future outcomes.
SAS Institute Inc.	**Visual Analytics** • Fraud solutions • Insurance & healthcare solutions • property & casualty • workers' compensation	• Interactively visualize, explore and communicate data discoveries • Transform structured and unstructured data into fact-based insights for better decisions • Monitor results and facilitate continuous refinement of your analytic models
Microsoft Corporation	Visual Analytics	• Sinclair Community College • University of Oregon
TIBCO Software	College Scheduler	• University of Arizona • Arizona State University
SAP AG	• Customer lifecycle • Campaigns and promotions optimization • Sales and purchasing planning	• Customer acquisition, cross-sell, up-sell, retention and next best activity • More targeted and effective promotions and campaigns • Creating forecasts for pricing and promotion analysis, store clustering, store location selection, and sales and purchasing planning. • Identifying market gaps, turning them into revenue.

nesses are using predictive analytics to analyze historical data and facts in order to better understand clients' needs, market potentials, products, suppliers, and partners. Predictive analytics is also utilized to identify potential risks and opportunities for a company (Lebied, 2016).

Most often Data Analytics is associated with corporate decision-making. However, analytics has applications well beyond the for-profit world of business. From banking to manufacturing, from retail to healthcare, data analytics is used to make breakthrough discoveries, to deliver better services, and enrich the customer experience. Corporations around the world are using analytics to gain various business benefits, including new revenue opportunities, improved operational efficiency, better customer service, more effective marketing, and competitive advantages over rivals. According to a recent study by Business Application Research Center (BARC), organizations that used Data Analytics reported an 8 percent increase in revenues as well as a 10 percent reduction in costs. Other benefits reported are better strategic decisions, better understanding of customers, and improved control of operation processes (Lebied, 2017).

Business Applications of Predictive Analytics

The market for Big Data analytics directly parallels the growth of Big Data. According to research firm IDC, worldwide revenue for Big Data analytics was $130 billion in 2016. That number is expected to reach $150.8 billion in 2017 and grow to more than $210 billion by 2020 representing a 56 percent increase in just four years. The industries driving much of this growth in 2017 are banking, discrete manufacturing, process manufacturing, federal/central government, and professional services. Together, these five industries will spend $72.4 billion on Big Data and business analytics solutions this year. They will also remain the top five industries in 2020 when their total investment will be $101.5 billion (IDC, 2017)

Predictive analytics is becoming a mainstream application as organizations increasingly look to forecast customer behavior, market trends, effective medical treatments and more. The business value gained from predictive analytics efforts can add up to significant amounts. Knowledge of what a particular customer is likely to buy next, which piece of manufacturing equipment might break down, etc. can pay dividends now.

Predictive Analytics is used to predict: stock prices, risk, delinquencies, accidents, health problems, hospital admissions, malfunctions, oil flow, electricity outages, sales, donations, clicks, cancellations, fraud, tax evasion, crime, approvals for government benefits, thoughts, intention, answers, opinions, lies, grades, dropouts, friendship, romance, pregnancy, divorce, jobs, quitting, wins, votes, and more (Siegel, 2016).

Table 5 (see appendix) highlights applications of analytics in different industries. The following summarizes Predictive Analytics business applications:

Healthcare

The health care industry has used analytics to analyze large amounts of information quickly in order to provide lifesaving diagnoses or treatment options in a timely manner. Walgreens is using data analytics to make its pharmacy operations as customer-focused as possible and to personalize interactions with customers and anticipate their needs. The company is using predictive analytics as part of patient assessments at its in-store health clinics. The analytics process is aimed at improving patient care and identifying potential health risks before they become issues (Stedman, 2017).

Airline Industries

The airline industries across the world are using analytics to predict flight delays, effectively drive customer loyalty programs, and decide how many tickets to sell at each price for a flight. Southwest and Alaska Airlines are among the top users of embraced analytics to bring changes in their way of working.

Banking, Financial, and Insurance

The banking and financial industries are using analytics in order to analyze the probabilities of risk and default. Moreover, analytics helps them to push their banking products based on customer's purchasing power. The financial market uses analytics in high frequency trading sentiment measurement, and pre-trade-decision-support analytics. PayPal is using predictive data analysis to help protect its users from fraud and stop fraudulent transactions before they are processed (Burns, 2016). The Security Exchange Commission (SEC) is using data analytics to monitor financial market activities and to catch illegal market activities. Insurance companies use analytics to enhance fraud detection and to provide faster service in the area of claims management. Life insurance companies are using predicts analytics to predict the likelihood an elderly insurance policy holder will die within a few years in order to trigger end-of-life counseling. Credit scoring is another well-known application for predictive analytics. Financial companies use a range of information to assess the likelihood of future credit payments being made.

Government

The government is using pattern recognition in images and videos for enhanced security and threat detection (Analytics Vidhya, 2015; Siegel, 2016). Other applications of analytics in government sector include: traffic control, route planning, intelligent transport systems, and congestion management (Gaitho, 2017). The Social Security Administration (SSA) is using analytics to study social disability claims for detection of suspicious or fraudulent claims. Moreover, analytics enables the SSA to process medical information rapidly and effectively for faster decision making.

Manufacturing

Analytics tools have been used in solving manufacturing challenges including demand forecasting, integrated business planning, supply collaboration and risk analysis, and in inventory management. Supply chain professionals have used Predictive analytics to improve supply chain efficiencies. Predictive analytics can help manufacturers to satisfy the increasing demands of consumers who expect products delivered exactly when promised. Supply chain professionals need a complete view of their supply chain as it exists now, but also being able to know where their supply chain needs to be. By applying predictive analytics tools to identify patterns and predict future events, manufacturers gain the ability to make better decisions that anticipate what their customers are asking for now, and will be asking for in the future. Data analytics is also used in self-driving cars and robots (DeAngelis, 2015). Figure 9 shows key benefits of Predictive Analytics in manufacturing.

Retail

Predictive analytics is also being used for contextual marketing and retailing. The retail industry takes advantage of data analytics for fraud reduction, timely analysis of inventory, and for optimizing staff using data from shopping patterns and local events, etc. Moreover, the industry is also using data analytics to determine customer responses or purchases and set up for up selling and cross selling opportunities. (Gaitho, 2017). For example Target uses predictive analytics to predict which customers had the most probability of rapidly becoming pregnant from shopping behavior (Salleh, 2013). The information is then used to contact prospects with offers related to the needs of a newborn's parents. Tesco is a large grocery store operating in 13 countries with headquarters in UK. The company uses predictive analytics to increase redemption rates of 100 million personalized coupons issued annually at its grocery cash registers across 13 countries.

Logistics

Logistic companies (UPS, DHL, and FedEx) have used analytics to reduce costs and improve their operational efficiency (Rosenbush and Stevens, 2015). Predictive analytics ensures ships stay on shipshape for cargo companies. For example, RightShip, a Melbourne-based cargo company, is using predictive analytics to more accurately assess if ships are ready to be sent out to the sea (DeAngelis, 2015).

Social Networks

Active usage of social networks for meeting new people is staggering. Social sites like Match.com, e-Harmony, OkCupid, Tinder, and Badoo use some very sophisticated predictive analytics to model and predict human attraction. They offer an interactive way for singles to meet other singles with whom they might otherwise never cross paths (Kalakota, 2014). Facebook uses analytics to Improve the precision of suggested people you may know and wish to link to (Siegel, 2016).

Sports

Competitive sports is a heavy user of predictive analytics. The application of analytics to a wide variety of sports is now standard practice. When signing players, selection committee analyzes hundreds

Figure 9. Key benefits of predictive analytics in manufacturing

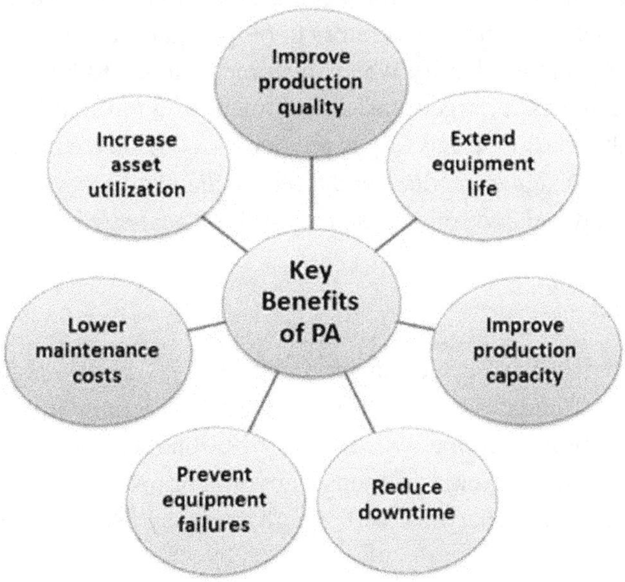

of detailed statistics from every player and every game, attempting to predict future performance and production. Some statistics are even obtained from game footage by using video recognition techniques.

Human Resources

HR Analytics was the initial term used to describe the effectiveness of HR programs. However, recently the other terms came into use specially, people analytics, talent analytics, and workforce analytics. People analytics has largely become the dominant term. People analytics applies math, statistics and predictive modeling to HR related data to predict patterns and make better decisions about all aspects of HR strategy with the objectives of improving organization performance. People analytics is being used to help more companies in their recruiting, compensation, performance management, and retention efforts (Rouse, 2017). Similarly, people analytics have been used to determine which employees are most likely to leave, valuate employees' performance, and decide employee's bonus. For example Hewlett-Packard has developed a predictive analytics application to forecast the probability of employees leaving (Salleh, 2013). U.S. special forces uses predictive analytics to determine which candidates will be successful and worthy of investing years of training. LinkedIn is also using predictive analytics to label one's profile with skills it predicts ones have from ones written contents. Wikipedia predicts which of its nearly million volunteer editors will discontinue their work (Siegel, 2016).

Marketing, Advertising and the Websites

Google is a heavy user of predictive analytics and is continuously changing the landscape of search with this technology. Using predictive analytics, Google Suggests, Google AutoComplete and Google Instant are generating search results instantly as users' type. Google further enhanced predictive search, serving as a personalized assistant that can predict your needs, wants, and deep desires. Netflix is also using predictive analytics to predict which movies a subscriber will like based on what he/she watched (Kalakota, 2014). British Broadcasting Company (BBC) receives millions of attempted posts on its websites. BBC predicts which comments will be approved for posting on its web site reducing total numbers of posts which needed to be screened by human moderators to only a quarter of a million. PayPal use customer written feedback on its web site to identify which customer intends to leave with 85 percent accuracy. Harbor Sweets applied analytics to target lapsed customers to win them back. The response rate was around 40 percent. Harrah's Casino in Las Vegas predicts how much a customer will spend over a long term. Elie Tahari, a fashion designer, predicts and forecasts demand for women's fashion line products. Finally, Pandora recommends related songs based on 400 musical attributes (Siegel, 2016).

Utilities

Predictive analytics is used in fault detection for safety and efficiency. Con Edison predicts energy distribution cable failure, and updates risk levels in New York City three times an hour. BNSF uses Predictive Analytics to predict broken train tracks. Argonne National Laboratory does predictive modeling of nuclear reactor failures. Finally, Nokia Siemens Networks improve service availability by predicting customer outage on its 4G wireless network with a high accuracy (Siegel, 2016).

Education

Officials at the University of Maryland, use predictive analytics to analyze student data including grades, demographics, financial aid, course schedules, and enrollment status to find at-risk students and improve retention rate. They believe predictive analytics enables officials to intervene with struggling students before it is too late. Analytics help officials identify bottle necks and problems such as a difficult class or other pressing issues that could lead students to drop out. Analytics is used to predict student success or failure. One of their findings is that students who enroll in a course very late tend not to perform well in that class. Therefore, the new school's policy is not to let any student to enroll in a class few days before the class start. The student can drop a class four days after the class starts without a penalty. The university is also using a data tool called Student Success Matrix that is developed by Predictive Analytics Reporting Framework. Using the analytics tool, system officials can determine whether a "C" grade in an introductory marketing course indicates a low chance of student to graduate in the major. Then, they use "Intrusive advising" to help student to improve grades or change majors. (Wells, 2017). University of Phoenix also predicts student success or failure in order to target intervention measures including advising and coaching. University of Melbourne uses a predictive model to identify which applications for research grants will be approved (Siegel, 2016).

SUMMARY AND CONCLUSION

Enterprises are continually employing new and old strategies to overcome industry challenges and remain relevant in the changing marketplace. Adapting to new environments, innovating new offerings and investing in cost-saving technologies are just a few avenues for transforming challenges into opportunities. Over the past five years, the sheer volume of data has grown exponentially and new analytics tools have been developed to turn this flood of unstructured, semi-structured, and structured data into insights. The amount of data available is providing enterprises with the information needed to operate more efficiently, effectively, and safely, consequently allowing them to overcome some of the challenging and disruptive obstacles. Utilization and management of the Big Data are increasingly becoming areas of competitive advantage. Predictive analytics software is one of the crucial tools that companies can use to obtain actionable information from the viable data. Hence, enterprises are adopting predictive analytics as one of the core technologies to be able to compete in the market.

As discussed in this paper, technology trends such as greater computational power, increased data storage capacity, the growth of cloud-based platforms, and advances in algorithms have all contributed to a breakthrough in the field of BI and are helping rapid advances in Predictive Analytics software. Predictive Analytics solutions allow organizations to predict trends and act on opportunities before they manifest. Companies that incorporate predictive analytics into their business intelligence strategies can realize significant benefits through more rapid identification of emerging opportunities and faster detection and correction of problems and issues.

However, as discussed in this paper, there are technological and organizational drawbacks to predictive analytics. The important ones are the amount of up-to-date data it requires and lack of in-house experts to implement the results. While this would not be an issue for larger organizations, smaller firms may not see as useful technology as a result.

Organizations around the world are operating in an increasingly complex and competitive environment. This paper identified contemporary challenges facing organizations and explored the potential of predictive analytics in addressing these challenges. Additionally, this paper proposed a conceptual framework for successful implementation of analytics in different organizations. Moreover, this study highlighted the applications of Predictive analytics across different industries such as banking, financial services, and insurance, government, healthcare, utilities, retail, logistics, and energy, among others. The paper also argued that organizations should consider analytics a strategic investment because adding new analytic functions affects an organization's existing applications, devices, services, and web sites. Important decisions such as the best way to deliver analytic content and report to customers and employees, and ensuring that analytic content is engaging must be made. Business leaders must also evaluate how a predictive analytics initiative will affect users (external and internal), existing applications and interfaces, and multiple stakeholders such as executives, managers, marketing and sales personnel.

REFERENCES

Analytics Vidhya. (2015). *13 Amazing Applications/Uses of data Science Today*. Retrieved September 21 from https://www.analyticsvidhya.com/blog/2015/09/applications-data-science/

Asllani, A. (2015). *Business Analytics with Management Science, Models and Methods*. Upper Saddle River, NJ: Pearson Education Inc.

Bughin, J. (2016). Big Data, Big Bang? *Journal of Big Data*, *3*(2).

Bughin, J. (2016). Big Data: Getting a Better Read on Performance. *McKinsey Quarterly*. Retrieved from https://www.mckinsey.com/industries/high-tech/our-insights/big-data-getting-a-better-read-on-performance

Burns, E. (2016). *How PayPal Fights Fraud with Predictive Data Analysis*. Retrieved from http://searchbusinessanalytics.techtarget.com/feature/How-PayPal-fights-fraud-with-predictive-data-analysis

Butler, C. (2017). 2017 State of Embedded Analytics Report. *Logi Analytics*. Retrieved from http://go.logianalytics.com/rs/793-ECD-841/images/2017%20State%20of%20Embedded%20Analytics_Logi_final.pdf

Carlos, A., Gomez-Uribe, & Hunt, N. (2016). The Netflix recommender system: Algorithms, business value, and innovation. *ACM Transactions on Management Information Systems*, *6*(4).

DeAngelis, S. F. (2015). *Predictive Analytics becoming a Mainstream Business Tool*. Retrieved from https://www.enterrasolutions.com/blog/predictive-analytics-becoming-a-mainstream-business-tool/

Decker, J. (2017). *Embedded Analytics for Dummies*. John Wiley & Sons, Inc.

Diebold, F. X. (2012). *On the Origin(s) and Development of the Term "Big Data," PIER Working Paper 12-037*. Penn Institute for Economic Research, Department of Economics, University of Pennsylvania. Retrieved from https://economics.sas.upenn.edu/sites/economics.sas.upenn.edu/files/12-037.pdf

Dubey, R., Gunasekaran, A., Childe, S. J., & Roubaud, D. (2017). Can Big Data and Predictive Analytics Improve Social and Environmental Sustainability? *Technological Forecasting and Social Change*.

Eckerson, W. (2016). *Embedded Analytics: The Future of Business Intelligence*. Eckerson Group. Retrieved from https://www3.technologyevaluation.com/research/white-paper/embedded-analytics-the-future-of-business-intelligence.html

Evelson, B., & Bennett, M. (2015). Quantify Tangible Business Value of BI. *Forrester*. Retrieved from http://www.lavastorm.com/assets/2015-Forrester-Quantify-Tangible-Business-Value-of-BI.pdf

Feki, M., Boughzala, I., & Wamba, S. F. (2016). Big Data Analytics-enabled Supply Chain Transformation: A Literature Review. *49th Hawaii International Conference on System Sciences*.

Gaitho, M. (2017). How Applications of Big Data Drive Industries. *SimpliLearn*. Retrieved from https://www.simplilearn.com/big-data-applications-in-industries-article

Gartner Report. (2015). Retrieved from http://www.gartner.com/newsroom/id/3130817

Gets, J., & Reinsel, D. (2013). *The Digital Universe in 2020*. IDC.

Henke, N.,Bughin, J., Chui, M., Manyika, J., Saleh, T., Wiseman, B., & Sethupathy, G. (2016). *The Age of Analytics: Competing in a Data-Driven World*. McKinsey Global Institute.

IDC. (2017). *Worldwide Semiannual Big Data and Analytics Spending Guide*. Retrieved from https://www.idc.com/getdoc.jsp?containerId=prUS42371417

Intel. (2017). *Guide to Getting Started with Advanced Analytics. Intel Planning Guide*. Retrieved from https://www.intel.com/content/www/us/en/analytics/getting-started-advanced-analytics-planning-guide.html

Kalakota, R. (2014). A Primer on Predictive Analytics. *inShare3*. Retrieved from https://practicalanalytics.co/predictive-analytics-101/

Lebied, M. (2016). Top 11 Business Intelligence and Analytics Trends for 2017. *Business Intelligence*. Retrieved from http://www.datapine.com/blog/business-intelligence-trends-2017/

Loshin, D. (2017). *Five Steps to Build Better Predictive Analytics Applications*. Retrieved from http://searchbusinessanalytics.techtarget.com/tip/Five-steps-to-build-better-predictive-analytics-applications

Loshin, D. (2017). *Ten Steps to Start Using Predictive Analytics Algorithms Effectively*. Retrieved from http://searchbusinessanalytics.techtarget.com/tip/Ten-steps-to-start-using-predictive-analytics-algorithms-effectively

Marr, B. (2015). Big Data: 20 Mind-Boggling Facts Everyone Must Read. *Forbes*. Retrieved from https://www.forbes.com/sites/bernardmarr/2015/09/30/big-data-20-mind-boggling-facts-everyone-must-read/#56a1b34e17b1

McAfee, A., & Brynjolfsson, E. (2012). Big Data: The Management Revolution. *Harvard Business Review*. Retrieved from https://hbr.org/2012/10/big-data-the-management-revolution

McNeill, D. (2014). *Analytics in Healthcare and the Life Sciences: Strategies, Implementation Methods and Best Practices*. Upper Sadler River, NJ: International Institute for Analytics.

Minelli, M., Chambers, M., & Dhiraj, A. (2013). *Big Data, Big Analytics: Emerging Business Intelligence and Analytic Trends for Today's Businesses*. Hoboken, NJ: John Wiley & Sons. doi:10.1002/9781118562260

Perrin, A. (2015). *One-fifth of Americans report going online-almost constantly*. Pew Research Center.

Rajpurohit, A. (2014). Has Predictive Analytics Crossed The Chasm? *Ventana Research*. Retrieved from https://www.kdnuggets.com/2014/05/has-predictive-analytics-crossed-chasm.html

Rosenbush, S., & Stevens, L. (2015). At UPS the Algorithm is the Driver. *The Wall Street Journal*. Retrieved from https://www.wsj.com/articles/at-ups-the-algorithm-is-the-driver-1424136536

Rouse, M. (2017). People Analytics (HR Analaytics). *TechTarget*. Retrieved from http://searchhrsoftware.techtarget.com/definition/human-resources-analytics-talent-analytics?vgnextfmt=print

Salleh, S. (2013). *Applying Predictive Analytics in Enterprise Decision Making*. Retrieved from

Siegel, E. (2016). *Predictive Analytics: The Power to Predict Who Will Click, Buy, Lie, or Die*. Hoboken, NJ: John Wiley & Sons, Inc.

Stedman, C. (2017). Eyeing the future with predictive analytics can pay dividends now. *TechTarget*. Retrieved from http://searchbusinessanalytics.techtarget.com/ehandbook/Predictive-data-analytics-advances-businesses-ahead-of-the-game

Taylor, P. (2012, June 19). Crunch Time for Big Data. *The Financial Times*.

Ventana Research. (2015). *Ventana Research Benchmark Research: Next-Generation Predictive Analytics*. Retrieved from http://www.iconresources.com/Icon/eMailer/IBM/Ventana-Research/Ventana-Research-on-Next-generation-Analytics-june-2015.pdf

Weiss, S. M., & Indurkhya, N. (1998). *Predictive Data Mining: A Practical Guide*. Morgan Kaufmann Publishers, Inc.

Wells, C. (2017). Maryland Universities to Use Data to Predict Student Success-or Failure. *The Baltimore Sun*. Retrieved from http://www.baltimoresun.com/news/maryland/education/bs-md-college-analytics-20160611-story.html

APPENDIX

Table 5. Application of predictive analytics in different industries

Industry	Organizations	Applications
Banks, Financial Institutions & Insurance	• Chase, Citigroup • London Stock Exchange • Capital • Citizen Bank • Rebellion Research • Allstate • Infinity Insurance • PayPal	• Generate a credit score –assessing person's credit worthiness. • Analyze the probabilities of risk and default • Predict which checks are fraudulent • Application approval and denials • Compliance and regulatory reporting • Trade surveillance • Predicting bodily injury liability • Detect the misuse of credit and debit cards • Protect users from fraud
Airlines	• Southwest Airlines • Alaska Airlines • Continental Airlines	• Decide how many tickets to sell at each price for a flight and predict flight delay • Decide which class of airplanes to buy • Effectively drive customer loyalty programs
Retail	• Target • Tesco	• Determine customer responses or purchases and set up for upselling and cross selling opportunities. • Merchandising and market basket analysis • Predict trends, recommend new products – and boost profitability. • Events and behavior-based targeting • Market and consumer segmentations
Healthcare	• Stanford University • Sisters of Mercy Health Systems • University of Pittsburgh Medical Center • Pfizer • Blue Cross Blue Shield of Tennessee	• Disease pattern and clinical trials data analysis • Identify changes in patient and provider behavior due to newly introduced legislation or pharmaceuticals. • Patient care quality and program analysis • Provide a rapid and conclusive overview of competitors, pricing, and substitute products when negotiating procurement of pharmaceuticals for hospitals, integrated care networks, and health insurers. • Drug discovery and development analysis
Marketing, Advertising & the Web	• Harbor Sweets • Target • Harrah's Las Vegas • Cox Communications • Elie Tahari • Pandora • Netflix • Google • Sun Microsystems	• Target lapsed customers to win them back • Predict how much a customer will spend over a long term • Predict propensity to buy • Forecast demand for women's fashion line products • Recommend related songs based on 400 musical attributes • Predict which new ads will get many bounces • Improve the number of leads per phone contact
Government, Nonprofit, and Education	• Social Security Administration • Internal Revenue Service • U.S. Postal Service • U.S. Armed Force • U.S. Department of Defense • University of Maryland • University of Phoenix • University of Melbourne • Chicago Police Department	• Streamline operations while giving the agency a more holistic view of criminal activity. • Improve traffic management & overcrowding administration. • Predict suspected incidence of contract fraud • Predict which students risk failing a course • Predict Which applications for research grants will be approved • Predict terrorist attacks and armed opposition group activities • Predicted which workers' compensation claims and payments are unwarranted.

continued on following page

Table 5. Continued

Industry	Organizations	Applications
Utilities	• Con Edison • BNSF • Argonne National Laboratory • Nokia Siemens Networks	• Predict energy distribution cable failure, and update risk levels • Predict fault detection for safety and efficiency • Predict broken train tracks • Predict customer outage
Human Resources	• Hewlett-Packard • U.S. Special Forces • Wikipedia • Amazon.com	• Determine which employees are most likely to leave. • Evaluate employees' performance. • Decide employee's bonus. • Predict which candidates will be successful • Predict the appropriate security access code of employees
Social Networks	• Match.com • e-Harmony • OkCupid • Tinder • Badoo • facebook	• Model and predict human attraction • Improve the precision of suggested people you may know and wish to link to
Logistics	• UPS • DHL • FedEx	• Determine the best routes to ship, the best suited time to deliver, the best mode of transport to choose • Supply chain management and analytics

Chapter 5
Developing Business Intelligence Product and Metacontent Map (BIP-Map)

Chin-Hoong Chee
Universiti Teknologi PETRONAS, Malaysia

ABSTRACT

A business intelligence (BI) system provides users with multi-dimensional information (a so-called "BI product") to support decision making. However, existing BI systems overlook the lineage metadata which supports individual data quality dimensions such as data believability and ease of understanding. Using a design science research paradigm, this chapter proposes and develops an integrated framework (known as BI product and metacontent map – "BIP-Map") to facilitate the traceability and accountability of BI products. Specifically, the business workflow layer of the integrated framework is modelled using business process modelling notation, and an information product map is used to model the second layer's information manufacturing process, whilst the third layer represents the metacontent detail of the data validation stage, from source system through to ETL, to the data warehousing stage. The integrated framework addresses individual-related data quality issues and builds user confidence by enhancing the traceability and accountability of a BI product.

INTRODUCTION AND RESEARCH MOTIVATION

In recent years, business intelligence (BI) tools have emerged as one of the top spending priorities for many CIOs (Gartner 2013a). It is reported that worldwide business intelligence software revenue surpassed US$12 billion dollars in 2012 (Gartner 2013b). Organisations are willing to invest heavily in BI because this technology enables companies to make fact-based decisions which can increase revenue, cut costs, and provide competitive advantage (Bogza & Zaharie 2008). According to Wixom and Watson (2010, p.14), business intelligence is "*a broad category of technologies, applications, and processes used for gathering, storing, accessing, and analysing data to help its users make better decisions*". In other words, BI is a system that allows users to leverage disparate data sources so that they can make informed

DOI: 10.4018/978-1-5225-5718-0.ch005

business decisions (Elbashir et al. 2008; Negash 2004). To do so, BI systems are designed to provide decision-makers with BI products[1] delivered at the right time, at the right place, and in the correct form (Negash 2004). A BI product is akin to manufacturing a physical product in the factory because most of the processes used in product quality-control are applicable in producing higher quality information (Ballou et al. 1998; Shankaranarayanan et al. 2003).

While the BI market appears vibrant and while the importance of BI systems is more widely accepted, a weakness of current systems is that data are treated too technically without considering the 'soft' aspects of the information; for instance, aspects such as data lineage and reliability are often ignored (Foshay 2005; Foshay et al. 2007; Shankaranarayanan et al. 2003). A data-driven BI system that concentrates mainly on data itself will yield lower levels of efficiency in business decision making (Ou & Peng 2006). This is because business decision-making is a complex process which involves not only hard data, such as sales volumes, but also other considerations such as the information manufacturing process and standard operating procedures (SOP) of the company. For example, any changes in the SOP or business workflow may affect the operations of the business which, in turn, affects how data are generated; indeed, such changes can affect the reliability of the BI product manufacturing process itself. Moreover, contemporary managers are forced to make optimised decisions in the shortest possible time in response to today's highly competitive and fast-paced business environment (Delen & Pratt 2006). Yet, business users still rely on IT to supply the metadata/metacontent[2], a time-consuming process which can delay them from acting/reacting promptly. A problem with current BI systems is that business users typically engage only at the complex analysis layer without access to adequate metacontent to support their decision-making. Dynamic decision-support demands adequate lineage metadata[3] as well as sufficient knowledge of business workflow and BI product manufacturing processes.

Due to inadequate lineage metadata in existing BI systems (Foshay 2005; Foshay et al. 2007), questions have been raised about the ability of business users who are not technically-savvy to understand the BI environment or to adequately comprehend the highly-granular information provided by BI technologies. Consequently, the problems associated with individual-related data-quality dimensions, such as ease of understanding, data believability, and accessibility, are becoming more pronounced (Wang & Strong 1996). Similarly, there are problems in understanding the relationships of all participants and processes for a business transaction (Tan et al. 2008). Therefore, the provision of comprehensive metadata to enhance the understanding of BI products has grown in importance (Foshay 2005; Foshay et al. 2007; Shankaranarayanan & Even 2006).

While 'metadata' has been defined as 'data about the data', this paper uses the definition suggested by Dempsey and Heery (1998, p. 155) who describe it as "data that is associated with objects which relieves their potential users of having full advance knowledge of their existence or characteristics." This definition addresses individual-related data quality challenges, especially BI product believability, ease of understanding, and metadata accessibility, all of which are paramount for heightening BI users' acceptance (Wang & Strong 1996; Foshay 2005; Foshay et al. 2007). As the quantity and complexity of corporate data has increased dramatically, and as data becomes more widely distributed throughout organisations, users at all management levels are required to make decisions in more responsive and dynamic ways (Shankaranarayanan et al. 2003). However, the perceived quality of data is affected by the way it is applied by users because the same data may be viewed in different perspectives by different people in different situations (Shankaranarayanan & Cai 2006). If users of data interpret the information incorrectly then there may be severe consequences to the business of an organisation. Thus, it is imperative that metadata should be implemented properly at various levels in a BI system in order to ensure that data are understood and used correctly when decisions are made.

Further, data governance and stewardship have been accorded particular prominence in many organisations recently because the quantity of corporate data continues to expand exponentially (Tallon 2013). In addition, regulatory mandates - such as the Sarbanes-Oxley (SOX) Act and Basel II - have increased the attention now being paid to data governance (Khatri & Brown 2010). However, a recent survey has indicated that most of the resources allocated by organisations to data governance provide little value (Aiken et al. 2011). To achieve better data governance it is important to help end-users access metacontent in order to make informed decisions that are also in compliance with regulatory requirements. However, while much literature has been published on the subjects of data quality and governance, little attention has been paid to the provision of comprehensive lineage metadata for the entire BI product manufacturing process. Although useful, the Verifiable Intelligence Products (VIP) framework developed by Zhu and Wang (2010) is targeted to the intelligence community, such as the Central Intelligence Agency of the USA, for the purpose of tracing the sources and production processes of an intelligence product. Their data emanates from a variety of external sources and are characterised by large volumes of semi-structured and unstructured data, so-called 'big data'. Their VIP framework does not take into account the internal, structured data common to an enterprise's BI systems. Drawing on the IP-Map of Shankaranarayan et al. (2003), Shankaranarayanan and Cai (2006) included a comprehensive metadata repository within the IP-Map framework to assist in computing data quality dimensions for implementation of total data quality management capabilities. While the metadata repository is helpful in communicating data quality metadata, it does not consider the specific metadata components for data validation, extraction, transformation, loading and storage in both the database and data warehouse of an organisation – component that are critical for better understanding of BI products.

Existing research has proposed that the management of both business and IT processes need to be integrated with BI in order to better manage business performance (Shi & Lu 2010). Therefore, in this paper we present an integrated framework of BI Product and Metacontent map ('BIP-Map') which serves as a mechanism to provide the context for the BI product. Specifically, through a design science research approach (Hevner & Chatterjee 2010) we integrate the modelling techniques used in business process modelling, the information product map (IP-Map) of total data quality management, and the metacontent representation so as to construct a three-layered integrated framework. Moreover, we demonstrate and validate the BIP-Map framework in the real-world setting of an online job advertising firm.

It is expected that this research will advance BI lineage research and, more broadly, that it will contribute to the field of data quality and governance. This research builds on and extends the foundational work of Shankaranarayan et al. (2003) by supplementing their IP-Map concept with business workflow and metadata associated with BI products. Shankaranarayan et al. (2003) focused on data-quality management but they did not consider other important aspects in data governance, such as business processes and metadata components. Thus, this research addresses these particular aspects of data governance which have been neglected in prior studies. Specifically, the integrated BIP-Map framework will assist BI stakeholders to make timely and informed decisions because the framework will enable users to better visualise how their business and information manufacturing processes are inter-related. In addition, the framework provides comprehensive metacontent that will allow users to better understand the business rules and metadata of the BI products from data validation through to the data warehousing stage before making any important decisions. Furthermore, the framework enables BI stakeholders to identify the critical parts of a process or system that may create the problem of poor data quality, and by doing so the business intelligence of an organisation can be improved continually.

The remainder of this paper is organised as follows. The next section provides the research paradigm and introduces the integrated BIP-Map framework and the relevant literature. In the following section we demonstrate the utility of the framework within the setting of an online job advertising firm, followed by interview findings with the key BI stakeholders of the firm. The final section provides a summary of the study; it reflects on the design science paradigm and highlights the research contributions.

RESEARCH PARADIGM

This study applies a design science research paradigm. According to Hevner et al. (2004), the objective of design science is to create artefacts (broadly defined, including constructs, models, methods, and instantiations) that are useful. This research demonstrates the applicability and utility of an integrated framework of BIP-Map (which is classified as a model) and a BIP-Map informed prototype system (i.e., an instantiation). The purpose of the design and development of these two artefacts is to enable the users to better understand the BI product and its manufacturing process and hence improve the efficiency and effectiveness of their decision-making. The design science paradigm aligns with this research's purpose perfectly given that the focus is to design and test artefacts that improve BI system understanding and use. Hevner et al.'s (2004) study specified a set of guidelines for the conduct and assessment of information systems (IS) design-science research that has been widely accepted. The detailed assessment of this study against Hevner et al.'s guidelines is provided in the final section of this paper.

INTEGRATED FRAMEWORK OF BIP-MAP

Based on business process modelling notation, information product map and metacontent, we develop the integrated framework known as a Business Intelligence Product and Metacontent Map (BIP-Map). The purpose of this integration is to produce a comprehensive framework which is able to enhance the traceability and accountability of BI products so that the end-users can make more informed and timely decisions for their business. As depicted in Figure 1, the BIP-Map is built as a multi-layered framework where the business processes/workflow, information modelling processes, and metacontent is integrated into three different layers, with business workflow as the first layer, information manufacturing as the second layer, and metacontent as the third layer. The following provides the relevant literature and justification of why these three layers are designed in this specific order.

A business process consists of "a set of activities that are performed in coordination in an organisational and technical environment to realise a business goal" (Weske 2007, p.5). It is crucial to identify clearly the activities and participants involved in a business workflow, since a BI product can only be analysed if its business workflow is being modelled correctly (Aguilar-Saven 2003). To represent the processes or workflows of an organisation, business process modelling notation[4] (BPMN) is commonly used so that current business processes or workflow may be analysed and improved in the future. In this research, BPMN, a well-supported standard modelling notation has been applied accordingly. BPMN has been unanimously endorsed as the de facto standard notation by the BPM Initiative Notation Working Group, which represents a large segment of the business workflow modelling community. After review-

Figure 1. High-level BIP-Map framework

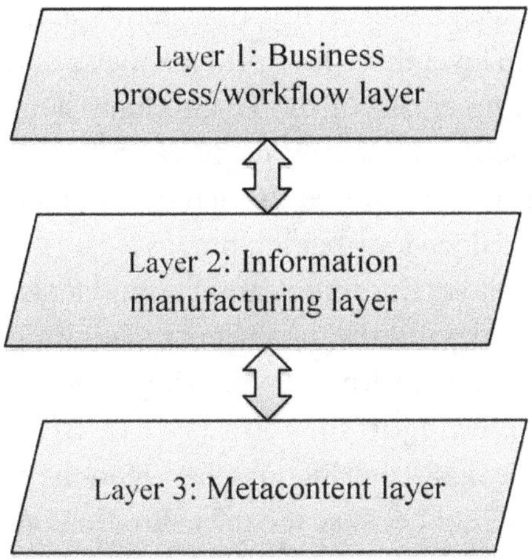

ing various notations and methodologies, the BPM Initiative Notation Working Group consolidates the best ideas from the divergent notations into a single, standard notation - BPMN. Based on flow-charting techniques, BPMN provides a standardised language for business and technical developers (Wang et al. 2006; White 2004). Thus, BPMN has been integrated into the BIP-Map framework. In other words, the BIP-Map layer one presents the business workflow to the users so that they can understand the relationship of all the participants and processes for a business transaction. Furthermore, when the activities and participants of a specific business workflow are defined at this layer, various manual tasks can be automated and, thus accomplished in a more efficient manner. It also has the added benefit of facilitating rapid changes and improvements to the business workflow. This can be achieved because the interaction of activities between different participants for a business workflow is indicated in this layer.

Although BPMN is a very useful modelling technique for managing business processes as it presents to the users a clear workflow of the transactions involved in the business, it does not, however, describe the manufacturing process of data. Therefore, users will not understand how corporate data are captured, processed, stored and utilised. This problem can be addressed, in part, by the use of an information product map[5] (IP-Map) which describes the manufacturing processes of data in a detailed manner. Originating from the total data quality management concept, the purpose of an IP-Map is to deliver high quality information to users by treating data and information in much the same way as other products used in the manufacturing industry (Wang 1998; Wang et al. 1998; Shankaranarayanan et al. 2000; Shankaranarayanan 2005). It allows people to comprehend, evaluate, and describe how information is compiled. However, a limitation of the IP-Map is that it does not provide descriptions of the business processes that are related to the manufacturing or utilisation of data in an organisation. So, users are still unable to identify the business processes that have an effect on corporate data. Therefore, the adoption of business process modelling and information product map will complement each other. Applying the IP-Map concept, BIP-Map layer two illustrates the information manufacturing processes so that users can identify how the data are being captured, processed, stored and utilised in order to produce better information products. Additionally, the IP-Map enables end-users to visualise the manufacture of an information product (Wang 1998; Wang et al. 1998; Shankaranarayanan et al. 2000; Shankaranarayanan 2005), and to appraise its data quality in order to implement continuous improvement (Fisher et al. 2006).

By providing the content and context of the data directly to users, the quality of the data, especially in terms of ease of understanding, data believability, traceability and accountability is greatly increased. Therefore, the purpose of BIP-Map layer three is to provide metacontent to users so they can understand the business rules and associated metadata of the BI products before using them to make decisions. Traditionally, metacontent is owned and used by technical personnel; but through the provision of a BIP-Map framework, business users are exposed to such metacontent in a timely manner which would improve their BI understanding and decision-making process. The metacontent of layer three is grouped into a few categories according to the entire information manufacturing processes, from data entry, extract, transform and load (ETL) stage, until the data warehousing stage (Ballard et al. 2006; Vaduva and Dittrich 2002). They include metacontent for data filtering/validation, data transformation, database, and for the data warehouse. By referring to the third layer of BIP-Map, BI users can know in detail how data are being validated by the data-filtering process when they are captured from source systems. Knowing how data are validated is vital because it can ensure that only data that are accurate and useful to the system are retained. Moreover, this layer is a useful reference for the technical personnel, such as database administrators and software developers, since metacontent is provided for the transformation of data from a database into a data warehouse. Table 1 provides a summary of the main components of the BIP-Map framework and the relevant literature which serve as the theoretical foundation of this research.

The advantage of having a hierarchical, integrated framework is that different levels of details are systematically segregated into different layers (from high-level BI products and business processes to the underlying information manufacturing processes). For decision-making, management users can understand the BI products that are supplied by the BI systems in a more efficient manner. Managers are able to drill down into the detailed information manufacturing layer and the associated metacontent layer in order to identify how the data are being captured, validated, processed, stored, transformed and generated throughout the organisation. Apart from this, the business workflow layer helps the technical BI developers/users to understand the business considerations behind certain data, whilst the informa-

Table 1. BIP-Map framework and the main components

BIP-Map layer	Main component	Representation method	Purpose	References
One	Business process/ workflow modelling	Business process modelling notation (BPMN)	Describe the activities and participants of a business workflow relating to the manufacturing of a BI product.	Weske 2007; White 2004; Wang et al. 2006
Two	Information manufacturing modelling	Information product map (IP-Map)	Describe the manufacturing processes related to the information product, so BI users are able to visualise the steps involved in capturing, processing, and storing that BI product.	Wang 1998; Wang et al. 1998; Shankaranarayanan et al. 2000; Shankaranarayanan 2005; Shankaranarayan et al. 2003
Three	Provision of metacontent	Metacontent for data filtering/validation, metacontent for data transformation, metacontent for database, and metacontent for data warehouse	Provide the metacontent information like business rules and metadata so BI users can know in detail how data are being validated by the data-filtering process from source systems to data warehousing stage.	Foshay 2005; Foshay et al. 2007; Ponniah 2001

tion manufacturing layer enables the business users to gain insight into the logic behind the information generated for them. Thus, the integrated BIP-Map framework enables users to have a comprehensive understanding of the BI products from the integrated perspectives of business workflows, information manufacturing and associated metacontent.

BIP-Map Demonstration

To illustrate the utility of the BIP-Map framework, a BIP-Map informed prototype has been developed in collaboration with an online job advertising firm. First, the system requirements for the executive BI Dashboard were gathered through a series of interviews with the key BI stakeholders. Next, the BI Dashboard was developed using PHP programming language and an open source BI tool, referred to as Business Intelligence and Reporting Tools (BIRT). Both the PHP and the BIRT technologies were used to query the data from the firm's Microsoft SQL Server database into the BI Dashboard. The BIP-Map was attached to the BI Dashboard where the users can click on the link located below any chart available in the BI Dashboard. The following sub-sections illustrate the three-layered BIP-Map framework based on a BI Dashboard of the online job advertising firm.

First Layer of BIP-Map: Business Process/Workflow Layer

Figure 2 shows an example of a graph available in the BI Dashboard that displays the total number of job advertisements posted by the online job advertising firm and its competitors. This graph enables the BI stakeholders to compare the amount of job advertisements posted by different competitors. It is important for them to identify the number of job advertisements posted each month so that they can execute the appropriate strategies to compete with the competitors.

When users click on the BIP-Map link located below the chart on the BI Dashboard, the first layer of the BIP-Map for that particular information will be invoked. This first layer is based on BPMN and is used to describe the business workflow that is related to the BI product. By referring to the first layer, end users can readily identify the activities and participants of a business workflow relating to the manufacturing of a BI product. Without this layer, a wrong decision could be made because different sets of data in the entire organisation could have similar attribute names and this might mislead users in simply using the data for conducting business decision making within the wrong context. Hence, understanding the business activities and participants involved is crucial. Figure 3 shows the first layer of a BIP-Map for the job competitor graph. It indicates how the job employers, customer service agents and data entry clerks are involved with the creation of a job advertisement in the firm. When the employer wants to create, update or delete a job advertisement, he can accomplish this by accessing the firm's website or contacting the customer service agent through phone or e-mail. The data entry clerks are responsible for entering the job advertisement details of their competitors into the system. As soon as the job advertisement details are available in the system, the management users will access the BI products to support their business analysis and decision-making. The activity represented by a dashed line is expandable, and users can click on it to access the second layer (information manufacturing layer) of the BIP-Map for that particular activity.

Figure 2. Job competitor's graph from BI dashboard

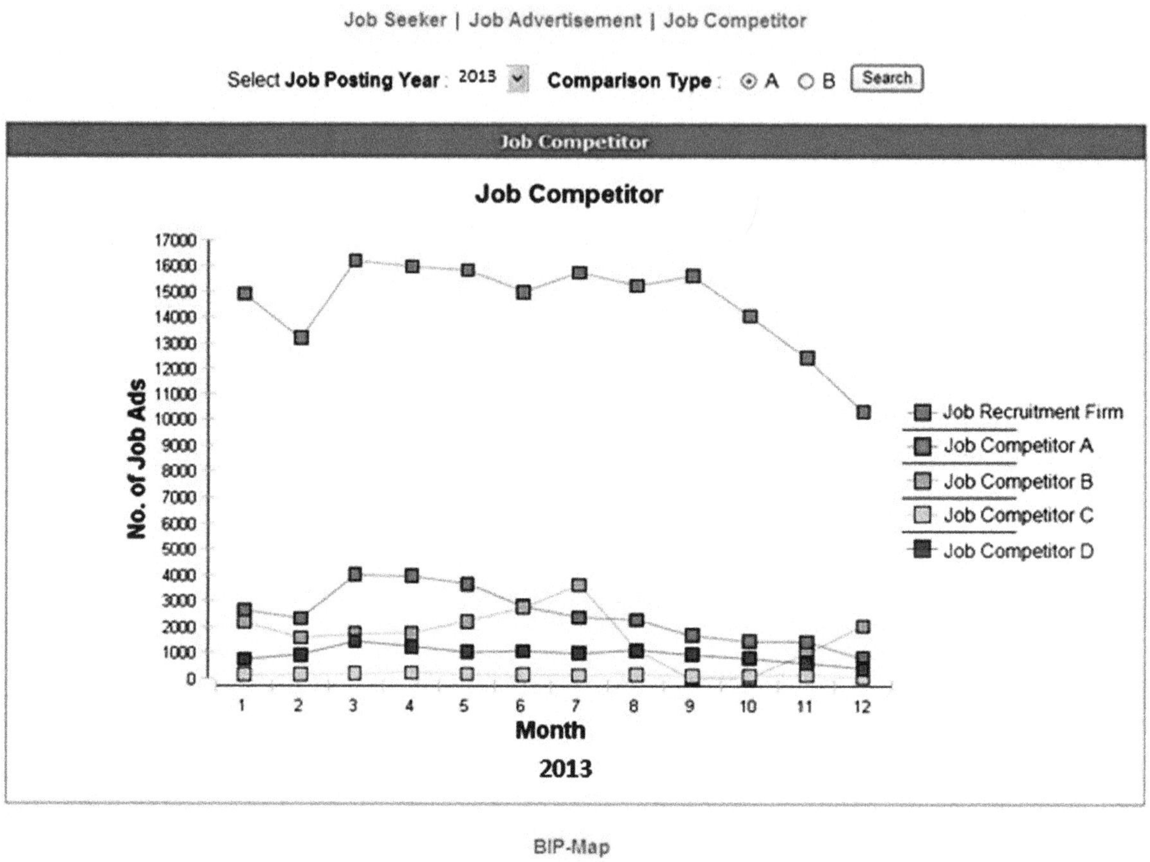

Second Layer of BIP-Map: Information Manufacturing Layer

When users click on any expandable process on the first layer of a BIP-Map, the second layer will then be invoked. The second layer is based on the information product map (IP-Map) of Wang (1998), Wang et al. (1998) and Shankaranarayanan et al. (2000). An IP-Map is used to describe the processes related to the information product, and users are able to visualise the steps involved in capturing, processing, and storing that product (Wang 1998; Wang et al. 1998; Shankaranarayanan et al. 2000; Shankaranarayanan 2005). This helps end-users to make good use of the data in their organisations for business analysis and decision-making. Similarly, it facilitates changes to improve the workflow of information processes when the users are able to identify how the data are being captured, processed, stored and utilised throughout the organisation. Figure 4 shows the second layer of a BIP-Map for the job competitor graph, which indicates the information manufacturing processes of all the job advertisements posted by the online job advertising firm and its competitors. The job advertisement can be created, updated and deleted by the job employer, customer service agent and data entry clerk. When they create or update a job advertisement, the job advertisement data will be captured and validated before it is created or updated in the database. If they delete a job advertisement, the job advertisement ID will be captured and verified before it is deleted from the database. Then, the data will be extracted, transformed and loaded (ETL)

Figure 3. First layer (business workflow) of BIP-Map for job competitor

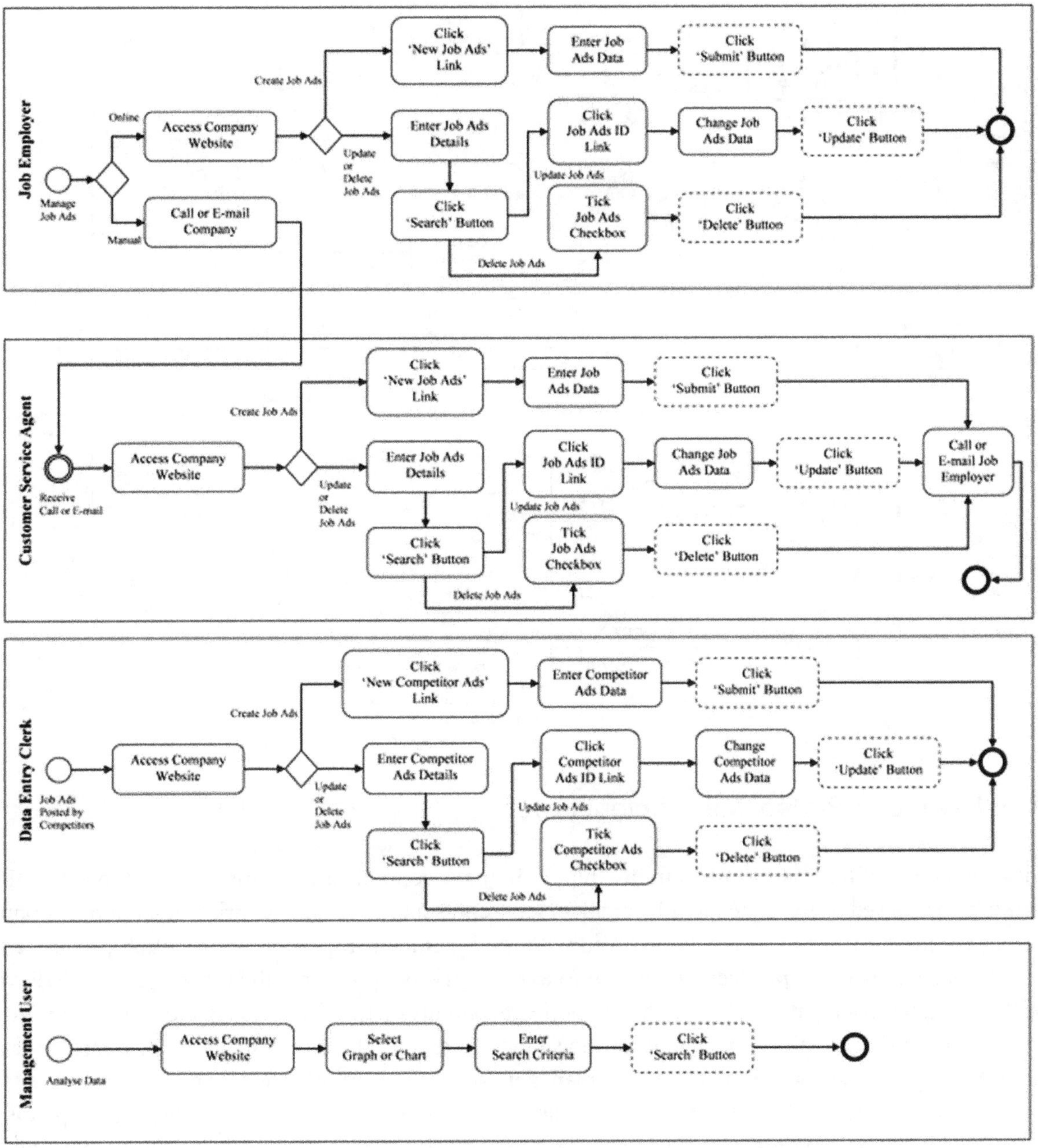

from the database into the data warehouse in a multi-dimensional form to support the decision-making process. When the management users view the information for BI reporting purpose, the search criteria will be captured and validated in order to retrieve the relevant data to be included in the BI product. The building block represented by a dashed line is expandable, and users can click on it to access the third layer (metacontent layer) of the BIP-Map for that particular building block.

Figure 4. Second layer (information manufacturing) of BIP-Map for job competitor graph

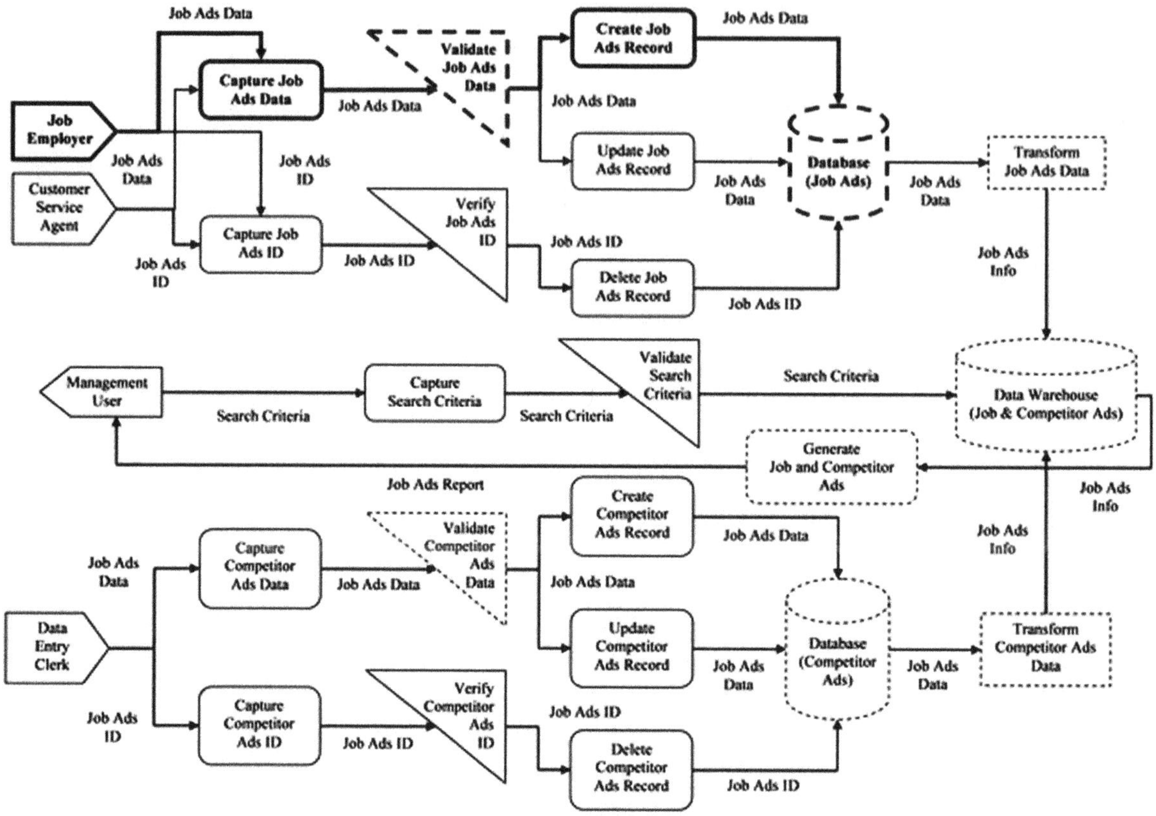

Third Layer of BIP-Map: Metacontent Layer

Clicking on one of the dashed line building blocks in the second layer of a BIP-Map will invoke a third layer which is based on the concept of BI metacontent representation, and comprises a set of metacontent such as business rules and metadata involved with the manufacturing of the information product from source systems to end BI products. Figures 5 to 8, respectively, represents the third layer of a BIP-Map for the job advertisement graph that shows the metacontent for the data entry/validation stage, metacontent for the ETL stage, metacontent for the storage of data in the database, and metacontent for the data warehouse. Based on this metacontent, managers are able to identify the business rules and criteria used to generate a report from the BI system. Knowing such information will help them more precisely interpret the reports and thus make informed decisions for their organisations. In addition, metacontent on the storage of data in databases and data warehouses are also a useful reference resource for the technical personnel to improve corporate data governance.

Framework Validation

This research puts forward an integrated BIP-Map framework and demonstrates the utility of the framework within an online job advertising setting in collaboration with JobCo, a medium-sized company

Figure 5. Third layer of BIP-Map for job advertisement graph (data entry/data validation)

Data	Description	Condition	Compulsory	Option
Job Position	- A name that describes the job.	- Not more than 25 alphanumeric characters.	Yes	-
Country	- A country for the job applicant to work.	- Select one option only.		- A list of countries.
State	- A state for the job applicant to work.			- A list of states for the selected country.
City	- A city for the job applicant to work.			- A list of cities for the selected state.
Job Responsibilities	- Information that describes what the job applicant needs to do.	- Not more than 500 alphanumeric characters.	No	-
Job Requirements	- Academic qualification and working experience that the job applicant needs to fulfill.			-
Application Deadline	- The job is closed for application on this date.	- A date that is greater than the current date. - The default selected date is 1 month later than the current date.	Yes	- A javascript calendar with date selection.
Advertisement Status	- Indicates whether the job advertisement is posted online or not. - Job advertisement that is saved but not posted online will not be displayed.	- Select one option only. - Default Value : Post Online		- Post Online - On Hold

Figure 6. Third layer of BIP-Map for job advertisement graph (ETL stage)

Database	ETL Process	Data Warehouse
advertisement Table advertisement_id — int advertiser_id — int original_posting_date — datetime advertisement_status_code — int **advertiser Table** advertiser_id — int industry_code — int **ref_industry Table** industry_code — int industry_name — varchar(255)	1. Create the **DimIndustry** dimension table. • DimIndustry.IndustryKey: Auto-generated • ref_industry.industry_code → DimIndustry.IndustryCode • ref_industry.industry_name → DimIndustry.IndustryName 2. Create the **DimAdvertiser** dimension table. • DimAdvertiser.AdvertiserKey: Auto-generated • advertiser.advertiser_id → DimAdvertiser.AdvertiserID 3. Create the **DimPostingDate** dimension table and **FactJobAdvertisement** fact table. • DimPostingDate.PostingDateKey: Auto-generated • advertisement.original_posting_date → DimPostingDate.PostingDate • YEAR(advertisement.original_posting_date) → DimPostingDate.PostingYear • DATENAME(MONTH, advertisement.original_posting_date) → DimPostingDate.PostingMonth • DAY(advertisement.original_posting_date) → DimPostingDate.PostingDay • DimAdvertiser.AdvertiserKey → FactJobAdvertisement. AdvertiserKey • DimIndustry.IndustryKey → FactJobAdvertisement.IndustryKey • DimPostingDate.PostingDateKey → FactJobAdvertisement. PostingDateKey • advertisement.advertisement_id → FactJobAdvertisement.AdvertisementID • advertisement.advertisement_status_code → FactJobAdvertisement. AdvertisementStatusCode	**FactJobAdvertisement Table** AdvertiserKey — int IndustryKey — int PostingDateKey — int AdvertisementID — int AdvertisementStatusCode — int **DimAdvertiser Table** AdvertiserKey — int AdvertiserID — int **DimIndustry Table** IndustryKey — int IndustryCode — int IndustryName — varchar(255) **DimPostingDate Table** PostingDateKey — int PostingDate — datetime PostingYear — int PostingMonth — varchar(50) PostingDay — int

based in Southeast Asia that provides services to thousands of corporate customers. A typical service provided by JobCo is online job advertisement posting on its websites. Its corporate customers (i.e. employers) can directly access the firm's online platform and post job advertisements, or alternatively, a customer service agent could post job advertisements on behalf of the employers. The firm also collects job advertising data of its main competitors and tracks its monthly sales performance against its competitors using a business intelligence tool.

To validate the usefulness of the BIP-Map, we engaged a panel of BI stakeholders of the online job advertising firm. Specifically, semi-structured interviews were conducted with the firm's seven BI stakeholders, who are also the key BI users of the medium-sized company. They included the regional process

Figure 7. Third layer of BIP-Map for job advertisement graph (database)

advertisement

Data	Description	Input Type	Data Source	Data Type	Data Code
advertisement_id	- An auto-generated number used to uniquely identify a job advertisement.	System Input	-	int	-
job_position	- A name that describes the job.		Job Position	varchar(50)	-
job_country	- A country for the job applicant to work.		Country		- Refer to Country List
job_state	- A state for the job applicant to work.		State	int	- Refer to State List
job_city	- A city for the job applicant to work.		City		- Refer to City List
job_responsibilities	- Information that describes what the job applicant needs to do.	Form Input	Job Responsibilities		-
job_requirements	- Academic qualification and working experience that the job applicant needs to fulfill.		Job Requirements	varchar(250)	-
application_deadline	- The job is closed for application on this date.		Application Deadline	datetime	-
advertiser_id	- A company or person who posted the job advertisement. - Automatically set by the system based on the user login ID.		-	int	- Refer to Advertiser List
original_posting_date	- A date that the job advertisement is posted online. - Automatically set by the system based on the system date.	System Input	-	datetime	-
advertisement_status_code	- Indicates whether the job advertisement is posted online or not. - Job advertisement that is saved but not posted online will not be displayed.		Advertisement Status	int	1 : Post Online 2 : On Hold

ref_industry

Data	Description	Data Type
industry_code	- An auto-generated number used to uniquely identify an industry.	int
industry_name	- A name that describes the industry.	varchar(255)

ref_advertiser

Data	Description	Data Type
advertiser_id	- An auto-generated number used to uniquely identify an advertiser.	int
industry_code	- As a foreign key to identify the industry of an advertiser.	

improvement manager, the quality and administration manager, the management information systems manager, the chief executive officer, the chief operations officer, the chief information officer, and the chief technology officer. The interview sought to elicit detailed opinions and comments specific to the subject of BIP-Map for the firm's BI systems. Unlike a focus group, an interview method is particularly suitable for this situation because it facilitates personal contact between participants but avoids the possibility of dominance by opinion-leaders, and so ensures democratic participation (Carson et al. 2001). Face-to-face interviews with BI stakeholders, each of which lasted 40 to 50 minutes, were conducted on scheduled times at their respective work sites. During the interview, the researchers demonstrated the working prototype of the BIP-Map and the interviewees were then asked to comment on the artefacts based on a pre-defined list of questions. Hence, it allowed for some latitude in getting detailed information from the interviewees during the interview but, at the same time, general questions could be asked so that all participants were treated in a consistent manner.

The feedback received was instructive and validated the BIP-Map framework. Interview panellists were unanimous in the view that that framework is useful for timely and informed business decision-making when it is integrated into a BI Dashboard. This is because a BIP-Map provides the BI users with lineage metadata – that is, a clear picture of the business workflow and the information manufacturing processes, and also a metacontent understanding on the data tabulated into the various BI reports. Moreover, the panellists recognised that a BIP-Map framework enables users to gain more insight into the displayed reports or charts in a BI Dashboard. One interviewee stated,

Figure 8. Third layer of BIP-Map for job advertisement graph (data warehouse)

FactJobAdvertisement					
Data	**Description**	**Input Type**	**Data Source**	**Data Type**	**Data Code**
AdvertiserKey	- A number used to uniquely identify an advertiser.	Extraction	- DimAdvertiser • AdvertiserKey	int	-
IndustryKey	- A number used to uniquely identify an industry.		- DimIndustry • IndustryKey		-
PostingDateKey	- A number used to uniquely identify a job posting date.		- DimPostingDate • PostingDateKey		-
AdvertisementID	- A number used to uniquely identify a job advertisement.		- advertisement • advertisement_id		-
AdvertisementStatusCode	- Indicates whether the job advertisement is posted online or not. - Job advertisement that is saved but not posted online will not be displayed.		- advertisement • advertisement_status_code		1 : Posted Jobs 2 : Not Posted Jobs

DimIndustry					
Data	**Description**	**Input Type**	**Data Source**	**Data Type**	**Data Code**
IndustryKey	- An auto-generated number used to uniquely identify an industry.	Generation	- Auto-Generated	int	-
IndustryCode	- The original number used to uniquely identify an industry.	Extraction	- ref_industry • industry_code		-
IndustryName	- A name that describes the industry.		- ref_industry • industry_name	varchar(255)	-

DimAdvertiser					
Data	**Description**	**Input Type**	**Data Source**	**Data Type**	**Data Code**
AdvertiserKey	- An auto-generated number used to uniquely identify an advertiser.	Generation	- Auto-Generated	int	-
AdvertiserID	- The original number used to uniquely identify an advertiser.	Extraction	- advertisement • advertisement_id		-

DimPostingDate					
Data	**Description**	**Input Type**	**Data Source**	**Data Type**	**Data Code**
PostingDateKey	- An auto-generated number used to uniquely identify a job posting date.	Generation	- Auto-Generated	int	-
PostingYear	- The year of a job posting date.	Transformation	- advertisement • original_posting_date		-
PostingMonth	- The month of a job posting date.			varchar(50)	-
PostingDate	- The day of a job posting date.			int	-

It helps in the understanding of how the information came about and provides a mechanism for improving the data capturing and information generation processes.

In other words, having such a three-layered integrated framework would allow BI users to readily identify data quality problems and the personnel responsible for each information product. One panellist pointed out that a BI Dashboard alone is not sufficient for users to fulfil the BI needs of their organisation. Therefore, the BIP-Map framework will serve as a comprehensive framework to address individual-related data quality issues, such as BI product believability, ease of understanding and metadata accessibility, and to provide detailed information that is important for prompt business analysis and timely decision-making. In addition, the panellists asserted that individual end-users may have only a limited knowledge of the information manufacturing process that underlies a particular BI product produced in the Dashboard. One interviewee mentioned that,

This (i.e. BIP-Map) provides the technical team with some form of documentation of the report structure which can be controlled in order to ensure the report's integrity. It is also useful when the technical personnel, unfamiliar with the reports, need to understand the logic behind the data. With the combination of the three layers, the technical personnel are able to understand the business considerations behind certain data, while the business personnel can get an insight into the logic behind the report information.

This indicates that BI users do not necessarily understand how the data in any BI report are being constructed from within the firm's information systems, yet, when making business decisions, it is risky to rely on data whose source has not been clearly identified. To summarise, it was clear from the validation feedback that a BIP-Map framework is a valuable framework that can assist BI users to understand the entire business workflow and information manufacturing process (together with the metacontent) of any BI product before they make any important decisions for their organisation.

CONCLUDING REMARKS AND CONTRIBUTIONS

This project applied a design science research paradigm (Hevner & Chatterjee 2010), and in this final section we show how the research fulfilled the seven guidelines for that paradigm as proposed by Hevner et al. (2004).

This study entailed the development of two artefacts. Referring to Hevner et al.'s Guideline 1 – design as an artefact, the initial artefact developed in this research was an integrated framework of Business Intelligence Product and Metacontent Map (BIP-Map) (i.e. a model). The second artefact was a BIP-Map informed prototype (i.e., an instantiation). The purposes of this research were to address the BI lineage problems and the individual-related data-quality issues and in this way we will be assisting BI users to better understand the BI products (Hevner et al.'s Guideline 2 – problem relevance). In achieving this, the designed artefacts have been strictly informed by, and incorporated with, three modelling and representation techniques; namely, the business process modelling notation (BPMN), the information product map (IP-Map), and the metacontent representation (Hevner et al.'s Guideline 5 – research rigour). The BIP-Map framework comprises three layers: the first layer adopts the business process model to describe both the business workflow and the participants involved. The second layer is an information product map which shows the information (i.e. BI product) manufacturing process and is constructed by expanding the first layer. The third layer represents the metacontent detail of the data validation stage at source system through to ETL, and the data warehousing stage.

In addition, the usefulness of the artefacts was validated via interviews by adhering to the interview methodology (Hevner et al.'s Guideline 3 – design evaluation and Guideline 5 – research rigour). The results of the framework validation will be used to refine the designed artefacts for future works. Such a build-and-evaluate loop will iterate several times before the final design artefacts are generated (Hevner et al.'s Guideline 6 – design as a search process). Moreover, this paper includes both the technical presentation and practical framing in terms of application in the online job advertising setting (Hevner et al.'s Guideline 7 – communication of research).

The designed artefacts are the major contribution of this research and as such they meet Guideline 4 – research contributions. The integration of the layers into one framework enables BI users to better understand BI products and so empowers them to respond promptly. In other words, this research explicitly addresses individual-related data-quality issues within a BI environment such as data believability, traceability, and accountability, issues that have not been addressed in earlier research but which can profoundly affect decision making. It proposes an integrated framework to provide business workflow and lineage information which helps users understand the BI product and its manufacturing process. The prior IP-Map of Shankaranarayan et al. (2003) did not consider the business workflow and the metacontent from data validation through to the data warehousing stage that are related to the manufacturing of BI products in an organisation. This study, therefore, fills the research gap and it represents an extension of the foundational IP-Map research of Shankaranarayan et al. (2003). It also addresses the data-quality, data-stewardship, and business process management aspects of data governance by ensuring that data can be trusted and that people can be made accountable for any data quality issues. Furthermore, the BIP-Map could serve as a framework for BI practitioners to identify business and information phases that may create data quality problems. Technical personnel will be able to understand the business considerations that underlie certain data, while business personnel can obtain insights into the logic used in the creation of BI reports. In short, the BIP-Map framework builds confidence in the BI product by clearly outlining lineage information. Future research could apply the proposed BIP-Map framework to other business settings and test the utility of the framework.

ACKNOWLEDGMENT

An earlier version of this paper was published at Journal of Database Management, IGI Global Publisher. The comments of the journal's anonymous reviewers are much appreciated.

REFERENCES

Aguilar-Saven, R. S. (2004). Business Process Modelling: Review and Framework. *International Journal of Production Economics*, *90*(2), 129–149. doi:10.1016/S0925-5273(03)00102-6

Aiken, P., Gillenson, M. L., Zhang, X., & Rafner, D. (2011). Data Management and Data Administration: Assessing 25 Years of Practice. *Journal of Database Management*, *22*(3), 24–44. doi:10.4018/jdm.2011070102

Ballard, C., Farrell, D. M., Gupta, A., Mazuela, C., & Vohnik, S. (2006). *Dimensional Modelling: In a Business Intelligence Environment*. New York: IBM.

Ballou, D. P., Wang, R. Y., Pazer, H., & Tayi, G. K. (1998). Modeling Information Manufacturing Systems to Determine Information Product Quality. *Management Science*, *44*(4), 462–484. doi:10.1287/mnsc.44.4.462

Bogza, R. M., & Zaharie, D. (2008). Business Intelligence as a Competitive Differentiator. *IEEE International Conference on Automation, Quality and Testing, Robotics*.

Carson, D., Gilmore, A., Gronhaug, K., & Perry, C. (2001). *Qualitative Research in Marketing*. London: Sage. doi:10.4135/9781849209625

Delen, D., & Pratt, D. B. (2006). An Integrated and Intelligent DSS for Manufacturing Systems. *Expert Systems with Applications*, *30*(2), 325–336. doi:10.1016/j.eswa.2005.07.017

Dempsey, L., & Heery, R. (1998). Metadata: A Current View of Practice and Issues. *The Journal of Documentation*, *54*(2), 145–172. doi:10.1108/EUM0000000007164

Elbashir, M. Z., Collier, P., & Davern, M. (2008). Measuring the Effects of Business Intelligence Systems: The Relationship between Business Process and Organisational Performance. *International Journal of Accounting Information Systems*, *9*(3), 135–153. doi:10.1016/j.accinf.2008.03.001

Fisher, C., Lauria, E., Chengalur-Smith, S., & Wang, R. (2006). *Introduction to Information Quality*. MIT Information Quality Program.

Foshay, N. (2005). *The Influence of End-User Metadata on User Attitudes toward, and Use of a Data Warehouse*. IBM, Somers.

Foshay, N., Mukherjee, A., & Taylor, A. (2007). Does Data Warehouse End-user Metadata Add Value? *Communications of the ACM*, *50*(11), 70–77. doi:10.1145/1297797.1297800

Gartner Press Release. (2013a). *Gartner Executive Program Survey of More Than 2,000 CIOs Shows Digital Technologies Are Top Priorities in 2013*. Retrieved from http://www.gartner.com/newsroom/id/2304615

Gartner Press Release. (2013b). *Gartner Says Worldwide Business Intelligence Software Revenue to Grow 7 Percent in 2013*. Retrieved from http://www.gartner.com/newsroom/id/2340216

Hevner, A., & Chatterjee, S. (2010). *Design Research in Information Systems: Theory and Practice*. New York: Springer. doi:10.1007/978-1-4419-5653-8

Hevner, A. R., March, S. T., Park, J., & Ram, S. (2004). Design Science in Information Systems Research. *Management Information Systems Quarterly*, *28*(1), 75–105. doi:10.2307/25148625

Howson, C. (2011). *Despite Successes, BI Adoption is Flat*. Retrieved from http://www.informationweek.com/news/software/bi/231902636

Khatri, V., & Brown, C. V. (2010). Designing data governance. *Communications of the ACM*, *53*(1), 148–152. doi:10.1145/1629175.1629210

Negash, S. (2004). Business Intelligence. *Communications of the Association for Information Systems*, *13*, 177–195.

Ou, L., & Peng, H. (2006). Knowledge and Process Based Decision Support in Business Intelligence System. *Proceedings of the First International Multi-Symposiums on Computer and Computational Sciences*. 10.1109/IMSCCS.2006.236

Ponniah, P. (2001). *Data Warehousing Fundamentals: A Comprehensive Guide for IT Professionals*. Wiley. doi:10.1002/0471221627

Sen, A. (2002). Metadata Management: Past, Present and Future. *Decision Support Systems*, *37*(1), 151–173. doi:10.1016/S0167-9236(02)00208-7

Shankaranarayanan, G. (2005). Towards Implementing Total Data Quality Management in a Data Warehouse. *Journal of Information Technology Management*, *16*(1), 21–30.

Shankaranarayanan, G., & Cai, Y. (2006). Supporting Data Quality Management in Decision-Making. *Decision Support Systems*, *42*(1), 302–317. doi:10.1016/j.dss.2004.12.006

Shankaranarayanan, G., & Even, A. (2006). The Metadata Enigma. *Communications of the ACM*, *49*(2), 88–94. doi:10.1145/1113034.1113035

Shankaranarayanan, G., Wang, R. Y., & Ziad, M. (2000). IP-MAP: Representing the Manufacture of an Information Product. In *Proceedings of the 2000 International Conference on Information Quality*. MIT.

Shankaranarayanan, G., Ziad, M., & Wang, R. Y. (2003). Managing Data Quality in Dynamic Decision Environments: An Information Product Approach. *Journal of Database Management, 14*(4), 14–32. doi:10.4018/jdm.2003100102

Shi, Y., & Lu, X. (2010). The Role of Business Intelligence in Business Performance Management. *3rd International Conference on Information Management, Innovation Management and Industrial Engineering*. 10.1109/ICIII.2010.522

Stock, D., & Winter, R. (2011). The Value of Business Metadata – Structuring the Benefits in a Business Intelligence Context. In A. d'Atri, M. Ferrara, J. F. George, & P. Spagnoletti (Eds.), *Information Technology and Innovation Trends in Organisations* (pp. 133–141). Heidelberg, Germany: Physica. doi:10.1007/978-3-7908-2632-6_16

Tallon, P. (2013). Corporate Governance of Big Data: Perspectives on Value, Risk, and Cost. *IEEE Computer Journal, 46*(6), 32–38. doi:10.1109/MC.2013.155

Tan, W., Shen, W., Xu, L., Zhou, B., & Li, L. (2008). A Business Process Intelligence System for Enterprise Process Performance Management. *IEEE Transactions on Systems, Man and Cybernetics. Part C, Applications and Reviews, 38*(6), 745–756. doi:10.1109/TSMCC.2008.2001571

Vaduva, A., & Dittrich, K. R. (2002). Metadata Management for Data Warehousing: Between Vision and Reality. *International Symposium on Database Engineering & Applications*, Grenoble, France.

Wang, R. (1998). A Product Perspective on Total Data Quality Management. *Communications of the ACM, 41*(2), 58–63. doi:10.1145/269012.269022

Wang, R., Lee, Y., Pipino, L., & Strong, D. (1998). Manage Your Information as a Product. *Sloan Management Review, 39*(4), 95–105.

Wang, R. Y., & Strong, D. M. (1996). Beyond Accuracy: What Data Quality Means to Data Consumers. *Journal of Management Information Systems, 12*(4), 5–34. doi:10.1080/07421222.1996.11518099

Wang, W., Ding, H., Dong, J., & Ren, C. (2006). A Comparison of Business Process Modelling Methods. *IEEE International Conference on Service Operations and Logistics, and Informatics Proceedings*, Shanghai, China.

Weske, M. (2007). *Business Process Management: Concepts, Languages, Architectures*. Berlin: Springer.

White, S. A. (2004). *Introduction to BPMN*. IBM Corporation.

Wixom, B., & Watson, H. (2010). The BI-Based Organisation. *International Journal of Business Intelligence Research, 1*(1), 13–28. doi:10.4018/jbir.2010071702

Zhu, H., & Wang, R. Y. (2010). *Information Quality Framework for Verifiable Intelligence Products. In Data Engineering: Mining, Information and Intelligence. Springer.*

ENDNOTES

1 Based on information product concept, a BI product refers to any reporting information that is provided to the BI users for decision-making where information is treated much like the products found in the manufacturing environment of any industry (Wang 1998; Wang et al. 1998; Shankaranarayanan et al. 2000; Shankaranarayanan et al. 2003; Shankaranarayanan 2005).

2 In this paper, the terms metadata and metacontent are used interchangeably.

3 According to Foshay et al. (2007), lineage metadata "tells the user about the original source of data in the warehouse and describes what has been done to the data prior to being loaded into the warehouse. Lineage information answers the user's questions: Where did this data originate, and what has been done to it?"(p.72)

4 A detailed explanation of the BPMN building blocks is included in Appendix 1.

5 A detailed explanation of the IP-Map building blocks is included in Appendix 2.

APPENDIX 1

The elements of business process modelling notation (BPMN) can be categorised into four basic groups, namely, *Flow Objects*, *Connecting Objects*, *Swimlanes*, and *Artefacts* (White 2004). The function of each element in the four groups is briefly described in Tables 2 to 5. The elements in the Flow Objects group are used to describe the occurrence of events and the execution of activities in a business process. The Connecting Objects group contains elements that connect all the objects together in order to indicate the flow and dependencies among the events and activities. The elements in the Swimlanes group categorise the activities to be conducted by different users into separate sections so that the interaction between all participants involved in a business process can be easily identified. The Artefacts group contains elements that are used to include additional information about how the activities are executed in a business process.

Table 2. BPMN flow objects

Flow Objects	Function
Event  Start Intermediate End	- Event is something that happens during the execution of a business process and it is categorised as Start, Intermediate, and End.
Activity 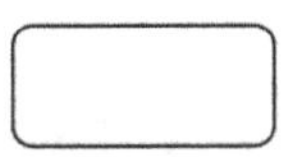	- Activity is the work performed in a business process.
Gateway 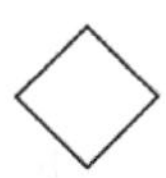	- Gateway is used to control the direction of flow for the activities in a business process.

Table 3. BPMN connecting objects

Connecting Objects	Function
Sequence Flow 	- Sequence Flow shows the order of activities being performed in a business process.
Message Flow 	- Message Flow shows the communication of messages between two different parties.
Association 	- Association is used to indicate the inputs and outputs of an activity.

Table 4. BPMN swimlanes

Swimlanes	Function
Pool 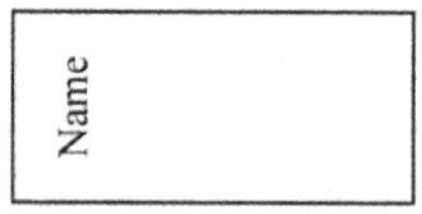	- A participant in a process is represented by a pool that acts as a graphical container for separating a set of activities.
Lane 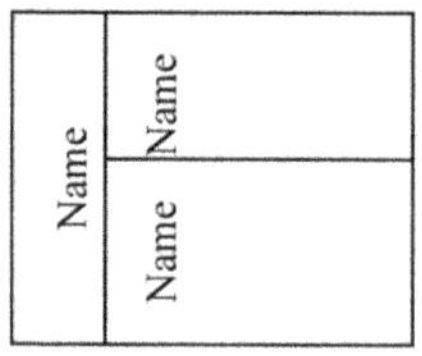	- The sub-section of a pool is called a lane and it separates the pool, either vertically or horizontally.

Table 5. BPMN artefacts

Artefacts	Function
Data Object 	- Data Object shows the data that are captured or generated by an activity.
Group 	- Group categorizes a set of activities together for the purpose of documentation or analysis.
Annotation 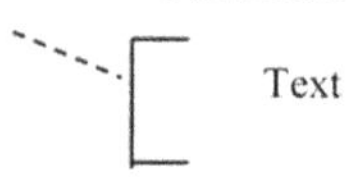	- Annotation provides extra details about an event or activity.

APPENDIX 2

The Information Product Map (IP-MAP) is a modelling technique for representing the manufacturing processes of the information products available in an organisation or industry (Wang 1998; Wang et al. 1998; Shankaranarayanan et al. 2000; Shankaranarayanan 2005). With an IP-MAP, users are able to visualise the entire information manufacturing chain and identify the critical parts that may create data quality problems. The function of each building block in the IP-MAP model is briefly described in Table 6. The *Source* and *Customer* blocks play the role of indicating the origin and destination of data so that users are able to identify all the providers and consumers of data. The *Processing*, *Data Quality* and *Decision* blocks are used to show the processes that the data have gone through, and the flow from one place to another, based on different scenarios. The *Data Storage*, *Business Boundary* and *IS Boundary* blocks specify where the data are being stored or transferred throughout the organisation.

Table 6. IP-MAP building blocks

Building Blocks	Function
Source Block 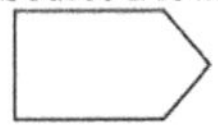	- Represents the source of raw data or input.
Customer Block 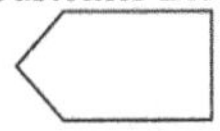	- Represents the consumer of an information product.
Processing Block 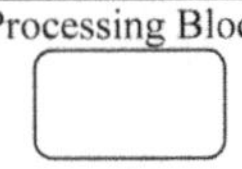	- Represents any manipulations, calculations, or combinations involving the raw input data or component data.
Data Quality Block 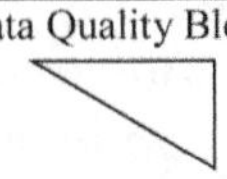	- Represents the checks for data quality on data items.
Decision Block 	- Used to capture different conditions to be evaluated and directs users to the appropriate procedures.
Data Storage Block 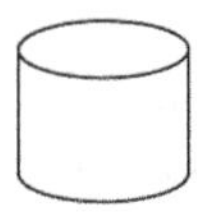	- Represents the capture of data in storage files or databases.
Business Boundary Block 	- Represents instances where the raw input data or component data are "handed over" by one business (organizational) unit to another unit.
IS Boundary Block 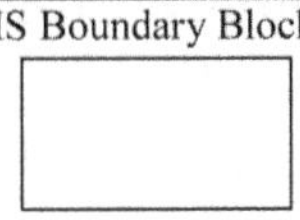	- Used to reflect the changes to raw or component data as they move from one information system to another information system.

Chapter 6
Business Intelligence Implementation Critical Success Factors

Ahad Zare Ravasan
Kharazmi University, Iran

Sogol Rabiee Savoji
Mehralborz Institute of Higher Education, Iran

ABSTRACT

Many organizations take business intelligence (BI) systems to improve their decision-making processes. Although many organizations have adopted BI systems, not all of these implementations have been successful. This chapter seeks to identify critical success factors (CSFs) that impact on the successful implementation of BI systems in organizations. So, at first, through literature review, 26 CSFs were identified. Following that, a questionnaire was developed and then filled out by domain experts who had at least three years of experience in BI implementation projects. Robust exploratory factor analysis (EFA) was run for data analysis, which finally classified 26 CSFs into four distinct groups termed as "organizational," "human," "project management," and "technical." The results of this study provide a very useful reference for scholars and managers to identify the relevant issues of BI projects in Iran.

INTRODUCTION

For future enterprises must compete in all aspects, the need to generate, collect and transform their data into actionable knowledge would be sensed more than ever (Delen & Demirkan, 2013). Therefore, almost all enterprises are involved in the process of adopting decision support systems to exploit data, return information more agile and better, and also improve analytical capabilities as a new valence for their services (Delen & Demirkan, 2013; Martins, Oliveira, & Popovič, 2013; Rouhani & Ravasan, 2014). Thus, the theme "business intelligence (BI)" is introduced as a response to current needs of businesses and consequently to solve managerial decision- making issues (Petrini & Pozzebon, 2009). Rather than having a unique and generally accepted definition, BI is typically used as an 'umbrella' term to describe

DOI: 10.4018/978-1-5225-5718-0.ch006

a process, or concepts and methods that improve decision making by using fact-based support systems. Many terms such as "*business intelligence*", "*business analytics*", "*big data*", "*data mining*", and "*data warehousing*" are often used interchangeably in the literature. Rouhani and Zare ravasan (2015) proposed a taxonomy for BI definitions approaches as managerial, technical, and system enabler main categories. BI has evolved because the amount of data generated through the internet and smart devices has grown exponentially altering how organizations and individuals use information(Larson & Chang, 2016). Regarding decision-support, BI intends to equip stakeholders with valuable information on decision-making process through data integration and analytical capabilities (Popovič, Hackney, Coelho, & Jaklič, 2012). Many analysts posit BI as the number one IT investment and the top-most priority for most chief information officers (CIOs) (Ishikiriyama, Miro, & Gomes, 2015; Işık, Jones, & Sidorova, 2012; Rouhani, Ashrafi, Zare, & Afshari, 2016; Wieder & Ossimitz, 2015; B. Wixom & Watson, 2010). By considering the top management concerns, it is not astonishing that BI has settled on the head of IT developments in recent years (Howson, 2008; Luftman & Ben-Zvi, 2010). One assumption is that it is becoming more pervasive within organizations and is affecting the way information is used, analyzed and applied. As a result, enterprises can lead, decide, measure, manage and optimize their performance to obtain superior efficiency and derive financial benefits (Hostmann, Rayner, & Friedman, 2006).

However, Rasmussen, Goldy, and Solli (2002) declared that the cost of buying and implementing BI software could vary from 50 thousand dollars to millions. Sahay and Ranjan (2008) and Ramamurthy, Sen, and Sinha (2008) also cited the tremendous cost of BI implementation in the organizational environment. Nonetheless, many organizations have invested significantly in BI systems to help them gain better information processing and make the best business decisions, but have seen only limited success in getting their business users to adopt them (Ocampo & MCSD, 2007). In a similar vein, Gartner revealed that more than 50 percent of BI projects have been accepted on a limited basis or have failed. There is anecdotal evidence that a significant number of companies have been unable to realize the expected benefits of BI and they sometimes even consider the BI initiative as a failure in itself (Chenoweth, Corral, & Demirkan, 2006; M. I. Hwang & Xu, 2005; Johnson, 2004). The Gartner group also warned that more than half of the Global 2000 enterprises would fail to realize the capabilities of BI and, hence, would lose market share to companies that could successfully apply BI systems (Dresner H. J., 2002). A survey of 142 companies, found that 41 percent of the respondents had experienced at least one BI project failure and only 15 percent of respondents believed that their BI initiative was a significant success (Hawking & Sellitto, 2010). Moss and Atre (2003) indicated that 60% of BI projects failed due to inadequate planning, poor project management, undelivered business requirements and so on.

While the goal of BI has been to facilitate business analytics, increase revenue and competitiveness, it can impose substantial costs for given enterprises. Hence, it indicates that adopting these systems should also be considered with caution by organizations from different aspects. Besides, it is evident that occurrence of an inconsistency and inappropriate assessment about influencing factors during the implementation process can lead projects into failure.

Despite its importance and aforementioned high failure rate, few studies have investigated the success or failure critical factors in the implementation of these systems (Jagielska, Darke, & Zagari, 2003). Therefore, empirical research is needed to shed more light on those CSFs influencing the implementation of BI systems. An understanding of the CSFs enables BI stakeholders to optimize their scarce resources and efforts by focusing on those significant factors that are most likely to aid successful system implementation (Yeoh & Koronios, 2010). Because the rate of BI systems implementation is raising in Iran and these projects, by their nature, are associated with a high failure rate, so it is of crucial importance to identify the CSFs in such projects. Therefore, this study intends to identify and classify the BI implementation CSFs in Iranian cases. For this purpose, through in-depth literature review, 26 critical success factors are identified, and a classification model is proposed using Robust Exploratory Factor Analysis (EFA). On the basis of this model, some recommendations can be made to avert failure or to avoid potential losses in future projects. In the final section, discussions are made about the implications of the new model and the identified factors.

LITERATURE REVIEW

CSFs are the characteristics, conditions or variables that can significantly impact on the success of a firm competing in a particular industry given the fact that the variables, conditions, and characteristics are well sustained, maintained or managed. A set of CSFs identified for the development of any major information system, such as a BI system, is fundamentally different from the set of interlinked detailed tasks which must be accompanied to ensure a project's completion (Dobbins, 2000; Yeoh, 2008). Although successful execution of CSFs may not guarantee the success of a project implementation admittedly, it can give a long run to the project (Vodapalli, 2009). Many of the success factors identified in the literature related to the successful implementation of BI are not unique to the BI environment. Many of these success factors can be applied to other IS projects and have been noted in the implementation of IT service management (ITSM) (Mohammadi, Ravasan, & Hamidi, 2015), enterprise resource planning (ERP) (Amid, Moalagh, & Zare Ravasan, 2012), Customer Relationship Management (CRM) (Kim, Lee, & Pan, 2002; Mankoff, 2001), knowledge management (Wong, 2005), and supply chain management (Ngai, Cheng, & Ho, 2004). In the context of Business Intelligence systems, CSFs can be perceived as a set of tasks and procedures that should be addressed to ensure BI systems accomplishment (Olszak & Ziemba, 2012). Studies are carried out to recognize success factors in business intelligence. The most important and relevant ones are summarized in this section.

Chen. et al. (2000) in a survey of 42 end-users found that user satisfaction played an important role in the success of a data warehouse. Sammon and Finnegan (2000) adopted a case study approach and identified the organizational prerequisites for the successful implementation of a firm's data warehouse. They found that the successful organizational factors associated with implementation were adopting a business-driven approach, management support, adequate resources including budgetary and skills, data quality, flexible enterprise model, data stewardship, strategy for automated data extraction methods/tools, integration of data warehouse with existing systems, and hardware/software proof of concept.

In another research, Wixom and Watson (2001) studied 111 organizations and found that data quality and system quality impacted significantly on data warehouse success with system quality being four times as important as data quality. They further identified that system quality was affected by management support, adequate resources, user participation and a skilled project team. Wixom and Watson (2001) in their work, measured both BI implementation factors and BI success factors. Through a review of the literature, the survey of data warehouse conference attendees and interviews of data warehouse experts, they developed a research model for data warehousing success. They addressed critical factors such as management support, adequate resources, user participation, team skills, system quality, data quality, source systems and development technologies in a particular model which is called BI success model. One shortcoming of the Wixom and Watson (2001) BI success model is the lack of strategic factors that influence the success of a BI project. Other scholars have emphasized the importance of organizational alignment (Chenoweth et al., 2006; Williams & Williams, 2010), apparently defined business objectives (M. I. Hwang & Xu, 2005; Watson, Fuller, & Ariyachandra, 2004) and an enterprise as a whole (Little Jr & Gibson, 2003; Sammon & Finnegan, 2000), as relevant success factors in a BI project.

However, one success factor that is particularly unique to BI is the need to integrate data from various source systems. The successful integration of data is dependent on the number and type of source systems, the quality of these systems, the accuracy of each system's data, the metadata, and the ability for the BI to interface with these systems (Sammon & Finnegan, 2000). The increase in the number and diversity of source systems has a direct impact on this success factor. Moalagh and Zare Ravasan (2012) suggest that one way of improving the quality of data sources is to integrate the heterogeneous sources through the implementation of an ERP system.

Some scholars proposed BI CSFs in the organization, environment, and project planning dimensions. They found solid support for organizational factors (H. G. Hwang, Ku, Yen, & Cheng, 2004). Ariyachandra and Watson (2006), analyzing CSFs for BI implementation, take account of two critical dimensions: process performance (i.e., how well the process of a BI system implementation went on), and infrastructure performance (i.e., the quality of the system and the standard of output). Process performance can be assessed concerning time-schedule and budgetary considerations while infrastructure performance is concerned with the quality of a system, the quality of information and system use. According to Hirsimäki (2017) and Yeoh and Popovic (2015), Yeoh and Koronios (2010), CSFs can be broadly classified into three dimensions: organizational, process, and technological. Organizational dimension entails such elements as committed management support and sponsorship, a clear vision, and a well-established business case. In turn, the process dimension is comprised of the business-centric championship and balanced team composition, business-driven and interactive development approach and user-oriented change management. Technological dimension is perceived to consist of elements such as business-driven, scalable and flexible technical framework, and sustainable data quality and integrity. In particular, Mesároš, Čarnický and Mandičák (2015) have identified and confirmed some of the most common BI key success factors which are necessary for successful implementation and use of BI. Based on the results of examination, they have identified seven key success factors of implementation and use of BI in enterprises: active involvement of a strong sponsor respectively of the project, BI competence center, high quality of the source data, close cooperation between solution users and the team of professional IT staff, enterprise-wide solution scope, corporate culture opened to change, properly selected analytical tools and promoting active use of available tools. Denic. et al. (2016) analyzed key success factors for business intelligence systems implementation based on a literature review, industrial presentations, and on the processing of data obtained from interviews with several companies. These factors include organizational, system, factors and data factors.

To sum up, the Appendix proposes a list of 26 critical success factors extracted from a literature review.

RESEARCH METHOD

The research steps, i.e., identifying CSFs, conducting instrument development, data collection, data analysis using robust EFA, are shown in Figure 1.

Figure 1. The research steps

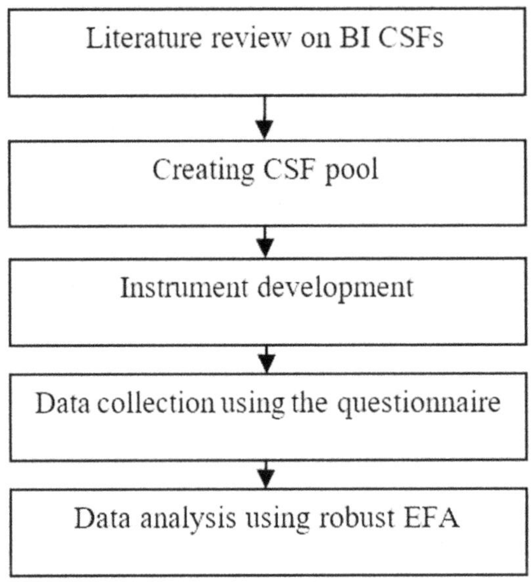

Instrument Development

A 26 items questionnaire has been developed by integrating factors identified through literature review. The survey instrument asked the respondents to rate the impact of 26 identified CSFs using a 9 point scale with items ranged from 1 (strongly low) to 9 (strongly high). Face or content validity of the questionnaire is conducted through the literature review and experts judgment. To ensure this, at first six BI implementation project managers of high academic levels and more than five-year experience reviewed the questionnaire. They had some comments on the length and the clarity of each question. Their suggestions were incorporated into the final version of the questionnaire. The content validity of the instrument was thereby addressed. Also, for evaluating the reliability of the questionnaire, the test-retest method was used. For conducting test-retest method, authors asked 15 project managers in a 14-day interval to participate in the study. The resulted Cronbach alpha estimated to be 0.85 (higher than 0.7) that implies good reliability of the instrument.

Data Collection and Sample Size

The target of this study was BI implementation project team members in Iranian industries which have at least three years of experience. In order to gather data from the companies, the following procedure was performed: first, the eligible companies and related team members were identified, and their contact information was gathered; second, authors asked them to participate in the study; third, the questionnaire was sent to them, and finally, they filled and replied the questionnaires. 185 questionnaires were sent, 132 questionnaires were gathered, and 122 usable questionnaires were used for the analysis (response rate: 0.66). The sample size of 122 seems to be adequate for conducting robust EFA (recommended ratio of 5:1). However, some authors argued that such ratios might be an oversimplification (MacCallum, Widaman, Preacher, & Hong, 2001).

RESULTS

EFA is a frequently used method to discover patterns of multidimensional constructs that are subsequently used for the development of measurement scales. Its primary objective is to reduce the number of observed variables to fewer factors to enhance interpretability and detect hidden structures in the data. Here, robust EFA (Treiblmaier & Filzmoser, 2010) was employed to perform the analysis. Robust EFA has many advantages over classical factor analyses in helping a researcher to choose the multitude of options, such as various types of data transformation, the choice of the factor extraction method, factor rotation, and the number of factors to be chosen. Also, it makes less restrictive assumptions about data distribution than classical factor analysis and reduces the influence of outliers, which finally leads to more valid results (Amid, Moalagh, & Zare Ravasan, 2012).

Before factor analysis, a test was conducted to verify the adequacy of the data for FA. The Kaiser-Meyer-Olkin (KMO) measure of sampling adequacy is the favorite measure for assessing the extent to which the indicators of a construct belong to one another. Large values for the KMO indicate that a factor analysis of the variables is a good idea. The KMO is 0.814 which is above the "Mediocre" threshold of 0.5. We also performed a Bartlett sphericity test, which was statistically significant ($p < 0.05$), indicating the eligibility of the data. Then, we used a Shapiro–Wilk test to determine whether our sample had a normal distribution. We found that none of our variables were normally distributed. Thus, principal component analysis (PCA) was our choice for the factor extraction method as proposed in robust EFA.

Another option should be selected for conducting robust EFA is factor rotation method. There are various rotation methods available for use in several widely used statistical software packages. Here, since it was reasonable to expect that the dimensions of BI implementation CSFs would correlate with one another, we used Oblimin rotation, which is proposed in robust EFA (Treiblmaier & Filzmoser, 2010). Also, other methods such as Varimax rotation usually results in a highly dominant first factor and a rather weak discrimination of the other factors according to their loadings that is not desired here. Finally, the number of factors to be extracted from the data should be determined. There are several ways for the purpose. A researcher may decide to use Eigen values higher than 1, a visual scree plot, or require a specific amount of variance to be explained by the factors. Here, Eigen values greater than one, and an absolute value of factor loading greater than 0.6 has been selected. It has been suggested that a factor loading higher than 0.60 on the ''parent factor'' and a loading of less than 0.40 on a ''foreign factor'' indicate convergent and discriminant validity of the constructs (Chin, Gopal, & Salisbury, 1997). As a result, 3 out of 26 factors were dropped from the initial pool and remained 23 factors were grouped into four components. The results can be seen in Table 1.

Extraction method used is Principle Component Analysis and the rotation method used is Oblimin.

Data Interpretation

To indicate the meaning of the components, they have been given short labels indicating their content. Since the results of this stage were open to several interpretations, we decided to use experts' opinions here. So, we invited five BI project managers and finalized components' name by discussion and general agreement. In this way, "Organizational", "Human Resources", "Project Management", and finally "Technical" are the names which have been assigned to the extracted components. The final results are shown in Table 2.

Table 1. The results of robust EFA

Factors	1	2	3	4
Ensure senior management support	0.91			
Well-Defined vision and clear goals for system and business	0.85			
Adequate resources including budgetary and human resources	0.88			
BI and business strategy alignment	0.83			
User support		0.88		
Participation end users		0.75		
Change management		0.91		
User training		0.88		
Managing users' expectations		0.80		
Strong project management			0.85	
Avoid deviation from the initial goals of the project			0.78	
Risk management			0.86	
project team Management			0.80	
Being flexible and responsive to change			0.83	
Strong partnership between the business and IT counterparts			0.78	
IT knowledge and technical skills of the project team			0.91	
Creating the data warehouse organization				0.88
Data management				0.76
Strong applications management in the organization				0.84
Identify user's specific issues and requirements				0.76
Appropriateness of technology with organization				0.82
Adequate and reliable technical architecture				0.80
Select the appropriate tools				0.86
% of variance	25.78	21.35	18.45	12.95
Cumulative %		47.13	65.58	78.53

DISCUSSION

The classification proposed in this study is somewhat compatible with the classification performed in previous studies for the critical success factors in the implementation of business intelligence systems. For instance, in a study by Yeoh (2008), critical success factors have been classified into three main groups: organizational, process and technology, which in this study process dimension has been divided into two distinct dimensions of project management and human management.

Considering the results, it can be understood that organizational component is the most important CSF group in the implementation of business intelligence systems which is in line with the results of previous work (e.g., H. G. Hwang et al., 2004). This component contains factors of senior management support of the projects, the management believes in the project and proper allocation of financial resources. Senior management support of projects in several studies is listed as one of the factors affecting

Table 2. Extracted components and their related factors

Component name	Factor ID	Factor name
F1: Organizational	OR01	Ensure senior management support
	OR02	Well-Defined vision and clear goals for system and business
	OR03	Adequate resources including budgetary and human resources
	OR04	BI and business strategy alignment
F2: Human Resources	HR01	User support
	HR02	Participation end users
	HR03	Change management
	HR04	User training
	HR05	Managing users' expectations
F3: Project Management	PM01	Strong project management
	PM02	Avoid deviation from the initial goals of the project
	PM03	Risk management
	PM04	Project team Management
	PM05	Being flexible and responsive to change
	PM06	Strong partnership between the business and IT counterparts
	PM07	IT knowledge and technical skills of the project team
F4: Technical	TC01	Creating the data warehouse organization
	TC02	Data management
	TC03	Strong applications management in the organization
	TC04	Identify user's specific issues and requirements
	TC05	Appropriateness of technology with organization
	TC06	Adequate and reliable technical architecture
	TC07	Select the appropriate tools

the successful implementation of business intelligence systems in the organizations (e.g., Chenoweth et al., 2006; Howson, 2006; Olbrich, Poppelbuß, & Niehaves, 2012; Yeoh & Koronios, 2010). If the implementation of business intelligence is tied and aligned with strategies of the organization, it will acquire the support of senior managers. Such support not only would facilitate the funding needed to provide hardware, software and human requirements but would also provide support for the executive team to reduce the resistance of personnel and people in the organization. This can be of a leveraging effect on the project success, and consequently, the proposed system would find a strategic position in the organization. Also according to the results, it can be said that a senior management support plays a very effective role in the successful deployment of the system. Apparently, if the senior management of the organization does not believe in the benefits arising from the establishment of these frameworks, they would not provide the needed support for the project and would doubt in right allocation of human and financial resources required to develop the project.

To strengthen the management believes in the project, it is necessary to hold relevant training courses, seminars, and workshops and establish the appropriate supporting managerial culture to raise their knowledge and awareness. By their nature, implementation of business intelligence system requires the involvement of a wide variety of stakeholders with diverse skills. However, this can be beneficial to the organization; but on the other hand, it may lead to different perspectives, each of which has their concerns. It may also lead to conflicts within the organization, which senior management should meet the challenge with conflict management as well as the appropriate and timely allocation of the available resources to the project. Another factor in the organizational component is BI alignment with business strategy. One of the problems in IT systems is that the information technology units cannot respond to the business requirements appropriately, and always it is stated as a challenge to the success of IT systems. Therefore, to achieve a sustainable competitive advantage, alignment between IT in general and business intelligence systems in particular with business requirements should be followed (Howson, 2006; Olbrich et al., 2012). By aligning IT and business, not only business strategies bring about growth and development of IT in organizations, but at the same time IT strategies also lead to a change in and reorientation of business strategies.

The next component affecting on the successful implementation of BI systems in organizations is the human factor. Employees' awareness is one of the most important factors to achieve success in BI project since that can reveal the importance of the system and also the necessity of its run for them in the organization. Besides, the factor may lead to the alignment of various organizational levels including operational and management levels. With implementing the system in an organization, it will reduce employees' resistance against the project and will facilitate dealing with the challenges as well. Employees' awareness can be achieved through staff training, so staff training should consistently be followed (Hanafizadeh & Ravasan, 2011). Because the implementation of BI systems requires some organizational changes, it is usually accompanied with the employees' resistance during implementation. Recognizing employees' disagreement patterns and staff involvement in the project, not only reduces their opposition level, but it can also raise the probability of project success (Knightsbridge, 2006; Olszak & Ziemba, 2012; Vodapalli, 2009). In the meantime, users' involvement in the process of development and implementation of the system and their support after "go live" will be highly instrumental. It should also be noted that unrealistic and implausible expectations should be avoided because if the real capabilities of the implemented system fell short of users' expectations, the users would resist it and not cooperate with others.

Project management is another component in the successful implementation of BI systems. In this regard, one of the most important factors is the strong project management in the organization. To carry out projects within approved cost and time, it is essential to avoid creeping the project' primary goals, which might baffle managers and employees (Ravasan & Mansouri, 2014; Watson et al., 2004). Also, given the fact that by their nature, the implementation of IT systems projects, are associated with a high risk, highly risk-taking managers in an organization can be effective in promoting the goals of the organization and the system. Another factor that is of great importance in this regard is the use of a strong project team. Knowledge and skills of the project team and users play a crucial part in the successful implementation of BI systems. A competent project team, consisting of managers, employees, and IT professionals, is essential to implement BI (B. H. Wixom & Watson, 2001; Yeoh, 2008). The project team should have both adequate technical and business knowledge. These different views in a project team preempt single orientation dimension and attend only to particular aspects. Also, it is essential to have a full-time project team in place to focus more on the project. Furthermore, project team members should be flexible and well-prepared to respond to possible changes during the project, even after the system "go live".

The last category affecting the successful implementation of business intelligence systems in organizations pertains to technical component. Deployment of business intelligence systems in organizations also poses a major challenge technically because it is needed to provide the required technical infrastructure and deployment of data warehouse, which is expensive, technically complicated and time-consuming (ESCC, 2009; Knightsbridge, 2006). Similarly, the data quality has to be controlled regarding its accuracy, precision, completeness, and compatibility of the data (Knightsbridge, 2006; Meister, 2009; Vesset, 2005; Vodapalli, 2009). One of the key factors in the development of information systems in general and business intelligence, in particular, is to accurately identify the users' requirements and integrate these requirements in the system. With regard to architecture, the proposed technical architecture for a system should be feasible and be capable of development, scalability, and compatibility with the existing architecture as well as be compatible with the technical status and infrastructure of the organization.

CONCLUSION

Traditional organizations often encounter issues such as data congestion and redundancy, lack of information, knowledge, and quality of the required reports. As a result, for timely decision-making by senior management in the minimum possible time, decision- making is usually adapted based on the experiences which in turn cause a higher risk or lower the output of decisions. Business intelligence is a tool used by organizations to collect and analyze structured and unstructured data, which is the right response to the challenges in question.

Despite all the benefits that can be derived from the BI system for organizations, the high failure rate is a real concern. Such a high rate of failure has led some researchers to seek out the causes of its implementation failure as well as identification of its critical success factors. This study has been conducted with this in mind and in response to this question: "What are the critical success factors in the implementation of BI systems?". To answer this question, the study enjoyed an in-depth literature review. Then, using data yielded by 122 questionnaires gathered through BI implementation project team members in Iranian industries, a robust EFA was conducted. Through this, 23 factors were categorized into four main components: "Organizational", "Human Resources", "Project Management", and finally "Technical" groups. Based on these findings, a framework was proposed for BI CSFs classification in Iranian industries, and finally, each main component was discretely discussed to give practitioners and academic researchers in the field a brilliant insight.

This study suffers from some limitations. One of the main limitations of the work is the limited number of available BI experts because Iranian organizations often are not mature enough to implement BI systems. This limitation turned data collection process into a cumbersome endeavor for authors. Also, this study is by no means exhaustive enough to address all issues related to BI success factors in Iran. It is also difficult to make generalizations based on the contents of the work done here, and relatively few articles could be found in most countries, especially in developing countries. As a potential topic for further research, the conceptual framework could be applied to other countries to investigate its applicability. Likewise, researchers may assume qualitative research methods such as case studies to investigate such factors in similar or different settings. The case study is a useful method in studying such a topic. Moreover, future work could focus on more specific areas such as project management, organizational structure or organizational culture impact on BI implementation projects so that more detailed and in-depth information or deep-rooted failure-success reasons could be identified. Moreover, future research can move beyond listing CSFs and explore the interrelationships between them. For example, it is worthwhile to investigate whether mismatches between factors such as management, processes, human resources, structures, and technology are the causes of these problems. It would also be valuable to relate CSFs to project phases.

REFERENCES

Amid, A., Moalagh, M., & Ravasan, Z. (2012). Identification and classification of ERP critical failure factors in Iranian industries. *Information Systems*, *37*(3), 227–237. doi:10.1016/j.is.2011.10.010

Ariyachandra, T., & Watson, H. J. (2006). Which data warehouse architecture is most successful? *Business Intelligence Journal, 11*(1), 4.

Chamoni, P., & Gluchowski, P. (2004). Integrationstrends bei Business-Intelligence-Systemen. *Wirtschaftsinformatik*, *46*(2), 119–128. doi:10.1007/BF03250931

Chen, L. D., Soliman, K. S., Mao, E., & Frolick, M. N. (2000). Measuring user satisfaction with data warehouses: An exploratory study. *Information & Management*, *37*(3), 103–110. doi:10.1016/S0378-7206(99)00042-7

Chenoweth, T., Corral, K., & Demirkan, H. (2006). Seven key interventions for data warehouse success. *Communications of the ACM*, *49*(1), 114–119. doi:10.1145/1107458.1107464

Chin, W. W., Gopal, A., & Salisbury, W. D. (1997). Advancing the theory of adaptive structuration: The development of a scale to measure faithfulness of appropriation. *Information Systems Research*, *8*(4), 342–367. doi:10.1287/isre.8.4.342

Delen, D., & Demirkan, H. (2013). Data, information and analytics as services. *Decision Support Systems*, *55*(1), 359–363. doi:10.1016/j.dss.2012.05.044

Denic, N., Vujovic, V., Filic, S., & Spasic, B. (2016). Analysis of key success factors for business intelligence systems implementation. *Fascicle of Management and Technological Engineering Structure, 42*, 30.

Dobbins, J. (2000). *On a Generalized CSF Process Model for Critical Success Factors Identification and Analysis* (PhD Thesis). George Washington University.

Dresner H. J., Buytendijk, F., Linden, A., Friedman, T., Strange, K. H., Knox, M., & Camm, M. (2002). *The business intelligence competency center: An essential business strategy.* Gartner Strategic Analysis Report.

Eckerson, W. W. (2005). *The Keys to Enterprise Business Intelligence: Critical Success Factors.* TDWI Report.

ESCC. (2009). Overview: Business Intelligence Reference Guide. U.S. Army Enterprise Solutions Competency Center.

Finucane, B., Bange, C., Mack, M., Vierkorn, S., & Keller, P. (2010). *The BI Survey 9 - The Customer Verdict. Business Application Reserach Center*. BARC.

Gile, K. (2003). *Success Factors for Implementing Enterprise Business Intelligence.* International User Conference. Business Objects.

Hanafizadeh, P., & Ravasan, A. Z. (2011). A McKinsey 7S model-based framework for ERP readiness assessment. *International Journal of Enterprise Information Systems*, *7*(4), 23–63. doi:10.4018/jeis.2011100103

Hawking, P., & Sellitto, C. (2010). Business Intelligence (BI) Critical Success Factors. *ACIS 2010 Proceedings*, 4. Retrieved from https://aisel.aisnet.org/acis2010/4

Hirsimäki, R. (2017). *Critical success factors for business intelligence system implementation* (Bachelor's thesis). Jyväskylä: University of Jyväskylä.

Hostmann, B., Rayner, N., & Friedman, T. (2006). *Gartner's Business Intelligence and Performance Management Framework.* Stamford, CT: Gartner.

Howson, C. (2006). Seven Pillars of BI Success: BI tools may be getting better, but technology is only part of the story. *Intelligent Enterprise-San Mateo*, *9*(9), 33.

Howson, C. (2008). *Successful Business Intelligence*. Editorial Mc Graw Hill.

Hwang, H. G., Ku, C. Y., Yen, D. V., & Cheng, C. C. (2004). Critical factors influencing the adoption of data warehouse technology: A study of the banking industry in Taiwan. *Decision Support Systems*, *37*(1), 1–21. doi:10.1016/S0167-9236(02)00191-4

Hwang, M. I., & Xu, H. (2005). A survey of data warehousing success issues. *Business Intelligence Journal, 10*(4), 7.

Ishikiriyama, C. S., Miro, D., & Gomes, C. F. S. (2015). Text Mining Business Intelligence: A small sample of what words can say. *Procedia Computer Science*, *55*, 261–267. doi:10.1016/j.procs.2015.07.044

Işık, Ö., Jones, M. C., & Sidorova, A. (2012). Business Intelligence Success: The Role of BI Capabilities and Decision Environment. *Information & Management*.

Jagielska, I., Darke, P., & Zagari, G. (2003). Business Intelligence systems for decision support: Concepts, processes and practice. *Conference of the International Society for Decision Support Systems*, 215-228.

Johnson, L.K. (2004). Strategies for Data Warehousing. *MIT Sloan Management Review, 45*(3), 9.

Jr, L., Grover, R., & Gibson, M. L. (2003). Perceived influences on implementing data warehousing. *IEEE Transactions on Software Engineering*, *29*(4), 290–296. doi:10.1109/TSE.2003.1191794

Kim, H.-W., Lee, G.-H., & Pan, S. L. (2002). *Exploring the Critical Success Factors for Customer Relationship Management and Electronic Customer Relationship Management Systems.* Paper presented at the ICIS.

Knightsbridge. (2006). *Getting Smart About BI: Best Practices Deliver Real Value.* BusinessWeek Research Services.

Larson, D., & Chang, V. (2016). A review and future direction of agile, business intelligence, analytics and data science. *International Journal of Information Management*, *36*(5), 700–710. doi:10.1016/j.ijinfomgt.2016.04.013

Luftman, J., & Ben-Zvi, T. (2010). Key issues for IT executives 2010: Judicious IT investments continue post-recession. *MIS Quarterly Executive*, *9*(4), 263–273.

MacCallum, R. C., Widaman, K. F., Preacher, K. J., & Hong, S. (2001). Sample size in factor analysis: The role of model error. *Multivariate Behavioral Research*, *36*(4), 611–637. doi:10.1207/S15327906MBR3604_06 PMID:26822184

Mankoff, S. (2001). *Ten Critical Success Factors for CRM*. Siebel System, White Paper.

Markarian, J., Brobst, S., & Bedell, J. (2007). *Critical Success Factors Deploying Pervasive BI*. Informatica, Teradata, Microstrategy.

Martins, C., Oliveira, T., & Popovič, A. (2013). Understanding the Internet banking adoption: A unified theory of acceptance and use of technology and perceived risk application. *International Journal of Information Management*.

Meister, C. (2009). *Successful Business Intelligence Implementation*. Auxis Inc.

Mesaros, P., Carnicky, S., & Mandicak, T. (2015). Key factors and barriers of business intelligence implementation. *US-China L. Rev.*, *12*, 220.

Moalagh, M., & Zare Ravasan, A. (2012). Developing a practical framework for assessing ERP post-implementation success using fuzzy analytic network process. *International Journal of Production Research*, *51*(4), 1236–1257. doi:10.1080/00207543.2012.698318

Mohammadi, M. M., Ravasan, A. Z., & Hamidi, H. (2015). Investigating Critical Success Factors in Implementing ITIL Framework: The Case of a Developing Country. *International Journal of Standardization Research*, *13*(1), 74–91. doi:10.4018/IJSR.2015010104

Moss, L. T., & Atre, S. (2003). *Business Intelligence Roadmap: The Complete Project Lifecycle for Decision-Support-Applications*. Addison-Wesley Professional.

Mukherjee, D., & D'Souza, D. (2003). Think phased implementation for successful data warehousing. *Information Systems Management*, *20*(2), 82–90. doi:10.1201/1078/43204.20.2.20030301/41473.11

Ngai, E. W. T., Cheng, T. C. E., & Ho, S. S. M. (2004). Critical success factors of web-based supply-chain management systems: An exploratory study. *Production Planning and Control*, *15*(6), 622–630. doi:10.1080/09537280412331283928

Ocampo, M. A. (2007). Overcoming the Barriers to Business Intelligence Success. *DM Review*, *17*(9), 24.

Olbrich, S., Poppelbuß, J., & Niehaves, B. (2012). *Critical Contextual Success Factors for Business Intelligence: A Delphi Study on Their Relevance, Variability, and Controllability*. Paper presented at the 2012 45th Hawaii International Conference on System Science (HICSS).

Olszak, C. M., & Ziemba, E. (2012). Critical Success Factors for Implementing Business Intelligence Systems in Small and Medium Enterprises on the Example of Upper Silesia, Poland. *Interdisciplinary Journal of Information, Knowledge, and Management*, *7*, 130–150. doi:10.28945/1584

Petrini, M., & Pozzebon, M. (2009). Managing sustainability with the support of business intelligence: Integrating socio-environmental indicators and organisational context. *The Journal of Strategic Information Systems*, *18*(4), 178–191. doi:10.1016/j.jsis.2009.06.001

Popovič, A., Hackney, R., Coelho, P. S., & Jaklič, J. (2012). Towards business intelligence systems success: Effects of maturity and culture on analytical decision making. *Decision Support Systems*.

Ramamurthy, K., Sen, A., & Sinha, A. P. (2008). An empirical investigation of the key determinants of data warehouse adoption. *Decision Support Systems*, *44*(4), 817–841. doi:10.1016/j.dss.2007.10.006

Rasmussen, N. H., Goldy, P. S., & Solli, P. O. (2002). *Financial business intelligence: trends, technology, software selection, and implementation*. John Wiley & Sons.

Ravasan, A. Z., & Mansouri, T. (2014). A FCM-Based Dynamic Modeling of ERP Implementation Critical Failure Factors. *International Journal of Enterprise Information Systems*, *10*(1), 32–52. doi:10.4018/ijeis.2014010103

Rouhani, S., Ashrafi, A., Zare, A., & Afshari, S. (2016). The impact model of business intelligence on decision support and organizational benefits. *Journal of Enterprise Information Management*, *29*(1), 19–50. doi:10.1108/JEIM-12-2014-0126

Rouhani, S., & Ravasan, A. Z. (2014). A practical framework for assessing business intelligence competencies of enterprise systems using fuzzy ANP approach. *International Journal of Applied Decision Sciences*, *8*(1), 52–82. doi:10.1504/IJADS.2015.066559

Rouhani, S., & Ravasan, A. Z. (2015). Multi-objective model for intelligence evaluation and selection of enterprise systems. *International Journal of Business Information Systems*, *20*(4), 397–426. doi:10.1504/IJBIS.2015.072736

Sahay, B. S., & Ranjan, J. (2008). Real time business intelligence in supply chain analytics. *Information Management & Computer Security*, *16*(1), 28–48. doi:10.1108/09685220810862733

Salmeron, J. L., & Herrero, I. (2005). An AHP-based methodology to rank critical success factors of executive information systems. *Computer Standards & Interfaces*, *28*(1), 1–12. doi:10.1016/j.csi.2004.09.002

Sammon, D., & Finnegan, P. (2000). The ten commandments of data warehousing. *ACM SIGMIS Database*, *31*(4), 82–91. doi:10.1145/506760.506767

Treiblmaier, H., & Filzmoser, P. (2010). Exploratory factor analysis revisited: How robust methods support the detection of hidden multivariate data structures in IS research. *Information & Management*, *47*(4), 197–207. doi:10.1016/j.im.2010.02.002

Vesset, D. (2005). *Bridging the IT and Business Needs Gap: Keys to Successful Business Intelligence Deployment*. IDC.

Vodapalli, T. K. (2009). *Critical Success Factors of BI Implementation.* IT University of Copenhagen. Retrieved from http://mit. itu. dk/ucs/pb/download/BI%20Thesis%20Report-New.pdf

Watson, H. J., Fuller, C., & Ariyachandra, T. (2004). Data warehouse governance: Best practices at Blue Cross and Blue Shield of North Carolina. *Decision Support Systems*, *38*(3), 435–450. doi:10.1016/j.dss.2003.06.001

Wieder, B., & Ossimitz, M.-L. (2015). The Impact of Business Intelligence on the Quality of Decision Making–A Mediation Model. *Procedia Computer Science*, *64*, 1163–1171. doi:10.1016/j.procs.2015.08.599

Williams, S., & Williams, N. (2010). *The profit impact of business intelligence* (1st ed.). Morgan Kaufmann.

Wixom, B., & Watson, H. (2010). The BI-based organization. *International Journal of Business Intelligence Research*, *1*(1), 13–28. doi:10.4018/jbir.2010071702

Wixom, B. H., & Watson, H. J. (2001). An empirical investigation of the factors affecting data warehousing success. *Management Information Systems Quarterly*, *25*(1), 17–32. doi:10.2307/3250957

Wong, K. Y. (2005). Critical success factors for implementing knowledge management in small and medium enterprises. *Industrial Management & Data Systems*, *105*(3), 261–279. doi:10.1108/02635570510590101

Yeoh, W. (2008). *Critical success factors for implementation of business intelligence systems in engineering asset management organisations (PhD).* University of South Australia.

Yeoh, W., & Koronios, A. (2010). Critical Success Factors for Business Intelligence Systems. *Journal of Computer Information Systems*, *50*(3), 23–32.

Yeoh, W., & Popovič, A. (2015). Extending the understanding of critical success factors for implementing business intelligence systems. *Journal of the Association for Information Science and Technology*, *67*(1), 134–147. doi:10.1002/asi.23366

APPENDIX

Table 3. CSFs identified from Literature review

ID	Critical Success Factors	Knightsbridge (2006)	Chenowet., et al. (2006)	Howson (2006)	Salmeron and Herrero (2005)	Vesset (2005)	Eckerson (2005)	Chamoni and Gluchowski (2004)	Watson, Fuller, and Ariyachandra (2004)	Gile (2003)	Mukherjee and D'Souza (2003)	Little and Gibson (2003)	Wixom and Watson (2001)	Chen., et al. (2000)	Sammon and Finnegan (2000)
1	Well-Defined vision and clear goals for system and business	✓				✓			✓	✓	✓				
2	Strong project management									✓					
3	Adequate resources including budgetary and human resources												✓		✓
4	BI and business strategy alignment			✓											
5	Creating the data warehouse	✓													
6	Data management	✓		✓		✓					✓	✓	✓		✓
7	Strong applications management in the organization			✓			✓	✓							
8	Avoid deviation from the initial goals of the project								✓						
9	Identify user's specific issues and requirements					✓			✓						
10	Risk management														
11	User support						✓								
12	Participation end users		✓								✓		✓	✓	
13	Change management		✓								✓				
14	Project team Management												✓		
15	IT skills of the project team												✓		
16	Appropriateness of technology with organization										✓				✓
17	Ensure senior management support		✓	✓							✓	✓	✓		✓

continued on following page

Table 3. Continued

18	Adequate and reliable technical architecture		✓	✓			✓								
19	Use iterative prototyping methodologies in development system														
20	user training	✓													
21	Select the appropriate tools			✓	✓										
22	Ability to match with business requirements														
23	Being flexible and responsive to change				✓										
24	Managing users' expectations					✓									
25	Strong partnership between the business and IT counterparts	✓		✓											
26	Use business and project management driven methodologies			✓											✓
ID	**Critical Success Factors**	**Hirsimäki (2017)**	**DENIC., et al. (2016)**	**Yeoh and Popovic (2015)**	**Mesároš, Čarnický and Mandičák (2015)**	**Olbrich, Poppelbuß, and Niehaves (2012)**	**Olszak and Ziemba (2012)**	**Hawking and Sellitto (2010)**	**Finucane., et al. (2010)**	**Yeoh and Koronios (2010)**	**ESCC (2009)**	**Vodapalli (2009)**	**Meister (2009)**	**Yeoh (2008)**	**Markarian, Brobst, and Bedell (2007)**
1	*Well-Defined vision and clear goals for system and business*	✓	■	✓	■	■	✓		■	✓		✓	✓	✓	
2	*Strong project management*	✓	✓					✓				✓			
3	*Adequate resources including budgetary and human resources*		✓	✓	■	✓									
4	*BI and business strategy alignment*	✓	✓		■	✓									
5	*Creating the data warehouse*								■	■	✓				
6	*Data management*	✓	✓	✓	✓	✓	✓	✓	✓	✓	✓	✓	✓	✓	✓
7	*Strong applications management in the organization*				■	✓			■	✓					

continued on following page

Table 3. Continued

8	Avoid deviation from the initial goals of the project														
9	Identify user's specific issues and requirements	✓	■	✓								✓			
10	Risk management											✓			
11	User support	✓	■	✓											
12	Participation end users	✓	✓	✓	✓	✓			■	■	✓				
13	Change management	✓	✓	✓	✓	✓	✓		■	✓		✓		✓	
14	Project team Management	✓	✓	✓					■	✓		✓		✓	✓
15	IT skills of the project team	✓			■	✓		■	✓						
16	Appropriateness of technology with organization											✓			
17	Ensure senior management support	✓	✓	✓	✓	✓			■	✓		✓			
18	Adequate and reliable technical architecture		■	✓	■	■	✓		■	✓		✓	✓	✓	
19	Use iterative prototyping methodologies in development system	✓	■	✓					■	■	✓		✓		
20	user training	✓	✓		■	■	✓					✓			
21	Select the appropriate tools	■	■	■	✓							✓			
22	Ability to match with business requirements							✓							
23	Being flexible and responsive to change	✓	■	✓											
24	Managing users' expectations											✓			
25	Strong partnership between the business and IT counterparts	✓	✓		✓	■	✓		■	■	✓				
26	Use business and project management driven methodologies								■	■	✓	✓		✓	

Chapter 7
Integration of Knowledge Management and Business Intelligence for Lean Organizational Learning by the Digital Worker

Selvi Kannan
Victoria University, Australia

Shah J. Miah
Victoria University, Australia

ABSTRACT

The polarization of global labor market, hunt for talent, need to adapt quickly to changing environment is pressuring businesses more than ever before on their performance. This is further snowballed with the development of digitalization, automation, robotization, and artificial intelligence that offer approaches for addressing enormous industry challenges. These challenges create a push for organizational decision makers to rethink on the management of work. Knowledge management (KM) is understood to encourage content management, collaboration with inclusion of organizational behavioral science, and of course technologies. Complementing BI with knowledge management (KM) system in an organization can account for lean and accelerated performance. In this chapter, the authors present their position and insights in the integration of KM and BI suited for the worker in the digital world which possibly encourages lifelong learning with the focus on adaptability.

INTRODUCTION

The objective of this chapter is to understand the relationship between business intelligence (BI) and knowledge management (KM) to address accelerated organizational performance. Hence, leading the discussions into how BI and KM can extend into lean organizational teaching and learning.

DOI: 10.4018/978-1-5225-5718-0.ch007

Knowledge Society framed by Drucker (1992) was understood in the scholarly world as the contemporary society. The challenge of the contemporary society can be described how organizations need to swiftly utilize their capabilities and networks to survive in the fast-paced digital world. As Davenport et al (1998) posit that intelligent knowledge is the power to survival in the competitive space. The complexity of this challenge is that expertise and new talent are shaped by the automation technologies. Essentially, it is driving organizations to look closer how the knowledge held and networks formed by individuals can be enhanced through effective KM with BI integrated for a more effective and shorter-oriented time for teaching and learning.

Managing knowledge and relevant management networks are relatively critical to organizations, thus it is important to posit a theoretical discussion on how business intelligence (BI) can be integrated with the knowledge teaching management (KTM) system in organization to optimise learning an organizational worker. Focusing on the on the role of technology, Alavi and Leidner's (2001) framework provides insight on perspectives of knowledge that can be optimised for learning. This framework lends toward supporting an integrated BI and KTM system. The framework of perspectives by Alavi and Leider (2001) drawn from the works of Huber (1991) and Nonaka (1994) can be seen in the table below.

The table above illustrates that effectuating of these knowledge perspectives in an organization is critical for it to be addressed from an individual level to a collective level. The authors argue that when this process occurs in a shared space then there is less need for contextual knowledge teaching and learning.

Thus integration with BI can aid this process and assist in creating the natural flow. However, literature on BI and KM integration has been few and far despite the emphasis by Herschel and Jones (2005) who emphasized the importance of KM and BI integration. Albescu, Pugna and Paraschiv (2008) who posit that it is important for organizations to respond to a fast-challenged business environment when investing to integrate their BI and KMS to exploit data in real time and enable smart decisions from teaching and learning. Both scholars Herschel and Jones (2005) and Albescu et al (2008) shed light on the various aspects of KM and BI and demonstrate that text mining and analysis of content is a shared connectedness. The fundamental issues raised by both these works was that practitioners were not able to primarily understand the difference between BI and KM. Perhaps if McKnight's (2002) viewpoint was taken that both KM and BI deal with intelligent content and that KM looks inwardly whilst BI looks at the application of the techniques, then maybe this would promote the better integration.

The rise of digitalization can deepen the position of KM and BI towards teaching and learning as it positions Cook and Cook's (2000) view that human analysis leads to strong decision-making process and cannot be replaced by technology. This fundamentally acknowledges the relationship of individuals in a shared context for effective teaching and learning.

Table 1. Perspectives of knowledge for KMT (adapted from Alavi & Leider, 2001)

Perspectives of Knowledge	KM System for Teaching & Learning
State of Mind	A space where experiences are shared and enabled.
An Object	Permitting the gathering, storage, distribution and renewal.
A Process	Acts as link between two or more for the relationship of teaching and learning. Permitting a way of flow.
A Condition of Access to Information	Ability to query, locate and access information with the diverse thought patterns and approaches.
A Capability	To enhance cognition and journey into insights.

IMPORTANCE OF BI

Business intelligence can be defined as a modern set of tools and techniques that gathers data and analyses that aid the managers, executives and members in an organization concerned on issues to help form a decision. Before the decision is derived at the engagement takes place on the sharing, exchange and learning. In other words, the transformation of data into information for an informed decision making is what business intelligence does (Martin, Miranda & V. 2014). BI as defined is the process of collection, selection and interpretation of external available information that is made sense to the organization through its positioning, performance and capability performance. The analytical process is then benchmarked with public sources for strategic possibilities for the organization (Albescu, Pugna and Paraschiv, 2008).

The BI architecture has four main components: data warehouse, business analytics, business performance management and user interface (Jongsawas 2016). Business Intelligence may involve popular CRM, ERP, Cloud computing, OLAP, Data Warehousing and many other intelligent techniques, technologies and applications.

As organizations get inundated with data from their external environment, the way to structure and manage it becomes ever so important. Realizing the use of business intelligence in a competitive way is vital for organizations.

The problem facing businesses is that they are experiencing the need to handle data on a mobile platform for real-time decision-making support and production of intelligent data for further analytics. Management areas that are seeing this emerging BI tools and techniques are predominately in agriculture, healthcare, supply chain, tourism and workforce. The analytics of these data are on both cloud and traditional storage.

Singh and Singh (2013) suggest that a key role of BI is to not only determine an organization's performance but also help differentiate the problems by integrating information and at the same time forecasting into the business future. This opens a whole new diverse range of challenges for organizations where managers are seeking for quality information in order to maintain that competitive advantage (Gangadharan and Swami, 2004). This is further supported by Polasky et al (2011) who states that for decision making support, there must be appropriate level of information made available. Therefore, the concept of BI is to create value and transform raw data into relevant information that assists in decision making towards organizational competitiveness. Whilst BI literature focuses on the systems, tools and techniques, mmanagement scholars have argued that knowledge held by employees is a key competitive resource (Davenport and Prusak, 1998; Argote & Ingram, 2000; Darroch, 2005; Marjanovic, 2013). It is the human knowledge that is the capital and that acts as both data and information. Given that key thinkers have pointed to the importance of skills and experience as a key competitive resource, it makes sense for organizations to investigate knowledge acquisition and knowledge transmission with a view to retaining knowledge resources (Kannan, 2016).

As scholars in the field of BI have pointed out that conceptualising the relationships to knowledge such as teaching, and learning is a new concept for BI solution developers (Shah, 2010). This concept of merging a systemized technological interception and implementation into work of humans raises challenges itself and the first challenge is the vital link of knowledge and managing that knowledge.

IMPORTANCE OF KM

In reviewing the KM literature, we can define knowledge sharing is the process of exchanging knowledge activities amongst the individuals in an organization. Knowledge sharing occurs when individuals possess knowledge, opinion or experience on a matter and are willing to share them with the organization. Knowledge sharing within an organization creates future benefits for the organization as well.

Rubenstein-Montano et al. (2001) assert that knowledge management is about more than putting in place technologies that enable knowledge sharing, but rather it is more the people and culture that are the determinants of success of this knowledge relationship. This means that at the group and organizational level there must be structural elements that support and include both culture and individuals so that tacit knowledge is captured and stored within the organization as explicit knowledge and is able to become organizational memory to be stored for future use.

This extraction and conversion premise has significant impact on the individual's behaviour in the organization and how they deal with the changes needing to be undertaken. Through complex -based enquiry, Rook (2013) established that mental models of staff and management determined those individual's actions within the organization. This is because mental models capture a person's understanding of what is happening within their world and is constructed from that individual's experiences and knowledge bases and concepts. Rook further asserts that a mental model has 'the capacity to influence, or effect, how a person acts. As such it is of benefit to the organization to be aware of these mental models to enhance their relationship in teaching and learning.

Taking this relationship of knowledge, knowledge management as Nonaka (1995) defines simply through the SECI Framework expressing it as a dynamic iterative process of knowledge creation, sharing and transfer in the spaces of socialisation, externalisation, combination and internalisation. The unique feature of Nonaka and Takeuchi's (1995 and 2004) SECI KM framework is that it emphasises that knowledge is a resource that needs to be created and continuously recreated for an organization to be competitively sustainable. Based on the findings using the principles of the SECI KM model (Nonaka & Takeuchi, 1995), the key theoretical implications incorporate both individual and organizational level contributions to the harnessing and transfer of knowledge for learning. Furthermore, the synthesis of tacit and explicit knowledge creates space for connectedness and interactiveness described as 'Ba' (Takeuchi & Nonaka, 2004). This framework also explicates the dynamism in the creation of knowledge and management processes, where stocks of knowledge flow in 'knowledge spaces', which describe the process of knowledge creation and encouragement of knowledge sharing between individuals and groups (Kannan, 2016).

As knowledge captured in systems is shared, the purposes extend further than sharing, there occurs within the individual a cognitive process of teaching and learning. There is scarce literature on how knowledge management plays a major role in BI and some argue that BI is a part of KM.

INTEGRATION OF BI AND KM FOR TEACHING AND LEARNING

Treading into the organizational learning space, it is argued that to gain competitive advantage in today's age of information, organizations realize that learning is a strategic tool required to keep one step ahead of their competition (Atak & Erturqut, 2010). Organizational learning refers to a process where individuals act on behalf of the organization when the outcomes expected are not in alignment with the actual outcomes. The process involves taking steps that enhances the effectiveness and efficiency of the organization thereby achieving expected outcomes (Wang & Ahmed, 2003). It is a learning process where knowledge transfer takes place within an organization and this knowledge sharing and transfer proves to be beneficial for the organization (Pakka 2015).

Digitalisation and globalization have both increased the need for responsiveness as well as the reach of such competition (Brown, 2011). The learning organization is therefore one in which all members are continuously learning from both the successes and the failures and using and sharing that knowledge to improve how things are done at the individual and group level and using that knowledge to improve the organization's performance and achieving its strategic goals and objectives. However, Brown (2011), draws differentiation to OL reflecting on the works of Argyris (2002); Schien (2004) and Senge (2006), saying that OLs can be framed in different schools of thought. For instance, Argyris (2002) provides the principle of double loop learning with its foundation in correcting errors by changing governing values and then the actions. Schein (2004) provides that culture within an organization is the sum total of an organization's total learning through its mistakes and Senge (2006) on the other hand contends that learning organization is one where all levels of employees collectively and continually are enhancing their capacity to create things they want. These three schools of thought are the culmination and application of experience and academic learnings and their application is intended to lead the organization to a continuous state of self-directed learning leading to positive growth and change in the individual, the team and the organization. (Brown, 2011).

Enlarging further on Senge's (2004) perspective of learning, the author draws on five disciplines. Senge's mental models refers to people's perceptions on how the world works, work practices and includes beliefs, mind sets and values. Rook (2013), citing (Miller, 2003; Senge, 2006; Starkey et al., 2004) provides that mental models access a person's understanding and that these models capture an individual's comprehension within a specific part of their mind and therefore understanding this from an organizational and management perspective is important, so they can access this and enhance their learning and engage in a mastery process. At an individual level, personal mastery refers to the individual being engaged and open to taking on their own professional development, attitudes and goals which at the organizational level are recognized and encouraged. Roper and Pettit, (2002) state that at this level individuals need to almost undertake their own 'mental models' and challenge previous assumptions, motivations, and work relationships to be open to changes required. Atak and Erturqut (2010) state that by attracting and retaining employees with high organizational commitment and then encouraging this during their employment, increases their commitment towards becoming a learning organization. Senge (1994), provides that if nothing else, a learning organization will help people embrace change and that people who embrace change are able to anticipate and adapt to change more readily.

Despite the rise of literature in organizational learning, very little has been discussed on Shulman's (1987) notion of knowledge and teaching that brings about learning. The author rightly points out that for learning to occur the fundamental knowledge base for teaching must be established. Such as identifying what and where are the knowledge sources; the process of the pedagogical reasoning and action moving beyond teaching paradigm but states must possess "intuitive credibility" (p.5). We assert that teaching and learning is a connected process flow that must be looked at with the integration of BI and KM.

At an organizational level, failure to attract and retain people willing to take on this self-reflection, development and commitment would likely lead to decline of true learning. From an organizational perspective, this connection of the human element of analysis through the lens of the organization's vision. This then through the techniques and tools available in BI help make the informed decision.

DISCUSSION

KM and BI Integrated to Encourage Learning

The above discussions show that human socialisation allows for the creation of new tacit knowledge from old tacit knowledge through social engagement. While tacit knowledge is difficult to capture, tacit knowledge that is expressed and diffused can be a tool to create competitive advantage (Kalkan, 2008; Mayfield, 2010). Hall (2006) has supported the notion that tacit knowledge is a tool to create competitive advantage, arguing that knowledge can be transferred through the socialisation and transformation of tacit knowledge into explicit knowledge. During the externalisation process, new tacit knowledge becomes explicit knowledge — embedded into documents or retrieval artefacts. This explicit knowledge is integrated with previously learned explicit knowledge to create new forms of explicit knowledge in a process called combination. This new explicit knowledge becomes tacit knowledge through the internalisation process. In this way, the transformation of knowledge is an iterative process with socialisation at its heart.

The diagram above conceptualises the dynamic learning process with organizational knowing for the digital worker. The heart of a digital worker is to innovate. Innovation is the key to gaining competitive advantage in the market for any organization. It is almost impossible to find any organization that does not innovate. Innovation leads to new ideas and concepts which leads to higher and a greater learning within and outside the organization. More the organization is open to innovations, more will be the employees' creativity skills and will lead to an increased participative decision making. Higher the acceptance of change and innovation, greater will be the probabilities of organizational learning. Organizational learning comes with innovation and change. (Rosa, Reza & Ali 2017) (Herschel & Jones 2005). Using this conceptualisation of knowledge, it is then vital to identify the core areas that BI can contribute.

Figure 1. Conceptualisation of organizational knowing

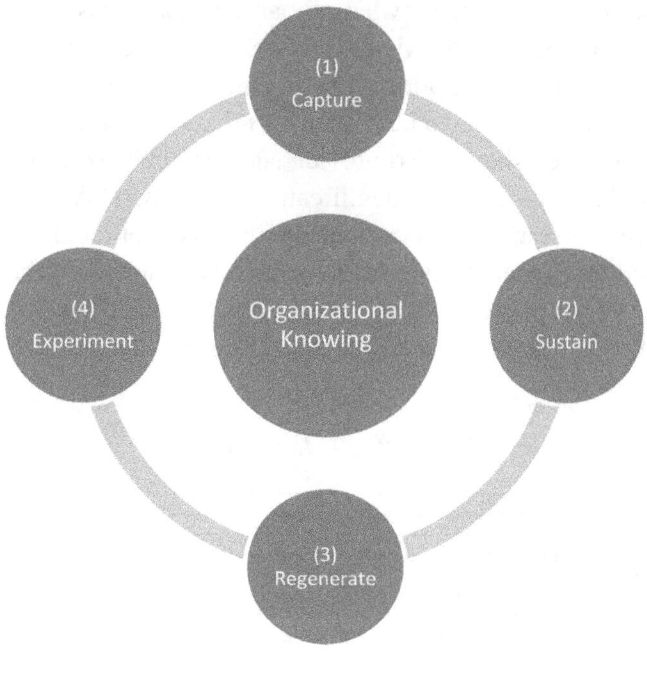

As per Nazemoff's (2014) intelligence design – the core areas of Financial Intelligence, customer intelligence, data intelligence and mastermind intelligence could the areas of focus of knowledge management in the organization. In the financial areas the knowledge gathered and codified can be on the organization's cash flow, profitability, accounting quality and productivity. In the customer focus, the knowledge gathered can be on the customer support, type of relationship and partnership. The focus for data can be on the internal systems, processes that are time and culture sensitive to the organization. Finally, in the mastermind intelligence, the focus on knowledge captured can be on ideas, decisions made and any other innovative.

Business Intelligence systems derive data from huge sources and transform these insightful data into valuable information that aids in effective decision making. They comprise of various tools, techniques and technologies that analyses the given data.

Business Intelligence Systems involve computing large amount of data. Organizations have a big data and sometimes it even exceeds the storage value of the organization. In such a situation, organizations look for innovative ways to gather, compute and analyse such data where innovation falls into the picture. Innovative ways of computing the information are found out through creativity and innovation, new practices are implemented that leads to organizational learning. (Hurley & Hult 1998; Fink, Yogev & Even, 2017).

Business Intelligence has come a long way today and has proven to be effective where it has been able to efficiently transform big data into valuable insights. It is essential to integrate the organizational processes and constructs with the BI tools to achieve the desired results. Knowledge transfer and innovation are some of the factors that will always be present to create organizational learning from BI tools. As human behaviour is a complex concept, and every individual is different from the other in many ways. To accommodate different individuals in an organization, organizations must develop cultures that accommodate differences and guide to what is required.

Akhavan & Husseini (2015) propose that feelings of identification with a team increases the chance of knowledge sharing and decreases knowledge hoarding. These same feelings would also be expected to apply to virtual teams. The problem of knowledge hoarding is also raised by Atieh and Samiei (2017) but in the context of retention of such knowledge and undocumented intellectual property when individuals leave an organization. The implication at the organizational level then means that management needs to include 'socialization channels to help team members obtain team values, norms, and shared cognitive schemata. Further they should also provide such channels so as result in 'shared language, closer interpersonal ties, shared norms, and identification with others' Akhavan & Husseini (2015).

Brown (2011) states that organizational development in this era of rapid technological advancement, means organizations need to constantly look for new models, new approaches and new techniques to keep ahead and competitive. As part of that competitive positioning, organizations realize that learning organizations can become strategic tools to ensure their growth and continuity.

Table 2. Intelligence design (source: Nazemoff, 2014, p.15)

Financial Intelligence	Reinvest and Regrow how you exceed revenue capacity
Customer Intelligence	Rethink and Redefine how you attract and maintain customers
Data Intelligence	Reinvent and Recreate the way you see, organize, collaborate, and interpret information
Mastermind Intelligence	Rewire the way your company communicates, operates, solves problems, interacts, creates, and innovates

The proposition of introducing virtual learning systems into an organization or even learning institution and what behaviours need to change in order to facilitate the change itself need to be considered. Factors such as attitude, perception, reinforcement and positive modelling are some of the elements that can enhance individual and group behaviour change. In this Liu et al (2007) talks about the 'social capital' that comes from on line communities and provides that at some point within this community, shared values and a form of mutual understanding will eventually benefit the user and provide support and socioemotional wellbeing' as well as provides positive relationships that form and provide a sense of community, engagement, and satisfaction.

From an organizational and learning perspective, management need to look at and develop perceptual change to remote participation. Management also need to put in place the systems able to manage how information can be captured and stored A framework that enables trust not only defines how individuals communicate in a shared space but that their behaviour is supported by the system.

CONCLUSION

Awareness of knowledge management as intellectual capital is increasingly placing more emphasis on knowledge as a strategic asset that needs to be managed efficiently in order for any benefits to be derived from it. Meso and Smith (2002) In looking at implementing KMS there are a number of processes, tools, systems, structures, techniques and methods for harnessing individual knowledge and sharing this, but these methods are not always guaranteed to achieve the desired outcomes. The presence of social structures also adds to the difficulties in managing these processes, Lauring and Selmer, (2002). Furthermore, although knowledge transfer within an organization begins at the individual level, this knowledge needs to extend and reach to the broader intercompany levels to be effective. That is, information needs to be shared between members, teams, divisions, etc. If learning organizations are defined by continuous learning, then it stands to reason that the transfer of knowledge needs to be present within the organizations systems in order for it to achieve such learning status.

The contribution made in this chapter is to highlight the importance of integrating KM and BI towards OL for the worker of tomorrow. There is definitely a gap in understanding the world of work of the emerging digital worker and the kind of knowledge as humans can contribute with further sophistication of BI. Managing knowledge in the digitalized space is a much need area of research. Further research would be required to conduct more-deeper investigation through developing a feasible systematic KM solution platform that operationalises the knowledge specifically for the importance of knowledge integration. Organizations taking the steps to cultivate intuition in their teaching and learning for competitive performance.

REFERENCES

Akhavan, P., Hosseini, S., Abbasi, M., & Manteghi, M. (2015). Knowledge-sharing determinants, behaviors, and innovative work behaviors: An integrated theoretical view and empirical examination. *Aslib Journal Of Information Management*, *67*(5), 562–591. doi:10.1108/AJIM-02-2015-0018

Albescu, F, Pugnam, I & Paraschiv, D, (2008), Business Intelligence and knowledge management – Technological support for strategic management in knowledge based economy. *Revista Informatica Economica, 4*(48).

Argote, L., & Ingram, P. (2000). Knowledge transfer: A basis for competitive advantage in firms. *Organizational Behavior and Human Decision Processes, 82*(1), 150–169. doi:10.1006/obhd.2000.2893

Argyris, C. (2002). Double-Loop Learning, Teaching, and Research. *Academy of Management Learning & Education, 1*(2), 206–218. doi:10.5465/AMLE.2002.8509400

Atak, M., & Erturgut, R. (2010). WCES-2010: An empirical analysis on the relation between learning organization and organizational commitment. Procedia - Social and Behavioral Sciences, 2, 3472-3476.

Brown, D. R. (2011). *An experiential approach to organization development*. Upper Saddle River, NJ: Prentice Hall.

Darroch, J. (2005). Knowledge management, innovation and firm performance. *Journal of Knowledge Management, 9*(3), 101–115. doi:10.1108/13673270510602809

Davenport, T. H., & Prusak, L. (1998). *Working knowledge: How organizations manage what they know*. Harvard Business School Press.

Drucker, P. F. (1992). *Managing for the future*. Oxford, UK: Butterworth-Heinemann.

Fink, L., Yogev, N., & Even, A. (2017). Business intelligence and organizational learning: An empirical investigation of value creation processes. *Information & Management, 54*(1), 38–56. doi:10.1016/j.im.2016.03.009

Gangadharan, G., & Swami, S. N. (2004). Business intelligence systems: design and implementation strategies. *Information Technology Interfaces, 2004. 26th International Conference on*, 139-144.

Hall, M. (2006). *Knowledge management and the limits of knowledge codification*. Academic Press.

Hall, M. (2006, May). Knowledge management and the limits of knowledge codification. *Journal of Knowledge Management, 10*(3), 117–126. doi:10.1108/13673270610670894

Herschel, R. T., & Jones, N. E. (2005). Knowledge management and business intelligence: The importance of integration. *Journal of Knowledge Management, 9*(4), 45–55. doi:10.1108/13673270510610323

Hurley, R. F., & Hult, G. T. M. (1998). Innovation, market orientation, and organizational learning: An integration and empirical examination. *Journal of Marketing, 62*(3), 42–54. doi:10.2307/1251742

Johnson, M., & Johnson, L. (2010). *Generation Inc - From Boomers to Linsters - Managing the Friction Between Generations at Work*. American Management Association.

Jongsawas, C. (2016). Managing big data in coal-fired power plants: A business intelligence framework. *Industrial Management & Data Systems, 116*(8), 1779–1799. doi:10.1108/IMDS-11-2015-0473

Jongsawas, C. (2016). Managing big data in coal-fired power plants: A business intelligence framework. *Industrial Management & Data Systems, 116*(8), 1779–1799. doi:10.1108/IMDS-11-2015-0473

Kalkan, V. D. (2008). An overall view of knowledge management challenges for global business. *Business Process Management Journal, 14*(3), 390–400. doi:10.1108/14637150810876689

Kalkan, V. D. (2008). An overall view of knowledge management challenges for global business. *Business Process Management Journal, 14*(3), 390–400.

Kannan, S. (2016). *Perspectives on knowledge retention and loss from expert attrition – An organisational case study* (Thesis). Melbourne, Australia.

Lauring, J., & Selmer, J. (2012). Knowledge sharing in diverse organisations. *Human Resource Management Journal, 22*(1), 89–105. doi:10.1111/j.1748-8583.2010.00158.x

Marjanovic, O. (2013). *Improving data-driven decision making through human entered knowledge sharing*. Paper presented at the 24th Australasian Conference on Information Systems.

Martin, A., Miranda, L.T., & V., P.V. (2014). A survey on recent research in business intelligence. *Journal of Enterprise Information Management, 27*(6), 831-66.

Mayfield, M. (2010). Tacit knowledge sharing: Techniques for putting a powerful tool in practice. *Development and Learning in Organizations, 24*(1), 24–26.

Meso, P., & Smith, R. (2000). A resource-based view of organizational knowledge management systems. *Journal of Knowledge Management, 4*(3), 224–234. doi:10.1108/13673270010350020

Miah, S.J. (2010). *A new semantic knowledge sharing approach for e-government systems*. Academic Press.

Nazemoff, V. (2014). *The Four Intelligences Of The Business Mind: How To Rewire Your Brain And Your Business For Success*. Academic Press.

Nonaka & Takeuchi. (1995). Toward middle-up-down management: accelerating information creation. *Sloan Management Review, 29*(3), 9-18.

Pakka, P. (2015). The role of Business Intelligence for internationalisation and organisational learning. Academic Press.

Polasky, S., Carpenter, S. R., Folke, C., & Keeler, B. (2011). Decision-making under great uncertainty: Environmental management in an era of global change. *Trends in Ecology & Evolution, 26*(8), 398–404. doi:10.1016/j.tree.2011.04.007 PMID:21616553

Rook, L. (2013). Mental Models: A Robust Definition. *The Learning Organization, 20*(1), 38–47. doi:10.1108/09696471311288519

Rosa, E., Reza, S., & Ali, C. E. (2017). Analysing the role of business intelligence, knowledge sharing and organisational innovation on gaining competitive advantage. *Journal of Workplace Learning, 29*(4), 250–267. doi:10.1108/JWL-07-2016-0070

Rubenstein-Montano, B., Liebowitz, J., Buchwalter, J., McCaw, D., Newman, B., & Rebeck, K. (2001). A systems thinking framework for knowledge management. Decision Support Systems, 31, 5-16.

Schein, E. H. (2004). *Organizational culture and leadership*. San Francisco: Jossey-Bass.

Senge, P., Smith, B., Kruschwitz, N., Laur, J., & Schley, S. (2008). *The Necessary Revolution - How Individuals and Organizations are Working Together to Create a Sustainable World*. London, UK: Nicholas Brealey Publishing.

Senge, P. M. (2006). *The fifth discipline: the art and practice of the learning organization*. London: Random House.

Shulman, L. S. (1987). Knowledge and teaching: Foundations of the new reform. *Harvard Educational Review*, *57*(1), 1–23. doi:10.17763/haer.57.1.j463w79r56455411

Singh, H., & Singh, B. P. (2013). Business Intelligence: Effective machine learning for business administration. *International Journal of IT Engineering and Applied Sciences Research*, *2*(1), 13–19.

Wang, C., & Ahmed, P. (2003). Organisational learning: A critical review. *The Learning Organization*, *10*(1), 8–17. doi:10.1108/09696470310457469

Section 2

Diversified Business Aspects and BI or Analytics Applications

Chapter 8
Culturally Sensitive Data Visualizations

Michael Gendron
Central Connecticut State University, USA

ABSTRACT

Organizations are undergoing significant changes in their business environment. Competing on a global scale means that organizations must better understand cultural issues of their customers, employees, and key stakeholders. As business analytics grows in importance, managers are sharing data visualizations to a variety of different cultures and beliefs. When creating culturally sensitive data visualizations, a set of best practices is required to assist managers to make timely and accurate decisions with the least possible cultural bias. This chapter aims to develop these best practices by analyzing cultural traits, communication habits, and other differences between the western and eastern global regions.

INTRODUCTION

There are significant challenges within the business environment as a result of globalization. Instead of only competing within their own geographic area, organizations are now competing in a global marketplace. According to some, "globalization today has become a matter of survival" (Firoz & Ramin, 2004). Part of that survival is business analytics. A foundation of good analytics is data visualization, which is essential to increase an organizations competitive advantage. Managers are now sharing data visualizations with a variety of key stakeholders, sometimes in countries with different perceptions. This paper is about trying to understand the impact of those perceptions and developing a set of best practices for culturally sensitive data visualizations. In short, the authors attempt to answer the question: How do today's managers create high quality visualizations that ensure cross-cultural competency?

The genesis of globalization in the United States and elsewhere can be traced back to the 1960s when the first rush occurred to enter foreign markets (Scher, Reuss, Frank, & Dorman, 2000). In order to set the stage, the authors have adopted Thomas Friedman's definition of globalization:

DOI: 10.4018/978-1-5225-5718-0.ch008

The inexorable integration of markets, transportation systems, and communication systems to a degree never witnessed before – in a way that is enabling corporations, countries, and individuals to reach around the world farther, faster, deeper, and cheaper than ever before. (Friedman, 2002)

The rise of interactions in the global market place has influenced us to do this research because the authors believe that for an enterprise to be competitive today, they must understand the culture-specific differences regarding phenomena and relations (Mintu, Calantone, & Gassenheimer, 1994) with those they are dealing with.

The target audience for the proposed best practices is middle level managers in multinational organizations. Specifically, the best practices are adapted for managers in service industries in the eastern and western regions – these are defined below. Culture significantly influences organizations competing across geographic boundaries with different values. Because of the variable influence of local norms and cultural differences the authors decided to create best practices for the western and eastern regions of the world.

Cultural sensitivity can have severe impact on an organization's ability to compete internationally. Too often organizations try implementing an existing product into a foreign market with disastrous results; the same can happen with data visualizations that are not sensitive to the local norms of the reader. No one is exempt from making blunders in this space, not even multi-billion dollar organizations. An example of an advertising blunder is when Kentucky Fried Chicken introduced their new slogan "Finger lickin' good" in China. That slogan translated to "eat your fingers off." The slogan had a negative impact on their business in China, both to their reputation and from a financial standpoint. Other multinational organizations such as Coca-Cola, Toyota, and Goodyear have made similar blunders (Hunt & Hodkin, 2012). While these examples are focused more on marketing, they accurately portray the potential consequences of overlooking the importance culture has in a global economy and to visualizations.

The Internet and Globalization Challenges

Over the past 25 years society has seen the change from a world where global communication was expensive and not always easy to do. The Internet has changed this dramatically and today even average citizens can interact in real-time with people around the world; extend that to multinational organizations that are able to instantly communicate globally. A major advantage of recent technology is that the time to communicate around the world with co-workers, decision-makers and others has decreased significantly (Chary, 2007). This new found freedom to communicate across the world has allowed businesses to expand internationally. Along with the relatively newly expanded and easy to tap marketplace, organizations face challenges like never previously seen in history.

Study Purpose

This study is based on an extensive literature review to determine the considerations for best practices for culturally sensitive data visualizations. The researchers aim to address the following question: How does culture influence a manager when viewing and interpreting data visualization? This topic is essential on the international business stage, due to globalization and the rise of multinational organizations. With best practices, organizations will be able to increase business productivity and cultural awareness. To ensure the proposed best practices are relevant, where possible every attempt was made to use literature published in the last ten years.

Data Visualization

To effectively report information, organizations create data visualizations. Data visualization is defined as "the presentation of data in a pictorial or graphical format. It enables decision-makers to see analytics presented visually, so they can grasp difficult concepts or identify new patterns" (SAS, 2016). Additionally, three reasons to use visualizations include:

1. A vast majority of people are visual learners. By providing representation of data graphically, most of us can arrive more quickly at the "ah-ha moment" – the instant someone sees a relationship in data that they once only suspected was there.
2. Big data used today causes complexities that make it harder to see relationships between data, particularly for non-technical personnel. Information visualization products can examine information from a wide variety of database sources and find relationships that can be nearly impossible to discern when the volume of data becomes overwhelming.
3. The process of manually querying a data repository is quite tedious and exacting (Freedman, 2006).

Businesses have a variety of uses for analytic visualizations. Whatever type of analytics, there is a common theme in that all analytics provide decision-makers with information to allow them to make better decisions. The questions become: How will different cultures view these data visualizations? Will managers in China draw the same conclusions as managers in the U.S.? Do things like color impact the interpretation of a visualization?

The importance of business intelligence, business analysis, and data visualization can all be traced back to the rise of globalization and the Internet. Kevin Plank, CEO, chairman and founder of Under Armour recently said "We believe data is the new oil. The companies that will win are the companies using math. As humans we make decisions but it's important we have the best information to make our decisions" (Charara, 2016).The need for culturally sensitive data visualization is directly related to organizations competing in new global markets. Consideration of globalization and data visualizations should not be discounted as doing so can lead to disastrous consequences. Cultural influence cannot be overlooked.

THE LITERATURE

While there was no directly relevant literature on cultural blunders caused by inappropriate data visualizations there was a large amount of advertising literature – our use of advertising as a proxy for data visualization is discussed below. What was found was that the need for culturally sensitive practices is apparent because of cultural blunders that multinational organizations committed in foreign markets. Examples of such blunders were given earlier. Also, the authors noted that literature on the ideal traits for data analyst did not mention that cultural sensitivity was needed to perform that role. These reasons reinforced our belief that the proposed best practices are needed.

Industry Sector and Audience

Once the need and demand for best practices was determined, the next step was to determine the target audience. We analyzed different levels of managers and determined that focusing on middle managers would allow our best practices to have the greatest impact. The advantages and disadvantages of targeting a specific industry sector were also evaluated. Using data from the U.S. Bureau of Economic Analysis, U.S. CENSUS and The First Research database led us to believe that our focus should be on the service industry. After breaking down the U.S. and Chinese economies by industry sector and viewing projections, the service industry was projected to remain the largest industry. Since the authors wanted to impact the largest part of these economies they chose the service sector. To further define our target audience, the authors divided the World into regions. The goal was to create one set of best practices when dealing with all cultures, but the research quickly showed this not possible. Due to cross-cultural differences, one set of best practices would not be feasible or applicable. Instead the work was broken down by a set of activities.

Using data from the U.S. Department of Commerce, the top five global economies by GDP were found. Those five countries were combined into two groups, resulting in western and eastern regions. The west region consisted of the U.S., U.K. and Germany, and the east region is China and Japan. The U.S. trade outputs and inputs in services were also examined using data from the U.S. Department of Commerce. Lastly, the GDP composition by industry sector was determined with data from the Central Intelligence Agency. Based on the data, the authors selected the dominant country in each region, starting with the U.S. in the western region. China was then selected as a focal point of the eastern region because it is the second largest economy, and conducts significant trade with and has a very different culture than the U.S

Use of Marketing/Advertising in This Research

Since there have been few studies performed on the cultural impact of data visualizations, advertising effectiveness was used as a proxy. How advertisement is viewed varies by culture. The literature clearly shows that advertisement should be adopted to fit each region. These differences share similar characteristics with data visualization. For example, color associations and how each culture views and perceives colors varies. Multiple studies found that each culture perceives colors differently (Firoz & Ramin, 2004) & (McCandless, 2009) The relationship between occupational background and color association is also important. Based on several studies (Wang & Or, 2015), occupational background affects how-colors are viewed. Color is a significant part of data visualizations and is significant in the proposed best practices.

To supplement the paucity of literature on the impact of culture on data visualization, advertising effectiveness was reviewed. When evaluating the U.S. and China, a common solution does not exist for advertising. Advertisements that appeal to low-context individualistic culture are effective in the U.S., while advertisements that appeal to the high-context collective culture will be more effective in China (Zhang & Neelankavil, 1997) & (Hunt & Hodkin, 2012). This is an important aspect to consider when designing a visual ad campaign, and which is important when creating best practices for data visualizations. Our supposition that the importance stressed in advertisements is also relevant to data visualizations is further supported by the following:

It would seem appropriate to predict, a priori, that culturally-congruent appeals, such as those that demonstrate collective or group benefits in China or those that illustrate individual benefits in the USA, are more effective in promoting the products or services in each country since such appeals conform to the prevailing cultural norms. (Hunt & Hodkin, 2012)

Globalization's Impact on Organizations

Thomas Friedman, a leading foreign affairs journalist, stated the current era of globalization started only 10 years ago. "Today's era of globalization is built around falling telecommunications costs – thanks to microchips, satellites, fiber optics and the Internet. These new technologies are able to weave the world together even tighter (Friedman T. L., 2000)." The Internet increased the ability to create data visualizations. Globalization creates the demand for culturally sensitive managers as well as culturally sensitive data visualizations. Organizations are increasingly implementing business intelligence visualizations to create competitive advantage. Globalization has forced organizations to create data visualizations for a variety of cultures.

Technology allows everyone to communicate and conduct business around the world with a click of a button. "Businesses positioned to operate internationally not only have the infrastructure in place to support global business operations, but they are also aware of the cultural differences between trading partners (Hunt & Hodkin, 2012)." Our research shows that while they are aware of the differences between trading partners, they may not possess the skills to create visualizations that give all partners the same message.

Communication Styles: High Context vs. Low Context

A key factor of cross-culture communications is perception, or how things are viewed. There are two major styles of cultures, high-context and low-context: (Hall, 1976)

- **High-context:** "is one in which little explicit message context is needed because most of the information is based in the context."
- **Low-context:** "...much explicit message should be said or written in communication because the context does not covey much meaning".

This ties directly into why cultures view data visualizations differently. Studies found that eastern countries are often high-context, compared to western countries which are low-context (Li & Putterill, 2007).

The differences in cross-cultural communication styles were analyzed to determine if each country had a high-context or low-context culture. Eastern countries are often considered high-context, while the U.S. and western regions are low-context. When creating a visualization to be presented to a high-context culture, there is little reason for explicit message context as they observe the message in the visualization. The visualization instead uses implicit messages to convey the target message. Inversely, a low-context culture requires significant explicit content to ensure the message is received (Bourne, 2016).

Culture

Culture was examined by using keywords such as: cultural sensitivities, cultural traits and dimensions, cross-cultural communication, and the overall cultural impact on the business environment. Culture has been widely researched in a variety of academic fields, including how it affects international business. There are two reasons for the increase in research on the cultural impact of international business that tie directly to globalization (Mintu, Calantone, & Gassenheimer, 1994):

1. To provide evidence addressing the generalizability of implications across borders.
2. To understand any culture-specific differences regarding phenomena and relations.

Cultural differences between regions were compared using Hofstede's cultural dimensions (see *Table 1*). This allowed us to compare and contrast the similarities and differences between the regions. Individualism versus collectivism was our key focus as it best summarizes the differences between the west and east. The culture dimensions provided a foundation in understanding culture, but to relate it to data visualization additional topics were considered. For instance, the relationship between globalization and cross-cultural communication were studied to determine if globalization results in cultural homogeneity or reinforces previously existing fault lines. Cultural homogeneity occurs when different cultures start to blend together, eventually creating one merged culture. If globalization reinforces fault lines, the cultures remain unique and separate (Fujimoto, Bahfen, & Fermelis, 2007).

To analyze how culture impacts data visualizations, the cultural differences in the U.S. and China were first found. To start, the authors used the cultural dimensions to compare and contrast the two countries. In the U.S., the power-distance dimension is not as important as it is in China. Managers in U.S. organizations are less likely to accept unequally distributed power than in China. Additionally, Chinese managers favor long-term orientation and collectivism compared to U.S. managers. Short-term orientation and individualism are much more important to U.S. managers and greatly affects how they conduct business. The two countries are similar on the dimension of uncertainty avoidance, as managers in both countries seem to feel threatened by unknown situations (Hofstede & Hofstede, 2005). They also appear to have similar beliefs on the masculinity/femininity dimension.

Table 1. Six cultural dimensions of work-related values adapted from (Hofstede, Hofstede, & Minkov, 2010)

Individualism versus collectivism	Individualism is the opposite of collectivism and represents the degree to which individuals are supposed to look after themselves or remain integrated into groups.
Power distance	The extent to which the less powerful members of institutions and organizations within a country expect and accept that power is distributed unequally.
Masculinity versus Femininity	Society where emotional gender roles are clearly distinct: Those with masculine traits are more assertive, tough, and focused on material success; Those exhibiting feminine traits are more modest, tender, and concerned with the quality of life.
Uncertainty Avoidance	The extent to which members of a culture feel threaten by ambiguous or unknown situations.
Long-Term versus Short-Term Normative Orientation	Represents the extent to which members of a culture are cognitively programed to accept delayed gratification of material, social, and emotional needs.
Indulgence versus Restraint	Society that allows relatively free gratification of basic and natural human drives related to enjoying life and having fun.

Culture: Differences and Sensitivity

A broad definition of cultural sensitivity is "being aware that cultural differences and sensitivity exist and have an effect on values, learning and behaviors" (Stafford, Lopes-DeFede, Bowman, Hanna, & Eking, 1997). Cultural sensitivity can be further defined as having two dimensions: surface and deep structure (Resnicow, 1999). Our best practices focus on the deep structure of culture by factoring in the numerous forces that influence a country's culture. Deep structure is defined as incorporating the cultural, social, historical, environmental and psychological forces that influence the target behavior in the proposed population (Resnicow, 1999).

A four-stage model useful in understanding cross-cultural sensitivity was developed for international business relationships (Shapiro, Ozanne, & Saatcioglu, 2008). Each stage represents a level of cultural sensitivity, including the necessary skills and benefits. This allows a manager to analyze the level of cultural sensitivity in an employee. The four stages are further explored in Table 2. Defining cultural sensitivity levels provides a framework to compare and contrast a managers' ability to implement the best practices for data visualization. Managers at a higher level will have an easier time implementing these standards as they have the knowledge needed to understand the importance of culture. This framework guided our creation of the east-west best practices.

Culture: Traits

The relationship between culture and business has been studied often. In this field Geert Hofstede, described the five cultural dimensions in 1980 which are (1) individualism-collectivism, (2) power distance, (3) masculinity-femininity, (4) uncertainty avoidance, and (5) Long-Term versus Short-Term Normative Orientation (Hofstede G., International Differences in Work-Related Values, 1980). It was expanded and

Table 2. Four stages of cultural sensitivity adapted from (Shapiro, Ozanne, & Saatcioglu, 2008)

Stages	Attitude & Cultural Depth	Cultural Sensitivity	Business Relationships & Strategies	Forms of Trust
1. Romantic sojourner	• Fascination • Shallow, daily contact, tourist	• Etic declarative & procedural knowledge	• Discrete, profit-based • Opportunistic	• Uncalculated risks • Naïve trust
2. Foreign worker	• Immersion in business culture • More realistic attitude • Ends in disenchantment and cultural shock	• Begin to develop emic knowledge • Initial emergence of scanning skills and enacted procedural knowledge	• Trail-and-error based but developing relationships • Constructed frames of meaning are tactical	• Competence, integrity, & reliability trust • Trust violation result in relationship dissolution
3. Skilled Worker	• Deeper cultural contact • Skillful diplomats • Evolution to outsider status	• Frustration ends as emic knowledge structures develop • Skillful enacted procedural knowledge and scanning	• Business-bounded relationships but expanding to interpersonal • Greater self-efficacy	• Reliability, integrity, and competence trust still important • Emerging benevolence trust
4. Partner	• Very deep immersion within the culture • Balanced and respectful yet re-enchanted	• Cultural reflexivity • Situated knowledge of cultural differences	• Negotiated business culture as a third way of knowing • High self-efficacy	• Benevolence trust • Relational trust • Other forms of trust become less important

a sixth dimension - Indulgence versus Restraint - was added (Hofstede, Hofstede, & Minkov, 2010). The six cultural dimensions are described in Table 1. These are useful in understanding the types of issues faced across cultures.

Using the culture dimensions created by The Hofstede Center, *Figure 1* compares the cultural dimensions between several major countries. This graph shows the differences on the various dimensions between the eastern and western regions of the World. The U.S. along with Germany and the U.K. appear to share similar values for each of the six dimensions, but differ greatly from China and Japan. Power Distance, Individualism, Uncertainty Avoidance, Orientation and Indulgence dimensions are viewed differently in the U.S. and China. Hofstede's cultural dimensions' show many significant differences between the eastern and western regions, validating the need for culturally sensitive visuals based on the viewer's region. Also validating our decision to examine the east-west dichotomy for our research.

Culture: Cross-Cultural Communication

An important factor in considering how to best convey meaning in data visualizations shared across the east/west boundaries is how cross-cultural communications differ. With the rise of the Internet, new communication methods including video conferencing, social media, and email have become common. These methods allow instant communication, thus increasing the frequency of cross-cultural communications in business. Furthermore, there are two schools of thought on how culture changes due to technology: (1) Technological progress causes cultural homogeneity, which at its simplest form is the diminishing of cultural diversity, and (2) technological progress reinforces cultural fault-lines [i.e. driving cultures apart (Lau & Murnighan, 1998)] (Fujimoto, Bahfen, & Fermelis, 2007). Further, it has been hypothi-

Figure 1. Measurement of Hofstede's cultural dimensions adapted from: (The Hofstede Centre, 2016)

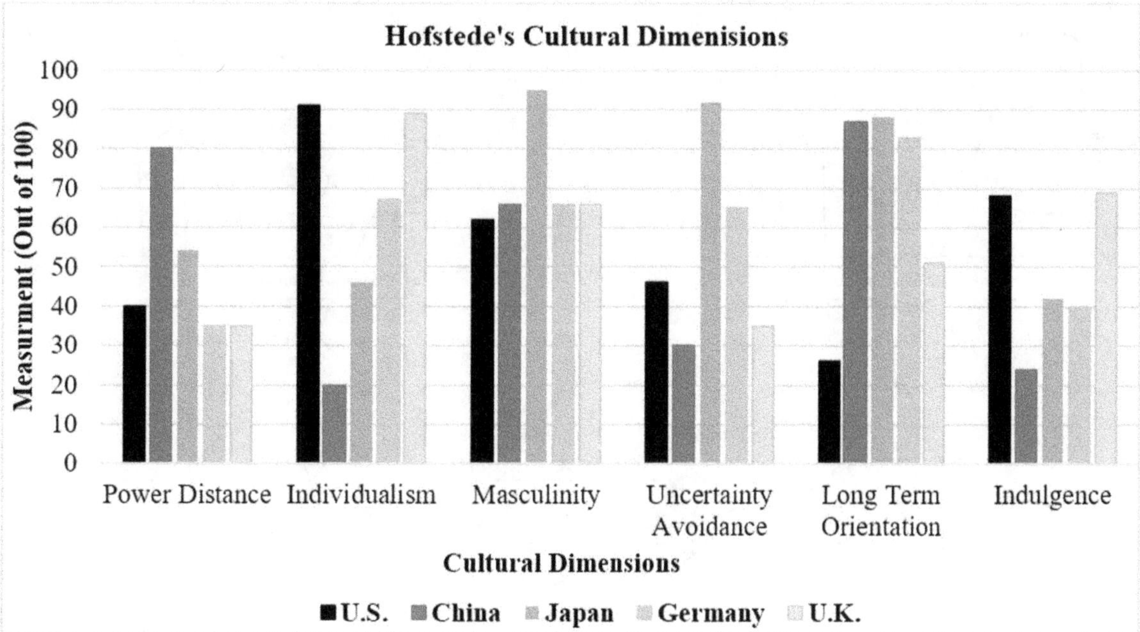

sized that cultural differences will migrate to the online world, increasing the demand for intercultural communication (Fujimoto, Bahfen, & Fermelis, 2007). As business communications are increasingly done online, cross-cultural sensitivity in communication needs to be a priority. Failure to take cultural influence into consideration will impact the organizations ability to communicate.

As seen in Figure 2, five factors influence intercultural communications: communication style, perception, culture, identities, and personality. We chose to focus on perceptions defined as: the way in which an individual receives and actively samples information from the surrounding environment (Vuckovic, 2008). It is essential that data visualization meet the viewer's ideal perception; without it, the information presented will be ineffective. These five factors tie back into Hofstede's six cultural dimensions as they share similar characteristics.

New communication methods have changed how cross-cultural communication is performed. Cultures are now starting to become more similar due to technological advances, yet retain some specific differences. For instance, the Chinese have adopted several western cultural themes such as clothing and entertainment, yet marketers need a different advertising campaign than in the western regions. The differences tie back to the cultural dimension individualistic versus collectivism. Studies have shown that advertising that focuses on individualistic benefits works best for the U.S. (Zhang & Neelankavil, 1997). The "Marlboro Man" an advertising campaign for the cigarette company Marlboro was extremely popular in the U.S. but lacked effectiveness in China due to it only showing individualistic benefits (Hunt & Hodkin, 2012).

Figure 2. Dynamic model of inter-cultural communication

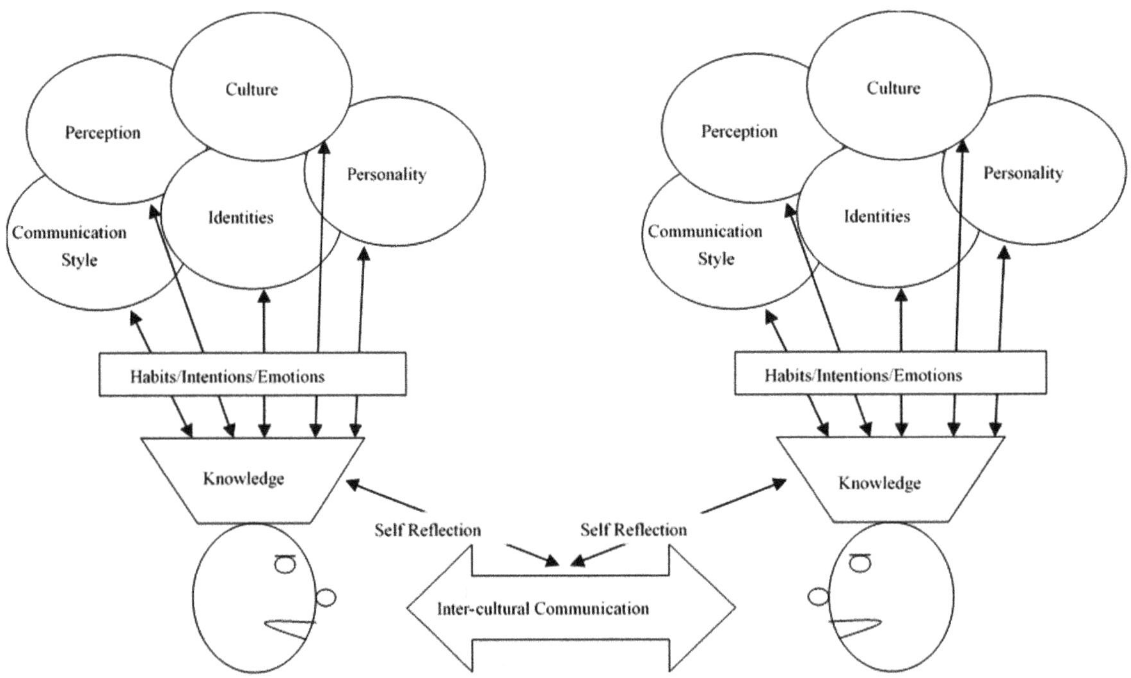

Culture: Communication

An example of the different cultural communication styles is:

A high-context speaker would expect the listeners to understand what the problem is without providing very specific information. Whereas in a low-context culture, the speaker is expected to be responsible for constructing a clear, direct, and unambiguous message that the listeners can decode easily (Bourne, 2016).

Not understanding the context of the presenter can result in misinterpretations and ultimately impact business decisions. This principal has significant impact on our recommendations for best practices.

An interesting view that motivates our best practices is highlighted in a study by Jonasson and Lauring in 2012. Danish and Chinese managers were studied during a business negotiation. The Danish manager believed that Chinese culture is too complex to understand, and that managers do not take initiative. The Chinese managers offer a differing view believing that western managers do not want to learn or see Chinese managers as equal partners. As seen in this study, not understanding cultural differences severely affects business transactions as neither party wants to try to understand the others culture. "Strategies for communication and human resource management that do not take into account essentialization processes may be scantly focused as a result (Jonasson & Lauring, 2012)". This concern is reflected in our proposed best practices.

Culture: Cross-Cultural Management

Cross-cultural management explains the behavior of people in organizations around the world and shows people how to work in organizations with employees and client populations from many different cultures (Adler, 2008). Research on cross-cultural management is faced with a very difficult decision. "An unstated question that has driven cross-cultural research is where the focus should be on understanding the past or shaping the future" (Fontaine, 2007).

Cross-cultural managers are faced with several limitations when managing employees of different cultures. Fontaine gives us three examples of these limitations which include:

1. Cross-cultural management is a matter of perspective. It would be useful if some further discussion leads scholars to a more complete list of perspectives and metaphors associated with these perspectives.
2. Cross-cultural management has, for reasons not entirely clear, not discussed in enough detail the dynamics of stereotyping.
3. Cultural values are pretty well understood but little is known about how to turn tacit knowledge into explicit knowledge or how the structure of the system influences behavior.

These limitations are a result of several cultural differences, including a manager's thinking style. The two most researched styles include the holistic and analytic approach (Nisbett, Peng, Choi, & Norenzayan, 2001). Eastern managers tend to take the holistic approach as "they make little use of categories and formal logic and instead focus on relations among objects and the context in which they interact. (Bower, 2000)". The analytic approach differs as a western manager (esp. in the U.S.) "looks for the traits of objects while largely ignoring their context, categorize items by applying formal logic and explicit rules, and try to resolve any contradictions that turns up" (Bower, 2000). The differing viewpoints on reasoning between east and west alters their perception of visualizations. To address these perceptions, visualizations will need to be changed to ensure the message is portrayed.

Cultural: Individualism vs. Collectivism

The cultural dimension, individualism versus collectivism greatly affects cross-cultural management. A manager from an individualist country, such as the U.S., will manage with a largely opposite style from the Chinese manager. The specific differences in these opposing cultures are shown in Table 3.

These differences make it clear that one set of practices are simply not appropriate. Instead the five countries were placed into two groups, European countries and the U.S. as the western group, and China and Japan as the eastern group. For this reason, the primary focus of our best practices for culturally sensitive data visualization's is for east and west interactions. While this may be too much of a generalization, the authors felt it was a good starting point for this research.

Data Generation and Visualization

Another area the authors focused on was to determine if data generation was impacted by an analyst's culture. It was found that a common start for data generation is to use data mining software. Data mining seeks to discover hidden facts contained in large databases (Freedman, 2006). As data mining increases in importance, several weaknesses in the process need to be addressed. One significant problem is the difficulty non-technical users have understanding and drawing conclusions from data mining results. A common solution is to create a summary of the important points but the better option is to present the data visually.

To expand the research to determine the cultural impact on data mining, the industry standard model, the Cross-Industry Standard Process for Data Mining (CRISP-DM) was analyzed (Mariscal, Marban, & Fernandez, 2010). Each step of the process is shown and defined in Table 4. We focused our proposed best practices on the deployment stage as it is when the data is organized and presented to a customer.

Table 3. Individualist Culture versus collective culture adapted from (Reynolds & Valentine, 2011)

Individualist Culture (U.S.)	Collective Culture (China)
1. Transaction oriented	1. Relationship oriented
2. Short-term goals	2. Long-term growth
3. Emphasis on content	3. Emphasis on context
4. Independent	4. Interdependent
5. Competitive, decision driven	5. Collaborative
6. Direct, explicit communication	6. Indirect circuitous communication
7. Personal accountability	7. Protection of face
8. Private offices	8. Open office plan
9. Linear time, impatient	9. Flexible time, patient

Table 4. Detailed breakdown of CRISP-DM model adapted from (Chapman, et al., 2010)

Business Understanding	Focuses on understanding the project objectives and requirements from a business perspective, then converting this knowledge into a data mining problem definition and a preliminary plan designed to achieve the objectives.
Data Understanding	Starts with initial data collection and proceeds with activities that enable you to become familiar with the data, identify data quality problems, discover first insights into the data, and/or detect interesting subsets to form hypotheses regarding hidden information.
Data Preparation	Covers all activities needed to construct the final dataset [data that will be fed into the modeling tool(s)] from the initial raw data. Data preparation tasks are likely to be performed multiple times and not in any prescribed order. Tasks include table, record, and attribute selection, as well as transformation and cleaning of data for modeling tools.
Modeling	Various modeling techniques are selected and applied, and their parameters are calibrated to optimal values. Typically, there are several techniques for the same data mining problem type. Some techniques have specific requirements on the form of data. Therefore, going back to the data preparation phase is often necessary.
Evaluation	Before proceeding to final deployment of the model, it is important to thoroughly evaluate it and review the steps executed to create it, to be certain the model properly achieves the business objectives. A key objective is to determine if there is some important business issue that has not been sufficiently considered. At the end of this phase, a decision on the use of the data mining results should be reached.
Deployment	Creation of the model is generally not the end of the project. Even if the purpose of the model is to increase knowledge of the data, the knowledge gained will need to be organized and presented in a way that the customer can use it. It often involves applying "live" models within an organization's decision making processes—for example, real-time personalization of Web pages or repeated scoring of marketing databases. [This should include data visualization.]

While out of scope of this article which focuses on the deployment stage of the CRISP-DM model, our research shows that the data analyst has multiple opportunities to add cultural bias. The other stages should probably also have best practices, In the deployment stage care must be taken to produce culturally sensitive data visualizations. The proposed best practices provide the next step in securing that sensitivity.

Issues Around Color and Its Use

There is a wide and varied literature on how color of objects and text are perceived in the east and west. The authors chose several salient articles for the literature review that best represented the goals of this study. We found that culture has a significant impact on how colors are viewed. The colors red and black stand out as significant in the literature. In the U.S. and most western countries, the color red is perceived as negative as it normally portrays a loss. In China, the color red is preferred as it is traditionally considered lucky. However, red should never be used to write a personal name in the east as it goes against Buddhist tradition (Firoz & Ramin, 2004). Further, the U.S. normally associates the color black with death, while China views white as the color of death.

Additional colors such as green and yellow are viewed differently by east and west countries as well (Firoz & Ramin, 2004). The careful consideration of the colors is key in our proposed best practices. One of the most complete studies on the cultural impact of color association was done by McCandless. The author completed a study on ten regions of the world determining how they view different colors (McCandless, 2009). Table 5 is a summary of the significant findings for western countries, and two eastern countries (China and Japan). Where nothing is listed, no significant impact was found in the literature for that region/country.

As shown in Table 5, colors such as green are viewed somewhat similarly by the westerners and the Chinese. Blue is perceived similarly between westerners and the Japanese in that they both see it positively.

Table 5. Colors in culture adapted from (McCandless, 2009)

Colors	West	China	Japan
Red	Power Boldness	Happiness Success/ fortune	Excitement Strength
Orange	Friendly Reliable Warmth	Learning Kinship	Enthusiasm Balance Energy
Yellow	Fun Peace	Royalty Respect	Joy Deceit
Green	Grow Natural Trust	Growth Life Infidelity	
Blue	Smart Progress Loyalty		Wealth Loyalty Purity
Black	Authority Power Overpowering	Nobility Class Mourning	Death Self-examination
White	Neutral Purity Vagueness	Truce Death Mourning	Death Mourning Humility

Even with these similarities, the color white is considered in almost diametrically opposite ways by the east and west. While the U.S. sees white being neutral and pure, China and Japan see it symbolizing death. This is a prime example of how different colors are perceived by cultures. This reinforces our conclusion that because the use of colors is extremely common in data visuals and because the target audience's perceptions will be impacted by color choice, color selection must be in our proposed best practices.

Literature Summary

We used a synthesis of recent journal articles focusing on topics such as; culture, culturally sensitive business practices, advertising effectiveness, data visualizations, globalization and cultural dimensions to develop our proposed data visualization best practices for east-west business interactions. We know that culture influences domestic and international organizations in all aspects of their business environment. For multinational organizations, the regions they compete in has great influence on their business environment. Our research focused on two distinct world regions: east and west. The eastern region consists of countries in eastern Asia, such as Japan and China. The western region is primarily countries in North America and two European countries, the U.K. and Germany as they share many cultural similarities. We then selected the largest country by economic metrics to represent each region. China representing the eastern region, and the U.S. the western region.

Impact of Color

Research has shown significant evidence that culture has an impact on color association. For example, the color red in China represents happiness and success, but in the western regions red portrays power and excitement except in accounting/financial domains where it is perceived as negative. Presenting a financial data visualization in the U.S. using the color red instantly portrays a financial loss, whereas in China, the same visualization might be viewed as lucky. Another example is the color black that can also be viewed differently in data visualizations. The color black in the U.S. is the standard color of font for businesses, yet it is associated with death in the east (McCandless, 2009). Further, black in the east can be associated with concepts like nobility, class, mourning or self-examination.

To fully understand the color preferences for the U.S. and China, a study was performed by Madden, Hewett and Roth to determine preferred colors for these two countries. The results of this study are shown in Figure 3. In this study, the 0 represents a deep dislike of the color, and 7 represents a strong preference. Both countries first choice was blue, while green, black and white where second, third and fourth choice respectively. When using different colors in visualizations, the color preferences of each culture should be used if feasible (Madden, Hewett, & Roth, 2000).

Business Practices and Target Audience

The impact culture has on the business environment cannot be overlooked. Each region of the world has varying traditions, customs, and business practices, all influenced by their culture. The Global Business Practice Model (Schuster & Copeland, 2008) was used to breakdown the cultural differences. The specific differences between China and U.S. are shown in Table 6.

As seen in Table 6, these two countries conduct business very differently. The key finding of the Schuster & Copeland study is that when creating data visualizations, the normal customs and traditions need to be followed before the visualization is shown to the target audience. Multinational companies such as Coca-Cola and Kentucky Fried Chicken have shown that the effects of insensitive business practices can be severely negative.

Figure 3. U.S. & China color preferences adapted from (Madden, Hewett, & Roth, 2000)

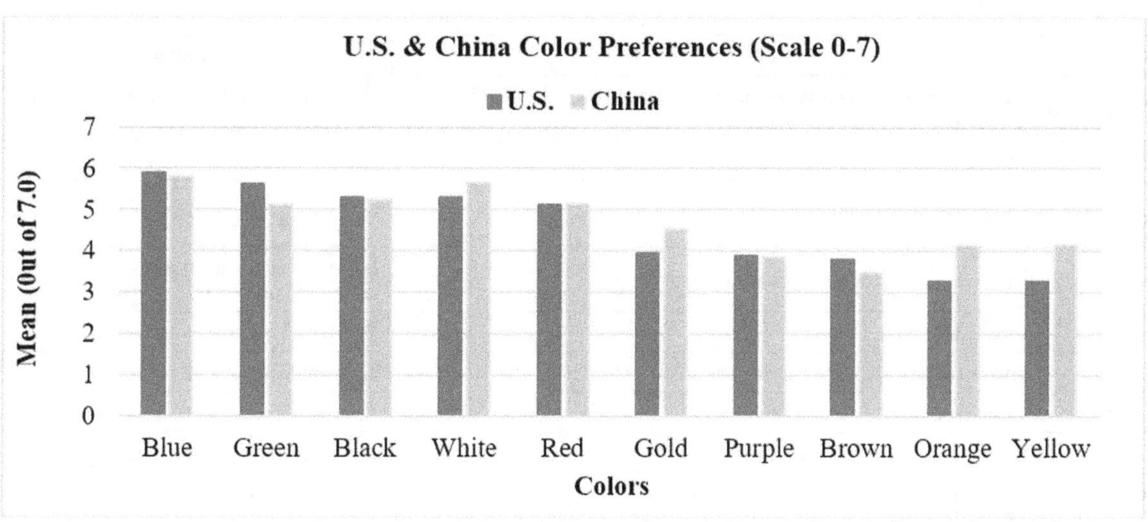

The increase of data visualization usage can be directly linked to globalization and the rising popularity of business analytics. Research suggest the advantages to using data visualizations are that the majority of people are visual learners, and due to the increased amount of data, relationships are harder to see clearly (Freedman, 2006). The need for culturally sensitive data visualizations is directly linked to the new global marketplace. Organizations are building relationships and sharing data visualizations with a variety of different cultures throughout the world.

RECOMMENDED BEST PRACTICES

The recommended set of best practices are targeted specifically towards middle managers, but should be implemented by every employee involved in the data visualization process. The recommended practices are placed in three activities; 1) preparing to create data visualizations, 2) designing data visualizations, and 3) presenting data visualizations. Since the authors believe it is necessary to narrow the proposed best practices in this first attempt at such work, these practices are targeted towards a U.S. organization sharing data visualizations to a Chinese audience. The best practices focus on middle managers who are responsible for implementing data visualizations.

Activity One: Preparing Data Visualizations

When preparing for a presentation, it is essential that all employees involved have a thorough understanding of the cultural differences between the U.S. and China. This includes the data analyst who collect, analyze, and create the visuals, as well as the managers responsible for the presentation. The best method to analyze the cultural differences between the two countries is using the six cultural dimensions, shown in *Table 1*. All employees need to understand the differences between an individualistic and col-

Table 6. U.S. & China business practice model adapted from (Schuster & Copeland, 2008)

	U.S.	China
Government	The government sets parameters and constraints to create the environment for doing business	Direct involvement of government in business as business partner
Law	Reliance on systems and procedures	Pragmatism or situational consideration
Hierarchy	Assumption of equality	Combination of assumption of equality and status differences
Privacy	Business and private matters are separate	Business and private matters are combined and part of one reality
Time	Fixed time	Flexible or "rubber" time
Flow	Time works in a linear fashion	Time works in a cyclical faction
Truth	Universal truth	Many truths exist at once
Words	Words have explicit meanings	Words have implicit meanings
Style	Communication is direct and forthright	Communication is indirect
Logic	Combination of formal deductive reasoning and alternative heuristic	Alterative heuristic

lectivist culture. For example: China being a collectivist culture prioritizes relationships and long term team building over task completion. The U.S. is an individualistic culture and is more apt to focus on short-term independent goals while improving individual skills (Hofstede, Hofstede, & Minkov, 2010).

By teaching employees how to understand cultural differences, their cultural intelligence skills are increased. This process is very time consuming and costly. However, if these skills are not taught, managers only need to look at the cultural blunders made by many multinational companies to see the possible negative consequences.

- **Best Practice One:** Know the culture of the target audience using a framework like that proposed by Hofstede.

Activity Two: Designing Data Visualizations

To effectively convey the content in visualizations, managers need to understand the differences between high-context and low-context cultures. As previously mentioned, China is a high-context culture, and the U.S. is a low-context culture. To ensure that content is received as desired by a Chinese audience, presentations need to be in a high-context style. The content needs to be conveyed entirely in the visualization providing an opportunity for the audience to interpret the content. However, the message should not be explicitly defined and provided to the audience, it must require the audience to interpret it. For example, pitching a partnership with a Chinese company by directly saying "invest now in my company" will result in a negative response. Instead, the presentation should show the benefits of investing in the company. This allows the audience to come to their own conclusions based on the information provided. A proper understanding of the differences between high-context and low-context culture, will reduce the risk of culturally insensitive data visualizations (Bourne, 2016).

Visualizations need to be appealing to the Chinese audience. Implementing their preferred colors and paying attention to how color is perceived will benefit the organization in two ways. First, the efficiency of designing the visualization will be increased as the analysts will know what colors to use. Second, the recommended colors will increase the likelihood of the desired response when sharing visualizations with a culturally different audience.

- **Best Practice Two:** Understand context and how color is interpreted by the target audience; design visuals accordingly.

Activity Three: Presenting Data Visualizations

When presenting data visualizations managers will have to adjust their message based on how the audience best receives information – high vs. low context. For example, in a high-context culture, nonverbal communication is as important as verbal communication. Displaying poor nonverbal communication skills can influence how the audience views and interprets data visualizations. Additionally, poor nonverbal communication skills can insult an audience (Bourne, 2016). Managers must always be sure the same message is being conveyed by their verbal and nonverbal language.

In China, the presentation style of a data visualization should be targeted towards a collective cultural audience. This is a significant change from presenting to a U.S. audience that is normally very individualistically oriented. The focus of the presentation should be on collective cultural traits such as, long-term goals and how it benefits the audience as a whole (Firoz & Ramin, 2004). The best recommendation when presenting data visualizations is to have managers learn and integrate themselves into the audience's culture. This is a broad, costly, and time-consuming recommendation, but is the best chance of an employee learning how to interact with the target culture and present visualizations that will be well received.

- **Best Practice Three:** Incorporate context into presentation style and delivery.

Summary of Best Practices for US vs. Chinese Interaction

A summary of the recommended best practices for a US company working with a Chinese company are shown in Table 7. These represent our synthesis of the literature used in this review. Organizations will see multiple benefits from implementing the proposed best practices. For example, an organization will decrease their chance of committing a cultural blunder when data visualizations are shared with another culture. Also, it will increase the cultural intelligence of employees, therefore increasing the effectiveness when creating data visualizations. These benefits will produce a better relationship between business partners, and thereby provide financial benefit to all involved.

CONCLUSION

This study's initial goal was to recommend a set of best practices to implement on a global scale. The researchers quickly understood that this was not feasible. Therefore, the scope of this initial study was narrowed by country, region, and industry sector. Based on the findings, the target was limited to the eastern and western regions. The U.S. was selected to represent the western region, and China was chosen for the eastern region. This instantly limits this study as it did not include countries in regions such as Africa, South America, Australia, and the Middle- east. Due to the unique culture in every country and region, these best practices may not completely apply to additional countries outside the western or

Table 7. Recommended best practices

Summary of Best Practices for Organization Conducting Business in China	
Activity	**Recommendation** *Notes*
Preparing Data Visualizations	**Best Practice One - Preparing Data Visualization** **Know the culture of the target audience using a framework like that proposed by Hofstede.** *Provide cultural background on the target audience to all employees associated with creating data visualizations. Especially examine the culture of both the receiving audience along these dimensions of collectivism and individualism*
Designing Data Visualizations	**Best Practice Two - Designing Data Visualizations** **Understand context and how color is interpreted by the target audience; design visuals accordingly.** *Know the receiving culture context – low vs. high*
Presenting Data Visualizations	**Best Practice Three - Presenting Data Visualizations** **Incorporate context into presentation style and delivery.** *Be cognizant of nonverbal and verbal communications and presentation style.*

eastern regions. This research provided a starting point for creating a set of best practices for countries in these two regions, but you would need to further examine a specific country to determine appropriate recommendations. All of that said, the proposed best practices have global applicability with the caveat that they may need to be adjusted for implementation in specific countries.

The proposed best practices were based on the national culture for each country, without taking into consideration the numerous cultural sub-groups. A country's culture can be broken down from the national culture to regional cultures, and further by religion, ethnic background or residency. The best practices may be limited in their overall effectiveness as the national culture may not represent the diverse cultural sub-groups. For example, the statistical research that was found supporting color association is limited in the number of participants and the region they reside in (Wang & Or, 2015). Due to the number of diverse cultural sub-groups in the U.S. and China, only the national culture of each country was analyzed. That is because the national culture seems to be most representative of commercial organizations.

The target audience was limited by the industry sector and the manager's position in the organization. This leads to limitations in implementing the best practices as the service sector is the dominate industry sector in the U.S. but not in China. The Chinese economy relies almost equally on both services and manufacturing (Central Intelligence Agency, 2015). The recommendations are targeted specifically to the services sector but with future research adapted to the manufacturing sector. In addition to focusing on the service sector, a specific service industry was not targeted. The services sector is comprised of many different industries, with culture effecting each one differently. Initially the aim of this study was to focus on the financial industry, but the authors quickly switched to the services sector due to a lack of available data. Additionally, the study was limited by not focusing on organizational factors, such as the organizational culture, structure, or the number of employees. Each factor can influence the effectiveness of our recommended best practices.

The authors note that a final limitation was the shortage of recent studies on the influence of culture in organizations. The cultures in the U.S. and China are constantly changing and adapting hence impacting the relevancy of our recommendations. We attempted to limit our research within the last ten years, but our timeframe expanded because of a lack of recent research. Many of the studies cited in our work need to be updated to reflect the changes caused by factors such as globalization. Notwithstanding all the limitations, the authors believe that our recommendations are applicable to today's organization doing business with a global partner from another country.

REFERENCES

Adler, N. (2008). *International Dimensions of Organizational Behavior* (5th ed.). Cincinnati, OH: South-Western.

Ardalan, K. (2008). Globalization and culture: Four paradigmatic views. *International Journal of Social Economics*, 513–534.

Bourne, J. S. (2016). Exploring Intercultural Communication Challenges: A Case Study on Chinese-English Interpreting. *China Media Research*, 14-24.

Bower, B. (2000). Culture of Reason: Thinking styles may take Eastern and Western routes. Society for Science & the Public, 56-58.

Cameron, R., & Molina-Azorin, J. F. (2011). The acceptance of mixed methods in business and management research. *The International Journal of Organizational Analysis*, *19*(3), 256–270. doi:10.1108/19348831111149204

Central Intelligence Agency. (2015). *The World Factbook*. Retrieved from Central Intelligence Agency: https://www.cia.gov/library/publications/the-world-factbook/fields/2012.html

Chapman, P., Clinton, J., Kerber, R., Khabaza, T., Reinartz, T., Shearer, C., & Wirth, R. (2010). *CRISP-DM 1.0*. SPSS.

Charara, S. (2016, March 14). *Under Armour CEO: Data is the new oil*. Retrieved from Wareable: http://www.wareable.com/under-armour/under-armour-health-data-connected-fitness-sxsw-2453

Chary, M. (2007). *Public Organizations in the Age of Globalization and Technology*. Springer + Business Media, LLC.

Cooper, H., & Hedges, L. V. (1994). *The handbook of research synthesis*. New York, NY: Russell Sage Foundation.

Corrigan, G. (2015). Talent: Attracting, Retaining, and Growing a Critical Yet Scarce Resource. *Business Intelligence Journal*, 17-24.

Creswell, J. W., & Clark, V. L. (2007). *Designing and Conducting Mixed Methods Research*. Thousand Oaks, CA: Sage.

Evans, J. R. (2016). *Business Analytics: Methods, models, and decisions* (2nd ed.). Upper Saddle River, NJ: Pearson Education.

Firoz, N. M., & Ramin, T. (2004). Understanding Cultural Variables is Critical to Success in International Business. *International Journal of Management*, 307–323.

Fontaine, R. (2007). Cross-Cultural Management: Six perspectives. *Cross Cultural Management*, *14*(2), 125–135. doi:10.1108/13527600710745732

Freedman, M. (2006). Information Visualization Brings Data into Shaper Focus. *Scientific Computing*, 24-25.

Friedman, T. (2002). *Longitudes & Attitudes*. Farrar, Straus & Grioux.

Friedman, T. L. (2000). *The Lexus and the Olive Tree*. New York, NY: Farrar, Staus, and Giroux.

Fujimoto, Y., Bahfen, N., Fermelis, J., & Härtel, C. E. J. (2007). The global village: Online cross-cultural communication and HRM. *Cross Cultural Management*, *14*(1), 7–22. doi:10.1108/13527600710718804

Gutierrez, B., Spencer, S. M., & Zhu, G. (2012). Thinking globally. leading locally: Chinese, Indian, and Western leadership. *Cross Cultural Management*, *19*(1), 67–89. doi:10.1108/13527601211195637

Hall. (1976). *Beyond Culture*. New York, NY: Anchor Press/Doubleday.

Hofstede, G. (1980). *International Differences in Work-Related Values*. Beverly Hills, CA.

Hofstede, G., & Hofstede, G. (2005). Cultures and Organizations: Software of the Mind (2nd ed.). New York, NY: McGraw-Hill.

Hofstede, G., Hofstede, G. J., & Minkov, M. (2010). *Cultures and Organizations: Software of the Mind*. McGraw-Hill.

House, R. J., Hanges, P. J., Javidan, M., Dorfman, P. W., & Gupta, V. (2004). *Culture, Leadership and Organizations The Globe Study of 62 Societies*. Thousand Oaks, CA: Sage.

Hult, G., Tomas, M., Ketchen, D. J. Jr, Griffith, D. A., Finnegan, C. A., Gonzalez-Padron, T., ... Cavusgil, S. T. (2008). Data equivalence in cross-cultural international business research: Assessment and guidelines. *Journal of International Business Studies*, *39*(6), 1027–1044. doi:10.1057/palgrave.jibs.8400396

Hunt, K. A., & Hodkin, W. (2012). The Criticality of Cultural Awareness in Global Marketing: Some Case Examples. *Journal of Business Case Studies*.

Jameson, K. A. (2005). Culture and Cognition: What is Universal about the Representation of Color Experience? *Journal of Cognition and Culture*, 294–347.

Jiang, Y. (2013). Business Negotiation Culture in China. *International Business Research*, 109–116.

John, R., & Schermerhorn, J. (2008). *Management* (9th ed.). John Wiley & Sons, Inc.

Jonasson, C., & Lauring, J. (2012). Cultural differences in use: the power to essentialize communication styles. *Journal of Communication Management*, 405-419.

Kirca, A. H., & Yaprak, A. (2010). The use of meta-analysis in international business research: Its current status and suggestions for better practice. *International Business Review*, *19*(3), 306–314. doi:10.1016/j.ibusrev.2010.01.001

Lau, D. C., & Murnighan, J. K. (1998). Demographic Diversity and Faultlines: The Compositional Dynamics of Organizational Groups. *Academy of Management Review*, 325–340.

Li, X., & Putterill, M. (2007). Strategy implications of business culture differences between Japan and China. *Business Strategy Series*, *8*(2), 148–154. doi:10.1108/17515630710685212

Lustig, I., Dietrich, B., Johnson, C., & Dziekan, C. (2010, November/December). *The Analytics Journey*. Retrieved from Analytics Magazine: http://www.analytics-magazine.org/november-december-2010/54-the-analytics-journey

Madden, T. J., Hewett, K., & Roth, M. S. (2000). Managing Images in Different Cultures: A Cross-National Study of COlor Meanings and Preferences. *Journal of International Marketing*, *8*(4), 90–107. doi:10.1509/jimk.8.4.90.19795

Mariscal, G., Marban, O., & Fernandez, C. (2010). A survery of data mining and knowledge discovery process models and methodologies. *The Knowledge Engineering Review*, *25*(02), 137–166. doi:10.1017/S0269888910000032

McCandless, D. (2009). *Information is Beautiful*. Collins.

Mesdag, M. (2000). Culture-sensitive adapation or global standardization - the duration-of-usage hypothesis. *International Marketing Review*, *17*(1), 74–84. doi:10.1108/02651330010314722

Mintu, A. T., Calantone, R., & Gassenheimer, J. B. (1994). Towards improving cross-cultural research: Extending Churchill's research paradigm. *Journal of International Marketing*, 5–23.

Nisbett, R. E., Peng, K., Choi, I., & Norenzayan, A. (2001). Culture and Systems of Thought: Holistic Versus Analytic Cognition. American Psychological Association, Inc.

Resnicow, K. (1999). *Cultural Sensitivity in Public Health: Defined and Demystified*. Academic Press.

Reynolds, S., & Valentine, D. (2011). *Guide to Cross-cultural Communication* (2nd ed.). Prentice Hall.

SAS. (2016, March 3). *Data Visualization What it is and why it matters*. Retrieved from SAS: http://www.sas.com/en_us/insights/big-data/data-visualization.html

Scher, A., Reuss, A., Frank, E., & Dorman, P. (2000). The ABCs of the Global Economy. *Dollars and Sense*, 26–32.

Schuster, C. P., & Copeland, M. J. (2008). Cultural theory in use: the instersection of structure, process and communication in business practice. *Journal of Public Affairs*, 261-280.

Shapiro, J. M., Ozanne, J. L., & Saatcioglu, B. (2008). An interpretive examination of the development of cultural sensitivity in international business. *Journal of International Business Studies*, *39*(1), 71–87. doi:10.1057/palgrave.jibs.8400327

Smith, A. (2013). Data visualisation and beyond: A multi-disciplinary approach to promote user engagement with official statistics. *Statistical Journal of the IAOS*, 173–185.

Stafford, J. R., Lopes-DeFede, A., Bowman, R., Hanna, J., & Eking, T. (1997). *Building cultural bridges*. Bloomington, IN: National Educational Services.

The Hofstede Centre. (2016, March 1). *Cultural Compass*. Retrieved from The Hofstede Centre: http://www.geert-hofstede.com/

The World Bank. (2015). *GDP at market price (current US$)*. Retrieved from The World Bank: http://data.worldbank.org/indicator/NY.GDP.MKTP.CD?order=wbapi_data_value_2014%20wbapi_data_value%20wbapi_data_value-last&sort=desc

The World Bank. (2016, April 1). *World Developement Indicators*. Retrieved from The World Bank: http://data.worldbank.org/data-catalog/world-development-indicators

U.S. Census Bureau. (2016). *Definition: NAICS 48-49 to 81, Services Sectors*. Retrieved from U.S. Census Bureau: http://www.census.gov/econ/services.html

U.S. Department of Commerce. (2015). *Industry Data from Bureau of Economic Analysis*. Retrieved from Bureau of Economic Analysis: http://www.bea.gov/iTable/iTable.cfm?ReqID=51&step=1#reqid=51&step=51&isuri=1&5114=a&5102=1

Vuckovic, A. (2008). Inter-cultural communication: A foundation of communicative action. *Multicultural Education & Technology Journal*, *2*(1), 47–59. doi:10.1108/17504970810867151

Wang, H., & Or, C. K. (2015). *A study of the relationship between color-concept association and occupational background for Chinese*. Elsevier.

Watson, H. J., Wixon, B. H., & Ariyachandra, T. (2013). Insights on Hiring for BI and Analytics. *Business Intelligence Journal*, 4-7.

Wells, D. (2008, April 8). *Business Analytics- Getting the Point.* Retrieved from BeyeNetwork: http://www.b-eye-network.com/view/7133

Xiumei, S., & Jinying, W. (2011). Cultural Distance between China and US across GLOBE Model and Hofstede Model. *International Business and Management*, 11-17.

Zhang, Y., & Neelankavil, J. P. (1997). The influence of culture on advertising effectiveness in China and the USA. *European Journal of Marketing*, *31*(2), 134–149. doi:10.1108/03090569710157106

Chapter 9
Building a Maturity Framework for Big Data Cybersecurity Analytics

Chi Minh Pham
Deakin University, Australia

ABSTRACT

In recent years, big data analytics has become widely applied in cybersecurity, leading to the novel approach of big data cybersecurity analytics. While some organizations have been adopting this new approach in tackling cybercrime, there are limited guidelines to which companies can refer. Therefore, the renowned maturity model concept, which offers a systematic approach for an organization to measure and improve its maturity level, is applied in this study. On the basis of a comprehensive literature review, this chapter proposes a maturity framework for big data cybersecurity analytics. This synthesized comprehensive maturity framework comprises seven dimensions across five stage levels—namely organization, human, infrastructure, data management, analytics application, governance, and security dimensions. Knowing which dimensions need to be improved and which pathway to follow ensures the successful implementation of big data cybersecurity analytics within organizations.

INTRODUCTION

Despite advances in technology, cybersecurity may not become obsolete over time because these advances simultaneously enable modern cybercriminals to employ breakthrough techniques to damage organizations (Jegede, 2016; Matrane, Talea, & Okar, 2014), and breaches and attacks have increased across organizational levels ranging from industries to government agencies. Therefore, the modern era of information complexity has led to not only increased big data volume, where petabytes and exabytes of information are transferred daily, but also increased breakthrough cyberattacks (Mahmood & Afzal, 2013).

DOI: 10.4018/978-1-5225-5718-0.ch009

According to Mahmood and Afzal (2013), cybersecurity includes techniques, processes, and methodologies aimed at thwarting illegal attacks and protecting systems and networks from damage. Security analytics is a specific technique used to detect cybercrimes and measure cybersecurity performance on a large (national or international) scale (Cybenko & Landwehr, 2012).

Big data empower security analytics by supplying available data types for correlation and processing in analytics for security purposes (Shackleford, 2016). In addition to analyzing structured data, big data analytics operates with bunches of semi-structured and unstructured data (e.g., security data such as text in log files, security events, and GPS locations), which confer invaluable information. Hence, big data, characterized by the four Vs—volume, velocity, variety, and veracity—can solve the challenging questions on data limitations and data set availabilities for validation. When traditional techniques cannot handle the complexity of cybersecurity attacks and crimes, the big data approach is a potential solution.

However, big data cybersecurity analytics (BDCA) is substantially different from other types of security analytics. BDCA includes functions such as technologies for integrating dissimilar data types, ETL tools, multidimensional analysis, and advanced data visualization applications (Sullivan, 2015). However, there are many fundamental components that need more development, presenting problems ranging from human resources and investment to IT architecture for capturing and storing data.

With these scenarios, both practical and research sectors are in need of clear guidelines that present a road map for the future of big data application in cybersecurity. To solve the problem, this study proposed a maturity framework for BDCA with systematic guidelines and staged evolutionary levels. The maturity framework might encourage organizations to implement big data platforms and develop business strategies, while providing a complete picture of big data development, particularly for cybersecurity purposes. This may motivate researchers to continue the innovation or identify a related sub-field that warrants investigation.

For this purpose, a maturity framework to describe the significant steps in the maturity pathway, and the effectiveness measurements of deploying BDCA in organization contexts, was developed. In addition, the model was transformed into a questionnaire that serves as a diagnostic tool to identify problems as well as measure capability maturity in BDCA programs in an organization.

The research contributes to the theory by introducing a wide range of indicators for the maturity framework in the field, and by placing indicators in a hierarchical level. Meanwhile, as a practical contribution, it assists organizations in evaluating their current programs against an ideal BDCA approach, so that they can identify gaps for improvement, as well as standardize the performance with other organizations in the industry.

The remainder of this paper is structured as follows. The next section provides a review of the relevant literature. The third section explains the research methodology before presenting the literature findings. In the subsequent section, the maturity framework for BDCA is outlined, followed by the conclusion and proposals for further research.

BACKGROUND AND LITERATURE REVIEW

The objective of this research was to develop a framework that guides organizations to reach maturity in their big data analytics platform for cybersecurity purposes. Figure 1 shows the three components of the research—big data analytics, cybersecurity, and maturity model.

Figure 1. Research components and relationships

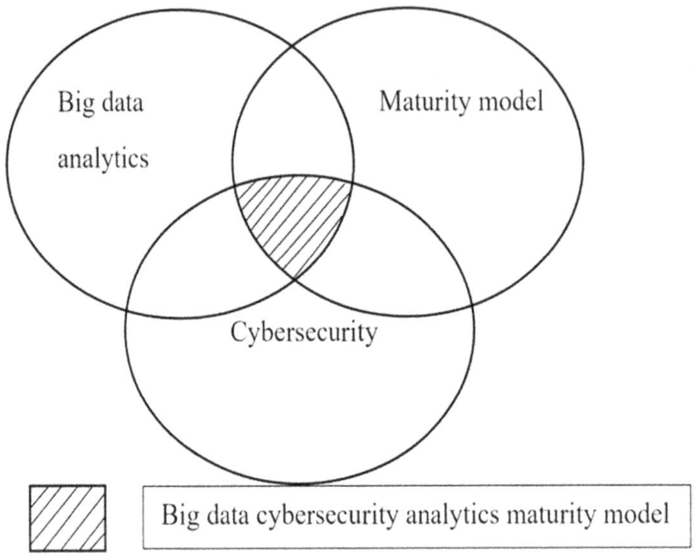

Big Data Analytics

Big data analytics requires significant social–technical dimensions to be mature in organizational contexts. Thamir and Theodoulidis (2013) accumulated comprehensive capability maturity models, which had been researched and conducted, and reviewed the maturity aspects addressed in these models. The current research of Foshay, Yeoh, Boo, Ong, and Mattie (2015) extended the work by adding more maturity studies from succeeding years, which provides the latest comprehensive review on the maturity framework for business intelligence. The dimensions included in the research of Foshay et al. (2015) are "organizational aspects" (including analytical process, organizational structure, governance, and cost-benefits); "technical aspects" (including technical infrastructure/tools and data architecture); and "human aspects" (including skill, training, sponsorship, and culture). These are key elements that the research needs to address for the intelligence analytics.

Cybersecurity

Musthaler (2013) stated that, in terms of security perspective, security analytics is the future trend of IT security. To handle cyber activities, logs, and network access, security information and event management (SIEM) technology systems collect and store extensive data and information of users, which can be analyzed to detect threats by applying big data analytics–based techniques (Musthaler, 2013). In addition, Musthaler (2013) claimed that, to evaluate the competence of security systems, analysts need to use the analyzed pattern of security issues and vulnerabilities to make the existing security controls effective to protect the organization.

Maturity Model

The maturity model concept, which was derived from Crosby (1979) and known as Crosby's Quality Management Maturity Grid, has a long history of development. Humphrey (1988) asserted that, to "accelerate the transition of advance technology and methods into practice," there are five levels of software engineering process maturity:

1. **Initial:** Until the process is under statistical control, no orderly progress in process improvement is possible;
2. **Repeatable:** A stable process with a repeatable level of statistical control by initiating rigorous project management of commitments, cost, schedule and changes;
3. **Defined:** The organization has defined the process, to ensure consistent implementation and provide a basis for better understanding;
4. **Managed:** Comprehensive process measurements, beyond those of cost and schedule performance; and
5. **Optimising:** The organisation now has a foundation for continued improvement and optimisation of the process (p. 74).

The revised capability maturity model by Paulk, Curtis, Chrissis, and Weber (1993) reinforces the predictability, effectiveness, and manageability-related developments of an IT asset (i.e., software) and boosts its maturity levels. This means that the new maturity framework ensures the continuous improvement of systems and activities, and that management needs to identify and acknowledge the current maturity level of the system, and what systems need to be achieved, as well as to compare with other peers and industry norms (Lainhart, 2000; Matrane et al., 2014).

METHODOLOGY

This research focused on developing a maturity framework for BDCA. There is no significant model that specializes in applying big data analytics to cybersecurity areas, but three components (i.e., big data analytics, security analytics, and capability maturity model) are common in research papers and maturity frameworks already developed. Hence, the findings of this paper aimed to fill the gaps and enhance the body of knowledge related to big data analytics–based cybersecurity.

To gain a definitive view, a detailed analysis of published research, which involved content analysis of each article, was undertaken. For this purpose, the research included three steps as follows:

Step 1: Identifying common and most reviewed papers by searching for the keywords "big data security analytics maturity model" in database sources (e.g., ProQuest, IEEExplore, Sciencedirect, Emerald, and Springerlink) and in a research engine (Google Scholar). Among these resources, only definitions and future outlooks of the technique were retrieved, and no maturity model was conducted.

Step 2: Collecting each key component of the research by searching separately for "big data" and "security analytics" related to the maturity model and by comparing and synthesizing the outcomes. Different keywords and their combinations were used to search in different sources in the databases. The combinations used for searching were:

- ◦ Big data analytics maturity model (framework).
- ◦ (Cyber)security (analytics) maturity model (framework).
- ◦ Keywords for dimensions of big data analytics (organizational, human, and technical features) that are key factors for the maturity model.

Step 3: Aggregating research papers into topic clusters and comparing the outcomes.

The initial outcome of the analysis showed that published papers on the big data analytics maturity model are limited. However, the outcome for "cybersecurity components" was acceptable, and included many papers and papers covering various domains required for a cybersecurity program. Nevertheless, additional industrial knowledge was required for the final model.

The next stage of the analysis was to repeat Step 1 of the method, but to expand it to practical searching tools (i.e., Google and Yahoo) to include potential practical applications in the field. The result of the next round showed that there are a few papers written by industrial experts on both the big data and the security components. Because of the lack of available resources for the analysis, industrial materials were included in the research as a guideline for the developed model. The outcome was investigated for each component, by considering the time frame of the research, the domain, and the detail in hierarchical maturity levels.

Review of the Big Data Analytics Maturity Model

Table 1 illustrates all contemporary research contributions to the big data analytics maturity model. The research period ranges from 2013 to 2016, but mostly from 2013 to 2014. Comuzzi and Patel (2016) conducted the first academic paper on the topic, but the knowledge is based only on previous practical models. Adapting the summative table of Comuzzi and Patel (2016) in Table 1, this research included the latest white paper of Dhanuka (2016) on the big data maturity model. That paper only mentions capability domains that an organization needs to cover to empower the big data platform, but no stages of the development are described, which makes it challenging for the organization to understand its performance.

Regarding the outcome of this component, the research identified that most of the models are online questionnaires containing generic information to diagnose the state of an organization. Only the models of Halper and Krishnan (2013), Nott and Betteridge (2014), and Comuzzi and Patel (2016) provided meaningful descriptions of maturity stages. Thus, the next part of this paper focuses on the content of these three models as key enablers.

Halper and Krishnan (2013) are the pioneering authors who proposed the benchmark guidelines for the big data maturity model. In this model, the authors designed five stages of the maturity pathway—"nascent," "pre-adoption," "early adoption," "corporate adoption," and "mature." However, between the early adoption and the corporate adoption stages, there is a gap called "chasm." This is described as a hurdle that organizations need to overcome, because it is a significant milestone and organizations need to allocate large amounts of time for it to mature. The proposed model of Nott and Betteridge (2014) from IBM is based on the experience perspective, and the ideas are general and less detailed than those of the first counterpart authors. Comuzzi and Patel (2016) also refined features of selected maturity models to design a new one, which is based on all the identified domains.

Moreover, different from the models of Halper and Krishnan (2013) and Nott and Betteridge (2014), where domains are addressed directly, the model of Comuzzi and Patel (2016) defines some specific

Table 1. Big data maturity dimensions (adapted from Comuzzi and Patel [2016])

Big data maturity domain	Halper and Krishnan (2013)	El-Darwiche, Koch, Meer, Shehadi, and Tohme (2014)	Radcliffe (2014)	Nott and Betteridge (2014)	IDC (2013)	Info-Tech (2013)	Knowledgent (2014)	Dhanuka (2016)
Strategic alignment	-	-	Vision, and strategy	Business strategy	Intent	Business focus	-	Vision, strategy
Process	-	Sponsorship	Values and metrics	-	Process	-	Operating model	Sponsorship
Data analysis	Analytics	Data driven decision-making	Analytics and visualization	-	-	-	Analytics	Data analytics
Management	Data management	Customer segmentation; data availability	Trust, privacy, data management	-	Data	Data type and quality	-	Program measurement
Organization people	Organization	Organizational capability	People and organizations	-	People	Staff	Business environment	Skill set, practice, leadership
Culture	-	-	-	Culture and execution	-	-	-	-
Governance	Governance	Governance	Governance	-	Management and governance	-	-	Governance and budgeting
Information technology/ management	-	-	Data source	Information	Technology	Technology	Core information discipline	Analytics tools
IT infrastructure	Infrastructure	-	-	Architecture	-	-	Technology platform	Storage infrastructure

domains and creates subsets for each domain to describe a feature of each subset. Levels in this model are numerated from 1 to 5, which avoids differences in names of previous models.

Regarding traditional research in intelligence analytics, the social–technical aspects (human, organizational, and technical aspects) are the main domains, and the subsets of each domain are considered of less importance (Foshay et al., 2015). However, big data analytics maturity frameworks do not follow this methodology precisely, even though they retain all necessary features. Regarding the existing models, all three models (Comuzzi & Patel, 2016; Halper & Krishnan, 2013; Nott and Betteridge, 2014) include the abovementioned organizational, technical, and human aspects. However, the classifications differ for the organizational aspects (strategy and vision, including cost benefit analysis as a consideration for an organizational investment; analytical application; and governance) and the technical aspects (infrastructure and data management). For example, the model of Halper and Krishnan (2013) lists each category separately, without acknowledging the general social–technical aspect, and the model of Comuzzi and Patel (2016) uses "strategy alignment domain" to describe the strategy and process, and "organization domain" to include the human and culture considerations. In contrast, Nott and Betteridge (2014)'s model includes a "culture and operational execution dimension," where the key information is about business processes and analytics approaches in organizations.

Regarding the human aspects (skills and training for employees to apply the big data platform for analytics), Nott and Betteridge (2014)'s model does not include training as a dimension of the maturity framework, and in the model of Halper and Krishman (2013), training is only listed in the chasm gap between Level 3 (early adoption) and Level 4 (corporate adoption). Thus, the latter model only considers staff skills when the organization needs the incorporation of business activities because staff in a unit need to understand functions of other units for a smooth business operational process or when the organization needs to employ new staff with demanding skill sets. As in these models, Dhanuka (2016) mentioned skill sets for staff—and training programs improve the analytical capabilities of staff. Only Comuzzi and Patel (2016) thoroughly described the human analytics element. In fact, organizations may need to recruit more experts to gain more knowledge and practical management. Russom (2011) explained that the lack of experts in this field results in the fact that implementation is not an easy task for organizations, which suggests that it is necessary to hire experts to work in key roles in the project. These experts assist to plan the training programs for employment as well as to implement big data analytics in the organization.

Table 2 shows that, because of the multidisciplinary characteristic of the research topic, analysis of the security component reveals that some similar dimensions are required but with additional features. For example, the organizational structure includes procedures and operational processes involved in the information security governance category. Humans are a pivotal part in the security operation of an organization; therefore, demanding skill sets for security concerns may require employees with awareness and competence in advanced security. In another analysis involving the security investment perspective, cost vs. benefit is discussed with third-party management of the security dimension.

Review of the Security Maturity Model

The most noticeable point in the analysis of the outcome (Table 2) is that these models are not up to date. These models were mostly designed for general security programs, and the time frame of the analysis was from 2001 to 2011. Nevertheless, although this type of model is not the focus of current research, its information is also important to review. The most recent is the model of Muthukrishnan and Palaniap-

Table 2. Summary of various security maturity models (developed by the author)

Topic	Model name	Reference	Description
Information security	Generic information security maturity model	Lessing (2008)	Eight famous maturity models, which tackled different aspects in the organization situation including process, documentation, protection, and software design, are gathered. After that, the features are combined and optimized.
	Cybersecurity maturity model	Deloitte (2014)	The paper described a full landscape of cybersecurity maturity for different industries. The increase in security requirement level depends on the context of an organization (e.g., media and SMEs have less security requirements than do the banking sectors and military). In general, the model plans to develop incident-response strategy, asset protection, and training, and employ applications to manage and detect threats. The maturity is demonstrated by the well-prepared, automated, and well-developed strategies in the cybersecurity landscape.
	Information security maturity model	NIST (2005)	The model covered all business dimensions. Five steps of the model include policies, procedures, implementation, test, and integration. With the model, authors argued that polices are essential to address all specific criteria.
	Information security maturity model	Saleh (2011)	The model concerns the compliance of security programs in organizations. Where policies and procedures tare needed to secure business, human factors and infrastructure development are factors of maturity in the security program.
	Information security maturity model	Alaboodi (2007)	The model takes into account technology, humans, and processes as main domains of the security posture, which assist the business performance and continuity. The technology/infrastructure layer is considered physical, and environmental security at the bottom line and moving up the hierarchy to a definite security layer. Three fundamental security processes are prevention, protection, and recovery. The human side captures the effect by sophistication and visibility indices.
Community cybersecurity	Community cybersecurity maturity model	White (2007)	The model is for national scale, and focuses are threat preventions, metrics, information sharing, training, technology, and testing. In the scope of the topic, this paper is useful to examine technology as an aspect that an organization should keep on a par with national infrastructure, as it enables applications toward national standards to protect the business. Information sharing is important as it reinforces and increases data sets and sizes, which increase the accuracy of validation.
Process orientation and risk reduction	Information security management maturity model	Canal (2004)	The increase in the level of investment in information security management processes can help to reduce technical threats and even internal risk if a significant maturity level (i.e., Level 4) is achieved. The optimized level (Level 5) is the realm for compulsory use and continuous improvements of process metrics.
Security metrics	Security metrics maturity model for operational security	Muthukrishnan and Palaniappan (2016)	Dashboard and intelligence are key elements of the model. The maturity model shows the evolution of analytics metrics from ad hoc to highly automated dashboards to detect threats as an organization-wide strategy.
Governance	Information security governance maturity model	William (2001)	Based on the security capability maturity model, the information security governance maturity model includes six stages including non-existent, initial, repeatable, defined, managed, and optimized. Key considerations are: risks management regarding processes, policies, responsibilities and awareness, incident response, and well-prepared reports addressing the whole organization.
Humans	Information security competence maturity model	Thomson and von Solms (2006)	The research focuses on human awareness and competence built and developed by training and educational programs, and how staff subsequently accumulate experience via organizational contexts to achieve the mature stage. The highest level of awareness is described as an employee who can work as second-nature behavior, and as a corporate culture state.
IT outsourcing	Maturity model for IT outsource relationship	Gottschalk and Solli-Sæther (2006)	Cloud computing is the most common feature of a big data platform where an organization cannot develop a data center by itself. Information outsourcing, external data, and systems integration are at critical risk level. The research conducts three stages that can support the compatibility of client and vendor capabilities in finance, infrastructure/human skills, and strategy alignment.
Resilience	Business resilience management model	Caralli, Allen, Curtis, White, and Young (2010)	The model is based on operational resilience processes in organizations, and includes the initial levels with various shortcomings where the whole picture is not well addressed to further development stages where statistical analysis is employed to measure the performance of processes.
Identity	Cloud computing identity maturity model	Palson Kennedy and Gopal (2010)	The maturity model describes access authority level in an organization, administration activities, and cost burden. The increase in authorizing level of access privilege can increase the security status, as well as reduce administration tasks and costs in the organization.

pan (2016), which focuses on an emerging feature—security metrics and intelligence. Because of the escalation of cybercrime, this research only recruited the latest models, considered competent to handle modern attacks, including those of Deloitte (2014) and Muthukrishnan and Palaniappan (2016). The current research also employed older models if they were relevant to the final model, and had subsections providing details for each category.

The Human Aspect From the Information Security Perspective

Thomson and von Solms (2006) developed a maturity model on information security competence, which enables organizations to characterize and generate employee awareness. Ideally, organizations provide training and educational programs for staff to reach the maturity competence. In the model, employee competence develops through four stages—(1) unconscious incompetence, (2) conscious incompetence, (3) conscious competence, and (4) unconscious competence—to finally reach corporate information security obedience. The external factors contributing to the development in each stage of the maturity level include raising awareness, training, education, and experience, respectively (Figure 2).

In addition, Thomson, von Solms, and Louw (2006) identified a relationship between information security and corporate culture in organizations. In the mature stage of Thomson and von Solms's model (2006), employees, after acknowledging information security, need to regard it as second nature in daily activities involved in information security practices and as the culture of the business— so-called corporate information security obedience (Thomson et al., 2006). Thus, for the human dimension of the current proposed model, employee competence is considered in both analytical skills (Halper & Krishman, 2013) and security awareness and competence (Thomson & von Solms, 2006).

Figure 2. Information security competence maturity model
(Thomson & von Solms, 2006)

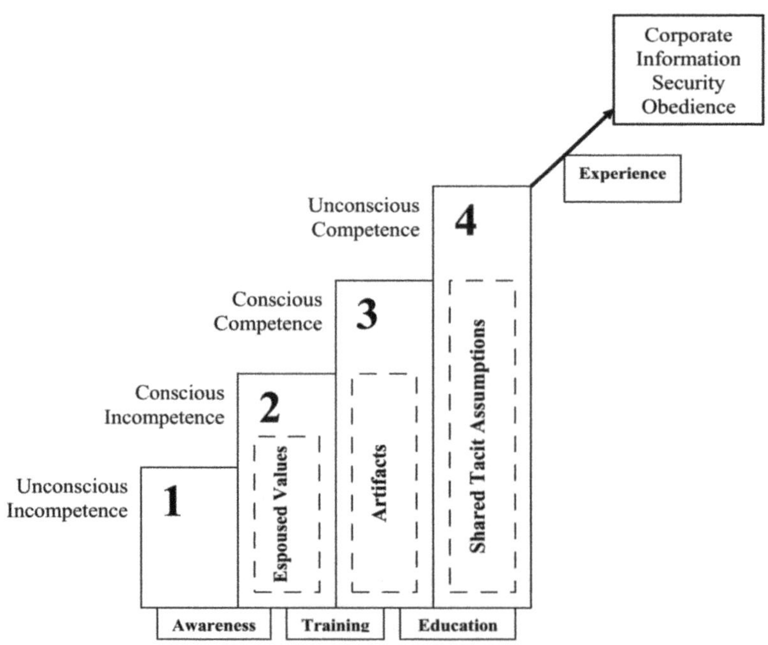

Security Dimension

Lessing (2008) identified eight famous maturity models that dealt with various aspects in the organization situation (including process, documentation, protection, and software design), then combined and optimized the features. The general maturity model includes five significant steps (Table 3). The shortcoming of that research is that the cyber element is not fully revealed; in addition, application of intelligence analytics for the security issue is not included in the papers.

Alaboodi (2007) worked on a model that includes humans, process components, and technology in layers as the infrastructure maturity framework for an organization. Key features on humans and processes are covered in other domains of the model, and the infrastructure is the only aspect to which the current model should refer.

Alternatively, on the basis of industrial practices, Deloitte (2014) composed a maturity model for cybersecurity contexts. In Deloitte's paper (2014), the major focus is the application of cybersecurity, and intelligence and cyber infrastructure are comprehensively described. In this framework, the details of capabilities and services of an organization need to be identified and in place to handle incidents and significantly reduce cyberattacks. Deloitte (2014) explained that, depending on the level of transaction confidentialities and time sensitiveness of an industry, higher levels of security maturity need to be satisfied. However, because of the details provided as a checklist to follow, organizations to some extent cannot achieve all items mentioned in this stage. Moreover, different industries require different standards and vulnerability levels, which makes it challenging for organizations to realize their levels.

Alternatively, Muthukrishnan and Palaniappan (2016) deployed a maturity model based on security metrics only. This model is only a generic description of metric/analytics competence in an organization, but is compatible with the details of Deloitte's cybersecurity maturity framework. Thus, the current research amalgamated Muthukrishnan and Palaniappan's (2016), Deloitte's (2014), and Lessing's (2008) works with specific key requirements to develop the security dimension for the framework.

Table 3. Generic information security maturity model (Source: Lessing, 2008)

Level	Characteristics
Level 1: Blind trusting Physical and environment focus	Physical security Lack of confidence Basic computer and network protection
Level 2: Repeatable Front-end system security	Critical review of organization Appoint security team Some level of confidence Formal security policies/procedure
Level 3: Defined Back-end system security	Initiation of security program Security architecture Stricter security controls Organization-wide policies/procedures
Level 4: Managed All-inclusive security awareness	Security testing Mitigate security weakness Information management Identity security threats
Level 5: Maintenance Definite proactive security	Full implementation of policies/procedures Consistent outcomes Automated security control

The community cybersecurity maturity model of White (2007) represents the community standard adopted by the current model, which ensures that maturity levels in the proposed model match the community (national or international) standards.

Governance Dimension

This dimension is well covered in the abovementioned big data maturity models, but in this section, the governance framework is of greater concern for security, because many standards are essential for effective governance in an organization. A significant feature of the model of Williams (2001) is that risks, vulnerabilities, and threats assessment and control are included in the scope of security governance. This research involved the procedures, policies, responsibilities, and accountabilities for IT security and continuous services. The security maturity models of NIST (2005) and Saleh (2011) also described the maturity level according to the procedures and policies in organizations. While NIST (2005) mentioned that policies are key requirements that lead to security improvement, Saleh (2011) focused on compliance at each level, where procedures and policies evolve and mature to adapt to all business activities. However, resilience in handling attacks is not described in detail.

Incident response is acknowledged as a key requirement for a complete security program, and enables an organization whose incident has been eradicated to recover the resources damaged in the incident. It is essential to find and fix the loophole to prevent the incident from reoccurring, as having the backup to restore the system without realizing the root cause is not a sustainable solution in the era of modern attacks (Talabis et al., 2014). Resilience is the key element that contributes to the effectiveness of a security system, as this feature demonstrates that the security system can handle incidents and that backup plans can recover the system immediately.

Caralli et al. (2010) developed a resilience management model, to improve the operational resilience process in organizations, which addresses the overall situation in security incidents. From the 'initial' to the 'optimizing' status (Levels 1 to 5), the operational resilience processes (so-called processes) in organizations evolve through initial (Level 1) resilience processes targeting specific but limited goals; defined and managed (Levels 3 & 4), refining and improving, processes, which are tailored to a standard that is consistent across units; and optimizing (Level 5) processes, which use statistics to measure the quality and performance of processes (Caralli et al., 2010). This feature is synthesized and displayed in the governance dimension of the final maturity model.

IT Outsourcing Dimension

'Cloud'-based services are a common platform for organizations that cannot build the data center by themselves (Russom, 2011). However, this also increases the risk of loopholes for attacks. Thus, an IT outsourcing relationship maturity model was designed to enable organizations to implement and develop in the situation. That research developed a three-stage model for the evolution of the outsourcing relationship, including (1) the cost stage, costs based on transactions and economic theory; (2) the resource stage, resources and competencies of the organization; and (3) the partnership stage, stakeholder and social exchange (Gottschalk & Solli-Sæther, 2006). This dimension is included in the proposed model as the first three stages (Levels 1, 2, & 3), because IT outsourcing (i.e., cloud infrastructure) constitutes the groundwork for organizations to optimize sources to reach the managed and optimizing stages. Therefore, organizations need to exploit these resources to gain the competitive advantage.

To increase the level of security when employing third-party platforms, protocol and identity management are addressed. The maturity stage of this is focusing on individual access level control and audit trail effectiveness, which can reduce administration tasks as well as transaction costs, and improve security levels (PalsonKennedy & Gopal, 2010).

Articulating the Maturity Models

Because of the variety of names and domains reported in different research papers, the current proposed framework synthesizes the reviewed big data maturity models by using the domains in the framework of Halper and Krishnan (2013) as a structural template (Table 4). This approach was adopted because the framework of Halper and Krishnan (2013) provides comprehensive descriptions, which can be used to articulate the other selected big data maturity frameworks.

The security domain is the main indicator to summarize all necessary features, but selected models for governance, resilience, process, human and identity features are allocated in suitable domains as shown above. Instead of having all information about security in a domain, human competence is allocated to the human domain, identity to the infrastructure domain, and governance and process policies–related elements to the governance domain of the final model.

A MATURITY FRAMEWORK FOR BIG DATA CYBERSECURITY ANALYTICS

Table 5, based on the comprehensive literature review, presents the synthesized comprehensive maturity framework for BDCA. In general, there are seven dimensions in the framework—namely, organization, human, infrastructure, data management, analytics application, governance, and security dimensions.

Table 4. Mapping the component maturity models into the final framework

Proposed framework domains (adapted from Halper and Krishnan [2013])	Big data maturity model domains (Table 1 summary)	Security maturity model domains (Table 2 summary)
Organization	Strategic alignment Culture	
Human	Organization people	Human
Infrastructure	IT infrastructure	Identity
Data management	IT management Management	
Analytics application	Data analysis	
Governance	Process Governance	Governance Resilience Process and risk
Security		Security metrics Information security Community security IT outsourcing

Table 5. Big data cybersecurity analytics maturity model

Dimension	Level 1: Initial	Level 2: Repeatable	Level 3 – Defined	Level 4 – Managed	Level 5: Optimizing
1/ Organization (vision and funding)	Big data analytics is discussed as choices of individuals, not an organization-wide perspective. Security programs such as responses to attacks are implemented but not continuous.	A common road map is defined, and organizations start to consider protecting investments. The mindset in traditional companies is experimental rather than organization-wide strategies. Analytics for the decision-making process is used with skepticism. Internet-based firms grasp the chance to implement and set up goals quickly.	More executives are interested in and involved in the project, with a wider scope of big data application; this also centralizes the management of all security-related issues Consideration about cost as a burden appears.	Organizations realize that analytics is a competitive differentiator—more practice of analytics for strategies. Having control over security requires monitoring systems The funding process is secured, and an ROI is in place for big data analytics.	Analytics is seen as a competitive weapon and the mindset is creative. The business is always looking for opportunities to use analytics in new ways and corporate big data as part of culture.
2/ Human (training, skill set, commercial, and culture)	Unconscious incompetence—staff are unaware of their roles in security and think about it as a hindrance rather than a benefit. Big data analytics is really new, so it is jointly limited use of data for analytics.	Conscious incompetence—information security awareness program to raise the awareness of information security roles and responsibilities and benefits from this.	Conscious competence—training program assists employees in learning vital skills, and applying this to hands-on activities. Employees can use big data analytics, but still lack knowledge, so hiring experts to train staff is essential.	Unconscious competence—long term learning is in place to upgrade employees' knowledge and attitude toward information security. Specific skill sets are required to operate big data technology, and skill sets also apply to security analytics; an education program is the choice for this.	Employees' behavior becomes second nature in daily activities and toward information security practices. Staffs can optimize experience to make innovative solutions for the organization.
3/ Infrastructure	Information architecture is fragmented. It is essential for data management to have an in-depth understanding of the new infrastructure to support critical big data components.	Installation, configuration and maintenance are defined There is a level of compliance to an enterprise standard, although the class of infrastructure may not be close to production or may be utilized for a basic use case Cloud performance: the organization starts with the initial role of individual level access, and even timely deprovisioning of login and access privileges can happen. Consolidating administration system to reduce cost from system administrators.	The standard for defined installation, configuration and maintenance appears. A typical infrastructure is a tier 2 production-class cluster that is installed and maintained in a data center or the cloud. Cloud performance: faster turn-around times on request that do not impede projects. Reduce administration tasks and operational costs.	The infrastructure and architecture of the big data ecosystem comply with backup and recovery or disaster recovery procedures. Organization infrastructure is a tier 1 production-class cluster that is installed and maintained in the data center, including cloud. Cloud performance: auditing by role and by person using the resources. Role-based security is auditable and trackable.	The organization has to manage the complexity of infrastructure. It employs new sources in both internal and external data. Cloud performance: reduction of deployment cost and faster internal development. Secured integration through extensible markup language. Enterprise-wide security strategy

continued on following page

Table 5. Continued

Dimension	Level 1: Initial	Level 2: Repeatable	Level 3 – Defined	Level 4 – Managed	Level 5: Optimizing
4/ Data management	Data warehouse exists, but data are continued to be collected. Data unification is unseen, leading to chaotic format and storage structure.	Some big data sources (which are typically internal) are identified and collected as part of an experimental process. Metadata and a defined end-state data architecture exist, but files are still in different formats.	Files are in different formats, but they potentially have division or enterprise standards for naming and storage management. The organization is moving at a fast pace to implement big data initiatives; they are aware of issues related to data quality and security.	The organization is always looking for new data to enhance its analytics; organizations can make forms of data, and sharing is a collaborative activity. Data soiling is minimized in this phase, and the organization sees values from all components of the data infrastructure.	The program is treated as a critical mission and given the right amount of staffing and skills. Data are shared across the organization.
5/ Analytics application	Silo analytics, for specific targets only. Structured data and predictive analytics are common at this stage.	Can involve outside consultation for analytics strategy. Explored some kinds of advanced analytics.	Internal data including unstructured ones (i.e., network monitoring, or using location data and unstructured social media data for isolated department analytics). Utilizing descriptive or even predictive analytics in its projects.	Analytics might be automated or integrated with the business process. Analytics supports the whole organization. Typically, the organization has a center of excellence (COE) in place, which serves different parts of the organization.	The mindset is to continually develop analytics, which makes use of all kinds of data, including real-time data. The visionary organization can connect the dots between new data and existing assets.
6/ Governance (together with operational resilience process)	IT risk is in an ad hoc manner, without following defined processes or policies. "Finger pointing" responses if detected. Informal responsibilities for continuous service.	Some approaches to risk assessment exist, but the process is still immature and developing. Security policies are being developed, but inadequate skills and tools are still being used. Fragmented approach to responsibilities for continuous service.	Risk assessment follows a defined process that is documented and available to all staff. IT security procedures are defined and fit into a structure for security policies and procedures. Management communicates consistently the need for continuous service.	Risk assessment is a standard procedure, and exceptions would be noticed by IT management. Security policies and practices are completed with specific security baselines. Responsibilities and standards for continuous service are enforced.	Risk assessment is under a structured, organization-wide process with good management. Security requirements are clearly defined, optimized, and included in a verified security plan. Continuous service plans and business continuity plans are integrated, aligned, and routinely maintained.
7/ Security (third-party element is for cloud outsource maturity only)	Ad hoc, chaotic individual efforts, poor measuring with very few processes, and inconsistent metrics. Contracting/third-party management (if any) with concerns on rights, responsibility, and risk preferences.	Some measurement processes exist; mostly non-repeatable, still highly ad hoc. Manipulating third-party resources (i.e., technical competence, aligning to business and relationship management).	Early adoption of SIEM (security information event management) system, establish process, more repeatable measurement. Considering third party as an alliance for intangible value and gaining the mutually compatible goals.	Establish a stable process and SIEM exist, basic dashboards exist, and repeatable measurement produced. Third party involved in defined process for security incident reporting.	Optimized, established, fully automated, and meaningful SIEM-based metrics exist. Comprehensive security metrics dashboard and periodic security posture report exist. Third-party collaborated incident-response testing.

For this final framework, available models in the literature review were assembled. According to Comuzzi and Patel (2016), big data maturity models always resemble and refine the common structure of previous maturity models. There are many common features that do not include any factors that may prevent alignment. Thus, it is convenient to classify and align different big data maturity models together. The only issue here is the determinant level of cloud outsourcing, which was based on the priority of this event in the implementation life cycle. Cloud infrastructure is built after a business case analysis and a third-party contract are approved; therefore, the IT outsource model was placed as the first three stages of the final framework before further applications.

Conversely, the main characteristics of cybersecurity maturity models are IT infrastructure development and application of analytics. This pattern is very similar to that of the maturity framework considered for the big data component. (The governance and security domains described in past research are based on significant security standards, such as ISO27001 and COBIT, and guided the current maturity standards, resulting in significant alignment with the final model).

To provide details of the construction procedure, the following descriptions reveal how the 'backbone framework' was articulated to its counterparts.

Organization Domain

This section is based mainly on the descriptions of Halper and Krishnan (2013). In addition, the ideas of Nott and Betteridge (2014) and of Comuzzi and Patel (2016) on strategy and road maps in big data analytics are adopted as this domain in Levels 1 and 2. Further, Saleh's (2011) statement about business attention to protection (considered as vision), is included in this domain.

Human Domain

The focus here is the competence of employees toward security in an organization, as described by Thomson and von Solms (2006). Also relevant is the suggestion by Thomson et al. (2006) and Comuzzi and Patel (2016) that an organization's culture is the reflection of human behavior, and if appropriate behavior is second nature, employee performances can reach the mature stage. Because application of big data analytics is more about software and solutions, which is included in the analytics application domain, only the culture of analytics application is included here. Comuzzi and Patel (2016) stated that there is an increasing positive trend in organizations toward the application from Level 1 to Level 5.

Infrastructure Domain

Big data infrastructure is a specific IT asset, and the domain is described using Halper and Krishnan's (2013) criteria in terms of the alignment of this infrastructure to the current state of the organization. This also requires that the infrastructure is suitable for various big data technologies. In addition, because most big data infrastructure systems employ the cloud platform for storage, the maturity model of cloud performance of PalsonKennedy and Gopal (2010) is mapped in this domain.

Data Management Domain

Data for big data analytics are the combination of internal and external data, even if formats differ between departments and divisions. The maturity is evaluated by the unified data strategy, and how an organization can use it as an organization-wide asset that can be shared and managed effectively. The content is described meticulously by Halper and Krishnan (2013), and only some minor ideas on polices and management extracted from the model of Comuzzi and Patel (2016) are added here.

Analytics Application Domain

In this section, Halper and Krishnan (2013) mapped the maturity by types of data employed in different stages, such as (a) simple structured data in initial levels, (b) other data such as semi-structured and unstructured data in moderate levels, and (c) various data types with techniques such as descriptive and predictive for organization purposes (e.g., process quality and security). Comuzzi and Patel (2016) comprehensively described the domain by considering the software applied in practice. This is the key feature acknowledged in this domain.

Governance Domain

This domain includes the governance guidelines of Halper and Krishnan (2013) for big data, the information security of Williams (2001), and the resilience operation process of Caralli et al. (2010). The ideas about governance of Comuzzi and Patel (2016) involve staff awareness about the role of big data; that feature is included in the human domain, so is not mapped here.

Security Domain

Muthukrishnan and Palaniappan (2016) described the maturity of security metrics by the development from ad hoc to SIEM measurement. In addition, Deloitte (2014) developed a detailed model for maturity in cybersecurity, which considered the latest analytics and intelligence techniques and standards for policies, and incident-response plans. Conversely, third-party management is an important standard, which can create loopholes if it is not carefully prepared. Gottschalk and Solli-Sæther (2006) underlined this feature in their outsource relationship maturity model. The summary and combination of these three papers constitute the main content of this domain.

CONCLUSION

This research examined and gathered the common features of various maturity models of big data analytics and of cybersecurity components. Various research papers were reviewed, and commonly described factors were considered important and included in the current maturity model. Thereafter, the factors of the two fields were combined to form a unique maturity model for BDCA.

In terms of research contribution, this study fills a research gap and provides a maturity model for BDCA. Many technique proposals for using big data analytics in cybersecurity exist, but without a comprehensive guideline for the implementation. This study represents one of the first studies that offers a comprehensive framework covering different dimensions, evolutionary stages of each dimension, and guidelines to proceed to the next level. It also lays a baseline foundation for future research.

Along with the maturity model, a diagnostic toolkit is provided to evaluate the maturity of BDCA practice. The diagnostic toolkit, with marking criteria, offers a convenient way to determine the maturity level of an organization. Details of the maturity model and the questionnaire are available at https://tinyurl.com/bdcsaMM.

In practical contexts, big data analytics in cybersecurity are a two-edged knife if executives use it carelessly. Despite the potential benefits of big data analytics, security attacks are diverse and fast escalating, which makes data complicated to analyses. Thus, security analytics should be an organization-wide continuous strategy and remain current to address potential issues to protect the organization. In this paper, the toolkit enables the organization to develop gap analysis and strategies for business improvement. It is also the benchmark for organizations to criticize their current positions and how they can proceed to a higher stage to handle and detect worldwide modern attacks. Hayden (2010) highlighted the need for increased alignments of common security controlling frameworks into a unique program to facilitate control and management. Therefore, it is applicable to standardize the security program by integrating the maturity model into the whole security program to evaluate the performance. In fact, the maturity of BDCA provides more powerful measurements for the security program in terms of policies, incident-response plans, and cyber-ecosystem safety. This is because security metrics in the context of regulatory compliance or conformance to other control structures support organizations to develop innovative measurements to cover situations and security performance indicators (Hayden, 2010).

Widespread cybercrime attacks make it challenging for an organization to solve the problem. It is desirable for organizations to have intelligence practices in place to enable recognition of cybercrime patterns and security information sharing among organizations, and real-time information and techniques to detect and prevent cyberattacks (Johnson, Badger, Waltermire, Snyder, & Skorupka, 2016; PwC, 2016). The maturity model contribution is regarded as a common standard for organizations to follow, which makes information sharing easier. The developed framework reinforces the confidence of organizations to proceed to a new desired approach with minimum risk. In the landscape of various cases of cyberattacks and security issues, the model is a basic guideline for security investment in an organization. Canal (2006) argued that security investment is averse to risk; maturity in security enables mitigation of risk factors, resulting in relevant economic benefits.

In terms of limitations, this research deployed a literature survey–based method, resulting in a rigid approach rather than significant outcomes derived from empirical analysis or design science research. This warrants validation from an expert panel or through a questionnaire survey. Moreover, the rapid changes in the digital era necessitate regular updates to the maturity model. In particular, social media analytics is an attractive and informative big data source but is challenging to exploit, which is not addressed in the chapter. Future research may apply the proposed model in real-world companies and test its usefulness.

In conclusion, this research offers an overarching framework with a systematic set of guidelines for the maturity of BDCA. It provides a structured road map for organizations to confidently invest in a new but potential platform, as all necessary features for BDCA development are captured and included. It is also a stepping stone for new research in terms of techniques and domains for future cybersecurity requirements.

REFERENCES

Alaboodi, S. S. (2007). *Towards evaluating security implementations using the Information Security Maturity Model (ISMM)* (Master's thesis). University of Waterloo.

Canal, V. A. (2004). *ISM3 1.0. Information security management maturity model*. Retrieved from https://pdfs.semanticscholar.org/64ac/1e4585056babd78d978827bf35eae78b5ff6.pdf

Caralli, R. A., Allen, J. H., Curtis, P. D., White, D. W., & Young, L. R. (2010). *CERT® resilience management model, version 1.0: Improving operational resilience processes* (Technical report). Retrieved from http://www.sei.cmu.edu/reports/10tr012.pdf

Comuzzi, M., & Patel, A. (2016). How organisations leverage big data: A maturity model. *Industrial Management & Data Systems*, *116*(8), 1468–1492. doi:10.1108/IMDS-12-2015-0495

Crosby, P. B. (1979). *Quality is free*. New York, NY: McGraw-Hill.

Cybenko, G., & Landwehr, C. E. (2012). Security analytics and measurements. *IEEE Security and Privacy*, *10*(3), 5–8. doi:10.1109/MSP.2012.75

Deloitte. (2014). *Cybersecurity: Empowering the CIO* (Report). Retrieved from https://www2.deloitte.com/au/en/pages/risk/articles/cyber-security.html

Dhanuka, V. (2016). *Hortonworks big data maturity model: The strategic path to accelerating business transformations* (White paper). Retrieved from http://hortonworks.com/wp-content/uploads/2016/04/Hortonworks-Big-Data-Maturity-Assessment.pdf

El-Darwiche, B., Koch, V., Meer, D., Shehadi, R., & Tohme, W. (2014). Big data maturity: An action plan for policymakers and executives. In B. Bilbao-Osorio, S. Dutta, & B. Lanvin (Eds.), *The global information technology report* (pp. 43–53). Geneva, Switzerland: World Economic Forum and INSEAD.

Foshay, N., Yeoh, W., Boo, Y. L., Ong, K.-L., & Mattie, D. (2015). A comprehensive diagnostic framework for evaluating business intelligence and analytics effectiveness. *AJIS. Australasian Journal of Information Systems*, 19.

Gottschalk, P., & Solli-Sæther, H. (2006). Maturity model for IT outsourcing relationships. *Industrial Management & Data Systems*, *106*(2), 200–212. doi:10.1108/02635570610649853

Halper, F., & Krishnan, K. (2013). *TDWI big data maturity model guide: Interpreting your assessment score* (Benchmark guide). Retrieved from http://www.pentaho.com/sites/default/files/uploads/resources/tdwi_big_data_maturity_model_guide_2013.pdf

Hayden, L. (2010). *IT security metrics: A practical framework for measuring security & protecting data*. New York, NY: McGraw-Hill Education.

Humphrey, W. S. (1988). Characterizing the software process: A maturity framework. *IEEE Software*, *5*(2), 73–79. doi:10.1109/52.2014

IDC. (2013). *Big data maturity tool*. Retrieved from http://csc.bigdatamaturity.com/

Info-Tech. (2013). *Big data maturity assessment tool.* Retrieved from https://www.infotech.com/research/ss/leverage-big-data-by-starting-small/it-big-data-maturity-assessment-tool

Jegede, A. E. (2016). Modern information technology, global risk, and the challenges of crime in the era of late modernity. In O. Nelson, B. R. Ojebuyi, & A. Salawu (Eds.), *Impacts of the Media on African Socio-Economic Development* (pp. 18–33). Hershey, PA: IGI Global.

Johnson, C., Badger, L., Waltermire, D., Snyder, J., & Skorupka, C. (2016). *Guide to cyber threat information sharing* (Special publication). Retrieved from http://nvlpubs.nist.gov/nistpubs/SpecialPublications/NIST.SP.800-150.pdf

Knowledgent. (2014). *Big data maturity assessment.* Retrieved from https://bigdatamaturity.knowledgent.com/

Lainhart, J. W. IV. (2000). COBIT™: A methodology for managing and controlling information and information technology risks and vulnerabilities. *Journal of Information Systems, 14*(Suppl. 1), 21–25. doi:10.2308/jis.2000.14.s-1.21

Lessing, M. M. (2008, September). *Best practices show the way to information security maturity.* Paper presented at the 6th National Conference on Process Establishment, Assessment and Improvement in Information Technology (ImproveIT 2008), Johannesburg, South Africa.

Mahmood, T., & Afzal, U. (2013). Security analytics: Big data analytics for cybersecurity—A review of trends, techniques and tools. In *Proceedings of the 2013 2nd National Conference on Information Assurance* (pp. 129–134). IEEE. 10.1109/NCIA.2013.6725337

Matrane, O., Talea, M., & Okar, C. (2014). Towards a new maturity model for information security management. *International Journal of Advanced Research in Computer Science and Software Engineering, 4*(6).

Musthaler, L. (2013). *Security analytics will be the next big thing in IT security* (Opinion). Retrieved from https://www.networkworld.com/article/2166806/infrastructure-management/security-analytics-will-be-the-next-big-thing-in-it-security.html

Muthukrishnan, S. M., & Palaniappan, S. (2016). Security metrics maturity model for operational security. In *2016 IEEE Symposium on Computer Applications & Industrial Electronics ISCAIE* (pp. 101–106). IEEE. 10.1109/ISCAIE.2016.7575045

NIST. (2005). *Program review for information security management assistance: Security maturity levels.* Retrieved from http://csrc.nist.gov/groups/SMA/prisma/security_maturity_levels.html

Nott, C., & Betteridge, N. (2014). Big data and analytics maturity model [Web log post]. Retrieved from http://www.ibmbigdatahub.com/blog/big-data-analytics-maturity-model

PalsonKennedy, R., & Gopal, T. (2010). Assessing the risks and opportunities of cloud computing—defining identity management systems and maturity models. In Trendz in Information Sciences & Computing (pp. 138–142). Academic Press.

Paulk, M. C., Curtis, B., Chrissis, M. B., & Weber, C. V. (1993). Capability maturity model, version 1.1. *IEEE Software, 10*(4), 18–27. doi:10.1109/52.219617

PwC. (2016). *Toward new possibilities in threat management.* Retrieved from http://www.pwc.com/gx/en/issues/cyber-security/information-security-survey/assets/gsiss-report-cybersecurity-privacy-possibilities.pdf

Radcliffe, J. (2014). *Leverage a big data maturity model to build your big data roadmap.* Retrieved from www.radcliffeadvisory.com/research/download.php?file=RAS_BD_MatMod.pdf

Russom, P. (2011). *Executive summary: Big data analytics.* Retrieved from https://tdwi.org/research/2011/09/~/media/TDWI/TDWI/Research/BPR/2011/TDWI_BPReport_Q411_Big_Data_Analytics_Web/TDWI_BPReport_Q411_Big%20Data_ExecSummary.ashx

Saleh, M. F. (2011). Information security maturity model. *International Journal of Computer Science and Security, 5*, 316–337.

Shackleford, D. (2016). *Using analytics to predict future attacks and breaches* (Press release). Retrieved from https://www.sans.org/reading-room/whitepapers/analyst/analytics-predict-future-attacks-breaches-36720

Sullivan, D. (2015). *Introduction to big data security analytics in the enterprise.* Retrieved from http://searchsecurity.techtarget.com/feature/Introduction-to-big-data-security-analytics-in-the-enterprise

Talabis, M., McPherson, R., Miyamoto, I., & Martin, J. (2014). *Information Security Analytics: Finding Security Insights, Patterns, and Anomalies in Big Data.* Syngress.

Thamir, A., & Theodoulidis, B. (2013). Business intelligence maturity models: Information management perspective. In *International Conference on Information and Software Technologies* (pp. 198–221). Academic Press. 10.1007/978-3-642-41947-8_18

Thomson, K.-L., & von Solms, R. (2006). Towards an information security competence maturity model. *Computer Fraud & Security, 2006*(5), 11–15. doi:10.1016/S1361-3723(06)70356-6

Thomson, K.-L., von Solms, R., & Louw, L. (2006). Cultivating an organizational information security culture. *Computer Fraud & Security, 2006*(10), 7–11. doi:10.1016/S1361-3723(06)70430-4

White, G. B. (2007). The community cyber security maturity model. In *40th Annual Hawaii International Conference on System Sciences* (pp. 99). Academic Press.

Williams, P. (2001). Information security governance. *Information Security Technical Report, 6*(3), 60–70. doi:10.1016/S1363-4127(01)00309-0

Chapter 10
Developing Strategic Capability Through Business Intelligence Applications:
A Case Study From the German Healthcare Insurance Industry

Martin George Wynn
University of Gloucestershire, UK

Daniel Brinkmann
University of Gloucestershire, UK

ABSTRACT

Company performance can be measured at all levels across an organization, and in the German healthcare industry, business intelligence systems play a crucial role in achieving this. For one major health insurance company (discussed here as an alias – AK Healthcare), the deployment of business intelligence applications has supported sustained growth in turnover and market share in the past five years. In this chapter, these tools are classified within an appropriate conceptual framework which encompasses the organization's information infrastructure and associated processes. Different components of the framework are identified and examples are given: systems infrastructure, data provision/access control, the BI tools and technologies, report generation, and information users. The use and integration of business intelligence tools in the strategy development process is then analyzed, and the key functions and features of these tools for strategic capability development are discussed. Research findings encompass system access, report characteristics, and end-users' capabilities.

INTRODUCTION

Many companies have made significant investment in enterprise-wide information systems in an attempt to work faster and smarter. However, software packages such as Enterprise Resource Planning (ERP), Customer Relationship Management (CRM) and Supply Chain Management (SCM) systems often produce large amounts of data but little information. Companies are beginning to explore the potential of

DOI: 10.4018/978-1-5225-5718-0.ch010

new Business Intelligence (BI) products and technologies, which can exploit their corporate databases to improve management control and assess the impact of key business decisions. A sound technology platform that supports integrated information systems is a key requirement that needs addressing as a company expands. To harness the full potential of corporate knowledge, the use of BI tools will be necessary in most market environments. Sound core systems and effective BI tools deployment are the pre-requisites for the management of corporate knowledge relating to new market and product development, quality standards enhancement and process improvement.

BI information and its exploitation for key decision-making can play a vital role in underpinning strategic choice and corporate profitability. Operational data must be processed, analysed and reported in order to control and measure the performance of a company and its management. Effective and timely business information is recognized as being essential for organizations to succeed, but also simply to exist in today's rapidly changing and challenging business environment (Lönnqvist & Pirttimäki, 2006). According to Pisello & Strassman (2003), companies can gain competitive advantage not just by focusing on implementing new technologies, but also by deploying technology to share, manage, and increase the level of knowledge throughout the organization.

To improve the BI process, senior management should be cognizant of the effects and impact of BI on their organization – and they can also be key players and stakeholders in the integration of BI tools into the strategy development process. Company performance can be comprehensively measured at all levels across an organisation, but BI tools can contribute to the management of knowledge in certain key strategic areas. They can be used to improve the way internal business processes are executed so that an organization performs the same activities better than its competitors (Hemmatfar, Salehi, & Bayat, 2010). They may also be applied to performance management to allow organizations to track, understand, and manage vital business information. Such improvements increase employee and customer satisfaction, quality and productivity, and decrease time to market.

This research focuses on the capabilities of Business Intelligence (BI) tools and technologies to support strategic knowledge management that enhances competitive advantage. It explores which BI technologies and tools are currently used within AK Healthcare (AKH), how they are used, how they can be classified, their interaction with the strategy development process, and the key elements of these tools that support effective knowledge management. The objectives of BI deployment are discussed and relevant BI products for AKH are reviewed.

THEORETICAL FRAMEWORK

Since Zuboff (1988) introduced the concept of automate-informate-transformate as a sequential process for applying technology in business, there have been many definitions and classifications of systems providing management information as the link between manual process automation and radical business transformation. The concept of management information systems (MIS) was central to many information systems strategies in the 1990s to "provide information for managing an organization" (Alter, 2002), by extracting and summarising data from transaction processing systems. Peppard (1993) took these concepts further by developing a grid for viewing application portfolios from a strategic perspective, and the early focus on mainly financial information was expanded to include a broader range of information to plan and control business operations. The balanced scorecard (Kaplan and Norton, 1992), for example, contains not only a financial view of a company, but also the customer view, internal operational information, and human resource perspectives such as innovation and learning. Since the turn of the century, the concept of Corporate Performance Management (CPM) systems has emerged, which Gartner defines as "the combination of methodologies, metrics, processes and systems used to monitor and manage the business performance of an enterprise" (Buytendijk *et al*, 2004). Business Intelligence tools and systems have emerged as the key technologies to facilitate CPM and help organizations to manage, develop, and communicate intangible assets such as information and knowledge. It is often considered essential for organizations operating in the current knowledge-based economy (Alnoukari, 2009). BI is discussed by Gansor, Totok, & Stock (2010) as an analytical process that transfers internal and external data into appropriate knowledge to support decision-making. The term BI has also been defined as the collection, saving, analysis, and provision of data to support the decision-making processes of a company (Seufert & Oehler, 2009).

This paper assumes that relevant strategic data will be stored in a structured way in a data warehouse – a "subject-oriented, integrated and time-variant collection of data in support of management's decisions" (Inmon, 2002, p. 31). This is most likely to be the case in organisations that do not have one large integrated software package – an enterprise resource planning system - fulfilling their systems needs, where there may be less of a business case for a data warehouse. It is more prevalent in organisations – like AKH – where a best of breed systems strategy has been pursued, resulting in a range of different applications and data sources. In such situations, the data warehouse (DWH) is often a key component of overall systems strategy; and it is also the base infrastructural element of a BI system, allowing storage and structuring of data from various systems and external sources, supporting the provision of key management information (Figure 1).

"Big Data" is another relevant concept - large volumes of data from different data sources that can be identified and analyzed with the help of BI applications. Similar to analytics, Big Data should allow the generation of findings and insights that provide business advantage (McAfee & Brynjolfsson, 2012); and Big Data may also relate to specific subject areas and be stored in sub-areas of the DWH, often termed "data marts".

Strategic BI technologies and tools can be characterized by their ability to significantly change the manner in which business is conducted, providing an organisation with discernible strategic benefit (Turban *et al.*, 2006). BI technologies are perceived as instruments that generate the knowledge that supports or changes an organisation's strategy (Wiseman, 1985). Eckerson (2005) argues that BI must be able to provide data mining, planning, and modelling tools. BI includes a set of concepts, methods, and processes designed to improve business decisions, using information from multiple sources and applying past experience to develop a more precise understanding of business dynamics (Maria, 2005). It integrates the analysis of data with decision-analysis tools, with the purpose of improving strategic decisions. Although these tools may be used across an organization, it is often in the financial and management accounting areas of the business where BI applications are most in evidence. It is often these departments that are at the centre of strategic planning and knowledge management for the organization as a whole.

BI also encompasses predictive and explorative analytics, often collectively termed business analytics (Weber & Fohrholz, 2013). These tools follow on from the early online application processing (OLAP) tools that emerged in the 1990s, and their use requires multi-dimensional arrays or cube structures within the DWH as well as the more traditional relational database structures. These cube structures often relate to specific subject areas (e.g. customer profitability) and may be held as individual data marts. Predictive analytics are often used to forecast financial developments or consolidation activities with

Figure 1. Typical systems architecture underpinning BI tools deployment

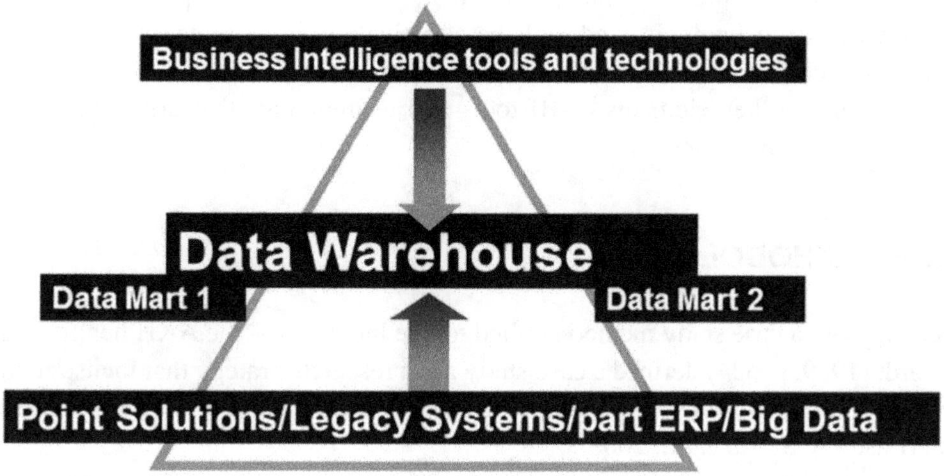

the aim of sustaining competitive advantage (Siegel, 2010). Explorative analytics, on the other hand, employ analytical and optimization methods to enable BI end-users to improve their understanding and interpretation of corporate data and information, and thereby generate new knowledge.

BI can change the way people work as individuals, in groups, and in the organization. People perform their work following business processes that are embedded in BI (Watson, 2010). Benefits attributed to BI may be non-financial and intangible, such as the improved quality and timeliness of information. Although such non-financial effects may lead to advantageous financial outcomes, there is often a time lag between the acquisition of information from BI and the related financial gain. Measuring BI benefits can thus be extremely difficult in practice (Lönnqvist & Pirttimäki, 2006). Carver & Ritacco (2006) conclude that the users of existing BI technologies and tools often emphasise that non-measurable benefits are worth more than measurable benefits. BI can be considered an essential component of a successful business in the current knowledge-based economy arena (Alnoukari, 2009). Changes in corporate-positioning or strategy can be implemented quickly for better and faster decision making. The business user's role is strengthened by reliance on effective information delivered via BI solutions. Whether acting upon a report as an end-user, or performing analytics as a business analyst or employee in management accounting, the BI end-user role provides flexibility for information delivery (Volitich, 2008).

The strategy development process is the essential top level activity where enhanced knowledge management can have a major strategic impact. This process can be divided into four sequential but overlapping steps: information analysis, strategy development, strategy implementation and strategy review (Fueglistaller *et al.*, 2005). By impacting upon this process, BI applications can make a major contribution to providing competitive advantage. For example, the incorporation of external data into BI applications and the DWH allows organizations to ascertain market reactions to competitors' sales campaigns. Health insurance companies may also develop and access critical information through BI tools deployment, in order to meet customer requirements in an increasingly complex world of processes and structures within the public healthcare sector. With this technology and business context as a backdrop, this article addresses three research questions (RQs), with specific reference to the AKH health insurance company:

- **RQ1:** How can BI technologies and tools be classified within an appropriate conceptual framework that encompasses the wider information management provision process?
- **RQ2:** How can BI technologies and tools be effectively used and integrated within the strategy development process?
- **RQ3:** What are the key elements of BI tools and technologies that are needed to support the knowledge management process?

RESEARCH METHODOLOGY

This research employs a case study method applied to one large case – the AKH health insurance company. Eisenhardt (1989, p. 534) defined a case study as "a research strategy that focuses on understanding the dynamics present within single settings." The case study can focus on a single case or a single organization (Easterby-Smith *et al.*, 2008).

The research questions were used to generate sets of sub-questions for one-to-one interviews with twelve AKH employees, most of which are BI tools users. For RQ1, 18 sub-questions were generated, there being 8 more for RQ2 and a further 11 for RQ3. An interpretivist paradigm was adopted to attempt to understand what is happening in the company, developing ideas and theory through induction from this interview data. Relevant concepts derived from existing literature were also incorporated into the analysis of findings. As Gray (2009) states, pre-existing theories or ideas are beneficial when approaching a problem. A qualitative methodology was chosen to explore and understand participant perspectives as shaped through their experiences and respective business roles and views (Creswell, 2009).

The case study is based on two sources of evidence: the direct observation of the events being studied, and the interviews of the persons involved in the events. The strength of a case study such as AKH is that it allows a large variety of evidence to be reviewed, such as documents, interview material, and observations that would not be available in a conventional historical study. Concerning the selection of the AKH interviewees, nine employee types were identified as being of primary interest with regard to answering the research questions. Appropriate employees were selected being either BI end-users or having access to certain BI outputs or solutions, such as reports or analysis platforms. Structured in-depth interviews were conducted with twelve employees between July and November 2013 in the company's Hanover offices. Interviews were audio-recorded, and these files were transcribed after each interview. Interviewees included the authorized agent of the CEO, marketing director, BI consultant, management accounting employees, director of management accounting, performance analysts, director of management accounting for health care, director of health care management, and the director of physical therapy.

The evidence from the one-to-one interviews was analysed in two phases as recommended by Miles and Huberman (1994). First, the replies to each of the 37 sub-questions were summarised and some specific, distinct responses were identified. Then these responses were organised and oriented around the main research questions and synthesised in a table that summarized the findings for each research question. This allowed the identification of key statements and attitudes regarding current BI applications and their deployment. The drivers of successful BI deployment in different business contexts were classified into different categories, allowing an initial positioning of interview material against each research question. This process was repeated several times, expanding and refining the interview material relevant to each RQ as the conceptual framework for analysis was developed and confirmed.

FINDINGS AND ANALYSIS

The case study findings are based on in-house observation and material from the twelve in-depth interviews with AKH staff noted above. The deployment of different BI technologies and tools in AKH is classified within an appropriate conceptual framework that helps us understand their role in the strategy development process, and also supports the identification of key features and functions that may further knowledge management within the organization.

The conceptual framework attempts to provide a mechanism for the classification and integration of BI technologies and tools at AKH (RQ1). Certain elements have been taken from the existing literature and have been further developed. This framework comprises five distinct layers: infrastructure, data provision/access control, BI tools deployment, reporting, and information receivers (Figure 2).

Infrastructure is the lowest layer in this framework. To develop qualitative reports and analyses, a consistent database has to be in place, and this is provided by the DWH. The interviewees stressed the importance of a common structure and definition for data drawn from different sources - internal operational systems and external scientific data bases, such as official health statistics of memberships or financial data for healthcare industry benchmarking. This data is organized in the DWH in aggregated forms for multidimensional cube access, as well as in relational forms to provide in-depth views and detailed in-

Figure 2. Conceptual framework for the classification of BI tools and technologies

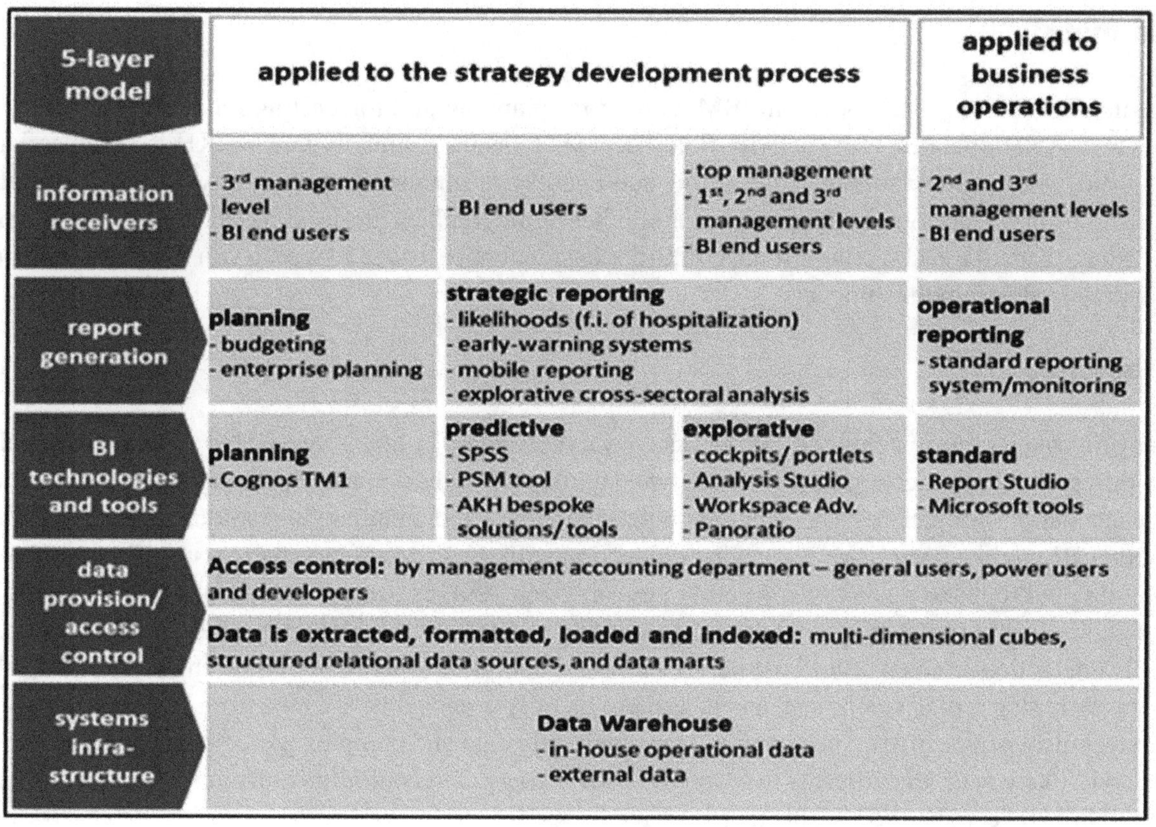

formation presentations. The harmonization of data from different data sources is a major requirement for developing consistent reports and analyses. In the past, this was accomplished only with significant manual intervention by management accounting employees. BI end-users can now access centralized common master data structures and dimensions. Ratios can be used that are commonly defined so that reports in different areas of the organization can be compared and cross-referenced. Management accountants, as well as a wider cross-section of end-users, are able to access appropriately structured data.

The *data provision/access control* layer is integrally linked to the access control function of the company's management accounting department, working in liaison with the corporate IT support function. All data on the DWH is potentially available to all end-users, and management accounting controls tools availability and access for BI end-users, who can access analysis platforms to develop individual reports. In addition, some BI end-users receive print reports from management accounting employees.

Regarding the *BI technologies and tools* layer, interview statements suggest a classification according to their purpose or role – *planning, predictive, explorative* or *standard/general*. These tools can collectively be referred to as "analytics", and some can be used for more than one of these purposes. For instance, Cognos BI products, which were mentioned most frequently by interviewees, deliver analytics that all BI end-users can use to answer key business questions, and they can be viewed as both explorative and standard tools. Users can also develop individual analyses for specific cases. In order to enhance these analytics, management accounting employees are often required to support BI end-users in finding appropriate answers to specific business questions. Some more detailed examples of these four main BI roles are given below.

Planning

Cognos TM1, a major BI tool from IBM, is used for planning and forecasting for all "activity fields" in which AKH operates. (An "activity field" denotes a business area in which AKH is commercially involved). The entire planning cycle and its sub-phases are supported by this software. Key variables relating to price, customer age structures and other demographics are used to calculate forecasts and spending plans for each activity field. Multi-dimensional cube based planning can also be developed and deployed within this product.

Predictive

The propensity score matching (PSM) BI system was developed in-house by AKH to compare and evaluate different customer cost groups. It is designed to identify and calculate likelihoods of hospitalization or cancellations for patients, and is based on past diagnoses and ambulant or stationary benefits. SPSS, another BI product from IBM, is used in conjunction with the PSM tool to analyze specific data abnormalities, and to make predictions. Another area in which AKH is using this technology is for artificial intelligence for purposes of future hospital accounting. A predictive model is being used to determine the likely interaction between future hospital services automation and operational requirements. The model is in the early stages of development, and has still to be fully tested and evaluated from both informational and technical perspectives. Such applications require big data and complex predictive analytics. This in turn will likely need amendments to corporate data strategy, and commitment from senior management to a plan for executing the insights that are gained.

Explorative

Explorative BI tools are evident in a number of forms in AKH, and this is the most widely used BI purpose in the company. These tools can be seen on screen as a "portlet", a "cockpit", or the "corporate dashboard", depending on which tool is used, and what job role the end-user has. All levels of business management have the opportunity to use these tools to apply corporate ratios and trends to explore individual regional developments. These tools enable BI users to generate data and develop reports individually, and to get preferred analyses for their areas of responsibility. Cockpits are helpful in combining graphic displays with relevant corporate trends in comprehensive summaries of specific data and information. From a knowledge management perspective, these are very powerful, allowing all data, functions, developments, trends, and navigation opportunities to be integrated into one cockpit.

To maximise benefits for end-users, cockpits and dashboards have to be carefully designed and tested. Both the design and contents have to be critically checked and evaluated by professional leaders and employees in the respective area for which the dashboards are intended. Dashboards have the primary goal of enabling quick and direct information access; they are user-friendly and graphic oriented applications, providing insights into abnormalities. These abnormalities are usually evident visually on screen via graphic display, and allow relevant questioning from business managers, providing further information from the underlying data. For each area relevant drivers have to be identified with key ratios to measure them. For instance, efficiency in a business area could be measured by ratios of productive and non-productive mail or case progression. The aim and content of a dashboard revolves around "telling a story" in the respective business area. The type of questions that such dashboards can address include the following:

1. How much work is generated directly from customers or other business areas and how efficiently is it processed?
2. What work backlogs do we have in our business area and when did they appear?
3. Are these backlogs growing or reducing, do they concern mail processing, case progression or other work, and what is the trend of progress within my team?

Figure 3 illustrates how a dashboard may be used to respond to such questions, typically for regional business managers or directors.

Cognos Analysis Studio is an example of a specific explorative tool in evidence within AKH. End-users find it generally easy-to-use, allowing reasonably complex queries. AKH analysts use this tool for multi-dimensional analysis and the exploration of large data sources. An interactive drag-and-drop function is often used for exploring and analyzing data and making data comparisons such as actual versus budgeted results. In addition, Panoratio provide a range of BI tools that also allow analysis of multi-dimensional data sources, such as those contained in an OLAP cube. These products are viewed as being of strategic value for AKH, in particular for healthcare analytics. They can provide a platform for rough and ready, "first-cut", analysis of business opportunities, using multi-dimensional cubes and aggregated data structures. In this context, Panoratio tools are used for business analytics by a wide range of end-users to experiment with data and develop individual scenarios and data portfolios.

Figure 3. A dashboard layout to answer relevant questions regarding mail processing and team performance

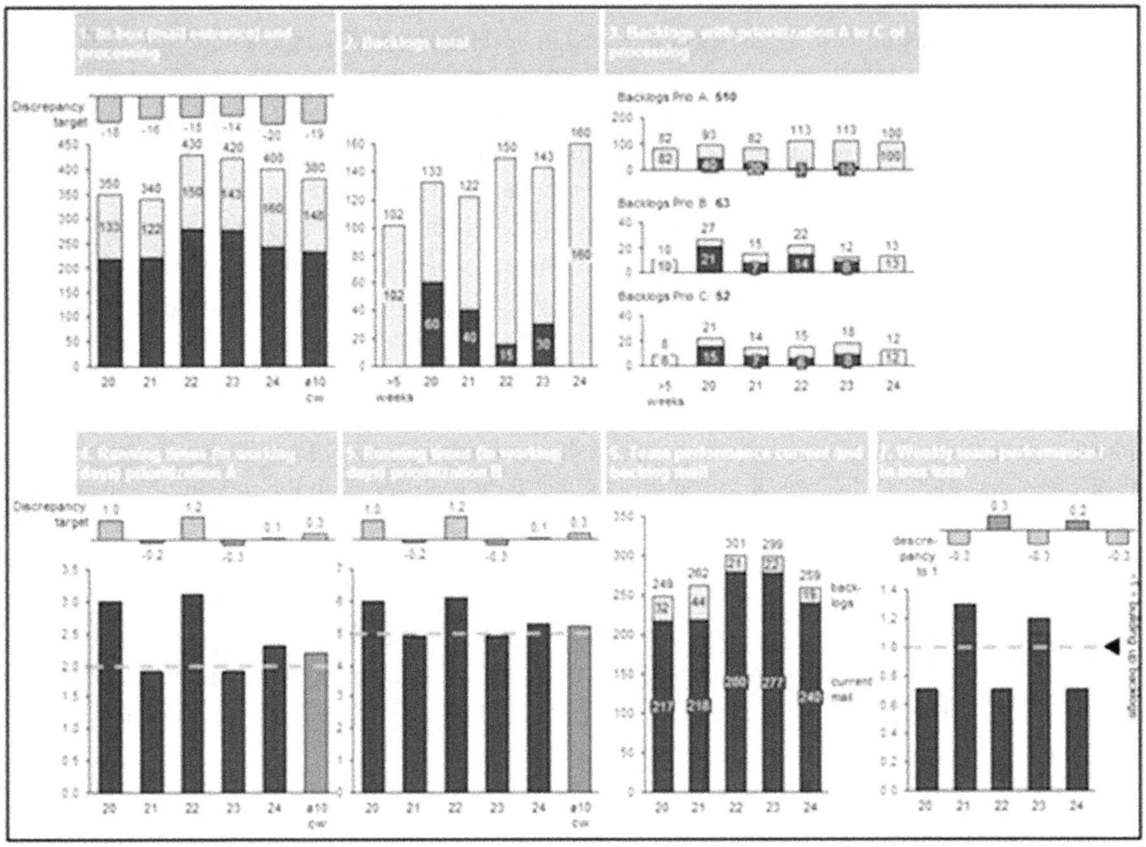

Standard

Cognos Report Studio is used for operational reporting, which is generally short-term-oriented and highly detailed. Clearly structured reports with relevant ratios are needed to serve different but related perspectives – for example, quality, cost-efficiency, and customer satisfaction. Reports are generally kept as simple as possible, and are easily managed and customised by end-users. This standard reporting and data monitoring function serves as the main information source for management and analysts in the business divisions, to view past activity on a short-term basis, based on previously defined relevant ratios and trend views.

Standard reports can also build upon and incorporate data from explorative dashboards such as those discussed in the above sub-section. For example, the explorative dashboard application may enable the regional business manager to see team performance information at employee level. This may lead him/her to ask questions regarding the nature of employees' tasks, whether further training or qualifications are necessary or which employees can function as best practice examples for other team members? Some of this data and information can be incorporated into standard reports developed in Cognos Report Studio.

The *report generation* layer concerns the output material - the business intelligence itself - generated by these tools. AKH is striving to provide top management with a panoramic view of information in an integrated reporting system. This includes external distribution, market and medical data from hospitals and doctors, which is summarized and cross-referenced. An example of advanced reporting capability which is more generally available in AKH is provided by Cognos Workspace Advanced, which is mainly used for explorative analytics. It allows basic developers, predominantly management accounting employees, to create reports and analyze different data sources in one interface. The product is designed to allow querying and analyses from a single interface, and it interacts with other Cognos products. It is used in business meetings to display structured overviews and trends, and can be manipulated to show further analysis and visual representations of information that aid decision processes in these meetings.

Mobile reporting from BI tools is a significant development being pursued at AKH. For certain tablet computers, mobile reports can be made available from the Cognos AKH systems. The company has developed tablet reporting solutions in the form of dashboards for the CEO, somewhat akin to the old concept of "executive information systems". From his tablet, the CEO can request detailed analytical reports and receive them more or less immediately, in real time. He can then customize the analytical views depending on what he needs to see, by swiping on the tablet. Improvements are being made in information availability, speedier report development, and optimal hardware utilization. It is expected that these developments in mobile BI, being piloted with the CEO, will be rolled out to support AKH's distribution and marketing functions. These mobile apps could be used, for example, to allow field based staff to enter doctor information that can then be transferred directly to the operational system for further analysis. So BI apps will be used for reporting, but also for field based data gathering and data entry.

The top layer in this model concerns the main users of this business intelligence information – the *information receivers*. This model refers to top management, operating at Board level, and then three further levels of management in the company, the first level being the most senior answering to Board directors. Planning reports and associated BI macros and applications are used by BI end- users and the third level of management. Strategic reporting is conducted by BI end-users, employing predictive analytics. It is likely that all levels of management will require increasing support from explorative analytics BI in future. BI outputs relating to business operations tend to be used by the second and third levels of management, as well as BI end-users (Figure 2).

We can now consider how BI tools and technologies can best be deployed and integrated within the strategy development process (RQ2). Based on the four phases of this process identified by Fueglistaller *et al.* (2005), interview analysis and internal documentation suggest objectives, BI activities and BI tools deployment for each phase (Figure 4). These tools are discussed in the context of their use at AKH, but others could be used in different business technology contexts. Some examples can be given to illustrate the overall picture given in Figure 4. In the *information analysis* phase, for example, SPSS serves as a predictive analysis tool for the calculation of probabilities and their relevant weightings. This encompasses possible customer cancellations and hospitalization rates. Such predictive data also aids the development of the appropriate strategy for relevant customers and thus optimizes AKH's business portfolio.

Central to the *strategy/concept development* phase, is the search for new activity fields and possible strategic direction changes. The definition of new project objectives, and any related process implications, is clarified at this stage. This is done with the help of explorative information searches, prediction models, and scenario generators. Panoratio is used to develop different scenarios for intervention. Concept development is supported by data analysis, using a number of BI tools, including Panoratio, SPSS and scenario generators.

In the *strategy implementation* phase, standardized monitoring from BI tools is used to show relevant ratios and cross-organisational implications for staff centrally involved in strategy development

Figure 4. Deployment of BI technologies and tools within the strategy development process (Phase -> Objectives->BI activity->BI tools deployed)

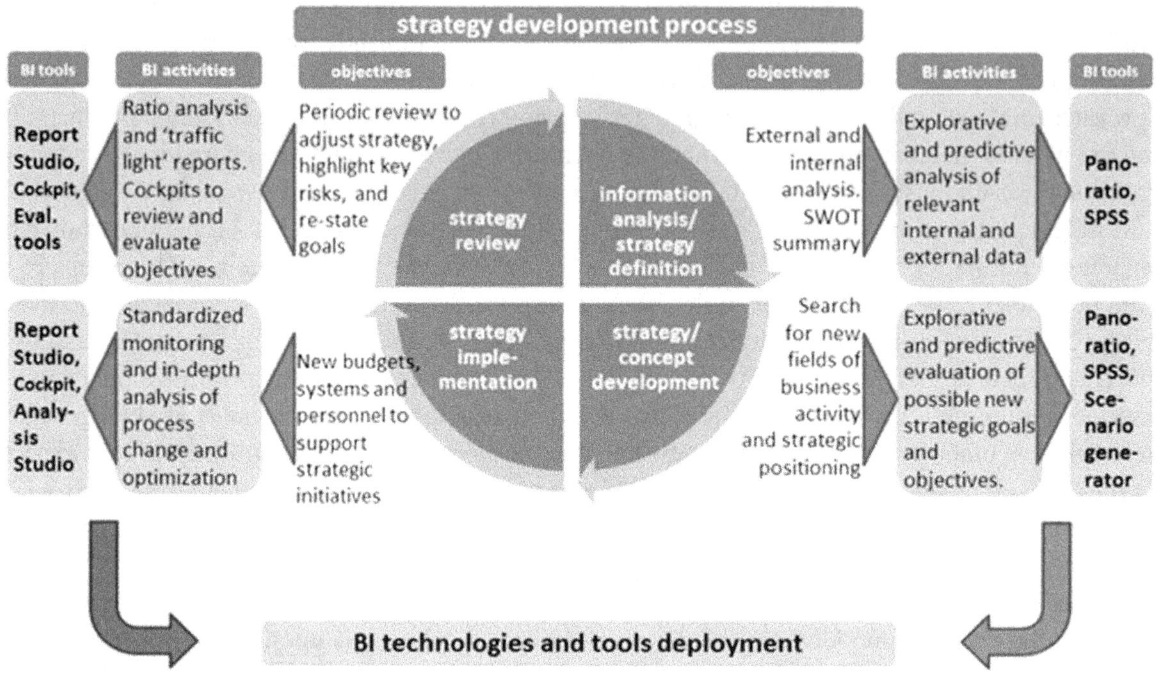

and implementation. Business strategy implementation is supported by reporting and monitoring that includes the relevant ratios to minimize uncertainties and support strategy evaluation. For standardized monitoring, Cognos Report Studio is used to provide access to all data packages – markets and customers, hospitals, doctors, pharmaceuticals and a number of related statistical ratios – and to prepare and present them appropriately. For more in-depth analyses, including countermeasure and adverse event impacts, explorative tools such as Cognos Analysis Studio and associated dashboards are used. The *strategy review* phase encompasses a number of periodical reviews which act as an early warning of any adverse results and analyses the potential impacts of appropriate countermeasures. Statistical evaluation BI tools, such as the PSM tool and Panoratio with its integrated statistical package, provide relevant ratios for achieving strategic objectives and milestones. In this way, the results of the strategy evaluation and review are communicated to the responsible divisions, for instance, health care management. A holistic evaluation of a healthcare project linked to overall strategy, for instance, will measures results to date against the defined financial objectives.

The role of these tools within the strategy development and implementation process can be illustrated in the context of the implementation of healthcare projects, which are developed and enhanced by different product teams. Current healthcare projects concern the insurance costs of certain medical conditions: depression, schizophrenia, and cardiac disease. They focus on the generation of cost or quality advantages and the targeted enhancement of healthcare structures in Germany. The basic conditions that are required in order to implement healthcare structures or models of specialized departments, hospitals, or cross-sectoral regional budgets in Germany can be found in Social Law regulations. AKH has to act within this political and legal framework. BI reports with traffic light systems of warnings and escalation mechanisms provide evidence of whether certain healthcare projects are successful or not. These mechanisms can be used as the basis for decisions to review or adjust initial strategy choices.

As regards the key elements of BI tools and technologies (RQ3), the interviews suggested a range of factors that might improve BI deployment for knowledge management. These factors can be divided into five components: *technology element, software product, ways of access, report characteristics*, and *BI end- user communication.*

Technology

Interview feedback highlighted the need for BI technologies to be efficient, user-friendly, and custom- fit to the market and specific business division needs. Aggregated data structures for performance analyses (such as Panoratio databases and subject specific data marts) play a crucial role in certain business areas. For further in-depth data analyses, relational data technologies have to be available primarily for management accounting employees and certain BI end-users.

Software Products

The Cognos BI software is viewed as providing fast and efficient functions with planning, standard and explorative tools, and mobile cockpits and dashboards. Data mining products can play a key role here; their objective is to extract knowledge from a data set or structure and their function involves data base and data management, model and inference building, visualization and online updating. AKH provides data mining solutions to find correlations in different activity fields such as the likelihood of the withdrawal of target customers or identifying excellence in care provision. The key employees are trained in statistics and in data sciences. Data mining can be exploited using SPSS in combination with social media analytical platforms. This is a new area of knowledge management that will use social media data in conjunction with BI tools to analyze social behavior characteristics and the needs and attitudes of customers. This should be conducted with due consideration of privacy protection.

Access

There are many ways to access reports or analysis templates. The delivery can be an active transmission with management accounting support. For instance, a management report may be delivered via email in pdf format by management accounting employees. However, there are other options for standard reporting handling and provision. The management of AKH is now using a self-provision function available via a Cognos portal, where reports are available in fixed pdf format. The Cognos Event Studio can also be automated to schedule report delivery immediately following weekly data synchronisation. Self-provision via a self-service portal with provision for end-user pick-up is becoming increasingly important as a means of access in AKH. Some employees have mobile access to pre-prepared reports and corporate ratios via tablets. An "Event Studio" is also in use in the management accounting division for receiving reports after the weekly or monthly data synchronisation process. This automatic data provision process will be expanded in the future to free up resources for more focused strategic BI tasks. It is intended to roll-out the self-service portal to all divisions, making a wide range of reports and analysis available to end-users.

Reports

Interview feedback highlighted the importance of standard reporting procedures, consistent definition and use of key ratios, and well communicated processes for report generation and access. The value of interactive graphics for report analysis was also emphasized. Statistical functions should be clearly defined to allow evaluations of, for example, specific health care projects. Reports should provide flexibility so that BI users and management can access multiple views, trends, or data.

The visualization of information and Big Data plays a crucial role in this context. This development is logical because it is difficult to get an overview of the amount of available data and to identify structures and correlations within it. Today, it is not possible to identify all relevant data patterns with automatic algorithms. The skills of employees are necessary for this process. Thus, it is important to focus on certain analysis activities and platforms. Graphic presentations afford the opportunity to visualize structures and trends, as opposed to simple tabulation. The visualization process can be structured in four steps: data integration, classification, sorting, and coloration. Visual BI with different visualization options will be an important area of development in AKH and in the wider BI world in the future.

BI Communication

The effective in-house communication of BI developments is crucial and it is intended to strengthen this in AKH in the coming years. Interview feedback suggested that communication with BI end-users and BI customers within the company has to be more custom-fit on the basis of the corporate policies and individual needs. This communication needs to be aligned with first-level product support, the training and qualification advancement of BI end-users, and even cultural aspects such as corporate mission and vision aspirations. These guidelines and requirements for using BI for effective knowledge management are summarized in Figure 5.

CONCLUSION

The BI tools and technologies discussed in this article constitute examples of both MIS and CPM systems. The benefits provided to companies such as AKH are manifold. These systems encompass a variety of performance information that is relevant to different functions and roles within the organization, and they provide performance information on a regular basis and typically at shorter time intervals than purely financial information. This allows corrective action to be taken when under-performance occurs, before it is too late. In this context, BI systems are more than a mere sub-set of management information systems. They comprise not only a technology component and the information provision noted above, but also a number of related processes – planning, prediction and exploration, as well as standard reporting. There are also often procedures and guidelines for best practice deployment of these concepts and technologies. Plans should be developed in line with forecasts and should be reviewed on a regular basis, and corrective action taken whenever they are off-course. Reports may include key performance indicators or similar metrics, and both high and low performances should be addressed by exception with the overall process providing opportunities for learning by benchmarking. BI systems

Figure 5. Factors to engender BI technology deployment for knowledge management

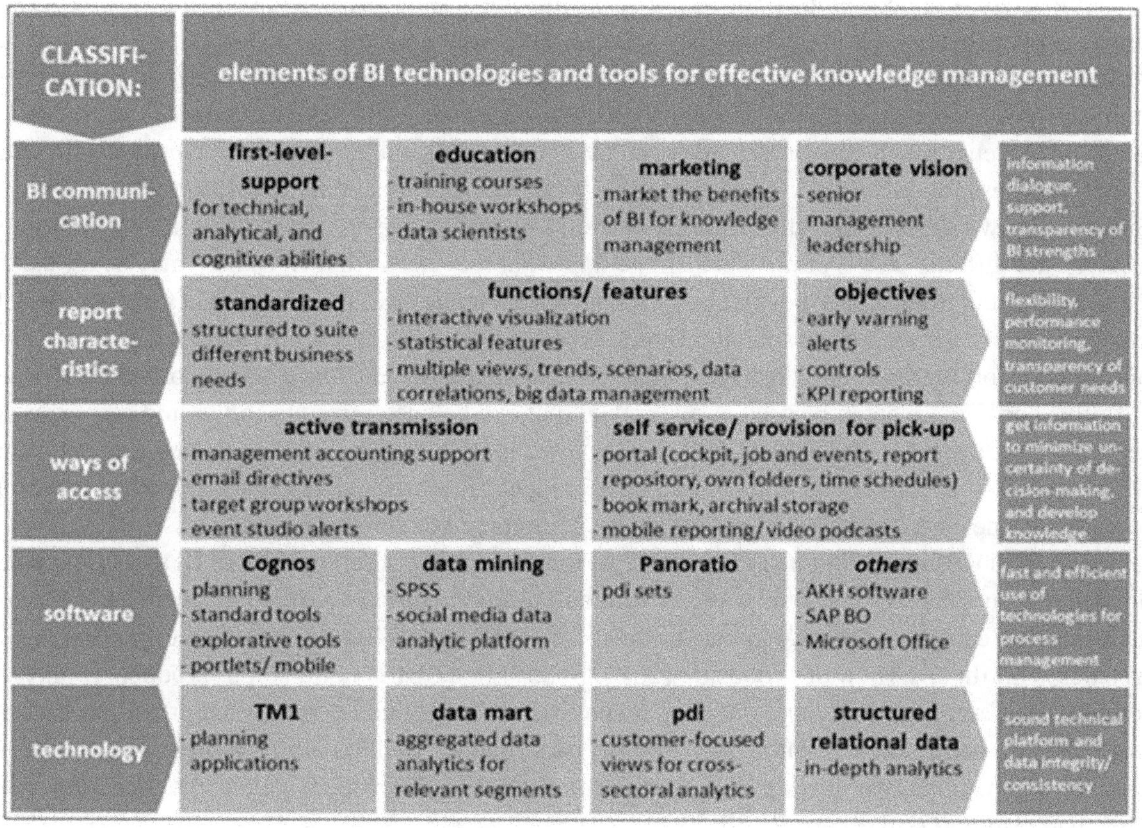

should provide information that is consistent and comprehensive and culminate in concise performance reports that are made available to senior management and/or the Board. The provision of up to date performance information should facilitate performance reviews and discussions at all levels and enable effective action to be taken at the right time.

However, the research findings discussed in this paper come with certain qualifications. The methodological decision to rely in the main on in-depth interviews comes at the cost of limited representation as compared to quantitative surveys, for example. Further limitations arise from the national and cultural setting of the empirical research stage. The fact that the empirical study was conducted in Germany means that results are potentially biased by the local culture or regional traditions. While goal-oriented activities are executed in a specific way in the AKH region in the north of Lower-Saxony, these objectives may be pursued in significantly different manner, even in nearby regions that can vary greatly with regard to culture or even religion.

Through the extensive transcripts, English translations, coding and use of interview materials, and internal inquiries, the results of the case study have been reviewed and confirmed from different positions within the company. To allow wider generalisations to be made, the emergent models need to be applied and cross-checked in other organizational contexts. For other companies like AKH, there is the opportunity to become a totally networked and intelligent company exploiting the benefits of an appropriate set of BI tools and technologies. The conceptual framework shown in Figure 2 can be used as a checklist to plan and monitor in-company BI deployment. Is there a technically sound and appropriately structured database underpinning BI operations? Is someone or some department playing the role of DWH manager to effectively control access to BI tools and data? Are you exploiting the full range of tools and technologies available? Whilst the *planning* and *standard* tools are reasonably well known and used, the *predictive* and *explorative* tools are less so, and this is where AKH has attained significant business benefit, as evidenced in the use of BI in the strategy development and implementation process. In a wider context, business processes have been enhanced through end-users creatively exploiting these tools to achieve their own goals aligned to corporate strategy. As regards report generation and the information receivers, are different levels of management getting what they need from BI? There may be a wealth of data available, but this needs to be effectively managed and made available in the right formats, using the appropriate tools. The enhanced analytical abilities of employees using BI tools and technologies should improve decision-making at all levels to engender process improvement and attain competitive edge.

To this end, Figure 5 can be used as a template that can be customized to individual organizational needs and circumstances. Whilst Figure 2 depicts *what* is required for effective BI deployment, Figure 5 illustrates *how* BI can be used. This is, however, specific to the AKH organizational context, and provides but one case example. Other authors have attempted to summarise and classify these factors. Gonzales (2011) identifies four main requirements for the successful deployment of BI tools for effective knowledge management - leadership, value, skill and infrastructure. In particular, steadfast and consistent leadership can play a key role in the sustainability of BI and its impact within an organisation. This resonates with the assertion of Woodside (2011, p. 557) that “BI is not a single product, application, program, user, area, or system, but rather an architecture of integrated systems that provides users with easy access to, and storage of, information for decision-making and learning.” It highlights the significance for organizations of bridging the gap between theoretical knowledge and its practical application for decision support (Guarda *et al.*, 2013).

BI products and their benefits for the organisation have to be marketed in-house to the professional business divisions. This may encompass a range of functions, processes and disciplines: new product development and innovation, for example, are becoming increasingly important to many organizations as they focus on new ideas capture, screening and prioritization to drive future growth, and BI tools can play a key role in these initiatives. Risk management is also now becoming an issue of strategic importance as increased regulation and the need for continuous improvement has brought renewed focus on strategic, process and programme risk management. Corporate governance is closely linked to risk management. There is now a significant amount of visibility and focus on the senior management team, who need to manage the business in a way that is both highly effective and compliant with regulations. This creates a need for information visibility and process control underpinned by sound knowledge management systems, of which BI tools are a key component. The ability to present the right information to the right people at the right time using well-constructed dashboards and analytical platforms is an important element of BI delivery. A single version of the “truth”, delivered on a well- integrated and secure BI technical platform through transparent data management, is a key element of successful BI deployment. BI integrates information utilities and a decision support system that can help organizations to manage, develop, and communicate their intangible assets embedded in corporate information and knowledge.

Davydov (2001) has noted that the key to providing management information “is to integrate the whole set of enterprise wide applications into a single integrated information network”. This is valid enough as an objective of corporate systems strategy, but the means by which it is achieved does not need to involve widespread systems replacement. For many companies, this level of investment is unrealistic; instead, a pragmatic approach - that maximizes the value of investments already made - is likely to find more support from senior management and the Board. As Sweet (2003) noted, "organisations are starting to look at additional technologies and methodologies, which could provide better insights. These include business intelligence (BI) solutions, data warehousing, and a variety of management techniques, some of which are directly supported by specialist applications". The BI strategy adopted at AKH is a good example of this approach.

More specifically, this research has focused on professional practice development, which was established using a mixture of theoretical and practical frameworks. Theory must be supplemented with daily business practice at AKH. The first steps have been taken, but an increase in BI end-users would further engender an IT-driven self-service with BI technologies and tools at their core. Together, top management and BI end-users can generate new strategic capabilities as the findings and analyses of the research questions showed. If awareness and creativity can be raised by using BI technologies and tools, then BI solutions will generate fast, simple, and diverse advantages for AKH. In the different business divisions, a broad portfolio of BI applications and analysis tools is supporting and enriching the way opportunities are identified, and how key strategic and operational decisions are made and implemented in a better informed, appropriately qualified, and more transparent manner.

REFERENCES

Alnoukari, M. (2009). Using Business Intelligence Solutions for Achieving Organization's Strategy: Arab International University Case Study. *Internetworking Indonesia Journal*, *1*(3), 11–16.

Alter, S. (2002). *Information Systems (the foundation of E-business)*. Prentice Hall, Pearson Education.

Buytendijk, F., Geishecker, L., & Wood, B. (2004). *Magic Quadrant for CPM Suites*. Gartner Research.

Carver, A., & Ritacco, M. (2006). *The Business Value of Business Intelligence – A Framework for Measuring the Benefits of Business Intelligence*. Business Objects.

Creswell, J. W. (2009). *Research Design. Qualitative, quantitative and mixed methods approaches* (3rd ed.). Thousand Oaks, CA: SAGE Publications, Inc.

Davydov, M. (2001). *Corporate Portals and e-Business Integration*. New York: McGraw-Hill.

Easterby-Smith, M., Thorpe, R., & Jackson, P. R. (2008). *Management Research: Theory and Research* (3rd ed.). London: SAGE Publications Ltd.

Eckerson, W. (2005). *Performance Dashboards: Measuring, Monitoring, and Managing Your Business*. Wiley.

Eisenhardt, K. M. (1989). Building Theories from Case Study Research. *Academy of Management Review*, *14*(4), 532–550.

Fueglistaller, U., Frey, U., Halter, F., & Hartl, R. (2005). Unternehmensführung 3 – Der Strategiefindungsprozess– Vorgehensmethodik zur Erarbeitung einer Strategie in vier Schritten. Study booklet of Europäische Fernhochschule Hamburg. UNFÜ 3/H, Hamburg.

Gansor, T., Totok, A., & Stock, S. (2010). *Von der Strategie zum Business Intelligence Competency Center (BICC) – Konzeption, Betrieb, Praxis* (1st ed.). Munich: Hanser; doi:10.3139/9783446424869

Gonzales, M. (2011). Success Factors for Business Intelligence and Data Warehousing Maturity and Competitive Advantage. *Business Intelligence Journal*, *16*(1), 22–29.

Gray, D. E. (2009). *Doing Research in the Real World* (2nd ed.). London: SAGE Publications Ltd.

Guarda, T., Santos, M., Pinto, F., Augusto, M., & Silva, C. (2013). Business Intelligence as a Competitive Advantage for SMEs. *International Journal of Trade. Economics and Finance*, *4*(4), 187–190.

Hemmatfar, M., Salehi, M., & Bayat, M. (2010). Competitive Advantage and Strategic Information Systems. *International Journal of Business and Management*, *5*(7), 158–169. doi:10.5539/ijbm.v5n7p158

Inmon, W. H. (2002). *Building the Data Warehouse*. J Wiley.

Kaplan, R. S., & Norton, D. P. (1992, January). The balanced scorecard: Measures that drive performance. *Harvard Business Review*, 71–80. PMID:10119714

Lönnqvist, A., & Pirttimäki, V. (2006). The Measurement of Business Intelligence. *Information Systems Management Journal*, *23*(1), 32–40. doi:10.1201/1078.10580530/45769.23.1.20061201/91770.4

Maria, F. (2005). *Improving the utilization of external strategic information* (Unpublished Master of Science Thesis). Tampere University of Technology.

McAfee, A. & Brynjolfsson, E. (2012, November). Besser entscheiden mit Big Data. *Harvard Business Manager,* 22-30.

Miles, M. B., & Huberman, A. M. (1994). *Qualitative Data Analysis: an Expanded Sourcebook*. Thousand Oaks, CA: SAGE Publications, Inc.

Peppard, J. (1993). *IT Strategy for Business*. London: Pitman Publishing.

Pisello, T., & Strassmann, P. (2003). *IT Value Chain Management – Maximizing the ROI from IT Investments.* The Information Economics Press.

Seufert, A., & Oehler, K. (2009). Business Intelligence & Controlling Competence (1st ed.). Berlin: Academic Press.

Siegel, E. (2010). *Seven Reasons You Need Predictive Analytics Today*. Prediction Impact, Inc.

Sweet, P. (2003, June). Looking before you leap. In *Corporate Performance Management.* Conspectus Report.

Turban, E., Leidner, D., McLean, E., & Wetherbe, J. (2006). *Information Technology for Management: Transforming Organizations in the Digital Economy* (5th ed.). J. Wiley and Sons.

Volitich, D. (2008). *IBM Cognos 8 Business Intelligence: The Official Guide* (1st ed.). New York: McGraw-Hill.

Watson, H. J. (2010). BI-based Organizations. *Business Intelligence Journal*, *15*(2), 4–6.

Weber, N., & Fohrholz, C. (2013). Wirtschaftliche Potenziale von Business Analytics – Ergebnisse einer explorativen Studie. *ERP Management*, *4*, 36–38.

Wiseman, C. (1985). *Strategic Information Systems*. Homewood, IL: Irwin.

Woodside, J. (2011). Business Intelligence Best Practices for Success. *Proceedings of the European Conference on Information Management*, 556-562.

Zuboff, S. (1988). *In the Age of the Smart Machine*. New York: Basic Books.

Chapter 11
Factors Influencing Managers' Use of Mobile Tablets:
An Exploratory Study

Shijia Gao
Monash University, Australia

William Yeoh
Deakin University, Australia

Siew Fan Wong
Sunway University, Malaysia

Edgar Alexander Bruno Kautzner
Monash University, Australia

ABSTRACT

In recent years mobile tablets are being used by many managers. Yet hitherto there is a lack of research on managerial use of the new mobile technology. Hence, this study aims to explore the factors that influence the use of mobile tablets by managers and how mobile tablets impact the use of other digital devices. Semi-structured interviews were conducted with a panel of mid- to high-level managers who had incorporated mobile tablets into their work routine. The findings reveal that mobile tablets are suitable for managerial tasks due to nine main factors: non-routineness, collaborative nature, time-critical, information-centric, mobility, user friendliness of the interface, reliability, connectivity, and autonomy. Also, the use of mobile tablets has significant impact on the use of other digital devices as well as traditional manual process of using pens and papers. This study fills in the research gap and provides a foundation to help managers establish a business case for or against mobile tablet use.

1. INTRODUCTION

In recent years, mobile technology such as iPads has become increasingly popular with overwhelming sales success (Hughes, 2013; Gartner, 2017). According to Gartner (2017), the worldwide sales of mobile tablets have reached 168 million units in 2016. The mobile technology permeates not only personal routines, but also work practices. In fact, the popularity of mobile tablets in workplaces has led to an

DOI: 10.4018/978-1-5225-5718-0.ch011

emerging and profitable enterprise tablet market (Endler, 2014). More importantly, contemporary managers are no longer tied to stagnant and heavy-duty desktop computers. Instead they are on-the-go with light-weight handheld tablets that contain necessary work information at finger-tips.

Two of the first researchers investigating the use of mobile technologies in business, Grover and Goslar (1993) found wide use of mobile phones among managers for routine activities. Tan and Sie (2015) revealed that Internet-based smartphone is undergoing rapid innovative changes. Mobile device allows managers to be efficient, multitask without disrupting others, respond immediately to messages, and work from anywhere (Middleton & Cukier, 2006). Managers use a range of portable devices to achieve convenience, mobility, input efficiency, and content readability (Karlson, Meyers, Jacobs, & Kane, 2009). Such technology is seen as disruptive because it frees people from tethered systems, such as landline phones and desktops, and provides users with ubiquitous access to people and information. The trend towards adoption of mobile devices such as tablets and smartphones in the workplace is strong and likely unstoppable (Harris, Ives, & Junglas, 2012). Yuan, Archer, Connelly, and Zheng (2010) found that managers work away from their primary working location for more than 30% of their work time. In Kim's (2008) study, the percentage even reached 60%. Puuronen and Savolainen (1997) argued this remote work is something mobile technology enables. Since managers spend more time away from their primary work location, Gebauer and Shaw (2004) confirmed they use mobile applications more often than other employees. Gebauer, Shaw, and Gribbins (2010) asserted that mobile technology will improve managers' performance when the characteristics of managerial tasks match those of mobile technology characteristics. One proposed reason why mobile technologies are widely adopted in the workplace is '*the old computing was about what computers could do; the new computing is about what users can do.*' (Shneiderman, 2003, p.2).

While some see mobile technology as a transformational tool, others call it a disruptive device (Prentice, 2010). Even though many managers are current business users of mobile tablets, the role of the devices within the managerial technology portfolio is still largely unknown. While prior studies (e.g., Gebauer & Shaw, 2004; Ioimo & Aronson, 2004; Liang, Huang, Yeh, & Lin, 2007; Tan & Sie, 2015) have investigated the use and impacts of conventional mobile technologies such as laptops, smartphones and personal digital assistants (PDA), there has been a relative dearth of research on the use of mobile tablets by managers. In response, due to the widespread managerial use of tablets in workplace (Endler, 2014), it is important to understand the work nature of managers and how these mobile devices fit into managers' work routine. Therefore, this research aims to understand the underlying factors influencing the use of mobile tablets by managers and how mobile tablets impact the use of other digital devices and media. Particularly, we focus on the nature of managerial work and the characteristics of mobile tablets that act as the influencers. To achieve the research objectives, we employed exploratory qualitative approach and conducted semi-structured interviews with a panel of mid to high-level managers who use mobile tablets in their work routine.

The remainder of this paper is structured as follows. The next section presents a literature review on the use of mobile tablets. The third section describes the qualitative research method. The fourth section provides the research findings. The fifth section discusses the findings, then follows the conclusion and future research.

2. LITERATURE REVIEW

2.1 Tablet Computer

A tablet computer (otherwise known simply as a "tablet", "tablet PC" or "slate") is a portable mobile device that was originally designed to provide the functionality of a computer with the portability, mobility and flexible data-input methods that are associated with pen-and-paper (Ozok, Benson, Chakraborty, & Norcio, 2008). Tablets are smaller and lighter than laptops, but bigger and heavier than smartphones or PDAs (McClard & Somers, 2000). According to Gartner, tablets are now common business tools, joining smartphones and laptops (Willis, 2011) and have been utilized for a range of business applications (McClard & Somers, 2000).

Although many tablets are designed to provide users with the option to use a detachable keyboard accessory, the primary input methods include tapping and pen-based methods (McClard & Somers, 2000). This represents a significant advantage of tablets over laptops in their portability and dependence from input devices such as a keyboard and mouse (Ozok et al., 2008).

As portability is a key benefit of tablets, a large amount of the design efforts and considerations have been focused around highly mobile occupations, including delivery-based roles and hospital workers (McClard & Somers, 2000). McClard and Somers (2000) stated that they enable spontaneous access to information and communication at anywhere. They also asserted that the characteristics of a tablet should conform to the way people conceptualize and use it (McClard & Somers, 2000). Ozok et al. (2008, p.329) noted however that usability studies concerning mobile tablet are lacking.

2.2 Studies on the Use of Mobile Devices

The use of mobile devices offers new opportunities for businesses (Basole, 2008) and can lead to numerous improvements including flexibility, efficiency, and effectiveness (Balasubramanian, Peterson, & Jarvenpaa, 2002) and can be a mediator of new experiences and social interactions (Mylonopoulos, & Doukidis, 2003). Perry, O'Hara, Sellen, Brown, and Harper (2001) outline four factors in the undertaking of tasks via mobile devices: planning, utilizing "dead time", accessing informational resources, and monitoring the activities of staff. Ubiquitous computing on a range of mobile and non-mobile devices is the "dominant vision" of the computer market (Mylonopoulos, & Doukidis, 2003) allowing constant access to information and individuals (Perry et al., 2001).

Information workers, such as managers use a range of computing devices including desktop and portable computers to achieve a balance of convenience, mobility, input efficiency and content readability during the course of their duties (Karlson et al., 2009). The introduction of mobile devices has not merely replaced previous technology, it also has a dramatic effect on the work routines of users, resulting in new experiences and user demands, and requiring frequent adaptation of practice to accommodate the technology (Mylonopoulos, & Doukidis, 2003).

Kelly and Scrape (2010) conducted a study where six staff members were issued with iPads. They found that the iPad has a high degree of usability and that staff members utilized the device primarily for e-mail, browsing the Internet, taking notes, consuming media, and file storage. A number of studies have also addressed topics relating to the use of iPad as a reading device. Batsell (2011) examined the overall news experience on iPads, and Pearson and Buchanan (2010) highlighted real-time document collaboration using iPads. Müller, Gove, and Webb (2012) conducted a market research survey involving written and video diaries, in-home interviews, and contextual inquiry observations. They found that email checking, playing games and social networking were the most popular activities on tablets. A case study by Sheng, Nah, and Siau (2005) found tablets to be used by publishing company employees to perform daily working activities such as accessing the company Intranet, checking and searching electronic catalogues, demonstrating products to customers, and taking notes. The findings suggest that tablets improve the working process, increase internal communication and knowledge sharing, and enhance sales and marketing effectiveness.

Since the tablet has been widely used in these different contexts, several researchers have investigated what characteristics of the tablet allow it to achieve such a wide adoption. McClard and Somers (2000) suggested that a tablet must have three characteristics to support general Web access and text-based communication: (1) the software must contain features perceived as useful, (2) it must be highly portable and comfortable to use, and (3) the screen and keyboard must be large enough to be usable. Pitt, Berthon, and Robson (2011) found some of its characteristics unique, or at least very different from other mobile devices: unique to the user, almost ideal screen size, very portable, 'always on and instant on', very long battery life, ease of use and a range of functions, such as accelerometer, GPS and gyroscope. They recommended that if developers and vendors can take full advantage of the characteristics, tablets will add significant business value to organizations. Also, how these characteristics can be utilized to support users well is becoming another interesting topic among researchers.

In sum, tablets have seen a wide use in many contexts for reasons ranging from user attitudes to its characteristics. None of these contexts from prior research are in a managerial setting. Whether these reasons and features apply to managerial use, and whether there is a fit between tablets' characteristics and managers' task needs, are topics worthy of investigation.

3. METHODOLOGY

Exploratory semi-structured interviews were used to collect the data since this technique enables detailed information to be gathered about the tablet usage habits of managers and allows follow-up questions to be asked for participants to elaborate on responses. The interviewee selection criteria were: (1) The participant is a manager who gets work done through others (Kotter, 1982)—that is, the participant is responsible for controlling or administering at least a group of staff; and (2) The participant is currently using an iPad as part of their work routine. iPad was chosen as the technology-in-use example in this study due to its dominance in the enterprise tablet market (Endler, 2014).

A panel of seven mid to high-level managers in Australia were included in the study. As shown in the participant demographic information in Table 1, there was a fairly even spread of public and private institutions (three and four respectively) and representation of a variety of industry sectors including retail, IT, advertising, education, professional services, and government. The interviews strictly complied with the university and national guidelines for ethical conduct of research involving humans. A condition of the university ethics committee approval for the interviews was anonymity for the individuals involved; accordingly identities have been disguised. The aggregated gender and age spread amongst the participants is representative of the manager population considered in this study; and the participants represented a broad spectrum of industries, organization sizes, and managerial roles.

An interview protocol (see Appendix) was developed for guiding the interview process to ensure each interview session follows a consistent structure and format; and hence, increase the reliability of

Table 1. Demographics of the panel

Identifier	Occupation	Sector	Industry	Organizational Size
U1	Director / Owner	Private	Fashion / Retail	SME
U2	Executive Manager	Private	IT	SME
U3	Group Manager	Private	Advertising	Large
U4	Manager	Public	Education	Large
U5	Director	Public	Education	Large
U6	Principal Consultant	Private	Professional Services	SME
U7	Director	Public	Government	Large

the data collected. A face-to-face interview was conducted with each interviewee lasted approximately an hour. With the permission of the participants, all interviews were recorded using an audio recording device. Hand-written notes were also taken to record the content of the interviews.

At the conclusion of each interview, the audio recording was transcribed verbatim into texts, and the notes taken were also typed into texts. The texts were loaded into NVivo, a qualitative data analysis software package designed to aid users in handling unstructured and semi-structured qualitative data, by supporting coding and analysis (Neuman, 2011). A thematic approach was employed to analyze the data. The process started with two researchers independently reading through each transcript and assigning codes to represent ideas that were found to be common amongst the participants. Then discussions took place where the two coders were able to challenge or confirm any questions or issues as they arose. The ability to frequently discuss during the data analysis process improved the consistency and reliability of the coding.

4. FINDINGS

We present the findings in two parts. Section 4.1 lays out the nature of managerial work along with how mobile tablets fit these tasks, which helps us to understand the factors influencing the use of mobile tablets by managers. Section 4.2 highlights how mobile tablets impact the use of other digital devices as well as traditional manual process of using pens and papers.

4.1 Factors Influencing Managerial Use of Mobile Tablets

The following presents the major influential factors that emerged from the data covering the nature of managerial work and the characteristics of mobile tablet that contribute to its use in managers' daily work.

Non-Routineness

The managers interviewed tended to display a fairly high level of non-routineness in their work activities. The structure of their day would be determined by numerous factors including opportunities, action items, issues, projects, and the general strategic direction of the organization. One manager mentioned that "*on a day-by-day basis, I don't really have a very regular schedule…and they change daily and weekly depending on what's going on*" (U3). Even the participant who could be described as more of an administrative manager and regularly performed tasks that were more routine in nature (e.g., order processing, e-mails) would adapt his routine depending on the staff present and the information requirements at a given point in time.

Collaborative Nature

The majority of the managers interviewed indicated that they worked with a large number of people (including subordinates, peers, and partners) during the course of their work activities. Collaborative and interdependent work was often required to complete a task. This collaboration involved discussions, contributing to or providing feedback on documents, and sharing of general responsibilities. The participants also undertook tasks that required managing, maintaining, and nurturing relationships with a large number of people. Mobile tablets with the relevant applications supported all these collaborative work. The devices give managers quick access to information and allow them to connect seamlessly with colleagues and customers.

Time-Critical

All participants interviewed indicated a high degree of urgency in their work tasks because completing certain tasks in a timely manner was of critical importance. An example of such a task is responding to a client or business partner. All respondents mentioned that they dealt with large volumes of e-mail on a daily basis, and they needed to manage this constantly to avoid it from "*getting out of hand*". In addition, some managers cited that work from subordinates and colleagues may require attention by the managers and therefore they needed to take actions quickly to avoid delay. One participant highlighted that "*the speed in which I can provide responses is critical*" (U7). Therefore, these managers depended heavily on mobile tablets to obtain the latest information and to respond accordingly.

Information-Centric

The tasks that the managers undertook as part of their work routine were information-centric such as presenting, exchanging, and consuming information. A significant amount of information gathering and research tasks were undertaken by all managers interviewed. Examples of these tasks were reading various documents, monitoring websites, and sourcing market and competitor information. In fact, significant preparation in the form of information gathering was required prior to undertaking business tasks including meetings. The high information-centricity of managerial tasks was also reflected in the amount of time the managers spent on communicating with others, either face to face, via e-mails, or in other forms. One manager commented, "*My pre-work and post-work engagement is around information. So I spend my life online and it's always looking at Twitter and reading and picking up signals about what's going on in the world around us. The more I can do that, the better I can do my job*" (U3).

Mobility

The managers indicated that a fairly high degree of mobility was required in the process of carrying out their work duties. They spent considerable amount of time working away from their primary work location (i.e., work desk) in places such as meeting rooms, boardrooms, and offices of other staff. The managers also did work from their home, other offices, while commuting, and in public locations such as cafés. So, mobile tablets, being extremely lightweight and portable, provide them with the mobility they needed. One participant mentioned that the advantage of the mobile tablet is that it is "*convenient, compact, [and] not heavy to hold*" (U1). They added that the device is smaller and more compatible with their lifestyle. One participant mentioned "*you can sit with your feet up on the lounge and you can really grasp it. The laptop is not like that*" (U1). Another participant (U2) likened the device to a clipboard, mentioning that it is "more natural" to grasp, carry around, and easy to show others. Other comments include that it is more discreet and can be used in more situations than a laptop.

User Friendliness of the Interface

The user interface of the mobile tablets was an important attribute that increases its user friendliness, particularly its large screen, on-screen keyboard, and touch interface. One participant (U1) referred to the touch screen as "*fantastic*" and "*much better than the mouse*". They mentioned that they were happy to forego a keyboard in place of the touch interface. Another participant added that the mobile tablet is "*more physical and controlled*". When compared with other devices with a keyboard, a number of participants indicated that the mobile tablet was arduous and not as user-friendly to type large amounts of text such as documents or long e-mails. The ability to easily scroll through documents was indicated by one participant: "*it's an easy interface to scroll through pages and work more fluidly*" and "*it's easier than having to go through a scroll down scroll up type [interface] (using the iMac)*" (U2). They stated that a mobile tablet is superior simply because it is easier to use.

Reliability

The mobile tablet was referred to as a reliable device by a number of participants. An attribute of the mobile tablet that was mentioned by most participants was the 'instant-on' feature with minimal time required for start-up of the device. In the words of one participant: "*It's just there. You want it, you press the button, and it's on. And that's what people want*" (U1). They also said that "*it doesn't go into any kind of sleep mode that takes another half an hour to get out of it*". Another participant outlined a practical example to illustrate this: "*for instance, I was in a car with a guy and we were trying to do something and he was able to get information very quickly whereas with the laptop, you have to open it up, boot it up. There's a delay. Whereas with the iPad, like a phone, the information is instant*" (U2). The reliability of the device was also mentioned in reference to the battery life, which was referred to as "*superior*" and "*incomparable*" to a laptop. The perceived reliability of the device in terms of reducing threats from viruses and malware was also mentioned. One participant perceived that there were "*no threats of viruses whatsoever, no threat of malware*" and that it "*doesn't slow your system down*".

Connectivity

The ability to connect to networks and the cloud capability of the mobile tablets allow the managers to access information from any location which facilitates the forming of a truly mobile office. This feature is extremely helpful because the majority of the tasks the managers did such as searching the Internet, e-mailing, and video conferencing required network connection. Also, the remote access of information also meant that there is less to lose if the device is damaged or lost.

Autonomy

The managers had a high level of autonomy and flexibility in the allocation of their time. They often arranged and prioritized their work activities depending on action items and issues that may arise during the course of their duties. According to a participant, "*so much stuff comes up on the moment in these sorts of roles that you have to shift things, shift priorities, rearrange your diary. Because there's an opportunity, or there's a fire going that you need to get on top of and resolve as quickly as you can before it turns into something disastrous*" (U7).

4.2 Disruptive Impact of Mobile Tablets

The introduction of mobile tablets into managerial work routines had a significant impact on the use of other digital devices including smartphones, desktop PCs, and laptops. Besides that, manual routines involving pen and paper were impacted too.

Work Laptops (Primary Device Used When Mobile)

Managerial work tasks previously undertaken with laptops were severely disrupted by mobile tablets when the managers were away from their primary work location. Examples of business tasks previously undertaken with laptops when mobile were content consumption and presentation and viewing and responding to e-mails. Since these tasks did not involve a significant amount of document creation, mobile tablets were a perfect match besides having additional advantages of mobility and instant-on capability. This resulted in a sharp decline in the use of laptops in favor of mobile tablets.

Desktop PCs / Laptops (Primary Device Used at the Primary Work Location)

The main device used at the primary work location (whether it is a laptop or PC) remained largely undisrupted by mobile tablets. This can be explained by the deficiencies of mobile tablets in serving as an effective device for document and content creation as well as manipulation.

Desktop PCs / Laptops (Primary Device Used at Home)

The use of desktop PCs or laptops for business tasks at home were significantly disrupted by mobile tablets because managers tended to perform less document intensive tasks while at home. Primarily, they only checked e-mails and typed short responses to e-mails, surfed the Internet, and read documents. In fact, a number of participants noted that they rarely used their desktop PCs / laptops at home since having mobile tablets.

Smartphones

Smartphones were moderately disrupted after the introduction of mobile tablets. The main reason was that smartphones are the only true 'always with you device' in the managerial device portfolio as they are small and highly portable. Additionally, they provide the ability to make phone-calls directly from the device. While smartphones remained the primary reference point for calendar, contacts, and portable music player functionality, mobile tablets can provide similar functions which suit the managers.

The context where smartphones have been largely disrupted by mobile tablets has to do with business-related mobile tasks such as viewing documents and writing e-mails, for which mobile tablets have a greater degree of fit. The reasons for this relate primarily to viewing difficulties caused by the screen size and various aspects relating to the interface as discussed in previous sections. In general, the participants cited using smartphones to the same degree while walking, but less in mobile contexts where they were stationary (such as while commuting, at a café, etc.). Nonetheless, the smartphone was regarded as the most discreet device and remained the primary choice when maximum privacy is sought.

Manual Tasks

Mobile tablets have somewhat disrupted other manual tasks such as using a pen and paper to take notes and use of a paper diary or address book to organize calendar and contact information. The benefits were largely centered on synchronization and ubiquitous access of information, the ability to search content, and the ability to share content with others. Some participants noted that this allowed them to better utilize information (e.g., notes) because it was able to be easily accessed. When using paper for this purpose, the content was more likely to be lost in a pile of information and never retrieved. It should be noted that severe disruption of pen and paper was observed in the case of one participant. They would use mobile tablets to take all business notes, manipulate contacts and calendars, etc., and had ceased using pen and paper in their work routine.

Media

Disruption of print media was also mentioned. A number of participants noted that they were far less likely to purchase a physical newspaper and would use mobile tablets as the primary source of news. The ability to browse through and easily locate information was mentioned as a key benefit of using mobile tablets for this purpose.

Other content delivery mechanisms including television were also somewhat disrupted. A number of participants cited that they would watch less television since acquiring mobile tablets. The ability to watch content on demand using applications such as ABC iView enabled users to watch programs on their time, without having to work around public broadcast schedules. This flexibility is likely to be especially important for managers who are time-poor and cannot commit to consuming content at a specific time during a given period. Table 2 summarizes the extent to which the managers felt their use of other media were disrupted with the iPads.

Table 2. Disruption of other digital devices

Use Context	Level of Disruption
Work laptops (primary device used when mobile)	Severely disrupted
Desktop PCs / laptops (primary device used at the primary work location)	Little to no disruption
Desktop PCs / laptops (primary device used at home)	Significantly disrupted
Smartphones	Moderately disrupted
Manual tasks	Somewhat disrupted
Media (newspaper and television)	Somewhat disrupted

5. DISCUSSION

This study contributes to the unexplored area of managerial technology use by exploring and providing a better understanding of the critical factors influencing managers' use of mobile tablets, and how mobile tablets affect the use of other digital devices and media. It makes two important contributions. First, it enriches our understanding of a new type of mobile technology use behavior in organizations. The existing literature (e.g., Gebauer & Shaw, 2004; Ioimo & Aronson, 2004; Liang et al., 2007; Tan & Sie, 2015) examines mainly conventional mobile devices such as laptops, PDAs and smart phones. Mobile tablets carry distinct features, thus requiring studies to understand their usage. This study thus contributes to technology use theory aspect by focusing on a new type of technology (i.e., mobile tablet).

Second, our study focuses on mid to high-level managers – a group that is seldom the target of study in researching technology use. In fact, the literature focuses only on individuals such as students, general household users and workers below the managerial level. While comparing to other user groups, managers may not be a large user group, but they represent an important party with the power to influence usage and selection of technology among workers in organizations. Bagozzi and Dholakia's (2006) concept of group norm in their goal-directed behavior model can explain the phenomenon where influential people such as managers can affect new technology selection among the subordinates. In other words, because the nature of managerial work differs substantially from other employees, the findings of this study provide direct and relevant insights specific for managers. Hence, by focusing on managers and mobile tablets, this study addresses two research gaps in the literature for mobile technology use.

The findings showed that managerial tasks involved a high degree of non-routineness where the work undertaken was largely determined by priority and urgency. Many tasks were also time-critical, thus requiring immediate actions. Additionally, the tasks were information-centric and required collaboration with others. The most significant tasks managers undertook using mobile tablets are document access and viewing, web surfing and consuming online content, e-mail access, note-taking, and calendar and contact management. To a lesser extent, the managers also used mobile tablets to perform social networking and presentations. Besides that, a mobile tablet has high degree of mobility and portability due to its size, form factor, and weight. The user-friendliness of the tablet interface was also a key aspect, especially the large screen, on-screen keyboard, and touch interface. Reliability considerations including the battery life, minimal start-up time required, and resistance to viruses were also taken into account by managers. Furthermore, its' general functionalities such as the applications ('apps') available for use, and the network connectivity were important to managers.

Overall, mobile tablets are suitable for managerial task due to the features of high mobility, easy accessibility, reliability, and abundance of available applications. The compact form factor and intuitive user interface were perceived by participants to be 'natural', comfortable to use, and less intrusive when used in the presence of others. In comparison to other devices, mobile tablets are more likely to be used by managers in a wider variety of situations, leading to greater utility and higher overall value to the managers. The characteristics of the device are a close fit with managers and the nature of the tasks they undertake when away from their primary work location.

The high level of mobile tablets use among managers has led to the 'disruption' of devices, especially laptops, when managers are away from their primary work location. While away, mobile tablets are used for content consumption and presentation as well as viewing and responding to e-mails. However, when managers are at their primary work location, they revert to desktops or laptops as the main device. The reasons being mobile tablets lack suitable applications to create, edit and manipulate business documents, and it is inconvenient to use the on-screen keyboards for large-scale text input. When managers do work from home, they also choose suitable devices depending on the tasks they want to perform. Adoption of mobile tablets also disrupts manual tasks using pens and papers such as taking notes, and organizing calendar and contact information. In short, there is a set of factors influencing managers' usage patterns of mobile tablets.

Along with other digital devices, the mobile tablets intrude into the managers' life and work routines. The managers favored devices that are less visible and would fade into the background. As the degree of intrusiveness increases, they will seek ways to make the devices less visible. Figure 1 ranks the degree of intrusiveness for four devices with desktop PCs on one end of the spectrum being most intrusive and the smartphones on the other end being the least intrusive. As technology develops, the continuum of intrusiveness will determine how physical characteristics of technology and the method of interaction with human evolve. With this comes the issue of social etiquette about acceptable and unacceptable behavior of technology use. Therefore, the key is to make human-technology interaction as natural as possible to minimize the degree of distraction of the users as well as others present.

6. CONCLUSION

This paper has explored and identified the factors influencing managerial use of mobile tablet and how mobile tablets impact the use of other digital devices through semi-structured interviews with managers who had incorporated mobile tablets into their work routine. The study has found that the mobile technology is suitable for managerial use due to a set of nine key factors: non-routineness, collaborative

Figure 1. Continuum of intrusiveness

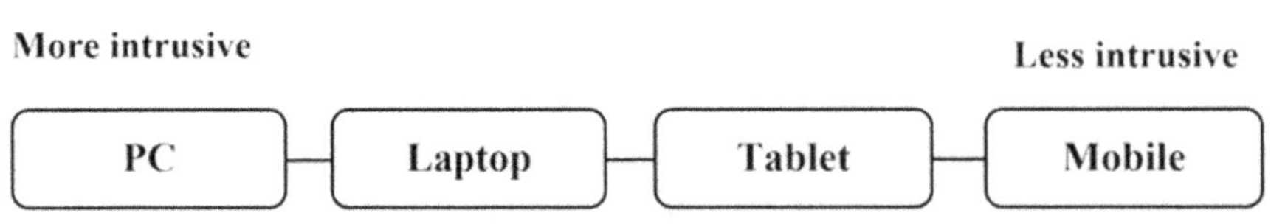

nature, time-critical, information-centric, mobility, user friendliness of the interface, reliability, connectivity, and autonomy. Furthermore, the study reveals that the adoption of mobile tablets affects the use of other digital devices as well as traditional manual method of employing pens and papers. In addition, this study contributes to practice by offering a solid basis to help managers establish a business case for mobile tablet adoption.

Like other research projects, this study has some limitations which also offer opportunities for future research. Firstly, a main limitation of this study relates to the nature of the exploratory qualitative approach, and so the findings are produced by replication logic rather than the sampling logic obtained from quantitative research. Hence, the factors identified serve as a good foundation for future quantitative studies such as survey into managerial use of mobile technology. Secondly, this study focused primarily on panel members who had experience with Apple's iPad, the most popular tablet in the workplace (Endler, 2014). There may have been some bias in responses that were not shared by those individuals familiar with other tablets. Nonetheless, the major functions and features of other vendors' mobile tables are somewhat similar to Apple's iPad. Future research could test the factors revealed in this paper using quantitative methods such as questionnaires.

ACKNOWLEDGMENT

An earlier version of this paper was presented at the 19th Pacific Asia Conference on Information Systems. The comments of the reviewers are appreciated.

REFERENCES

Bagozzi, R. P., & Dholakia, U. M. (2006). Antecedents and purchase consequences of customer participation in small group brand communities. *International Journal of Research in Marketing*, *23*(1), 45–61. doi:10.1016/j.ijresmar.2006.01.005

Balasubramanian, S., Peterson, R., & Jarvenpaa, S. (2002). Exploring the implications of m-commerce for markets and marketing. *Journal of the Academy of Marketing Science*, *30*(4), 348–361. doi:10.1177/009207002236910

Basole, R. (2008). *Enterprise mobility: Applications, technologies and strategies*. Amsterdam: IOS Press.

Batsell, J. (2011). Intrigued, but not immersed: Millennial students analyze the iPad's performance as a news platform. In *International Symposium on Online Journalism*. University of Texas at Austin.

Endler, M. (2014). iPad dominates enterprise tablet market. *InformationWeek*. Retrieved May 15 2016 from InformationWeek website: http://www.informationweek.com/mobile/mobile-devices/ipad-dominates-enterprise-tablet-market/d/d-id/1113813?piddl_msgpage=1#msgs

Gartner. (2017). *Gartner forecasts flat worldwide device shipments until 2018*. Retrieved June 19 2017 from Gartner Newsroom website: http://www.gartner.com/newsroom/id/3560517

Gebauer, J., & Shaw, M. J. (2004). Success factors and impacts of mobile business applications: Results from a mobile e-procurement study. *International Journal of Electronic Commerce*, *8*(3), 19–41.

Gebauer, J., Shaw, M. J., & Gribbins, M. L. (2010). Task-technology fit for mobile information systems. *Journal of Information Technology*, *25*(3), 259–272. doi:10.1057/jit.2010.10

Grover, V., & Goslar, M. (1993). Toward an empirical taxonomy and model of evolution for telecommunications technologies. *Journal of Information Technology*, *8*(3), 167–176. doi:10.1057/jit.1993.23

Harris, J., Ives, B., & Junglas, I. (2012). IT consumerization: When gadgets turn into enterprise IT tools. *MIS Quarterly Executive*, *11*(3), 99–112.

Hughes, N. (2013). *Apple has sold 170M iPads to date, implying sales near 15M in September quarter*. Retrieved May 15 2016 from AppleInsider website: http://appleinsider.com/articles/13/10/23/apple-has-sold-170m-ipads-to-date-implying-sales-near-15m-in-sept-quarter

Ioimo, R. E., & Aronson, J. E. (2004). Police field mobile computing: Applying the theory of Task-Technology Fit. *Police Quarterly*, *7*(4), 403–428. doi:10.1177/1098611103251113

Karlson, A. K., Meyers, B. R., Jacobs, A., Johns, P., & Kane, S. K. (2009). Working overtime: Patterns of smartphone and PC usage in the day of an information worker. In H. Tokuda, M. Beigl, A. Friday, A. J. B. Brush, & Y. Tobe (Eds.), *Pervasive Computing* (pp. 398–405). Redmond, WA: Springer. doi:10.1007/978-3-642-01516-8_27

Kelly, J., & Schrape, J. (2010). 100 days with an iPad: Lessons learnt and apps acquired. In Curriculum, Technology & Transformation for an Unknown Future, Sydney, Australia.

Kim, S. H. (2008). Moderating effects of job relevance and experience on mobile wireless technology acceptance: Adoption of a smartphone by individuals. *Information & Management*, *45*(6), 387–393. doi:10.1016/j.im.2008.05.002

Kotter, J. P. (1982). *The general managers*. New York: Free Press.

Liang, T.-P., Huang, C.-W., Yeh, Y.-H., & Lin, B. (2007). Adoption of mobile technology in business: A fit-viability model. *Industrial Management & Data Systems*, *107*(8), 1154–1169. doi:10.1108/02635570710822796

McClard, A., & Somers, P. (2000). Unleashed: Web tablet integration into the home. *Proceedings of the SIGCHI Conference on Human Factors in Computing Systems*. 10.1145/332040.332042

Middleton, C. A., & Cukier, W. (2006). Is mobile email functional or dysfunctional? Two perspectives on mobile email usage. *European Journal of Information Systems*, *15*(3), 252–260. doi:10.1057/palgrave.ejis.3000614

Müller, H., Gove, J., & Webb, J. (2012). Understanding tablet use: A multi-method exploration. *Proceedings of the 14th International Conference on Human-Computer Interaction with Mobile Devices and Services*.

Mylonopoulos, N. A., & Doukidis, G. I. (2003). Introduction to the special issue: Mobile business: Technological pluralism, social assimilation, and growth. *International Journal of Electronic Commerce*, *8*(1), 5–22.

Neuman, W. L. (2011). *Social research methods: Qualitative and quantitative approaches* (7th ed.). Pearson/Allyn and Bacon.

Ozok, A. A., Benson, D., Chakraborty, J., & Norcio, A. F. (2008). A comparative study between tablet and laptop PCs: User satisfaction and preferences. *International Journal of Human-Computer Interaction, 24*(3), 329–352. doi:10.1080/10447310801920524

Pearson, J., & Buchanan, G. (2010). Real-time document collaboration using iPads. In *Proceedings of the third workshop on Research advances in large digital book repositories and complementary media.* Toronto: ACM.

Perry, M., O'Hara, K., Sellen, A., Brown, B., & Harper, R. (2001). Dealing with mobility: Understanding access anytime, anywhere. *ACM Transactions on Computer-Human Interaction, 8*(4), 323–347. doi:10.1145/504704.504707

Pitt, L., Berthon, P., & Robson, K. (2011). Deciding when to use tablets for business applications. *MIS Quarterly Executive, 10*(3), 133–139.

Prentice, S. (2010). *CEO advisory: Seize the iPad opportunity now.* Gartner Publisher.

Puuronen, S., & Savolainen, V. (1997). Mobile information systems – Executives' view. *Information Systems Journal, 7*(1), 3–20. doi:10.1046/j.1365-2575.1997.00002.x

Sheng, H., Nah, F. F. H., & Siau, K. (2005). Strategic implications of mobile technology: A case study using value-focused thinking. *The Journal of Strategic Information Systems, 14*(3), 269–290. doi:10.1016/j.jsis.2005.07.004

Shneiderman, B. (2003). *Leonardo's laptop: Human needs and the new computing technologies.* MIT Press.

Tan, W. K., & Sie, M. S. (2015). The impact of personal innovativeness on product aesthetics and self-connection with brand: A case study of mobile phone users. *Behaviour & Information Technology, 34*(3), 316–325. doi:10.1080/0144929X.2014.952777

Willis, D. A. (2011). *iPad and beyond: The media tablet in business.* Retrieved March 11 2016 from Gartner website: http://www.gartner.com/technology/research/ipad-media-tablet/

Yuan, Y., Archer, N., Connelly, C. E., & Zheng, W. (2010). Identifying the ideal fit between mobile work and mobile work support. *Information & Management, 47*(3), 125–137. doi:10.1016/j.im.2009.12.004

APPENDIX

Interview Protocol

Icebreaker

Include approximately two minutes of 'small talk' to develop a rapport with the participant.

- Not to mention iPads at this point as this might distract the participant when answering the questions in the next section.

Background Information

Aim of Questioning: To gain important information about the current role and responsibilities of the respondent.

- Can you please describe your role in your organization? In your answer you can discuss your areas of responsibility and accountability.
- Can you please describe the hierarchy / chain of command in your organization? You can talk about staff you manage, who you report to, and the tasks you undertake during your work activities.
- What would be a typical day at work for you? Do you work out of the office? From home?

Transitional Question

- How do you use information technology in your role? What business tasks do you use technology to complete?

Acquisition

Aim of Questioning: To obtain data to answer the following question: Are iPads replacing pre-existing personal computers, or simply adding to the devices at a manager's disposal?

- What devices do you currently use as part of your work routine? (Please consider Desktop PCs, Laptops, Netbooks, Tablets and Smartphones). How many of each device do you have?
- Tell me about your iPad. Please discuss the model, length of use, etc.
- What were the circumstances surrounding you acquiring the iPad? What would you say was the main reason you came to use the device?
- What were your first impressions of the device? When and why did you consider using the device for business?
- Do any of your managers, colleagues, subordinates, or business contacts use iPads to carry out business tasks? Is there any distinct resistance or support from others in the organization towards iPads?

Utilization

Aim of Questioning: To obtain data to answer the following question: What tasks are managers using iPads for? Why?

- What would you say are the main business tasks for which you use your iPad to complete?
- For what tasks do you favor iPads over other devices? Why?
- How have your usage habits changed since acquisition of the iPad? Are you currently using the device differently to how you initially utilized it?
- What tasks do you feel are unsuitable for iPads?
- What would be the main situations (or locations) where you use your iPad?

Aim of Questioning: To obtain data to answer the following question: Are iPads more suited for certain tasks undertaken by managers than other technologies such as laptops, netbooks and smartphones?

- Before you acquired your iPad, what devices were you using to complete business tasks? Please consider devices you use at work *and* at home that you use for work. Describe how and why you used each device.
- How have you changed your daily work routine since acquiring an iPad?
- What devices are you using less or have you ceased to use since the acquisition of the iPad?

Aim of Questioning: To obtain data to answer the following question: Where do iPads fit into the current managerial technology portfolio?

- Do you feel that iPads enable you to perform your job more efficiently or effectively? What tasks do you feel that you are able to perform better with the use of an iPad? Do you feel that you are able to make better use of your time?
- How would you like to / do you intend to use iPads in the future for work-related tasks?
- Are you using the iPad differently to how you originally expected?
- What non-work tasks do you use your iPad for? Does anyone else use your iPad for non-work tasks?

Chapter 12
Mind the Gap:
From Analytics to Action in Student Retention

Qing Huang
La Trobe University, Australia

Nilupulee Nathawitharana
La Trobe University, Australia

Kok-Leong Ong
La Trobe University, Australia

Susan Keller
La Trobe University, Australia

Damminda Alahakoon
La Trobe University, Australia

ABSTRACT

The issue of student attrition is a complex one and has been an area of research interest among education researchers. Recently, education researchers are proposing to tap into the large amount of student data that are housed within the institution's data warehouse. This big student data of demography, learning journey, and their interactions with the institution presents a rich source of insights that can be discovered using advanced analytics. Consequently, education researchers have put forward predictive models, suggest the use of data triggers and dashboards aimed at improving student retention. This however has been met with limited success to date. From experience, there remains a gap between the analytics and the operationalization of the analytics. Consequently, this gap needs to be addressed to achieve student retention. The authors propose a dual framework to close this gap. While this framework was developed in the context of creating a solution for student attrition, it is sufficiently generalizable to analytical solutions for problems around student learning.

DOI: 10.4018/978-1-5225-5718-0.ch012

1. INTRODUCTION

Student attrition is one of the biggest challenges facing universities worldwide. The cost of student attrition is high, impacting not only individual students but also universities and society as a whole. Higher education (Johnson, Brett, & Deary, 2010) facilitates upward social mobility with university graduates enjoying higher incomes over their lifetimes Education is also a powerful enabler of social and economic development in both developed and developing countries. From the university prospective, student attrition not only results in direct loss of revenue, but it can damage a university's reputation and undermine its aspirations for increasing access and equity to higher education.

There has been a lot of research over the past fifty years into the determinants of student attrition. Several theoretical models have been proposed, notably those put forward by (Tinto, 1987) and (Bean & Metzner, 1985). These theories informed us of the reasons behind students leaving higher education and have since being used by universities to implement preventive programs. Unfortunately, though, these programs have not led to substantial improvements in student retention according to (Seidman, 2005)

There are many reasons for the disappointing outcome. One of them is the increase in the diversity and mobility of student cohorts (Tremblay, 2013), which has made the task a lot more challenging and resource intensive. Furthermore, the research to date has also confirmed the issue of student attrition and retention to be a challenging and complex issue, often with factors interlaced by that of an individual, or the social and organization environment. These combination of factors mean that intervention that are effective in one context may not be so in another. For example, an individual's previous academic success, level of commitment to current study as well emotional intelligence scores have all been shown to be correlated or are predictors of attrition (Sparkman, Maulding, & Roberts, 2012). Yet social factors, including the support of family, friends and community also play a part in retention and hence, attrition. It is also further recognized that the broad attrition and retention outcome from a university is also very much tied to the social, economic and political environment that the university operates in (Seidman, 2005). To further complicate the issue, the university as an organization also contribute to the student's success. The influencing factors can include the university's location, student-staff interaction, the cohort characteristics, the learning environment provided, as well as the fit of the university's teaching model to the students' learning needs (Seidman, 2005). These factors all play a role in triggering a student's decision to leave a course, or the university altogether.

Consequently, a key message that we synthesized from current works is that these factors all contribute to predicting attrition and that, we should not look at a subset of factors in isolation. In other words, if attrition is to be meaningfully understood and purposefully managed, then the institution needs to implement their student success strategies, policies, and actions with specific social, cultural and organizational context in mind. Yet to do this is no simply feat. Recent developments in managing attrition has started to lean towards the use of data driven models in formulating strategies, policies and delivery of interventions (Wagner & Longanecker, 2016). It is very promising and research into the use of data to manage attrition is starting to get traction, particularly in this age of 'big data'. However, progress in this area is also hampered by the lack of reliable data and clear data analysis methods to inform the university's approach and methodology to manage their own attrition issue. This situation is an interesting one because universities are traditionally forerunners of new ideas and development but not so in this case if we draw parallels between student retention and customer retention in customer-facing industries.

Yet, they share a lot of parallels. The big student data that university has includes the student demography, the student's learning journey, as well as their interaction with the learning organization. This corresponds very well with the big customer data that many commercial organizations have, i.e., the customer data that parallels student demography details, the customer's purchase history that maps well against the student's learning journey and the social media interaction of customers that is akin to the students' interaction with systems like the University's network and the LMS. In the case of customer-facing industries, many have been early adopters of data and analytics, producing many success stories in recent years (Jahromi, Stakhovych, & Ewing, 2015). Although the technology aspects of data driven decision making is already well-tested, most higher education institutions are yet to be in-step with industry developments (Abrahams, 2010). In fact, (Jones, 2007)'s study showed that universities are only slowly becoming aware of the need to create central repositories of their big student data. That said, institutions can now benefit from the well-tested methods that customer-facing industries have developed over the years.

The important question is whether institutions are ready to tap into the potential benefits that data and analytics will bring to them. It appears that this is becoming a non-question as digital disruptors represented strongly by the MOOCs are now at the door step of traditional institutions in the form of new learning paradigms (Kaplan & Haenlein, 2016). And they are primarily digital in their operations forcing traditional institution models to change so as to keep up with the MOOCs as well as their traditional competitors (Lahtinen & Weaver, 2015). For an institution to move towards a data driven paradigm however, the process is one that requires careful preparation and institution-wide support. This is crucial if a data driven strategy to retention and attrition management is to be successful. Indeed, the shift is a very challenging one, as it often involves a series of changes (not to mention the resources that go into implementing the change) to the institution's current information systems, BI/analytics strategy, administrative and academic procedures and even, organizational structure and culture. Without doubt, these complexities hinder the deployment of a data and analytical driven strategy with many carrying 'half-baked' solutions that held back what the approach can truly deliver in terms of outcomes.

Of course, the gap and challenge is not restricted to the issue of student retention but more broadly the implementation of data analytics within institutions. (Macfadyen & Dawson, 2012) found that a lack of preparation and capacity to resolve the complicated changes required by the adoption process prevented institutions from making significant use of data and analytics for learning (or learning analytics). In 2014, Ferguson *et al.*, revisited the issue and described how the ROMA framework (Ferguson et al., 2014) can be used as a step-by-step process to the institutional adoption of learning analytics. These research pointed out the need for a more systematic and holistic approach to help institutions implement a learning analytics strategy in which student retention is a component of. Even so, delivering and managing student success is a complex and challenging task. As mentioned, the understanding of attrition factors in one context does not necessarily translate to another in practice due to a range of factors involved. This stems from the gap that exist between the analytics and the operationalization of the analytics, including the implementation and use among staff on the ground. Consequently, this gap needs to be addressed so that the proper systems, processes and relevant 'buy-in' can be achieved to see the change that brings in the investment in analytics for student retention.

In this chapter, we propose a dual-framework consisting of (i) a holistic analytical solution approach that can be implemented by a (ii) systematic process. The first presents the guidelines to bridging the big student data to the specific problem(s) to be addressed and the later outlines how any such solution can be implemented to the effect of being measurable, or where impact can be demonstrated. While this framework was developed in the context of creating a solution for student attrition, it is sufficiently generalizable to analytical solutions for problems around student learning.

2. BACKGROUND

2.1 Definitions of Student Attrition and Student Retention

Across the literature about student attrition and student retention, the two terms have been used interchangeably. Many considers them two sides of the same coin although they have their distinction. For student attrition, the term refers to the departure of a student before completion of a course. However, this departure may be to start a new course at the same University, or it may an unofficial intermission. As a result, student attrition isn't as straightforward. To further complicate matters, research has shown that the features of student attrition are different at different stages. For example, commencing students are most vulnerable to withdrawing and the triggers (or reasons) are different to those who withdrew from the same course at other points in time.

Regardless of how or why attrition occurs, it is measured by an 'attrition rate'. This measure is defined by institutions to track and monitor the attrition of interest, such as intra-year attrition rate and between-year attrition rate. High attrition rate of any type will have a large impact on universities. The most direct impact would be the significant loss of revenue and sunk cost associated with the development of a course. More importantly, a high attrition rate damages the university's reputation as these leavers may potentially communicate dissatisfaction with their university experience to family, work and social networks.

Student retention, on the other hand, is about combating student attrition, i.e., to retain students. At the institution level, student retention could refer to keeping them within the institution until they successfully complete a course, or to retain a certain particular student group to support the institution's mission to the community. Yet as the same time, student retention as the course level is about keeping the student in the same course until they complete, which may not always be the ultimate goal of student retention at the Univeristy level. Hence as with the different attrition types, there are different student retention perspective and often, it is about the attrition types that one wants to address that drives the retention strategies.

In the big student data context, if any of these retention strategy is to be data-driven, then the right data and analytical framework must be identified. Further, this development of an analytical solution should also be designed in a way that operationalized well with the stakeholders of the operational environment such as the staff, the existing procedures and the current information systems in place.

2.2 Approaches for Student Retention

For the above reasons, the starting point is to understand the specific context in which the attrition factors are analysed. It is with this correct understanding that institutions can then take actions to retain students, which is often accomplished by allocating resources to conduct certain interventions. Learning from the experience of customer analytics, student retention will be better if the exact and personal concerns of the student is addressed. Yet every institution is limited by the resources available to conduct specific interventions and it would be unrealistic to intervene on a large population. This means there is a need to allocate resources in a more targeted manner.

Currently, the most widely-adopted approach is to identify a group of students who are deem at risk of attrition from the student data that is available to the organization unit responsible for managing attrition (Aulck, Velagapudi, Blumenstock, & West, 2016; Dietz-Uhler & Hurn, 2013; Sajjadi et al., 2017). By analyzing the historical data, the students whom are displaying patterns of attrition are identified and the biggest group is where the intervention resources are deployed. Such interventions are the only touch-point in which retention effort is visible to the students. Behind the scenes, intervention involves the complex decisions on how to best allocate human resources, facilities as well as the selection of appropriate intervention actions. Underpinning these is not just a comprehensive strategy to guide the process but also the correct data and analytics to support it.

2.3 Challenges

In the ideal situation, it is expected that many of the 'at-risk' students will be retained once the appropriate interventions are delivered with the correct understanding and strategy. In practice, this continues to be a challenge. In part, we attribute this to the fact that the studies reporting retention outcomes have been conducted in isolation and does not take a holistic view to implementing retention solutions. For example, we have seen reports of exploring attrition factors from within the institution. e.g., psychological (Richardson, Abraham, & Bond, 2012), as well as exploring attrition factors from outside, e.g., social (Bayer, Bydzovská, Géryk, Obsivac, & Popelinsky, 2012). We have also seen a technology approach where new advanced modelling techniques are used to better identify 'at-risk' students (Xing, Guo, Petakovic, & Goggins, 2015) to research on effective intervention actions by (Michels, 2016). Yet, it is hard to find research that tries to provide an overarching framework to present a way to encapsulate these isolated piece-wise solutions into a system that can be operationalized. As pointed out by (Eckerson, 2012), this is about the ability of the institution to undertake change management as part of deploying a data driven and analytical approach, which means ensuring that the right data, information systems architecture, and people & culture are in place.

Recently, there has been attempts to provide a holistic approach, such as the ROMA framework by (Ferguson et al., 2014). There are also a number of case studies of analytics implementation, such as the Open University of UK, the University of Technology, Sydney (Clow, 2014) and the Course Signals at Purdue (Arnold & Pistilli, 2012). Among them, the Course Signals project at Purdue University is well-known for being a pioneer in using analytics to improve student retention. However, it has not yet been deployed across the entire university despite the significant investment over a nine-year period (Ferguson et al., 2014) suggesting that barriers do exist when scaling up a system. Purdue is not alone in having road blocks with their analytics implementation. The Open University in UK has faced barriers for decades (Macfadyen & Dawson, 2012) as well.

Worse, as student population grows and the among of digital data now exploding within learning environments, this big student data phenomenon has added another layer of complexity that further reinforces the case for a holistic approach that takes into account, the various facets and factors of attrition in order to deliver a retention solution that is mapped well to the operational environment in practice. Specifically for the analytics and BI systems, this means making sure that the technology is well-aligned to the context in which the relevant features are extracted from the data warehouse (or the relevant data sources). While for operational reasons, there needs to be a strategy that allows one to deploy the system to fit the unique structure and workflow of the operational unit. That said, we recognize that the institutional context, culture, workflow, etc., is diverse. Hence, in search of a holistic approach, we found that the similarity among the diverse institutions lies in the student lifecycle.

The student lifecycle while different across institutions, presents sufficient common concepts to develop an over-arching framework to guide the use of big student data to operationalizing analytical solutions for specific attrition outcomes. At the same time, it is sufficiently generalizable to enable other kinds of solutions for problems pertaining to a student within a learning institution.

3. ANALYTICS FOR RETENTION: A HOLISTIC DATA-DRIVEN STUDENT RETENTION MODEL

As shown in Figure 1, there are a number of key questions to be answered in order to understand attrition and to conduct intervention. In understanding attrition, key questions to ask include when one drops off from a course include "who", "when" and "why". The answers to these questions helps us learn from the past and informs our ability to understand the triggers thereby allowing us to identify the candidates who are likely to leave, why and of course, who when and how to intervene. This not only aids understanding but also helps us in building the appropriate analytics model for the context and operation environment.

When explored in depth, the answers to these questions are not straightforward, possibly requiring a number of data analysis. This was made more difficult by the fact that we now operate in an environment where access to higher education is now available to a more diverse cohort in terms of demographical and social background. Furthermore, the disruption brought about by the change to curriculum design, delivery, assessment and evaluation over the years (Morgan, 2013) has added another layer of complexity to the challenge of finding the real answers for why a student left a course.

Consequently, attrition types are far more wide-ranging and is influenced by more factors than before. One way to help understand the causes and to identify the symptoms that led to a specific attrition event is to identify the attrition points over time. An attrition point is where an attrition event takes place. This reference point allows us to work out the timeframe in the lead up to this event and to aid in identifying the symptoms and causes that triggered the attrition. The symptoms and causes identified in this timeframe will help answer various questions about the type of attrition and to inform the subsequent design of the strategy to deliver the retention.

Figure 1. Key questions to be answered for student attrition and retention

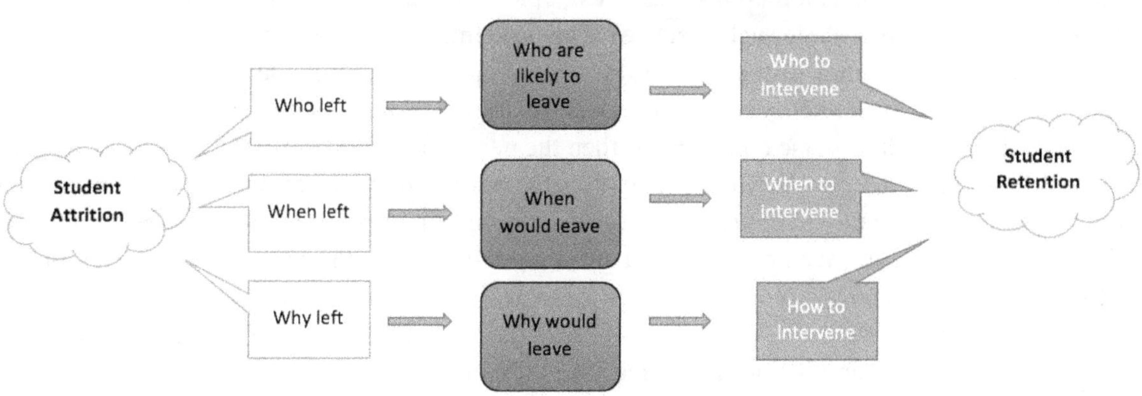

As we can see in Figure 1, there are multiple attrition points so a boundary is needed to decide on the ones that are of interest. Fortunately, there is an overarching timeframe to this, i.e., the student lifecycle. The student lifecycle gives us a meaningful context within which attrition events are to be considered. It is specific to each student, as we shall present next by suffice to say, this student lifecycle is also the link between the dual framework that we present in this chapter.

3.1 Student Lifecycle: The Context of Attrition and Retentions

The reason that the student lifecycle is specific to each student is because there are various start and end points possible. A student lifecycle (Morgan, 2013) could start when student was a prospect making the first contact with the institution, or when the student commences his or her study via a transfer from another institution. Similarly, an end point can be marked by a student finishing a course, transferred out of the course or has left the learning environment. Hence, the first question before undertaking any analytics or even in deciding on the student data to drive any attrition or retention operation is to determine the kind of student lifecycle that an institution is interested in exploring. This in turn leads to the attrition type that the institution is interested in undertaking. For most institutions and the attrition types of interest, the start and end points are well-aligned to the academic calendar and makes it easy in terms of stakeholder communication and alignment to existing information systems. In addition, it also makes the case for any new analytics projects to be easily project managed, giving stakeholders concrete dates and milestones to work with.

Some of the milestones can be further designated as checkpoints, to help design the intervention strategy, the targets for intervention and the protocol. For a specific attrition type, a check point can be determined to allow for sufficient lead time to pre-empt the attrition event. As an example, a checkpoint was set before the attrition point as shown in Figure 2. Usually this will provide sufficient lead time to preempt the attrition event. A checkpoint can also be set towards the end of the timeframe so that more up to date data about the symptoms and causes can be collected for future use regarding various attrition types.

3.2 Attrition Timeframe and Intervention Checkpoint

An attrition type could occur at multiple time points. Each time when it occurs, we have an attrition event that could lead to various attrition points. As an example, Australian institutions have an attrition type call ‘census’ that has two or three such events over an academic year. The ‘census’ attrition is a type of attrition that happens as a result of students deciding that a course wasn’t suitable and decided to withdraw usually by transferring to another course. If this is the attrition type and that the event of interest is in the first semester in which this course commences, then the next step is to identify the attrition time frame.

The attrition time frame, as shown in Figure 2, is the period in the lead up to an attrition event. An attrition event occurs because symptoms and causes are building up, ultimately triggering the event. Any intervention should be taken before the attrition event is triggered but an intervention should only start if sufficient causes and symptoms are identified to avoid interventions targeting the wrong student. Having an attrition time frame allows us to answer two questions:(i) from when we should start looking for symptoms and causes; and (ii) when to undertake “just-in-time” intervention.

Although this is a data centric framework that assist with identifying the intervention, the framework also carries with it a wealth of other information such as the ability to identify time points for symptoms

Figure 2. Attrition linked to student lifecycle and academic calendar

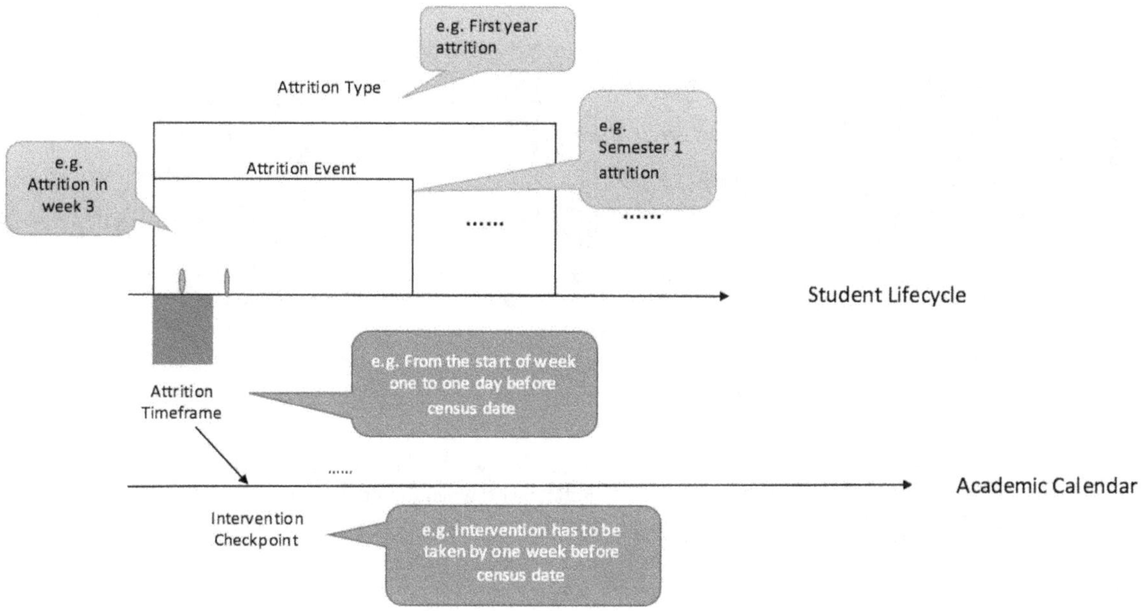

and cause, the identification of checkpoints and attrition points, and how to schedule these in practice. What is not obvious though is one has to estimate the amount of time required to carry out an intervention. There needs to be sufficient time between the checkpoint and the attrition point to allow implementation of the desired intervention. Otherwise, the analytics implementation is likely to fail or unable to deliver the results desired. In asking about the amount of time needed to implement an intervention, questions such as "who", "when", and "how" will also be answered particularly if there was an iterative process of designing an intervention based on the analytics.

The figure also helps to unpack more questions to be asked. This includes

- How large should the timeframe be in the lead up to an attrition point?
- What are the symptoms and causes that will trigger an attrition event?
- Where should checkpoints be placed?
- What is the intervention strategy and design w.r.t the checkpoint?
- What design should be undertaken?
- What are the evaluation criteria to assess the outcomes of the intervention?

Given the data-centric approach of this framework, the answer obviously lies in the data. In particular, we should be using the big student data within the learning environment to assist us through the four stages of developing data-driven intervention: understanding, targeting, intervening and intelligence refinement, as shown in Figure 3. Each stage is informed and driven by data, which flow from one stage to the next with feedback delivered in the form of an update via a closed data flow loop. We will unpack the details of each stage next.

Figure 3. Holistic data-driven student retention approach

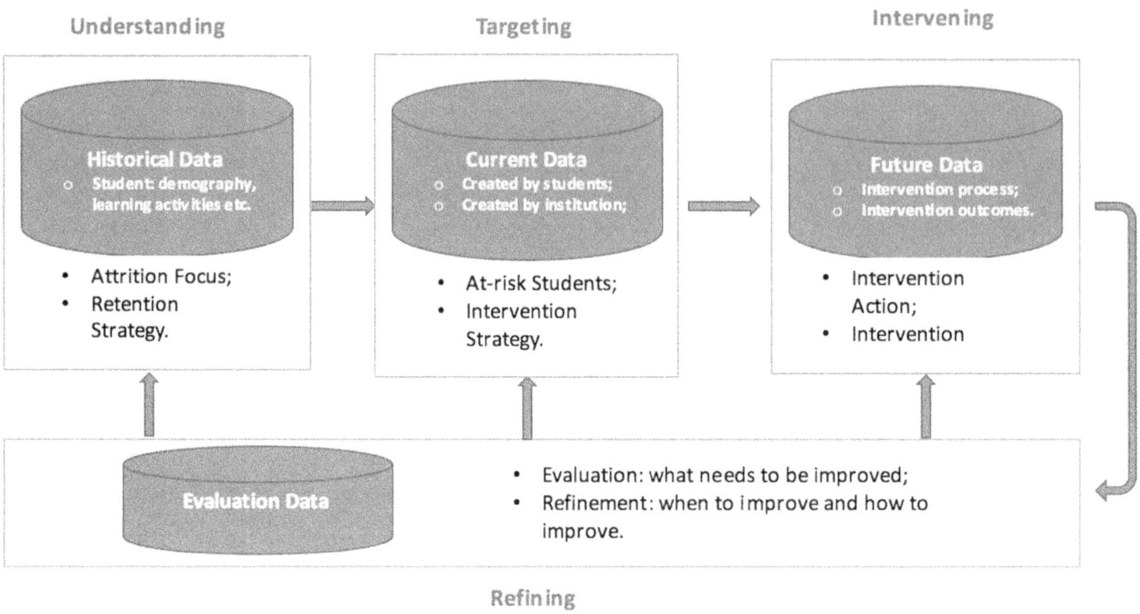

3.2.1 Stage One: Understanding

The first stage initiates the process of finding answers to the key questions raised in order to understand the attrition of interest from the past. This includes learning from observations of others through existing literature to understand the various questions that arises from the framework, including the distinct features that are understood to be triggers of a possible attrition event. Of course, this is unlikely to be sufficient given that each institution is structurally and culturally different. This is where the knowledge from the literature is to be discussed and contextualized. As shown in Figure 4, input from various stakeholders within the institution should be obtained and married with the learnings from the literature. This can be as simple as an analysis of the institution's attrition based on the methodology proposed, or it could be more complex analytical tasks undertaken through an analysis of the big student data (e.g., student profiling, course profile attribution, etc.) and then drawing parallels from the extant literature.

Regardless of the analysis, the goal is to identify the features or establish the student profiles that are strongly correlated to the attrition event for the institution. These analyses could be undertaken in any way from the data, and by no means does it need to be using advanced analytics techniques. More importantly, sourcing the correct data for the analysis to support the reasons for the attrition event is more important. In saying that, the nature of big student data mans that this step of investigating or the attempt to seek answers will require iteratively investigating the data to establish the clear evidence from the data to explain the attrition event of interest. This information can then be corroborated within the literature. While the outcomes may differ, it also helps to bring about questions on how a particular methodology from the literature should be modified to suit. Consequently, this brings about a much improved and informed approach to designing any intervention going forward.

On those occasions where the outcomes from the student of one's data doesn't lead to any similarity in the current literature, this would be a major 'red-flag' to the institution interested in an implementation

Figure 4. Contextualised understanding of attrition in institution

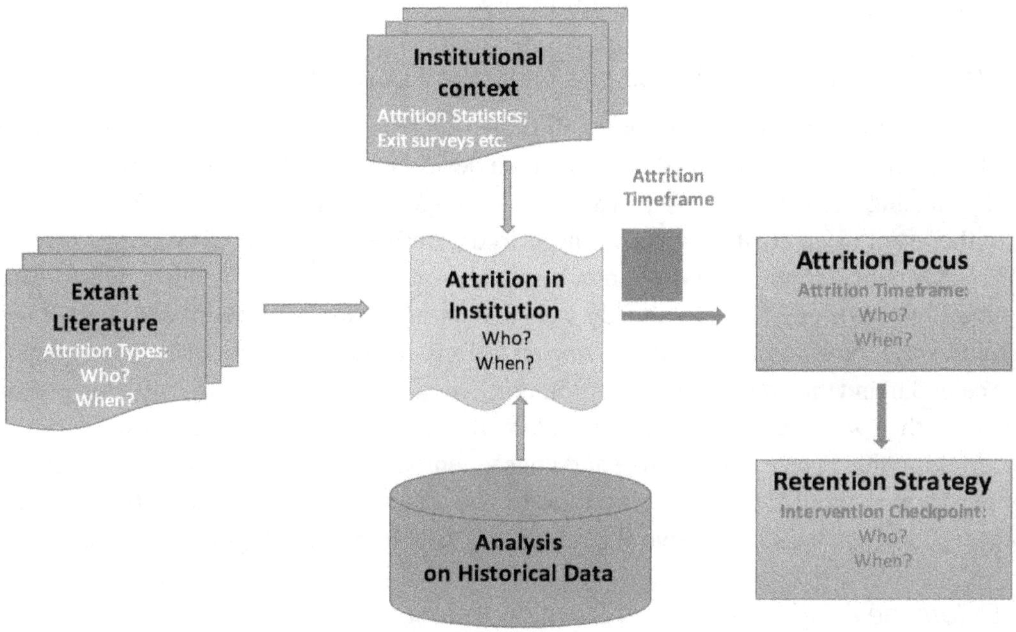

for operational purposes. In that case, it is likely that the project should be re-scoped as a trial or one that is undertaken as a research study rather than one that is to be moved into an institution wide implementation for operational purposes. At this juncture, the question of course is how unique and special this intervention is likely to be. Quite possibly, this can also include asking questions on what the risk and ROI may be if the institution were to attempt something that isn't been studied in the field yet. As a research or trial, the risk is definitely lower and possibly opening up to new discoveries. If that is one such intent for the institution, then that would be a problem. Otherwise, if the system is operationally focused, this stage will ensure that there is sufficient information to guide the implementation. Against Figure 2 and Figure 4, this stage involves three main steps.

Step 1: Identify Attrition Types, Events and Points

The first step is to identify what data the institution has to allow them to identify the different attrition types, attrition events and attrition points as per Figure 2. In the earlier "census" attrition example, we can expect this attrition to have an event which we call "semester 1" and "semester 2". For the "semester 2" event, this "census" attrition type is likely to have attrition points in Week 3 (as evidenced by the student) where further analysis show that this was concentrated around those Week 3 that has the first assessment due. While this example was drawn from the authors' own institutional experience, it is clear that the specific week and other factors will change the nature of attrition even for the same attrition type. Hence, the need for a strong data evidenced approach supported by the appropriate analytics is crucial here. The analytics and the data that we spoke of here need not necessarily be the same data that is ultimately used in the implementation of the intervention, which is an important point to note too. The individual situation therefore is guided by what is shown in Figure 3, where the iterative process is required to move through the four stages until we arrive at an understanding that will support the specific institution and the specific cohort that it wants to target.

Step 2: Identify Attrition Time Frames and Intervention Checkpoints

Once the various attrition types, events and points are identified, we should move to focus on the attrition type that an institution wants to address and then develop further details to support the intervention design. The starting point in this case, as we would suggest, is the timeframe. For an attrition point relating to the event of an attrition type, we need to determine what kind of timeframe do we have to work on this. Of course there will be a number of factors at play. Notably, is this a new intervention or was it a modification of one that was already well-understood. This in turn will determine how feasible those activities will be given the available time and if any resourcing is possible. If we map this to an academic calendar and that we are trying to prototype a new intervention for the attrition type we would like to address, then we need to source for the data within the organization that will support the feasibility of undertaking this in terms of the time and consequently, the resources and stakeholder availability. Once these various factors are well synchronized to one another can we then realistically undertake the development of a retention strategy that fits within that timeframe that Figure 2 depicts.

Step 3: Determine Attrition Focus and Develop Retention Strategy

The last step is to develop a plan for the attrition of interest. If a specific attrition type has not been determined in Step 2 but rather a formulation of various attrition types to consider, then this step will evaluate the possible attrition that the university would like to address to which the intervention (or retention) strategy can be developed. In developing the intervention strategy, a major focus will be on the feasible options available following the evaluation of the timeframes and other resources. This is the step to also assign resources around the strategy that was developed and to create accountability for the various stakeholders in terms of their role in this. On paper, this may seem straightforward but this is not the case for many institutions, particularly where multiple institution units are involved.

3.2.2 Stage Two: Targeting

The first stage is about "design" and that design is to be mainly driven by the student and institutional data they have. The aim is to understand the institution's own specific attrition problem and to help focus how they can address the problem in their own context. Up to this point, it may be possible that dealing with just a single attrition type may still land us with a big cohort of students. In this stage, this is where we aim to become more targeted in our delivery of the intervention. Despite that the cohort are all at risk by the data and indicators, we should still be identifying the targets that will give the most "ROI" for each intervention delivered. This comes back to the fact that the institution is likely to be resource constrained and time constrained, notwithstanding the intervention designed formulated in the previous stage. For example, an intervention design for a specific attrition type may require a one-on-one session with a course advisor or an academic staff. In this case, this is not a matter of throwing resources at the problem as it doesn't make practical sense. Therefore, this stage within the framework is about deciding who we should be targeting so that these resources are best assigned to deliver the best result for the outcome sought.

One strategy is to rank targets for intervention and deploy them based on the probability of success, or by a retention value matrix that the institution may establish. In other words, once targets are identified, it is important to run intervention selectively on the ones where the institution feel confident of achieving retention or if a target has high retention value, e.g., reflects the institution's social responsibility. Resources can also be ranked such that high ranked targets get the most effective resources while lower ranked targets are diverted to other forms of support. For example, a highly ranked target may be intervened by a face-to-face session with an academic whereas as a lower ranked target may be contacted by a general staff, or simply an electronic communication. As a result, this is the stage to further refine the resource allocation plan (previously developed in Stage 1) and to develop the details of each role that a stakeholder would have in undertaking the intervention. In developing these roles, key outcomes expected should be clearly articulated and ways to measure them should be in place. Training to staff is essential as the tight coordination between units is usually the weakest link for any intervention design and constant monitoring needs to be undertaken as well.

Last but not least, it is also important to ensure the any ranking mechanism developed is well-thought through as identifying the right target for intervention is just as important as the training among stakeholders to undertake the right intervention. There are two ways to identifying targets. The first is through human judgement based on what was learned from the literature and from past experience. The alternative is to use technology, particularly in the area of data analytics. It is highly possible that an institution starting out with student retention may depend largely on human judgement of possible targets, but as the institution matures its learning analytics set up, it is likely to be able to develop capacity for a fully automated and data driven set up instead. Either case, once targets are identified, we are able to move to the third stage.

3.3.3 Stage Three: Intervening

At this stage, intervention is undertaken based on the established strategies, allocated resources, and processes already established in the first two stages. Once intervention starts, an important element to ensure the success of intervention is to make sure that all outcomes from the undertaking of the planned intervention are recorded. Preferably, this should be in some purpose built digital data capture system so that the outcomes can be part of the data repository to feed and update the big student data within the institution. If not and especially for an institution that is just embarking on their retention strategy, Stage 1 and 2 may need to consider and resource the implementation of such a system on top of staff training to use the system to record any intervention outcome. For an institution that is starting out on their learning analytics journey, this can be a simple system or even a well-designed manually data entry system. The crucial aspect of this is to iteratively improve on its component so as to advance the institution's capability as a whole. The data captured, while not for the current intervention, will help capture any feedback and misses to allow the next intervention to be recalibrated or improved thus, improving the efficacy of the intervention.

In terms of what data should be captured for evaluation, we need to first revisit the evaluation criteria and its design. In setting up any evaluation criteria, the key questions to ask includes

- What needs to be evaluated and why.
- How to evaluate including evaluation measures, mechanisms and schedule etc.
- How the results to be used for refinement.

The first question considers the objective (or purpose) of having a specific evaluation. This is essential to closing the loop and allows us to

- Refine the institution's specific understanding of attrition, including how it differs between the literature and practice; the suitability of the historical data used in the analysis; the identification of attrition types and events; the calibration of attrition time frames, and so on.
- Refine our targeting methodology, including what student profiles are at-risk; what behaviours and external factors should be flagged; what techniques should be adopted in identifying targets.
- Refine the intervention, including whether the intervention points are appropriate; the suitability of the services delivered and demand levels; how intervention data should be recorded, etc.
- Refine the evaluation and refinement process, including what needs to be evaluated; how to evaluate and how to utilise the results, etc.

While these are the main questions, additional institutionally specific questions can also be asked and these would involve the stakeholders to evaluate auxiliary matters related to the attrition type, such as improvements to the teaching design or administrative process relating to the attrition type.

Once the objective of an evaluation is clarified, the next question to answer is how to evaluate, of which the answer largely relies on if the institution carries the right data to allow the evaluation. Unless one knows where to source the data for evaluation, a good evaluation measure without the available data is as worthless as not having one. This question is an important one because there are many cases where the data is simply not available. Hence, this step allows evaluation measures to be adjusted before implementation commences. It also means if the required data is absent, the institution is able to put in place mechanisms to capture the data required going forward in the next iteration.

Evaluation schedule is another important aspect to be considered when setting evaluation. Should this be done as each intervention takes place, or should it be done at set points in the student lifecycle to facilitate a holistic update to the system in place? Calibrating piece-wise may be easier but lacks a holistic approach. On the other hand, a full review of all interventions and their interactions should be considered at some point to ensure that the broad intent of managing attrition isn't lost and the system is still aligned to the institution's policies, goals and aspirations. Finally, the value as well as effectiveness of evaluation lie in how the results will be used for refinement. This will be elaborated in the final stage – refining.

3.2.4 Stage Four: Refining

As with any systems, the key to their success is seldom in the first iteration but rather through iterations of improvements. Therefore, this stage implements the two critical tasks that allow the institution to continuously improve on its processes: (i) evaluation and (ii) refinement; both which goes hand in hand since unless we evaluate, we won't know what and where in the system that needs refinement.

Evaluation is critical because it is at this stage where stakeholders question the progress of interventions, the problems encountered and most importantly, whether the system worked as intended. As already discussed in the previous stage, the evaluation outcomes will determine what needs to be improved (or refined). Once the items for refinement are identified, then questions such as how to approach each refinement, the resources required to implement a refinement and how each should be charted as a project so there is a responsible entity to manage the refinement are undertaken.

As shown in Figure 3, the refinement process is also data-driven, which uses data from various sources as the input according to the evaluation objectives and the evaluation output will be fed back to each stage for refinement including the refining stage itself. That is to refine the understanding of attrition, the targeting of at-risk students, the intervening procedure as well as the refining process. Data input for evaluation comes from all previous stages and other relevant sources, including the new attrition and retention statistics from any current interventions that may be running.

4. RETENTION IN ACTION: A SYSTEMATIC ANALYTICAL-DRIVEN STUDENT RETENTION PROCESS

In this dual-framework, the first focused on the design aspects of an intervention while the second framework is about the steps that an institution should take to build and execute a successful intervention. This means ensuring that the intervention design can be well situated in the institutional environment. Our experience a retention project in an Australian university has shown that the main challenge in adopting a data driven or analytics driven intervention is the difficulties of ensuring that all the required components are ready. This means that the strategy, data, and systems (including tools, people, facilities and services) must be ready for to undertake the intervention.

Roadblocks in any of these elements will hamper the potential power of running a successful data or analytics-driven intervention. For example, without a holistic retention strategy ready, the project is unlikely to be funded by the relevant institution units. Without the relevant data being available it is impossible to apply any analytics. Without the system tools being ready the analytical outcomes cannot be properly delivered to inform the intervention strategy, and without the skilled people ready, system tools and services cannot be effectively used to inform and conduct any action. The purpose of the second framework is thus to focus any implementations on two important phases: the 'get-ready' phase and the 'in-action' phase. The extent to which each required component is ready correlates to the range of actions that can actually be taken, and we have summarized this in Figure 5.

4.1 Get-Ready Phase (Enable)

In this phase, the implementation is about making sure that the institution as a whole is ready to deliver the intervention and that the resources committed well deliver the best return. We begin with an understanding of the attrition and explored the various angles guided by the first framework in Section 3.

Figure 5. Systematic Analytical-driven Student Retention Process

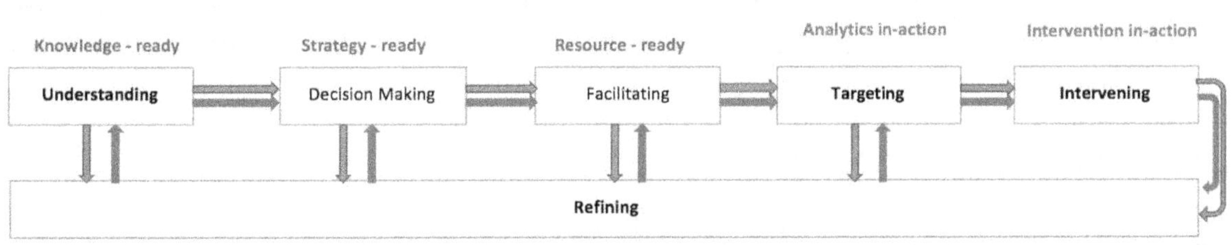

The purpose of this is to ensure that the institution and stakeholders as a whole is “knowledge ready”. It is also the basis that all stakeholders be able to share a common understanding of the purpose of the intervention and what outcomes are sought in this process.

The same documentation of all these insights can also be used to make the case to any project sponsor for any attrition-intervention to be delivered. In this case, the same document would have articulated the detailed information necessary to make the business case for developing such an intervention and to seek commitment and support from any relevant executive committess within the institution. It also ensures that proper resourcing can be committed and for the project leader to be able to deliver the promised outcomes. In that sense, this is about moving from “knowledge ready” to being “decision ready”, an important step for any successful implementation of the system.

Once an intervention is officially sponsored, it is then possible to move into execution. As a first step of that execution, the project lead should be looking at ensuring that all required and funded resources are ready. This “resource ready” step includes a number of factors which we have already highlighted earlier in our discussion of the first framework but now we consider them from an implementation point of view. This includes

- Becoming “data ready” – any data driven solutions should ensure that the relevant data is available and the setup to getting the data from various units or from the institution’s ICT data department is organised. At this stage, the relevant data requests and data sample should be clearly documented and made available to the data sponsor in advanced. In addition, this is also the stage where any data capture required, including the details of what data to capture should be negotiated with the relevant support unit as well as the data ethics or privacy unit on whether the institution has legal rights to use the student data for such purpose.
- Becoming “system ready” – here we are referring to an intervention as a system so this includes lining up the various resources to ensure that they are ready to implement the intervention. In particular, the required software tools should be set up and tested for use among the stakeholders. Usually there will be a range of tools so their ability to work with one another needs to be thoroughly investigated as this stage, including setting up access to ensure that every stakeholder has access to the correct subset of tools. Furthermore, any analysis that needs to be undertaken with the data analyst should be clarified and all integration among the units to deliver the results are clearly documented as a set of protocols.
- Becoming “people ready” – while we have mentioned this as the last element, the human factor is obviously the most critical. In particular, if an existing human resource is being deployed for any intervention project, there needs to be proper change management plans in place to allow for buy-in from those who are to undertake the intervention. There may be a high chance as well that such change will involve technical upgrades, new workflows and new systems to deal with and therefore, providing the appropriate support and training to allow for staff to become ready for the task is just as important. After all, a poorly executed intervention will not do any data driven approaches justice.

4.2 In-Action Phase

Once all the enabling components are ready, we can the move into the “in-action” phase where the intervention is in fact implemented. At this stage and like many project management theory, this phase is about executing all the planned intervention with the resources that were lined up. It is in this phase where the intervention is 'live' and various institutional units should now be undertaking their respective roles. The key actions undertaken here includes

- **Targeting:** Which is likely to be data driven or analytics driven in identifying the students at risk and possibly a 'risk score' calculated to help decide if the specific student at risks of a specific attrition type should be undergoing intervention.
- **Intervening:** This is the step that is likely a combination of information systems and human interaction with the student at risk. Depending on what the intervention design is, this is the step were learning education theory is used to maximise the retention outcome of that at-risk student.
- **Refining:** Strictly speaking not a part of the intervention but an important step in the action phase so that there is additional data to support better targeting and intervention design going forward. Of course, this "in action" step assumes that the institution is committed to a long-term investment of using a data driven and analytics driven approach to its operations. That in turn requires outcomes of initiating such projects which brings us to the question of how to evaluate and improve (refine) each intervention for longer term success.

5. EVALUATION AND IMPROVEMENTS

The last step in the "in action" phase is worth some additional discussion. As new data is gathered from the implementation, there is new insights that can be gained regardless of the intervention's outcome. If the intervention works, there should be a postmortem on identifying the critical success factors and documented for the institution. If the intervention didn't, the same study should be undertaken to identify where the fail points are and how to avoid this in the next iteration. Specifically, we want to highlight a few key areas to focus on evaluating and improvements. They include

- Improving targeting strategy of at-risk students – obviously, this is an important area to focus on as having the right students to intervene in a resource and time limited situation means we want to focus on the students that will deliver the best retention outcomes. If there is any data driven or analytics driven approaches used in this area, then questions on whether the predictive model or the data analysis is suitable should be considered and improvements identified.
- Improving intervention design – a major part of intervention is to achieve retention so clear indicators of retention success needs to be identified and designed in a way that is measurable. In its simplest form, this means thinking about what we are measuring in the context of the attrition type but it can also extend to evaluating if every step of the intervention is appropriate and if we require additional measures to determine the appropriateness of a particular intervention step. Evaluation here could also refer to the suitability of the human resource or a particular system that was used in a specific intervention design and extends to the entire workflow as well. In fact, the evaluation of this particular step is itself a separate project when we begin unpacking these factors that all needed proper resourcing to investigate.
- Improving evaluation design – of course, the evaluation process to undertake all of the above should also be a subject of constant review to ensure that the institution is indeed getting the right

benefit for their investment and that the outcomes sought are indeed been achieved. Also, the same attrition type and strategy will deliver different results at different time points and therefore, how to evaluate is a consideration that should be revisited every time the intervention is to be undertaken. Furthermore, how to conduct such evaluation at a reasonable cost and time should also be evaluated as is the case with whether any evaluation undertaken constructively feeds to advancing the outcomes of any data and analytics projects such as one as complex as this.

5. CONCLUSION

In this paper, we present our preliminary work on a dual framework that aims to provide important design guidance and implementation guidance towards realizing a solution that will deliver true data driven or analytics driven outcomes. As noted in the literature, data and analytics have been touted heavily as a game-changing solution for many organizations and while there is truth in this statement, a lot has not been mentioned in terms of the other critical success factors to make that success. The learning institutions, with its complex structure and large amount of student data is a great exemplar where the success of learning analytics is of great interest to education researchers but yet at the same time, we are seeing few success stories at the institutional level. As recent literature starts to acknowledge, there is more to the predictive model and as in the case of this paper, the discussion of these two frameworks to allow for any analytical models to be deployed will take up a large amount of focus and resources to begin with. Getting these right is equally important as the data analytics to be deployed if not, more important from the success perspective.

At the research level, this chapter highlights the importance of having a holistic data-driven approach to achieving an organizational outcome, particularly if the environment is complex and the stakeholders varied. While we have focused our discussion here on one specific problem – student attrition – the discussions here could apply to other learning problems and can be seen as a framework that can be generalized to solving other learning problems through a data driven and data analytics approach. There are great opportunities here as institutions start to realize that they are the custodian of big data about students in the national they are situated in. As success at the institutional level develops over time, we imagine there may be a time where the big student data can be effectively utilized by government for future education policies planning and design. That's where the potential of big data of students lie but until then, any institutions considering a big data implementation should consider design and implementation frameworks to guide their process.

REFERENCES

Abrahams, D. A. (2010). Technology adoption in higher education: A framework for identifying and prioritising issues and barriers to adoption of instructional technology. *Journal of Applied Research in Higher Education*, *2*(2), 34–49. doi:10.1108/17581184201000012

Arnold, K. E., & Pistilli, M. D. (2012). Course signals at Purdue: Using learning analytics to increase student success. *Proceedings of the 2nd international conference on learning analytics and knowledge*. 10.1145/2330601.2330666

Aulck, L., Velagapudi, N., Blumenstock, J., & West, J. (2016). *Predicting student dropout in higher education.* arXiv preprint arXiv:1606.06364

Bayer, J., Bydzovská, H., Géryk, J., Obsivac, T., & Popelinsky, L. (2012). *Predicting Drop-Out from Social Behaviour of Students.* International Educational Data Mining Society.

Bean, J. P., & Metzner, B. S. (1985). A conceptual model of nontraditional undergraduate student attrition. *Review of Educational Research*, *55*(4), 485–540. doi:10.3102/00346543055004485

Clow, D. (2014). Data wranglers: human interpreters to help close the feedback loop. *Proceedings of the Fourth International Conference on Learning Analytics and Knowledge.* 10.1145/2567574.2567603

Dietz-Uhler, B., & Hurn, J. E. (2013). Using learning analytics to predict (and improve) student success: A faculty perspective. *Journal of Interactive Online Learning*, *12*(1), 17–26.

Eckerson, W. W. (2012). *Secrets of Analytical Leaders.* Technics Publications.

Ferguson, R., Clow, D., Macfadyen, L., Essa, A., Dawson, S., & Alexander, S. (2014). Setting learning analytics in context: overcoming the barriers to large-scale adoption. *Proceedings of the Fourth International Conference on Learning Analytics And Knowledge.* 10.1145/2567574.2567592

Jahromi, A. T., Stakhovych, S., & Ewing, M. (2015). Customer Churn Models: A Comparison of Probability and Data Mining Approaches. *Proceedings of the 2013 World Marketing Congress.*

Johnson, W., Brett, C. E., & Deary, I. J. (2010). The pivotal role of education in the association between ability and social class attainment: A look across three generations. *Intelligence*, *38*(1), 55–65. doi:10.1016/j.intell.2009.11.008

Jones, C. (2007). *Institutional repositories: content and culture in an open access environment.* Elsevier. doi:10.1533/9781780631110

Kaplan, A. M., & Haenlein, M. (2016). Higher education and the digital revolution: About MOOCs, SPOCs, social media, and the Cookie Monster. *Business Horizons*, *59*(4), 441–450. doi:10.1016/j.bushor.2016.03.008

Lahtinen, M., & Weaver, B. (2015). *Educating for a digital future–Walking three roads simultaneously: one analog and two digital.* Paper presented at the Lunds universitets utvecklingskonferens, 2015.

Macfadyen, L. P., & Dawson, S. (2012). Numbers are not enough. Why e-learning analytics failed to inform an institutional strategic plan. *Journal of Educational Technology & Society*, *15*(3), 149–163.

Michels, L. J. (2016). *Prudence and Persistence: Personality in Student Retention.* Academic Press.

Morgan, M. (2013). *Improving the Student Experience: A practical guide for universities and colleges.* Routledge.

Richardson, M., Abraham, C., & Bond, R. (2012). Psychological correlates of university students' academic performance: A systematic review and meta-analysis. *Psychological Bulletin*, *138*(2), 353–387. doi:10.1037/a0026838 PMID:22352812

Sajjadi, S., Shapiro, B., McKinlay, C., Sarkisyan, A., Shubin, C., & Osoba, E. (2017). *Finding Bottlenecks: Predicting Student Attrition with Unsupervised Classifier.* arXiv preprint arXiv:1705.02687

Seidman, A. (2005). *College student retention: Formula for student success*. Greenwood Publishing Group.

Sparkman, L., Maulding, W., & Roberts, J. (2012). Non-cognitive predictors of student success in college. *College Student Journal*, *46*(3), 642–652.

Tinto, V. (1987). *Leaving college: Rethinking the causes and cures of student attrition*. ERIC.

Tremblay, K. (2013). *OECD assessment of higher education learning outcomes (AHELO). In Modeling and measuring competencies in higher education* (pp. 113–126). Springer. doi:10.1007/978-94-6091-867-4_8

Wagner, E., & Longanecker, D. (2016). Scaling Student Success with Predictive Analytics: Reflections After Four Years in the Data Trenches. *Change: The Magazine of Higher Learning*, *48*(1), 52–59. doi:10.1080/00091383.2016.1121087

Xing, W., Guo, R., Petakovic, E., & Goggins, S. (2015). Participation-based student final performance prediction model through interpretable Genetic Programming: Integrating learning analytics, educational data mining and theory. *Computers in Human Behavior*, *47*, 168–181. doi:10.1016/j.chb.2014.09.034

Section 3

Emerging Areas of BI Research and Its Growth

Chapter 13
Tailorable Technologies for Improving Business Intelligence Systems:
Small Business Decision Maker's Perspective

Shah J. Miah
Victoria University, Australia

ABSTRACT

The Australian farm-based businesses can be benefited from specially designed applications for cost-effective operation while maximizing profits to survive in economic and environmental crises. For decision support, existing business intelligence systems (BIS) approaches scarcely deal with specific user's provisions to adjust changing situations in decision making, without extra technical exertions. In this chapter, the authors describe a conceptual framework of tailorable BIS solution that is based on case study findings in that the highlighted requirements are relevant to address changing situations through enhancing end user's engagement. The activities of end user's engagement supported through the use of tailorable features that reinforce a shift from the traditional BIS process to a new provision where business owners can actively involve in adjusting their features to their decision support.

INTRODUCTION

Although the growth of small and medium sized enterprises (SMEs) has been considered of paramount importance to accelerate local and national economy, the issues of SMEs are not often prioritised for their research problems. Many prior studies identify requirements of computer based applications for improving managers' performance in selected areas, but application developments research is limited for specially-designed decision systems. The decision systems are mainly for meeting the information demand of smart owners/managers, whose primary function is not information system development but

DOI: 10.4018/978-1-5225-5718-0.ch013

to engage and actively involved in lower-end development utilising their own knowledge from SMEs (Ray, 1994; Khan and Khan, 1992; Duan and Xu, 2009).

In SMEs of rural business domains, most of the small or family-based farms are classified as owner operated and their productivity of the businesses are overwhelmingly depended on managers/owners' innovation (Mustafa, 2012) in particular for decision making. By tradition, the SMEs are defined as relatively small size industry that is (a) actively managed by its owners, (b) highly personalised, (c) largely local in its area of operations, and (d) largely dependent on an internal source of capital to finance its growth (Baumback, 1988). Traditional applications used for smart owners/managers' decision support are still emergent and underdeveloped, specially to accommodate immediate changes for enhancing decision support. Therefore it is of paramount to investigate the requirements of specially-designed applications of decision support of smart owners/managers.

As the demand of business intelligence systems (BIS) have been increased in organisational decision support, the umbrella term used to describe data warehousing, knowledge management, data mining, collaborative systems, online analytical processing, and various types of decision support systems (DSS) (Gibson et al, 2004). BIS can be considered as the combination of processes and technologies to assist in decision making for managers. The BIS systems have been well-recognized for enhancing the effectiveness of information organisation and provide comprehensive decision support mechanism to meet all levels of decision demands through applications such as decision support systems, query and reporting, online analytical processing (OLAP), statistical analysis, forecasting, and data mining (Stasieńko, 2010). This implies that BIS has influence to operationalise as data-driven DSS[1] applications (Power, 2007). Over the past decades, as data driven DSS, BISs have been shown its potential use for decision support for turning business data into support information. Most of the current BIS solution frameworks are designed to support executive managements (Singh,Watson, and Watson, 2002). A decision-making situation relevant to business operations can be more important to keep track of end-level business matters such as resource allocations, in order to cutting-down costs while maximising profits continuously in businesses. Our study focuses on the perspective of designing such BIS that can be classified as data-driven DSS for meeting the demand of smart manager/business owners in the rural business domain.

In context of application development, relatively few studies have addressed decision support issues of SMEs managers/business owners. Our target case highlights the small businesses with less than 10 employees that are located in rural areas. These businesses are mainly based on family owned or operated small farming business. Cox (1996) and Kerr (2004) suggest that most decision support applications for small-farm business owners were based on research models that have the primary aim of discovering and understanding relationships between data, or applied pre-defined models used as decision support mechanisms. Although these applications generate reports from range of data sources, they provide limited user provisions to adjust the changes in decision making.

Most of the cases, the applications hold inappropriate provisions for decision makers and they have lack of features of situational support due to rigid analyses or employing analytics tools, in the face of changing business needs. Most of the cases, these solutions need ongoing reengineering effort to incorporate new information in the system. User factors such as a limited fit with their specific context of decision making problems, differences in problem definition between users and application designers, and poor usability, generally only compound this situation. Dauan and Xu (2009) described that managers of small businesses have often been dissatisfied with software packages because of the inability of these to adapt well to their business needs (Heikkila et al., 1991). In-house development of decision support applications is often not straightforward as they associate with potential lack of completeness in the identification and definition of the problem particularly in more complex problems and spreadsheet based (Janvrin and Morrison, 2000).

A purely adoptive approach of decision support such as BIS applications, for meeting both SMEs changing demand and manager's dynamic requirements can be of significance matter. In their analysis on historical importance of DSS research. Hosack et al. (2012) suggested that decision support development research needs shift the focus to delivering more customer-centric solution. For IS development, Iivari and Iivari (2011) have analysed existing literature on UCD (User-Centred Design) methods used in IS development. The authors suggested four aspects of user-centredness, namely, a focus on the system user; a focus on user work-centredness; a focus on user involvement; and a focus on system personalisation. In addition, Iivari and Iivari (2011) mention that the extension of work-centredness to activity-centredness could be a good UCD research challenge for the future.

From a technological point of angle, purely adoptive approach so called a tailorable design theory (Germonprez, Hovorka and Gal, 2011; Germonprez, Hovorka and Collopy, 2007), in that the technology (e.g. IS applications) contains dynamic, recognisable components and conventions for enabling users to tailor features. This theory offers user-customisable features so that they can easily be adapted to a user's particular needs, activities or within their settings (Iivari and Iivari, 2011). In our study, we aim to address the issues of changing demand and manager's dynamic requirements for small business owners, through the use of the tailorable design concept (Germonprez et al. 2011). Our arguments are based on an empirical study of developing a BIS and the key aspect is to empower business owners/managers by providing a re-adjustable technology so that they can address the changing demands and stay up-to-date in business operations.

The remainder of this paper is organized as follows. The next section provides background facts on the tailorable design perspectives, BIS and targeted SMEs decision support aspects. The section after that provides detail of adopted method in the study. The next section presents the BIS solution framework for meeting the operational demand of small business owners. We then provide detail of the empirical studies which demonstrate its use in a small scale. The discussion and conclusion section highlights with summary, contributions and limitations, and formulate directions for future research.

STUDY BACKGROUND

Target Context of Small and Medium Businesses (SMEs)

SMEs have been defined as business organisations that employ less than 50 people and been considered as significant contributors to national economic (MacGregor and Vrazalic, 2005). Eikebrokk and Olsen (2009) suggest that SMEs hold several definitions and meanings due to their global diversity and characteristics. Conrad and Darren (2009) explain that the main reason why SME definition varies particularly from industry to industry; county to country; size to size and number of employee to number of employee is to reflect industry, country, size and employment differences accurately. Some studies define the SMEs in terms of manpower, management structure and capital investment limit (Arowomole, 2000). According to Jasra et al. (2011), SMEs represent businesses that are not a public limited company. The Australian Bureau of Statistics reported (2014) more than 1.2 million businesses classified as small businesses due to not just their size, but also by other major distinguishing unique factors that set them apart from large businesses. For the SMEs in rural or regional areas, Studies suggest that regional areas are classified as inner and outer regions, remote and very remote areas (Australian Bureau of Statistics, 2014). Determining the classification of a region is based on a formula which primarily relies on the measures of proximity to services in terms of physical distance, and population size (MacGregor and Vrazalic, 2005). Rather than inner and outer regional areas, our study presented in this paper focuses on family or owner operated farm-based small businesses in remote and rural areas as the businesses located in these areas in Australia contribute 50% of the national export income (Keniry, 2003). This particular domain of SMEs holds significant research attention over the past decades (Kerr, 2004; Kuhlmann and Brodersen, 2001) as innovations are always of paramount to keep holding traditional practices with new management strategies in order to cut costing while maximising profits to survive recent economic and environmental crises.

For data-driven decision support applications two schools of thoughts were appeared within this domain of rural businesses: first focuses on scientific process optimisation orientation (such as improving production system in farming businesses (e.g. Darby-Dowman et al. 2000; Recio et al. 2003) and second involves business improvement e.g. issues of business practice improvement, such as user uptake on DSS applications (Kuhlmann and Brodersen, 2001; Little, 2004; Lynch and Gregor, 2004; Walker, 2002). Reasons for the noted poor adoption rate, most of the cases, suggest that the data-driven DSS applications for this type of small businesses have unfamiliar options to decision makers, mainly lack of frequently updating options and are inflexible for users. Our study attempts to address these issues.

Past studies directly related to decision support applications in the domain of SMEs can been viewed in three different directions of studies: success factors and evaluation-oriented studies; specific decision support development oriented studies and studies that are various issues on DSS. Table 1 illustrates example studies in these directions. The first group of studies explore on user determinants of the decision support applications and their effectiveness and success factors in the context of the small business, while second group of studies focuses on solving or optimising business operations through the decision support solutions. The third group of studies are highlighted various issues and new provisions of decision support applications development. Our study is relevant to the third direction. For the specific small business problems, many data-driven DSS solutions offered help for business decision makers to gain a competitive advantage, data exchange and meet other strategic enterprise objectives (Lin et al. 2012). However, these applications are not connected to address the underlying issues of enhancing managers involvements and meeting own requirements. Our study aims to outline provision of a new technology in a form of BIS in order to develop specific decision support application for internal resource management. The focus is to enhance production while minimising cost and effective use of internal resources. The solution is aimed to offer user options for secondary activities to business owners or managers. Gupta and Raj (2013) emphasise on adoption of new technological solution for the end users of SMEs, when assessing the opportunities of using cloud computing-based business solution. This view is supportive to our study as we intend to develop a BIS for internal resource management of rural small business, in that embedded provisions will be based on the tailorable design (Germonprez, Hovorka and Gal 2011).

BIS and Tailorable Design Technology

BI has been described as both a process and a product in the literature. The process refers to methods that organisations utilise to develop useful information, or intelligence, that can help them survive in business. The product refers to information production that offers organisations to predict the behaviour of their customers, suppliers, products, services, and the general business environment with a degree of

Table 1. Three directions of DSS studies in SMEs Research

Main Research Tends in IS Development for SMEs	Example Sub-Topics
Success factor and evaluation studies for SMEs	Success of personal DSS (Raymond, L., Bergeron, F. 1992) Success of BI systems (Popovič, Hackney, Coelho, and Jaklič, 2012) Evaluating DSS using TAM (Dulcic, Pavlic and Silic, 2012) Adoption of IT for decision making (Yang and Fu, 2008)
Specific DSS applications for SMEs	Inventory DSS (Chaudhry, Salchenberger and Beheshtian, 1996) Credit scoring DSS (Tsaih, Liu, Liu and Lien 2014) DSS for financial management (Zopounidis, Doumpos and Matsatsinis, 1997) DSS for manufacturing SMEs (Lin, Nagalingam, Kuik and Murata, 2012)
Other issues of DSS applications for SMEs	Issues of knowledge cultivating for DSS (Li, Zhu and Pan, 2010) Issues of cloud based DSS (Gupta and Raj, 2013) Issues of risk management (Bajo, Borrajo, De Paz, Corchado and Pellicer, 2012)

certainty (Jourdan, Rainer and Marshall, 2012). Our study focuses on process view as we intend to outline a method of decision support so organisation or business owners can have support from their internal business data. Small business owners deserve benefits from the process that is specially-designed so that they can have more flexible in-house solution to meet their changing and situational demand. Business owners can play roles for technical activities in their own right during ongoing system operation and recreation of decision support application. Germonprez et al. (2011) introduce an IS theory related to tailorable system design in that a system undergoes primary design process where features are built in prior to general release and then end users engage in a secondary design process "where functions and content emerge during interaction, modification, and embodiment of the system in use" (pp.662). Germonprez et al. (2011) describe a case study in that end users are engaged as designers, framed by dualities in behaviours including planned and emergent behaviours, and participatory and reifying behaviours that can be seen as an extension work on tailorable systems, investigating processes of secondary design in a highly interactive system suited to support user engagement. We extend the idea through developing specific features of BIS, in that the option to conduct secondary activities is promising, in the SMEs research in particular for decision support applications development.

BI and decision support systems have been introduced for the welfare of small business managers by offering information access, model analysis and supporting tools (Meensel et al. 2012). Multiple data-driven applications have been offered to address various issues such as for inventory issues (Chaudhry, Salchenberger and Beheshtian, 1996), manufacturing issues (Lin, Nagalingam, Kuik and Murata, 2012), and credit scoring issues (Tsaih, Liu, Liu and Lien, 2014). However, as the complexity of decisions increases due to changes of market regulation or farming conditions, managers increasingly lack the necessary expertise to make decisions that integrate the range of issues involved (Meensel et al. 2012; Walker, 2002). The pre-modelled or simulation based decision support has widely failed to fulfil user expectations due to mismatches with system's features (Meensel et al. 2012; Kerr, 2004). Many studies report on the poor uptake such as for the agricultural decision support within the context of owner operated small businesses (McCown, 2004). Niu's et al. (2013) view, although is for supporting manager's cognition through situation retrieval model, the view is not supportive to ongoing adjustment according to business owners' preference. The tailorablity of planning and analysis functions of emergency preparation has been discussed in a small scale of a DSS development project, but the development project (de Walle and Turoff, 2008) did not come up with a complete technological solution or a framework that can addressing end users secondary or tailoring issues. This issue are the central focus in our study.

RESEARCH CONTEXT AND METHOD

The identified problem context was related to dairy farming businesses. The Queensland Department of Primary Industries established a project for improving farming system so called 'Sustainable Dairy Farm Systems for Profit' to address the impact of deregulation on farm owners (Chataway, Walker and Callow 2010). In the project various alternative farming systems were investigated through the use of physical models linked with commercial objectives (Callow, Gobius and Hetherington 2005). One important objective of the project was to improve business owners' decision support approaches, particularly with regard to maximizing profits with minimal costing. To achieve this, it is essential to address the requirement of developing an effective method to improve farming practices. We identified dairy business owner' current decision making needs in relation to the management of milk protein concentration as being worthy of detailed consideration. Meeting industry standards for milk protein concentration throughout the year is particularly challenging for dairy farmers/business owners in northern Australia (Australian Dairy Industry in Focus 2008) due to inherent features of the sub-tropical environment (temperature, humidity, forage quality) and their impact on lactating animals. As a number of quality factors, including milk protein concentration (Parker, Woodford and Woods 2000) impact on milk volume pricing, business owners receive penalties and/or price incentives for milk of different processing standard. In the context of a deregulated industry, small improvements in milk quality can lead to significant differences in financial incomes. Dairy farmers need to consider decision making approaches that can enhance production and take advantage of incentives offered by factories, for example with respect to milk protein concentration. Employing a BIS can be of paramount to business owners decision making specifically for operating a profitable business by taking advantage of factory incentives.

Based on our analysis on decision support solution technologies and to meeting complexity of the practical problems it is realised that the functional deliverables could be better accomplished through prototyping method. The prototyping method is well-known for BIS solutions development (Rouibah and Ould-ali, 2002) as the method provides options to adjust their delivery requirements and business owner's expectations. To accommodate the development we employed a straightforward life cycle for developing the BIS solution that is composed of analysis, designing, development and evaluation phases. The adapted BI life-cycle is similar to the BI development life-cycle proposed by Gangadharan and Swami (2004) in that development phases were defined, such as: analysis, designing, development, deployment and evaluation. We did not use the deployment phase due to scope limitation in our project. The table 2 provides the details of activities in the four distinctive phases.

DEVELOPMENT OF TAILORABLE BIS

The central issues of BIS solutions such as limited options to meet industry demands and lack of option to include necessary expertise to make effective business owners' decisions are considered. Previous BI studies focus on analytics issues through developing associated technologies such as data warehouses, multi-dimensional techniques for data extraction, OLAP, query and reporting algorithms (Stasienho,

Table 2. Descriptions of the phases of BI life-cycle

Phases	Details
Analysis	Project identified problem definition and tailorable design components to achieve the target benefits by the business owners. The project also identified primary and secondary activities for decision support within the scope of the BI development project. We conducted three focus group meetings.
Design	Project outlined a BI process that provides functional deliverables through selected technologies. We used tailorable features to accommodate the knowledge sharing and other situational realities. We conducted prototyping in three different phases. Phase 1 provided stakeholders provisions within their business situations, phase 2 heled outline the primary and secondary boundaries of their activities and phase 3 helped allocate appropriate features for the entire design within two modules.
Development	Project modelled the full process that offer two access modules and flow of information across for providing appropriate decision support. We used ontology modelling to develop the data/knowledge repository.
Evaluation	Project evaluated the use of the BI features adapted in the system. We focus on the common factors such as preceded usefulness and ease of use. Focus group interviews were utilised to conduct the evaluation study it is one of the well-known evaluation method for DSS solution (Haghighi, Burstein, Zaslavsky, and Arbon, 2013).

2012). User oriented issues in the application layer are largely ignored as Hosack et al. (2012) argued that the end-user oriented issue became an obvious in DSS development. A tailorable technology provides dynamic components that enable users to modify and make the technology fit to specific business context through its features (Germonprez et al., 2007). As discussed earlier, to support decision making for effective internal resource management we outline a framework that offers two modules. The first module is mainly for the business owners to add/modify and allocate appropriate decision making factors that will be linked to extraction, transformation and loading (ETL) into data warehouse for the business managers. The second module is for managers who are responsible for assessing resource allocation and appropriate conditions for the everyday use, as the data warehouse will be ready for delivering data through the ETL layer. For the purpose of prototyping we used a simple SQL query to link to DMP table. Figure 1 shows the two modules within the BIS system for outlining the decision support within a specific business situation.

The proposed tailorable BIS solution allows two groups of users through the selection of the system components, within the primary architecture controlling its integrity. The primary environment remains in its original form (i.e. in its primary design state) for any action of tailoring at first level by business owners at seasons or reasons basis and second level by managers at daily basis. In addition, the primary form recognizes both user groups as intentional users to tailor the system through its features that suits their specific business contexts. When the business owners accommodate appropriate decision makings parameters (DMP) and setup rules and suggestions for further use, the managers module is ready for interaction for their own information support development. For instance, in a case of milk protein enhancement, dairy farmers have different feeding strategies for their cows depending on the season and their specific farming practices. As such, the status of these practices needs to be monitored to ensure appropriate decision making. In this particular example, the outcome variable would be milk protein enhancement. Decision making factors as identified in Chapter Five are the Dry matter, Feed values, Water management, Herd management, Heat stress management, and Breed management that have various influence on quality milk production (e.g. higher protein). According to the decision-making rules setup based on particular seasons or reasons by business owners, managers can obtain the decision support information (by selecting appropriate set of DMP within the scope for target improvement) that

Figure 1. BIS solution framework in that business owner's decision-making situation can be adjusted for managers to produce timely and quality information for decision support aid
(DMP= decision making parameters, ETL: extraction, transformation and loading)

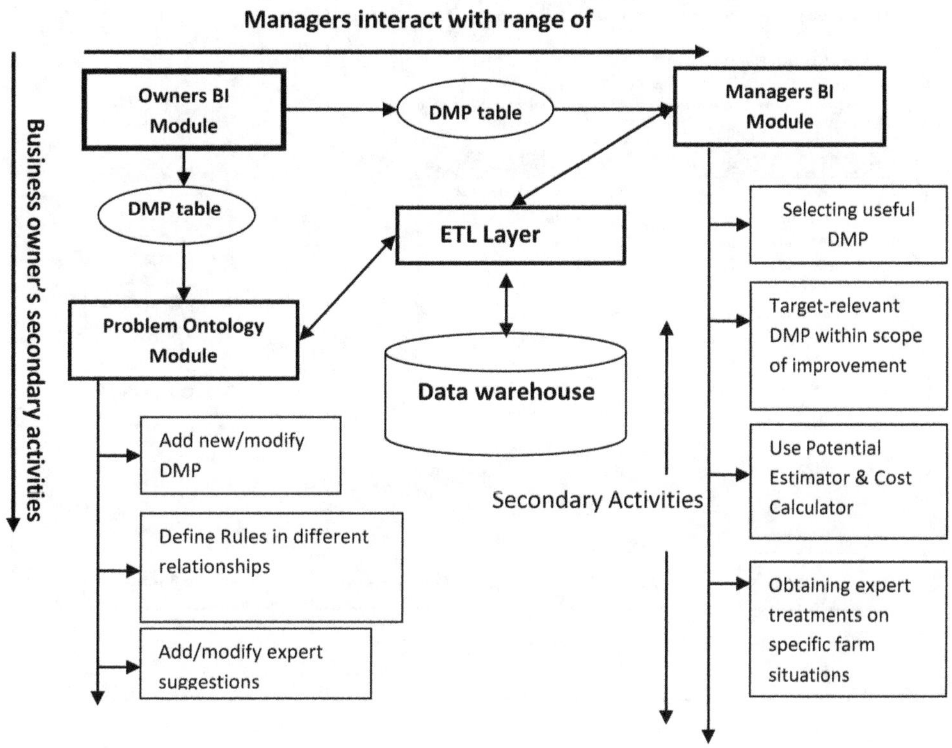

is extracted and transformed through the current conditions. Developing the BI provision in the system three key features were outlined for small business users.

These are as follows:

1. Features for situation specific customisation

Situation specific customisation in decision systems development is an important matter for designers. The system should have dynamic provisions for adding or modifying decision making parameters to meet changing requirements without requiring intermediate design stages. In design research, Germonprez et al. (2011) described a case of behaviour design research in that a secondary view is proposed to consider users as designers in their own right during the ongoing creation and recreation of application to adjust with problem space. Figure 2 illustrates options for adding or modifying decision making parameters to meet changing requirements.

2. Features for knowledge sharing

It is important to employ features for knowledge sharing specially for incorporating expertise and knowledge support on effective practices for relevant decision support aids. The feature represents a pro-

Figure 2. Problem ontology allowing parameters adding and modifications

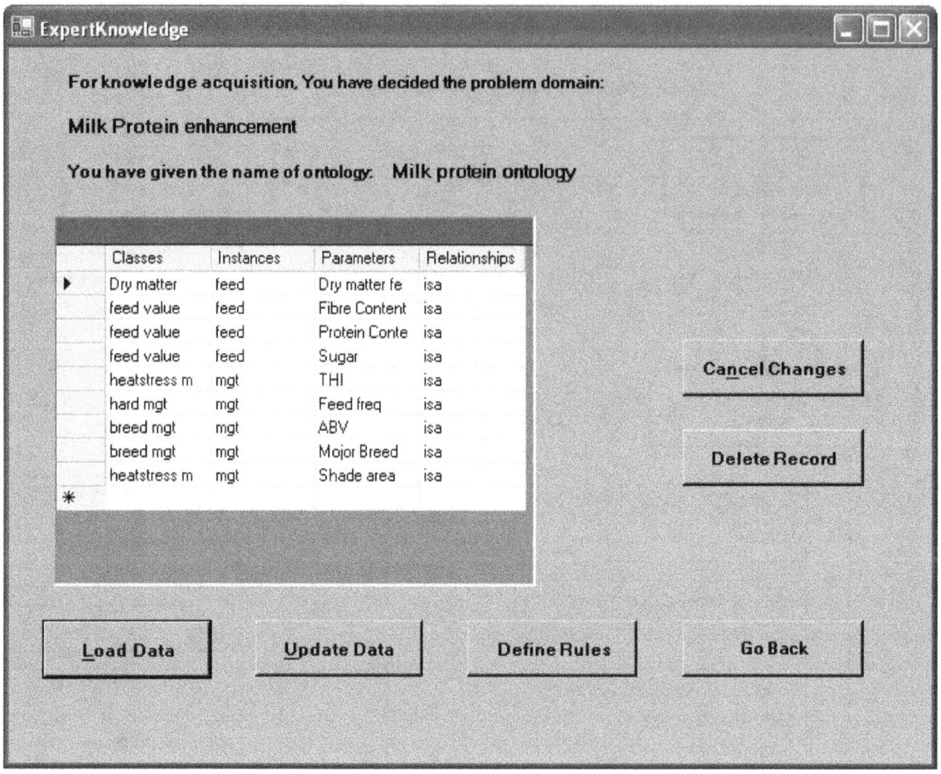

cess for business owners' involvement to incorporate new knowledge into practice. Extensible knowledge representations such as contextual graphs that allow for updating without re-engineering may be used to add dynamism to a DSS (Sherwell et al., 2005). Figure 3 shows user logon for the business owners and managers for their access to secondary features as shown in the figure 1.

Figure 3. User logins for specific options of design

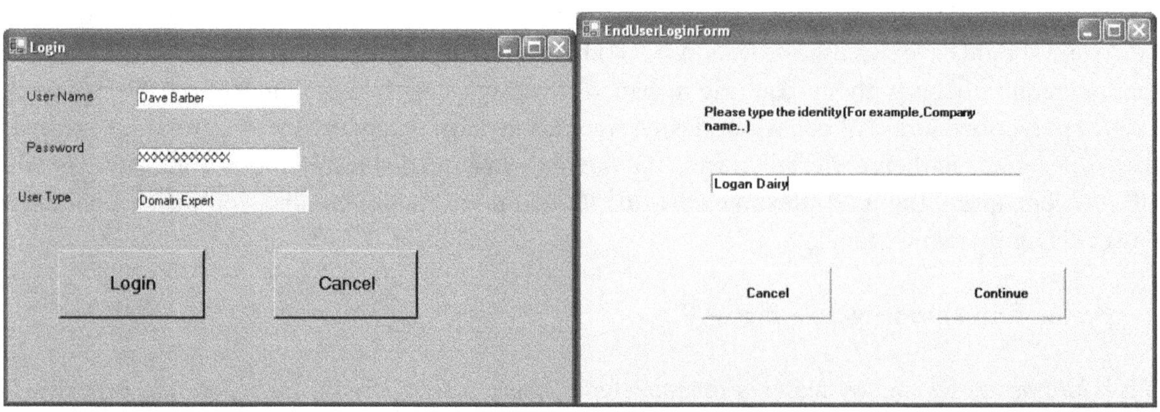

3. Features for practice based secondary design facilities

It is important to accommodate decision makers' practical consequences into decision-making context. For instance, in dairy farming, the study articulated practical decision making 'rules of thumb' that are significant for decision support design. In design research this reality can also be informed through the idea of secondary design Germonprez et al. (2011) in that the design perspective recognizes user's behaviours and contexts change over time and when solutions are engaged and customised by users in their work or problem space. Figure 4 shows how business owner add/modify and develop decision making rules in business practices.

EMPRICAL EVALUATION CONTEXT

Adopting BIS must meet the demands and offer benefits such as for quality of business information provided, powerful tools for data analysis and representation, lower cost of decision making, web based accessibility, increased efficiency and effectiveness of the decisions (Tutunea and Rus, 2012). In our case, the BIS provided the following benefits specially for internal resource allocation aiming at cutting cost for profit maximisation: Farm owners and managers have provisions for adjusting decision making

Figure 4. Domain experts adding decision support rules

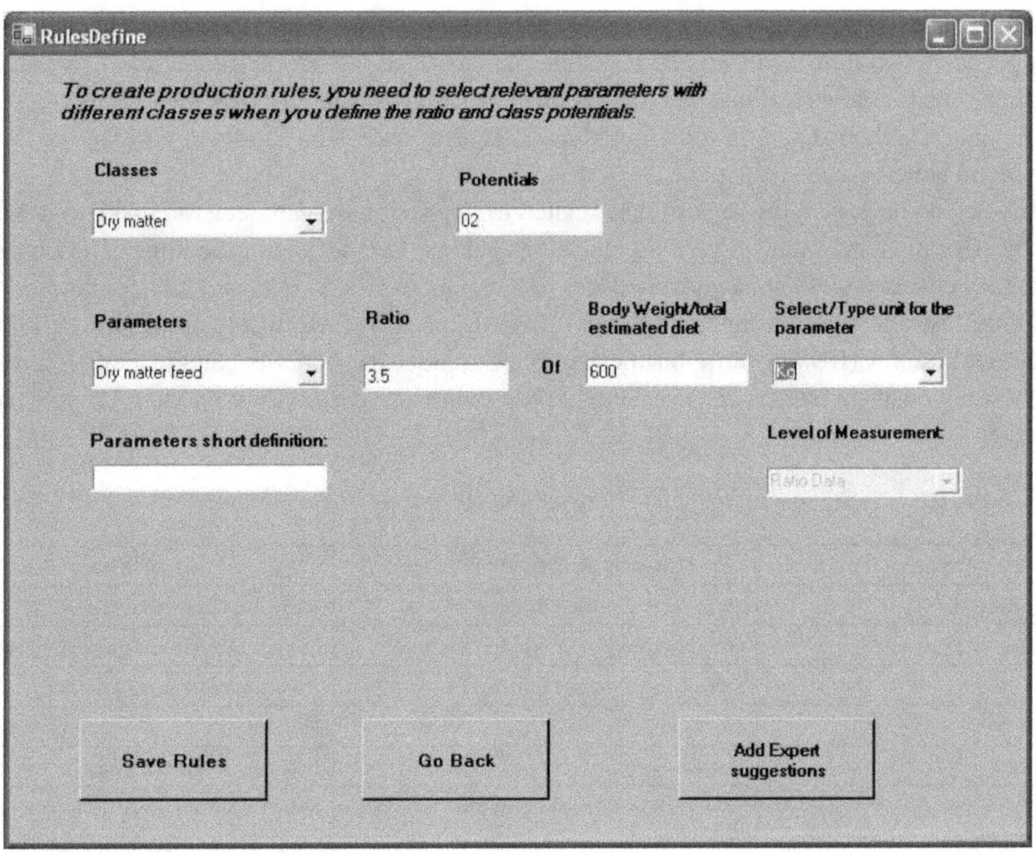

factors into considerations of decision support; Farm owners have options for knowledge sharing for improving managers' decision making; Farm owners can draw decision support situations needed for everyday operations in particular seasons.

We compared the developed prototype with an established similar BI application developed for financial knowledge management (Cheng, Lu and Sheu, 2009) which is able to extract, transform and load financial data. The following table (table 3) shows the comparison with our proposed framework.

Focus group technique has been used for acquiring rich qualitative data when evaluating decision support applications (Haghighi et al. 2013). We used the focus group technique since there was an opportunity for a face-to-face meeting with the group of stakeholders to evaluate the validity of the BI process that has been developed.

DISCUSSION AND CONCLUSION

BI should be referred through appropriate use of decision support technology to collect and effectively convert information to improve business decision making. The study described the useful provision of tailorable features for BIS solution design that may better address limitations of traditional decision support approaches for small business owners as they are static, model based and inflexibility of system that resulted in a poor user uptake. In relation to improve user uptake, two main issues were highlighted in the study and these are seen as lack of the necessary expertise to make decisions and user uptake to develop their decision support. The tailorable features discussed in the chapter were suitable for addressing the issues. For instance, Jourdan et al. (2012) suggest four distinct BI research categories after a comprehensive literature review on BI research. The artificial intelligence category offers algorithms and applications for classifications and prediction. The benefits category deals with how organisations could use data warehousing, data mining and an enterprise wide BI systems to achieve some measurable financial benefit.

The decision category represents studies related to improving overall decision making and includes such subjective matters of data modelling, decision-making, and decision modelling. The implementation category covers project management issues in a variety of BI contexts including data warehousing, data mining, customer relationship management (CRM), enterprise resource planning (ERP), knowledge management systems (KMS), and e-business projects. Under the benefits category our research dealt with how small business owners can use data for their own effective decision making. Using a tailorable

Table 3. Contrast between an existing BI solution and proposed BIS

Criteria	Cheng et al. (2009) BI solution	Proposed BIS solution
Key purposes	Financial knowledge extraction	Internal resource management
Techniques	Ontology based for knowledge modelling	Ontology based for knowledge modelling
Ability	Extract, transform and load data.	Extract, transform and load data.
System	Prototype	Prototype
Target users	Domain expert	Business owners and managers
Key issues	Integration of decision support and knowledge management	Knowledge sharing and decision support collaboration

technology, the proposed approach outlined a process framework to address secondary design roles of the business owners and managers. In this research, the needs of flexibility in both activities by the users within non-technical boundaries are outlined to instantly obtain their appropriate decision support. We have demonstrated this through an example of the approach that addressed northern Australian dairy industry deregulation case.

In this chapter, we developed an specially-designed BIS application development perspective and through this it is argued that the tailorable technology embedded in any BIS will have implications for small businesses related to production systems, because the decision making aspect in the production systems in the types of businesses such as livestock-based rural business are very similar.

We developed a prototype solution for representing a process demonstration in a small scale method. Further study is required to address this challenge, including database management issues for fully developing the BI solution. In addition, examining associated risks and opportunities relevant to the proposed approach would also be an interesting study area for its further evaluation in different decision making situations of businesses. The prototype is a proof-of-concept demonstration with an initial evaluation with key stakeholders, but without its great details. The solution model and the development approach cannot be useful in similar businesses in different scales. Therefore, further research can be designed for investigating the aspect more intimately in other non-farming SMEs. Thus, the contribution of this study can be considered as an important benchmark in the domain of BIS solutions for SMEs.

REFERENCES

Australian Bureau of Statistics. (2014). Available at: www.abs.gov.au

Australian Dairy Industry in Focus. (2008). Available at: http://www.dairyaustralia.com.au/Our-Dairy-Industry/~/media/Publications/Australian Dairy Industry in Focus/2008/AustralianDairyIndustryInFocus2008.ashx?la=en

Bajo, J., Borrajo, M. L., De Paz, J. F., Corchado, J. M., & Pellicer, M. A. (2012). A multi-agent system for web-based risk management in small and medium business. *Expert Systems with Applications*, *39*(8), 6921–6931. doi:10.1016/j.eswa.2012.01.001

Baumback, C. (1988). *How to Organize and Operate a Small Business*. Prentice Hall.

Callow, M. N., Gobius, N., & Hetherington, G. (2005). Development of profitable milk production systems for northern Australia: An analysis of intensification of current systems. *AFBM Journal*, *2*, 24–37.

Chae, B. (2014). A complexity theory approach to IT-enabled services (IESs) and service innovation: Business analytics as an illustration of IES. *Decision Support Systems*, *57*, 1–10. doi:10.1016/j.dss.2013.07.005

Chataway, R. G., Walker, R. G., & Callow, M. N. (2010). Development of profitable milk production systems for northern Australia: A field assessment of the productivity of five potential farming systems using farmlets. *Australian Journal of Experimental Agriculture*, *50*, 246–264.

Chaudhry, S. S., Salchenberger, L., & Beheshtian, M. (1996). A small business inventory DSS: Design development, and implementation issues. *Computers & Operations*, *23*(1), 63–72. doi:10.1016/0305-0548(95)00004-6

Cheng, H., Lu, Y. C., & Sheu, C. (2009). An ontology-based business intelligence application in a financial knowledge management system. *Expert Systems with Applications*, *36*(2), 3614–3622. doi:10.1016/j.eswa.2008.02.047

Cox, P. G. (1996). Some issues in the design of Agricultural Decision Support Systems. *Agricultural Systems*, *52*(2-3), 355–381. doi:10.1016/0308-521X(96)00063-7

Darby-Dowman, K., Barker, S., Audsley, E., & Parsons, D. (2000). A two-stage stochastic programming with resource model for determining robust planting plans in horticulture. *The Journal of the Operational Research Society*, *51*(1), 83–89. doi:10.1057/palgrave.jors.2600858

Duan, Y., & Xu, M. (2009). Decision Support Systems in Small Businesses. In Encyclopedia of information science and technology (2nd ed.). Hershey, PA: IGI Global. doi:10.4018/978-1-60566-026-4.ch155

Dulcic, Z., Pavlic, D., & Silic, I. (2012). Evaluating the Intended Use of Decision Support System (DSS) by Applying Technology Acceptance Model (TAM) in Business Organizations in Croatia. *Procedia: Social and Behavioral Sciences*, *58*, 1565–1575. doi:10.1016/j.sbspro.2012.09.1143

Gangadharan, G. R., & Swamy, N. S. (2004). Business intelligence systems: design and implementation strategies. *Proceedings of 26th International Conference on Information Technology Interfaces*. Available at: http://ieeexplore.ieee.org/

Germonprez, M., Hovorka, D., & Collopy, F. (2007). A theory of Tailorable Technology Design. *Journal of the Association for Information Systems*, *8*(6), 351–367. doi:10.17705/1jais.00131

Germonprez, M., Hovorka, D., & Gal, U. (2011). Secondary Design: A Case of Behavioral Design Science research. *Journal of the Association for Information Systems*, *12*(10), 662–683. doi:10.17705/1jais.00278

Gibson, M., Arnott, D., & Carlsson, S. (2004). Evaluating the Intangible Benefits of Business Intelligence: Review & Research Agenda. *Proceeding of the Decision Support in an Uncertain and Complex World: The IFIP TC8/WG8.3 International Conference*, 295-305.

Gupta, P., Seetharaman, A., & Raj, J. R. (2013). The usage and adoption of cloud computing by small and medium businesses. *International Journal of Information Management*, *33*(5), 861–874. doi:10.1016/j.ijinfomgt.2013.07.001

Haghighi, D. P., Burstein, F., Zaslavsky, A., & Arbon, P. (2013). Development and evaluation of ontology for intelligent decision support in medical emergency management for mass gatherings. *Decision Support Systems*, *54*(2), 1192–1204. doi:10.1016/j.dss.2012.11.013

Hayman, P. T., & Easdown, W. J. (2002). An ecology of a DSS: Reflections on managing wheat crops in the North-eastern Australian grains region with WHEATMAN. *Agricultural Systems*, *74*(1), 57–77. doi:10.1016/S0308-521X(02)00018-5

Hedgebeth, D. (2007). Data-driven decision making for the enterprise: An overview of business intelligence applications. *Vine*, *37*(4), 414–420. doi:10.1108/03055720710838498

Heikkila, J., Saariner, T., & Saaksjarvi, M. (1991). Success of software packages in small business: An exploratory study. *European Journal of Information Systems*, *1*(3), 159–169. doi:10.1057/ejis.1991.31

Hosack, B., Hall, D., Paradice, D., & Courtney, J. F. (2012). A Look Toward the Future: Decision Support Systems Research is Alive and Well. *Journal of the Association for Information Systems*, *13*(5), 315–340. doi:10.17705/1jais.00297

Iivari, J., & Iivari, N. (2011). Varieties of user-centredness: An analysis of four systems development methods. *Information Systems Journal*, *21*(2), 125–153. doi:10.1111/j.1365-2575.2010.00351.x

Jourdan, Z., Rainer, R. K., & Marshall, T. E. (2012). Business Intelligence: An Analysis of the Literature. *Information Systems Management*, *25*(2), 121–131. doi:10.1080/10580530801941512

Keniry, J., Blums, A., Notter, E., Radford, E., & Thomson, S. (2003). *Regional business – a plan for action*. Department of Transport and Regional Services. Available at: www.rbda.gov.au/action_plan

Kerr, D. V. (2004). Factors influencing the development and adoption of knowledge based decision support systems for small, owner operated rural businesses. *Artificial Intelligence Review*, *22*(2), 127–147. doi:10.1023/B:AIRE.0000045503.74951.7a

Khan, E. H., & Khan, G. M. (1992). Microcomperters and small business in Bahrain. *Industrial Management & Data Systems*, *92*(6), 297–304. doi:10.1108/02635579210015400

Kuhlmann, F., & Brodersen, C. (2001). Information technology and farm management: Developments and perspectives. *Computers and Electronics in Agriculture*, *30*(1-3), 71–83. doi:10.1016/S0168-1699(00)00157-5

Li, X., Zhu, Z., & Pan, X. (2010). Knowledge cultivating for intelligent decision making in small & middle businesses. *Procedia Computer Science*, *1*(1), 2479–2488. doi:10.1016/j.procs.2010.04.280

Lin, H. W., Nagalingam, S. V., Kuik, S. S., & Murata, T. (2012). Design of a Global Decision Support System for a manufacturing SME: Towards participating in Collaborative Manufacturing. *International Journal of Production Economics*, *136*(1), 1–12. doi:10.1016/j.ijpe.2011.07.001

Little, J. D. (2004). Models and managers: The concept of decision calculus. *Management Science*, *50*(12), 1841–1853. doi:10.1287/mnsc.1040.0267

Lynch, T., & Gregor, S. (2004). Use participation in decision support systems development: Influencing system outcomes. *European Journal of Information Systems*, *13*(4), 286–301. doi:10.1057/palgrave.ejis.3000512

MacGregor, R. C., & Vrazalic, L. (2005). A basic model of electronic commerce adoption barriers: A study of regional small businesses in Sweden and Australia. *Journal of Small Business and Enterprise Development*, *12*(4), 510–527. doi:10.1108/14626000510628199

Malhotra, R., & Temponi, C. (2010). Critical decisions for ERP integration: Small business issues. *International Journal of Information Management*, *30*(1), 28–37. doi:10.1016/j.ijinfomgt.2009.03.001

McCown, R. L. (2002). Changing systems for supporting farmers decisions: Problems, paradigms, and prospects. *Agricultural Systems*, *74*(1), 179–220. doi:10.1016/S0308-521X(02)00026-4

Meensel, J. V., Lauwers, L., Kempen, I., Dessein, J., & Huylenbroeck, G. V. (2012). Effect of a participatory approach on the successful development of agricultural decision support systems: The case of Pigs2win. *Decision Support Systems*, *54*(1), 164–172. doi:10.1016/j.dss.2012.05.002

Mustafa, Y. (2012). Helping small businesses identify their it application needs, a simple tool. *Issues in Information Systems*, *13*(1), 11–16.

Niu, L., Lu, J., Zhang, G., & Wu, D. (2013). FACETS: A cognitive business intelligence system. *Information Systems*, *38*(6), 835–862. doi:10.1016/j.is.2013.02.002

Parker, A., Woodford, K., & Woods, E. (2000). *Deregulation and restructuring in the Queensland dairy industry*. School of Natural and Rural Systems, the University of Queensland, Brisbane, Australia.

Popovič, A., Hackney, R., Coelho, P. S., & Jaklič, J. (2012). Towards business intelligence systems success: Effects of maturity and culture on analytical decision making. *Decision Support Systems*, *54*(1), 729–739. doi:10.1016/j.dss.2012.08.017

Power, D. (2007). What are the features of a data-driven DSS? *DSS News, 8*(4). Available at: http://dssresources.com/faq/pdf/135.pdf

Ray, C. M., Harris, T. M., & Dye, J. L. (1994). Small business attitudes toward computers. *Journal of End User Computing*, *6*(1), 16–25. doi:10.4018/joeuc.1994010102

Raymond, L., & Bergeron, F. (1992). Personal DSS success in small enterprises. *Information & Management*, *22*(5), 301–308. doi:10.1016/0378-7206(92)90076-R

Recio, B., Rubio, F., & Criado, J. A. (2003). A decision support system for farm planning using AgriSupport II. *Decision Support Systems*, *36*(2), 189–203. doi:10.1016/S0167-9236(02)00134-3

Rouibah, K., & Ould-ali, S. (2002). PUZZLE: A concept and prototype for linking business intelligence to business strategy. *The Journal of Strategic Information Systems*, *11*(2), 133–152. doi:10.1016/S0963-8687(02)00005-7

Sherwell, B. W., Gonzalez, A. J., & Nguyen, J. (2005). Contextual Implementation of Human Problem-solving Knowledge in a Real-World Decision Support System. *Proceedings of the Conference on Behavior Representation in Modeling and Simulation*. Available at: http://cc.ist.psu.edu/BRIMS2013/archives/2005/papers/05-BRIMS-025.pdf

Singh, S. K., Watson, H. J., & Watson, R. T. (2002). EIS support for the strategic management process. *Decision Support Systems*, *33*(1), 71–85. doi:10.1016/S0167-9236(01)00129-4

Stasieńko, J. (2010). Business Intelligence as a Decision Support System. In G. Setlak & K. Markov (Eds.), Methods and Instruments of Artificial Intelligence (pp. 141–148). Rzeszow, Poland: Academic Press.

Tsaih, R., Liu, Y. J., Liu, W., & Lien, Y. L. (2014). Credit scoring system for small business loans. *Decision Support Systems*, *38*(1), 91–99. doi:10.1016/S0167-9236(03)00079-4

Tutunea, M. F., & And Rus, R. V. (2012). Business intelligence solutions for SMEs. *Procedia Economics and Finance*, *3*, 865–870. doi:10.1016/S2212-5671(12)00242-0

Walker, D. H. (2002). Decision support, learning and rural resource management. *Agricultural Systems*, *73*(1), 113–127. doi:10.1016/S0308-521X(01)00103-2

Yang, X., & Fu, J. (2008). Review of IT/IS Adoption and Decision-Making Behavior in Small Businesses. *Tsinghua Science and Technology*, *13*(3), 323–328. doi:10.1016/S1007-0214(08)70052-X

ENDNOTE

1 Hedgebeth (2007) described the data driven DSS (one of the five classes as defined by Power (2007): model-driven, data-driven, communications-driven, document-driven, and knowledge-driven) within a perspective of business intelligence application development. Power (2007) described data-driven DSS "provide(s) operational and strategic business intelligence using internal company data and sometimes external data". We accept that a general view of BIS that can be defined as a data driven DSS and holds useful features to support the smart manager's demand in rural SMEs context.

Chapter 14
Design Methods of Strategic Decision Support Solutions for B2C Business Managers

Madhury Khatun
Victoria University, Australia

Shah J. Miah
Victoria University, Australia

ABSTRACT

This chapter reviews methods to develop a decision support system (DSS) for small business managers. The primary objective is to support managers, making strategic decisions for achieving competitive advantages in the business-to-consumer (B2C) e-commerce environment. Many researchers in the DSS domain utilized various methods to design information systems (IS) solution, mostly intended for large businesses. None of the researchers have considered the business environment as a knowledge source for DSS development of small business strategic decision support needs. User-centered design (UCD) and design science research (DSR) method were adopted for DSS development. DSR was appropriate because it addresses the real-world application environment where research problem or opportunity are defined. Multiple case studies and web content analysis were carried out for understanding business problems, needs, and system requirements. This study used the qualitative and descriptive data analysis methods. The findings suggested developing a DSS solution to meet the small business strategic needs.

INTRODUCTION

The analysis and design of Decision Support Systems (DSS) is a multifaceted activity that points toward exploiting of suitable methodologies for modelling decision processes (Brandas, 2011). This chapter describes various system development approaches to select suitable method(s) for a small business DSS development. The DSS is targeted to enhance small business owner/manager strategic decision-making competencies. The idea is to provide an option to managers using analytical knowledge to update competitive features on their websites within the business-to-consumer (B2C) e-commerce dynamic

DOI: 10.4018/978-1-5225-5718-0.ch014

environment. DSS is the area of information system (IS) discipline focused on systems that support and improve managerial decision-making (Arnott & Pervan, 2012).

A DSS is vital for this study related to addressing small business issues and needs because it can provide potential solutions to organisational problems (Arnott & Pervan, 2012). The DSS also can assist in improving managerial, strategic decision-making competencies (Arnott & Pervan, 2012; Power, 2016), and can help decision-makers understand underlying issues in a system (Wienclaw, 2008). Therefore, a DSS can help managers make better decisions (Pick, 2008; Wienclaw, 2008).

One of the vital roles of a manager in an organisation involves in making most productive decisions within the business environment and implementing them for the profitable business outcome. Making a productive decision is relatively a hard task for small business managers in the dynamic business environment (Power, 2010). Predominantly, decision making may difficult for most small businesses in the B2C e-commerce environment, where millions of consumers have the opportunity to direct dealings with companies on their websites and can evaluate products and services until choosing one site (Haag & Cummings, 2009). Also, global products and services are produced and delivered to customers in a technologically sophisticated electronic trading environment where markets change rapidly, and consumer demands are high (Power, Sharda & Kulkarni, 2007). Thus, the business processes are complex and competitive oriented (Alalwan, 2013). B2C e-commerce highly visible, as it directly interacts with more than several millions of consumers through websites (Haag & Cummings, 2009). This changing environment influences both problems and opportunities for businesses. Thus, managers as decision-makers require analysing problems in such environment (Hall, 2008). Consequently, appropriate decisions and actions are required by the decision makers in such situation (Hall, 2008).

The majority of Australian small businesses in the B2C sector have been experiencing significant issues in the running productively in their online businesses that were identified through multiple case studies before a DSS solution development. In this environment, effective decision-making could be impossible without the use of appropriate technical support that can assist selecting competitive features on small business websites. The adoption of competitive website features would help a small business to reach potential customers to increase sell online. These discussions suggest designing a purpose-specific DSS solution that is essential for owners/managers in making the strategic decision in such environment. The research objective of this study is:

What are the most appropriate methods to develop a small business DSS for their strategic business needs?

This chapter is organised as follows. First, it discusses the background of the chapter. Next, it explains the practical problems of small businesses and DSS requirements, and method used for requirement analysis. Then, it discusses various DSS development approaches to identify the most suitable methods for small business DSS development, and finally, presents a conclusion with further research direction.

BACKGROUND

DSS research has been established as a well-recognised practice in IS research field. Its dedication is promised to improving decision-making process and practice through the application of appropriate technologies (Miah & McKay, 2016). DSS is significant for this study as it usually focuses on the effectiveness (such as decision) rather than efficiency (such as search & measurement) in helping decision-making processes (Eom, 2007). In small business context, it may assist owners/managers for enhancing their strategic decision-making process and capabilities using an innovative DSS solution artefact because a DSS mainly helps human decision-making processes that are integrated into the organisational context and known as the new application domain (Angehrn & Jelassi, 1994). A DSS is also a comprehensive tool in IS discipline that can assist to improve decision-making processes in an organisation (Alyoubi, 2015). Decision-making is a process of choosing among alternative courses of action for attaining an organisational goal (Tariq & Rafi, 2012).

In spite of this, no research so far focused on designing a DSS for a small business strategic decision-making needs in the B2C e-commerce environment through the analysis of environmental factors (e.g., competitors). Likely, a review of literature published between 1990-2005 by Arnott and Pervan (2012) found that only a few researchers (10%) designed DSS for strategic decision-making perspective, and just for large business. For example, *Arnott (2004, p. 252-3) developed a personal DSS (PDSS) type when a large semi-government authority was faced with a problem of housing its administrative staff and used a strategic DSS project over its six-week life.* Moreover, earlier research related to small businesses had focused on social and economic issues rather than technological developments (Duan & Xu, 2009). Duan and Xu (2009) also argued that the focus of researchers mainly in the small business manufacturing sector was generally on the use of a DSS at the operational decision-making rather than at the strategic decision-making context.

General benefits of DSS are to assist better decision-making process at various phases within the business environment and to assist decision makers in making better decisions (Pick, 2008). The vital role of the DSS is to support all phases of the decision-making process (Sprague & Carlson, 1982). Sometimes, a DSS does not provide better decisions, but the decision process can be improved, for instance, decision makers might be achieved their goals with less effort within a time frame, and in some cases requiring the better documentation, thus, decision process improvements may provide improved decisions (Pick, 2008). The next section describes user issues, needs and analysis methods on DSS requirements.

PRACTICAL PROBLEM CONTEXT AND DSS REQUIREMENT ANALYSIS METHODS

This research was evolutionary, exploratory and centred on the practical problem and real business context, such as focused on the small business online system and strategic decision-making issues in the B2C e-commerce environment. Thus, prior to DSS solution development, multiple case studies were carried out with small business owners/managers from the online retail sector in Australia. The intention was to identify business internal issues and system requirements, and to recognise how owners/managers can address their problems strategically in such environment to make their websites interactive. This method was considered as the investigation and analysis of internal environment of small businesses and related factors. Summary of findings from case studies is discussed and analysed later using the MRT (Mintzberg, Raisinghani & Theoret, 1976) model in the conceptual DSS solution framework as shown in Figure 1.

This study also carried out the web content analysis before the innovative DSS solution design and development to identify issues of the small business existing e-commerce system, such as to determine the issues on adoption levels of small business website features against those of their overseas competitors as shown in Figure 2. The process is termed as the system analysis and requirements for a small business DSS development in the B2C e-commerce environment. This method can also be characterised the investigation and analysis of external organisational environment of small businesses and one of the significant external factors. The external factor was considered the overseas competitor who sell to Australia through their websites. Using the MRT model in the conceptual DSS framework, this section provides an analysis to rationalise small business internal issues related to their strategic decision-making competencies within the B2C e-commerce environment. This analysis helped to identify the small business problems, needs, and DSS requirements.

The overall methodology for developing this study was the design science research (DSR). The DSR was considered appropriate because this method assists in addressing the real-world application environment in which the research problem or opportunity is illustrated (Hevner, March, Park, & Ram, 2004). Design science (DS) has also become an essential and widely used approach within the IS research communities (Leukel, Mueller & Sugumaran, 2014). The primary purpose of the DSR is to design a system for the solution of a problem (Dresch, Lacerda & Antunes, 2015), and design is the fundamental process to the IS discipline (March & Storey, 2008).

This study adopted constructivist research philosophy and the overall approach of this study was qualitative (Miah, Ahsan, & Msimangira, 2014) and descriptive analysis methods (Henver et al., 2004). The strategy of enquiry by employing case study method with multiple cases, web content analysis, and focus group method. Constructivist research provides practical guidelines for understanding a context with various perspectives and diversities and generates theories. The constructivist research approach often combines with interpretivism and is typically seen as an approach to qualitative research (Creswell, 2013).

In the context of small business owners/managers strategic decision-making processes and making improved decisions, a conceptual DSS framework is constructed theoretical basis and based on the MRT model for strategic decision-making. This model is shown in Figure 1.

This model has been well-known in the strategic management literature. Many influential factors are associated with decision-making processes that are also part of this model, and one of the factors is environmental forces. Another factor related to decision process is comprehension cycles to understand and process information and this factor also addressed by this model (Power, 2009). These are other reasons that motivated this study to adopt MRT model for small business DSS requirements analysis.

This study was considered the B2C e-commerce environment and associated internal and external factors that force to retail industry changes. Thus, the study had been processed information in different cycles to understand the small business problems, needs, and DSS requirements. These activities were involved in information processing through multiple case studies and analysis of small business website

Figure 1. A conceptual DSS framework

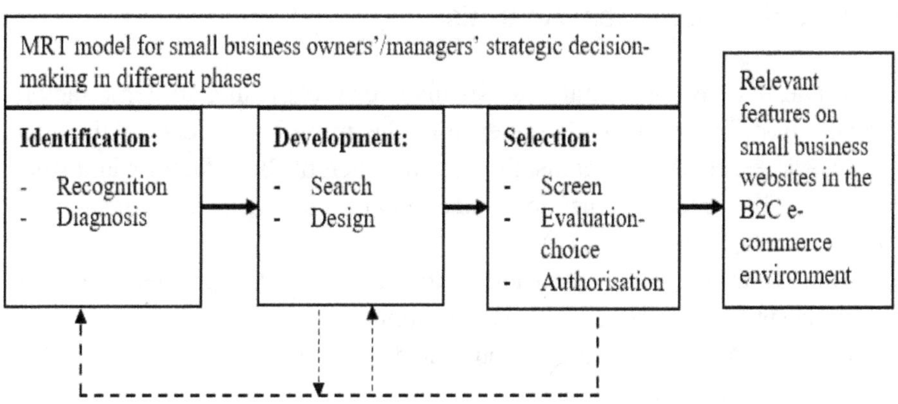

features. Finally, owners/managers were participated in processing information using the functional DSS artefact prototype and evaluating it to test the usability and efficiency of the prototype related to their strategic needs.

MRT model consists of three phases: identification, development and selection phases for management strategic decision-making processes in the business environment. The findings from case studies have been discussed and analysed using the phases of MRT model in the conceptual DSS framework to determine how small business owners/managers have been accomplished their strategic decisions at different phases in the B2C e-commerce environment, particularly in the selection of competitive features on their websites. These phases are described in the following sections.

Identification Phase

This phase comprises two routines: recognition and diagnosis. The 'recognition routine' initiates the decision-making process by recognising problems and opportunities for organisations within the business environment. In the problem 'recognition routine', this study found that all owners/managers had awareness and knowledge regarding online shopping problem in Australia. However, the majority had lack competencies and knowledge to address the problem. In the opportunity 'recognition routine' stage, although the majority of small business owners/managers expressed their opportunities to increase sales via websites, however, their strategies were incompatible to accomplish such opportunity.

In the 'diagnosis routine,' further information is required for decision makers to define and clarify the previously recognised problem or opportunity. In the small business perspective, additional information is crucial for owners/managers in strategic decision-making in the B2C e-commerce environment to clarify and address the challenges that they have been experiencing in such context. A strategic decision focuses on analysing or assessment in both the internal and external business environments and associated factors (De Wit & Meyer, 2010; Mintzberg et al., 1976). It also involves in qualitative judgments, using intuition and finally making rules or decisions (Bonczek, Holsapple & Whinston, 2014). However, many owners/managers lack awareness and analytical knowledge about internal and external business environment and associated environmental factors. Mainly, this inadequacy was showing in the B2C e-commerce environment. The analytical knowledge and its acquisition from the business environment are essential for improving business performance and remain competitive in the online business environment. Knowledge acquisition also associates with knowledge sources whether it can find internally or externally (Oliver, 2008).

Internal Factors and Requirement Analysis

Characteristically, internal environmental analysis involves recognising strategic factors crucial to the success of an organisation. This analysis also determines the importance of each of these factors, identifies the strengths and weaknesses of the organisation against each of these factors, and finally, preparing a strategic advantage profile for the organisation, and comparing it with profiles of successful competitors in the industry (Srivastava & Verma, 2012).

Small business internal factors were considered to analyse the real problem tracking. These factors include owners/managers as system users' concern about strategic decision-making competencies in the B2C e-commerce environment and issues continue on their existing system related to adoption level of website features. Additional internal factors had considered in this study including owner/manager knowledge and awareness about the business environment and associated factors (e.g., competitors). Moreover, how they can use their skills and knowledge for making the effective decision (e.g., significant internal factor) in the selection of relevant features on their websites. This study also considered internal strengths of small businesses and how they used them to maximise opportunities, and how they address their internal issues in the B2C e-commerce environment.

Although majority small businesses had a greater range of products as their internal resources, only one company had a strategy to provide relevant information on its website through which consumer interactions can be maximised. The majority small business internal weakness was lacked skills using advanced technology, and their strategies were unlike to counter this weakness. The most significant internal issue was the lack of understanding and analytical knowledge about the business environment. While the majority owners/managers believed that their opportunity is to increase sales via websites, their strategies were irrelevant to exploit such opportunity. In the perspective of external threat analysis, the most were known their external threat as competitors, but they had lack strategies to address such risk. Moreover, many were not attentive and interested in overseas competitors who sell to Australia. Only a few were concentrated on local competitors.

In the concept of owner/manager strategic decision-making competencies (critical internal factor) that this study was counted to analyse, mainly, how they select relevant features on their websites in the dynamic B2C e-commerce environment. This study found that the majority businesses had lack own strategies to choose and maintain competitive functional features on their sites. Most relied on web designers or consultants who are the secondary decision makers. Even, nearly all businesses had lack awareness about the adoption level features of their overseas competitor websites through they sell to Australia. The most of them had lack awareness and knowledge what features are available on their sites. Most small business owners/managers were occupied with everyday business operations, and they had no time for own research and development. Likewise, Buxton and Walton (2014) recognised that small businesses might find it challenging to collect market research data, due to limited time.

External Factors and Requirement Analysis

In the context of analysing the external business environment and associated factors, some researchers were considered some factors including new technologies, customers, suppliers, the economy, competitions and government policies (Thierauf, 1988; Pedersen & Sudzina, 2012; Rosenblatt, 2014). This study looked at small businesses who have to deal with overseas competitors, a significant external factor, and who can compete via their websites through the Internet.

From the B2C e-commerce perspective, the online environment must be attractive, with adequate features so the consumers can choose, perform, and enjoy their shopping experience (Abdallah & Jaleel, 2015; Bilgihan & Bujisic, 2015). One of the significant challenges that small business owners/managers have been encountering in forming strategies for creating their e-commerce website effective that found through case studies. The lack of strategy formation is centred on the selection and implementation of competitive features on their websites. This study does concern about the analysis of the external business environment and associated factors. Thus, it carried out an investigation at what extent small businesses adopted features on their websites against those of their overseas competitors. The study found that significantly lower of adoption levels of Information, Communication, Transaction, and Distribution related relevant features on small business websites than those of their overseas competitors who sell to Australia. The results are shown in Figure 2.

Figure 2. Problem finding through web content analysis

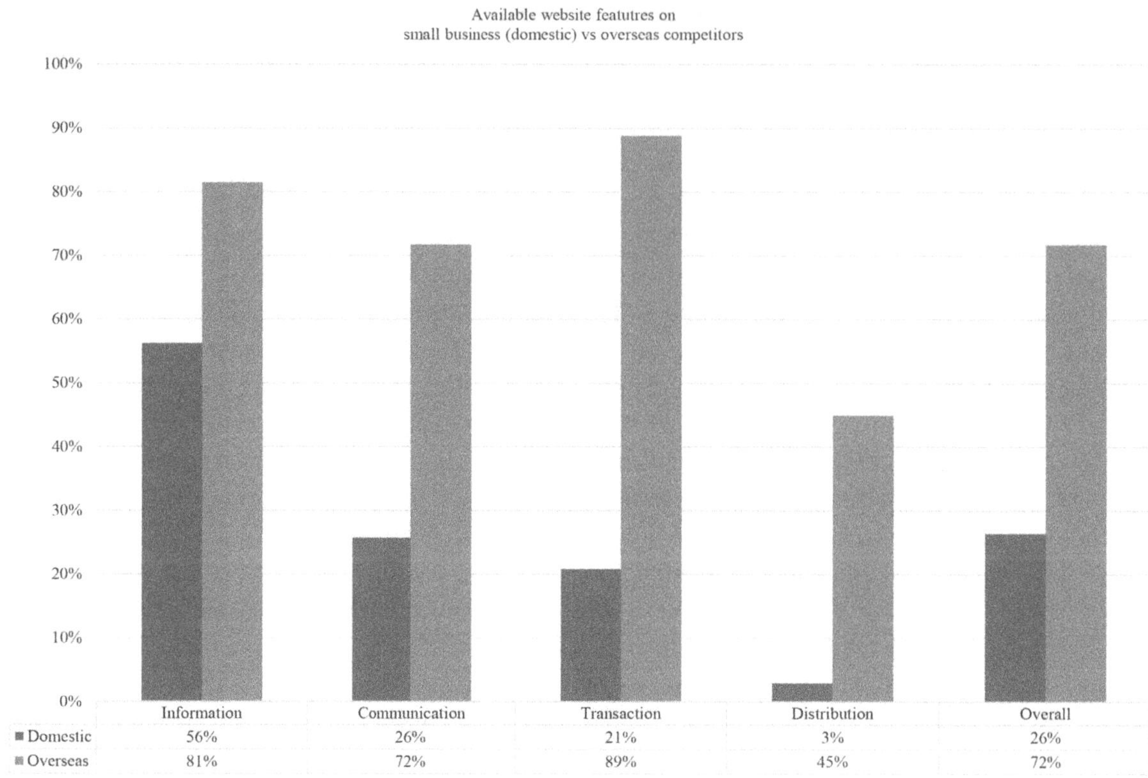

Practical issues discussed above acknowledge to design and development of a DSS solution to address the small business problems in the online retail environment. The DSS can assist in enhancing owners/managers strategic decision-making competencies to select and implement more competitive features on their websites in the B2C e-commerce environment and ultimately can maximise their sales online.

Development Phase

The development phase of MRT model involves a set of activities that generate one or more solutions. This phase has two routines. First is the 'search routine' that aims at finding ready-made solutions. Second is the 'design routine' that seeks information to develop new solutions or modify ready-made ones. In this phase, owner/managers can formulate or develop a decisions model, set the criterion for the choice, and search for alternatives. This study noticed that small business owners/managers had lack knowledge about the business environment that is significant for making strategic decisions to achieve organisational goals. Strategic decisions made by owners/managers were irrelevant to address the problems and opportunities. This study also found that many owners/managers are predominantly busy, and they had no time to participate, response and engaged in research and development activities.

Consequently, this study was initiated to design and development of a new DSS with the involvement of small business owners/managers. Given that, this study was adopted the user-centred design environment (UCDE) method, as developed by Miah et al. (2014) for the overall DSS design and development, as well as evaluation of the artefact with the involvement of owners/managers as end-users. According to

Miah et al. (2014), the significant characteristics of the UCDE method are: the secondary design activities that focus on decision-support parameters (such as issues); the conduct of a comparative analysis of current and desired states; and its ability to obtain expert analysis and generate reports for business decision-making.

Selection Phase

Mintzberg et al. (1976) suggested that the 'selection phase' of MRT model as shown in conceptual DSS framework is typically a multi-stage iterative process of decision making. Three routines emerged from this phase: screen, evaluation-choice, and authorisation. The selection phase starts with a 'screening routine,' which is activated to eliminate any impractical alternatives. Next, the best choice is selected, through a process of analysis, in the 'evaluation-choice routine.' Finally, the decision goes through the 'authorisation routine.' This activity involves an authorised decision-maker for making the strategic decision that relates to the selection of competitive website features. Competitive features for small business websites were categorised based on the business information, communication, transaction, and distribution (ICDT) provisions within the B2C e-commerce context by adopting Angehrn's (1997) ICDT model. This ICDT categories website features were recommended by Burgess (2016) for Australian small business websites. These categories of website features are presented in the Appendix. A prototype method was used for the small business DSS solution development and evaluation. A prototype is a smaller-scale representation or working model of the user's requirements, or a system development method in IS research field (Haag & Cummings, 2009).

Consequently, these activities were involved assimilating knowledge through analysing the external and internal business environment and related factors of small business organisations in the B2C e-commerce environment and system requirements activities. Evolving from the development phase of MRT model, next section discusses the system development approaches for the small business DSS solution design and development.

DSS DEVELOPMENT APPROACHES

Many approaches have been formed for system development in the IS research. The most frequently used method is the system development life cycle (SDLC) (Kroenke, Bunker & Wilson, 2014). The SDLC approach involves a long-term focused with many stages (Turban, 2007) for a large project (Kroenke et al., 2014). The small business strategic decision-making problem context in the dynamic B2C e-commerce environment, SDLC was unsuitable for the DSS design and development because this method is used for the massive project and the process taking a long time. Evolutionary prototyping method was suitable for the small business DSS design and development. The evolutionary development considers set of causes, which are some forces or factors that motivate users to the DSS adaptation process, and leads to evolution. Causal factors can be originated from the business environment and can be cognatic factors to the decision maker (Arnott, 2004) that the current study was centred. The evolutionary prototyping is based on the user-centred system design and development principles (Gulliksen et al., 2005). Prototyping was an appropriate approach because it is a smaller-scale working model of the user's requirements, or a system development method in information system research (Haag & Cummings, 2009). Likely, the small business DSS was a small-scale application that was developed and focused on finding the small business website issues for the purpose of providing the systematic solution.

Evolutionary Prototyping System Development Approach

As asserted by Chen and Lee (2003), the objective of cognitive decision support is to help managers in their decision making from human cognitive aspects, for instance, thinking, being familiar with the environment, understanding and predicting, and fully reusing their experience. Among these aspects, decision makers' situation awareness and mental models are considered to be two vital requirements for decision making, predominantly in the ill-structured and dynamic decision situations with uncertainties, and time limit. These researchers also identified that decision making is becoming increasingly difficult in the contemporary business environment where a cognitive style or a mental model plays a significant role that assists a decision maker for understanding business environments and ill-structured problems. Therefore, situation awareness by managers about the business environment is becoming a critical factor to make a productive decision (Niu, Lu & Zhang, 2009). Moreover, *Cognitive styles are also known as knowledge representation technique of human mental models that have received wide research attention in DSS researchers (Niu et al., 2009, p. 42).* The term cognition comprises general processes by which particular information is attended, transformed, stored, and retrieved (Rogers, O'Brien & Fisk, 2013).

A typical example of cognatic causes of DSS evaluation is when managers learn more about the decision task by using the system and interacting with a system analyst. They also think of new system requirements through the conversation with another manager or can come from a consultant if the consultant is a domain expert rather than an information system expert. Also, attending conferences, seminars and training courses could provide a cognitive cause of DSS evolution. These interactions and participation influence managers in thinking about the DSS. Finally, the decision task may lead to ideas that cause evolutionary changes to the system (Arnott, 2004).

In the small business context, many owners/managers have no interactions with system analysts and other managers, as the majority small businesses are owner-operated, and an owner is the primary decision-maker. Owners/managers are busy at most of the time, therefore, have no time and resources for attending conferences, seminars and training courses, in addition to research and development. Thus, this study initiated to develop a user-friendly DSS to assist owners/managers to improve their decision-making competencies in the B2C e-commerce environment where most of them have no skills in using advanced technology, who are the primary users of the system.

The main advantage of evolutionary system development approach is that phases of this method are related to producing the quick prototype system that is fully functional (Kroenke et al., 2014). Evolutionary prototyping is a special case of iterative prototypes in which the prototype evolves into part or all of the final system (Beaudouin-Lafon & Mackay, 2003). Evolutionary system development is an iterative process using the user-centred development (UCD) approach, which allows continuous iterations with users (Seffah, Gulliksen & Desmarais, 2005). These authors also recommended that design solutions need to be evaluated by users before they are made final. An iteration should contain a proper analysis of the user needs and the context of use, a design phase with suggestions for modifications and a redesign following the assessment results. An iteration could be as short as half an hour, as long as it contains all three steps of design, evaluation, and redesign.

This study was chosen evolutionary prototyping approach through updating the small business website features against those of their overseas competitors that originate from the analysis of external business environmental factors (Figure 2). This study also investigated owners/managers' cognatic causal factors through multiple case studies to analysed internal issues and needs. These investigations represent the evidence of initial requirement of system development with the interactions of system users and the researcher (as a domain expert). The small business owners/managers again involved in the evaluation phase of the novel DSS prototype development using focus group method. These activities are aligned with UCD principles with user (owner/manager) direct contributions to initial system requirements phase and the final evaluation phase of the innovative DSS development.

Using UCD Principles for Small Business DSS Design, Development and Evaluation

Although DSS has been commonly a successful concept that has been implemented in several forms over the last decades (Arnott & Dodson, 2008). Many researchers found that they did not always bring a practical outcome for their target users (Arnott & Pervan, 2014; Arnott & Pervan, 2012, Arnott & Dodson, 2008; Hosack, Hall, Paradice, & Courtney, 2012). Researchers found that the many failures of DSS project due to unfit design methods and the lack of user involvement in the design process (Nelson, 2007; Dwivedi et al., 2015). Also, the lack understanding their reality in the design process that creates inequality between the end user and designer motivations, and incompetent implementation methods (Arnott & Dodson, 2008; Arnott & Pervan, 2012). UCD principles adopted for the small business DSS development are discussed in this section.

The method of DSS design and development has traditionally established the importance of the decision, the system, or the support part of the systems (Courbon 1996). In such concepts, various methods have been proposed for DSS design and development including decision-centred design, system-centred design, support-centred design, and UCD. The decision-centred design focuses on the portfolio management. The system-centred design comes from the software engineering field and is viewed as a model-based and data-based system (data and model combination). In the context of the support-centred design, the paradigm suggests early implementation and testing of the system to provide necessary support to users. Finally, in the UCD method, the main principles include beginning with a significant decision problem, using a short life cycle, evolving the system with multiple cycles and evaluating constantly. Moreover, the UCD approach ensures not only decision-making tasks but also considers the decision-makers' involvement in the decision-making process (Zarate, 2013). Thus this study adopted the MRT model to analyse the case study results and realised the small business strategic decision-making processes in the B2C e-commerce environment.

UCD is also considered as a sociotechnical approach, which is guided by philosophies. There is no specific methods or processes are required for the design. The idea is to attempt the design using knowledge and willing to utilise social and cognitive analysis of human activities (Baek, Cagiltay, Boling, & Frick, 2008). UCD, besides, focused on cognatic causal factors to the decision maker. Cognatic style referred as the knowledge representation technique of human mental model also regarded as the situation awareness by managers about the business environment. Thus, the analysis of business environment is a critical factor to make a productive decision (Niu et al., 2009). Knowledge representation suggests the requirement of knowledge formalising in a symbolic form, and to find a symbolic expression that can be interpreted (Klein & Methlie, 1995).

There were various dimensions of user-centredness in the UCD literature. According to Gulliksen et al. (2005), UCD is based on following fundamental principles. These include user focus, active user involvement, evolutionary system development, simple design representations, prototyping, evaluate use in context, explicit and conscious design activities, a professional attitude, usability champion, holistic design, process customisation, and a user-centred approach. Likewise, an analysis of literature by Iivari and Iivari (2011) enabled four dimensions of user-centredness in the UCD literature: UCD as the user focus; UCD as user work-centeredness; UCD as user involvement; and UCD as system personalisation.

UCD as user work-centredness focuses on the relationship between people, technology, work requirements and organisational constraints in work settings, where people are with a set of skills and shared practices based on their experience of working with others. UCD as system personalisation focuses on the diversity of users use the system (Iivari & Iivari, 2011). These two dimensions were unsuitable for small business DSS development because the majority businesses are owner-operated, and they have lack skills of using advanced technology.

The UCD as 'user-focus' and 'user involvements' were appropriate for small business DSS development for the following reasons. This form of UCD places the person at the centre, and emphasis on the number of users use the system. Thus, when the system has one or only a few users, it is reasonably easy to detect them and to match the system according to their needs (Iivari & Iivari, 2011). This form of UCD is also *focusing on cognitive factors (such as perception, memory, learning, problem-solving, etc.,) as they come into play during people's interactions with the interface (Shahar, GorenBar, Boaz, & Tahan, 2006, p. 119).* This UCD is as well to take every individual user's capabilities into consideration and fully satisfy his or her needs related to the system to be developed (Iivari & Iivari, 2011). These researchers also found in the early literature, where most studies viewed 'UCD as user involvement' is an integral part of UCD method for DSS design and development. Many researchers also suggested for DSS development with the engagement of industry and decision makers (Arnott, 2006; Arnott & Pervan, 2012; Hosack et al., 2012). In IS design, user involvement is expected to lead to more accurate user requirements, features that meet the user needs, a greater acceptance of the system, and enhanced ease of use (Mao, Vredenburg, Smith, & Carey, 2005). A researcher also concluded that success in DSS design is associated with user involvement, which can be effective for appropriate method selection (Courbon, 1996). Therefore, in the UCD method, users' support and involvement are significant in developing products to match their requirements (Miah, 2004), where an appropriate set of web features were suggested for accessibility by students in the higher education sector.

Consequently, the involvement of small business owners/managers was vital in the initial phase of the DSS design and development and the final stage of DSS evaluation. For problem identifications and system requirements, initially, case studies and web content analysis were conducted. The owner/manager understanding, knowledge, and analytical skills about the business environment and associated environmental factors were investigated through multiple case studies. These activities represented the investigation of the situation awareness (SA) and mental model (Niu et al., 2009) of small business decision makers that are required for the successful system design and development related to their business needs. Finally, the involvement of owners/managers was vital for evaluating the DSS prototype artefact for confirming its usability and usefulness to end-users.

Supported on the above discussions, also for small business decision support requirements, the UCD as user-focused and involvements were suitable methods for DSS design, development and evaluation by employing the evolutionary prototyping approach of the direct participation of small business owners/managers as primary users.

CONCLUSION

This chapter reviewed the DSS design methods in the theoretical concept of the small business DSS development and evaluation. Various system development approaches were discussed in this chapter aimed at selecting suitable method(s) for the DSS artefact development and evaluation. The chapter also discussed real issues of small businesses within the B2C e-commerce environment using the MRT model in the conceptual DSS framework. Problems were identified through web content analysis and multiple case studies. These activities were considered as problem identification and system requirements analysis prior the small business DSS development. The significant issues were identified as the lack of realisation of their business goals, and skills using advanced technology for the improvement of strategic decision-making competencies in their business needs. The findings from case studies also produced the problem definitions related to many owners/managers' inadequate knowledge about internal and external business environment and associated factors that are significant for meeting the strategic decision-making requirements. These issues recognise a clear need for designing a context-specific practical DSS solution.

Many approaches have been employed for system development in the IS research. The most commonly used method is the SDLC. The small business strategic decision-making problem context in the dynamic B2C e-commerce environment, SDLC was unsuitable for the system design and development because this method is used for the vast project and the process has taken a long time. The evolutionary prototyping approach was suitable for the small business solution design and development because evolutionary development considers set of causes, such as, forces or factors that motivate users to DSS adaptation process. Causal factors can be originated from the business environment or can be cognatic causal factors to the decision maker that involved user-centred DSS design and development. A prototype was an appropriate method because it is a smaller-scale system development working model in IS research that was selected for small-scale DSS development for small business managers.

Ultimately, the small business DSS solution artefact was designed and developed primarily adopting the UCD principles, focusing on user-specific needs. In such concept, involvements of small business owners/managers were vital for the artefact design, development, and evaluation through the evolutionary prototyping approach that this study was adopted. The study contribution goes to the field of DSS research as the objective of this research is to enhance the current theory and practices relevant to the knowledge-based personal DSS design. Personal DSS is defined as a small scale IS development for a manager or a small number of independent users to support their decision-making tasks (Arnott, 2008).

Further Research Direction

DSR has not been fully developed in the small business domain, particularly from a strategic decision-making perspective. Future research should explore feedback cycles across several iterations for artefact evaluation. In the present study, the scope of the DSR research was to evaluate the short-term outcomes through the focus group sessions. However, more in-depth analysis of evaluation findings and further evaluation rounds may show the transitional and long-term impacts of the DSS that will have flexible implications for research and practice.

ACKNOWLEDGMENT

This paper is an extended form of a previously published article in the *International Journal of Business Intelligence Research*. Authors are thankful to reviewers and editor for providing constructive feedback to improve the chapter.

REFERENCES

Abdallah, S., & Jaleel, B. (2015). Website appeal: Development of an assessment tool and evaluation framework of e-marketing. *Journal of Theoretical and Applied Electronic Commerce Research*, *10*(3), 45–62. doi:10.4067/S0718-18762015000300005

Abdul-Muhmin, A. G. (2011). Repeat purchase intentions in online shopping: The role of satisfaction, attitude, and online retailers' performance. *Journal of International Consumer Marketing*, *23*(1), 5–20. doi:10.1080/08961530.2011.524571

Alalwan, J. A. (2013). A taxonomy for decision support capabilities of enterprise content management systems. *The Journal of High Technology Management Research*, *24*(1), 10–17. doi:10.1016/j.hitech.2013.02.001

Alavi, M., & Henderson, J. C. (1981). An evolutionary strategy for implementing a decision support system. *Management Science*, *27*(11), 1309–1323. doi:10.1287/mnsc.27.11.1309

Albert, W., & Tullis, T. (2013). *Measuring the user experience: Collecting, analysing, and presenting usability metrics*. Elsevier Inc.

Alyoubi, B. A. (2015). Decision support system and knowledge-based strategic management. *Procedia Computer Science*, *65*, 278–284. doi:10.1016/j.procs.2015.09.079

Angehrn, A. (1997). Designing mature Internet business strategies: The ICDT model. *European Management Journal*, *15*(4), 361–369. doi:10.1016/S0263-2373(97)00016-9

Angehrn, A. A., & Jelassi, T. (1994). DSS research and practice in perspective. *Decision Support Systems*, *12*(4), 267–275. doi:10.1016/0167-9236(94)90045-0

Arnott, D. (2004). Decision support systems evolution: Framework, case study and research agenda. *European Journal of Information Systems*, *13*(4), 247–259. doi:10.1057/palgrave.ejis.3000509

Arnott, D. (2006). Cognitive biases and decision support systems development: A design science approach. *Information Systems Journal*, *16*(1), 55–78. doi:10.1111/j.1365-2575.2006.00208.x

Arnott, D., & Dodson, G. (2008). Decision support systems failure. In F. Burstein & C. W. Holsapple (Eds.), *Handbook on decision support systems 1* (pp. 763–790). Berlin: Springer. doi:10.1007/978-3-540-48713-5_34

Arnott, D., & Pervan, G. (2012). Design science in decision support systems research: An assessment using the Hevner, March, Park, and Ram guidelines. *Journal of the Association for Information Systems*, *13*(11), 923–949. doi:10.17705/1jais.00315

Arnott, D., & Pervan, G. (2014). A critical analysis of decision support systems research revisited: The rise of design science. *Journal of Information Technology*, *29*(4), 269–293. doi:10.1057/jit.2014.16

Ayed, M. B., Ltifi, H., Kolski, C., & Alimi, A. M. (2010). A user-centered approach for the design and implementation of KDD-based DSS: A case study in the healthcare domain. *Decision Support Systems*, *50*(1), 64–78. doi:10.1016/j.dss.2010.07.003

Baek, E.-O., Cagiltay, K., Boling, E., & Frick, T. (2008). User-centered design and development. In I. J. Spector, M. Merrill, J. van Merrienboer, & M. Driscoll (Eds.), *Handbook of research on educational communications and technology* (pp. 660–668). New York: Routledge/Taylor & Francis Group.

Beaudouin-Lafon, M., & Mackay, W. (2003). Prototyping tools and techniques. In A. Sears & J. A. Jacko (Eds.), *Human-computer interaction: Development process* (pp. 121–142). Boca Raton, FL: CRC Press/Taylor & Francis Group.

Bilgihan, A., & Bujisic, M. (2015). The effect of website features in online relationship marketing: A case of online hotel booking. *Electronic Commerce Research and Applications*, *14*(4), 222–232. doi:10.1016/j.elerap.2014.09.001

Bonczek, R. H., Holsapple, C. W., & Whinston, A. B. (2014). *Foundations of decision support systems*. New York: Academic Press.

Brandas, C. (2011). Decision support systems development: A methodological approach. *Journal of Applied Business Information Systems*, *2*(4), 151–158.

Bullot, A., & Hornbrook, S. (2015). *GST: Online purchases – What will be caught and when? Tax Alert*. Retrieved from https://www2.deloitte.com/nz/en/pages/tax-alerts/articles/gst-online-purchases-what-will-be-caught-and-when.html

Burgess, S. (2016). Representing small business web presence content: The web presence pyramid model. *European Journal of Information Systems*, *25*(2), 110–130. doi:10.1057/ejis.2015.4

Buxton, M., & Walton, N. (2014). The Internet as a small business e-commerce ecosystem. In E. Lacka, H. Chan & N. Yip (Eds.), E-commerce platform acceptance: Suppliers, retailers, and consumers (pp. 79-100). Cham: Springer. doi:10.1007/978-3-319-06121-4_5

Chen, J. Q., & Lee, S. M. (2003). An exploratory cognitive DSS for strategic decision making. *Decision Support Systems*, *36*(2), 147–160. doi:10.1016/S0167-9236(02)00139-2

Courbon, J.-C. (1996). User-centered DSS design and implementation. In P. Humphreys, L. Bannon, A. McCosh, P. Migliarese, & J.-C. Pomerol (Eds.), *Implementing systems for supporting management decisions: Concepts, methods, and experiences* (pp. 108–123). Boston, MA: Springer. doi:10.1007/978-0-387-34967-1_8

Creswell, J. W. (2013). *Research design: Qualitative, quantitative, and mixed methods approaches*. Thousand Oaks, CA: Sage Publications Ltd.

De Wit, B., & Meyer, R. (2010). *Strategy process, content, context: An international perspective*. Cengage Learning EMEA.

Deloitte. (2013). *Global powers of retailing 2013 retail beyond*. Retrieved from http://www.deloitte.com/assets/DcomAustralia/Local%20Assets/Documents/Industries

Dresch, A., Lacerda, D. P., & Antunes, J. A. V. (2015). *Design science research: A method for science and technology advancement*. Springer International Publishing.

Duan, Y., & Xu, M. (2009). Decision support systems in small businesses. In M. Khosrow-Pour (Ed.), *Encyclopaedia of information science and technology* (2nd ed.; pp. 974–977). Hershey, PA: Information Science Reference. doi:10.4018/978-1-60566-026-4.ch155

Dwivedi, Y. K., Wastell, D., Laumer, S., Henriksen, H. Z., Myers, M. D., Bunker, D., & Srivastava, S. C. (2015). Research on information systems failures and successes: Status update and future directions. *Information Systems Frontiers*, *17*(1), 143–157. doi:10.100710796-014-9500-y

Eom, S. B. (2007). *The development of decision support systems research: A bibliometrical approach*. Lewiston, NY: Edwin Mellen Press.

Gulliksen, J., Göransson, B., Boivie, I., Blomkvist, S., Persson, J., & Cajander, Å. (2005). Key principles for user-centred systems design. In A. Seffah, J. Gulliksen, & M. C. Desmarais (Eds.), *Human-centered software engineering: Integrating usability in the software development lifecycle* (Vol. 8, pp. 17–36). Springer. doi:10.1007/1-4020-4113-6_2

Haag, S., & Cummings, M. (2009). *Information systems essentials*. New York: McGraw Hill/Irwin.

Hall, D. J. (2008). *Decision makers and their need for support. In Handbook on decision support systems 1: Basic theme* (Vol. 1, pp. 83–102). Berlin: Springer. doi:10.1007/978-3-540-48713-5_5

Hevner, A., March, S. T., Park, J., & Ram, S. (2004). Design science in information systems research. *Management Information Systems Quarterly*, *28*(1), 75–105. doi:10.2307/25148625

Hosack, B., Hall, D., Paradice, D., & Courtney, J. F. (2012). A look toward the future: Decision support systems research is alive and well. *Journal of the Association for Information Systems*, *13*(5), 315–340. doi:10.17705/1jais.00297

Iivari, J., & Iivari, N. (2011). Varieties of user-centredness: An analysis of four systems development methods. *Information Systems Journal*, *21*(2), 125–153. doi:10.1111/j.1365-2575.2010.00351.x

Irvine, B., Richardson, D., Fear, J., & Denniss, R. (2011). *The rise and rise of online retail. Technical Brief (8)*. Canberra, Australia: The Australia Institute.

Keen, P. G., & Scott, M. (1978). *Decision support systems: An organisational perspective*. Addison-Wesley.

Klein, M., & Methlie, L. B. (1995). *Knowledge-based decision support systems with applications in business*. West Sussex, UK: John Wiley & Sons Ltd.

Kroenke, D., Bunker, D., & Wilson, D. (2014). *Experiencing MIS*. Pearson Australia.

Kwee-Fah, L. (2016). Towards addressing persistent risk perceptions in online shopping. *Skyline Business Journal*, *12*(1), 1–10.

Lacka, E., Chan, H. K., & Yip, N. (2014). *E-commerce platform acceptance: Suppliers, retailers, and consumers*. Dordrecht: Springer International Publishing. doi:10.1007/978-3-319-06121-4

Leukel, J., Mueller, M., & Sugumaran, V. (2014). *The state of design science research within the BISE community: An empirical investigation.* Paper presented at the 35th International Conference on Information Systems (ICIS 2014), Auckland, New Zealand. Retrieved from https://www.researchgate.net/publication/289595575

Mao, J.-Y., Vredenburg, K., Smith, P. W., & Carey, T. (2005). The state of user-centered design practice. *Communications of the ACM*, *48*(3), 105–109. doi:10.1145/1047671.1047677

March, S. T., & Storey, V. C. (2008). Design science in the information system discipline: An introduction to the special issue on design science research. *Management Information Systems Quarterly*, *32*(4), 725730. doi:10.2307/25148869

Markus, M. L., & Mao, J.-Y. (2004). Participation in development and implementation-updating an old, tired concept for today's IS contexts. *Journal of the Association for Information Systems*, *5*(11), 14. doi:10.17705/1jais.00057

Miah, S., & McKay, J. (2016, September). *A new conceptualisation of design science research for DSS development*. Paper presented at the 20th Pacific Asia Conference on Information Systems (PACIS), Taiwan.

Miah, S. J. (2004). Accessibility improvement of multicultural educational web interface by using the user centred design (UCD) approach. *Journal of Issues in Informing Science and Information Technology*, *4*, 99–108.

Miah, S. J. (2008). *An ontology-based design environment for rural decision support* (Unpublished doctoral dissertation). Griffith University, Australia.

Miah, S. J. (2009). End user as application developer for decision support. In *Proceedings of American Conference on Information Systems*. San Francisco, CA: AMCIS. Retrieved from http://aisel.aisnet.org/amcis2009/142

Miah, S. J., Ahsan, K., & Msimangira, K. A. (2014). An approach of purchasing decision support in healthcare supply chain management. *Operations and Supply Chain Management*, *6*(2), 43–53.

Miah, S. J., Kerr, D., & von Hellens, L. (2014). A collective artefact design of decision support systems: A design science research perspective. *Information Technology & People*, *27*(3), 259–279. doi:10.1108/ITP-04-2012-0041

Mintzberg, H., Raisinghani, D., & Theoret, A. (1976). The structure of" unstructured" decision processes. *Administrative Science Quarterly*, *21*(2), 246–275. doi:10.2307/2392045

Mohapatra, S. (2012). *E-commerce strategy: Text and cases*. London: Springer.

Nelson, R. R. (2007). IT project management: Infamous failures, classic mistakes, and best practices. *MIS Quarterly Executive*, *6*(2), 67–78.

Niu, L., Lu, J., & Zhang, G. (2009). *Cognition-driven decision support for business intelligence: Models, techniques, systems, and applications*. New York: Springer-Verlag. doi:10.1007/978-3-642-03208-0

Okoli, C., & Carillo, K. (2012). The best of adaptive and predictive methodologies: Open source software development, a balance between agility and discipline. *International Journal of Information Technology and Management, 11*(1-2), 153–166. doi:10.1504/IJITM.2012.044071

Oliver, J. (2008). Knowledge management practices to support continuous improvement. *Journal of Knowledge Management Practice*, *9*(4), 1–14.

Pedersen, E. R. G., & Sudzina, F. (2012). Which firms use measures? *International Journal of Operations & Production Management*, *32*(1), 4–27. doi:10.1108/01443571211195718

Pick, R. A. (2008). Benefits of decision support systems. In F. Burstein & C. W. Holsapple (Eds.), *Handbook on decision support systems 1: Basic themes* (pp. 719–730). Berlin: Springer. doi:10.1007/978-3-540-48713-5_32

Poon, P.-L., & Lau, A. H. (2006). The present B2C implementation framework. *Communications of the ACM*, *49*(2), 96–103. doi:10.1145/1113034.1113036

Power, D. (2009). *Are strategic decision processes structured?* Retrieved from http://dssresources.com/faq/index.php?

Power, D., Sharda, R., & Kulkarni, U. (2007). Understanding decision support systems for global enterprises. In U. Kulkarni, D. Power, & R. Sharda (Eds.), *Decision support for global enterprises* (Vol. 2, pp. 3–14). Boston, MA: Springer. doi:10.1007/978-0-387-48137-1_1

Power, D. J. (2010). *Do small businesses need DSS?* Retrieved from http://dssresources.com/faq/index.php?action=artikel&id=200

Power, D. J. (2016). Computerized decision support case study research: Concepts and suggestions. In J. Papathanasiou, N. Ploskas, & I. Linden (Eds.), *Real-world decision support systems case studies: Integrated series in information systems* (Vol. 37, p. 113). Cham, Switzerland: Springer International Publishing. doi:10.1007/978-3-319-43916-7_1

PwC. (2012). *The future of retail: Consumer adaptive retailing*. Retrieved from http://www.pwc.com.au/industry/retail-consumer/

Rogers, W. A., O'Brien, M. A., & Fisk, A. D. (2013). Cognitive engineering to support successful aging. In D. L. John & K. Alex (Eds.), *The Oxford handbook of cognitive engineering* (p. 286). New York: Oxford University Press.

Rosenblatt, H. J. (2014). *Systems analysis and design*. Cengage Learning.

Seffah, A., Gulliksen, J., & Desmarais, M. C. (2005). *Human-centered software engineering-integrating usability in the software development lifecycle* (Vol. 8). Dordrecht, The Netherlands: Springer. doi:10.1007/1-4020-4113-6

Sensis. (2013). *Sensis® e-business report, 2013: The online experience of small and medium enterprises*. Retrieved from: http://about.sensis.com.au/IgnitionSuite/uploads/docs

Shahar, Y., Goren-Bar, D., Boaz, D., & Tahan, G. (2006). Distributed, intelligent, interactive visualization and exploration of time-oriented clinical data and their abstractions. *Artificial Intelligence in Medicine*, *38*(2), 115–135. doi:10.1016/j.artmed.2005.03.001 PMID:16343873

Sprague, R. H. Jr, & Carlson, E. D. (1982). *Building effective decision support systems*. Englewood Cliffs, NJ: Prentice-Hall: Prentice-Hall.

Srivastava, R., & Verma, S. (2012). *Strategic management: Concepts, skills, and practices*. Delhi, India: PHI Learning Pvt. Ltd.

Sullivan, F. (2012). *Australian and New Zealand shopping market and digital insights July 2012*. Retrieved from http://www.pwc.com.au/industry/retail-consumer/assets/Digital-Media-Online-Shopping-Jul12.pdf

Tariq, A., & Rafi, K. (2012). Intelligent decision support systems: A framework. *Information and Knowledge Management*, *2*(6), 12–20.

Thierauf, R. J. (1988). *User-oriented decision support systems: Accent on problem finding*. Englewood Cliffs, NJ: Prentice-Hall, Inc.

Todd, A. (2012). *Get your business online now! Be part of Australia's eCommerce revolution*. Sydney: Hachette Australia.

Turban, E. (2007). *Decision support and business intelligence systems*. Upper Saddle River, NJ: Prentice-Hall, Inc.

Turban, E., Sharda, R., & Delen, D. (2011). *Decision support and business intelligence systems*. Pearson Education India.

Wienclaw, R. A. (2008). *Decision support systems*. Retrieved from http://o-search.ebscohost.com.library.vu.edu.au/login.aspx

World Trade Organisation. (2013). E-commerce in developing countries: Opportunities and challenges for small and medium-sized enterprises. Geneva, Switzerland: World Trade Organization.

Zaraté, P. (2013). *Tools for collaborative decision-making*. London, UK: John Wiley & Sons. doi:10.1002/9781118574690

KEY TERMS AND DEFINITIONS

Case Study: A case study is a sophisticated method to assist researchers in identifying the real business problems and needs that support practical solution design to improve business performance.

Decision Support System: A DSS is an applied area within the IS discipline that focuses on solution design to support and improve managerial decision making.

Prototyping: A prototyping is a small-scale system development method in the IS domain, and particularly focused on user requirements.

Small Business: A small business is mainly owner-operated. In some cases, they have less than twenty employees in the Australian small business context.

Strategic Decisions: Strategic decisions are significant for a business to remain competitive within the business environment. The strategic decision is information-based decision that is sourced from the business environment with the analysis of environmental factors that are influencing the decision makers for making productive business decisions.

User-Centered Design: A user-centered design (UCD) is a system design philosophy and methods that places users at the center of the design process. Therefore, system users have significant contributions from the stage of planning, designing the system requirements, testing, and implementation of the system.

APPENDIX

Table 1. Website feature categories

ICDT model-based website feature categories in B2C e-commerce environment	
Information (I)-based website features	**Subcategory of features**
Contact details	Business name, email address, location with map, telephone and fax numbers
Business information	Product and service descriptions, static product reviews, product catalogue, policies and mission statements, company and employee background, privacy policy, customer testimonials, business images and videos, print order form
Added value	Frequently ask questions (FAQ), product use instructions, financial calculator
Communication (C)-based website features	**Subcategory of features**
Contact the business	Email form, email order form, customer enquiry form, and sign up for newsletter form
Reviews	Customer posting reviews direct to website
Social networking	Bulletin board, blogs, etc.
Transaction (T)-based website features	**Subcategory of features**
Online database	Real-time catalogue, online ordering, automatically record customer preferences
Payment	Real-time credit card payment, Internet banking, online voucher redemption, PayPal
Distribution (D)-based website features	**Subcategory of features**
Web-based distributions	Online download of digital goods or contents, software
E-services	Online digital product delivery information, online physical product tracking information

(Data Source: Burgess, 2016)

Section 4

Emerging Large and Huge BI Platforms and Applications

Chapter 15
Transformative Analytics and Logistics Pricing:
How Business Intelligence Can Inform Logistics

Jeffrey Drue Peck Jr.
Central Connecticut State University, USA

Michael S. Gendron
Central Connecticut State University, USA

Tera Black
Central Connecticut State University, USA

ABSTRACT

Raw materials and products are moved and created globally through complex supply chains. Within those supply chains, logistics is what enables the goods to move through distribution and reach the end consumer. Being such a widely used process, this is what motivates the researchers to examine the logistics portion of the supply chain from an analytical perspective and attempt to determine the relationship between various market forces and their impact on the cost of logistics. This will be accomplished with transformative analytics techniques, such as multivariate regression modeling focusing on areas such as directionality and precipitation. That should enable logistics managers, researchers, and others to better understand the factors that go into the cost of logistics services, and thus impact pricing of goods dependent on those services. In a world where logistics managers rely heavily on "gut feel," utilizing business intelligence and analytics can better enable decision making.

INTRODUCTION

Raw materials and products are moved and created globally through complex supply chains. Within those supply chains, logistics is the engine that enables raw materials and finished goods to move from the various suppliers to the manufacturer, through distribution and to the end consumer. This phenomenon drives pricing of goods and is what motivates the researchers to examine the logistics portion of the

DOI: 10.4018/978-1-5225-5718-0.ch015

supply chain. This research determines the relationship between various market forces and their impact on logistics cost. This area is ripe for transformative analytic techniques that will enable logistics managers, researchers and others to better understand the cost of logistics services and thus impact pricing of goods dependent on those services.

Based on the survey conducted by Accenture in 2014, more than one-third of the respondents reported being engaged in serious conversations to deploy analytics in supply chain management; and three out of ten already have an initiative in place to implement analytics. (Wang, Gunasekarana, Ngai, & Papadopoulos, 2016) The direct result of understanding external forces is to reduce transaction costs in logistics and procurement, one of a company's main activities in any industry (Nechaeva, Andrianova, & Sandriev, 2016). In this paper, the researchers will set forward the current and future research of the Central Connecticut State University School of Business Supply Chain and Logistics Research Forum (SCLF). The SCLF will extend the understanding of logistics pricing analytics and create techniques to enable managers within this industry to better innovate.

The current study explained in this paper looks at full truck load (FTL) pricing using a dataset provided by a US-based supply chain business intelligence company North American Supply Chain Analytics Company (NASCA)[1]. The goal is to create more accurate pricing and to determine the significance of various external factors. Logistics managers often operate by "gut feel" rather than data to support their decisions (NASCA, 2016) (Kersten, 2008). While decisions supported by business intelligence (BI) may not be able to replace the seasoned logistics manager, BI should be able to support managers in their quest to reduce costs and improve services within their company, all of which benefit the end-consumer.

A major milestone that must be considered in all logistics research is the signing of the US Motor Carrier Act (MCA) of 1980. MCA opened the door for the trucking industry to "become the responsive and innovative transportation mode it is today—capturing more than 70 percent of total freight revenue." (Schulz, 2015) Now the industry faces constant regulatory challenges covering everything from emissions pollution to the number of hours of sleep for drivers. Due to the "hub-and-spoke" networks, hours of service regulations have not had a direct effect on the industry. Rather there has been a "trickle down" effect as it forces the sector to hire additional drivers further contributing to the driver shortage and resulting in increases in pay, and resultant costs across the entire industry. Also, contributing to the industry's driver shortage is the increased scrutiny of drivers in terms of safety, environments, security regulations, economics, changing demographics, and difficulty marketing jobs to younger people and minorities. Some in the industry feel that the Federal Motor Carrier Safety Administration (FMCSA) focuses "almost exclusively on safety without regard for cost or adverse effects for trucking companies or their shipper customers." (Schulz, 2015). All of these factors have influenced the researchers at the SCLF desire to better understand logistics pricing.

Before continuing on to the current research, it is important that the researchers' perspective on supply chain and logistics management is understood as this impacts their perspective and motivation. As business analysts and information systems specialists, the staff at SCLF take an information flow perspective on the interaction and transaction costs with in the supply chain. This perspective is in line with the Global Supply Chain Forum as the researchers look at the supply chain as a set of information flows as given in Figure 1 – Information Flow View of Supply Chain Processes. (Supply Chain Management Institute, 2008)

Taken together these cross-functional and cross-organizational processes depend on correct, timely, and cost-effective logistics. The researchers believe that taking this approach sets the stage for a large and transformative foundation for the work by SCLF staff.

Figure 1. Information Flow View of Supply Chain Processes; adapted from (Supply Chain Management Institute, 2008)

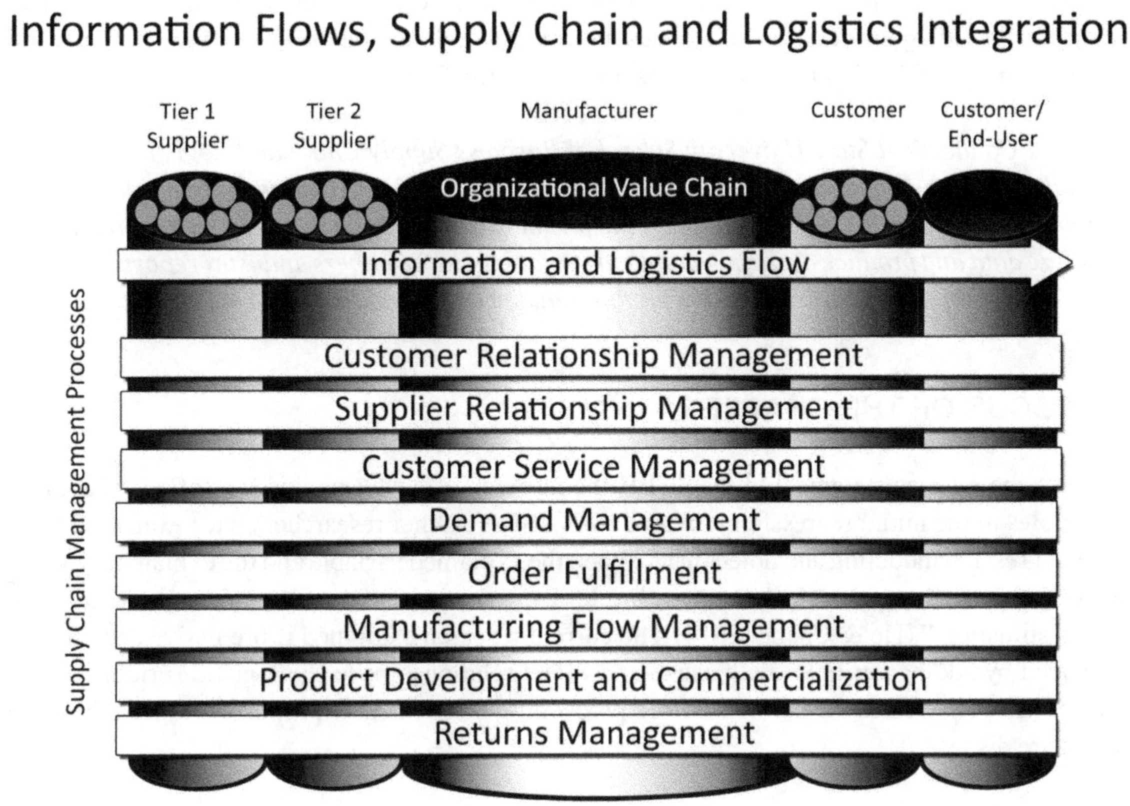

BACKGROUND

Often the concepts of supply chain and logistics are confused (Lambert, Garcia-Dastugue, & Croxton, 2008). This confusion extends to agreement about which processes should be included and where logistics fits. The SCLF emphasis on information flows supports transformation through the use of extensive logistics analytics. The basis for this research includes:

- Transportation and logistics have impact far beyond their cost, but just like a 5-cent washer can take a racecar out of a race, the slightest service failure in shipping can have major effects (Elleff, 2004). Good logistics analytics should minimize those service failures.
- According to The State of Logistics Report, logistics costs are 7.85% of the United States Gross Domestic Product (GDP) or $1.408 trillion (Schultz, 2016). Even a small increase in predictive accuracy will have a substantial impact to real dollars.
- By impacting logistics within the supply chain, and by understanding how external forces impact costs, more accurate BI will help logistics managers to optimize processes, minimize shipping times and bring improvements to this essential component of supply chain management.

Supply Chain and Logistics Forum

The newly formed SCLF provides a platform for the researchers to analyze areas that impact truck logistic pricing, thus providing information to logistics managers to aid their decision-making. The goals of this research forum are embodied in the mission statement of the SCLF:

The Central Connecticut State University School of Business Supply Chain and Logistics Forum exists to do analytical research and support the logistics industry. Its focus is to identify market forces that impact the supply chain. To further that goal, the forum works with industry partners to create projects that analyze data and produce academic output in the form of white papers, industry reports, and journal articles. These outputs are widely distributed through academic and industry channels.

MAIN FOCUS OF THE CHAPTER

In line with the mission statement of the SCLF, the researchers have examined the effect of adding two new variables to the initial regression provided by NASCA[2]. Other researchers have examined this area utilizing regression modeling and noted that, "When the explained variable and the explanatory variables have a cause-and-effect relationship and high relevance, the regression method can make a relatively accurate estimation." (He & Chang, 2014) The current research examined if predictive accuracy could be enhanced by adding variables with cause-and-effect relationships to the logistics pricing to the initial model (models 1R and 1D below). Before proceeding on to the new proposed models, the two new variables are discussed.

Directionality

It is easy to assume that directionality of shipments will not impact logistics costs. However, research by Tanaka suggests that does not hold true. Pricing for identical shipments from west-to-east and east-to-west are asymmetrical. (Tanaka, 2014) The average freight cost per Twenty-foot Equivalent Unit are different based on direction of transport. The Twenty-Foot Equivalent is defined as the unit of the capacity of a container ship, a container terminal, and the statistics of the container transit in a port (Embassy Freight, 2016). An example of this asymmetry (although outside the United States) is shipments from Asia to the United States cost about 1.78 times shipments in the opposite direction, and the cost from Asia to Europe is about 1.33 times the opposite direction. This could be caused by different types of shipping modalities (e.g. air, ship, rail, train), or there could be other unexplained reasons.

Further support for examining directionality is Tanaka's work in Japan. While this is not in the United States, it is within one country. Tanaka studied freight rates by relative pairs within 47 prefectures in Japan. To examine if the two-way freight rates are asymmetric, Tanaka used a t-test. The tests showed a significant difference, and that shipping costs are significantly asymmetrical. Another test used was the Shapiro-Francia test to assess whether the distribution between shipping methods was normal (see Table 1 - Directional Balance). This resulted in the discovery that the distributions are not normal with the export of truck transport. These results suggest trucking is asymmetrical, while freight rates for rail and ship seem to be relatively symmetrical.

Table 1. Directional balance

Mode	No. of Obs.	Mean (n)	S.D.	t-test for Zero Mean	Shapiro-Francia Test for Normality
Air	398	0.1	.99	0.038	0.02
Railway	266	0.04	0.83	0.432	0.00001
Ship	132	0.007	1.04	0.938	0.05
Truck	12,059	0.02	0.94	0.002	0.183
All	12,855	0.03	0.94	0.0005	0.217

Note: Directional balance is the positive log of freight rates from the prefecture *r* to prefecture *s* relative to that from *s* to *r*; S.D. standard deviation; t-test shows p-values for the null hypothesis of zero mean; Shapiro-Francia test shows p-values for the null hypothesis of normality.

Tanaka shows that it is not only the major factors such as fuel and mileage that impact overall cost, but directionality has impact on logistics price. The data presented by Tanaka supported the researchers examining directionality within the United States sample for truck-based logistics pricing.

Weather

In November 2012, the U.S. Department of Transportation sponsored a study that presents a methodology for estimating the cost of weather delays to the trucking industry (Krechmer, Perry, Destro, & Gallaher, 2012)(see Table 2 - Adapted Truck Cost Component Model). According to the study, each of the six categories making up truck costs carries a corresponding percentage of the total cost. Since each category is impacted by weather differently, an effect factor was established to account for this susceptibility. This study suggests that fixed costs such as equipment are less susceptible (less than 1.0) to weather while fuel and overhead are more vulnerable (greater than 1.0). The weighted average column shows how weather impacts cost overall. According to the US Department of Transportation study, the freight market has an approximate value of $574 billion annually, with weather related delays costing 1.6 percent, or approximately $8.7 billion. This study goes on to explain the results may seem immaterial on a percentage-basis, but the actual dollar values are quite significant.

The U.S. Department of Transportation study observed and analyzed five types of weather events across the country: snow, rain, ice, visibility, and wind. The impact of each type of weather event on truck delays was assessed as part of its analysis both individually and in combination with others. These delay

Table 2. Adapted truck cost component model

Expense Category	Portion of Total Expense	Weather Effect Factor	Weighed Effect
Labor	0.38	1	.038
Equipment	0.14	0.66	0.0924
Fuel	0.25	1.2	0.3
Overhead	0.17	1.05	0.1785
Margin	0.06	1	0.06

impacts were then applied to truck operating costs which had been broken down and weighted. The U.S. Department of Transportation study provides some initial evidence that weather does in fact influence logistics costs, and therefore the researchers added precipitation into the model as a proxy for weather.

SCLF Analysis With New Variables

The SCLF has undertaken its current study by adding the variables directionality and weather to the initial model provided by NASCA. NASCA's model used distance, month-of-shipment, and equipment type. The initial regression model was used as a basis for comparison, except the data was split by truck-type as the regression models were found to be more accurate. The goal was to see if either of the additional variables caused a perceptible increase in predictive accuracy. The researchers are concerned that any predictive increases should be weighed against the ongoing cost of attaining the additional variables. The researcher's recommendations about whether to use these new variables is in the conclusion of this phase of the research found below.

Dataset

NASCA's data set consisted of 803,858 records containing only FTL shipments from flatbed, dry, and refrigerated trucks from 2008 to 2014. Shipments were limited to the 48 contiguous United States. Intra-metropolitan shipments were excluded (i.e. only long haul FTL shipments were analyzed). Flatbed truck data was also excluded since there were very few flat-bed records; this left only FTL refrigerated and dry shipping records. This left a final dataset (n=654,834) to which the various regression models were applied (see Table 3 - NASCA Truck Type Percentages).

Descriptive statistics were analyzed. The number of records by delivery-month (see Figure 2 - Month Distribution by Equipment Type) and by distance (see Figure 3 - Distance Distribution by Equipment Type) show that the number of records by delivery-month is relatively evenly distributed between dry and refrigerated truck types.

New Variables Transformation

Steps needed to be taken in order to include directionality and precipitation into the regression models:

- Directionality was derived through a geometric conversion of the latitude and longitude of the pickup and delivery locations. This conversion created a number from 1-8 that equated to a bearing of the eight winds on a compass rose.

Table 3. NASCA truck type percentages

Truck Type	Number of Records	Percentage
Dry	233,585	36.2%
Refrigerated	412,249	63.8%
Total	654,834	100%

Figure 2. Month distribution by equipment type

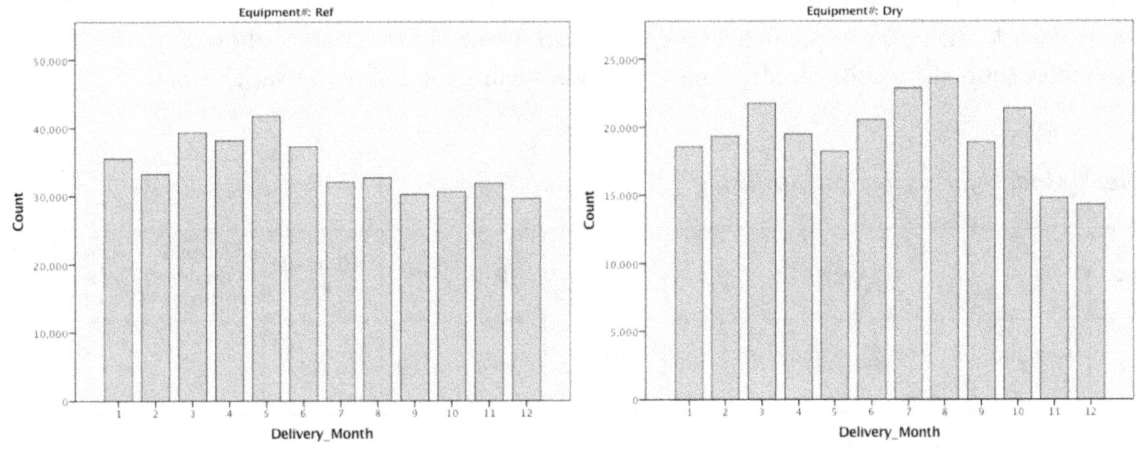

Figure 3. Distance distribution by equipment type

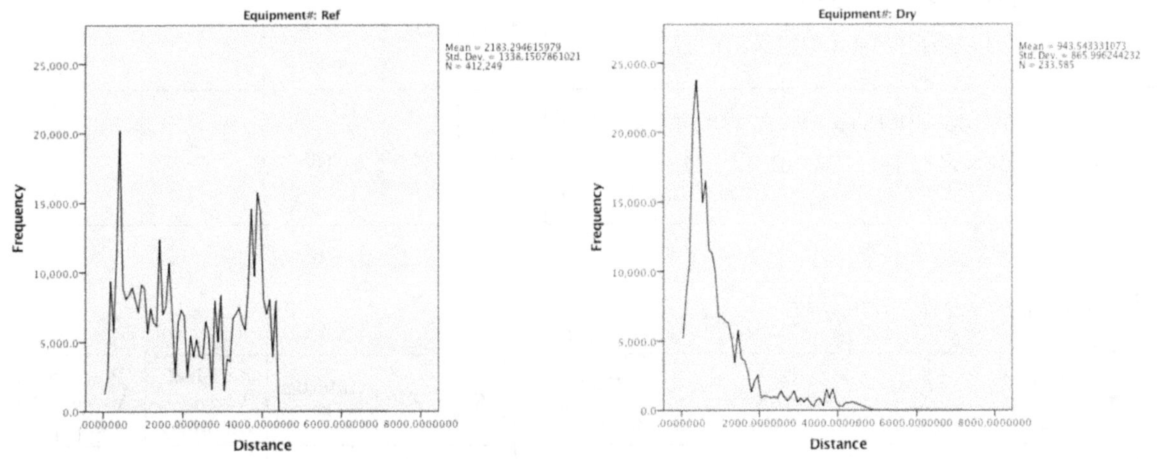

- Precipitation was obtained from the National Oceanic and Atmospheric Administration (NOAA) weather data. This data was obtained in a series of files segmented by day which were then mapped to the original NASCA dataset.

Regressions

The researchers used multi-variate linear regression to determine the relationship between truck prices and the variables described above. The predictability of the models evaluated were assessed using:

- Adjusted R-squared
- P-values/P-P plot
- Residual plots

The regression models and other data in Table 4 – Models for Refrigerated Trucking and Table 5 - Models for Dry Trucking give the information necessary for comparing models. The regression formulas show how truck price ($\hat{y}$) was predicted for each model. None of the variables showed multicollinearity. These tables show the results for all regression models using the following variable set:

Table 4. Models for refrigerated trucking

Model	Regression	R	R^2	Adjusted R^2	Original Variables *DIS MON*	Prec. Added *PRE*	Direct. Added *DIR*
1R	$\hat{y} = 240.212 + (1.207 \times DIS) + (13.865 \times MON)$	.898	0.807	0.807	x		
2R	$\hat{y} = 225.352 + (1.208 \times DIS) + (13.675 \times MON) + (4.956 \times PRE)$	.899	.808	.808	x	x	
3R	$\hat{y} = 774.432 + (1.133 \times DIS) + (13.420 \times MON) + (-96.843 \times DIR)$	.905	.819	.819	x		x
4R	$\hat{y} = 757.146 + (1.134 \times DIS) + (13.249 \times MON) + (4.154 \times PRE) + (-95.561 \times DIR)$	.905	.820	.820	x	x	x

Table 5. Models for dry trucking

Model	Regression	R	R^2	Adjusted R^2	Original Variables *DIS MON*	Prec. Added *PRE*	Direct. Added *DIR*
1D	$\hat{y} = 302.697 + (1.019 \times DIS) + (-13.437 \times MON)$	.778	.605	.605	x		
2D	$\hat{y} = 285.812 + (1.027 \times DIS) + (-13.404 \times MON) + (3.131 \times PRE)$	.781	.609	.609	x	x	
3D	$\hat{y} = 729.041 + (1.009 \times DIS) + (-11.639 \times MON) + (-91.049 \times DIR)$	.800	.640	.640	x		x
4D	$\hat{y} = 714.922 + (1.016 \times DIS) + (-11.566 \times MON) + (1.773 \times PRE) + (-90.590 \times DIR)$	.803	.644	.644	x	x	x

- **DIS:** Distance expressed in Km (original regression);
- **MON:** Month of delivery expressed as an integer corresponding to the month number (original regression);
- **PRE:** Precipitation expressed in inches (new variable);
- **DIR:** Directionality expressed in a numeric value (new variable).

Models 1R (refrigerated shipments) and 1D (dry shipments) are the original models use by NASCA split by truck type. Each subsequent model can be referenced in Table 4. Models for Refrigerated Trucking, and Table 5. Models for Dry Trucking. Taking each model type separately (dry vs refrigerated) residual and p-p plots are provided:

- Figure 4 - Model 1R Graphs shows residual outliers and a fairly significant range between Y and $\hat{y}$. The residual also shows better prediction closer to the mean. The p-p plot shows a fairly linear distribution across the expected and cumulative probabilities with slightly less predicate accuracy around 0.8.
- Figure 5 - Model 1D Graphs shows a similar pattern with a greater number of outliers. The p-p plot also shows better predictive accuracy around the middle of the data and extreme ends.

The graphs demonstrate some noise and inaccuracy within the predictability in the original models (1R and 1D). There were similar results from all other models, therefore for brevity no further graphics are shown.

Three additional multiple linear regressions were performed by truck type (i.e., dry and refrigerated) for the variables added to the original model (precipitation and directionality). As can be seen in Table 4. Models for Refrigerated Trucking and Table 5. Models for Dry Trucking. There was additional predictive effect by adding precipitation and/or directionality to the original (1R and 1D) models. The r^2

Figure 4. Model 1R Graphs

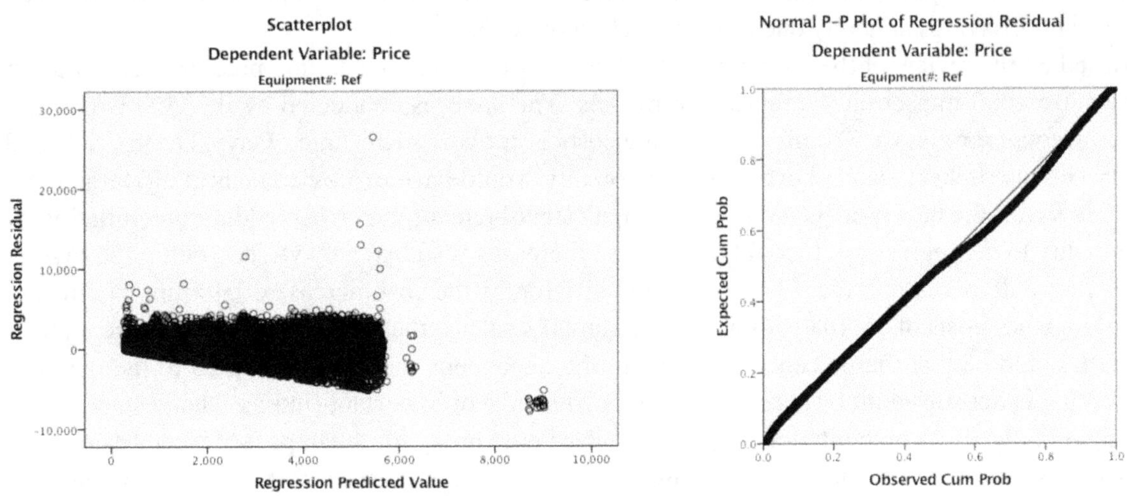

Figure 5. Model 1D Graphs

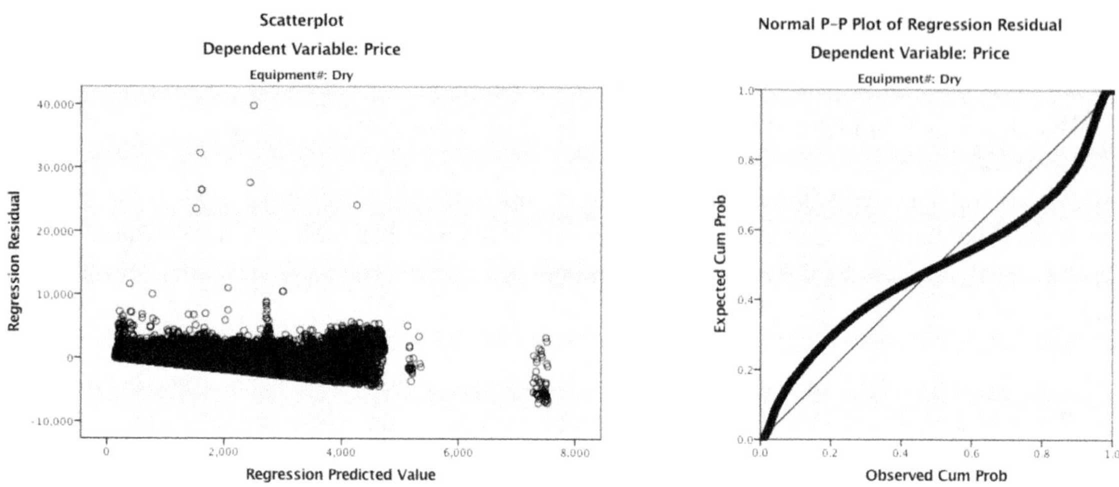

increase shows an improvement over the original model for both dry and refrigerated truck types. When comparing the percent increase alongside the plots, they illustrate that the increase was large enough to consider adding directionality and precipitation.

SOLUTIONS AND RECOMMENDATIONS

The original models yielded an r^2 of 0.807 (1R) and 0.605 (1D). These are substantial, and the goal is to make this model even more accurate without overfitting it. While it was hypothesized that integrating directionality and precipitation into the regression would greatly enhance the prediction of truck pricing estimates, the researchers only saw a slight increase in r^2. Even though on the face, there did not appear to be a significant increase in r^2. Each small percentage increase in prediction has the potential of substantial savings annually due to its impact on the GDP.

Based on the review of the literature, the researchers believed that adding precipitation should have had a substantial impact on the regression models. The analysis conducted by the U.S. DoT, weather delays account for almost \$9 billion in trucking costs every year. (Krechmer, Perry, Destro, & Gallaher, 2012) The researchers also believe that directionality would have expressed a similarly large increase in r^2. However, the new models did not see a significant increase in r^2 when adding precipitation or directionality to the regression. It could be that cost increases is statistically washed out in the regression so only a small increase in the r^2 is shown. Said differently, the cost increase of \$9 billion compared to a total logistics costs of \$1.408 trillion is such a small variance that it may not show a large increase in the r^2. It could be that the percentage change in the dependent variables compared to the overall cost of trucking is not substantially significant. That by itself is an important finding when estimating truck pricing. Finally, using precipitation may not be an accurate proxy for the impact of weather on logistics.

The most expanded models with the highest r^2 for refrigerated and dry truck price estimations tell us the following:

- **Refrigerated Model Including DIS, MON, PRE and DIR (4R):**
  - There is a base cost of $757.12 for all shipments
  - Each increase of 1Km adds $1.13
  - Each increase in the month of the year (e.g. January-February; February-March; etc.) adds $13.25
  - Each increase of precipitation by 1mm adds $4.15
  - As the direction of shipment goes from north, around the compass, the cost decreases by $95.56
- **Dry trucking Model Including DIS, MON, PRE and DIR (4D):**
  - There is a base cost of $714.92 for all shipments
  - Each increase of 1Km adds $1.02
  - Each increase in the month of the year (e.g. January-February; February-March; etc.) subtracts $11.57
  - Each increase of precipitation by 1mm adds $1.77
  - As the direction of shipment goes from north, around the compass, the cost decreases by $90.59

The final model yields some interesting results for both refrigerated and dry trucks. The findings appear to give these results:

- Both dry and refrigerated trucing have similar base costs, with refrigerated base costs being slightly more expensive (approximately 6%) than more than dry base costs.
- The increase in distance (Km), both dry and refrigerated trucking appear similar with refrigerated being about 10% more expensive then dry trucking. This seems seem reasonable since refrigerated trucking is more expensive than dry trucking.
- The month of year is not what was expected with a positive linear relationship where refrigerated trucking increases from January, through December at a rate of $95.56 per month and dry trucking increased $11.57 per month. This will require further investigation.
- It is interesting to note that as precipitation increased by 1mm, refrigerated trucking price increased at 2.3 times the rate of dry trucking
- As direction change from north to any other direction (e.g. south to north) the cost of shipping cost decreased between $95.56 and $90.59.

It is apparent to the researchers that the data needs further analysis using an analysis of variance approach to examine interactions between and within variables.

The researchers understand that there was a smaller than expected improvement and that further testing is needed to determine if the change in r^2 warrants the cost of collecting those data and adding them to the dataset or if there is a better technique to estimate truck pricing. It appears that these data should be analyzed using an analysis of variance to determine any within and between group interactions. Also, the researchers would be remiss not to mention this small increase could substantially impact the portion of GDP represented by this change. The SCLF's next step, described below, is to extend its research to include more global weather events.

Next Steps

The researchers are currently involved in a study examining the impact of specific weather events on shipping costs. These include widespread environmental events. This study will examine the impacts of environmental events on the logistics industry. This study will examine global environmental events such as:

- **Polar Vortex:** Large area of low pressure and cold air surrounding both of the Earth's poles (National Oceanic and Atmospheric Administration, 2016)
- Numerous hurricane events from 2008-2016
- El Nino 2008-2016
- Large storm events
- Wildfires

Using these events allows the researchers to compare similar event types to determine if the impact of these environmental phenomena is the same from year-to-year.

FUTURE RESEARCH DIRECTIONS

As the researchers look forward to the best ways to predict shipping costs, there are several areas under consideration and that drive SCLF research. These include:

- **Operational Costs of Trucking:** The American Transportation Research Institute published an analysis of operational costs in the trucking industry in years 2008-2013. Its research objective was to generate more precise cost metrics. This was accomplished by a standardized survey methodology that gathered data for the assessment of motor carrier operational costs. The results were split into two general categories vehicle based and drive based to remain consistent with previous surveys. Additionally, this survey contains information from trips that span between 100 miles or less and over 1,000 per trip as well as five different US regions. Trip type and regions guided the researchers in the creation of regressions. (American Transportation Research Institute, 2014).
- **Local vs Long Haul Shipping:** Local and long haul shipping are two different worlds within the logistics industry. According to the Bureau of Transportation Statistics, most freight shipments by value and tonnage move less than 250 miles. In 2002, more than half the value of all Commodity Flow Survey shipments ($4.5 trillion), moved in local and short-haul shipments which are critical to state and metropolitan area economies. During the past decade, local and short-haul shipments grew 41 percent by value, 16 percent by weight, and 19 percent by ton-miles. Shipments traveling over 250 miles grew faster—51 percent by value, 34 percent by weight, and 36 percent by ton-miles. It is also noted that on average there is a $920 pricing difference per ton between short haul and long haul shipping. The average price per ton of a shipment traveling less than 250 miles is $510 per ton and more than 250 miles averages $1,430 per ton. (United States Department of Transportation, 2002)

- **Regulatory events:** The researchers are interested in understanding the impact of two major regulatory events impacting shipping prices:
    - Hours of service changes and the 34-hour restart (Federal Motor Carrier Safety Administration, 2016).
    - Use of electronic logging devices.
    - Within current shipping methodologies, it is becoming common place for the drivers to be required to electronically keep track of events such as time on the road, hours of sleep, etc. This has been noted in the hours of service regulations by the FMCSA on December 18, 2014. For property-carrying drivers, there are numerous regulatory issues of interest.
- **Influence of Unemployment on Freight Prices:** In his 2013 dissertation, Alex Sanchez of West Virginia University, analyzes private datasets of truckload (TL) rates and publicly available data such as diesel fuel costs, unemployment rates, wages, population, and gross state product. The information was used to understand trends in TL price and was evaluated with the use of exploratory spatial data analysis and visualization techniques to gain valuable insights. Time series analysis and spatial econometric analysis were conducted to forecast TL prices.
- A distinguishing characteristic of Sanchez's model is it allows for various outputs based on numerous scenarios. This differs from traditional models that provide only a single output based on the inputs. Therefore, testing can be conducted on different inputs under several modeling parameters and visualized into a map. "The proposed model can calculate the impact on the dependent variable in a specific location, when changing an independent variable at one specific location." Sanchez concludes that exploratory spatial data analysis reveals a relationship between territory area and TL prices. Therefore, the researchers believe that this is an area where further analysis should be performed.
- **LTL Pricing:** In order to keep up with the ever-changing pricing landscape of the less-than-truckload (LTL) market, research published in the Journal of Transportation Management provides a means of modernizing previously outdated research. In 1993, the University of Tennessee's Center for Logistics Research published a study called "Pricing for the Nineties: An Examination of LTL Motor Carrier Pricing Practices and Suggestions for Improvements by Shipper Customers." Then in 2002, the management consulting firm Norbridge, Inc., followed up with its own analysis of LTL motor carrier pricing. (Defee, Hanna, & Overstreet, 2011) The underlying premise of this research is that the long-established practice of price discounting against base rates established using the National Motor Freight Classification had become meaningless. Norbidge's work intends to bring LTL pricing more in line with the current realities of freight costs and subsequent rates (at the time). However, due to the apparent lack of substantial research specifically on LTL pricing, the focus was on a qualitative, grounded theory methodology. Instead of analyzing available data sets, the research team conducted semi-structured interviews among key stakeholders across three industry segments: shippers, carriers, and 3PL. Analysis of all the interviews resulted in the emergence of five core themes which the researchers believe are ripe for further investigation: Base rates should be re-indexed, benchmark pricing, freight classification rules, density based pricing, and potential industry leadership change.
- **Nationwide Freight Generation Models:** Despite the substantial impact truck transportation has on economic competitiveness, freight transportation planning models are typically not as well developed as passenger transportation planning models. (Novak, Guo, Hodgdon, & Aultman-Hall, 2008) While the effects of spatial dependencies due to location of infrastructure, natural re-

sources, production facilities, and geographic and/or demographic attributes within specific traffic analysis zones are documented in the domain of transportation planning, these dependencies tend to be largely ignored in freight planning models. Additional recommendations from Novak's study include extensive research regarding spatial relationships, transportation network variables, and traffic analysis zones. (Novak, Guo, Hodgdon, & Aultman-Hall, 2008)

- **Self-driving Trucks:** There is much discussion of how self-driving trucks will impact the logistics industry. Some say that these self-driving trucks are years away and will be used for long-haul applications only. While Lana Batts, co-president of driver-screening firm Driver iQ and a former president of the Truckload Carriers Association says "Ain't never going to happen…The so-called "safety Nazis' will kill it before it ever gets tested. They dislike drivers, but they dislike driverless trucks even more." (Cullen, 2015) There are others that suggest that within a decade 1.7 million truck drivers jobs will be at risk of being replaced by self-driving trucks, particularly those of the long haul drivers, because there "isn't much judgment involved and it's a fairly controlled environment." (Kitroeff, 2016)

CONCLUSION

The SCLF's recently completed work adding directionality and precipitation is promising and delivers highly predictive models for estimating FTL truck pricing. While it may seem that the small changes in predictive accuracies are insignificant, the potential impact is large in real dollar terms. From the researchers' literature review, there are many expected benefits from accurately predicting shipping prices, and there are many opportunities for future research. These benefits have been described to the researchers by logistics managers when they deal with supply chain issues. With the current research completed, the SCLF is on to examining wide-spread weather events.

Potential future work at the SCLF was described above. All of the SCLF research has many pull-through-benefits including:

- Logistics prices are often based on "gut" feel of logistics managers. Wolfgang Kersten discusses in the Global Logistics Management text, that "In practice, a lot of issues have to be solved by gut feeling and pragmatism." (Kersten, 2008) The contribution of the ongoing business analytics transformation is better management through decisions supported by data rather than just intuition.
- Getting a better handle on shipping process should smooth out undesired fluctuations in the supply chain and has the potential for more stable pricing for the consumer. For example, if it is known that a regulatory event is coming and its possible to estimate its impact to shipping process, the logistics manager may be able to better manage shipment costs within the supply chain.
- Leveraging the shipping process from a business intelligence prospective will allow a better understanding on how different variables (distance, direction, precipitation, regulation, etc.) impact the overall pricing and create a method for more shipping costs.

The SCLF has been created to do research in these vital areas that can provide transformative business intelligence methods that will better allow logistics managers to estimate costs. These increased predictive techniques will flow to more stable and lower cost to the consumer.

ACKNOWLEDGMENT

An earlier version of this paper was published in the *International Journal of Business Intelligence Research.* The comments of the reviewers are appreciated.

REFERENCES

American Transportation Research Institute. (2014). *An Analysis of the Operational Costs of Trucking: 2014 Update*. American Transportation Research Institute.

Cullen, D. (2015). *The self-driving truck: The human factor*. Fleet Owner.

Defee, C., Hanna, J. B., & Overstreet, R. (2011, January). LTL Pricing: Looking Back to the Future. *Journal of Transportation Management, 22*(2), 45–58. Retrieved from https://www.researchgate.net/publication/256524025_LTL_pricing_Looking_back_to_the_future

Elleff, S. A. (2004). Glue, grease and conduit. *The Journal of Commerce*, 17.

Embassy Freight. (2016, October 30). *TEU (Twenty Foot Equivalent Unit)*. Retrieved from Logistics Glossary: http://www.logisticsglossary.com/term/teu/

Federal Motor Carrier Safety Administration. (2014, December 18). *Summary of Hours of Service Regulations*. Retrieved 2016 7, February, from Federal Motor Carrier Safety Administration: https://www.fmcsa.dot.gov/regulations/hours-service/summary-hours-service-regulations

Federal Motor Carrier Safety Administration. (2016, November 11). *Summary of H ours of Service Regulations*. Retrieved from United States Department of Transportation: https://www.fmcsa.dot.gov/regulations/hours-service/summary-hours-service-regulations

He, F.-b., & Chang, J. (2014). Combined forecasting of regional logistics demand optimized by genetic algorithm. *Grey Systems: Theory and Application*.

Kersten, W. (2008). *Global Logistics Management: Sustainability, Quality, Risks*. Berlin, Germany: Erich Schmidt Verlag GmbH & Co KG.

Kitroeff, N. (2016). *Robots could replace 1.7 million American truckers in the next decade*. Retrieved from Los Angeles Times: http://www.latimes.com/projects/la-fi-automated-trucks-labor-20160924/

Krechmer, D., Perry, N., Destro, L., & Gallaher, S. (2012). *Weather Delay Costs to Trucking. Cambridge Systematics & FTR Associates*. Washington, DC: U.S. Department of Transportation.

Lambert, D. M., Garcia-Dastugue, S. J., & Croxton, K. L. (2008). The Role of Logistics Managers in the Cross-Functional Implementation of Supply Chain Management. *Journal of Business Logistics, 29*(1), 113–132. doi:10.1002/j.2158-1592.2008.tb00071.x

National Oceanic and Atmospheric Administration. (2016). *What is the Polar Vortex?* Retrieved from National Weather Service: http://www.nws.noaa.gov/om/cold/polar_vortex.shtml

Nechaeva, P. A., Andrianova, N. V., & Sandriev, D. S. (2016). Trnasaction Costs in the Interaction of Logistics and Marketigng in Procurement. Academy of Strategic Management, 53-60.

Novak, D., Guo, F., Hodgdon, C., & Aultman-Hall, L. (2008, October 29). Nationwide Freight Generation Models: A Spacial Regression Approach. *Networks and Spatial Economics*, 23–41.

Sanchez, A. (2013). *Investigation of Truckload Prices in the US: Exploritory Analysis, Forecast Methods, and the Influence of Unemployment on Freight Prices. West Virginia University, Department of Civil and Environmental Engineering*. ProQuest LLC.

Schultz, J. D. (2016). 2016 State of Logistics Report. *Logistics Management*, 22-25.

Schulz, J. D. (2015, March). Trucking Regulation: Carriers push back, shippers to pay. *Logistics Management*, 52-60.

Supply Chain Management Institute. (2008). Supply Chain Management: Processes, Partnerships, Performance (D. Lambert, Ed.). Sarasota, FL: Supply Chain Management Institute.

Tanaka, K. (2014). *Directional imbalance of freight rates.* Institute of Developing Economies.

United States Department of Transportation. (2002). *Length of Haul*. Retrieved from Bureau of Transportation Statistics: http://www.rita.dot.gov/bts/programs/freight_transportation/html/length_of_haul.html

United States Department of Transportation. (2016, November 11). *Electronic Logging Devices and Hours of Service Supporting Document.* Retrieved from Federal Motor Carrier Safety Administration: https://www.fmcsa.dot.gov/hours-service/elds/electronic-logging-devices-and-hours-service-supporting-documents

Wang, G., Gunasekarana, A., Ngai, E., & Papadopoulos, T. (2016). Big data analytics in logistics and supply chain management: Certaininvestigations for research and applications. *International Journal of Production Economics*, *176*, 98–110. doi:10.1016/j.ijpe.2016.03.014

ENDNOTES

1 NASCA: is a pseudonym for a supply chain analytics company that provided access to its data and original concept paper which is the basis for model one in the paper.

2 The NASCA concept paper provided the initial regression model used in this research.

Chapter 16
Depicting Data Quality Issues in Business Intelligence Environment Through a Metadata Framework

Te-Wei Wang
University of Illinois at Springfield, USA

Yuriy Verbitskiy
University of South Australia, Australia

William Yeoh
Deakin University, Australia

ABSTRACT

Modern business intelligence systems depend highly on high quality data. The core of data quality management is to identify all possible sources of data quality problems. To achieve this goal, an extensive metadata infrastructure is the most promising solution. Through theoretical metadata model investigation, the authors identified a set of data quality dimensions by carefully examining the data quality management principles and applied those principles to current BI environment. They summarize the analysis by proposing a BI data quality framework.

INTRODUCTION

Recently Business Intelligence (BI) market has experienced high growth and BI technologies have consistently received attention by many Chief Information Officers (Gartner, 2015). BI is "a broad category of technologies, applications, and processes used for gathering, storing, accessing, and analysing data to help its users make better decisions". In a typical BI environment, data from different sources are extracted, transformed and loaded (ETL) into an Enterprise Data Warehouse (EDW) and, from there, are used for reporting across the organization (see Figure 1). During this process, data quality plays a

DOI: 10.4018/978-1-5225-5718-0.ch016

Figure 1. Main business intelligence stages

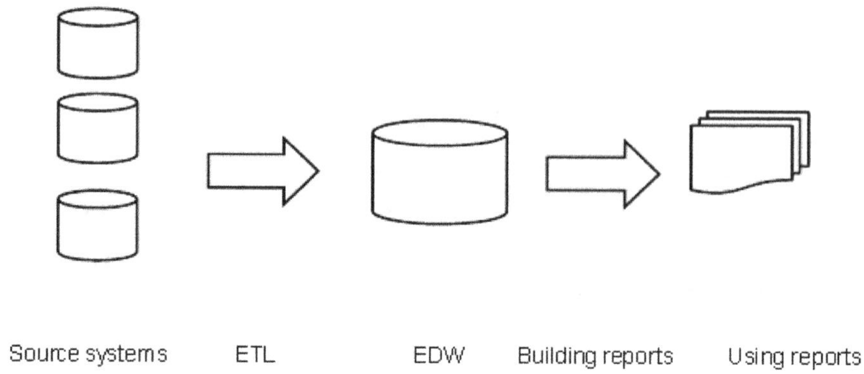

critical role in BI success since poor data quality can hinder business decisions at all levels of the organization (Daniel et al. 2008; Khatri and Brown, 2010). Being very complex at the same time, data quality is an issue that costs billions of dollars (Khatri and Brown, 2010; Vassiliadis, 2000) because data used in the BI environment are used for decision making at every organizational levels and various business processes (Ballou and Tayi, 1999).

In general, there are two main sources of data quality issues involved in BI projects. The first is rooted in the source systems. There are always data quality issues where data do not conform to business requirements even after extensive testing by business users and IT developers. The second source of data quality problem resides on the entire BI processes. By integrating data from the source systems BI projects create new requirements for the existing data. Now the data should conform not only to the original source system requirements but also to new business requirements gathered for the BI project (Ballou and Tayi, 1999). It is a major task of the BI processes to drive more data exploration and analysis, thereby exposing all existing data quality issues, even those which were not considered before. BI processes may themselves become the source of data quality issues because they involve very complex operations with the data during all BI stages.

In a typical BI process such as the one showing in Figure 1, the ETL represents the first key challenge for any BI project, "70% of the risk and effort in the DW/BI project comes from this step" (Kimball et al., 2008). The main reason for this is because during this step data with a different structure and designed for a different operational purpose are brought into one place and transformed in such a way as to enable them to be integrated and used together (Ballou and Tayi, 1999). It is challenging to address varying levels of data quality across source systems or even within one source system (Daniel, 2008).

The second risk for data quality is the database designed for the EDW. Database design for an EDW mainly depends on the business requirements for decision making, the structure of the available data in the source systems and quality levels of the source data. The database design process is extremely complex in its own right involving understanding of the source data and related business processes, analysing business requirements, and ensuring naming conventions and data integration through using conforming dimensions and facts.

The next step is report building. Production of reports may not seem risky in terms of data quality if the data in the EDW conform to business requirements, but this BI process has its own reasons for concern. Full understanding of original business requirements for the EDW data set, EDW data set structure, related business processes and specific report requirements are the main factors for a successful report development process. Merely to understand the data structure in the EDW can be a challenge since it usually stores multidimensional, integrated data that were designed to be used for different purposes. Presenting the data in the simplest way is another challenge. It requires solid knowledge of the available BI Reporting tools.

After the report development process is finished with the reports being approved by the corresponding business unit, there comes the last BI stage – using the reports. Even during this stage there is a risk of data quality issues appearing, especially when the report is used widely across the organization. Some users do not understand the objective of the report or some of its content. Some users might find that the report functionality does not meet their needs and requires modification. Some users might claim that the data in the report are wrong. These issues are related to business users' understanding of the data and their experience with the Reporting tools. Adequate training as well as specific information related to the report is required.

For BI projects to succeed it is important to ascertain where the data quality issues originate in order to respond to them appropriately and also to inform all stakeholders involved in the BI projects about their sources. BI will expose and amplify data quality issues along the way but will not show BI as a source of all data quality issues. For data quality issues to be fixed in source systems requires appropriate business processes, tools and staff. It is useful to discuss responsibilities and possible actions at the beginning of the BI project in case critical issues are found later.

Data quality represents a huge risk for BI implementation. It is essential for BI to have comprehensive data quality management, to show the status of data quality across all BI stages starting from source systems and ending with the use of reports. Otherwise BI implementation will always have issues with business confidence in data quality and common understanding within the organization of data quality issues and their sources.

There is a need for a framework that will assist with general BI issues, and address data quality in particular. This paper advocates that gathering, managing and providing BI metadata regarding data quality to all relevant types of users - technical and business users - is the best possible technical solution. Metadata serves as a mechanism that provides the context about the data within the BI environment (Tvrdíková, 2007) and the context about different elements of the BI environment. Without metadata the data and the BI environment itself cannot be understood properly (Inmon et al., 2008). In fact, Gartner argues that metadata management is one of the most important functionalities that the BI environment should deliver (Richardson et al., 2008).

In this paper we focus on data quality issues that originate from BI processes. We also discuss general principles of data quality management in the BI environment, present the key metadata elements and show how they can be applied to support data quality management in BI. In brief, this paper presents discussion and findings regarding the following research questions:

1. What data quality issues does Business Intelligence face?
2. What are the general data quality management principles for BI?
3. How can BI Metadata infrastructure support data quality management?

We address question 1 and 2 above through literature review. Then, an exemplar metadata model is presented to illustrate the feasibility of using a metadata model for quality management purpose. The remainder of this paper has been structured as follows. The next section provides a review of related work before elaborating on the data quality issues in the BI environment. The fourth section then outlines the data quality management principles. In the fifth section the authors present and discuss the metadata framework addressing data quality issues in the BI environment. The final section provides a summary of the research.

RELATED WORK

There have been several studies addressing data quality issues in the BI environment. It is common to use some metadata for dealing with data quality issues in BI (Daniel et al., 2008; Vassiliadis, 2000; Vassiliadis et al., 1999; Foshay et al., 2007; Rodic and Baranovic, 2009; Li and Osei-Bryson, 2010; Farinha et al., 2009; Gao et al., 2006). Some researchers acknowledge the characteristics of the BI environment which require them to focus on specific data quality dimensions (Ballou and Tayi, 1999; Vassiliadis et al., 1999; Foshay et al., 2007; Li and Osei-Bryson, 2010). However, not all previous work focused on dealing with data quality issues as such; some work focused on other topics in the data quality area like prioritisation of data quality enhancement in the data warehouse (Ballou and Tayi, 1999) and overall understanding of data quality across the organizations in specific industries (Gao et al., 2006).

There are literatures linking metadata model with data quality. Jarke et al. (1999) described a tool that presents metadata quality information and, therefore, allows analysing the status of metadata information stored in the metadata repository with ease. In the work of Vassiliadis et al. (1999) and Jarke et al. (1999), the authors proposed a wide-ranging metadata model with an added quality metamodel. This metadata model covers information about the data warehouse in three perspectives: conceptual, logical and physical. The extensive metadata model was enhanced by adding quality information about each object of the metadata model. The quality model also allows the user to distinguish between subjective quality goals and objective quality factors.

In addition, the idea of providing quality metadata about the data from which reports are generated is investigated in Daniel et al. (2008). Focusing on three quality dimensions (completeness, consistency and confidence) the authors proposed the use of quality-aware reports which allow users to get the quality status of the report, to change the report output by tuning quality indicators and to share quality related feedback. Also, implementation of data quality processes based on metadata and integrated into the ETL process is described in Rodic and Baranovic (2009). Data quality processes are proposed to be implemented by using data quality rules applied in two certain parts of the BI environment (Staging area of ETL and EDW). This approach is suggested for situations where data quality tools are not available or there is difficulty with data quality tool integration. To address the challenge of constant changes in the quality of BI components (source systems, processes, etc.) and in the users' requirements, Li and Osei-Bryson (2010) proposed a mechanism to capture and present quality changes to relevant end-users. For this they suggested two new services in the data warehouse architecture – Quality Factory, that stores quality information, and Quality Notification Service, that is responsible for notifying interested end-users. However, there is little literature that has explicitly addressed the data quality issues in the entire BI manufacturing process from source systems to report generation. In other words, a comprehensive management mechanism for both quality factory and quality notification system has not been addressed.

DATA QUALITY ISSUES IN THE BI ENVIRONMENT

Often, data quality is referred to as information quality with the main goals of "*meeting business requirements*" (Richardson et al. 2008) or "*satisfying data usage requirements*" (Khatri and Brown, 2010). This definition conforms to a widely accepted understanding of data quality as being multidimensional (Gao et al., 2006) since there are many aspects of meeting business requirements. Data quality issues may appear at any stage of the BI cycle (Figure 2). If during the implementation of any BI stage the requirements are not fully understood or not implemented appropriately, the result will not meet the business requirements. In the end it does not matter what the exact reason is for a wrong number in the end user's report, but in order to manage data quality we certainly need to understand all data quality sources. Finally, if the user of the report does not have full confidence in the data presented, does not understand what it means and does not have any tools to further investigate their concerns, than he might think that there is a data quality issue even when this might not the case. Derived from Figure1, Figure 2 shows all BI stages as sources of data quality issues. Based on Figure 2, the detailed explanation of data quality issues at each stage of BI manufacturing process are as follows.

ETL Development

Before starting to build the next ETL implementation technical staff needs to audit the source data (perform data profiling). Following this they are able to present the results of data profiling to business users

Figure 2. Main business intelligence stages as data quality sources

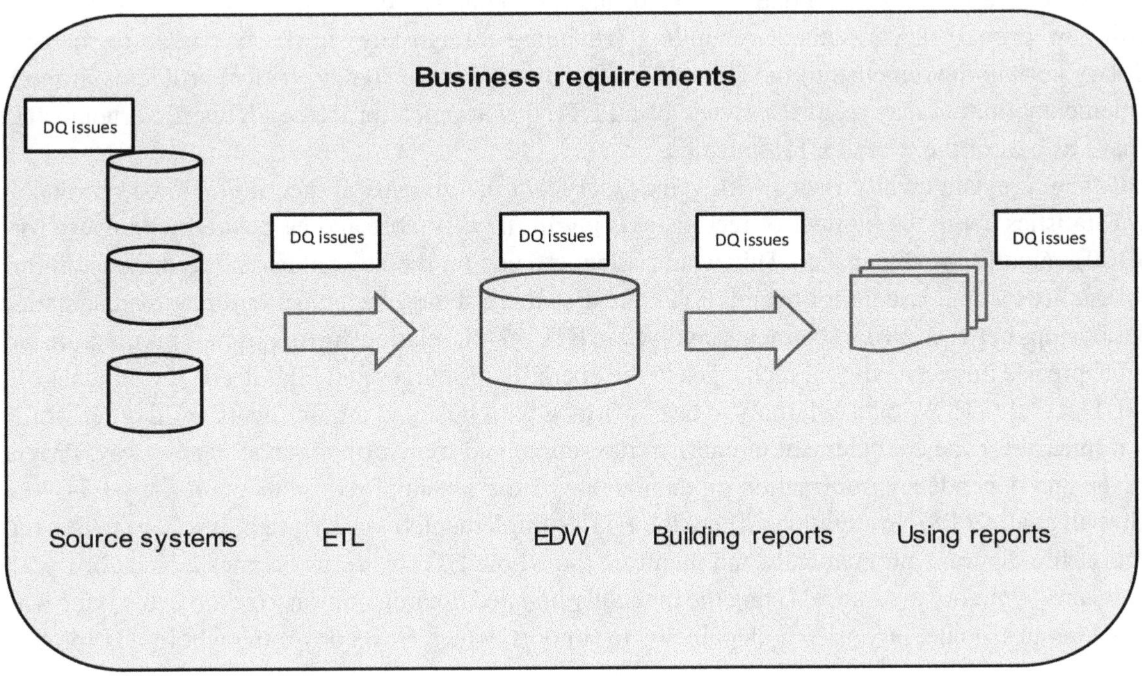

in order to validate the business requirements in terms of data quality, enabling them to decide how to implement the ETL in the most effective way. The challenge here is that technical staff must have regular data profiling results for every significant ETL stage and as a result to have profiling results before and after the ETL process as regularly as required (e.g. daily). This allows the data quality to be constantly monitored during the ETL process and to be communicated directly to business users if required.

Having data profiling statistics for ETL greatly assists with implementing comprehensive data quality processes. It is proposed to have a centralized dimensional data model called Error Event Schema to record all errors during the ETL process (Kimball et al., 2010). Similarly we believe that it is necessary to have *overall ETL statistics* which stores not only errors but also all major profiling results during the ETL process to allow monitoring of data quality through time and to pick up new issues that arise in source systems or during the ETL process.

Another required data quality statistic is related to relationships between the fact table and the dimension. It is a quite common situation, especially immediately after building a new fact table, to find that a number of records in the fact table do not have corresponding values in the dimension. This usually happens because of a mismatch between data used for populating the fact table and data used for populating the dimension. It means that there are data quality issues in one of the sources. In this situation the predefined foreign key (e.g. '-1') in the fact table is assigned and it relates to a specific "Unknown" record in the dimension. Getting the total number of unknown records in the fact table related to the specific dimension can be implemented simply by counting records with the foreign key value equal to '-1'. This *"Unknown" statistic* is an essential candidate to be included in the overall ETL statistics. Ideally there should not be any unknown records in the fact table but it is a long-term goal that cannot be achieved in a short term and that is why it requires constant monitoring.

It is also possible to have records in the fact table whose foreign keys are not associated with any primary keys in the dimension due to an error in ETL. This happens when the dimension gets rebuilt (with new primary keys) without rebuilding (changing foreign keys in the fact table to match new primary keys in the dimension) the fact tables. This type of issue signals critical problems in the ETL implementation that may require a review of all ETL development processes. This is a crucial statistic to have as part of the overall ETL statistics.

If there are data quality issues with values that form the dimension then it would be reasonable to have statistics about the number of records existing in the fact table and associated with every (or top 10/100) value in the dimension. This would allow a focus on the key values in the dimension for the data quality testing. Except for overall ETL statistics there should be a clear automatic presentation of relationships between all data elements involved in ETL – ETL relationship diagram. This diagram would enable precise impact analysis for changes in the operational sources and ETL itself. It would also allow the ETL result – EDW data column – to be confirmed with business requirements or, in other words, to get a lineage for the data element to confirm the source and transformations along the way. Providing lineage and dependency information on data is one of the essential requirements for any ETL system (Kimball et al., 2008). In situations where the ETL is implemented via scripting, it is hard to deliver the relationship diagram automatically and therefore the whole ETL process becomes a black box without any means of quality assurance. Using the manually updated documentation to resolve this issue usually results in out-of-date, inconsistent documents to support, which slows down the whole ETL process.

EDW Design

During this stage EDW modellers identify and analyse the corresponding business process, determine the grain of the fact table and identify candidate dimensions and fact measures (Kimball et al., 2008). In addition they have to implement data integration strategy using conformed dimensions and conformed facts.

Each fact table is designed to assist with a particular business process. Identifying and understanding the business process can be challenging in a large organization. Designing the new fact table is an even more complex task. It is important to store information about each business process (and associated business requirements) implemented in the EDW and information about each related fact table (e.g. description of the main goal of the fact table and for what purposes it can be used). This helps to clarify business requirements behind each fact table and gives a picture of how each business process is covered in the EDW. This and other EDW specific information can be stored in overall EDW statistics.

Fact table grain is the level of detail in the fact table and is the key to understanding the fact table. In order to properly determine the grain for the future fact table it is necessary to not only analyse the business requirements but also to check what data is available in the source systems. The general rule here is to design the fact table with the lowest grain possible (Kimball et al., 2008). There are many factors involved which may lead the DW team to a different decision (e.g. performance, business requirements, simplicity or existing grain in other similar fact tables). Therefore it is very important to provide information about the grain of the fact table in the overall EDW statistics. Each fact table has a number of joined dimensions and fact measures. This information together with the grain defines the fact table. Having that information in the overall EDW statistics allows users to see how business requirements associated with particular business processes were implemented in the EDW.

Report Development

The next source of data quality issues is the report development process. If a report developer does not fully understand business requirements or is not confident about the relationship between data in the EDW then it is highly likely that the resulting report will not meet expectations. Understanding business requirements is not only about having sufficient documentation. It is also about knowing what data is available in the EDW, its data structure, and main features. For instance, the grain of the fact table is the key information for the report developer when he builds the report based on the corresponding fact table. The report developer might think that he groups the data at some level when in fact he groups the data at another level simply because he does not know the grain of the related fact table. At the same time determining and describing the grain for complex data sets of the report is also important.

Describing the report content becomes increasingly difficult when more data are available in the EDW. Powerful reporting tools allow working with complex data using complex aggregations and presenting them in different ways (e.g. lists, crosstabs, charts, maps) but they do not help with selecting the most transparent presentation method. Even describing the data sets in the report can be challenging depending on the complexity of data involved and filters applied.

Report Use

At the last stage when report users are using reports data quality issues may still arise. Mainly these relate to situations where report users misunderstand the main goal of the report, and misuse the information presented in the reports.

One way of dealing with this issue is to provide additional information or metadata required for the report user to understand the report. This metadata should contain the context of the report (e.g. report purpose, audience, and usage information), information about related business processes and data quality information. Another way is to provide a mechanism to allow the user to give feedback about the report (similar to the approach in Daniel et al., 2008). That feedback is not the real indicator since it represents only the user's opinion about his understanding of the report. The user might think that he does not understand the report correctly when in fact he does but is not completely confident, or, he might think that he understands the report completely when in reality he does not.

In brief, data quality issues, originating from the BI processes, indicate weak data quality management in the BI environment. They show that within BI processes there are problems with understanding the business requirements or with ensuring that business requirements are implemented correctly during each major BI stage. In order to deal with data quality issues it is important to assist all related users with understanding business requirements and their implementation during the BI processes.

Some data quality issues can be easily identified by having the necessary statistics automatically gathered from BI processes (e.g. overall ETL statistics) and some data quality issues cannot be identified easily even with gathering sufficient statistics (e.g. overall EDW statistics). Even if the statistics do not show the data quality issues explicitly, it is still critical to have those statistics in order to assist with general awareness of the BI environment and data quality status. Having all data quality information in one place would show where data quality issues exist and where there are no such issues and should make clear who is responsible for fixing data quality issues. It will also assure all involved stakeholders that data quality is constantly monitored and therefore they can be confident of the BI system. Consequently, the possibility of adopting BI in the organization would be increased.

DATA QUALITY MANAGEMENT AND ITS PRINCIPLES

Data quality issues need to be addressed through practicing quality management principles. By data quality management we mean establishment of tools, information and business processes that facilitate data quality management. Data quality management must have tools that deliver *integrated* data quality information in an *open* way to all participants involved in the BI processes. Data quality management should have *consistency* in business processes across different BI stages as well as in *delivery* and *integration* principles of data quality. Data quality management processes must have *consistent responsibilities* principles and embed strong *assurance* principles. By principles we mean high level requirements for the data quality management process. Each of these principles defines the requirements for the corresponding data quality tools, information or business processes.

Integration

Comprehensive data quality management is possible only with having all data quality related information incorporated in one place. It allows engagement of different types of users in the same data area, to see others' progress and have confidence in data quality. Integrated data quality allows us to automate or semi-automate data quality processes, which can be helpful between BI stages and/or between different teams involved.

Integrated metadata describes elements of the BI environment at different BI stages and represents a foundation for data quality integration. It connects different elements of the BI environment and hence provides lineage and dependency capabilities for data in the BI environment. Data quality information is a part of the overall integrated BI metadata. In other words, data quality management requires integrated data quality information which in itself requires sound integrated BI metadata. All this demands tight integration with BI databases, which store data as they move though ETL stage, come into the EDW and appear on the end-user report.

Responsibility

Acknowledging the fact that responsibility for data quality is dispersed across the organization, there is a need for a common rule for sharing this responsibility. We propose a principle of consistency in responsibility for data quality across the organization – responsibility rests with the unit which has oversight of the area that is a source (upstream to the BI process) of data quality issues.

Openness/Transparency

Data quality results from any BI stage should be easily accessible by anyone in the organization to provide confidence to all involved users and, especially, to business users, and to increase awareness of existing data quality sources and processes of managing data quality in the BI environment.

Consistency

To make data quality more comprehensible by all types of users the data quality information should be based on a consistent data structure across the BI environment. There needs to be a consistent way of storing, and delivering data quality information and a clear way of analysing data quality information.

Delivery (One Stop Shop)

In terms of delivery data quality information should be easily accessible from the BI environment. On opening a BI report the user wants to see the overall status of the report in terms of data quality and if required to get quality details about particular data elements presented in the report.

Assurance

Assurance practices needs to be embedded into each data quality management process. The whole data quality management process should be based on best practice and independent quality assurance ideally performed by an external party. Quality assurance can be performed by an internal party depending on the cost-benefit of using the external party.

METADATA FRAMEWORK TO SUPPORT DATA QUALITY MANAGEMENT

Earlier we defined metadata as a mechanism for describing elements of the BI environment and data. Having metadata infrastructure that gathers processes and furnishes relevant metadata information to all types of users allows them to efficiently manage and share the knowledge about the BI environment. It seems reasonable to have a broad BI metadata system that will, in addition to other metadata information, provide data quality information. Thus a data quality initiative would be a part of overall metadata strategy. Below we describe major metadata elements that represent a basis for data quality metadata in the BI environment.

As we mentioned earlier, data quality has many dimensions. These dimensions can be represented as the attributes for describing data quality. Examples of these dimensions include consistency, completeness, confidence, freshness, coherence and accuracy (Daniel et al., 2008; Ballou and Tayi, 1999; Vassiliadis et al., 1999; Foshay et al., 2007; Jarke et al., 1999).

Based on data quality issues that we identified earlier, we propose the following main metadata elements for the metadata data quality model. Each BI stage has three core metadata elements that should be used for designing a data quality model of the related BI stage. Some of the metadata elements appear to be the same in different BI stages. It means that the same metadata element may have different data quality attributes depending on the BI stage e.g. a table element in source systems would have different data quality attributes from a table element in the EDW.

If design of the metadata data quality model is based on a dimensional approach then each BI stage would represent a business process while main metadata elements would represent compulsory dimensions for each fact table that represents the corresponding business process (BI stage). Below is an example of how an *ETL relationship diagram* can be implemented using proposed core metadata elements (Figure 4). Each relationship within the ETL processes would have a number of source data elements and a number of destination data elements. All data elements would be uniquely identified by a value in the database, table and column dimensions. The relationship dimension will have attributes about a business rule (if applicable) and about transformation implemented along the way. Relationship fact table will allow the definition of many source and destination data elements for each particular relationship. The relationship Role dimension would store a role of the data element in the relationship, for instance,

Figure 3. Main metadata elements for data quality model

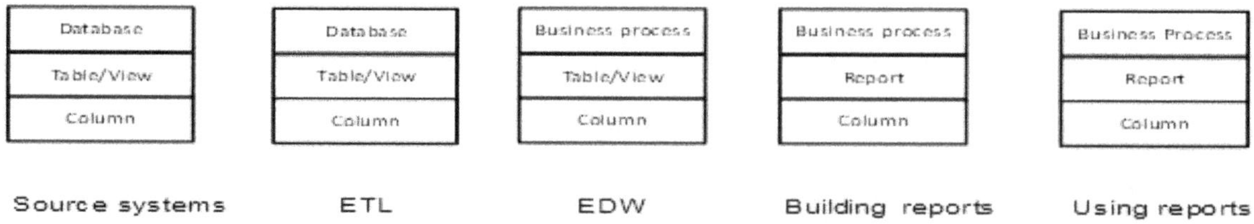

Figure 4. Example of ETL relationship diagram

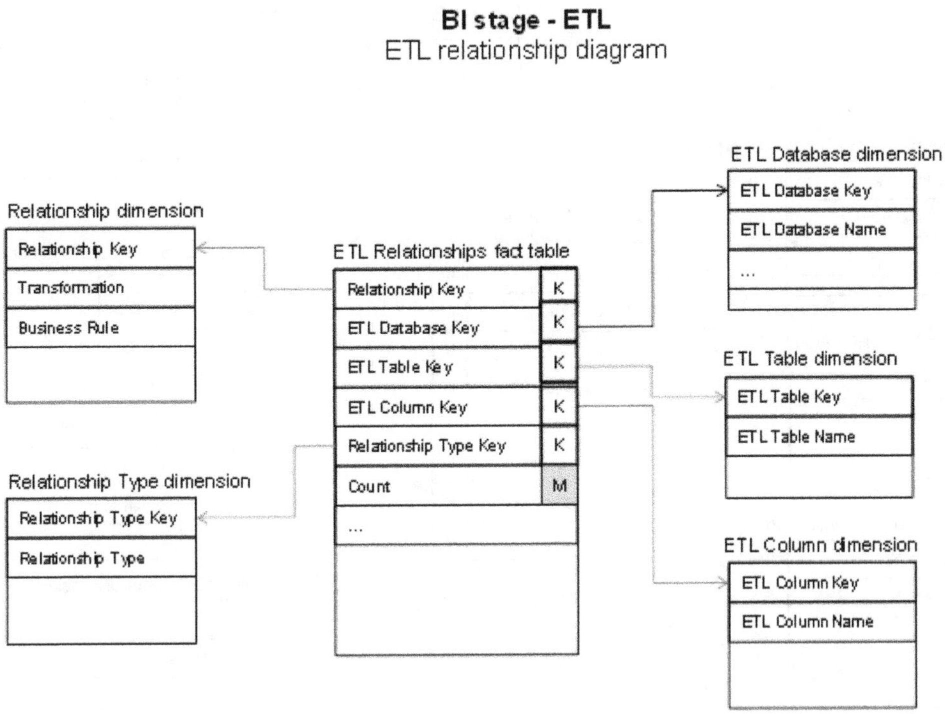

source data element or destination data element. The "Count" measure would have a constant value of '1' in order to allow counting data elements involved in the relationships.

As well as describing particular BI stage, proposed metadata elements can be used to describe relationships between elements of the BI environment existing in different BI stages. For example, consider a connection between the EDW BI stage and the Building reports BI stage which is implemented by storing the relationship between Column element on the report and source Column elements from the EDW (Figure 5). Each Column element in the report is a transformation of one or many Column elements from the EDW. Information about transformation and corresponding business rule is stored in the Relationship dimension. This model provides a lot of insightful information e.g. a list of all EDW tables used for the report, a list of all reports dependent on a particular EDW table and how business processes in the reporting area are correlated with the business process in the EDW.

CONCLUSION

Data quality represents a massive risk for the BI effort. BI processes have to incorporate steps for dealing with data quality issues originating from source systems and assure data quality within BI processes. Comprehensive data quality management is a necessity for BI success in the organization. But data quality management is not only about monitoring and fixing data quality issues. It is also about educating all types of BI users about data quality, data and the BI environment.

Figure 5. Example of connection between BI stages

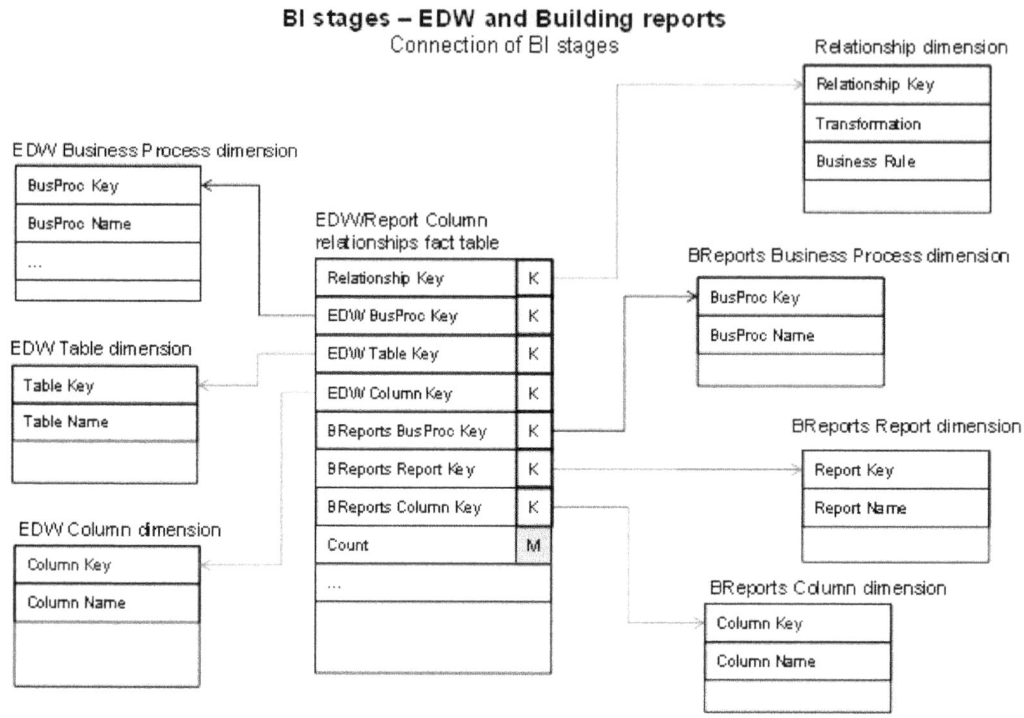

In this paper we have discussed data quality as being a main indicator for meeting business requirements. We discussed major sources of data quality issues, presented particular examples and outlined the information required to deal with given data quality issues. Furthermore, we recommended key principles to assist with the development of a comprehensive data quality management process. In addition, use of a metadata framework has been proposed as a main technical solution for data quality management with key metadata elements. Accordingly, we presented examples of the proposed metadata elements for describing data quality information across the BI environment. Combined, these ideas and proposals represent a methodology for comprehensive management of data quality in the BI environment.

ACKNOWLEDGMENT

An earlier version of this paper was published in the *International Journal of Business Intelligence Research*. The comments of the reviewers are appreciated.

REFERENCES

Ballou, D. P., & Tayi, G. K. (1999). Enhancing Data Quality in Data Warehouse Environments. *Communications of the ACM*, *42*(1), 73–78. doi:10.1145/291469.291471

Daniel, F., Casati, F., Palpanas, T., & Chayka, O. (2008). Managing Data Quality in Business Intelligence Applications. *Proceedings of the VLDB Endowment.*

Farinha, J., Trigueiros, M. J., & Belo, O. (2009). Using inheritance in a metadata based approach to data quality assessment. *Proceedings of the first international workshop on Model driven service engineering and data quality and security*, 1-8. 10.1145/1651415.1651417

Foshay, N., Mukherjee, A., & Taylor, A. (2007). Does data warehouse end-user metadata add value? *Communications of the ACM*, *50*(11), 70–77. doi:10.1145/1297797.1297800

Gao, J., Lin, S., & Koronios, A. (2006). Data Quality in Engineering Asset Management Organizations – Current Picture in Australia. *Proceedings of 1st World Congress on Engineering Asset Management.*

Gartner. (2015). *Gartner Executive Program Survey of More Than 2,000 CIOs Shows Digital Technologies Are Top Priorities in 2013.* Stamford, CT: Author.

Inmon, W., O'Neil, B., & Fryman, L. (2008). *Business Metadata - Capturing Enterprise Knowledge.* Burlington, VT: Morgan Kaufmann.

Jarke, M., Jeusfeld, M. A., Quix, C., & Vassiliadis, P. (1999). Architecture and quality in data warehouses: An extended repository approach. *Information Systems*, *24*(3), 229–253. doi:10.1016/S0306-4379(99)00017-4

Khatri, V., & Brown, C. V. (2010). Designing data governance. *Communications of the ACM*, *53*(1), 148–152. doi:10.1145/1629175.1629210

Kimball, R., Ross, M., Thornthwaite, W., Mundy, J., & Becker, B. (2008). *The Data Warehouse Lifecycle Toolkit: Practical Techniques for Building Data Warehouse and Business Intelligence Systems* (2nd ed.). John Wiley & Sons.

Li, Y., & Osei-Bryson, K.-M. (2010). Quality factory and quality notification service in data warehouse. *Proceedings of the 3rd workshop on information and knowledge management*, 25-32. 10.1145/1871902.1871907

Nichols, D. M., Chan, C., & Bainbridge, D. (2008). A lightweight metadata quality tool. *Proceedings of the 8th ACM/IEEE-CS joint conference on Digital libraries*, 385-388. 10.1145/1378889.1378957

Richardson, J., Schlegel, K., Hostmann, B., & McMurchy, N. (2008). *Magic Quadrant for Business Intelligence Platforms.* Gartner.

Rodic, J., & Baranovic, M. (2009). Generating data quality rules and integration into ETL process. *Proceedings of the ACM twelfth international workshop on Data warehousing and OLAP*, 65-72. 10.1145/1651291.1651303

Tvrdíková, M. (2007). Support of Decision Making by Business Intelligence Tools. *Proceedings of the 6th International Conference on Computer Information Systems and Industrial Management Applications.* 10.1109/CISIM.2007.64

Vassiliadis, P. (2000). Data Warehouse Modeling and Quality Issues. Athens, Greece: National Technical University of Athens.

Vassiliadis, P., Bouzeghoub, M., & Quix, C. (1999). Towards Quality-Oriented Data Warehouse Usage and Evolution. In M. Jarke & A. Oberweis (Eds.), *Advanced Information Systems Engineering* (pp. 164–179). Springer Heidelberg. doi:10.1007/3-540-48738-7_13

Wixom, B., & Watson, H. (2010). The BI-Based Organization. *International Journal of Business Intelligence Research*, *1*(1), 13–28. doi:10.4018/jbir.2010071702

Chapter 17
Strategy, Action Plan, and Approaches for Business Intelligence in Banking and Mining

Hafeez Niazi
University of South Australia, Australia

ABSTRACT

This case study will analyze the critical success factors and key matters related to the deployment of BI deployment in different organizations. Different organizations have different approaches to making BI available for different business users, divisions, and departments. Data visualization is also one of the important factors which will provide user better reflection of data rather than make them confuse about organization data with too much information in the reports and dashboards. Data quality and diverse standards, which make BI famous in the different organizations, are also analyzed during the investigation of both organizations used in this case study. The case study analysis also shows how BI maturity, governance, and framework are key factors involved in the successful deployment of the BI in different organizations.

BACKGROUND

Business Intelligence (BI) is becoming the part of strategy and vision in most of the organisations. Information and knowledge are essential assets to any organisations, where BI is utilising both to provide business values and strategic advantages to companies in competitive environments. BI is significant for the organization and its managers to view business performance and make right decisions on right time (Price, 2006). BI is established a set of technologies and processes, which used to explore, analyse structured and unstructured data to find different trends and pattern of organisational traditional and operational data.

DOI: 10.4018/978-1-5225-5718-0.ch017

BI makes the information available at the lowest level so organisation takes the benefits out for their operational data sources by integrating, analysing and presenting it online in a timely fashion in the form of a dashboard, reports and alerts. Before BI things were different and there were no processes involved which can lead to continuous improvement cycle. Things were done manually, costly and time-consuming fashion even though there were still latencies and discrepancies found in data. Processes were not agile and did one change can be a massive task. Business manager and users didn't have trust in the data when making decisions. Organisations were lacking the flexibility of selecting data dynamically through different time frames for operational and historical data point in time. BI implementation changes significantly by taking a requirement from users rather than building the solution on assumptions. For the successful deployment of BI depends on the technical skills and awareness of the business users of the organisations and how much time current spend on finding, accessing and analysing the operational source data. Implementation of BI also involved the business user roles and department they belong to regarding data availability and governance. Successful implementation of BI provides the completeness and accuracy of data at any point in time. It also provides the summary and detailed level of information by drilling and navigating to different reports from manager and business users perspective. Business Intelligence successful deployment depends on the BI framework, system architecture (Hardware and Software), data standards, data quality, BI strategy, visions and BI project lifecycle. With the technological advancements in ICT, BI is also adopting those changes with the trend of Big Data and Predictive Analytics as part of successful BI strategies and implementation.

RESEARCH MOTIVATION

The BI approach enables organisations to make decisions at the right time to achieve a competitive advantage. Acknowledgement of CSFs is essential for organisations successfully implement BI (Naderinejad, Jafar & Poorebrahimi, 2014). The CSFs include communication, collaboration, innovation, adaptability and leadership. A lack of information and communication can result in costly failures where 60% of companies lose value after five years, 30% have no increase in value and only 10% increase in value (Rud, 2009). Success or failure is not necessarily associated with BI implementation, but instead is determined by organisational and environmental factors (Olbrich, Poppelbub & Niehaves, 2012). The revenue generated from BI platforms reached US$10.5 billion worldwide in 2010 and 80% of BI projects fail (Jafartarokha & Teymournejada, 2012). A BI system is not simply a combination of software and hardware; it requires suitable infrastructure and resources for the longer term. Organisations generate enormous amount of data from external and internal sources but need to present meaningful information to their business users. This information must be clean and based on relevant data because data quality issues alone cost United States businesses over US$600 billion a year (Isik, Jones & Sidorova, 2013).

RESEARCH METHODOLOGY

This research is an explanatory case study that is used for theory building and to verify and validates the discoveries as part of field data findings around BI methodology, contributions of division, and CSFs. The main aim is to conduct semi-structured interviews with people with diverse expertise within the organisation to investigate the research questions in details. To examine and explore these questions, the exploratory case study is conducted for two organisations from diverse industries (Banking and Mining). The grouping of two different industries will provide a better understanding of real-world and theoretical issues related to BI. By examining and working for both organisations, the primary objective is the deployment of BI across all business units and most of the business users.

RESEARCH OBJECTIVE

The goal of this research is to explore and identify the followings:

- Establishing BI methodology within mining and banking organsiation
- The participation of different business units
- The main key factors for the BI implementation

RESEARCH QUESTIONS

To discover, BI implementation phases and factors involved in diverse organisations and divisions involvement about successful deployment of BI.

1. How are various organisations establishing their BI methodology to fulfil the requirements of their business?
2. What are the contributions of divisions and participation from IT in BI?
3. What are the critical factors involved in successful implementation of BI?

LITRATURE REVIEW

BI brings the creation and innovation how to present the data in organisations to make the business value out of it. World famous companies are using BI to evaluate their benefits of activities. Western Digital annual sales are about $3billion, using BI to manage inventory, customer relationship and supply chains to reduce company cost about 50%. On the other hand Continental Airlines, which was about to bank corrupt back in the 1990s, invested in BI about $30 million to improve BI business process and customer service, within six years turnover went high up to $500 million with ROI of more than 1,000%. CompUSA one of the leading sellers of computer equipment and software earned ROI more than $6 million after using BI to analyse its sales trends (Wrembel, 2012). BI offers organisation to evaluate business information to maintain, expand and improve management resolutions across business accomplishments (Elbashir et al., 2008). BI is the primary significance for most of the organisation because of quickly increasing of diverse data, volume and velocity (Isik, Jones & Sidorova, 2013).

BI leaders need to work on the enhancement of existing enterprise data warehouse architecture, information framework and big data technologies to align their agility with organisation visions and strategy. It will also help the organisation to represent the trends to deliver information through clouds on by using social media data and operational data on to smartphone and tablets devices to align and move the new technologies trends. In past, most of the analysis and reports were using existing logical data warehouse without looking to market segmentation of customers and predictive analysis by the current data. How different organisations such as Wal-Mart, Harrah's, Marriot and Capital One are running their business on the abilities to analyse and get data through BI and predictive analytics (Viaene & Viaene, 2008). Investment in BI and analytics will be substantial for the organisations to handle volume, velocity, variety and validity of data challenges (Neil, 2013). Organisation's involvement with new technologies to bring data for BI and predictive analytics will provide them with the advantage on their competitors. Advancement of technologies will provide companies to share their information on mobile and clouds to survive in the challenging market towards collaborative decision making where companies are moving and adopting BI. Gartner's yearly survey reflects that BI is a top priority and investment in BI is still continuous, and it is not going to stop in coming years. Innovations are coming to BI technologies even BI is becoming prime examples are enterprise metadata management, semantic information services and natural languages questions answering in BIM's Watson technology. In past two years, the Mobile BI is becoming more popular technologies with compatibility with IPads and Androids smartphone and tablets. Investment in BI as SaaS is also increasing because of the business hosts applications such as CRM and Web analytics. Different vendors like SAP, QlikTech, Tibco and Panorama are adding social software capabilities to their BI platforms to collaborate with social media. Most of the applications are providing the semantic layer of a single repository to enforce information governance in their Organisations. By adding enterprise metadata management capabilities will make organisations capable of managing their metadata and save more than $1 million on data related issues. Logical Data Warehouse (LDW) will be evolving by the end of 2015, and most of the organisations will be moving towards that for their predictive analytics as compared to Traditional Data Warehouse (TDW) which will be used for operational reporting only (Andreas, 2012).

BI was giving the current picture without giving any information about the future where an organisation can concentrate and invest on the concern areas as part of their investment in the competitive market. It will help the organisation to cope with growing volumes of data and bring transparency to their customers, partners and suppliers.

COLLECTING AND MANAGING DATA

For the business intelligence (BI) case study, I have used different data collection techniques to acquire the required information. My personal work experience and as the employee for both organisations (Banking and Mining) in this case, I have not face any significant challenges to access the required information with organisation's permission. On the other hand, if someone from outside is analysing and conducting as a case study, it was difficult to get access to required information of the organisation's BI documents. Most of the information I have acquired comes from the existing BI documentation for both organisations, which includes gap analysis, emails, agenda, presentation, BI strategy documentation, lesson learned documents, project meeting and minutes. I have also conducted an informal meeting with the familiar technical people involve in the implementation to ask the different question to confirmed my questionnaires, which will be easy to understand for the technical and business users at the same time as well. The informal meetings with professional people will give you the more insight of the real world scenario rather than get the single picture. There are limitations, and constraints involve with questionaries and surveys. Business users and technical people may forget to answer the specific question about some important issues during that period. Questionaries and investigation can end up with some open ended question which generates the significantly amount of data and participant will not answer the survey question and even turn-up for the interviews can lead to unpredictable analysis. I have also used audio tapes and take some notes during interview session by the permission of interviewee.

After collecting the data, second phase is to manage the collecting data so it will be easy to find the relevant documents and evidence uses for the case. The managing step required to divide data into separate collection depending on their source of information (Win, 2008). Database design to categorise data into information and set of protocols for questioners and surveys needs to be considered. I have classified data into the different section like if it's coming from organisations documents and computer files with the data acquired from the article, reports and books. All gathered information was recorded and documented for future use and if something is modify or change that is also reflects in the material for better understanding and management of the collected data. Managing and categorization will help to maintain the chain of evidence which required compiling the conclusion by research questions and propositions. I have used questionnaires and survey option to divide different people with diverse business and technical skills to get different information for my case analysis. These two possibilities are not that time consuming and pricey to compare with other methods and easy to manage and maintain the right data. Some challenges are using this approach with the number of people response and completeness if the questionnaire and surveys.

STRENGTH, WEAKNESSES, AND UNIT OF ANALYSIS

BI is becoming the top priority for most of the organisations to have a strategic advantage in the competitive market. Every organisation is implementing or either thinking of to deploy BI in their department and divisions. BI spending is increased from 13.4 percent level to 10.5 billion in 2010, and 49% of the companies are seeing applying BI solution (Ong, Siew & Wong, 2011). BI is on the top agenda for most of the organisations because of that CIOs spend more than $1 million on BI projects in 2008, and 24% of the projects are identified as successful projects (Anjariny & Zeki, 2011). BI market is getting larger with the growth rate of 23%, which shows the turnover around US$3.3 billion only in Asia Pacific region (Yeoh & Koronios, 2010). Two organisations selected but from diverse industries like banking and mining. As I was involved as BI developer in the implementation of BI in both organisations, so it required personal experience, ideas and implementation from the IT industries experts from the different background using giant IT companies like Oracle, SAS and Microsoft. By having a comparison of various industries will give more in-depth knowledge about BI strategic importance and implementation.

The case study concentrated on large organisations from various industries although similar concept can be applied to small firms when implementing BI. It requires further analysis to determine if the outcome remains the same. There are partial numbers of studies but not enough related to improving the performance of existing BI infrastructure. There are also less number of studies and work presented where companies can avoid the massive budget coast to BI projects when organisations short in budget.

ETHICAL ISSUES

If private enterprise collect all information about an individual can cause ethical concerns but on the other hand for the organisations itself, the privacy ethics is not a concern (Demila et al., 2012). Data collections about facts and figures about individuals and organisations, where it should not be released as part of a case study which can cause information breach later. Ethical issues which involve Data Warehousing, and Business Intelligence are very complex (Hackathron, 2005). Organisations should define company policies for developers about customer data and account number information. Organisations data become significant and critical when its contract with regulatory observance managing personal information and financial reporting data. The most important things to consider for the business users and developers when disclosing personal information and organisation information unintentionally, which can lead to identity theft of customer, employees and any strategic information belongs to the organisations itself. In recent years several major companies confirm that several million personal information has been stolen, which includes social security number, date of births, license numbers, credit card numbers, addresses and family member information. That is a very important matter for companies that business depends on customer trust if they lose that confidence they will lose the whole business. Organisations should prepare themselves for the worse and define some practical steps to handle these situations accordingly.

- Awareness about ethical issues those are significant for the organisations business, which will allow understanding boundaries, guidelines, objective and directions
- Collection of information and identification what is relevant to the organisation by maintaining, securing and providing appropriate access to the external and internal business users
- Define some guidelines and rules what is and what is not ethical for the organisation
- Be aware what's happening in the current world and around you, then try to make and adjust policies according to that
- Develop a culture in organisation to discuss and recommend some feedback on companies ethics
- Make it transparent where information is available for certain level of people
- Make it Confidential so only individuals with appropriate privileges can access that information
- Take recommendation from legal experts to make a proper approach towards legal issues

DISCUSSION AND FINDINGS

Issue Identification and Analysis

One of the significant findings is that organisation are making the robust move towards BI implementation by integrating with governance and IT infrastructure. The case study also indicates that organisation are concentrating more on BI reporting, KPI and performance matrix but less support for predictive analytics. BI dashboard and reports mostly used by managers, experience business users but less number of operational business users are utilising it. The case study also reflects that most the reports accessed at month end (EOM) and some of the reports on the daily basis depending on the department involvement in business operations. Both organisations were using ETL tool to transform, load and improve the quality of data but there is less concentration and work done towards initial data discoveries and data conditions issues reside in the source system. The data storage in centralise data warehouse is also becoming the primary concern because data is growing on daily basis and nightly process are taking the considerable longer amount of time to complete compared to previous years. One of the other findings where both organisations still using old legacy reporting tools and still there is no move towards to merge and transform all existing old reports into the new BI tool and remove all the additional reports, which are not required. By analysing both organisations, one of the findings was that they were not following any BI implementation maturity model which will help the organisation to improve, compare, efficient, measurement and management of the BI environment. Another finding was the lack of information about BI in organisations, which can overcome by involving all business units, departments and divisions must be involved in persistent communication and information distribution among business users for awareness and educating them about BI. The top management and standard system owner support and funding required for successful implementation for any BI projects. The case study analysis founds that both organisations struggling to find and allocate persistent budget for BI projects, especially in the time of global financial crisis and when organisations profits are going down the line. Both organisations developed usage tracking system for BI reports and dashboard to see whether business users are using the BI solution or not and also present in front of steering committee the trend line of business users for using the system effectively. It was also analysed that banking organisation was giving training, and awareness workshops to the corporate user on the other hand mining organisation were lacking those grounds; that's why most business users were unaware of any BI program is running in the organisation. Another significant finding was any top functional or business manager were allocated to the project office, which will overlook the business goals, strategies and any political disputes to resolve within the business and project team. The case study found that both organisations were lacking internal BI experts, developers and analytics to train and handover from BI contractors to the permanent employees of the organisations. By analysing both organisations, different stakeholders identified which can influence the successful project completion. The main stakeholders identified includes, organisation project and portfolio management team, business analyst, business user, application power user of the source system, enterprise information architect, program manager and executive sponsor and the departmental manager leading the project. One of the other findings was that both organisation problems could be reflected with TOP implementation framework including technology, organisation and people. In technology feature, all the BI business goals can be set to align with organisation strategy and vision, which are lacking in both organisations regarding proper BI maturity model. Organisational feature reflects all the BI infrastructure, governance and support mechanism to support the BI project and solution, which is also lacking in term of standardisation and to support BI solution. In people feature where business users, power users needs to be involved through training and top management engagement through discussion and presentation for quick wins also seemed to be lacked in both organisations at the higher level.

Solutions

The first resolution is BI strategy, to address most of the issues highlighted and identified, the organisation needs to build and implement BI Strategy. It will allow an organisation to align their strategy with their goals and vision by creating preeminent use of the information through tactical and operational decision making. A consultant from Deloitte explained that BI strategy would help organisations to bring the forces together which constrain business operations like people, process and technology in a collaborative environment to deliver successful BI implementation. Efficient BI strategy will ensure that business strategy, investment and enterprise objectives and BI are aligned with each other to address most common issues face by BI implementation (Pant, 2009).

According to Figure 1, it explained that BI strategy should include processes, technology, governance, a framework to deliver business value for organisations according to their visions and goals. The different steps to implement successful BI strategy:

Figure 1. BI aligning with BI strategy (Pant, 2009)

- Produce business case
- Buy in document from senior executives what to be delivered
- Set up criteria for successes
- Agree to preeminent practices and standards
- Generate the gap analysis resenting the current and future state
- Develop Governance mechanism
- Iterative implementation with parallel implementation
- Proven framework and methodologies
- BI framework which includes People, Processes and Technologies
- Constraints and assumptions must be documented
- Better decision for better business performance in business context
- KPI
- BI Architecture
- Data Quality
- Data integration
- Data architecture

The second resolution is Business Intelligence Competency Centre (BICC), It will help organisations to engaged IT and business divisions by involving different stakeholders and from various levels of organisations to ensure the implementation of BI application. BICC can be defined as dedicated Business and IT expertise accountable for establishing, organising, owning the BI strategy and agenda

(Safeer & Safar, 2011). BICCs is responsible for distributing high rate implementation of complete BI lifecycle by the consolidation of skill, information and knowledge (Boyer et al., 2010). BICC also help to generate and distribute the established practices and implement BI standards by improving the cost of services, training, support, hardware and software licensing. BICC is comprised of different components including BI Centre of Practice, BI Department, BI Community, BI Centre of Excellence, BI Centre of Knowledge, BI Community of Practice, BI Technology Services and Data Mining and Information Delivery. BICC will help the implementation of BI solutions by:

- Increase efficiency and quality if BI across every level of business through standards and reusability
- Different business case for diverse projects
- BI deployments with higher value and less cost
- Business user adoption to ensure its success
- Close gaps between business and IT deliveries
- Enable enhanced technology management and business agility
- IT combines business, IT and analytics
- Governance mechanism to measure BI success
- Align success of matrix by working with business sponsors

Action Plan

Action plan to develop and deliver with BI strategy and on the later stage when BI strategy will be mature organisation can add BICC as part of its BI strategy. BI strategy will help organisations to find out all departments and division those are doing transformational projects, operational reports and massive usage of excel sheets. This will also provide organisations to develop a rapid implementation development for BI applications which will offer quick wins to get the top management interest towards BI. BI strategy will help to find out the main stack holders and business users and try to engage them in making the successful implementation of BI. Many organisations are still struggling to implement BI strategic initiatives, and 67% Organisations are still complaining about a lack of time, budget and resources applied to it (Boyer et al., 2010). BI strategy will help to understand; it will provide you with the medium to get there. BI strategy will assist organisations to develop the framework to understand (how, why and what) the needs and consideration about its strategy.

- Produce business case to understand the current situation and define scope done
- Buy in document from senior executives what to be delivered, so it will be easy to determine target and milestones to achieve at the end of each phase of the project
- Set up criteria for successes and how to measure and define success in term of organisations mission, goals and strategy
- Define and implement different practices and standards around data and development so it will be easy to combine different development phases to support the solution.
- Generate the gap analysis to finds the differences on various aspects to present the clear picture to the top management what we were at and where we are going now.
- Develop Governance mechanism to define the different level of access to different people. It will also help to identify the data owners for accountability and traceability.

- It will help organisation define Agile and Iterative approach to handling the changes in the middle of and end of development through a proper change request mechanism
- Proven framework and methodologies to approach BI and ETL development to manage data loss, backup and rollbacks for different transactions at different level
- BI framework which includes People, Processes and Technologies
- Constraints and assumptions must be documented
- KPI will help to provide the insights on serious matter to measure progress, and it will contribute to measure performance against defined targets
- BI Architecture, which defines data sources, perform integration (ETL), Data Marts and Presentation Layer for analytics and reporting
- Data Quality, it will highlight the data issues at the level of origin or by performing data quality audit through different tools to achieve data quality and owned trust by the business users
- Data integration to gather all the various data sources at one platform through ODS and EW layer to define data marts and transform various data into exact shape
- Data architecture to provide business-specific attributes names rather than technical and physical name acquired from the data sources

HYPOTHESIS FOR THE RESEARCH QUESTIONS

H1: Making BI Available for Every One Across Different Divisions and Departments

After analysing both industries regarding BI initiative towards BI implementation start from a single business unit and then its roll over to other business units. This approach is adopted in both banking and mining organisations in terms to improve the awareness towards BI strategy. Different BI tools provide different abilities, and not all of them share the same characteristics (Isik, Jones & Sidorova, 2013). One of the findings of the case study about the organisation to provide data and report access to different users depends on the requirements comes from data governance team. In the Mining company there was no plan and thinking involved in providing the restriction to the BI reports and analysis to the business users but on the other hand, banking sector implemented major restriction around reports and data level security. The organisational cross-functional team must be created to make the BI strategy on the right track from the start (Richardson & Herschel, 2012). It's important to define and plan the architecture well in advance for BI implementation which will deliver confidence to the executive managers and business users.

H2: BI Dashboard and Reports With Drilling Capabilities and Detailed Level Analysis With BI

Both organisations produce reports with the requirements provided by different business units but lack regarding presenting reports with detailed analysis rather than just the reports itself. Organisation's executives and lead business subject areas experts use dashboards to understand the company's performance in an efficient way (Price, 2006). In both organisations, mostly reports are developed according to an end of the month (EOM) and daily snapshot approach, where data is taken from different data sources. One of the findings was in both organisations that most of the subject area experts view BI is just another reporting tool. In both organisations business users and executives provides training so they can better understand and utilise the operational reports. In both banking and mining organisations reports were carefully developed by developers, and better visualisation techniques were used by business analysts and subject area experts to publish BI dashboard and reports on companies' BI Portal. One of the main factors of successful BI solution is to provide predictive analysis, which both organisations used in this case study were missing. Predictive analysis about customer, products and customer behaviour will provide executives to make best and effective decisions on right time.

H3: BI Success Comes With Superior Data Quality in Organisations

For the successful implementation of BI, Organisation's division and business users have confidence about data comprehensive and accurateness. Integration of different systems is the major challenge for the organisations (Isik, Jones & Sidorova, 2013). It is assessed that most of the BI project flops due to data quality issues, which cost US$600 billion dollars to US businesses a year. One of the findings in this case study that combining different sources systems and provide precise information in the timely fashion is one of the main priorities of the organisation. The effective BI solution in NASA implemented through data integration of diverse data (Maluf et al., 2006). This is one of the core challenges organisations are facing, which requires data analysis and data discoveries to find the holes in underlying data and make them accurate. Organisations are using BI deployment to classify the data quality issues in their different sources systems (Morabito, Stohr & Genc, 2013).

H4: Agile and Flexible Environment and Architecture for Successful Deployment of BI

One of the main findings of Banking and Mining organisations that both are using entirely different approaches to creating data marts and denormalise start schema for the BI reports. The mining organisation approached towards loading data into the target tables in two phases. First phase staging schema load all the information from the source system, where all the transformation was already performed on the source system through database Views. In second phase enterprise warehouse (EW) load data and creating dimensions and facts from staging schema tables. The data is used for staging schema to create dimensions and facts, but the main problem with this approach was that it was not agile for disaster recovery (DR) processes if mappings stopped or error out in the middle of the night. On the other hand banking, organisation approach towards data loading was quite agile and flexible if something is broken in the middle of data loads. In banking organisation data ware house was divided into four phase, which involves landing, staging, ELT and EW schemas. In landing schema, all data is loaded from the sources, and then in staging the current and previous data from landing tables was used to perform in DR processes if something is broken. The final phase was almost the same like mining EW schema, where different data marts were created for a different set of BI reports. Organisation business environments varying so quickly and BI will provide proficiencies to absorb those changes into the existing business environment on time efficiently and effectively (Isik, Jones & Sidorova, 2013). Integration and infrastructure are the most important thing to make the BI foundation right at the start. BI provides the tractability to the organisation to point differences and gap in the business processes and guide organisations to select the core technology which is supported by the BI operations (Andreas, 2012). In this case study findings were that banking and mining organisations both are doing the same to achieve the gaps, discrepancies and data quality issues with the help of BI tools and their infrastructure technologies.

H5: Effective Decision Support System (DSS) With the Successful Deployment of BI

Organisations can make well-organized choices under the umbrella of BI, where decisions can be made more efficiently on the live and accurate data. In the past decisions support system was autonomous and has the fragile relationship with other systems in the organisation, which is overcome by the BI implementations (Ghazanfari, Jafari & Rouhani, 2011). By merging different analysis of data with the assistance of BI, will provide the organisations to develop proficient decision support system with comparative, premeditated and logical decisions (Li, Shue & Lee, 2008; Zeng & Duan, 2012). BI will provide dynamic organisations learning through innovation of new internal and external processes (Zeng & Duan, 2012). For the implementation of decision-making model organisations should move towards BI (Fatemah & Connie, 2009). In the case study of banking and mining, both organisations are massively using BI to support their operational and business reports. It is also found that there is less focus to move towards proper decision support system, which will provide business users to enhance internal knowledge, business process and procedures.

H6: Governance, Maturity, and Operational Framework for Successful BI Foundation

Analysing banking and mining organisations as part of this case study, one of the finding was that both companies lack the governance and operational framework. The result of that both companies was finding the key complications to implement governance and operational support after the deployment of dashboard and analysis. The successful deployment of BI in organisations needs to have proper governance and operational support [26]. Governance will support the entire BI program, which will oversee all programs phases, responsibilities for BI requirements and data stewards for underlying data for different department and divisions. Organisation's governance framework is dynamic for supporting BI applications and its usage in large organisations (Hammani & Alkhadldi, 2012).Operational support for the BI architecture, which will resolve production issues related to the BI and separated from operation systems support. Organisational maturity is also one of the key factors to consider when considering different BI solutions (Ong, Siew & Wong, 2011). One of the findings in the case study is that banking and mining organisations were not following any maturity models to improve and enhance the efficiency of BI. There are different maturities models exist in the market; most famous ones are Gartner and TWDI, which will allow the companies to align their framework, goals, visions and tactics according to their strategic goals. The detailed analysis of banking and mining organisations also provide the insight where there were a different set of awareness levels and standards were adopted at different levels of the organisations. Business Intelligence Competency Center (BICC) is the essential factor to provide BI awareness and standardisation to all stakeholders at all levels of organisations (Safeer & Zafar, 2011). BICC helps the organisations to accomplish and implement BI strategy, which aligns with organisations business goals. The detailed analysis of both banking and mining organisations reflect there is no project management office, or any business unit looks after the implementation of the BI even after its implementation to measure the performance and milestones achievements.

CONCLUSION

The BI will help organisations to move away from spreadsheet BI solutions towards more interactive resolutions where executive have more controlled and better view of the organisational performance and decision making. The exploratory case study disclosed different challenges involved in the implementation of BI solutions, which includes data quality, data governance, infrastructure for BI components, commitment from the common system owners, the interactivity of the BI reports and BI maturity models. It also focuses the areas where companies need to recruit and trained internal staff, BI experts and developer for ongoing support and development after the BI systems deployment. BI implementation is not only concentrate on technical perspective but also planning, which involves different BI maturity models, Business Intelligence Competency Center (BICC) and one of the organisation manager appointed in project office to improve and support efficiency and competence of their BI system deployment. BI preparation also includes the legacy systems and other old BI reporting tools used within the organisation to replace with the new BI efficient tool implementation. For the successful implementation of BI solution is the involvement and sponsorship from the top management which will help organisations to align their goals, visions and strategies for strategic advantages. Cross-functional division and business user involvement will contribute to capturing the precise requirements at the start of the successful deployment of BI solution. The successful implementation of BI comes with how the business measures the success? Which can be measured against the organisation's defined goals and business case for each phase of the project? BI implementation and adoption is growing, and it is still evolving in the global market. Organisation should take measure to implement BI strategy, which will have the competency to adopt changes and intended to be agile. BI execution starts with the high-level overview, which will have guidelines, set of rules, what we are preparing to construct, how we will plan to build and how user requirements can be met with the success of BI deployment. BI strategy must involve traditional system owners and key stakeholders to identify the business drivers and needs to win the confidence of the main organisation sponsors. Developed and maintain the user's usage of BI reports and dashboard to determine the adoption of BI. Established BI framework metrics, which will help organisations to align strategic goals with operational activities, identify and target specific problems and issues with BI context, evaluate the current situation, establish existing skills and technologies to support the successful execution of BI system. The primary objective of the BI is remaining within time and budget constraints and delivering the right information to the right people at right time.

REFERENCES

Andreas, B. (2012). Hype Cycle for Business Intelligence, 2012. *Gartner*. Retrieved from http://my.gartner.com/portal/server.pt?open=512&objID=260&mode=2&PageID=3460702&resId=2570415&ref=QuickSearch&sthkw=Hype+Cycle+for+Business+Intelligence

Andreas, S., & Josef, S. (2005). Enhanced business intelligence - supporting business processes with real-time business analytics. *Database and Expert Systems Applications, 2005. Proceedings. Sixteenth International Workshop on.*

Anjariny, A., & Zeki, A. (2011). Development of model for assessing organizations' readiness toward successful Business Intelligence systems. *Research and Innovation in Information Systems (ICRIIS), 2011 International Conference on.*

Azma, F., & Mostafapour, M. A. (2012). Business intelligence as a key strategy for development organizations. *Procedia Technology*, *1*(12), 102–106. doi:10.1016/j.protcy.2012.02.020

Boyer, J., Frank, B., Green, B., Harris, T., & Vanter, K. (2010). Business Intelligence Strategy, A Practical Guide for Achieving BI Excellence. *IBM*. Retrieved from http://public.dhe.ibm.com/common/ssi/ecm/en/imm14076usen/IMM14076USEN.PDF

Demilia, B., Peded, M., Jorgensen, K., & Subramanian, R. (2012). The ethics of BI with private and public entities. *Communications of the IIMA*, *12*(2), 13.

Elbashir, M. Z., Collier, P. A., & Davern, M. J. (2008). Measuring the effects of business intelligence systems: The relationship between business process and organizational performance. *International Journal of Accounting Information Systems*, *9*(3), 135–153. doi:10.1016/j.accinf.2008.03.001

Fatemeh, M., & Connie, Z. (2009). A Decision-making Model to Choose Business Intelligence Platforms for Organizations. *Intelligent Information Technology Application, 2009. IITA 2009. Third International Symposium on.*

Ghazanfari, M., Jafari, M., & Rouhani, S. (2011). A tool to evaluate the business intelligence of enterprise systems. *Scientia Iranica*, *18*(6), 1579–1590. doi:10.1016/j.scient.2011.11.011

Hackathorn, R. (2005). Ethics in business intelligence, A practical approach. *TERADATA*. Retrieved from http://online7.net/download/696

Hammami, S., & Alkhaldi, F. M. (2012). *Enhancing BI Systems Application Through the Integration of IT Governance and Knowledge Capabilities of the Organization. In Business Intelligence and Agile Methodologies for Knowledge-Based Organizations: Cross-Disciplinary Applications* (pp. 161–182). IGI Global.

Işık, Ö., Jones, M. C., & Sidorova, A. (2013). Business intelligence success: The roles of BI capabilities and decision environments. *Information & Management*, *50*(1), 13–23.

Jafartarokha, M., & Teymournejada, E. (2012). Using Association Rules for Evaluating and Predicting Risk Factors in Business Intelligence System. *Business Intelligence Journal*, *5*(2), 383.

Li, S.-T., Shue, L.-Y., & Lee, S.-F. (2008). Business intelligence approach to supporting strategy-making of ISP service management. *Expert Systems with Applications*, *35*(3), 739–754. doi:10.1016/j.eswa.2007.07.049

Maluf, D., Bell, D., Ashish, N., Putz, P., & Gawdiak, Y. (2006). Business Intelligence in Large Organizations: Integrating Which Data? In F. al Esposito (Ed.), *Foundations of Intelligent Systems* (Vol. 4203, pp. 248–257). Springer Berlin Heidelberg. doi:10.1007/11875604_28

Morabito, J., Stohr, E. A., & Genc, Y. (2013). Enterprise Intelligence: A Case Study and the Future of Business Intelligence. In Principles and Applications of Business Intelligence Research (pp. 47-67). IGI Global.

Naderinejad, M., Jafar, T. M., & Poorebrahimi, A. (2014). Recognition and Ranking Critical Success Factors of Business Intelligence in Hospitals - Case Study: Hasheminejad Hospital. *International Journal of Computer Science and Information Technology*, *6*(2), 121–129.

Neil, N. (2013). Agenda Overview for Analytics, Business Intelligence and Performance Management. *Gartner*. Retrieved from http://my.gartner.com/portal/server.pt?open=512&objID=260&mode=2&PageID=3460702&resId=2293025&ref=QuickSearch&sthkw=Agenda+Overview+for+Analytics%2C+Business+Intelligence+and+Performance+Management%2C+2013

Ong, I., Siew, P., & Wong, S. (2011). Assessing organizational business intelligence maturity. *Information Technology and Multimedia (ICIM), 2011 International Conference on.*

Olbrich, S., Poppelbuß, J., & Niehaves, B. (2012). Critical Contextual Success Factors for Business Intelligence: A Delphi Study on Their Relevance, Variability, and Controllability. *System Science (HICSS), 2012 45th Hawaii International Conference on*, 4148-415. doi:10.1109/ICIMU.2011.6122732

Pant, P. (2009). Business Intelligence (BI), How to build successful BI strategy. *Deloitte*. Retrieved from http://www.loria.fr/~ssidhom/UE909R/1_BI_strategy.pdf

Popovič, A., Hackney, R., Coelho, P. S., & Jaklič, J. (2012). Towards business intelligence systems success: Effects of maturity and culture on analytical decision making. *Decision Support Systems*, *54*(1), 729–739. doi:10.1016/j.dss.2012.08.017

Price, D. A. (2006). The Dawn of a New ERA. *DM Review*, *16*(2), 18–22.

Ramanigopal, C. S., Palaniappan, G., & Mani, A. (2012). Business intelligence for competence in consumer packaged good industry. *International Journal of Marketing and Technology*, *2*(5), 84–105.

Richardson, J., & Herschel, G. (2012). BI Strategy Gap Leads to Suboptimal Outcomes. *Gartner*. Retrieved from http://my.gartner.com/portal/server.pt?open=512&objID=260&mode=2&PageID=3460702&resId=1958615&ref=QuickSearch&sthkw=BI+Strategy+Gap+Leads+to+Suboptimal+Outcomes

Rud, O. P. (2009). *Business Intelligence Success Factors: Tools for Aligning Your Business in the Global Economy*. Hoboken, NJ: John Wiley & Sons.

Safeer, M., & Zafar, S. (2011). Impact of business intelligence competency center in success/ failure of B.I. applications. *Multitopic Conference (INMIC), 2011 IEEE 14th International.* 10.1109/INMIC.2011.6151486

Viaene, S., & Viaene, S. (2008). Linking Business Intelligence into Your Business. *IT Professional*, *10*(6), 28–34. doi:10.1109/MITP.2008.128

Williams, S., & Williams, N. (2007). *Business-centric business intelligence development with the BI pathway method. In The Profit Impact of Business Intelligence* (pp. 65–95). San Francisco: Morgan Kaufmann. doi:10.1016/B978-012372499-1/50005-3

Wrembel, R. (2012). The Business Value of Business Intelligence. In M.-A. Aufaure & E. Zimányi (Eds.), *Business Intelligence* (Vol. 96, pp. 27–62). Springer Berlin Heidelberg. doi:10.1007/978-3-642-27358-2_2

Yeoh, W., & Koronios, A. (2010, Spring). Critical success factors for business intelligence systems. *Journal of Computer Information Systems*, *50*(3), 23–32.

Yin, R. (2008). *Case Study Research Design and Methods* (4th ed.). SAGE Inc.

Zeng, L., Li, L., & Duan, L. (2012). Business intelligence in enterprise computing environment. *Information Technology Management*, *13*(4), 297–310. doi:10.100710799-012-0123-z

APPENDIX A

Interview Questionnaire 22: Questions

1. How BI data collection strategies handled
2. How data marts and enterprise warehouse layer relates to BI functionality to support data
3. How BI success is defined in the organisation compared to other projects
4. How Agile the BI environment is, its adopting the changes
5. How technological architecture and data standards defined
6. What sort of data is used for BI
7. Who is responsible for data collections
8. What strategies are employed
9. What sort of data qualities analysis implemented
10. User access and permission are set for row level and data level security
11. How Data Governance will be achieved and look after
12. BI is making any contribution to risk management and decision support
13. What business function and operations support by BI implementation
14. How many ETL and BI tools are used and distributed
15. How common system owners are committed and supported for BI
16. How business users are involved in the BI implementation and which stage
17. How training and workshops arrange to support new BI toll implementation
18. How Project office is driving and helping for BI solution
19. How BI strategy and Maturity is aligning with BI goals
20. How data visualisation is handling for the reports and dashboard
21. What approach of analysis and data model performed
22. What are the challenges and troubles faced during implementation of BI
23. What quick wins plans and any potential functional areas address
24. How usage tracking is monitored or implemented to reflect business user are using the solution
25. Which area of BI is more concentrating factor, views about cost and time

Positions and Title for Questionnaire

Business Manager, Common System Owner, Principal Consultant, Senior BI Developers, Teams Lead, Technical Architect, Project Manager, System Manager, Infrastructure and Support Manager

APPENDIX B

Survey: Business Intelligence Making the Difference in Organisation

Instruction: This survey is to reflect how Business Intelligence (BI) is helping your organisation? Please specify your favorite response by placing a tick in the required box of your choice, the survey will complete in approximately 10 minutes. (Table 1).

Table 1.

Statement	Strongly Agree	Agree	Strong Disagree	Disagree	Not Sure	None
Confidence on the data shown in reports						
Time efficient information analysis						
Access to the required information available						
Reports and Dashboard availability						
Operational and Financial Reports respond timely						
Required training and guides are useful						
Provide the required information for all levels of the department						
Single point of right data						
Changed information at the source reflect rapidly to the front end						
Helping decision making						
Provide enough information required						
User friendly and data visualization						
Data security issues for confidential information						
Business requirements keep changing						

Positions and Title for Survey

IT Staff, Experienced Business Users, Executive Users, Business Analyst, Functional Manager, Power Users

APPENDIX C

Consent Form

Title: Business Intelligence Critical Success Factors and Its Importance in the Organisation

Purpose

The main purpose of the questionnaires to acquire the information about different factors involved in business intelligence deployment and implementation in organisation. It will provide better understanding from business users perspective and what are their thoughts about the BI solution provided and to present diverse approaches from the industry experts. There are no funding allocated to produce result for this case study and complaints and suggestions can be provided to the case investigator.

Participants

By signing the consent form participants will be asked to complete the questionnaire, which will not take more than 30 minutes. Many of the questions are open ended questions and user can be answered what they think is the best suitable answers; the data will be store and presented accordingly without changing it. As participant your opinions are valuable for this case study analysis.

Risks

There are no risks engage by participating and providing input for the case study analysis.

What Will Happen the Information Provided by You

Data and results will be used by the organisation by itself to improve the different processes involved in the industry and to present the data for the case study. The participant name and response will not be shown and keep it anonymous to provide privacy and confidentiality. The data will be provide unique coding style to keep the obscurity and any data will not be available to those are not involved in the project directly and secure by encryption to keep the confidentiality.

Consent

I confirm that I have read and understand the information provided and explained to me. I intentionally presume there are no risks involved and understand that I can pull out my consent and suspend participation at any time without penalty and with no reasons. I have indicated my willingness of my own free will and taking part in this case study.

Participant Signature: ______________________________
Date:____________________________
Case Study Investigator: Hafeez Niazi
Date: 15th of October 2013

Thank you for your participation!

Hafeez Niazi
niahu001@mymail.unisa.edu.au

APPENDIX D: EVIDENCE COLLECTED EXTERNALLY

Figure 2. Activity Spend more time on (Skvorc and Rabuzin 2012)

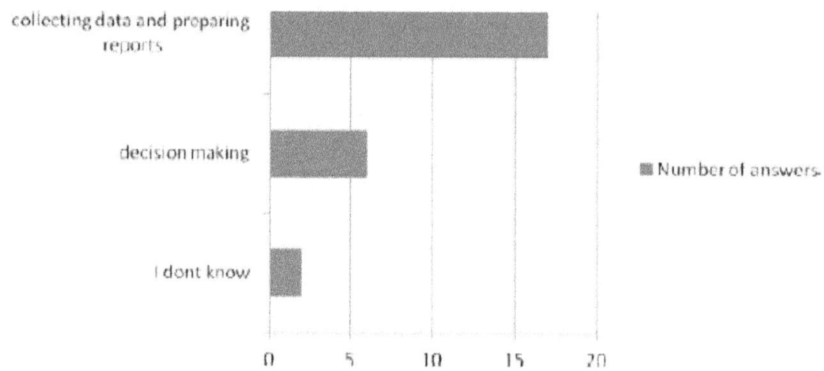

Figure 3. Is company ready to implement BI? (Skvorc and Rabuzin 2012)

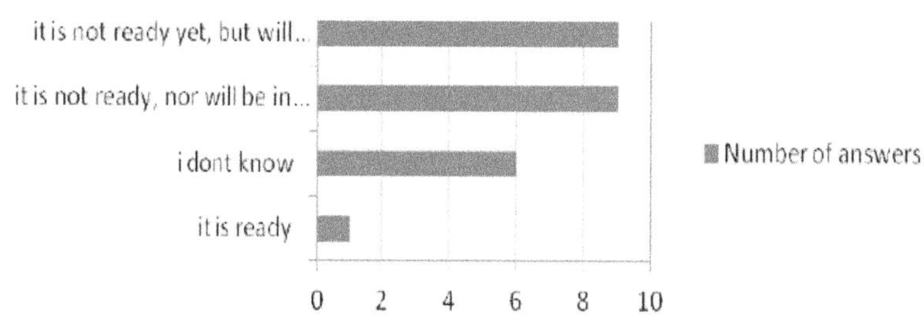

Figure 4. The reason BI is not implemented in the company (Skvorc and Rabuzin 2012)

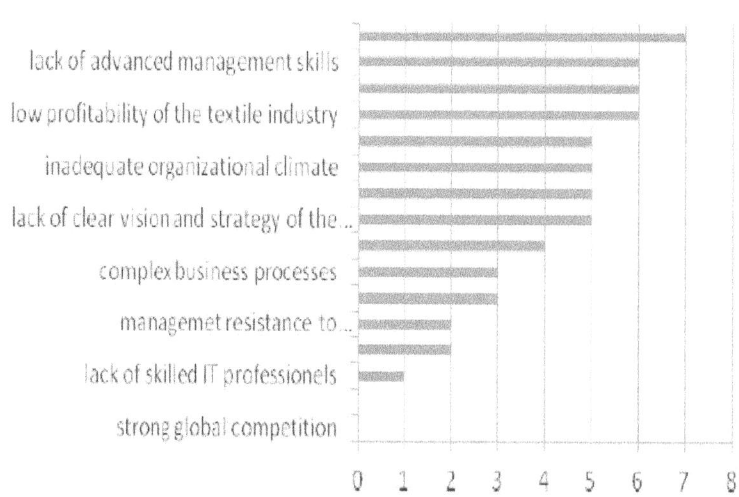

Figure 5. Level of Measurement and Correlations (Işık at el. 2013)

Construct level measurement statistics and correlation of constructs.

Construct	Composite reliability	AVE[a]	Risk Mgmt	Flexibility	Data quality	Integration	User access quality	Decision types	Information characteristics	BI success
Risk management	0.87	0.69	**0.831**							
Flexibility	0.94	0.81	0.586	**0.900**						
Data quality	0.85	0.49	0.410	0.546	**0.700**					
Integration	0.87	0.63	0.594	0.533	0.520	**0.794**				
User access quality	0.87	0.69	0.619	0.583	0.629	0.558	**0.831**			
decision type	0.47	0.45	0.066	0.262	0.200	0.085	0.110	**0.671**		
Information characteristics	0.83	0.70	0.176	0.051	0.101	0.111	0.196	0.041	**0.837**	
BI success	0.93	0.59	0.441	0.464	0.356	0.560	0.550	0.103	0.142	**0.768**

Figure 6. Job Functions, Classification and Orientation (Ramakrishnan at el. 2012)

Demographic	No. of respondents	Percentage of respondents
Primary job function		
Overall management of BI	13	20.6
Developing BI architecture and infrastructure	20	31.7
Evaluating and purchasing of new BI Technologies	1	1.6
Systems maintenance and operations	4	6.3
BI competency center employee	1	1.6
Business analyst	7	11.1
Business user	1	1.6
Others	16	24.2
BI orientation		
Technical	44	69.8
Business	99	30.2

Chapter 18
A Study of Business Intelligence Strategy Development by Large Organizations

Carmine Sellitto
Victoria University, Australia

Paul Hawking
Hawking Solutions, Australia

ABSTRACT

Organizations have adopted business intelligence solutions with a mixed degree of benefits. Some businesses highlight significant outcomes, while others identify limitations or shortfalls in the benefits derived. Notably, the alignment of business strategy with the adoption of business intelligence processes has been an important predictor of firms being able to achieve organizational wide benefits. The chapter uses a case study approach to document the informational needs achieved through aligning organizational strategy and the adoption of business intelligence solution at two distinct companies. The adoption approaches used by each firm, although different, reflect the important areas in which business intelligence is most useful—strategic alignment, governance, and information presentation.

INTRODUCTION

Sourcing appropriate information that is timely, accurate, complete and relevant enables people to be confident and effective when it comes to business decision-making (Isik et al., 2013). Organizational decision-makers have historically relied on data derived from business transaction systems— systems that over time increased in both number and complexity as the organization expanded. Indeed, as such systems became more widely implemented, so increased the challenges of not only sourcing the appropriate data, but also integrating the data to enable its interpretation for decision-making processes (Hawking & Sellitto, 2017). In order to address these integration problems, firms implement whole-of-company Enterprise Resource Planning (ERP) systems. ERP systems allowed corporations to be more process effective, enabling them to achieve significant efficiencies as a result of transactions being

DOI: 10.4018/978-1-5225-5718-0.ch018

aligned with one cross functional system that captured and stored and in a standardized manner (Davenport et al, 2003). Notably, such systems provide businesses with the essential information technology infrastructure that allows them to achieve growth, be competitive in their industry sector and manage process innovation (Chou et al., 2005).

The implementation of ERP systems resulted in numerous legacy systems being replaced, hence, addressing the integration issues. However, important issues persist in regards to analyzing the corporate data— particularly where legacy systems are still used. Hawking and Sellitto (2017) suggest that the persistence of legacy systems might be due to resource limitations not enabling complete integration or even a deficiency of these legacy functions in the new ERP system. Clearly, the persistence of organizational legacy systems that provide important data in management's decision making activities needs to be addressed as an integration issue. Arguably, data sourced from legacy systems will require alignment and integration with data captured by ERP systems— reflecting the corporate data pool that can be analyzed and accommodated in appropriate report formats. Furthermore, as people's informational needs underpin decision-making capacity, so have newer forms of computing technology systems resulted to directly facilitate this important activity. These computing systems embody a variety of offerings that include Data Mining (DM), Knowledge Discovery (KD), Collaborative Systems (CS) and Business Analytics (BA). The term Business Intelligence (BI) is proposed as a moniker that can be used to include all of the proceeding systems (Gibson et al., 2004; Olszak & Ziemba, 2007; Hawking & Sellitto, 2017).

For numerous organizations Business Intelligence has been a post-ERP systems implementation feature, allowing them to gain a deeper understanding of not only their data, but also processes and transactions. Howson (2007, p.2) defines Business Intelligence an activity that "...allows people at all levels of an organization to access, interact with, and analyse data to manage the business, improve performance, discover opportunities, and operate efficiently". Indeed, the analysis of organizational can result in improved productivity and competitive advantage— particularly over other firms in a similar industry sector that have not achieved the same level of information system adoption (Watson and Wixom, 2007; Luftman & Ben-Tvi, 2010). Moreover, Business Intelligence might be considered to factor for companies to be competitive in agile and ever-changing markets and sectors (Luftman & Ben-Tvi, 2010; Watson & Wixom, 2007).

Although the concept of Business Intelligence has been reported for a number of years, limited research has examined Business Intelligence strategy and its support for organizational decision makers. The paper contributes to this important theme through two cases that examined the practices and experience of Business Intelligence strategy development and enactment. The strategies presented can provide insights for not only industry practitioners, but also researchers and industry bodies.

BACKGROUND

Organizational benefits associated with adopting Enterprise Resource Planning (ERP) systems lead to enhanced business performance (Hawking & Sellitto, 2015). Corporations can use ERP systems to potentially attain competitive advantage over industry rivals— a feat which might be sustained over relatively long periods of time Davenport et al., 2003). Furthermore, according to Hawking et al. (2011), ERP-derived benefits will underpin the business processes across the organizational departments enabling greater efficiencies. Davenport et al (2003), indicates that ERP implantation embodies three discrete business maturity phases that reflects how the organization has achieved system integration (Integrate), process optimization (Optimize) and the ability to use ERP systems to disseminate information (Informate). This concept of maturity directly affects the firm's personnel and organizational processes which interact with the ever-changing business environment. ERP system adoption and maturity can also considered from four distinct perspectives that address (Accenture, 2013):

- **Systems Consolidation:** Where systems are simplified and consolidated around a common platform resulting in reduced information technology costs and risk.
- **Process Integration:** Business processes are streamlined, standardized, automated and supported by the ERP system. This results in improved efficiencies and effectiveness.
- **ERP Enabled Business Optimisation:** The transformation of business activities that are supported by the ERP system allow the firm to achieve operational excellence.
- **Innovative Capabilities:** Differentiated capabilities leading to a competitive advantage can be achieved through the leveraging of the improved business processes and operating models facilitated by the ERP system.

How firms use their ERP systems can directly contribute to organizational effectiveness allowing the company to directly improve industry competitiveness through the salient differentiation of their offerings. Executive management personnel have been noted to valued ERP systems the most for the improved decision-making capabilities it provides (Harris & Davenport, 2006). Indeed, executive management had strong motives for leveraging the system to improve the value of the data captured so it was of higher quality— internally to the firm or with external entities. It has been suggested that the accessibility of the data across a broad range of business functions provides an increased degree of process integration allowing data to be transparently available to executive management in decision making roles (Bucher et al., 2009; Rouhani et al., 2016).

As companies experience progressive maturity in their ERP systems use, so might there be an expected improvement in overall business capabilities and value-adding activities. According to Hawking and Sellitto (2010), numerous corporations have implemented Business Intelligence modules as an extension of their ERP system, reflecting how a system might mature over time and with progressive bolt-on software functionality. Clearly, the use of Business Intelligence by an organization aligns with the Informate stage suggested by Davenport et al. (2003) and can be viewed as enabling the various Innovative Capabilities alluded to by Accenture (2013). Aligned with a desire to extract organizational data to improve business capabilities, many companies have identified that data or information analytics applications can be aggressively used to further assisting them in not only their everyday operations, but also for future strategic directions (Hawking & Sellitto 2010; Elragal 2014). Raber et al. (2013) reiterate the notion that Business Intelligence has evolved from being considered an application providing a firm with analytical capabilities, to one where it is viewed as being of strategic importance.

Gartner (2014) identified that Chief Information Officers (CIO) considered data analytics and Business Intelligence implementation an important technology priority. Typically organizations will store data in a variety of formats and use traditional and new analytical tools so as to gain deeper insights of their business workings (Sellitto and Hawking 2015). Furthermore, this analysis allows a firm to better understand their operations, customers, affiliates and brands— which further elevates the value of Business Intelligence as a data management and analytics tool. Grenier (2013) suggests that firms are well positioned to undertake a real-time analysis of their data, presenting outcomes via dashboards and visualization, allowing people to quickly gain important insights.

A company might use Business Intelligence in a diverse manner to attain various benefits in order to assert influence in their industry sector. However, although Business Intelligence might be viewed as desirable by executives, many companies do encounter uncertainty in the post-implementation environment (Hawking & Sellitto, 2015). Some companies may not be rewarded with the anticipated adoption benefits— with some firms perceiving projects to be failures (Chenoweth et al., 2006). Biere (2011) suggests that the data generated by some Business Intelligence projects can be irrelevant, inaccurate and lack currency— making the practical value of Business Intelligence outputs fall short of user requirements. Business Intelligence best practice enables companies to use mapping approaches to fully leverage Business Intelligence initiatives (Grublješič & Jaklič, 2014). Within the traditional management of Business Intelligence, firms should identify relevant Critical Success Factors (CSF) allowing them to achieve project expected outcomes (Yeoh et al., 2008; Harrison, 2012). Another approach is the use of maturity models that directly reflect the evolution of how firms can practically use Business Intelligence (Hawking and Sellitto, 2015). Maturity models are noteworthy and embody elements that enable companies to purposely direct executive activities so as to leverage the management of corporate data— maximizing the benefits of their Business Intelligence initiatives. Maturity models have been noted to be of high relevance and importance if enacting Business Intelligence strategy (Lahrmann et al., 2011).

When considering the needs a Business Intelligence strategy, the focus should be on identifying business requirements and stakeholder expectations. This focus will invariably underpin the subsequent implementation of a comprehensive and process-driven Business Intelligence solution that enables an organization to raise the effectiveness of enterprise-wide decision making (Boyer et al., 2010; Pant, 2009). Raber et al. (2013) suggests that the literature examining the nexus between Business Intelligence implementation and organizational strategy is under reported— indeed even neglected. Arguably, for many organizations the non-alignment of their Business Intelligence strategy to business objectives can be a contributing factor in not realizing the expected benefits of their Business Intelligence initiatives. Clearly, the documentation of industry strategies associated with Business Intelligence initiatives is not only desirable, but allows both researchers and practitioners to gain a more appropriately understanding of the salient issues involved.

In examining the literature there is a lack of reporting of how different companies develop and implement their Business Intelligence strategies. Although a Business Intelligence strategy is consider an essential component for ensuring the success of Business Intelligence initiatives it appears that strategies differ significantly from company to company. It is important that different approaches are documented in order to gain a better understanding of factors to achieve effective Business Intelligence.

RESEARCH METHOD

The paper reports on research that examined the adoption of strategies associated with Business Intelligence solutions in two Australian firms. We used case studies to record the findings. According to Meyers (2013: p. 78) case study research "...uses empirical evidence from one or more organizations where an attempt is made to study the subject matter in context. Multiple sources of evidence are used, although most of the evidence comes from interviews and documents". Case studies provide the opportunity to study topics of interest in a context required by researchers (Yin, 2014)— underpinning a better understanding and comprehension of findings. Irani and Love (2008) strongly support the use of case studies to investigate different aspects of information systems. A number of researchers have used the case study approach to investigate different aspects of Business Intelligence adoption, implementation and subsequent use (Spruit et al., 2014; Alekh et al., 2013; Vuksic, 2013; Hawking & Sellitto, 2017).

The data collection originated from multiple sources that included the perusal of public record documents, content analysis of industry presentations and interviews of company stakeholders. The inclusion of a diverse range of data sources in research has been referred to as meaningful matter by allowing researchers to draw conclusions or inferences about a particular phenomenon (Krippendorf, 2004). The conducting of interviews with company stakeholders used the responsive interview approach (Rubin & Rubin, 2005) where people selected for interview have specialized knowledge about the research domain or issue. The paper reports the summary of interviews as a narrative and highlights the important aspects of the research issue being investigated.

CASE STUDIES

Company A

Company A is an Australian energy provider focused on infrastructure maintenance and electricity distribution. The company supplies electricity to some 800,000 customers in regional areas and 330,000 customers located in more highly populated urban areas. The company had a revenue stream of just over AUD$1 billion in 2015 and employed some 2,000 employees.

In the early 1990s, the company continually faced challenges in the provision of electricity to customers via an infrastructure network that required continual maintenance. It had numerous information systems in place that supported their infrastructure maintenance programs and assisted with keeping costs in check. However, this became more and more difficult as the company had numerous disparate information systems that hindered the integration of company-wide business processes, which in turn impacted on timely access to important information. The integration of business processes was also a major issue as they lacked standardization. Over time the number of information technology systems and their associated costs increased significantly. The decision was made to implement SAP's Enterprise Asset Management (EAM) functionality to address many of the issues. To further support the company's needs, additional functionality was subsequently introduced through the expansion of the ERP system with modules that included Works and Asset Management, Resource Planning and Scheduling, Logistics, Accounting and Human Resources. Furthermore, the SAP ERP system was configured to best support the requirements of the electricity utility business.

Even though the company had implemented the SAP ERP system they were still finding it difficult to retrieve information for reporting to support decision making. The reason for this was that the ERP system had not replaced all of their existing systems. The information from the remaining legacy systems was required to be integrated with the information from the ERP system for reporting purposes. Hence, the company invested in two different Business Intelligence solutions, SAP and Business Objects to address this problem. However issues arose as employees needed to retrieve reports from both Business Intelligence solutions and there was limited integration of information between the two. This resulted in monthly key performance indicator reports being developed and reported via spread sheets. It soon became evident that many of the Business Intelligence reports were not strategically aligned to support executive decision making.

Information Management Strategy

Around the late 2000s, an Information Management Strategy was developed in order to address their Business Intelligence implementation. This aimed to:

- Implement a single version of the enterprise-wide data warehouse to facilitate analysis of data associated with operational and strategic operations.
- Strategically align reporting to ensure that only relevant and intelligent data was reported.
- Improve financial information and data to support consolidation, planning and forecasting.
- Ensure that the right information was provided to the right people at the right time through web-based portals.
- Retire Business Objects to consolidate report environments and reduce IT costs.

The Information Management Strategy had six key components—

Information Hierarchy

Information Hierarchy addressed stakeholder information requirements. Notably, the information that was available was aligned with a person's management position and embodied various performance indicators. The identified performance indicators enhanced individual accountability and influenced behavior. There were two aspects to the information definitions requirements; Performance Management information (Grow the Business) and Decision and Operation Support information (Manage the Business). The Performance Management information related to performance measures supporting value-based management that utilized a Balance Scorecard approach. Accordingly, the key performance measures were related to financial and non-financial performance (Financial, Assets, Customers, Processes and People). Notably, the information required was aggregated information used to support high-level management decision making.

The company identified a number of dependent factors that were associated with Information Hierarchy requirements. These factors were concerned with gaining buy-in or support from people at the performance management and operations management level. It was considered essential that all levels of management were supportive of the proposed information hierarchy to ensure its adoption across the company.

Another factor was the use of the performance measures, which were dependent on the availability and reliability of data used to calculate these measures. This was to be achieved by the creation of a central repository that stored organizational data by subject area. To ensure there was a change in corporate behavior, business processes and supporting technology needed to be aligned to the firm's strategic objectives. A change management process was implemented to ensure staff understood these expectations, an issue that was reinforced through staff appraisal and compensation schemes.

Reporting Strategy

Reporting Strategy embodied the principles and processes allowing appropriate delivery of information to end users. The strategy had three features that included Enterprise Requirements, Efficiency and Preferences and Technical Requirements. The Enterprise Requirements provided guidelines for the priority/

criteria associated with report development. Criteria were aligned with business justification and the relationship to performance measures. The Efficiency and Preference feature allowed appropriate report design, data visualization and subsequent distribution. Report design and visualization guidelines were developed to assist with standardization and facilitated end user learning. This influenced how the report was distributed and when the information needed to be updated. The Technical Requirements were related identifying and defining the technical infrastructure needed to support the Reporting Strategy.

Governance Model

The Governance Model aligned with the information governance roles within the firm and was found to enhance the information technology value for business units. The roles within the Governance Model comprised of a formal structure reflecting the Business Process Champions, SAP Business Intelligence Technicians, Business Analysts and external Implementation Partners when required. One of the responsibilities of the governance team was to develop a process to evaluate the reports needed by end users and management.

Application Strategy

The Application Strategy was responsible for providing the Business Intelligence environment so as to deliver consistent and high quality data to IT applications and the subsequent information to users. This included the implementation of an Enterprise Data Warehouse (EDW) to store data that supported the various business units. This ensured information integrity across the various data repositories that could be accessed by user friendly reporting tools. The repository environment ensured consistency of information and data quality across the reporting tools. All these reporting tools could be accessed through a single common environment:

Furthermore, executive information access through dashboards enabled users to drill down to greater levels of business detail. The EDW provided a standardized Business Intelligence environment which reduced duplicate processes while minimizing the handling of data and improved overall data integrity. It enabled those previously responsible for collecting and transforming the data to spend more time on data analysis. There was also a reduction in costs associated with only needing to use a reporting system with a standardized interface environment. Part of this standardization was achieved through the use of SAP's pre-configured Business Content function.

Business Intelligence Architecture

The Business Intelligence Architecture was designed on the principles of scalability and reusable architecture to facilitate future business needs such as mergers and acquisitions. It was considered essential to avoid future performance issues.

The implementation of the architecture was designed from a top down perspective and adopted a phased incremental approach. Although there were long term goals, there were also a number of "quick wins" identified. The company acknowledged that unknown reporting requirements existed and these would evolve over time. An initial priority was the establishment of the Subject Area Repositories to provide a "single version of the truth". A longer term priority was the implementation financial budgeting, planning and consolidation functionality.

Company B

Company B was a fast moving consumer goods (FMCG) company focusing on health and hygiene products. The company operated in 55 countries, involving more than 42,000 employees and had revenue in excess of $US19.7 billion.

Around 2000, the company commenced implementing SAP's ERP system to support its global operations. The staged implementation included financial, sales and distribution, materials management modules. To facilitate global standardization and integration, the firm designed a template to apply to its business processes— with data being located in a single data center in Wisconsin (USA). As part of the ERP system's implementation a Business Intelligence (SAP BW - data warehouse) and Advanced Planner and Optimiser (SAP APO) were also implemented. Customer Relationship Management (CRM) was subsequently in place by late 2005. The Company has approximately 41,000 SAP users globally. The SAP Business Intelligence implementation was designed to support the firm's customer engagement, supply chain processes and finance activities. A Business Intelligence system was implemented for each of the four regions and another to consolidate the information globally. These were implemented based on the global standardization template it designed to facilitate the consolidation of information. By 2007 these Business Intelligence environments were storing 21 terabytes of data and were growing by 500 million records per week.

By 2007, the Business Intelligence solution the company had implemented was facing a number of issues. Although the Business Intelligence solution that had been introduced was based on a standardized template, inconsistent master data issues were still prevalent across the regions. This data inconsistency problem was typically exacerbated by what might be considered to be poor Business Intelligence governance in and across the locations the firm operated. End users perceived the data to be inaccurate and did not adequately understand how to use the available reporting tools. The volume of data being extracted from source systems, stored and analyzed was degrading query performance. People using the systems complained that responses to reporting queries were taking too long and, in many cases, timing out or reports were not arriving at all. This resulted in end users doubting the validity of the data which was presented to them, resulting in some users developing "work-arounds" such as downloading data from the ERP system directly to Microsoft Excel, editing and reformatting.

This loss of faith in the Business Intelligence solution resulted in management questioning the value proposition of their SAP supplied system, with information technology staff being subsequently asked to continually re-evaluate alternative Business Intelligence solutions. Indeed, the company had invested significantly in their ERP system and needed to leverage the data analysis capabilities provided to directly assist people with their decision making. The capability of the Business Intelligence solution to deliver reliable information across organizational, geographic, and systems boundaries was viewed critical to the Company's ability to deliver on its global business plan. Accordingly, in 2008 the company developed a Business Intelligence Strategy.

Business Intelligence Strategy

The strategy had four key elements that directly addressed:

- Business Strategy Alignment— this element involved aligning the information technology portfolio with the business reporting objectives, goals and strategies.

- Technology and Innovation— this element included the development of a portal for reporting and analytical needs, leveraging intuitive Business Intelligence tools, expanding self service capabilities and develop processes to enhance data accuracy.
- Capability— this element addressed the issue of developing training strategies to build Business Intelligence capability.
- Execution, Governance and Resource Management— this element involved aligning and governing Business Intelligence to the information technology business portfolio.

Business Strategy Alignment

An important aspect of the Company's Business Intelligence Strategy related to directly aligning technology with business reporting. The company realized that part of the issues with end user experiences was the poor performance of their Business Intelligence implementation. There were also higher expectations among personnel that data needed to be analyzed in near real time. They considered implementing their Business Intelligence on a more powerful technology platform in terms of processing power and storage, but this was deemed to be too expensive. In 2007, SAP in conjunction with their hardware partners developed an in-memory technology appliance (Business Intelligence Accelerator (BIA)) to radically enhance the performance of their Business Intelligence solution. The Company implemented BIA and reported a 60% increase in Business Intelligence query performance with some queries being 120 times faster.

Technology and Innovation

The Company's Business Intelligence Strategy included the development of a portal for reporting needs. The company realized that there was a number of issues associated with end user experiences associated accessing various reports. A single portal for all reporting needs including management reporting and integrated dashboards was developed.

The purpose of the portal was to improve the discovery and use of information available through the different reporting tools. This was facilitated through single user sign-on allowing them to access the underlying systems. The portal was configured to conveniently align a person's organizational role to reporting functionality— enabling end users to quickly access the reports most relevant to their daily tasks. At the same time there was the functionality to view the entire reporting catalogue that was supported through an advanced portal search feature. In addition there were links to report documentation and quick reference guides. The company developed standardized guidelines and templates for report development to reduce the development process and facilitate use of the portal. This standardization included layout, use of graphics and visualizations, terminology and color guidelines.

Capability

Another one of the key elements of the Business Intelligence Strategy was to develop training strategies to build the Business Intelligence capability. Prior to the development of the firm's Business Intelligence strategy it was estimated that more than 300 reports had been developed which users would seldom access. In addition, of end users ran reports but were not aware of the related data that could be further analyzed with a different set of reporting tools. It was identified that to effectively implement the Business Intelligence Strategy that the skill sets and capabilities of functional and technical analysts and end users would need to be directly improved. This led to the development of the Capability element of the Business Intelligence Strategy. The objectives of the training were to eliminate skill based barriers so as to be able to directly access the correct information to support decision making. Processes and procedures needed to be developed to ensure that end users knew how to use a particular reporting tool when it was made available to them.

The Company investigated three different options for the delivery of training. Due to diverse range of staff utilizing Business Intelligence and the amount of time required to complete all the training it was decided to analyze the SAP training materials to determine which knowledge was appropriate for the different end-user activities. This enabled the company to develop Business Intelligence training specific to a person's role within the organization. The Business Intelligence training areas included:

- Information Technology— developed for data warehouse development and support teams, including data warehouse functional analysts.
- Business Information Consumers— aimed at report developers, business leads, end users, power users, reporting key users.
- Management— developed for executives working at the layer 4 and 5 level within the firm.

A blended approach to training was implemented involving a combination of instructor led training, self-paced learning, computer based training and web based instruction.

Execution, Governance and Resource Management

The company established a Business Intelligence Steering Committee to implement and monitor their Business Intelligence Strategy. This committee provided enterprise wide governance and leadership in the overseeing the introduction of standardized business processes— processes that typically reflected FMCG industry best practices.

DISCUSSION

Each of the firms can be considered to have mature Business Intelligence scenarios. Their Business Intelligence initiatives evolved overtime as a result of previous initiatives not meeting expectations. When both company's Business Intelligence strategies are compared there are a number of commonalities which are evident.

Strategic Alignment

Business Intelligence is expected to support the corporate strategy— hence, a Business Intelligence strategy would have a component which focused on alignment of Business Intelligence initiatives and corporate strategy. This is reflected in both case studies. Company A's Information Hierarchy component of their Business Intelligence strategy focused on supporting decision making within the company while Company B's strategy a had Business Strategy Alignment component.

Solutions and Processes

Another important component of a Business Intelligence strategy are the tools, solutions, architectures and processes that need to be adopted to support Business Intelligence. Both companies had components in their strategy to reflect this. Company A had elements that aligned with Application Strategy/ Business Intelligence Architecture, while Company B had a decided feature that addressed Technology and Innovation. Notably, the solutions implemented and the respective approaches undertaken differed for each company.

Governance

Both companies included a component in their strategy responsible for the management of their Business Intelligence initiatives. For both companies a formal structure was in place that included key stakeholders— allowing a Business Intelligence strategy to be implemented and pertinent activities to be made a priority.

Information Presentation

Although each company strategies differed slightly in this area there were still important tenets that reflected the same underlying principles. This ensured that information was available in a prescribed format and the intended organizational users had the required skills to access, explore and analyze this information.

Each of the components identified across these four areas are high level and would most likely be found in most Business Intelligence strategies firms may have adopted. However, how these components would have evolved from after implementation would differ significantly between companies— particularly across industry sectors (this is reflected in the included case studies).

CONCLUSION

Business Intelligence strategy is an essential component of a successful Business Intelligence initiative. The case studies documented in this paper provide examples of Business Intelligence strategies. Both strategies include components related to Strategic Alignment, Solutions and Processes, Governance and Information Presentation. However, how these components were implemented in each company differs significantly.

REFERENCES

Accenture. (2013). *Value Realization – Capturing Business Value, Faster, from SAP Solutions*. Accenture.

Alekh, D., Maheshwari, N., & Kalicharan, S. (2013). A Business Intelligence Technique for Forecasting the Automobile Sales using Adaptive Intelligent Systems (ANFIS and ANN). *International Journal of Computers and Applications*, *74*(1), 7–13.

Biere, M. (2011). *The new era of enterprise business intelligence*. Boston: IBM Press.

Boyer, J., Frank, B., Green, B., Harris, T., & van De Vanter, K. (2010). *Business intelligence strategy: A practical guide for achieving BI excellence*. MC Press.

Bucher, T., Gericke, A., & Sigg, S. (2009). Process-centric business intelligence. *Business Process Management Journal*, *15*(3), 408–429. doi:10.1108/14637150910960648

Chenoweth, T., Corral, K., & Demirkan, H. (2006). Seven key interventions for data warehouse success. *Communications of the ACM*, *49*(1), 114–119. doi:10.1145/1107458.1107464

Chou, D. C., Tripuramallu, H. B., & Chou, A. Y. (2005). BI and ERP integration. *Information Management & Computer Security*, *13*(5), 340–349. doi:10.1108/09685220510627241

Davenport, T., Harris, J., & Cantrell, S. (2003). *The Return of Enterprise Solutions: The Director's Cut*. Accenture.

Elragal, A. (2014). ERP and Big Data: The Inept Couple. *Procedia Technology*, *16*, 242–249. doi:10.1016/j.protcy.2014.10.089

Gartner. (2014). *Flipping to Digital Leadership: The 2015 CIO Agenda*. Gartner.

Gibson, M., Arnott, D., & Carlsson, S. (2004). Evaluating the Intangible Benefits of Business Intelligence: Review & Research Agenda. *Proceedings of the Decision Support in an Uncertain and Complex World: The IFIP TC8/WG8.3 International Conference*, 295-305.

Grenier, L. (2013). *The Evolving Role of Data in Decision-making. Economist Intelligence Unit*. London, UK: EIU.

Grublješič, T., & Jaklič, J. (2014). Three Dimensions of Business Intelligence Systems Use Behavior. *International Journal of Enterprise Information Systems*, *10*(3), 62–76. doi:10.4018/ijeis.2014070105

Harris, J., & Davenport, T. (2006). *New Growth From Enterprise Systems*. Accenture.

Harrison, E. (2012). Critical Success Factors of Business Intelligence System Implementations: Evidence from the Energy Sector. *International Journal of Enterprise Information Systems*, *8*(2), 1–13. doi:10.4018/jeis.2012040101

Hawking, P., Jovanovic, R., & Sellitto, C. (2011). Business Intelligence Maturity in Australia. *Proceedings of the Americas Conference of Information Systems (AMCIS)*.

Hawking, P., & Sellitto, C. (2010). Business Intelligence (BI) Critical Success Factors (2010). *ACIS 2010 Proceedings*. Retrieved from http://aisel.aisnet.org/acis2010/4

Hawking, P., & Sellitto, C. (2015). Business Intelligence Strategy: A Utilities Company Case Study. *International Journal of Enterprise Information Systems*, *11*(1), 1–12. doi:10.4018/ijeis.2015010101

Hawking, P., & Sellitto, C. (2017). Business Intelligence Strategy: Two case Studies. *International Journal of Business Intelligence Research*, *8*(2), 17–30. doi:10.4018/IJBIR.2017070102

Howson, C. (2007). *Successful Business Intelligence: Secrets to Making BI a Killer App*. McGraw-Hill Professional.

Irani, Z., & Love, P. (2008). *Evaluating Information Systems in the Public and Private Sectors*. Oxford, UK: Elsevier.

Isik, O., Jones, M., & Sidorova, A. (2013). Business intelligence success: The roles of BI capabilities and decision environments. *Information & Management*, *50*(1), 13–23. doi:10.1016/j.im.2012.12.001

Krippendorff, K. (2004). *Content Analysis: An Introduction to its Methodology*. Beverly Hills, CA: Sage Publications.

Lahrmann, G., Marx, F., Winter, R., & Wortmann, F. (2011). Business Intelligence Maturity: Development and Evaluation of a Theoretical Model. *Proceedings of HICSS*. 10.1109/HICSS.2011.90

Luftman, J., & Ben-Tvi, T. (2010). Key issues for IT executives 2010: Judicious IT investments continue post-recession. *MIS Quarterly Executive*, *9*(4), 263–273.

Myers, M. D. (2013). *Qualitative Research in Business and Management* (2nd ed.). London: Sage.

Olszak, C. M., & Ziemba, E. (2007). Approach to building and implementing Business Intelligence Systems. *Interdisciplinary Journal of Information, Knowledge, and Management*, *2*, 135–148. doi:10.28945/105

Pant, P. (2009). *Business Intelligence: How to build successful BI strategy*. Deloitte Consulting. Available at http://www.deloitte.com/assets/Dcom-SouthAfrica/Local%20Assets/Documents/Business%20intelligence%20that%20aligns%20with%20enterprise%20goals.pdf

Raber, D., Wortmann, F., & Winter, R. (2013). Towards The Measurement Of Business Intelligence Maturity. *Proceedings of ECIS 2013*.

Rouhani, S., Ashrafi, A., Ravasan, A. Z., & Afshari, S. (2016). The impact model of business intelligence on decision support and organizational benefits. *Journal of Enterprise Information Management*, *29*(1), 19–50. doi:10.1108/JEIM-12-2014-0126

Rubin, H. J., & Rubin, I. S. (2005). *Qualitative interviewing: The art of hearing data* (2nd ed.). Thousand Oaks, CA: Sage. doi:10.4135/9781452226651

Sammon, D., & Finnegan, P. (2000). The ten commandments of data warehousing. *ACM SIGMIS Database*, *31*(4), 82–91. doi:10.1145/506760.506767

Spruit, M., Vroon, R., & Batenburg, R. (2014). Towards healthcare business intelligence in long-term care: An explorative case study in the Netherlands. *Computers in Human Behavior*, *30*, 698–707. doi:10.1016/j.chb.2013.07.038

Vuksic, V., Bach, M., & Popovic, A. (2013). Supporting performance management with business process management and business intelligence: A case analysis of integration and orchestration. *International Journal of Information Management*, *33*(4), 613–619. doi:10.1016/j.ijinfomgt.2013.03.008

Watson, H. J., & Wixom, H. (2007). Enterprise agility and mature BI capabilities. *Business Intelligence Journal*, *12*(3), 13–28.

Yeoh, W., Koronios, A., & Gao, J. (2008). Managing the Implementation of Business Intelligence Systems: A Critical Success Factors Framework. *International Journal of Enterprise Information Systems*, *4*(3), 79–94. doi:10.4018/jeis.2008070106

Yin, R. (2014). *Case Study Research, Design and Methods* (5th ed.). Newbury Park, CA: Sage Publications.

KEY TERMS AND DEFINITIONS

Business Intelligence: A solution that allows people at all levels of an organization to gain a deeper understanding of not only their data, but also processes and transactions allowing them to improve organizational performance.

Business Intelligence Strategy: A plan of action to maximize the impact of business intelligence on an organization.

Business Objects: One of the leading business intelligence vendors which was acquired by SAP.

Critical Success Factors: Factors that need to be identified and managed to ensure the success of a project.

Enterprise Resource Planning (ERP) Systems: A real-time modular information system responsible for automating and managing transactions associated with a company's core business processes.

Maturity Model: A business tool to assess the capabilities of an organization in regards to a particular phenomenon.

Online Transaction Processing (OLTP): Information systems responsible for transaction processing.

SAP: A leading vendor of ERP systems and business intelligence.

Compilation of References

Abdallah, S., & Jaleel, B. (2015). Website appeal: Development of an assessment tool and evaluation framework of e-marketing. *Journal of Theoretical and Applied Electronic Commerce Research*, *10*(3), 45–62. doi:10.4067/S0718-18762015000300005

Abdul-Muhmin, A. G. (2011). Repeat purchase intentions in online shopping: The role of satisfaction, attitude, and online retailers' performance. *Journal of International Consumer Marketing*, *23*(1), 5–20. doi:10.1080/08961530.2011.524571

Abrahams, D. A. (2010). Technology adoption in higher education: A framework for identifying and prioritising issues and barriers to adoption of instructional technology. *Journal of Applied Research in Higher Education*, *2*(2), 34–49. doi:10.1108/17581184201000012

Accenture. (2013). *Value Realization – Capturing Business Value, Faster, from SAP Solutions*. Accenture.

Adelman, S. (2015). Why Big Data Means Big Opportunity for the Travel Industry. *Forbes*. Retrieved from https://www.forbes.com/sites/ibm/2015/07/09/why-big-data-means-big-opportunity-for-the-travel-industry/#5528576b21a5

Adler, N. (2008). *International Dimensions of Organizational Behavior* (5th ed.). Cincinnati, OH: South-Western.

Aguilar-Saven, R. S. (2004). Business Process Modelling: Review and Framework. *International Journal of Production Economics*, *90*(2), 129–149. doi:10.1016/S0925-5273(03)00102-6

Aiken, P., Gillenson, M. L., Zhang, X., & Rafner, D. (2011). Data Management and Data Administration: Assessing 25 Years of Practice. *Journal of Database Management*, *22*(3), 24–44. doi:10.4018/jdm.2011070102

Akhavan, P., Hosseini, S., Abbasi, M., & Manteghi, M. (2015). Knowledge-sharing determinants, behaviors, and innovative work behaviors: An integrated theoretical view and empirical examination. *Aslib Journal Of Information Management*, *67*(5), 562–591. doi:10.1108/AJIM-02-2015-0018

Alaboodi, S. S. (2007). *Towards evaluating security implementations using the Information Security Maturity Model (ISMM)* (Master's thesis). University of Waterloo.

Alalwan, J. A. (2013). A taxonomy for decision support capabilities of enterprise content management systems. *The Journal of High Technology Management Research*, *24*(1), 10–17. doi:10.1016/j.hitech.2013.02.001

Alavi, M., & Henderson, J. C. (1981). An evolutionary strategy for implementing a decision support system. *Management Science*, *27*(11), 1309–1323. doi:10.1287/mnsc.27.11.1309

Albert, W., & Tullis, T. (2013). *Measuring the user experience: Collecting, analysing, and presenting usability metrics*. Elsevier Inc.

Albescu, F, Pugnam, I & Paraschiv, D, (2008), Business Intelligence and knowledge management – Technological support for strategic management in knowledge based economy. *Revista Informatica Economica, 4*(48).

Alekh, D., Maheshwari, N., & Kalicharan, S. (2013). A Business Intelligence Technique for Forecasting the Automobile Sales using Adaptive Intelligent Systems (ANFIS and ANN). *International Journal of Computers and Applications*, *74*(1), 7–13.

Allee, V., & Schwabe, O. (2011). *Value Networks and the true nature of collaboration*. ValueNet Works and Verna Allee Associates.

Alnoukari, M. (2009). Using Business Intelligence Solutions for Achieving Organization's Strategy: Arab International University Case Study. *Internetworking Indonesia Journal*, *1*(3), 11–16.

Alter, S. (2002). *Information Systems (the foundation of E-business)*. Prentice Hall, Pearson Education.

Alyoubi, B. A. (2015). Decision support system and knowledge-based strategic management. *Procedia Computer Science*, *65*, 278–284. doi:10.1016/j.procs.2015.09.079

American Transportation Research Institute. (2014). *An Analysis of the Operational Costs of Trucking: 2014 Update*. American Transportation Research Institute.

Amid, A., Moalagh, M., & Ravasan, Z. (2012). Identification and classification of ERP critical failure factors in Iranian industries. *Information Systems*, *37*(3), 227–237. doi:10.1016/j.is.2011.10.010

Analytics Vidhya. (2015). *13 Amazing Applications/Uses of data Science Today*. Retrieved September 21 from https://www.analyticsvidhya.com/blog/2015/09/applications-data-science/

Andreas, B. (2012). Hype Cycle for Business Intelligence, 2012. *Gartner*. Retrieved from http://my.gartner.com/portal/server.pt?open=512&objID=260&mode=2&PageID=3460702&resId=2570415&ref=QuickSearch&sthkw=Hype+Cycle+for+Business+Intelligence

Andreas, S., & Josef, S. (2005). Enhanced business intelligence - supporting business processes with real-time business analytics. *Database and Expert Systems Applications, 2005. Proceedings. Sixteenth International Workshop on.*

Angehrn, A. (1997). Designing mature Internet business strategies: The ICDT model. *European Management Journal*, *15*(4), 361–369. doi:10.1016/S0263-2373(97)00016-9

Angehrn, A. A., & Jelassi, T. (1994). DSS research and practice in perspective. *Decision Support Systems*, *12*(4), 267–275. doi:10.1016/0167-9236(94)90045-0

Anjariny, A., & Zeki, A. (2011). Development of model for assessing organizations' readiness toward successful Business Intelligence systems. *Research and Innovation in Information Systems (ICRIIS), 2011 International Conference on.*

Ardalan, K. (2008). Globalization and culture: Four paradigmatic views. *International Journal of Social Economics*, 513–534.

Argote, L., & Ingram, P. (2000). Knowledge transfer: A basis for competitive advantage in firms. *Organizational Behavior and Human Decision Processes*, *82*(1), 150–169. doi:10.1006/obhd.2000.2893

Argyris, C. (2002). Double-Loop Learning, Teaching, and Research. *Academy of Management Learning & Education*, *1*(2), 206–218. doi:10.5465/AMLE.2002.8509400

Ariyachandra, T., & Watson, H. J. (2006). Which data warehouse architecture is most successful? *Business Intelligence Journal*, *11*(1), 4.

Arnold, K. E., & Pistilli, M. D. (2012). Course signals at Purdue: Using learning analytics to increase student success. *Proceedings of the 2nd international conference on learning analytics and knowledge*. 10.1145/2330601.2330666

Arnott, D. (2004). Decision support systems evolution: Framework, case study and research agenda. *European Journal of Information Systems*, *13*(4), 247–259. doi:10.1057/palgrave.ejis.3000509

Arnott, D. (2006). Cognitive biases and decision support systems development: A design science approach. *Information Systems Journal*, *16*(1), 55–78. doi:10.1111/j.1365-2575.2006.00208.x

Arnott, D., & Dodson, G. (2008). Decision support systems failure. In F. Burstein & C. W. Holsapple (Eds.), *Handbook on decision support systems 1* (pp. 763–790). Berlin: Springer. doi:10.1007/978-3-540-48713-5_34

Arnott, D., & Pervan, G. (2012). Design science in decision support systems research: An assessment using the Hevner, March, Park, and Ram guidelines. *Journal of the Association for Information Systems*, *13*(11), 923–949. doi:10.17705/1jais.00315

Arnott, D., & Pervan, G. (2014). A critical analysis of decision support systems research revisited: The rise of design science. *Journal of Information Technology*, *29*(4), 269–293. doi:10.1057/jit.2014.16

Asllani, A. (2015). *Business Analytics with Management Science Models and Methods*. Upper Sadler River, NJ: Pearson Education, Inc.

Asllani, A. (2015). *Business Analytics with Management Science, Models and Methods*. Upper Saddle River, NJ: Pearson Education Inc.

Atak, M., & Erturgut, R. (2010). WCES-2010: An empirical analysis on the relation between learning organization and organizational commitment. Procedia - Social and Behavioral Sciences, 2, 3472-3476.

Aulck, L., Velagapudi, N., Blumenstock, J., & West, J. (2016). *Predicting student dropout in higher education*. arXiv preprint arXiv:1606.06364

Australian Bureau of Statistics. (2014). Available at: www.abs.gov.au

Australian Dairy Industry in Focus. (2008). Available at: http://www.dairyaustralia.com.au/Our-Dairy-Industry/~/media/Publications/Australian Dairy Industry in Focus/2008/AustralianDairyIndustryInFocus2008.ashx?la=en

Ayed, M. B., Ltifi, H., Kolski, C., & Alimi, A. M. (2010). A user-centered approach for the design and implementation of KDD-based DSS: A case study in the healthcare domain. *Decision Support Systems*, *50*(1), 64–78. doi:10.1016/j.dss.2010.07.003

Azma, F., & Mostafapour, M. A. (2012). Business intelligence as a key strategy for development organizations. *Procedia Technology*, *1*(12), 102–106. doi:10.1016/j.protcy.2012.02.020

Baek, E.-O., Cagiltay, K., Boling, E., & Frick, T. (2008). User-centered design and development. In I. J. Spector, M. Merrill, J. van Merrienboer, & M. Driscoll (Eds.), *Handbook of research on educational communications and technology* (pp. 660–668). New York: Routledge/Taylor & Francis Group.

Bagozzi, R. P., & Dholakia, U. M. (2006). Antecedents and purchase consequences of customer participation in small group brand communities. *International Journal of Research in Marketing*, *23*(1), 45–61. doi:10.1016/j.ijresmar.2006.01.005

Bajo, J., Borrajo, M. L., De Paz, J. F., Corchado, J. M., & Pellicer, M. A. (2012). A multi-agent system for web-based risk management in small and medium business. *Expert Systems with Applications*, *39*(8), 6921–6931. doi:10.1016/j.eswa.2012.01.001

Balasubramanian, S., Peterson, R., & Jarvenpaa, S. (2002). Exploring the implications of m-commerce for markets and marketing. *Journal of the Academy of Marketing Science*, *30*(4), 348–361. doi:10.1177/009207002236910

Ballard, C., Farrell, D. M., Gupta, A., Mazuela, C., & Vohnik, S. (2006). *Dimensional Modelling: In a Business Intelligence Environment*. New York: IBM.

Ballou, D. P., & Tayi, G. K. (1999). Enhancing Data Quality in Data Warehouse Environments. *Communications of the ACM*, *42*(1), 73–78. doi:10.1145/291469.291471

Ballou, D. P., Wang, R. Y., Pazer, H., & Tayi, G. K. (1998). Modeling Information Manufacturing Systems to Determine Information Product Quality. *Management Science*, *44*(4), 462–484. doi:10.1287/mnsc.44.4.462

Basole, R. (2008). *Enterprise mobility: Applications, technologies and strategies*. Amsterdam: IOS Press.

Batsell, J. (2011). Intrigued, but not immersed: Millennial students analyze the iPad's performance as a news platform. In *International Symposium on Online Journalism*. University of Texas at Austin.

Baumback, C. (1988). *How to Organize and Operate a Small Business*. Prentice Hall.

Bayer, J., Bydzovská, H., Géryk, J., Obsivac, T., & Popelinsky, L. (2012). *Predicting Drop-Out from Social Behaviour of Students*. International Educational Data Mining Society.

Bean, J. P., & Metzner, B. S. (1985). A conceptual model of nontraditional undergraduate student attrition. *Review of Educational Research*, *55*(4), 485–540. doi:10.3102/00346543055004485

Beaudouin-Lafon, M., & Mackay, W. (2003). Prototyping tools and techniques. In A. Sears & J. A. Jacko (Eds.), *Human-computer interaction: Development process* (pp. 121–142). Boca Raton, FL: CRC Press/Taylor & Francis Group.

Biere, M. (2011). *The new era of enterprise business intelligence*. Boston: IBM Press.

Bilgihan, A., & Bujisic, M. (2015). The effect of website features in online relationship marketing: A case of online hotel booking. *Electronic Commerce Research and Applications*, *14*(4), 222–232. doi:10.1016/j.elerap.2014.09.001

Bogza, R. M., & Zaharie, D. (2008). Business Intelligence as a Competitive Differentiator. *IEEE International Conference on Automation, Quality and Testing, Robotics*.

Bonczek, R. H., Holsapple, C. W., & Whinston, A. B. (2014). *Foundations of decision support systems*. New York: Academic Press.

Bourne, J. S. (2016). Exploring Intercultural Communication Challenges: A Case Study on Chinese-English Interpreting. *China Media Research*, 14-24.

Bower, B. (2000). Culture of Reason: Thinking styles may take Eastern and Western routes. Society for Science & the Public, 56-58.

Boyer, J., Frank, B., Green, B., Harris, T., & Vanter, K. (2010). Business Intelligence Strategy, A Practical Guide for Achieving BI Excellence. *IBM*. Retrieved from http://public.dhe.ibm.com/common/ssi/ecm/en/imm14076usen/IMM14076USEN.PDF

Boyer, J., Frank, B., Green, B., Harris, T., & van De Vanter, K. (2010). *Business intelligence strategy: A practical guide for achieving BI excellence*. MC Press.

Brandas, C. (2011). Decision support systems development: A methodological approach. *Journal of Applied Business Information Systems*, *2*(4), 151–158.

Brown, D. R. (2011). *An experiential approach to organization development*. Upper Saddle River, NJ: Prentice Hall.

Bucher, T., Gericke, A., & Sigg, S. (2009). Process-centric business intelligence. *Business Process Management Journal*, *15*(3), 408–429. doi:10.1108/14637150910960648

Bughin, J. (2016). Big Data, Big Bang? *Journal of Big Data, 3*(2).

Bughin, J. (2016). Big Data: Getting a Better Read on Performance. *McKinsey Quarterly*. Retrieved from https://www.mckinsey.com/industries/high-tech/our-insights/big-data-getting-a-better-read-on-performance

Bullot, A., & Hornbrook, S. (2015). *GST: Online purchases – What will be caught and when? Tax Alert*. Retrieved from https://www2.deloitte.com/nz/en/pages/tax-alerts/articles/gst-online-purchases-what-will-be-caught-and-when.html

Bulygo, Z. (2015). How Netflix Uses Analytics To Select Movies, Create Content, and Make Multimillion Dollar Decisions. *Kiss Metrics*. Retrieved from https://blog.kissmetrics.com/how-netflix-uses-analytics/

Burgess, S. (2016). Representing small business web presence content: The web presence pyramid model. *European Journal of Information Systems*, *25*(2), 110–130. doi:10.1057/ejis.2015.4

Burns, E. (2016). *How PayPal Fights Fraud with Predictive Data Analysis*. Retrieved from http://searchbusinessanalytics.techtarget.com/feature/How-PayPal-fights-fraud-with-predictive-data-analysis

Burton, B. (2009). *Toolkit: Maturity checklist for business intelligence and performance management*. Stamford, CT: Gartner Research.

Butler, C. (2017). 2017 State of Embedded Analytics Report. *Logi Analytics*. Retrieved from http://go.logianalytics.com/rs/793-ECD-841/images/2017%20State%20of%20Embedded%20Analytics_Logi_final.pdf

Buxton, M., & Walton, N. (2014). The Internet as a small business e-commerce ecosystem. In E. Lacka, H. Chan & N. Yip (Eds.), E-commerce platform acceptance: Suppliers, retailers, and consumers (pp. 79-100). Cham: Springer. doi:10.1007/978-3-319-06121-4_5

Buytendijk, F., Geishecker, L., & Wood, B. (2004). *Magic Quadrant for CPM Suites*. Gartner Research.

Callow, M. N., Gobius, N., & Hetherington, G. (2005). Development of profitable milk production systems for northern Australia: An analysis of intensification of current systems. *AFBM Journal*, *2*, 24–37.

Camarinha-Matos, L. M. (2009). Collaborative networked organizations: Status and trends in manufacturing. *Annual Reviews in Control*, *33*(3), 199–208. doi:10.1016/j.arcontrol.2009.05.006

Camarinha-Matos, L. M., & Afsarmanesh, H. (2005). Collaborative networks: A new scientific discipline. In *Collaborative Networks and their Breeding Environments* (pp. 193–204). New York: Springer-Verlag. doi:10.1007/0-387-29360-4

Camarinha-Matos, L. M., & Afsarmanesh, H. (2005). Collaborative networks: A new scientific discipline. *Journal of Intelligent Manufacturing*, 4–5.

Camarinha-Matos, L. M., & Afsarmanesh, H. (2007). A comprehensive modeling framework for collaborative networked organizations. *Journal of Intelligent Manufacturing*, *18*(5), 529–542. doi:10.100710845-007-0063-3

Camarinha-Matos, L. M., & Afsarmanesh, H. (2008). On reference models for collaborative networked organizations. *International Journal of Production Research*, *46*(9), 2453–2469. doi:10.1080/00207540701737666

Camarinha-Matos, L. M., Afsarmanesh, H., Galeano, N., & Molina, A. (2009). Collaborative networked organizations - Concepts and practice in manufacturing enterprises. *Computers & Industrial Engineering*, *57*(1), 46–60. doi:10.1016/j.cie.2008.11.024

Camarinha-Matos, L. M., Afsarmanesh, H., & Ollus, M. (2005). *Virtual Organizations: Systems and Practices*. New York: Springer. doi:10.1007/b102339

Camarinha-Matos, L. M., Afsarmanesh, H., & Ollus, M. (2008). *Methods and Tools for Collaborative Networked Organizations*. New York: Springer. doi:10.1007/978-0-387-79424-2

Cameron, R., & Molina-Azorin, J. F. (2011). The acceptance of mixed methods in business and management research. *The International Journal of Organizational Analysis*, *19*(3), 256–270. doi:10.1108/19348831111149204

Canal, V. A. (2004). *ISM3 1.0. Information security management maturity model.* Retrieved from https://pdfs.semanticscholar.org/64ac/1e4585056babd78d978827bf35eae78b5ff6.pdf

Caralli, R. A., Allen, J. H., Curtis, P. D., White, D. W., & Young, L. R. (2010). *CERT® resilience management model, version 1.0: Improving operational resilience processes* (Technical report). Retrieved from http://www.sei.cmu.edu/reports/10tr012.pdf

Carlos, A., Gomez-Uribe, & Hunt, N. (2016). The Netflix recommender system: Algorithms, business value, and innovation. *ACM Transactions on Management Information Systems*, *6*(4).

Carson, D., Gilmore, A., Gronhaug, K., & Perry, C. (2001). *Qualitative Research in Marketing*. London: Sage. doi:10.4135/9781849209625

Carver, A., & Ritacco, M. (2006). *The Business Value of Business Intelligence – A Framework for Measuring the Benefits of Business Intelligence.* Business Objects.

Central Intelligence Agency. (2015). *The World Factbook.* Retrieved from Central Intelligence Agency: https://www.cia.gov/library/publications/the-world-factbook/fields/2012.html

Chae, B. (2014). A complexity theory approach to IT-enabled services (IESs) and service innovation: Business analytics as an illustration of IES. *Decision Support Systems*, *57*, 1–10. doi:10.1016/j.dss.2013.07.005

Chamoni, P., & Gluchowski, P. (2004). Integration trends in business intelligence systems: An empirical study based on the business intelligence maturity model. *Wirtschaftsinformatik*, *46*(2), 119–128. doi:10.1007/BF03250931

Chapman, P., Clinton, J., Kerber, R., Khabaza, T., Reinartz, T., Shearer, C., & Wirth, R. (2010). *CRISP-DM 1.0.* SPSS.

Charara, S. (2016, March 14). *Under Armour CEO: Data is the new oil.* Retrieved from Wareable: http://www.wareable.com/under-armour/under-armour-health-data-connected-fitness-sxsw-2453

Chary, M. (2007). *Public Organizations in the Age of Globalization and Technology.* Springer + Business Media, LLC.

Chataway, R. G., Walker, R. G., & Callow, M. N. (2010). Development of profitable milk production systems for northern Australia: A field assessment of the productivity of five potential farming systems using farmlets. *Australian Journal of Experimental Agriculture*, *50*, 246–264.

Chaudhry, S. S., Salchenberger, L., & Beheshtian, M. (1996). A small business inventory DSS: Design development, and implementation issues. *Computers & Operations*, *23*(1), 63–72. doi:10.1016/0305-0548(95)00004-6

Cheng, H., Lu, Y. C., & Sheu, C. (2009). An ontology-based business intelligence application in a financial knowledge management system. *Expert Systems with Applications*, *36*(2), 3614–3622. doi:10.1016/j.eswa.2008.02.047

Chen, J. Q., & Lee, S. M. (2003). An exploratory cognitive DSS for strategic decision making. *Decision Support Systems*, *36*(2), 147–160. doi:10.1016/S0167-9236(02)00139-2

Chen, L. D., Soliman, K. S., Mao, E., & Frolick, M. N. (2000). Measuring user satisfaction with data warehouses: An exploratory study. *Information & Management*, *37*(3), 103–110. doi:10.1016/S0378-7206(99)00042-7

Chenoweth, T., Corral, K., & Demirkan, H. (2006). Seven key interventions for data warehouse success. *Communications of the ACM*, *49*(1), 114–119. doi:10.1145/1107458.1107464

Chin, W. W., Gopal, A., & Salisbury, W. D. (1997). Advancing the theory of adaptive structuration: The development of a scale to measure faithfulness of appropriation. *Information Systems Research*, *8*(4), 342–367. doi:10.1287/isre.8.4.342

Chou, D. C., Tripuramallu, H. B., & Chou, A. Y. (2005). BI and ERP integration. *Information Management & Computer Security*, *13*(5), 340–349. doi:10.1108/09685220510627241

Clow, D. (2014). Data wranglers: human interpreters to help close the feedback loop. *Proceedings of the Fourth International Conference on Learning Analytics and Knowledge*. 10.1145/2567574.2567603

Comuzzi, M., & Patel, A. (2016). How organisations leverage big data: A maturity model. *Industrial Management & Data Systems*, *116*(8), 1468–1492. doi:10.1108/IMDS-12-2015-0495

Cooper, H., & Hedges, L. V. (1994). *The handbook of research synthesis*. New York, NY: Russell Sage Foundation.

Corrigan, G. (2015). Talent: Attracting, Retaining, and Growing a Critical Yet Scarce Resource. *Business Intelligence Journal*, 17-24.

Courbon, J.-C. (1996). User-centered DSS design and implementation. In P. Humphreys, L. Bannon, A. McCosh, P. Migliarese, & J.-C. Pomerol (Eds.), *Implementing systems for supporting management decisions: Concepts, methods, and experiences* (pp. 108–123). Boston, MA: Springer. doi:10.1007/978-0-387-34967-1_8

Cox, P. G. (1996). Some issues in the design of Agricultural Decision Support Systems. *Agricultural Systems*, *52*(2-3), 355–381. doi:10.1016/0308-521X(96)00063-7

Creswell, J. W. (2009). *Research Design. Qualitative, quantitative and mixed methods approaches* (3rd ed.). Thousand Oaks, CA: SAGE Publications, Inc.

Creswell, J. W. (2013). *Research design: Qualitative, quantitative, and mixed methods approaches*. Thousand Oaks, CA: Sage Publications Ltd.

Creswell, J. W., & Clark, V. L. (2007). *Designing and Conducting Mixed Methods Research*. Thousand Oaks, CA: Sage.

Crosby, P. B. (1979). *Quality is free*. New York, NY: McGraw-Hill.

Cullen, D. (2015). *The self-driving truck: The human factor*. Fleet Owner.

Cybenko, G., & Landwehr, C. E. (2012). Security analytics and measurements. *IEEE Security and Privacy*, *10*(3), 5–8. doi:10.1109/MSP.2012.75

Danesh, M. (2012). Design and implementation of a framework for process management in service oriented organizations using service zones. Ottawa: Academic Press.

Danesh, M. H., Raahemi, B., Kamali, S. M., & Richards, G. (2013). A framework for process and performance management in service oriented virtual organizations. *IJCISIM*, 203-215.

Danesh, M. H., Raahemi, B., & Kamali, M. A. (2011). A frameweork for process management in service oriented virtual organizations. *7th International Conference on Next Generation Web Services Practices*, 12-17.

Daniel, F., Casati, F., Palpanas, T., & Chayka, O. (2008). Managing Data Quality in Business Intelligence Applications. *Proceedings of the VLDB Endowment.*

Darby-Dowman, K., Barker, S., Audsley, E., & Parsons, D. (2000). A two-stage stochastic programming with resource model for determining robust planting plans in horticulture. *The Journal of the Operational Research Society*, *51*(1), 83–89. doi:10.1057/palgrave.jors.2600858

Darroch, J. (2005). Knowledge management, innovation and firm performance. *Journal of Knowledge Management, 9*(3), 101–115. doi:10.1108/13673270510602809

Davenport, T. (2013, December). Analytics 3.0. *Harvard Business Review*, 13.

Davenport, T. H., & Prusak, L. (1998). *Working knowledge: How organizations manage what they know*. Harvard Business School Press.

Davenport, T., Harris, J., & Cantrell, S. (2003). *The Return of Enterprise Solutions: The Director's Cut*. Accenture.

Davydov, M. (2001). *Corporate Portals and e-Business Integration*. New York: McGraw-Hill.

de Bruin, T., Rosemann, M., Freeze, R., & Kulkarni, U. (2005, November–December). *Understanding the main phases of developing a maturity assessment model*. Paper presented at the Australasian Conference on Information Systems (ACIS), Sydney, Australia.

De Wit, B., & Meyer, R. (2010). *Strategy process, content, context: An international perspective*. Cengage Learning EMEA.

DeAngelis, S. F. (2015). *Predictive Analytics becoming a Mainstream Business Tool*. Retrieved from https://www.enterrasolutions.com/blog/predictive-analytics-becoming-a-mainstream-business-tool/

Decker, J. (2017). *Embedded Analytics for Dummies*. John Wiley & Sons, Inc.

Defee, C., Hanna, J. B., & Overstreet, R. (2011, January). LTL Pricing: Looking Back to the Future. *Journal of Transportation Management, 22*(2), 45–58. Retrieved from https://www.researchgate.net/publication/256524025_LTL_pricing_Looking_back_to_the_future

Delen, D., & Demirkan, H. (2013). Data, information and analytics as services. *Decision Support Systems, 55*(1), 359–363. doi:10.1016/j.dss.2012.05.044

Delen, D., & Pratt, D. B. (2006). An Integrated and Intelligent DSS for Manufacturing Systems. *Expert Systems with Applications, 30*(2), 325–336. doi:10.1016/j.eswa.2005.07.017

Deloitte. (2013). *Global powers of retailing 2013 retail beyond*. Retrieved from http://www.deloitte.com/assets/DcomAustralia/Local%20Assets/Documents/Industries

Deloitte. (2014). *Cybersecurity: Empowering the CIO* (Report). Retrieved from https://www2.deloitte.com/au/en/pages/risk/articles/cyber-security.html

Demilia, B., Peded, M., Jorgensen, K., & Subramanian, R. (2012). The ethics of BI with private and public entities. *Communications of the IIMA, 12*(2), 13.

Dempsey, L., & Heery, R. (1998). Metadata: A Current View of Practice and Issues. *The Journal of Documentation, 54*(2), 145–172. doi:10.1108/EUM0000000007164

Denic, N., Vujovic, V., Filic, S., & Spasic, B. (2016). Analysis of key success factors for business intelligence systems implementation. *Fascicle of Management and Technological Engineering Structure, 42*, 30.

Dhanuka, V. (2016). *Hortonworks big data maturity model: The strategic path to accelerating business transformations* (White paper). Retrieved from http://hortonworks.com/wp-content/uploads/2016/04/Hortonworks-Big-Data-Maturity-Assessment.pdf

Diebold, F. X. (2012). *On the Origin(s) and Development of the Term "Big Data," PIER Working Paper 12-037*. Penn Institute for Economic Research, Department of Economics, University of Pennsylvania. Retrieved from https://economics.sas.upenn.edu/sites/economics.sas.upenn.edu/files/12-037.pdf

Dietz-Uhler, B., & Hurn, J. E. (2013). Using learning analytics to predict (and improve) student success: A faculty perspective. *Journal of Interactive Online Learning, 12*(1), 17–26.

Dobbins, J. (2000). *On a Generalized CSF Process Model for Critical Success Factors Identification and Analysis* (PhD Thesis). George Washington University.

Dresch, A., Lacerda, D. P., & Antunes, J. A. V. (2015). *Design science research: A method for science and technology advancement.* Springer International Publishing.

Dresner H. J., Buytendijk, F., Linden, A., Friedman, T., Strange, K. H., Knox, M., & Camm, M. (2002). *The business intelligence competency center: An essential business strategy.* Gartner Strategic Analysis Report.

Drucker, P. F. (1992). *Managing for the future.* Oxford, UK: Butterworth-Heinemann.

Duan, Y., & Xu, M. (2009). Decision Support Systems in Small Businesses. In Encyclopedia of information science and technology (2nd ed.). Hershey, PA: IGI Global. doi:10.4018/978-1-60566-026-4.ch155

Dubey, R., Gunasekaran, A., Childe, S. J., & Roubaud, D. (2017). Can Big Data and Predictive Analytics Improve Social and Environmental Sustainability? *Technological Forecasting and Social Change.*

Dulcic, Z., Pavlic, D., & Silic, I. (2012). Evaluating the Intended Use of Decision Support System (DSS) by Applying Technology Acceptance Model (TAM) in Business Organizations in Croatia. *Procedia: Social and Behavioral Sciences, 58*, 1565–1575. doi:10.1016/j.sbspro.2012.09.1143

Dwivedi, Y. K., Wastell, D., Laumer, S., Henriksen, H. Z., Myers, M. D., Bunker, D., & Srivastava, S. C. (2015). Research on information systems failures and successes: Status update and future directions. *Information Systems Frontiers, 17*(1), 143–157. doi:10.100710796-014-9500-y

Easterby-Smith, M., Thorpe, R., & Jackson, P. R. (2008). *Management Research: Theory and Research* (3rd ed.). London: SAGE Publications Ltd.

Eckerson, W. (2016). *Embedded Analytics: The Future of Business Intelligence.* Eckerson Group. Retrieved from https://www3.technologyevaluation.com/research/white-paper/embedded-analytics-the-future-of-business-intelligence.html

Eckerson, W. W. (2005). *The Keys to Enterprise Business Intelligence: Critical Success Factors.* TDWI Report.

Eckerson, W. (2005). *Performance Dashboards: Measuring, Monitoring, and Managing Your Business.* Wiley.

Eckerson, W. W. (2012). *Secrets of Analytical Leaders.* Technics Publications.

Eisenhardt, K. M. (1989). Building Theories from Case Study Research. *Academy of Management Review, 14*(4), 532–550.

Elbashir, M. Z., Collier, P., & Davern, M. (2008). Measuring the Effects of Business Intelligence Systems: The Relationship between Business Process and Organisational Performance. *International Journal of Accounting Information Systems, 9*(3), 135–153. doi:10.1016/j.accinf.2008.03.001

El-Darwiche, B., Koch, V., Meer, D., Shehadi, R., & Tohme, W. (2014). Big data maturity: An action plan for policymakers and executives. In B. Bilbao-Osorio, S. Dutta, & B. Lanvin (Eds.), *The global information technology report* (pp. 43–53). Geneva, Switzerland: World Economic Forum and INSEAD.

Elleff, S. A. (2004). Glue, grease and conduit. *The Journal of Commerce*, 17.

Elragal, A. (2014). ERP and Big Data: The Inept Couple. *Procedia Technology, 16*, 242–249. doi:10.1016/j.protcy.2014.10.089

Embassy Freight. (2016, October 30). *TEU (Twenty Foot Equivalent Unit)*. Retrieved from Logistics Glossary: http://www.logisticsglossary.com/term/teu/

Endler, M. (2014). iPad dominates enterprise tablet market. *InformationWeek*. Retrieved May 15 2016 from InformationWeek website: http://www.informationweek.com/mobile/mobile-devices/ipad-dominates-enterprise-tablet-market/d/d-id/1113813?piddl_msgpage=1#msgs

Eom, S. B. (2007). *The development of decision support systems research: A bibliometrical approach*. Lewiston, NY: Edwin Mellen Press.

ESCC. (2009). Overview: Business Intelligence Reference Guide. U.S. Army Enterprise Solutions Competency Center.

Evans, J. R. (2016). *Business Analytics: Methods, models, and decisions* (2nd ed.). Upper Saddle River, NJ: Pearson Education.

Evelson, B., & Bennett, M. (2015). Quantify Tangible Business Value of BI. *Forrester*. Retrieved from http://www.lavastorm.com/assets/2015-Forrester-Quantify-Tangible-Business-Value-of-BI.pdf

Farinha, J., Trigueiros, M. J., & Belo, O. (2009). Using inheritance in a metadata based approach to data quality assessment. *Proceedings of the first international workshop on Model driven service engineering and data quality and security*, 1-8. 10.1145/1651415.1651417

Fatemeh, M., & Connie, Z. (2009). A Decision-making Model to Choose Business Intelligence Platforms for Organizations. *Intelligent Information Technology Application, 2009. IITA 2009. Third International Symposium on*.

Federal Motor Carrier Safety Administration. (2014, December 18). *Summary of Hours of Service Regulations*. Retrieved 2016 7, February, from Federal Motor Carrier Safety Administration: https://www.fmcsa.dot.gov/regulations/hours-service/summary-hours-service-regulations

Federal Motor Carrier Safety Administration. (2016, November 11). *Summary of H ours of Service Regulations*. Retrieved from United States Department of Transportation: https://www.fmcsa.dot.gov/regulations/hours-service/summary-hours-service-regulations

Feki, M., Boughzala, I., & Wamba, S. F. (2016). Big Data Analytics-enabled Supply Chain Transformation: A Literature Review. *49th Hawaii International Conference on System Sciences*.

Feo, J. D., & Barnard, W. (2003). *Juran Institute Six Sigma Breakthrough and Beyond: Quality Performance and Breakthrough Methods*. McGraw-Hill Professional.

Ferguson, R., Clow, D., Macfadyen, L., Essa, A., Dawson, S., & Alexander, S. (2014). Setting learning analytics in context: overcoming the barriers to large-scale adoption. *Proceedings of the Fourth International Conference on Learning Analytics And Knowledge*. 10.1145/2567574.2567592

Fiammante, M. (2009). *Dynamic SOA and BPM: Best Practices for Business Process Management and SOA Agility*. IBM Press.

Fink, L., Yogev, N., & Even, A. (2017). Business intelligence and organizational learning: An empirical investigation of value creation processes. *Information & Management*, *54*(1), 38–56. doi:10.1016/j.im.2016.03.009

Finucane, B., Bange, C., Mack, M., Vierkorn, S., & Keller, P. (2010). *The BI Survey 9 - The Customer Verdict. Business Application Reserach Center*. BARC.

Firoz, N. M., & Ramin, T. (2004). Understanding Cultural Variables is Critical to Success in International Business. *International Journal of Management*, 307–323.

Fisher, C., Lauria, E., Chengalur-Smith, S., & Wang, R. (2006). *Introduction to Information Quality*. MIT Information Quality Program.

Folan, P., & Browne, J. (2005). A review of performance measurement: Towards performance management. *Computers in Industry*, *56*(7), 663–680. doi:10.1016/j.compind.2005.03.001

Fontaine, R. (2007). Cross-Cultural Management: Six perspectives. *Cross Cultural Management*, *14*(2), 125–135. doi:10.1108/13527600710745732

Foshay, N. (2005). *The Influence of End-User Metadata on User Attitudes toward, and Use of a Data Warehouse*. IBM, Somers.

Foshay, N., Mukherjee, A., & Taylor, A. (2007). Does Data Warehouse End-user Metadata Add Value? *Communications of the ACM*, *50*(11), 70–77. doi:10.1145/1297797.1297800

Foshay, N., Yeoh, W., Boo, Y. L., Ong, K.-L., & Mattie, D. (2015). A comprehensive diagnostic framework for evaluating business intelligence and analytics effectiveness. *AJIS. Australasian Journal of Information Systems*, 19.

France, H. (2013). *Case Study*. Yellowfin International Pty Ltd. Retrieved from https://portal.yellowfinbi.com/Document.i4?DocumentId=242108

Franco-Santos, M., Kennerley, M., Micheli, P., Martinez, V., Mason, S., Marr, B., ... Neely, A. (2007). Towards a definition of a business measurement system. *International Journal of Operations & Production Management*, *27*(8), 784–801. doi:10.1108/01443570710763778

Fraser, P., Moultrie, J., & Gregory, M. J. (2002). The use of maturity models/grids as a tool in assessing product development capability. *IEEE International Engineering Management Conference (IEMC 2002): Managing Technology for the New Economy*. 10.1109/IEMC.2002.1038431

Freedman, M. (2006). Information Visualization Brings Data into Shaper Focus. *Scientific Computing*, 24-25.

Friedman, T. (2002). *Longitudes & Attitudes*. Farrar, Straus & Grioux.

Friedman, T. L. (2000). *The Lexus and the Olive Tree*. New York, NY: Farrar, Staus, and Giroux.

Fueglistaller, U., Frey, U., Halter, F., & Hartl, R. (2005). Unternehmensführung 3 – Der Strategiefindungsprozess– Vorgehensmethodik zur Erarbeitung einer Strategie in vier Schritten. Study booklet of Europäische Fernhochschule Hamburg. UNFÜ 3/H, Hamburg.

Fujimoto, Y., Bahfen, N., Fermelis, J., & Härtel, C. E. J. (2007). The global village: Online cross-cultural communication and HRM. *Cross Cultural Management*, *14*(1), 7–22. doi:10.1108/13527600710718804

Gaitho, M. (2017). How Applications of Big Data Drive Industries. *SimpliLearn*. Retrieved from https://www.simplilearn.com/big-data-applications-in-industries-article

Gangadharan, G. R., & Swamy, N. S. (2004). Business intelligence systems: design and implementation strategies. *Proceedings of 26th International Conference on Information Technology Interfaces*. Available at: http://ieeexplore.ieee.org/

Gangadharan, G., & Swami, S. N. (2004). Business intelligence systems: design and implementation strategies. *Information Technology Interfaces, 2004. 26th International Conference on*, 139-144.

Gansor, T., Totok, A., & Stock, S. (2010). *Von der Strategie zum Business Intelligence Competency Center (BICC) – Konzeption, Betrieb, Praxis* (1st ed.). Munich: Hanser; doi:10.3139/9783446424869

Gao, J., Lin, S., & Koronios, A. (2006). Data Quality in Engineering Asset Management Organizations – Current Picture in Australia. *Proceedings of 1st World Congress on Engineering Asset Management.*

Garter. (2018). *IT Glossary*. Retrieved from https://www.gartner.com/it-glossary/business-intelligence-bi/

Gartner I. T. Glossary. (2018). *Embedded Analytics*. Retrieved from https://www.gartner.com/it-glossary/embedded-analytics

Gartner Press Release. (2013a). *Gartner Executive Program Survey of More Than 2,000 CIOs Shows Digital Technologies Are Top Priorities in 2013*. Retrieved from http://www.gartner.com/newsroom/id/2304615

Gartner Press Release. (2013b). *Gartner Says Worldwide Business Intelligence Software Revenue to Grow 7 Percent in 2013*. Retrieved from http://www.gartner.com/newsroom/id/2340216

Gartner Report. (2015). Retrieved from http://www.gartner.com/newsroom/id/3130817

Gartner. (2011, April 20). *Gartner says worldwide business intelligence, analytics and performance management software market surpassed the $10 billion mark in 2010*. Retrieved from https://www.gartner.com/newsroom/id/1642714

Gartner. (2014). *Flipping to Digital Leadership: The 2015 CIO Agenda*. Gartner.

Gartner. (2015). *Gartner Executive Program Survey of More Than 2,000 CIOs Shows Digital Technologies Are Top Priorities in 2013*. Stamford, CT: Author.

Gartner. (2016, October 17). *Gartner survey of more than 2,500 CIOs charts the rise of the digital ecosystem* [Press release]. Retrieved from https://www.gartner.com/newsroom/id/3481117

Gartner. (2017). *Gartner forecasts flat worldwide device shipments until 2018*. Retrieved June 19 2017 from Gartner Newsroom website: http://www.gartner.com/newsroom/id/3560517

Gebauer, J., & Shaw, M. J. (2004). Success factors and impacts of mobile business applications: Results from a mobile e-procurement study. *International Journal of Electronic Commerce*, *8*(3), 19–41.

Gebauer, J., Shaw, M. J., & Gribbins, M. L. (2010). Task-technology fit for mobile information systems. *Journal of Information Technology*, *25*(3), 259–272. doi:10.1057/jit.2010.10

Germonprez, M., Hovorka, D., & Collopy, F. (2007). A theory of Tailorable Technology Design. *Journal of the Association for Information Systems*, *8*(6), 351–367. doi:10.17705/1jais.00131

Germonprez, M., Hovorka, D., & Gal, U. (2011). Secondary Design: A Case of Behavioral Design Science research. *Journal of the Association for Information Systems*, *12*(10), 662–683. doi:10.17705/1jais.00278

Gets, J., & Reinsel, D. (2013). *The Digital Universe in 2020*. IDC.

Ghazanfari, M., Jafari, M., & Rouhani, S. (2011). A tool to evaluate the business intelligence of enterprise systems. *Scientia Iranica*, *18*(6), 1579–1590. doi:10.1016/j.scient.2011.11.011

Gibson, M., Arnott, D., & Carlsson, S. (2004). Evaluating the Intangible Benefits of Business Intelligence: Review & Research Agenda. *Proceeding of the Decision Support in an Uncertain and Complex World: The IFIP TC8/WG8.3 International Conference*, 295-305.

Gibson, M., Arnott, D., & Carlsson, S. (2004). Evaluating the Intangible Benefits of Business Intelligence: Review & Research Agenda. *Proceedings of the Decision Support in an Uncertain and Complex World: The IFIP TC8/WG8.3 International Conference*, 295-305.

Gibson, C., & Nolan, R. (1974). Managing the four stages of EDP growth. *Harvard Business Review*, *1*, 76–88.

Gile, K. (2003). *Success Factors for Implementing Enterprise Business Intelligence.* International User Conference. Business Objects.

Gonzales, M. (2011). Success Factors for Business Intelligence and Data Warehousing Maturity and Competitive Advantage. *Business Intelligence Journal, 16*(1), 22–29.

Gordijn, J., & Akkermans, J. M. (2003). Value-based requirements engineering: Exploring innovative e-commerce ideas. *Requirements Engineering*, 114–134.

Gottschalk, P., & Solli-Sæther, H. (2006). Maturity model for IT outsourcing relationships. *Industrial Management & Data Systems, 106*(2), 200–212. doi:10.1108/02635570610649853

Graser, F., Jansson, K., Eschenbacher, J., Westphal, I., & Negretto, U. (2005). Towards Performance Measurement in Virtual Organizations. In *Collaborative Networks and Their Breeding Environments* (pp. 301–310). New York: Springer-Verlag. doi:10.1007/0-387-29360-4_31

Graser, F., Westphal, I., & Eschenbaecher, J. (2005). *Roadmap on VOPM challenges on operational and strategic level.* ECOLEAD.

Gray, D. E. (2009). *Doing Research in the Real World* (2nd ed.). London: SAGE Publications Ltd.

Grenier, L. (2013). *The Evolving Role of Data in Decision-making. Economist Intelligence Unit.* London, UK: EIU.

Grossmann, W., & Rinderle-Ma, S. (2015). *Fundamentals of Business Intelligence, Data-Centric Systems and Applications.* Springer. doi:10.1007/978-3-662-46531-8

Grover, V., & Goslar, M. (1993). Toward an empirical taxonomy and model of evolution for telecommunications technologies. *Journal of Information Technology, 8*(3), 167–176. doi:10.1057/jit.1993.23

Grublješič, T., & Jaklič, J. (2014). Three Dimensions of Business Intelligence Systems Use Behavior. *International Journal of Enterprise Information Systems, 10*(3), 62–76. doi:10.4018/ijeis.2014070105

Guarda, T., Santos, M., Pinto, F., Augusto, M., & Silva, C. (2013). Business Intelligence as a Competitive Advantage for SMEs. *International Journal of Trade. Economics and Finance, 4*(4), 187–190.

Gulliksen, J., Göransson, B., Boivie, I., Blomkvist, S., Persson, J., & Cajander, Å. (2005). Key principles for user-centred systems design. In A. Seffah, J. Gulliksen, & M. C. Desmarais (Eds.), *Human-centered software engineering: Integrating usability in the software development lifecycle* (Vol. 8, pp. 17–36). Springer. doi:10.1007/1-4020-4113-6_2

Gupta, P., Seetharaman, A., & Raj, J. R. (2013). The usage and adoption of cloud computing by small and medium businesses. *International Journal of Information Management, 33*(5), 861–874. doi:10.1016/j.ijinfomgt.2013.07.001

Gutierrez, B., Spencer, S. M., & Zhu, G. (2012). Thinking globally. leading locally: Chinese, Indian, and Western leadership. *Cross Cultural Management, 19*(1), 67–89. doi:10.1108/13527601211195637

Haag, S., & Cummings, M. (2009). *Information systems essentials.* New York: McGraw Hill/Irwin.

Hackathorn, R. (2005). Ethics in business intelligence, A practical approach. *TERADATA*. Retrieved from http://online7.net/download/696

Haghighi, D. P., Burstein, F., Zaslavsky, A., & Arbon, P. (2013). Development and evaluation of ontology for intelligent decision support in medical emergency management for mass gatherings. *Decision Support Systems, 54*(2), 1192–1204. doi:10.1016/j.dss.2012.11.013

Hall, M. (2006). *Knowledge management and the limits of knowledge codification.* Academic Press.

Hall. (1976). *Beyond Culture.* New York, NY: Anchor Press/Doubleday.

Hall, D. J. (2008). *Decision makers and their need for support. In Handbook on decision support systems 1: Basic theme* (Vol. 1, pp. 83–102). Berlin: Springer. doi:10.1007/978-3-540-48713-5_5

Hall, M. (2006, May). Knowledge management and the limits of knowledge codification. *Journal of Knowledge Management, 10*(3), 117–126. doi:10.1108/13673270610670894

Halper, F., & Krishnan, K. (2013). *TDWI big data maturity model guide: Interpreting your assessment score* (Benchmark guide). Retrieved from http://www.pentaho.com/sites/default/files/uploads/resources/tdwi_big_data_maturity_model_guide_2013.pdf

Hammami, S., & Alkhaldi, F. M. (2012). *Enhancing BI Systems Application Through the Integration of IT Governance and Knowledge Capabilities of the Organization. In Business Intelligence and Agile Methodologies for Knowledge-Based Organizations: Cross-Disciplinary Applications* (pp. 161–182). IGI Global.

Hanafizadeh, P., & Ravasan, A. Z. (2011). A McKinsey 7S model-based framework for ERP readiness assessment. *International Journal of Enterprise Information Systems, 7*(4), 23–63. doi:10.4018/jeis.2011100103

Haq, I., & Schikuta, E. (2010). Aggregation patterns of service level agreements. *8th International Conference on Frontiers of Information Technology*, 1-40.

Harris, D. (2017). A Guide to Embedded Analytics: Use Cases and Benefits. *Software Advice.* Retrieved from https://www.softwareadvice.com/resources/embedded-analytics-definition-and-examples/#benefits

Harris, J., & Davenport, T. (2006). *New Growth From Enterprise Systems.* Accenture.

Harris, J., Ives, B., & Junglas, I. (2012). IT consumerization: When gadgets turn into enterprise IT tools. *MIS Quarterly Executive, 11*(3), 99–112.

Harrison, E. (2012). Critical Success Factors of Business Intelligence System Implementations: Evidence from the Energy Sector. *International Journal of Enterprise Information Systems, 8*(2), 1–13. doi:10.4018/jeis.2012040101

Hasson, F., Keeney, S., & McKenna, H. (2000). Research guidelines for the Delphi survey technique. *Journal of Advanced Nursing, 32*(4), 1008–1015. PMID:11095242

Hawking, P., & Sellitto, C. (2010). Business Intelligence (BI) Critical Success Factors (2010). *ACIS 2010 Proceedings.* Retrieved from http://aisel.aisnet.org/acis2010/4

Hawking, P., & Sellitto, C. (2010). Business Intelligence (BI) Critical Success Factors. *ACIS 2010 Proceedings*, 4. Retrieved from https://aisel.aisnet.org/acis2010/4

Hawking, P., Jovanovic, R., & Sellitto, C. (2011). Business Intelligence Maturity in Australia. *Proceedings of the Americas Conference of Information Systems (AMCIS).*

Hawking, P., & Sellitto, C. (2015). Business Intelligence Strategy: A Utilities Company Case Study. *International Journal of Enterprise Information Systems, 11*(1), 1–12. doi:10.4018/ijeis.2015010101

Hawking, P., & Sellitto, C. (2017). Business Intelligence Strategy: Two case Studies. *International Journal of Business Intelligence Research, 8*(2), 17–30. doi:10.4018/IJBIR.2017070102

Hayden, L. (2010). *IT security metrics: A practical framework for measuring security & protecting data.* New York, NY: McGraw-Hill Education.

Hayman, P. T., & Easdown, W. J. (2002). An ecology of a DSS: Reflections on managing wheat crops in the North-eastern Australian grains region with WHEATMAN. *Agricultural Systems*, *74*(1), 57–77. doi:10.1016/S0308-521X(02)00018-5

He, F.-b., & Chang, J. (2014). Combined forecasting of regional logistics demand optimized by genetic algorithm. *Grey Systems: Theory and Application.*

Hedgebeth, D. (2007). Data-driven decision making for the enterprise: An overview of business intelligence applications. *Vine*, *37*(4), 414–420. doi:10.1108/03055720710838498

Heikkila, J., Saariner, T., & Saaksjarvi, M. (1991). Success of software packages in small business: An exploratory study. *European Journal of Information Systems*, *1*(3), 159–169. doi:10.1057/ejis.1991.31

Hemmatfar, M., Salehi, M., & Bayat, M. (2010). Competitive Advantage and Strategic Information Systems. *International Journal of Business and Management*, *5*(7), 158–169. doi:10.5539/ijbm.v5n7p158

Henke, N., Bughin, J., Chui, M., Manyika, J., Saleh, T., Wiseman, B., & Sethupathy, G. (2016). *The Age of Analytics: Competing in a Data-Driven World.* McKinsey Global Institute.

Henke, N.,Bughin, J., Chui, M., Manyika, J., Saleh, T., Wiseman, B., & Sethupathy, G. (2016). *The Age of Analytics: Competing in a Data-Driven World.* McKinsey Global Institute.

Herschel, R. T., & Jones, N. E. (2005). Knowledge management and business intelligence: The importance of integration. *Journal of Knowledge Management*, *9*(4), 45–55. doi:10.1108/13673270510610323

Hevner, A. R., March, S. T., Park, J., & Ram, S. (2004). Design Science in Information Systems Research. *Management Information Systems Quarterly*, *28*(1), 75–105. doi:10.2307/25148625

Hevner, A., & Chatterjee, S. (2010). *Design Research in Information Systems: Theory and Practice*. New York: Springer. doi:10.1007/978-1-4419-5653-8

Hirsimäki, R. (2017). *Critical success factors for business intelligence system implementation* (Bachelor's thesis). Jyväskylä: University of Jyväskylä.

Hofstede, G., & Hofstede, G. (2005). Cultures and Organizations: Software of the Mind (2nd ed.). New York, NY: McGraw-Hill.

Hofstede, G. (1980). *International Differences in Work-Related Values*. Beverly Hills, CA.

Hofstede, G., Hofstede, G. J., & Minkov, M. (2010). *Cultures and Organizations: Software of the Mind*. McGraw-Hill.

Hosack, B., Hall, D., Paradice, D., & Courtney, J. F. (2012). A Look Toward the Future: Decision Support Systems Research is Alive and Well. *Journal of the Association for Information Systems*, *13*(5), 315–340. doi:10.17705/1jais.00297

Hostmann, B., Rayner, N., & Friedman, T. (2006). *Gartner's Business Intelligence and Performance Management Framework*. Stamford, CT: Gartner.

House, R. J., Hanges, P. J., Javidan, M., Dorfman, P. W., & Gupta, V. (2004). *Culture, Leadership and Organizations The Globe Study of 62 Societies*. Thousand Oaks, CA: Sage.

Howson, C. (2011). *Despite Successes, BI Adoption is Flat*. Retrieved from http://www.informationweek.com/news/software/bi/231902636

Howson, C. (2006). Seven Pillars of BI Success: BI tools may be getting better, but technology is only part of the story. *Intelligent Enterprise-San Mateo*, *9*(9), 33.

Howson, C. (2007). *Successful Business Intelligence: Secrets to Making BI a Killer App*. McGraw-Hill Professional.

Howson, C. (2008). *Successful Business Intelligence*. Editorial Mc Graw Hill.

Hughes, N. (2013). *Apple has sold 170M iPads to date, implying sales near 15M in September quarter*. Retrieved May 15 2016 from AppleInsider website: http://appleinsider.com/articles/13/10/23/apple-has-sold-170m-ipads-to-date-implying-sales-near-15m-in-sept-quarter

Hult, G., Tomas, M., Ketchen, D. J. Jr, Griffith, D. A., Finnegan, C. A., Gonzalez-Padron, T., ... Cavusgil, S. T. (2008). Data equivalence in cross-cultural international business research: Assessment and guidelines. *Journal of International Business Studies*, *39*(6), 1027–1044. doi:10.1057/palgrave.jibs.8400396

Humphrey, W. S. (1988). Characterizing the software process: A maturity framework. *IEEE Software*, *5*(2), 73–79. doi:10.1109/52.2014

Hunt, K. A., & Hodkin, W. (2012). The Criticality of Cultural Awareness in Global Marketing: Some Case Examples. *Journal of Business Case Studies*.

Hurley, R. F., & Hult, G. T. M. (1998). Innovation, market orientation, and organizational learning: An integration and empirical examination. *Journal of Marketing*, *62*(3), 42–54. doi:10.2307/1251742

Hwang, M. I., & Xu, H. (2005). A survey of data warehousing success issues. *Business Intelligence Journal, 10*(4), 7.

Hwang, H. G., Ku, C. Y., Yen, D. V., & Cheng, C. C. (2004). Critical factors influencing the adoption of data warehouse technology: A study of the banking industry in Taiwan. *Decision Support Systems*, *37*(1), 1–21. doi:10.1016/S0167-9236(02)00191-4

IDC. (2013). *Big data maturity tool*. Retrieved from http://csc.bigdatamaturity.com/

IDC. (2017). *Worldwide Semiannual Big Data and Analytics Spending Guide*. Retrieved from https://www.idc.com/getdoc.jsp?containerId=prUS42371417

Iivari, J., & Iivari, N. (2011). Varieties of user-centredness: An analysis of four systems development methods. *Information Systems Journal*, *21*(2), 125–153. doi:10.1111/j.1365-2575.2010.00351.x

Info-Tech. (2013). *Big data maturity assessment tool*. Retrieved from https://www.infotech.com/research/ss/leverage-big-data-by-starting-small/it-big-data-maturity-assessment-tool

Inmon, W. H. (2002). *Building the Data Warehouse*. J Wiley.

Inmon, W., O'Neil, B., & Fryman, L. (2008). *Business Metadata - Capturing Enterprise Knowledge*. Burlington, VT: Morgan Kaufmann.

Intel. (2017). *Guide to Getting Started with Advanced Analytics*. Intel Planning Guide. Retrieved from https://www.intel.com/content/www/us/en/analytics/getting-started-advanced-analytics-planning-guide.html

Ioimo, R. E., & Aronson, J. E. (2004). Police field mobile computing: Applying the theory of Task-Technology Fit. *Police Quarterly*, *7*(4), 403–428. doi:10.1177/1098611103251113

Irani, Z., & Love, P. (2008). *Evaluating Information Systems in the Public and Private Sectors*. Oxford, UK: Elsevier.

Irvine, B., Richardson, D., Fear, J., & Denniss, R. (2011). *The rise and rise of online retail. Technical Brief (8)*. Canberra, Australia: The Australia Institute.

Ishikiriyama, C. S., Miro, D., & Gomes, C. F. S. (2015). Text Mining Business Intelligence: A small sample of what words can say. *Procedia Computer Science*, *55*, 261–267. doi:10.1016/j.procs.2015.07.044

Işık, Ö., Jones, M. C., & Sidorova, A. (2012). Business Intelligence Success: The Role of BI Capabilities and Decision Environment. *Information & Management*.

Işık, Ö., Jones, M. C., & Sidorova, A. (2013). Business intelligence success: The roles of BI capabilities and decision environments. *Information & Management*, *50*(1), 13–23.

Isik, O., Jones, M., & Sidorova, A. (2013). Business intelligence success: The roles of BI capabilities and decision environments. *Information & Management*, *50*(1), 13–23. doi:10.1016/j.im.2012.12.001

Jafartarokha, M., & Teymournejada, E. (2012). Using Association Rules for Evaluating and Predicting Risk Factors in Business Intelligence System. *Business Intelligence Journal*, *5*(2), 383.

Jagielska, I., Darke, P., & Zagari, G. (2003). Business Intelligence systems for decision support: Concepts, processes and practice. *Conference of the International Society for Decision Support Systems*, 215-228.

Jahromi, A. T., Stakhovych, S., & Ewing, M. (2015). Customer Churn Models: A Comparison of Probability and Data Mining Approaches. *Proceedings of the 2013 World Marketing Congress*.

Jameson, K. A. (2005). Culture and Cognition: What is Universal about the Representation of Color Experience? *Journal of Cognition and Culture*, 294–347.

Jarke, M., Jeusfeld, M. A., Quix, C., & Vassiliadis, P. (1999). Architecture and quality in data warehouses: An extended repository approach. *Information Systems*, *24*(3), 229–253. doi:10.1016/S0306-4379(99)00017-4

Jegede, A. E. (2016). Modern information technology, global risk, and the challenges of crime in the era of late modernity. In O. Nelson, B. R. Ojebuyi, & A. Salawu (Eds.), *Impacts of the Media on African Socio-Economic Development* (pp. 18–33). Hershey, PA: IGI Global.

Jiang, Y. (2013). Business Negotiation Culture in China. *International Business Research*, 109–116.

John, R., & Schermerhorn, J. (2008). *Management* (9th ed.). John Wiley & Sons, Inc.

Johnson, C., Badger, L., Waltermire, D., Snyder, J., & Skorupka, C. (2016). *Guide to cyber threat information sharing* (Special publication). Retrieved from http://nvlpubs.nist.gov/nistpubs/SpecialPublications/NIST.SP.800-150.pdf

Johnson, L.K. (2004). Strategies for Data Warehousing. *MIT Sloan Management Review, 45*(3), 9.

Johnson, M., & Johnson, L. (2010). *Generation Inc - From Boomers to Linsters - Managing the Friction Between Generations at Work*. American Management Association.

Johnson, W., Brett, C. E., & Deary, I. J. (2010). The pivotal role of education in the association between ability and social class attainment: A look across three generations. *Intelligence*, *38*(1), 55–65. doi:10.1016/j.intell.2009.11.008

Jonasson, C., & Lauring, J. (2012). Cultural differences in use: the power to essentialize communication styles. *Journal of Communication Management*, 405-419.

Jones, C. (2007). *Institutional repositories: content and culture in an open access environment*. Elsevier. doi:10.1533/9781780631110

Jongsawas, C. (2016). Managing big data in coal-fired power plants: A business intelligence framework. *Industrial Management & Data Systems*, *116*(8), 1779–1799. doi:10.1108/IMDS-11-2015-0473

Jourdan, Z., Rainer, R. K., & Marshall, T. E. (2012). Business Intelligence: An Analysis of the Literature. *Information Systems Management*, *25*(2), 121–131. doi:10.1080/10580530801941512

Jr, L., Grover, R., & Gibson, M. L. (2003). Perceived influences on implementing data warehousing. *IEEE Transactions on Software Engineering*, *29*(4), 290–296. doi:10.1109/TSE.2003.1191794

Kalakota, R. (2014). A Primer on Predictive Analytics. *inShare3*. Retrieved from https://practicalanalytics.co/predictive-analytics-101/

Kalkan, V. D. (2008). An overall view of knowledge management challenges for global business. *Business Process Management Journal*, *14*(3), 390–400.

Kalkan, V. D. (2008). An overall view of knowledge management challenges for global business. *Business Process Management Journal*, *14*(3), 390–400. doi:10.1108/14637150810876689

Kamali, S. M., Richards, G., Danesh, M. H., & Raahemi, B. (2012). A framework for performance measurement in service oriented virtual organizations: A value network approach to collaborative performance measurement. SciTePress.

Kannan, S. (2016). *Perspectives on knowledge retention and loss from expert attrition – An organisational case study* (Thesis). Melbourne, Australia.

Kaplan, A. M., & Haenlein, M. (2016). Higher education and the digital revolution: About MOOCs, SPOCs, social media, and the Cookie Monster. *Business Horizons*, *59*(4), 441–450. doi:10.1016/j.bushor.2016.03.008

Kaplan, R. S., & Norton, D. P. (1992, January). The balanced scorecard: Measures that drive performance. *Harvard Business Review*, 71–80. PMID:10119714

Karlson, A. K., Meyers, B. R., Jacobs, A., Johns, P., & Kane, S. K. (2009). Working overtime: Patterns of smartphone and PC usage in the day of an information worker. In H. Tokuda, M. Beigl, A. Friday, A. J. B. Brush, & Y. Tobe (Eds.), *Pervasive Computing* (pp. 398–405). Redmond, WA: Springer. doi:10.1007/978-3-642-01516-8_27

Karvonen, I., Salkari, I., & Ollus, M. (2005). *Collaborative Networks and their Breeding Environments*. New York: Springer-Verlag. doi:10.1007/0-387-29360-4_20

Keen, P. G., & Scott, M. (1978). *Decision support systems: An organisational perspective*. Addison-Wesley.

Kelly, J., & Schrape, J. (2010). 100 days with an iPad: Lessons learnt and apps acquired. In Curriculum, Technology & Transformation for an Unknown Future, Sydney, Australia.

Keniry, J., Blums, A., Notter, E., Radford, E., & Thomson, S. (2003). *Regional business – a plan for action*. Department of Transport and Regional Services. Available at: www.rbda.gov.au/action_plan

Kerr, D. V. (2004). Factors influencing the development and adoption of knowledge based decision support systems for small, owner operated rural businesses. *Artificial Intelligence Review*, *22*(2), 127–147. doi:10.1023/B:AIRE.0000045503.74951.7a

Kersten, W. (2008). *Global Logistics Management: Sustainability, Quality, Risks*. Berlin, Germany: Erich Schmidt Verlag GmbH & Co KG.

Khan, E. H., & Khan, G. M. (1992). Microcomperters and small business in Bahrain. *Industrial Management & Data Systems*, *92*(6), 297–304. doi:10.1108/02635579210015400

Khatri, V., & Brown, C. V. (2010). Designing data governance. *Communications of the ACM*, *53*(1), 148–152. doi:10.1145/1629175.1629210

Kim, H.-W., Lee, G.-H., & Pan, S. L. (2002). *Exploring the Critical Success Factors for Customer Relationship Management and Electronic Customer Relationship Management Systems*. Paper presented at the ICIS.

Kimball, R., Ross, M., Thornthwaite, W., Mundy, J., & Becker, B. (2008). *The Data Warehouse Lifecycle Toolkit: Practical Techniques for Building Data Warehouse and Business Intelligence Systems* (2nd ed.). John Wiley & Sons.

Kim, S. H. (2008). Moderating effects of job relevance and experience on mobile wireless technology acceptance: Adoption of a smartphone by individuals. *Information & Management*, *45*(6), 387–393. doi:10.1016/j.im.2008.05.002

Kirca, A. H., & Yaprak, A. (2010). The use of meta-analysis in international business research: Its current status and suggestions for better practice. *International Business Review*, *19*(3), 306–314. doi:10.1016/j.ibusrev.2010.01.001

Kitroeff, N. (2016). *Robots could replace 1.7 million American truckers in the next decade*. Retrieved from Los Angeles Times: http://www.latimes.com/projects/la-fi-automated-trucks-labor-20160924/

Klein, M., & Methlie, L. B. (1995). *Knowledge-based decision support systems with applications in business*. West Sussex, UK: John Wiley & Sons Ltd.

Klynveld Peat Marwick Goerdeler. (2009). *Does your business intelligence tell you the whole story?* Academic Press.

Knightsbridge. (2006). *Getting Smart About BI: Best Practices Deliver Real Value*. BusinessWeek Research Services.

Knowledgent. (2014). *Big data maturity assessment*. Retrieved from https://bigdatamaturity.knowledgent.com/

Kort, C., & Gordijn, J. (2007). *Handbook of Ontologies for Business Interaction*. IGI Global.

Kotter, J. P. (1982). *The general managers*. New York: Free Press.

Koushik, R. (2011). Analyze This! Analytics Explained and Applied. *Capgemini*. Retrieved from https://www.capgemini.com/gb-en/2011/05/analyse-this-analytics-explained-and-applied/

Krechmer, D., Perry, N., Destro, L., & Gallaher, S. (2012). *Weather Delay Costs to Trucking. Cambridge Systematics & FTR Associates*. Washington, DC: U.S. Department of Transportation.

Krippendorff, K. (2004). *Content Analysis: An Introduction to its Methodology*. Beverly Hills, CA: Sage Publications.

Kroenke, D., Bunker, D., & Wilson, D. (2014). *Experiencing MIS*. Pearson Australia.

Kuhlmann, F., & Brodersen, C. (2001). Information technology and farm management: Developments and perspectives. *Computers and Electronics in Agriculture*, *30*(1-3), 71–83. doi:10.1016/S0168-1699(00)00157-5

Kwee-Fah, L. (2016). Towards addressing persistent risk perceptions in online shopping. *Skyline Business Journal*, *12*(1), 1–10.

Lacka, E., Chan, H. K., & Yip, N. (2014). *E-commerce platform acceptance: Suppliers, retailers, and consumers*. Dordrecht: Springer International Publishing. doi:10.1007/978-3-319-06121-4

Lahrmann, G., Marx, F., Winter, R., & Wortmann, F. (2011). Business intelligence maturity: Development and evaluation of a theoretical model. In *44th Hawaii International Conference on* (pp. 1–10). IEEE.

Lahrmann, G., Marx, F., Winter, R., & Wortmann, F. (2010). Business intelligence maturity models: An overview. *Proceedings of the VII Conference of the Italian Chapter of AIS*.

Lahrmann, G., Marx, F., Winter, R., & Wortmann, F. (2011). Business Intelligence Maturity: Development and Evaluation of a Theoretical Model. *Proceedings of HICSS*. 10.1109/HICSS.2011.90

Lahtinen, M., & Weaver, B. (2015). *Educating for a digital future–Walking three roads simultaneously: one analog and two digital.* Paper presented at the Lunds universitets utvecklingskonferens, 2015.

Lainhart, J. W. IV. (2000). COBIT™: A methodology for managing and controlling information and information technology risks and vulnerabilities. *Journal of Information Systems*, *14*(Suppl. 1), 21–25. doi:10.2308/jis.2000.14.s-1.21

Lambert, D. M., Garcia-Dastugue, S. J., & Croxton, K. L. (2008). The Role of Logistics Managers in the Cross-Functional Implementation of Supply Chain Management. *Journal of Business Logistics*, *29*(1), 113–132. doi:10.1002/j.2158-1592.2008.tb00071.x

Larson, D., & Chang, V. (2016). A review and future direction of agile, business intelligence, analytics and data science. *International Journal of Information Management*, *36*(5), 700–710. doi:10.1016/j.ijinfomgt.2016.04.013

Lau, D. C., & Murnighan, J. K. (1998). Demographic Diversity and Faultlines: The Compositional Dynamics of Organizational Groups. *Academy of Management Review*, 325–340.

Lauring, J., & Selmer, J. (2012). Knowledge sharing in diverse organisations. *Human Resource Management Journal*, *22*(1), 89–105. doi:10.1111/j.1748-8583.2010.00158.x

Lebied, M. (2016). Top 11 Business Intelligence and Analytics Trends for 2017. *Business Intelligence*. Retrieved from http://www.datapine.com/blog/business-intelligence-trends-2017/

Lessing, M. M. (2008, September). *Best practices show the way to information security maturity*. Paper presented at the 6th National Conference on Process Establishment, Assessment and Improvement in Information Technology (ImproveIT 2008), Johannesburg, South Africa.

Leukel, J., Mueller, M., & Sugumaran, V. (2014). *The state of design science research within the BISE community: An empirical investigation.* Paper presented at the 35th International Conference on Information Systems (ICIS 2014), Auckland, New Zealand. Retrieved from https://www.researchgate.net/publication/289595575

Liang, T.-P., Huang, C.-W., Yeh, Y.-H., & Lin, B. (2007). Adoption of mobile technology in business: A fit-viability model. *Industrial Management & Data Systems*, *107*(8), 1154–1169. doi:10.1108/02635570710822796

Lincoln, Y. S., & Guba, E. G. (1985). *Naturalistic inquiry*. Newbury Park, CA: Sage.

Lin, H. W., Nagalingam, S. V., Kuik, S. S., & Murata, T. (2012). Design of a Global Decision Support System for a manufacturing SME: Towards participating in Collaborative Manufacturing. *International Journal of Production Economics*, *136*(1), 1–12. doi:10.1016/j.ijpe.2011.07.001

Linstone, H. A., & Turoff, M. (2002). *Delphi method: Techniques and applications*. Addison-Wesley.

Li, S.-T., Shue, L.-Y., & Lee, S.-F. (2008). Business intelligence approach to supporting strategy-making of ISP service management. *Expert Systems with Applications*, *35*(3), 739–754. doi:10.1016/j.eswa.2007.07.049

Little, J. D. (2004). Models and managers: The concept of decision calculus. *Management Science*, *50*(12), 1841–1853. doi:10.1287/mnsc.1040.0267

Li, X., & Putterill, M. (2007). Strategy implications of business culture differences between Japan and China. *Business Strategy Series*, *8*(2), 148–154. doi:10.1108/17515630710685212

Li, X., Zhu, Z., & Pan, X. (2010). Knowledge cultivating for intelligent decision making in small & middle businesses. *Procedia Computer Science*, *1*(1), 2479–2488. doi:10.1016/j.procs.2010.04.280

Li, Y., & Osei-Bryson, K.-M. (2010). Quality factory and quality notification service in data warehouse. *Proceedings of the 3rd workshop on information and knowledge management*, 25-32. 10.1145/1871902.1871907

Long, J. (2008). *ITIL Version 3 at a Glance*. New York: Springer.

Lönnqvist, A., & Pirttimäki, V. (2006). The Measurement of Business Intelligence. *Information Systems Management Journal*, *23*(1), 32–40. doi:10.1201/1078.10580530/45769.23.1.20061201/91770.4

Loshin, D. (2017). *Five Steps to Build Better Predictive Analytics Applications*. Retrieved from http://searchbusinessanalytics.techtarget.com/tip/Five-steps-to-build-better-predictive-analytics-applications

Loshin, D. (2017). *Ten Steps to Start Using Predictive Analytics Algorithms Effectively*. Retrieved from http://searchbusinessanalytics.techtarget.com/tip/Ten-steps-to-start-using-predictive-analytics-algorithms-effectively

Luftman, J., & Ben-Tvi, T. (2010). Key issues for IT executives 2010: Judicious IT investments continue post-recession. *MIS Quarterly Executive*, *9*(4), 263–273.

Luftman, J., & Ben-Zvi, T. (2010). Key issues for IT executives 2010: Judicious IT investments continue post-recession. *MIS Quarterly Executive*, *9*(4), 263–273.

Lustig, I., Dietrich, B., Johnson, C., & Dziekan, C. (2010, November/December). *The Analytics Journey*. Retrieved from Analytics Magazine: http://www.analytics-magazine.org/november-december-2010/54-the-analytics-journey

Lynch, T., & Gregor, S. (2004). Use participation in decision support systems development: Influencing system outcomes. *European Journal of Information Systems*, *13*(4), 286–301. doi:10.1057/palgrave.ejis.3000512

MacCallum, R. C., Widaman, K. F., Preacher, K. J., & Hong, S. (2001). Sample size in factor analysis: The role of model error. *Multivariate Behavioral Research*, *36*(4), 611–637. doi:10.1207/S15327906MBR3604_06 PMID:26822184

Macfadyen, L. P., & Dawson, S. (2012). Numbers are not enough. Why e-learning analytics failed to inform an institutional strategic plan. *Journal of Educational Technology & Society*, *15*(3), 149–163.

MacGregor, R. C., & Vrazalic, L. (2005). A basic model of electronic commerce adoption barriers: A study of regional small businesses in Sweden and Australia. *Journal of Small Business and Enterprise Development*, *12*(4), 510–527. doi:10.1108/14626000510628199

Madden, T. J., Hewett, K., & Roth, M. S. (2000). Managing Images in Different Cultures: A Cross-National Study of COlor Meanings and Preferences. *Journal of International Marketing*, *8*(4), 90–107. doi:10.1509/jimk.8.4.90.19795

Mahmood, T., & Afzal, U. (2013). Security analytics: Big data analytics for cybersecurity—A review of trends, techniques and tools. In *Proceedings of the 2013 2nd National Conference on Information Assurance* (pp. 129–134). IEEE. 10.1109/NCIA.2013.6725337

Malhotra, R., & Temponi, C. (2010). Critical decisions for ERP integration: Small business issues. *International Journal of Information Management*, *30*(1), 28–37. doi:10.1016/j.ijinfomgt.2009.03.001

Maluf, D., Bell, D., Ashish, N., Putz, P., & Gawdiak, Y. (2006). Business Intelligence in Large Organizations: Integrating Which Data? In F. al Esposito (Ed.), *Foundations of Intelligent Systems* (Vol. 4203, pp. 248–257). Springer Berlin Heidelberg. doi:10.1007/11875604_28

Mankoff, S. (2001). *Ten Critical Success Factors for CRM.* Siebel System, White Paper.

Mao, J.-Y., Vredenburg, K., Smith, P. W., & Carey, T. (2005). The state of user-centered design practice. *Communications of the ACM*, *48*(3), 105–109. doi:10.1145/1047671.1047677

March, S. T., & Storey, V. C. (2008). Design science in the information systems discipline: An introduction to the special issue on design science research. *Management Information Systems Quarterly*, *32*(4), 725–730. doi:10.2307/25148869

Maria, F. (2005). *Improving the utilization of external strategic information* (Unpublished Master of Science Thesis). Tampere University of Technology.

Mariscal, G., Marban, O., & Fernandez, C. (2010). A survery of data mining and knowledge discovery process models and methodologies. *The Knowledge Engineering Review*, *25*(02), 137–166. doi:10.1017/S0269888910000032

Marjanovic, O. (2013). *Improving data-driven decision making through human entered knowledge sharing*. Paper presented at the 24th Australasian Conference on Information Systems.

Markarian, J., Brobst, S., & Bedell, J. (2007). *Critical Success Factors Deploying Pervasive BI*. Informatica, Teradata, Microstrategy.

Markus, M. L., & Mao, J.-Y. (2004). Participation in development and implementation-updating an old, tired concept for today's IS contexts. *Journal of the Association for Information Systems*, *5*(11), 14. doi:10.17705/1jais.00057

Marr, B. (2015). Big Data: 20 Mind-Boggling Facts Everyone Must Read. *Forbes*. Retrieved from https://www.forbes.com/sites/bernardmarr/2015/09/30/big-data-20-mind-boggling-facts-everyone-must-read/#56a1b34e17b1

Martin, A., Miranda, L.T., & V., P.V. (2014). A survey on recent research in business intelligence. *Journal of Enterprise Information Management, 27*(6), 831-66.

Martins, C., Oliveira, T., & Popovič, A. (2013). Understanding the Internet banking adoption: A unified theory of acceptance and use of technology and perceived risk application. *International Journal of Information Management*.

Matrane, O., Talea, M., & Okar, C. (2014). Towards a new maturity model for information security management. *International Journal of Advanced Research in Computer Science and Software Engineering*, *4*(6).

Mayfield, M. (2010). Tacit knowledge sharing: Techniques for putting a powerful tool in practice. *Development and Learning in Organizations*, *24*(1), 24–26.

McAfee, A. & Brynjolfsson, E. (2012, November). Besser entscheiden mit Big Data. *Harvard Business Manager,* 22-30.

McAfee, A., & Brynjolfsson, E. (2012). Big Data: The Management Revolution. *Harvard Business Review*. Retrieved from https://hbr.org/2012/10/big-data-the-management-revolution

McCandless, D. (2009). *Information is Beautiful*. Collins.

McClard, A., & Somers, P. (2000). Unleashed: Web tablet integration into the home. *Proceedings of the SIGCHI Conference on Human Factors in Computing Systems*. 10.1145/332040.332042

McCown, R. L. (2002). Changing systems for supporting farmers decisions: Problems, paradigms, and prospects. *Agricultural Systems*, *74*(1), 179–220. doi:10.1016/S0308-521X(02)00026-4

McNeill, D. (2014). *Analytics in Healthcare and the Life Sciences: Strategies, Implementation Methods and Best Practices*. Upper Sadler River, NJ: International Institute for Analytics.

Meensel, J. V., Lauwers, L., Kempen, I., Dessein, J., & Huylenbroeck, G. V. (2012). Effect of a participatory approach on the successful development of agricultural decision support systems: The case of Pigs2win. *Decision Support Systems*, *54*(1), 164–172. doi:10.1016/j.dss.2012.05.002

Meister, C. (2009). *Successful Business Intelligence Implementation*. Auxis Inc.

Mesaros, P., Carnicky, S., & Mandicak, T. (2015). Key factors and barriers of business intelligence implementation. *US-China L. Rev.*, *12*, 220.

Mesdag, M. (2000). Culture-sensitive adapation or global standardization - the duration-of-usage hypothesis. *International Marketing Review*, *17*(1), 74–84. doi:10.1108/02651330010314722

Meso, P., & Smith, R. (2000). A resource-based view of organizational knowledge management systems. *Journal of Knowledge Management*, *4*(3), 224–234. doi:10.1108/13673270010350020

Mettler, T., & Rohner, P. (2009). Situational maturity models as instrumental artifacts for organizational design. *Proceedings of 4th International Conference on Design Science Research in Information Systems and Technology*. 10.1145/1555619.1555649

Miah, S. J. (2008). *An ontology-based design environment for rural decision support* (Unpublished doctoral dissertation). Griffith University, Australia.

Miah, S., & McKay, J. (2016, September). *A new conceptualisation of design science research for DSS development*. Paper presented at the 20th Pacific Asia Conference on Information Systems (PACIS), Taiwan.

Miah, S.J. (2010). *A new semantic knowledge sharing approach for e-government systems*. Academic Press.

Miah, S. J. (2004). Accessibility improvement of multicultural educational web interface by using the user centred design (UCD) approach. *Journal of Issues in Informing Science and Information Technology*, *4*, 99–108.

Miah, S. J. (2009). End user as application developer for decision support. In *Proceedings of American Conference on Information Systems*. San Francisco, CA: AMCIS. Retrieved from http://aisel.aisnet.org/amcis2009/142

Miah, S. J., Ahsan, K., & Msimangira, K. A. (2014). An approach of purchasing decision support in healthcare supply chain management. *Operations and Supply Chain Management*, *6*(2), 43–53.

Miah, S. J., Kerr, D., & von Hellens, L. (2014). A collective artefact design of decision support systems: A design science research perspective. *Information Technology & People*, *27*(3), 259–279. doi:10.1108/ITP-04-2012-0041

Michels, L. J. (2016). *Prudence and Persistence: Personality in Student Retention*. Academic Press.

Middleton, C. A., & Cukier, W. (2006). Is mobile email functional or dysfunctional? Two perspectives on mobile email usage. *European Journal of Information Systems*, *15*(3), 252–260. doi:10.1057/palgrave.ejis.3000614

Miles, M. B., & Huberman, A. M. (1994). *Qualitative data analysis* (2nd ed.). Thousand Oaks, CA: Sage.

Miles, M. B., & Huberman, A. M. (1994). *Qualitative Data Analysis: an Expanded Sourcebook*. Thousand Oaks, CA: SAGE Publications, Inc.

Minelli, M., Chambers, M., & Dhiraj, A. (2013). *Big Data, Big Analytics: Emerging Business Intelligence and Analytic Trends for Today's Businesses*. Hoboken, NJ: John Wiley & Sons. doi:10.1002/9781118562260

Mintu, A. T., Calantone, R., & Gassenheimer, J. B. (1994). Towards improving cross-cultural research: Extending Churchill's research paradigm. *Journal of International Marketing*, 5–23.

Mintzberg, H., Raisinghani, D., & Theoret, A. (1976). The structure of" unstructured" decision processes. *Administrative Science Quarterly*, *21*(2), 246–275. doi:10.2307/2392045

Moalagh, M., & Zare Ravasan, A. (2012). Developing a practical framework for assessing ERP post-implementation success using fuzzy analytic network process. *International Journal of Production Research*, *51*(4), 1236–1257. doi:10.1080/00207543.2012.698318

Mohamed, U. A., Galal-Edeen, G. H., & El-Zoghbi, A. A. (2010). Building integrated oil and gas B2B e-commerce hub architecture based on SOA. *International Conference on e-Education, e-Business, e-Management, and e-Learning*, 599-608. 10.1109/IC4E.2010.138

Mohammadi, M. M., Ravasan, A. Z., & Hamidi, H. (2015). Investigating Critical Success Factors in Implementing ITIL Framework: The Case of a Developing Country. *International Journal of Standardization Research*, *13*(1), 74–91. doi:10.4018/IJSR.2015010104

Mohapatra, S. (2012). *E-commerce strategy: Text and cases*. London: Springer.

Morabito, J., Stohr, E. A., & Genc, Y. (2013). Enterprise Intelligence: A Case Study and the Future of Business Intelligence. In Principles and Applications of Business Intelligence Research (pp. 47-67). IGI Global.

Morgan, M. (2013). *Improving the Student Experience: A practical guide for universities and colleges*. Routledge.

Moss, L. T., & Atre, S. (2003). *Business Intelligence Roadmap: The Complete Project Lifecycle for Decision-Support-Applications*. Addison-Wesley Professional.

Mukherjee, D., & D'Souza, D. (2003). Think phased implementation for successful data warehousing. *Information Systems Management*, *20*(2), 82–90. doi:10.1201/1078/43204.20.2.20030301/41473.11

Müller, H., Gove, J., & Webb, J. (2012). Understanding tablet use: A multi-method exploration. *Proceedings of the 14th International Conference on Human-Computer Interaction with Mobile Devices and Services.*

Mustafa, Y. (2012). Helping small businesses identify their it application needs, a simple tool. *Issues in Information Systems*, *13*(1), 11–16.

Musthaler, L. (2013). *Security analytics will be the next big thing in IT security* (Opinion). Retrieved from https://www.networkworld.com/article/2166806/infrastructure-management/security-analytics-will-be-the-next-big-thing-in-it-security.html

Muthukrishnan, S. M., & Palaniappan, S. (2016). Security metrics maturity model for operational security. In *2016 IEEE Symposium on Computer Applications & Industrial Electronics ISCAIE* (pp. 101–106). IEEE. 10.1109/ISCAIE.2016.7575045

Myers, M. D. (2013). *Qualitative Research in Business and Management* (2nd ed.). London: Sage.

Mylonopoulos, N. A., & Doukidis, G. I. (2003). Introduction to the special issue: Mobile business: Technological pluralism, social assimilation, and growth. *International Journal of Electronic Commerce*, *8*(1), 5–22.

Naderinejad, M., Jafar, T. M., & Poorebrahimi, A. (2014). Recognition and Ranking Critical Success Factors of Business Intelligence in Hospitals - Case Study: Hasheminejad Hospital. *International Journal of Computer Science and Information Technology*, *6*(2), 121–129.

National Oceanic and Atmospheric Administration. (2016). *What is the Polar Vortex?* Retrieved from National Weather Service: http://www.nws.noaa.gov/om/cold/polar_vortex.shtml

Nazemoff, V. (2014). *The Four Intelligences Of The Business Mind: How To Rewire Your Brain And Your Business For Success*. Academic Press.

Nechaeva, P. A., Andrianova, N. V., & Sandriev, D. S. (2016). Trnasaction Costs in the Interaction of Logistics and Marketigng in Procurement. Academy of Strategic Management, 53-60.

Negash, S. (2004). Business Intelligence. *Communications of the Association for Information Systems*, *13*, 177–195.

Neil, N. (2013). Agenda Overview for Analytics, Business Intelligence and Performance Management. *Gartner*. Retrieved from http://my.gartner.com/portal/server.pt?open=512&objID=260&mode=2&PageID=3460702&resId=2293025&ref=QuickSearch&sthkw=Agenda+Overview+for+Analytics%2C+Business+Intelligence+and+Performance+Management%2C+2013

Nelson, R. R. (2007). IT project management: Infamous failures, classic mistakes, and best practices. *MIS Quarterly Executive, 6*(2), 67–78.

Neuman, W. L. (2011). *Social research methods: Qualitative and quantitative approaches* (7th ed.). Pearson/Allyn and Bacon.

Ngai, E. W. T., Cheng, T. C. E., & Ho, S. S. M. (2004). Critical success factors of web-based supply-chain management systems: An exploratory study. *Production Planning and Control, 15*(6), 622–630. doi:10.1080/09537280412331283928

Nichols, D. M., Chan, C., & Bainbridge, D. (2008). A lightweight metadata quality tool. *Proceedings of the 8th ACM/IEEE-CS joint conference on Digital libraries*, 385-388. 10.1145/1378889.1378957

Nisbett, R. E., Peng, K., Choi, I., & Norenzayan, A. (2001). Culture and Systems of Thought: Holistic Versus Analytic Cognition. American Psychological Association, Inc.

NIST. (2005). *Program review for information security management assistance: Security maturity levels.* Retrieved from http://csrc.nist.gov/groups/SMA/prisma/security_maturity_levels.html

Niu, L., Lu, J., & Zhang, G. (2009). *Cognition-driven decision support for business intelligence: Models, techniques, systems, and applications.* New York: Springer-Verlag. doi:10.1007/978-3-642-03208-0

Niu, L., Lu, J., Zhang, G., & Wu, D. (2013). FACETS: A cognitive business intelligence system. *Information Systems, 38*(6), 835–862. doi:10.1016/j.is.2013.02.002

Nonaka & Takeuchi. (1995). Toward middle-up-down management: accelerating information creation. *Sloan Management Review, 29*(3), 9-18.

Nott, C., & Betteridge, N. (2014). Big data and analytics maturity model [Web log post]. Retrieved from http://www.ibmbigdatahub.com/blog/big-data-analytics-maturity-model

Novak, D., Guo, F., Hodgdon, C., & Aultman-Hall, L. (2008, October 29). Nationwide Freight Generation Models: A Spacial Regression Approach. *Networks and Spatial Economics*, 23–41.

Ocampo, M. A. (2007). Overcoming the Barriers to Business Intelligence Success. *DM Review, 17*(9), 24.

Office of Government Commerce. (2007). *Service Design.* London: UK Government, Cabinet Office.

Office of Government Commerce. (2007a). *Continual Service Improvement.* London: Cabinet Office, UK Government.

Okoli, C., & Carillo, K. (2012). The best of adaptive and predictive methodologies: Open source software development, a balance between agility and discipline. *International Journal of Information Technology and Management, 11*(1-2), 153–166. doi:10.1504/IJITM.2012.044071

Olbrich, S., Poppelbuß, J., & Niehaves, B. (2012). *Critical Contextual Success Factors for Business Intelligence: A Delphi Study on Their Relevance, Variability, and Controllability.* Paper presented at the 2012 45th Hawaii International Conference on System Science (HICSS).

Olbrich, S., Poppelbuß, J., & Niehaves, B. (2012). Critical Contextual Success Factors for Business Intelligence: A Delphi Study on Their Relevance, Variability, and Controllability. *System Science (HICSS), 2012 45th Hawaii International Conference on*, 4148-415. doi:10.1109/ICIMU.2011.6122732

Oliver, J. (2008). Knowledge management practices to support continuous improvement. *Journal of Knowledge Management Practice, 9*(4), 1–14.

Olszak, C. M., & Ziemba, E. (2007). Approach to building and implementing Business Intelligence Systems. *Interdisciplinary Journal of Information, Knowledge, and Management*, *2*, 135–148. doi:10.28945/105

Olszak, C. M., & Ziemba, E. (2012). Critical Success Factors for Implementing Business Intelligence Systems in Small and Medium Enterprises on the Example of Upper Silesia, Poland. *Interdisciplinary Journal of Information, Knowledge, and Management*, *7*, 130–150. doi:10.28945/1584

Ong, I., Siew, P., & Wong, S. (2011). Assessing organizational business intelligence maturity. *Information Technology and Multimedia (ICIM), 2011 International Conference on.*

Ou, L., & Peng, H. (2006). Knowledge and Process Based Decision Support in Business Intelligence System. *Proceedings of the First International Multi-Symposiums on Computer and Computational Sciences.* 10.1109/IMSCCS.2006.236

Ozok, A. A., Benson, D., Chakraborty, J., & Norcio, A. F. (2008). A comparative study between tablet and laptop PCs: User satisfaction and preferences. *International Journal of Human-Computer Interaction*, *24*(3), 329–352. doi:10.1080/10447310801920524

Pakka, P. (2015). The role of Business Intelligence for internationalisation and organisational learning. Academic Press.

PalsonKennedy, R., & Gopal, T. (2010). Assessing the risks and opportunities of cloud computing—defining identity management systems and maturity models. In Trendz in Information Sciences & Computing (pp. 138–142). Academic Press.

Pant, P. (2009). Business Intelligence (BI), How to build successful BI strategy. *Deloitte*. Retrieved from http://www.loria.fr/~ssidhom/UE909R/1_BI_strategy.pdf

Pant, P. (2009). *Business Intelligence: How to build successful BI strategy*. Deloitte Consulting. Available at http://www.deloitte.com/assets/Dcom-SouthAfrica/Local%20Assets/Documents/Business%20intelligence%20that%20aligns%20with%20enterprise%20goals.pdf

Parker, A., Woodford, K., & Woods, E. (2000). *Deregulation and restructuring in the Queensland dairy industry*. School of Natural and Rural Systems, the University of Queensland, Brisbane, Australia.

Paulk, M. C., Curtis, B., Chrissis, M. B., & Weber, C. V. (1993). Capability maturity model, version 1.1. *IEEE Software*, *10*(4), 18–27. doi:10.1109/52.219617

Pearson, J., & Buchanan, G. (2010). Real-time document collaboration using iPads. In *Proceedings of the third workshop on Research advances in large digital book repositories and complementary media*. Toronto: ACM.

Pedersen, E. R. G., & Sudzina, F. (2012). Which firms use measures? *International Journal of Operations & Production Management*, *32*(1), 4–27. doi:10.1108/01443571211195718

Peffers, K., Tuunanen, T., Rothenberger, M., & Chatterjee, S. (2008). A Design Science Research Methodology for Information Systems Researc. *Journal of Management Information Systems*, 45–77.

Peppard, J. (1993). *IT Strategy for Business*. London: Pitman Publishing.

Perrin, A. (2015). *One-fifth of Americans report going online-almost constantly*. Pew Research Center.

Perrin, A. (2015). *One-fifth of Americans Report Going Online-Almost Constantly*. Pew Research Center.

Perry, M., O'Hara, K., Sellen, A., Brown, B., & Harper, R. (2001). Dealing with mobility: Understanding access anytime, anywhere. *ACM Transactions on Computer-Human Interaction*, *8*(4), 323–347. doi:10.1145/504704.504707

Petrini, M., & Pozzebon, M. (2009). Managing sustainability with the support of business intelligence: Integrating socio-environmental indicators and organisational context. *The Journal of Strategic Information Systems*, *18*(4), 178–191. doi:10.1016/j.jsis.2009.06.001

Phillips, J. (2014). *Analytics 3.0: The Era of Impact*. International Institute for Analytics. Retrieved from https://www.sas.com/content/dam/SAS/en_us/doc/event/The-Era-of-Impact-127837.pdf

Pick, R. A. (2008). Benefits of decision support systems. In F. Burstein & C. W. Holsapple (Eds.), *Handbook on decision support systems 1: Basic themes* (pp. 719–730). Berlin: Springer. doi:10.1007/978-3-540-48713-5_32

Pisello, T., & Strassmann, P. (2003). *IT Value Chain Management – Maximizing the ROI from IT Investments*. The Information Economics Press.

Pitt, L., Berthon, P., & Robson, K. (2011). Deciding when to use tablets for business applications. *MIS Quarterly Executive*, *10*(3), 133–139.

Polasky, S., Carpenter, S. R., Folke, C., & Keeler, B. (2011). Decision-making under great uncertainty: Environmental management in an era of global change. *Trends in Ecology & Evolution*, *26*(8), 398–404. doi:10.1016/j.tree.2011.04.007 PMID:21616553

Ponniah, P. (2001). *Data Warehousing Fundamentals: A Comprehensive Guide for IT Professionals*. Wiley. doi:10.1002/0471221627

Poon, P.-L., & Lau, A. H. (2006). The present B2C implementation framework. *Communications of the ACM*, *49*(2), 96–103. doi:10.1145/1113034.1113036

Popovič, A., Hackney, R., Coelho, P. S., & Jaklič, J. (2012). Towards business intelligence systems success: Effects of maturity and culture on analytical decision making. *Decision Support Systems*, *54*(1), 729–739. doi:10.1016/j.dss.2012.08.017

Popovič, A., Hackney, R., Coelho, P. S., & Jaklič, J. (2012). Towards business intelligence systems success: Effects of maturity and culture on analytical decision making. *Decision Support Systems*.

Power, D. (2007). What are the features of a data-driven DSS? *DSS News*, *8*(4). Available at: http://dssresources.com/faq/pdf/135.pdf

Power, D. (2009). *Are strategic decision processes structured?* Retrieved from http://dssresources.com/faq/index.php?

Power, D. J. (2010). *Do small businesses need DSS?* Retrieved from http://dssresources.com/faq/index.php?action=artikel&id=200

Power, D. J. (2016). Computerized decision support case study research: Concepts and suggestions. In J. Papathanasiou, N. Ploskas, & I. Linden (Eds.), *Real-world decision support systems case studies: Integrated series in information systems* (Vol. 37, p. 113). Cham, Switzerland: Springer International Publishing. doi:10.1007/978-3-319-43916-7_1

Power, D., Sharda, R., & Kulkarni, U. (2007). Understanding decision support systems for global enterprises. In U. Kulkarni, D. Power, & R. Sharda (Eds.), *Decision support for global enterprises* (Vol. 2, pp. 3–14). Boston, MA: Springer. doi:10.1007/978-0-387-48137-1_1

Prentice, S. (2010). *CEO advisory: Seize the iPad opportunity now*. Gartner Publisher.

Price, D. A. (2006). The Dawn of a New ERA. *DM Review*, *16*(2), 18–22.

Puuronen, S., & Savolainen, V. (1997). Mobile information systems – Executives' view. *Information Systems Journal*, *7*(1), 3–20. doi:10.1046/j.1365-2575.1997.00002.x

PwC. (2012). *The future of retail: Consumer adaptive retailing.* Retrieved from http://www.pwc.com.au/industry/retail-consumer/

PwC. (2016). *Toward new possibilities in threat management.* Retrieved from http://www.pwc.com/gx/en/issues/cyber-security/information-security-survey/assets/gsiss-report-cybersecurity-privacy-possibilities.pdf

Rabelo, R. J., Gusmeroli, S., Arana, C., & Nagellen, T. (2006). The Ecolead ICT infrastructure for collaborative networked organizations. In *Network-Centric Collaboration and Supporting Frameworks* (pp. 451–460). Boston: Springer. doi:10.1007/978-0-387-38269-2_47

Raber, D., Wortmann, F., & Winter, R. (2013). Towards The Measurement Of Business Intelligence Maturity. *Proceedings of ECIS 2013.*

Radcliffe, J. (2014). *Leverage a big data maturity model to build your big data roadmap.* Retrieved from www.radcliffeadvisory.com/research/download.php?file=RAS_BD_MatMod.pdf

Rajpurohit, A. (2014). Has Predictive Analytics Crossed The Chasm? *Ventana Research.* Retrieved from https://www.kdnuggets.com/2014/05/has-predictive-analytics-crossed-chasm.html

Ramamurthy, K., Sen, A., & Sinha, A. P. (2008). An empirical investigation of the key determinants of data warehouse adoption. *Decision Support Systems, 44*(4), 817–841. doi:10.1016/j.dss.2007.10.006

Ramanigopal, C. S., Palaniappan, G., & Mani, A. (2012). Business intelligence for competence in consumer packaged good industry. *International Journal of Marketing and Technology, 2*(5), 84–105.

Rasmussen, N. H., Goldy, P. S., & Solli, P. O. (2002). *Financial business intelligence: trends, technology, software selection, and implementation.* John Wiley & Sons.

Ravasan, A. Z., & Mansouri, T. (2014). A FCM-Based Dynamic Modeling of ERP Implementation Critical Failure Factors. *International Journal of Enterprise Information Systems, 10*(1), 32–52. doi:10.4018/ijeis.2014010103

Ray, C. M., Harris, T. M., & Dye, J. L. (1994). Small business attitudes toward computers. *Journal of End User Computing, 6*(1), 16–25. doi:10.4018/joeuc.1994010102

Raymond, L., & Bergeron, F. (1992). Personal DSS success in small enterprises. *Information & Management, 22*(5), 301–308. doi:10.1016/0378-7206(92)90076-R

Recio, B., Rubio, F., & Criado, J. A. (2003). A decision support system for farm planning using AgriSupport II. *Decision Support Systems, 36*(2), 189–203. doi:10.1016/S0167-9236(02)00134-3

Resnicow, K. (1999). *Cultural Sensitivity in Public Health: Defined and Demystified.* Academic Press.

Reynolds, S., & Valentine, D. (2011). *Guide to Cross-cultural Communication* (2nd ed.). Prentice Hall.

Riabacke, M., Danielson, M., & Love, E. (2012). State-of-the-Art Prescriptive Criteria Weight Elicitation. *Advances in Decision Sciences, 2012*, 1–24. doi:10.1155/2012/276584

Richardson, J., & Herschel, G. (2012). BI Strategy Gap Leads to Suboptimal Outcomes. *Gartner.* Retrieved from http://my.gartner.com/portal/server.pt?open=512&objID=260&mode=2&PageID=3460702&resId=1958615&ref=QuickSearch&sthkw=BI+Strategy+Gap+Leads+to+Suboptimal+Outcomes

Richardson, J., Schlegel, K., Hostmann, B., & McMurchy, N. (2008). *Magic Quadrant for Business Intelligence Platforms.* Gartner.

Richardson, M., Abraham, C., & Bond, R. (2012). Psychological correlates of university students' academic performance: A systematic review and meta-analysis. *Psychological Bulletin*, *138*(2), 353–387. doi:10.1037/a0026838 PMID:22352812

Rodic, J., & Baranovic, M. (2009). Generating data quality rules and integration into ETL process. *Proceedings of the ACM twelfth international workshop on Data warehousing and OLAP*, 65-72. 10.1145/1651291.1651303

Rogers, W. A., O'Brien, M. A., & Fisk, A. D. (2013). Cognitive engineering to support successful aging. In D. L. John & K. Alex (Eds.), *The Oxford handbook of cognitive engineering* (p. 286). New York: Oxford University Press.

Rook, L. (2013). Mental Models: A Robust Definition. *The Learning Organization*, *20*(1), 38–47. doi:10.1108/09696471311288519

Rosa, E., Reza, S., & Ali, C. E. (2017). Analysing the role of business intelligence, knowledge sharing and organisational innovation on gaining competitive advantage. *Journal of Workplace Learning*, *29*(4), 250–267. doi:10.1108/JWL-07-2016-0070

Rosenblatt, H. J. (2014). *Systems analysis and design*. Cengage Learning.

Rosenbush, S., & Stevens, L. (2015). At UPS the Algorithm is the Driver. *The Wall Street Journal*. Retrieved from https://www.wsj.com/articles/at-ups-the-algorithm-is-the-driver-1424136536

Rouhani, S., Ashrafi, A., Zare, A., & Afshari, S. (2016). The impact model of business intelligence on decision support and organizational benefits. *Journal of Enterprise Information Management*, *29*(1), 19–50. doi:10.1108/JEIM-12-2014-0126

Rouhani, S., & Ravasan, A. Z. (2014). A practical framework for assessing business intelligence competencies of enterprise systems using fuzzy ANP approach. *International Journal of Applied Decision Sciences*, *8*(1), 52–82. doi:10.1504/IJADS.2015.066559

Rouhani, S., & Ravasan, A. Z. (2015). Multi-objective model for intelligence evaluation and selection of enterprise systems. *International Journal of Business Information Systems*, *20*(4), 397–426. doi:10.1504/IJBIS.2015.072736

Rouibah, K., & Ould-ali, S. (2002). PUZZLE: A concept and prototype for linking business intelligence to business strategy. *The Journal of Strategic Information Systems*, *11*(2), 133–152. doi:10.1016/S0963-8687(02)00005-7

Rouse, M. (2017). People Analytics (HR Analaytics). *TechTarget*. Retrieved from http://searchhrsoftware.techtarget.com/definition/human-resources-analytics-talent-analytics?vgnextfmt=print

Rubenstein-Montano, B., Liebowitz, J., Buchwalter, J., McCaw, D., Newman, B., & Rebeck, K. (2001). A systems thinking framework for knowledge management. Decision Support Systems, 31, 5-16.

Rubin, H. J., & Rubin, I. S. (2005). *Qualitative interviewing: The art of hearing data* (2nd ed.). Thousand Oaks, CA: Sage. doi:10.4135/9781452226651

Rud, O. P. (2009). *Business Intelligence Success Factors: Tools for Aligning Your Business in the Global Economy*. Hoboken, NJ: John Wiley & Sons.

Russom, P. (2011). *Executive summary: Big data analytics*. Retrieved from https://tdwi.org/research/2011/09/~/media/TDWI/TDWI/Research/BPR/2011/TDWI_BPReport_Q411_Big_Data_Analytics_Web/TDWI_BPReport_Q411_Big%20Data_ExecSummary.ashx

Safeer, M., & Zafar, S. (2011). Impact of business intelligence competency center in success/ failure of B.I. applications. *Multitopic Conference (INMIC), 2011 IEEE 14th International*. 10.1109/INMIC.2011.6151486

Sahay, B. S., & Ranjan, J. (2008). Real time business intelligence in supply chain analytics. *Information Management & Computer Security*, *16*(1), 28–48. doi:10.1108/09685220810862733

Sajjadi, S., Shapiro, B., McKinlay, C., Sarkisyan, A., Shubin, C., & Osoba, E. (2017). *Finding Bottlenecks: Predicting Student Attrition with Unsupervised Classifier.* arXiv preprint arXiv:1705.02687

Saleh, M. F. (2011). Information security maturity model. *International Journal of Computer Science and Security, 5*, 316–337.

Salleh, S. (2013). *Applying Predictive Analytics in Enterprise Decision Making*. Retrieved from

Salmeron, J. L., & Herrero, I. (2005). An AHP-based methodology to rank critical success factors of executive information systems. *Computer Standards & Interfaces*, *28*(1), 1–12. doi:10.1016/j.csi.2004.09.002

Sammon, D., & Finnegan, P. (2000). The ten commandments of data warehousing. *ACM SIGMIS Database*, *31*(4), 82–91. doi:10.1145/506760.506767

Sanchez, A. (2013). *Investigation of Truckload Prices in the US: Exploritory Analysis, Forecast Methods, and the Influence of Unemployment on Freight Prices. West Virginia University, Department of Civil and Environmental Engineering*. ProQuest LLC.

SAS. (2016, March 3). *Data Visualization What it is and why it matters*. Retrieved from SAS: http://www.sas.com/en_us/insights/big-data/data-visualization.html

Schein, E. H. (2004). *Organizational culture and leadership*. San Francisco: Jossey-Bass.

Scher, A., Reuss, A., Frank, E., & Dorman, P. (2000). The ABCs of the Global Economy. *Dollars and Sense*, 26–32.

Schultz, J. D. (2016). 2016 State of Logistics Report. *Logistics Management*, 22-25.

Schulz, J. D. (2015, March). Trucking Regulation: Carriers push back, shippers to pay. *Logistics Management*, 52-60.

Schuster, C. P., & Copeland, M. J. (2008). Cultural theory in use: the instersection of structure, process and communication in business practice. *Journal of Public Affairs*, 261-280.

Seffah, A., Gulliksen, J., & Desmarais, M. C. (2005). *Human-centered software engineering-integrating usability in the software development lifecycle* (Vol. 8). Dordrecht, The Netherlands: Springer. doi:10.1007/1-4020-4113-6

Seidman, A. (2005). *College student retention: Formula for student success*. Greenwood Publishing Group.

Sen, A. (2002). Metadata Management: Past, Present and Future. *Decision Support Systems*, *37*(1), 151–173. doi:10.1016/S0167-9236(02)00208-7

Senge, P. M. (2006). *The fifth discipline: the art and practice of the learning organization*. London: Random House.

Senge, P., Smith, B., Kruschwitz, N., Laur, J., & Schley, S. (2008). *The Necessary Revolution - How Individuals and Organizations are Working Together to Create a Sustainable World*. London, UK: Nicholas Brealey Publishing.

Sensis. (2013). *Sensis® e-business report, 2013: The online experience of small and medium enterprises*. Retrieved from: http://about.sensis.com.au/IgnitionSuite/uploads/docs

Seufert, A., & Oehler, K. (2009). Business Intelligence & Controlling Competence (1st ed.). Berlin: Academic Press.

Shaaban, E., Helmy, Y., Khedr, A., & Nasr, M. (2011). Business intelligence maturity models: Toward new integrated model. In *Proceedings of The International Arab Conference on Information Technology (ACIT '11)*. Riyadh, Saudi Arabia: Academic Press.

Shackleford, D. (2016). *Using analytics to predict future attacks and breaches* (Press release). Retrieved from https://www.sans.org/reading-room/whitepapers/analyst/analytics-predict-future-attacks-breaches-36720

Shahar, Y., Goren-Bar, D., Boaz, D., & Tahan, G. (2006). Distributed, intelligent, interactive visualization and exploration of time-oriented clinical data and their abstractions. *Artificial Intelligence in Medicine*, *38*(2), 115–135. doi:10.1016/j.artmed.2005.03.001 PMID:16343873

Shankaranarayanan, G., Wang, R. Y., & Ziad, M. (2000). IP-MAP: Representing the Manufacture of an Information Product. In *Proceedings of the 2000 International Conference on Information Quality*. MIT.

Shankaranarayanan, G. (2005). Towards Implementing Total Data Quality Management in a Data Warehouse. *Journal of Information Technology Management*, *16*(1), 21–30.

Shankaranarayanan, G., & Cai, Y. (2006). Supporting Data Quality Management in Decision-Making. *Decision Support Systems*, *42*(1), 302–317. doi:10.1016/j.dss.2004.12.006

Shankaranarayanan, G., & Even, A. (2006). The Metadata Enigma. *Communications of the ACM*, *49*(2), 88–94. doi:10.1145/1113034.1113035

Shankaranarayanan, G., Ziad, M., & Wang, R. Y. (2003). Managing Data Quality in Dynamic Decision Environments: An Information Product Approach. *Journal of Database Management*, *14*(4), 14–32. doi:10.4018/jdm.2003100102

Shapiro, J. M., Ozanne, J. L., & Saatcioglu, B. (2008). An interpretive examination of the development of cultural sensitivity in international business. *Journal of International Business Studies*, *39*(1), 71–87. doi:10.1057/palgrave.jibs.8400327

Sheng, H., Nah, F. F. H., & Siau, K. (2005). Strategic implications of mobile technology: A case study using value-focused thinking. *The Journal of Strategic Information Systems*, *14*(3), 269–290. doi:10.1016/j.jsis.2005.07.004

Sherman, R. (2015). *Business Intelligence Guidebook: From Data Integration to Analytics* (1st ed.). Kindle Edition.

Sherwell, B. W., Gonzalez, A. J., & Nguyen, J. (2005). Contextual Implementation of Human Problem-solving Knowledge in a Real-World Decision Support System. *Proceedings of the Conference on Behavior Representation in Modeling and Simulation*. Available at: http://cc.ist.psu.edu/BRIMS2013/archives/2005/papers/05-BRIMS-025.pdf

Shi, Y., & Lu, X. (2010). The Role of Business Intelligence in Business Performance Management. *3rd International Conference on Information Management, Innovation Management and Industrial Engineering*. 10.1109/ICIII.2010.522

Shneiderman, B. (2003). *Leonardo's laptop: Human needs and the new computing technologies*. MIT Press.

Shulman, L. S. (1987). Knowledge and teaching: Foundations of the new reform. *Harvard Educational Review*, *57*(1), 1–23. doi:10.17763/haer.57.1.j463w79r56455411

Shu, W., & Chuang, M. Y. (2007). Service Innovation in the Context of Business Web: Enterprise Web Resource Planning as a Strategic Tool for Inreasing Service Value. *Service Science*, 45–77.

Siegel, E. (2010). *Seven Reasons You Need Predictive Analytics Today*. Prediction Impact, Inc.

Siegel, E. (2016). *Predictive Analytics: The Power to Predict Who Will Click, Buy, Lie, or Die*. Hoboken, NJ: John Wiley & Sons, Inc.

Simpson, E. S. C., & Weiner, J. A. (Eds.). (1989). *The Oxford encyclopaedic English dictionary*. Oxford, UK: Clarendon Press.

Singh, H., & Singh, B. P. (2013). Business Intelligence: Effective machine learning for business administration. *International Journal of IT Engineering and Applied Sciences Research*, *2*(1), 13–19.

Singh, S. K., Watson, H. J., & Watson, R. T. (2002). EIS support for the strategic management process. *Decision Support Systems*, *33*(1), 71–85. doi:10.1016/S0167-9236(01)00129-4

Smith, A. (2013). Data visualisation and beyond: A multi-disciplinary approach to promote user engagement with official statistics. *Statistical Journal of the IAOS*, 173–185.

Sparkman, L., Maulding, W., & Roberts, J. (2012). Non-cognitive predictors of student success in college. *College Student Journal*, *46*(3), 642–652.

Sprague, R. H. Jr, & Carlson, E. D. (1982). *Building effective decision support systems*. Englewood Cliffs, NJ: Prentice-Hall: Prentice-Hall.

Spruit, M., Vroon, R., & Batenburg, R. (2014). Towards healthcare business intelligence in long-term care: An explorative case study in the Netherlands. *Computers in Human Behavior*, *30*, 698–707. doi:10.1016/j.chb.2013.07.038

Srivastava, R., & Verma, S. (2012). *Strategic management: Concepts, skills, and practices*. Delhi, India: PHI Learning Pvt. Ltd.

Stafford, J. R., Lopes-DeFede, A., Bowman, R., Hanna, J., & Eking, T. (1997). *Building cultural bridges*. Bloomington, IN: National Educational Services.

Stasieńko, J. (2010). Business Intelligence as a Decision Support System. In G. Setlak & K. Markov (Eds.), Methods and Instruments of Artificial Intelligence (pp. 141–148). Rzeszow, Poland: Academic Press.

Stedman, C. (2017). Eyeing the future with predictive analytics can pay dividends now. *TechTarget*. Retrieved from http://searchbusinessanalytics.techtarget.com/ehandbook/Predictive-data-analytics-advances-businesses-ahead-of-the-game

Stock, D., & Winter, R. (2011). The Value of Business Metadata – Structuring the Benefits in a Business Intelligence Context. In A. d'Atri, M. Ferrara, J. F. George, & P. Spagnoletti (Eds.), *Information Technology and Innovation Trends in Organisations* (pp. 133–141). Heidelberg, Germany: Physica. doi:10.1007/978-3-7908-2632-6_16

Strickland, J. (2015). *Analytics: is it more than a buzzword?* Retrieved from https://bicorner.com/2015/09/16/analytics-is-it-more-than-a-buzzword/

Sullivan, D. (2015). *Introduction to big data security analytics in the enterprise*. Retrieved from http://searchsecurity.techtarget.com/feature/Introduction-to-big-data-security-analytics-in-the-enterprise

Sullivan, F. (2012). *Australian and New Zealand shopping market and digital insights July 2012*. Retrieved from http://www.pwc.com.au/industry/retail-consumer/assets/Digital-Media-Online-Shopping-Jul12.pdf

Supply Chain Council. (2010). *Supply Chain Operations Reference model overview: Version 10*. Author.

Supply Chain Management Institute. (2008). Supply Chain Management: Processes, Partnerships, Performance (D. Lambert, Ed.). Sarasota, FL: Supply Chain Management Institute.

Sweet, P. (2003, June). Looking before you leap. In *Corporate Performance Management*. Conspectus Report.

Talabis, M., McPherson, R., Miyamoto, I., & Martin, J. (2014). *Information Security Analytics: Finding Security Insights, Patterns, and Anomalies in Big Data*. Syngress.

Tallon, P. (2013). Corporate Governance of Big Data: Perspectives on Value, Risk, and Cost. *IEEE Computer Journal*, *46*(6), 32–38. doi:10.1109/MC.2013.155

Tanaka, K. (2014). *Directional imbalance of freight rates*. Institute of Developing Economies.

Tan, W. K., & Sie, M. S. (2015). The impact of personal innovativeness on product aesthetics and self-connection with brand: A case study of mobile phone users. *Behaviour & Information Technology*, *34*(3), 316–325. doi:10.1080/0144929X.2014.952777

Tan, W., Shen, W., Xu, L., Zhou, B., & Li, L. (2008). A Business Process Intelligence System for Enterprise Process Performance Management. *IEEE Transactions on Systems, Man and Cybernetics. Part C, Applications and Reviews*, *38*(6), 745–756. doi:10.1109/TSMCC.2008.2001571

Tariq, A., & Rafi, K. (2012). Intelligent decision support systems: A framework. *Information and Knowledge Management*, *2*(6), 12–20.

Taylor, P. (2012, June 19). Crunch Time for Big Data. *The Financial Times*.

Thamir, A., & Theodoulidis, B. (2013). Business intelligence maturity models: Information management perspective. In *International Conference on Information and Software Technologies* (pp. 198–221). Academic Press. 10.1007/978-3-642-41947-8_18

The Hofstede Centre. (2016, March 1). *Cultural Compass*. Retrieved from The Hofstede Centre: http://www.geert-hofstede.com/

The World Bank. (2015). *GDP at market price (current US$)*. Retrieved from The World Bank: http://data.worldbank.org/indicator/NY.GDP.MKTP.CD?order=wbapi_data_value_2014%20wbapi_data_value%20wbapi_data_value-last&sort=desc

The World Bank. (2016, April 1). *World Developement Indicators*. Retrieved from The World Bank: http://data.worldbank.org/data-catalog/world-development-indicators

Thierauf, R. J. (1988). *User-oriented decision support systems: Accent on problem finding*. Englewood Cliffs, NJ: Prentice-Hall, Inc.

Thompson, O. (2004). *Business intelligence success, lessons learned*. Retrieved from http://www.technologyevaluation.com/Research/ResearchHighlights/ExecutiveView/2004/01/research_notes/MI_EV_XOT_01_29_04_1.asp

Thomson, K.-L., & von Solms, R. (2006). Towards an information security competence maturity model. *Computer Fraud & Security*, *2006*(5), 11–15. doi:10.1016/S1361-3723(06)70356-6

Thomson, K.-L., von Solms, R., & Louw, L. (2006). Cultivating an organizational information security culture. *Computer Fraud & Security*, *2006*(10), 7–11. doi:10.1016/S1361-3723(06)70430-4

Tinto, V. (1987). *Leaving college: Rethinking the causes and cures of student attrition*. ERIC.

Todd, A. (2012). *Get your business online now! Be part of Australia's eCommerce revolution*. Sydney: Hachette Australia.

Treiblmaier, H., & Filzmoser, P. (2010). Exploratory factor analysis revisited: How robust methods support the detection of hidden multivariate data structures in IS research. *Information & Management*, *47*(4), 197–207. doi:10.1016/j.im.2010.02.002

Tremblay, K. (2013). *OECD assessment of higher education learning outcomes (AHELO). In Modeling and measuring competencies in higher education* (pp. 113–126). Springer. doi:10.1007/978-94-6091-867-4_8

Tsaih, R., Liu, Y. J., Liu, W., & Lien, Y. L. (2014). Credit scoring system for small business loans. *Decision Support Systems*, *38*(1), 91–99. doi:10.1016/S0167-9236(03)00079-4

Turban, E. (2007). *Decision support and business intelligence systems*. Upper Saddle River, NJ: Prentice-Hall, Inc.

Turban, E., Leidner, D., McLean, E., & Wetherbe, J. (2006). *Information Technology for Management: Transforming Organizations in the Digital Economy* (5th ed.). J. Wiley and Sons.

Turban, E., & Sharda, R. (2008). Introduction to business intelligence. In E. Turban, R. Sharda, D. Delen, & D. King (Eds.), *Business intelligence* (2nd ed.; pp. 9–16). New York, NY: Pearson Prentice Hall.

Tutunea, M. F., & And Rus, R. V. (2012). Business intelligence solutions for SMEs. *Procedia Economics and Finance*, *3*, 865–870. doi:10.1016/S2212-5671(12)00242-0

Tvrdíková, M. (2007). Support of Decision Making by Business Intelligence Tools. *Proceedings of the 6th International Conference on Computer Information Systems and Industrial Management Applications*. 10.1109/CISIM.2007.64

U.S. Census Bureau. (2016). *Definition: NAICS 48-49 to 81, Services Sectors*. Retrieved from U.S. Census Bureau: http://www.census.gov/econ/services.html

U.S. Department of Commerce. (2015). *Industry Data from Bureau of Economic Analysis*. Retrieved from Bureau of Economic Analysis: http://www.bea.gov/iTable/iTable.cfm?ReqID=51&step=1#reqid=51&step=51&isuri=1&5114=a&5102=1

United States Department of Transportation. (2002). *Length of Haul*. Retrieved from Bureau of Transportation Statistics: http://www.rita.dot.gov/bts/programs/freight_transportation/html/length_of_haul.html

United States Department of Transportation. (2016, November 11). *Electronic Logging Devices and Hours of Service Supporting Document*. Retrieved from Federal Motor Carrier Safety Administration: https://www.fmcsa.dot.gov/hours-service/elds/electronic-logging-devices-and-hours-service-supporting-documents

Vaduva, A., & Dittrich, K. R. (2002). Metadata Management for Data Warehousing: Between Vision and Reality. *International Symposium on Database Engineering & Applications*, Grenoble, France.

Vassiliadis, P. (2000). Data Warehouse Modeling and Quality Issues. Athens, Greece: National Technical University of Athens.

Vassiliadis, P., Bouzeghoub, M., & Quix, C. (1999). Towards Quality-Oriented Data Warehouse Usage and Evolution. In M. Jarke & A. Oberweis (Eds.), *Advanced Information Systems Engineering* (pp. 164–179). Springer Heidelberg. doi:10.1007/3-540-48738-7_13

Ventana Research. (2015). *Ventana Research Benchmark Research: Next-Generation Predictive Analytics*. Retrieved from http://www.iconresources.com/Icon/eMailer/IBM/Ventana-Research/Ventana-Research-on-Next-generation-Analytics-june-2015.pdf

Vesset, D. (2005). *Bridging the IT and Business Needs Gap: Keys to Successful Business Intelligence Deployment*. IDC.

Viaene, S., & Viaene, S. (2008). Linking Business Intelligence into Your Business. *IT Professional*, *10*(6), 28–34. doi:10.1109/MITP.2008.128

Vidhya, A. (2015). *13 Amazing Applications/Uses of data Science Today*. Retrieved from https://www.analyticsvidhya.com/blog/2015/09/applications-data-science/

Vodapalli, T. K. (2009). *Critical Success Factors of BI Implementation*. IT University of Copenhagen. Retrieved from http://mit. itu. dk/ucs/pb/download/BI%20Thesis%20Report-New.pdf

Volitich, D. (2008). *IBM Cognos 8 Business Intelligence: The Official Guide* (1st ed.). New York: McGraw-Hill.

Vuckovic, A. (2008). Inter-cultural communication: A foundation of communicative action. *Multicultural Education & Technology Journal*, *2*(1), 47–59. doi:10.1108/17504970810867151

Vuksic, V., Bach, M., & Popovic, A. (2013). Supporting performance management with business process management and business intelligence: A case analysis of integration and orchestration. *International Journal of Information Management*, *33*(4), 613–619. doi:10.1016/j.ijinfomgt.2013.03.008

Wagner, E., & Longanecker, D. (2016). Scaling Student Success with Predictive Analytics: Reflections After Four Years in the Data Trenches. *Change: The Magazine of Higher Learning*, *48*(1), 52–59. doi:10.1080/00091383.2016.1121087

Walker, D. H. (2002). Decision support, learning and rural resource management. *Agricultural Systems*, *73*(1), 113–127. doi:10.1016/S0308-521X(01)00103-2

Wang, C., & Ahmed, P. (2003). Organisational learning: A critical review. *The Learning Organization*, *10*(1), 8–17. doi:10.1108/09696470310457469

Wang, G., Gunasekarana, A., Ngai, E., & Papadopoulos, T. (2016). Big data analytics in logistics and supply chain management: Certaininvestigations for research and applications. *International Journal of Production Economics*, *176*, 98–110. doi:10.1016/j.ijpe.2016.03.014

Wang, H., & Or, C. K. (2015). *A study of the relationship between color-concept association and occupational background for Chinese*. Elsevier.

Wang, R. (1998). A Product Perspective on Total Data Quality Management. *Communications of the ACM*, *41*(2), 58–63. doi:10.1145/269012.269022

Wang, R. Y., & Strong, D. M. (1996). Beyond Accuracy: What Data Quality Means to Data Consumers. *Journal of Management Information Systems*, *12*(4), 5–34. doi:10.1080/07421222.1996.11518099

Wang, R., Lee, Y., Pipino, L., & Strong, D. (1998). Manage Your Information as a Product. *Sloan Management Review*, *39*(4), 95–105.

Wang, W., Ding, H., Dong, J., & Ren, C. (2006). A Comparison of Business Process Modelling Methods. *IEEE International Conference on Service Operations and Logistics, and Informatics Proceedings*, Shanghai, China.

Wang, Z., Chu, D., & Xu, X. (2010). Value network based service choreography design and evolution. In *E-Business Engineering, IEEE International Conference*, (pp. 495-500). Los Alamitos, CA: IEEE.

Watson, H. J., Wixon, B. H., & Ariyachandra, T. (2013). Insights on Hiring for BI and Analytics. *Business Intelligence Journal*, 4-7.

Watson, H. J. (2010). BI-based Organizations. *Business Intelligence Journal*, *15*(2), 4–6.

Watson, H. J., Ariyachandra, T. R., & Matyska, R. J. Jr. (2001). Data warehousing stages of growth. *Information Systems Management*, *18*(3), 42–50. doi:10.1201/1078/43196.18.3.20010601/31289.6

Watson, H. J., Fuller, C., & Ariyachandra, T. (2004). Data warehouse governance: Best practices at Blue Cross and Blue Shield of North Carolina. *Decision Support Systems*, *38*(3), 435–450. doi:10.1016/j.dss.2003.06.001

Watson, H. J., & Wixom, H. (2007). Enterprise agility and mature BI capabilities. *Business Intelligence Journal*, *12*(3), 13–28.

Weber, N., & Fohrholz, C. (2013). Wirtschaftliche Potenziale von Business Analytics – Ergebnisse einer explorativen Studie. *ERP Management*, *4*, 36–38.

Weiss, S. M., & Indurkhya, N. (1998). *Predictive Data Mining: A Practical Guide*. Morgan Kaufmann Publishers, Inc.

Wells, C. (2017). Maryland Universities to Use Data to Predict Student Success-or Failure. *The Baltimore Sun*. Retrieved from http://www.baltimoresun.com/news/maryland/education/bs-md-college-analytics-20160611-story.html

Wells, D. (2008, April 8). *Business Analytics- Getting the Point*. Retrieved from BeyeNetwork: http://www.b-eye-network.com/view/7133

Weske, M. (2007). *Business Process Management: Concepts, Languages, Architectures*. Berlin: Springer.

Westphal, I., Thoben, K. D., & Seifert, M. (2007). Measuring Collaboration Performance. In *Virtual Organizations: Establishing The Foundation Of Collaborative Networks* (Vol. 243, pp. 33–42). Boston: Springer. doi:10.1007/978-0-387-73798-0_4

Westphal, I., Thoben, K. D., & Seifert, M. (2010). Managing collaboration performance to govern virtual organizations. *Journal of Intelligent Manufacturing*, *21*(3), 311–320. doi:10.100710845-008-0182-5

Wetherbee, C. (2014). *Optimizing Your Agency's Business Processes through Analytics*. Retrieved from http://slideplayer.com/slide/1606960/

White, G. B. (2007). The community cyber security maturity model. In *40th Annual Hawaii International Conference on System Sciences* (pp. 99). Academic Press.

White, S. A. (2004). *Introduction to BPMN*. IBM Corporation.

Wieder, B., & Ossimitz, M.-L. (2015). The Impact of Business Intelligence on the Quality of Decision Making–A Mediation Model. *Procedia Computer Science*, *64*, 1163–1171. doi:10.1016/j.procs.2015.08.599

Wienclaw, R. A. (2008). *Decision support systems*. Retrieved from http://o-search.ebscohost.com.library.vu.edu.au/login.aspx

Williams, P. (2001). Information security governance. *Information Security Technical Report*, *6*(3), 60–70. doi:10.1016/S1363-4127(01)00309-0

Williams, S., & Williams, N. (2007). *Business-centric business intelligence development with the BI pathway method. In The Profit Impact of Business Intelligence* (pp. 65–95). San Francisco: Morgan Kaufmann. doi:10.1016/B978-012372499-1/50005-3

Williams, S., & Williams, N. (2010). *The profit impact of business intelligence* (1st ed.). Morgan Kaufmann.

Willis, D. A. (2011). *iPad and beyond: The media tablet in business*. Retrieved March 11 2016 from Gartner website: http://www.gartner.com/technology/research/ipad-media-tablet/

Wiseman, C. (1985). *Strategic Information Systems*. Homewood, IL: Irwin.

Wixom, B. H., & Watson, H. J. (2001). An empirical investigation of the factors affecting data warehousing success. *Management Information Systems Quarterly*, *25*(1), 17–32. doi:10.2307/3250957

Wixom, B. H., & Watson, H. J. (2010). The BI-based organization. *International Journal of Business Intelligence Research*, *1*(1), 13–28. doi:10.4018/jbir.2010071702

Wong, A. (2013). What is Embedded Analytics? *Logi Analytics*. Retrieved from https://www.logianalytics.com/bi-trends/what-is-embedded-analytics/

Wong, K. Y. (2005). Critical success factors for implementing knowledge management in small and medium enterprises. *Industrial Management & Data Systems*, *105*(3), 261–279. doi:10.1108/02635570510590101

Woodside, J. (2011). Business Intelligence Best Practices for Success. *Proceedings of the European Conference on Information Management*, 556-562.

World Trade Organisation. (2013). E-commerce in developing countries: Opportunities and challenges for small and medium-sized enterprises. Geneva, Switzerland: World Trade Organization.

Wrembel, R. (2012). The Business Value of Business Intelligence. In M.-A. Aufaure & E. Zimányi (Eds.), *Business Intelligence* (Vol. 96, pp. 27–62). Springer Berlin Heidelberg. doi:10.1007/978-3-642-27358-2_2

Xing, W., Guo, R., Petakovic, E., & Goggins, S. (2015). Participation-based student final performance prediction model through interpretable Genetic Programming: Integrating learning analytics, educational data mining and theory. *Computers in Human Behavior*, *47*, 168–181. doi:10.1016/j.chb.2014.09.034

Xiumei, S., & Jinying, W. (2011). Cultural Distance between China and US across GLOBE Model and Hofstede Model. *International Business and Management*, 11-17.

Yang, X., & Fu, J. (2008). Review of IT/IS Adoption and Decision-Making Behavior in Small Businesses. *Tsinghua Science and Technology*, *13*(3), 323–328. doi:10.1016/S1007-0214(08)70052-X

Yeoh, W. (2008). *Critical success factors for implementation of business intelligence systems in engineering asset management organisations (PhD)*. University of South Australia.

Yeoh, W., & Koronios, A. (2010). Critical Success Factors for Business Intelligence Systems. *Journal of Computer Information Systems*, *50*(3), 23–32.

Yeoh, W., & Koronios, A. (2010, Spring). Critical success factors for business intelligence systems. *Journal of Computer Information Systems*, *50*(3), 23–32.

Yeoh, W., Koronios, A., & Gao, J. (2008). Managing the Implementation of Business Intelligence Systems: A Critical Success Factors Framework. *International Journal of Enterprise Information Systems*, *4*(3), 79–94. doi:10.4018/jeis.2008070106

Yeoh, W., & Popovič, A. (2015). Extending the understanding of critical success factors for implementing business intelligence systems. *Journal of the Association for Information Science and Technology*, *67*(1), 134–147. doi:10.1002/asi.23366

Yin, R. (2008). *Case Study Research Design and Methods* (4th ed.). SAGE Inc.

Yin, R. (2014). *Case Study Research, Design and Methods* (5th ed.). Newbury Park, CA: Sage Publications.

Yin, R. K. (2003). *Case Study Research: Design and Methods*. Newbury Park, CA: Sage.

Yuan, Y., Archer, N., Connelly, C. E., & Zheng, W. (2010). Identifying the ideal fit between mobile work and mobile work support. *Information & Management*, *47*(3), 125–137. doi:10.1016/j.im.2009.12.004

Zaraté, P. (2013). *Tools for collaborative decision-making*. London, UK: John Wiley & Sons. doi:10.1002/9781118574690

Zeng, L., Li, L., & Duan, L. (2012). Business intelligence in enterprise computing environment. *Information Technology Management*, *13*(4), 297–310. doi:10.100710799-012-0123-z

Zhang, Y., & Neelankavil, J. P. (1997). The influence of culture on advertising effectiveness in China and the USA. *European Journal of Marketing*, *31*(2), 134–149. doi:10.1108/03090569710157106

Zhu, H., & Wang, R. Y. (2010). *Information Quality Framework for Verifiable Intelligence Products. In Data Engineering: Mining, Information and Intelligence. Springer.*

Zuboff, S. (1988). *In the Age of the Smart Machine*. New York: Basic Books.

About the Contributors

Shah J. Miah is an Associate Professor of Information Systems (IS) and Coordinator of the Master of Business Analytics and Bachelor of Business Information Systems Management. Prior to this position, he had academic positions at the University of the Sunshine Coast, Griffith University and James Cook University, Australia. Dr. Miah is the author/editor of over 100 publications including research books, conference proceedings, book chapters, journal articles, and refereed conference articles. Dr. Miah's publication appeared in the premier, and top-tier IS journals, including Information and Management, Information Technology & People, Information Systems, Telematics and Informatics, Australasian Journal of Information Systems, Knowledge-Based Systems. Dr Miah has become one of the influential academics in the IS discipline, having coordinated and contributed to many international, national and local conferences, including Americas Conference on Information Systems, Australasian Conference on Information Systems, Pacific Asia Conference on Information Systems, International Conference on Semantic, Knowledge, and Grid.

William Yeoh is the Director for IBM Centre of Excellence in Business Analytics at Deakin University. He is a leading researcher in Business Intelligence and Analytics field. He has published over 70 refereed articles in high-tier journals and the top five Information Systems conferences. He is the current Editor-in-Chief of the International Journal of Business Intelligence Research. Dr Yeoh has won numerous awards including the ICT Educator of the Year Gold Award (2017), internationally-competitive IBM Faculty Awards (2016 & 2017), Deakin's Vice-Chancellor Award for Value Innovation (2016), and Faculty Excellence in Research Award (2017). Moreover, his mentored team was crowned the World Champion at the 2016 IBM Watson Analytics Global Competition held in Las Vegas.

* * *

Mohsen Attaran is the 2004-05 Millie Ablin Outstanding Professor of Management at California State University, Bakersfield. He obtained his Ph.D. in Systems science with specialization in Operations Management and Business Forecasting from Portland State University. He is the author/co-author of three books, over one hundred papers, and ten commercial software packages. His research has been widely published in the major professional journals in his field. Professor Attaran has been a consultant for public and private organizations and has conducted numerous in-house workshops and seminars for Fortune 500 companies including Chevron Western Business Unit, Shell Oil Co., Texaco USA, Arco Oil and Gas, Phillips Laboratory, Mission Energy, and Bechtel. He has over 20 years of business experience as an entrepreneur, and developer. He is the founder and president of IES, Inc. a web and Mobile App

Development Company with more than 4,000 clients in 48 states. He has founded, launched and managed several businesses in his career in a variety of technological fields including a Telehealth Doctor Visits; a subscription based virtual business, and a non-profit organization with the aim of closing the gender gap in coding.

Sharmin Attaran is an Associate Professor of Marketing at Bryant University. She obtained her PhD in Marketing and Entrepreneurship from the University of Illinois at Chicago, her MBA from California State University Bakersfield, and her BA in Economics from UCLA. Dr. Attaran is an expert in the field of Digital Marketing and enjoys researching how technology aids marketing communication and marketing education. She also runs a successful digital marketing consulting business aiming at refining marketing strategies for businesses.

Tera Black has over 10 years of experience in business, marketing, and human resources. She is currently the marketing and communications manager for Jefferson Radiology, a leader in New England's radiology services and care. During her career, she has participated in and lead a variety of data analysis projects pertaining to human resources and marketing information and decisions. She is a recent graduate of Central Connecticut State University's Masters in Business Administration program with a specialization in business analytics.

Daniel Brinkmann is a professional management accountant working in the health insurance industry in Germany. He attained his Doctoral degree at the University of Gloucestershire in 2015.

Chin-Hoong Chee is currently doing his PhD study at Universiti Teknologi PETRONAS. He was a Lecturer in Universiti Tunku Abdul Rahman (UTAR), Malaysia. He received his Master of Computer Science (by research) from the same university. His main research areas are in business intelligence and information quality. Before joining the academic, he worked as a Programmer in a few software companies.

Mohammad Danesh is currently an Enterprise Architect at the Royal Bank of Canada and a researcher at the University of Toronto where he is exploring Modeling IT/IS Capabilities to design Adaptive Enterprise Architectures including Capability Boundary Analysis, Capability Bundling and Deployment, Reasoning on Capability Flexibility/Rigidity, and Analysis & Evaluation of Flexibility in Software Architecture.

Shijia (Caddie) Gao is a lecturer at the Faculty of Information Technology, Monash University. She received her PhD degree in Business Information Systems from the University of Queensland Business School. Her research interests include business intelligence, decision support systems, decision theory, financial information systems, risk management, business process management, and knowledge management. Her research has appeared in Decision Support Systems, International Journal of Information Management, The Australasian Journal of Information Systems, Journal of Knowledge Management, Journal of Decision Systems, Journal of Database Management, Expert Systems with Applications, among others.

Michael Gendron has over 40 years of industry and academic experience in information systems. He has held positions such as CIO for a large health maintenance organization, and as a research analyst for a state health department. He holds his Ph.D. in Information Science with specializations in Information Decision Systems and Health Policy and Management from the State University of New York at Albany. His current position is as Professor of Management Information Systems at CCSU.

Paul Hawking was an Associate Professor in the College of Business at Victoria University in Melbourne, Australia. He is now the principal consultant for Hawking Solutions focusing on SAP business intelligence solutions. Paul has published extensively on topics associated with enterprise resource planning systems, and business intelligence related to SAP solutions. His knowledge and experience in these areas is widely acknowledged by both academia and industry. Paul was the first academic to become a SAP Mentor. Further details about Paul can be found at https://www.hawking.solutions/.

Qing Huang is a PhD in Business Analytics at La Trobe Business School. She obtained her Honours in Information Technology with first class at Deakin University. Her main research area include learning analytics, customer analytics.

Amin Kamali received his B.Sc. in Industrial Engineering, from Sharif University of Technology, in 2010. He then joined University of Ottawa, where he finished his M.Sc. in Systems Science, in 2012. His current research interests include Business Process and Performance Management, Business Intelligence, Data Mining, and Machine Learning applications in the organizations. He currently works at IBM Canada, as Digital Transformation Technical Analyst.

Edgar Kautzner is an experienced technologist, analytics consultant and educator based in Melbourne, Australia. He holds a Bachelor of Information Technology and Systems and a Master of Business Information Systems (Honours) with H1 honours from Monash University. The original paper entitled "How and why do managers use iPads? An exploratory study of the usage motivations, nature of use, and suitability of iPads for management tasks" was written by Edgar as part of his Master's thesis under the supervision of Prof. David Arnott and Dr. Shijia Gao from Monash University.

Madhury Khatun is a doctoral candidate in the College of Business at Victoria University, Australia. She completed her MBA from AIS, New Zealand. She also completed her postgraduate and undergraduate degrees in Physics from the University of Dhaka, Bangladesh. Her research areas of interest include decision support systems (DSS) design for small businesses, user-centred and knowledge-based information system design.

Nilupulee Nathawitharana is a PhD candidate at the La Trobe Business School and a member of the La Trobe Centre for Data Analytics and Cognition. Her research interests lie in text analytics, data mining, and business intelligence and her PhD research aim at addressing challenges and limitations in current document representation and text analytics techniques by incorporating semantics. Nilupulee graduated from the University of Colombo School of Computing, Sri Lanka with a first class honours degree in Computer Science. She obtained Master of Science in Enterprise Applications Development by Sheffield Hallam University, United Kingdom. Before commencing research at La Trobe University, she worked as a Teaching Assistant and a Tutor at Deakin University. Nilupulee also worked as a Senior

Software Engineer in Sri Lanka and possesses more than six years working experience in the software industry. Nilupulee is currently employed as a Research and Teaching Assistant at La Trobe University, and for the past five years worked in a number of Text Analytics projects.

Kok-Leong Ong has attracted over $620,000 in research grant related to data analytics research and has to date, received over 427 citations from his publications of over 70 conferences and journal papers. He has a h-index of 12 and an i10-index of 16 according to Google Scholar. Kok-Leong has served in over 50 Program Committees of international conferences related to analytics, including the prestigious KDD (2015 and 2017) and PAKDD (2006 and 2018). He is also a Steering Committee Member of AusDM since 2010. Kok-Leong has co-chaired in various roles in different conferences since 2006 and has served as a reviewer for over 20 journals throughout his academic career. He is currently a Section Editor of Business Analytics with the Australasian Journal of Information Systems (ABDC A) and has also served as an industry judge for the Victoria iAwards and the SAP-RMIT University Analytics Competition. In addition, Kok-Leong has received a best paper award in 2007 and has two invited papers in 2003 and 2012. He was also an invited speaker at the recent Emerging Big Data Technologies Summit 2016. Besides academic measures, Kok-Leong's research has also demonstrated real-life impact. For example, his work on using analytics to improve community well-being was featured by the European Commission in Science for Environmental Policy and many of his papers were ranked by Altmetric to be in the top 25% and 5% of publications.

Jeffrey Peck Jr. is currently carving out his experience within the information technology industry with a variety of analyst roles in his skillset. His current position is as a Product Analyst on a software development team at 3M in their Health Insurance Systems division, but also has experience in the banking industry from an IT perspective. He is a recent graduate of Central Connecticut State University's Masters in Business Administration program specializing in Business Analytics.

Chi Pham, Master of Information Systems at Deakin University of Australia. His research interests include business analytics, cyber security and IS adoption and usage.

Bijan Raahemi received his Ph.D. in Electrical and Computer Engineering from the University of Waterloo, Canada, in 1997. Prior to joining the Telfer School of Management as an Associate Professor in Management Information Systems and Technology, Dr. Raahemi held several research positions in the telecommunications industry, including Nortel and Alcatel, focusing on computer networks architectures and services, dynamics of internet traffic, systems modelling, and performance analysis. Professor Raahemi's work has appeared in peer-reviewed journals and conferences papers. He also holds several patents in data communications. His current research interests include data mining and knowledge discovery, information systems, business intelligence, data communications networks and services, service oriented architecture, systems modelling, and performance analysis. Dr. Raahemi established the Knowledge Discovery and Data mining (KDD) Research Laboratory comprising of graduate students and researchers from multidisciplinary areas of E-Business Technology, Systems Science, and Engineering.

Sogol Rabiee Savoji received her master degree in Information Technology engineering from Mehralborz University. Her research interests include Enterprise Resource Planning Systems, Business Intelligence, and Business Process Management.

Gregory Richards conducts research into organizational performance management, Business Intelligence and Business Analytic practices and outcomes in public and private sector organizations. He leads the Centre for Business Analytics and Performance that explores emerging technical and social issues related to analytics, Internet of Things and Artificial Intelligence. He also coordinates the BDO/Interis Public Sector Performance Management research cluster that examines performance strategies unique to public management.

Carmine Sellitto is an academic at Victoria University in the Information Systems discipline. He is also affiliated as a research associate with the Centre for Applied Informatics, as well as the Institute for Sport, Exercise Science and Active Living (ISEAL). Dr. Sellitto has published widely and some of his 150 peer-reviewed publications have been on topics associated with education and learning, management and technology, tourism, e-business & Internet-marketing, sport technology and small business technology adoption.

Tewei Wang is an educator and a practitioner in the area of information systems. Currently, he is an association professor at the University of Illinois Springfield (UIS). He is also an independent consultant in the area of Business Intelligence. In the past five years, he has served as an executive advisor for a software company called Smart eVision International, Inc. He teaches for the Management Information Systems department at UIS. His two main areas of teaching are Database Management and Systems Analysis and Design. Dr. Wang is also an experienced online teacher. He started to teach online and has developed online teaching materials since 2005. In additional to his full-time teaching job at UIS. He has also taught part-time or during summer for many Universities around the world, including Ming-Chi University of Technology (Taiwan), Northern Illinois University, and Shanghai Dianji University (China). Dr. Wang is also an active researcher. His publications show up in academic journals such as Decision Support Systems, and Journal of Database Management. The majority of his research is cross-disciplinary and is related to decision making, and data analytics. He is an active member in the Association of Information Systems (AIS). He currently serves on the Educational Committee at AIS. Dr. Wang received his Ph. D. in management from Southern Illinois University at Carbondale. He also has a Master of Science in Mechanical Engineering from University of Missouri - Rolla (currently, Missouri Science and Technology University). His undergraduate degree was complete at Ming-Chi University of Technology (Taiwan, Republic of China). His native language is Chinese and speaks fluent English. He can also communicate very well in Spanish. He is passionate in taking on new adventures and share his knowledge and experiences with his friends, his colleagues, his students, and communities around the world.

Siew Fan Wong is an adjunct professor with Sunway University, Malaysia. She received her PhD degree in MIS from the University of Houston, Texas. Her research interests involve organizational IT strategy, information privacy and business analytics. Her publications have appeared in journals such as the Journal of Global Information Management, International Journal of Information Management, Government Information Quarterly and Industrial Management & Data Systems.

Martin Wynn worked for 20 years in industry as an IT professional, including 10 years as IT Director at HP Bulmer Drinks Ltd, now part of the Heineken Group. Since his return to academia in 2002, he has focused on post graduate research supervision and knowledge transfer activities with local industries. He has supervised over 20 industry based projects which have implemented a range of new technologies in local companies, including integrated systems packages, business intelligence solutions and portal based e-business applications.

Ahad Zare Ravasan is an Assistant Professor of Information Systems at Kharazmi University, Tehran, Iran. He received his MSc and PhD in Information Technology Management at Allameh Tabataba'i University, Tehran, Iran .Ahad has published a number of papers in acclaimed journals, such as the Expert Systems with Applications, Information Systems, International Journal of Production Research, Telecommunication Systems, Production Planning and Control, Scientia Iranica, International Journal of Data Warehousing and Mining, Strategic Outsourcing; An International Journal and International Journal of Enterprise Information Systems to name only a few. His key research interests include ERPs, artificial neural networks' applications in practice, business process outsourcing, business intelligence, Requirements Engineering, and IT Service management.

Index

A

analytics 18, 21-39, 55, 57-60, 64-86, 113, 132, 142, 144, 156, 164-168, 170, 173, 175, 178-180, 186-187, 190-191, 193, 218, 220-227, 229, 231, 234, 239, 243, 275-277, 306, 308, 310-311, 327-328

B

BI 2, 10, 21-22, 27-28, 31-32, 34-35, 37, 44-53, 55-61, 66-67, 70, 72-74, 79, 85, 91-94, 96-105, 112-117, 120-122, 130-137, 184-191, 193-199, 220, 222, 241-243, 245, 248-249, 276, 291-295, 298-302, 305-317, 321-322, 324, 327
BI implementation 44-46, 49, 52, 55-58, 60-61, 112-117, 121-122, 293, 306-307, 310-311, 314, 317
big data 21-25, 32, 65-68, 73-74, 81, 85, 93, 113, 136, 164-168, 170, 174-175, 178-180, 186, 190, 196, 219, 234, 306-307
big data analytics 22, 67, 74, 81, 164-168, 170, 178-180
business environment 27, 45, 67, 92, 131, 142, 147, 154-155, 185, 241, 254-256, 258-265, 272, 315, 328
Business intelligence (BI) 1-2, 21-22, 25, 31, 36, 39, 44-46, 66, 70, 72, 74, 76, 78, 85, 91, 94, 97, 101, 104, 112-115, 118-121, 130-132, 136, 144, 146, 166, 184-186, 192-193, 199, 238-239, 266, 275-276, 288-289, 291-292, 295, 302, 305-306, 308, 310, 312, 316-317, 321-322, 326-336, 339
business intelligence maturity (EBIM) model 44-45
Business Intelligence strategy 326-327, 329, 333-336, 339
Business Objects 330, 339
business workflow 91-97, 99, 102, 104

C

case studies 44, 51, 56, 121, 222, 254-259, 263-265, 329-330, 335-336
case study 51, 61, 114, 121, 184, 188-189, 197, 205, 238, 242, 257, 263, 271, 305-311, 314-317, 322-323, 326, 329-330
Cognitive analytics 28, 30
competitive advantage 4, 24, 45-46, 64, 66, 76, 85, 91, 120, 132-133, 135, 142, 146, 174, 185, 187, 241, 306, 327
Critical Success Factors (CSFs) 52, 112, 114-115, 118, 121, 233-234, 305, 322, 329, 339
cultural differences 143, 146-148, 150-151, 155-157
cybersecurity 164-168, 173-175, 178-180

D

data mining 21, 29, 57, 59, 66, 69, 72, 74, 113, 152, 186, 195, 239, 248, 313, 327
data quality 91-95, 103, 105, 111, 114-115, 121, 291-302, 305-306, 315-317, 332
data-driven 3, 36, 92, 221, 223, 225-226, 231, 234, 239, 241-242
decision support system 198, 254, 271, 316
Delphi 44, 49-53, 60-61
Descriptive analytics 28, 67-68, 72
design science 2, 91, 93-94, 104, 180, 254, 257
diagnostic analytics 29, 68-69
directionality 275, 278-280, 283-284, 288
DSS 239-242, 244, 246, 254-258, 260-265, 271, 316

E

embedded analytics 21-23, 31-39, 70, 73
end users 32, 39, 44, 73, 97, 241-243, 331-335
Enterprise Resource Planning (ERP) systems 2, 326-327, 339
evolutionary prototyping 261-262, 264-265
experts 45, 49-53, 55, 57, 60, 85, 112, 114, 116-117, 121, 168, 170, 247, 309, 311, 314-315, 317, 322

G

German Healthcare 184

H

higher education 219-220, 223, 264
Hofstede 147-150, 157

I

information manufacturing 91-98, 100, 102-104, 111
Insurance Industry 184
interview 51-52, 56, 58, 94, 102, 104, 188, 190, 193, 195-197, 205-206, 216, 309, 321, 330

K

Kentucky Fried Chicken 143, 155
knowledge management 114, 130, 133, 136-137, 185-187, 189, 191, 195-198, 239, 248

L

logistics 83, 86, 275-280, 284, 286, 288, 330

M

manager 10, 14, 102, 143, 148, 151-152, 159, 192, 198, 205-207, 216, 239-240, 242, 254-255, 258-259, 262-265, 276, 306, 311, 317, 321-322
managerial use 202-203, 205-206, 212-213
maturity framework 44, 164-167, 170, 173, 175, 178
maturity model 45-46, 49, 61, 164-165, 167-168, 170, 172-174, 178-180, 311, 339
metadata 9-10, 14, 91-93, 96, 100, 102-103, 115, 291, 293-294, 298-302, 308
mobile tablet 202, 204, 206, 208, 211-213
mobile technology 202-203, 211-213

N

Networked Organizations 2-3, 7

O

Online Transaction Processing (OLTP) 339
organization 1-4, 6, 22, 24-25, 29-31, 34, 39, 45-46, 49-60, 65, 68-70, 72, 76, 79, 84, 86, 115, 119-121, 130-137, 143, 156-159, 164-166, 168, 170, 173-175, 178-180, 184-190, 196, 205-206, 219, 221, 228, 291-293, 297-299, 301, 305, 326-329, 335, 339

P

performance measurement 1-4, 6, 17
precipitation 275, 280, 283-284, 288
predictive analytics 29-30, 35-38, 57, 64-65, 69-86, 186, 190, 193, 306, 308, 310
Prescriptive analytics 30, 69
prototyping 11, 22, 243-244, 261-262, 264-265, 271

R

regression modeling 275, 278
Robust Exploratory Factor Analysis (EFA) 112, 114

S

SAP 79, 308, 330, 332-335, 339
Service Oriented Architecture 2
small business 238, 240-242, 245, 248, 254-265, 271
small business owners 240, 242, 248, 256-260, 263-265
SMEs 3, 17, 238-242, 249
SOA-based BPM 2, 4
Strategic Capability 184
strategic decisions 38, 81, 186, 254, 258, 260, 272
strategic knowledge management 185
strategy 21, 24, 36, 45, 48-49, 57, 66, 78, 84, 114, 120, 170, 178-180, 184-190, 193-195, 198-199, 220-224, 228-229, 231, 257, 259, 297, 300, 305-308, 311-314, 316-317, 326-327, 329, 331-336, 339
student retention 218-223, 226, 229, 231
successful deployment of the BI 305
supply chain 2-3, 5, 7, 30, 69, 82, 114, 132, 184, 275-278, 288, 333

T

tailorable design 240-241

U

User-Centered Design 240, 254, 260, 272

V

virtual organizations 1, 3-4, 17
VO 1-5, 7-8, 14, 16-17

W

web content analysis 254, 256-257, 260, 264-265
website features 255-258, 261-262

www.ingramcontent.com/pod-product-compliance
Lightning Source LLC
LaVergne TN
LVHW060405300926
849162LV00006B/1353